SOVIET DISUNION

SOVIET DISUNION

A History of the Nationalities Problem in the USSR

BOHDAN NAHAYLO AND
VICTOR SWOBODA

THE FREE PRESS
A Division of Macmillan, Inc.
NEW YORK

The Free Press
A Division of Macmillan, Inc.
866 Third Avenue, New York, N.Y. 10022

First American Edition 1990

Printed in the United States of America

printing number
2   3   4   5   6   7   8   9   10

Library of Congress Cataloging-in-Publication Data
Nahaylo, Bohdan.
  Soviet disunion: a history of the nationalities problem in the USSR / Bohdan Nahaylo and Victor Swoboda. — 1st American ed.
      p.   cm.
  Includes bibliographical references.
  ISBN 0-02-922401-2
  1. Soviet Union—Ethnic relations.   2. Soviet Union-History—1917-   3. Ethnology—Soviet Union.   I. Swoboda, Victor.
II. Title.
DK33.N26   1990
947.004—dc20   89-71502
                                                                        CIP

Contents

═══

List of Illustrations

List of Maps

═══

THE SOVIET UNION

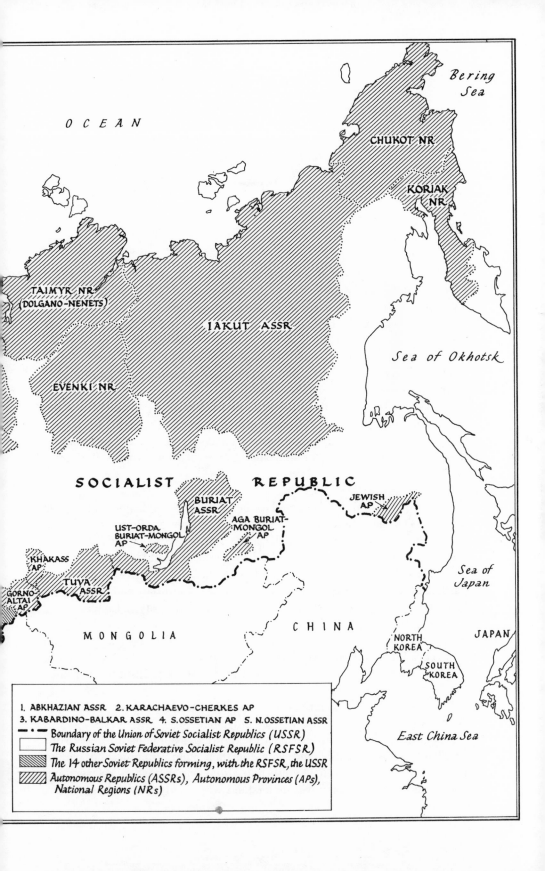

O C E A N

Bering Sea

CHUKOT NR

KORIAK NR

TAIMYR NR (DOLGANO-NENETS)

IAKUT ASSR

Sea of Okhotsk

EVENKI NR

S O C I A L I S T   R E P U B L I C

BURIAT ASSR

JEWISH AP

UST-ORDA BURIAT-MONGOL AP

AGA BURIAT-MONGOL AP

KHAKASS AP

TUVA ASSR

GORNO-ALTAI AP

Sea of Japan

MONGOLIA

C H I N A

JAPAN

NORTH KOREA

SOUTH KOREA

East China Sea

1. ABKHAZIAN ASSR   2. KARACHAEVO-CHERKES AP
3. KABARDINO-BALKAR ASSR 4. S.OSSETIAN AP 5. N.OSSETIAN ASSR
–·– Boundary of the Union of Soviet Socialist Republics (USSR)
☐ The Russian Soviet Federative Socialist Republic (RSFSR)
▨ The 14 other Soviet Republics forming, with the RSFSR, the USSR
▨ Autonomous Republics (ASSRs), Autonomous Provinces (APs),
  National Regions (NRs)

Acknowledgements

Bohdan Nahaylo wishes to express his gratitude to the Director of Radio Liberty, Dr Enders Wimbush, and the management of Radio Free Europe and Radio Liberty for generously granting him sabbatical leave to enable him to work on this book and for allowing him full access to RFE/RL's marvellous research facilities. He would also like to thank all his colleagues in the RFE/RL research departments and broadcast services who helped him with his numerous queries or provided photographs, and to express his admiration for their expertise and the work they are doing.

He also wishes to thank Bob Farrell and David Allis, the editors of the invaluable *Report on the USSR*, and Iwanka Rebet and the RFE/RL library staff, especially Inna Burger and her colleagues in the Current Information Service, and Elena Schluter in Radio Liberty's Red Archive Periodical Section.

Victor Swoboda is greatly indebted to the Director of the School of Slavonic and East European Studies of the University of London, Professor Michael Branch, for facilitating his research for the present work; and he is also very grateful to the School's Librarian, Dr J. E. O. Screen, and his staff, for their help. He is likewise greatly obliged to the staff of the British Library, in particular to Dr Christine Thomas, and to the Librarian and staff of the School of Oriental and African Studies Library, University of London.

Both authors express their warmest gratitude to Dr Edward Kasinec of the New York Public Library, Ms Tamara Maripuu of Estonian House, London, and Mr Endel Aruja, Librarian and Archivist of the Tartu Institute, Toronto, for their very kind help.

We also wish to thank our editors for their understanding when deadlines slipped by, and for their help and encouragement.

And of course, we would also like to acknowledge our immense debt to our respective wives Petrusia and Rita for their help, support and patient forbearance; Bohdan Nahaylo also hopes that one day when Maksym and Emma see this book they will understand why daddy was always so busy working.

Introduction

One of the most dramatic developments since Mikhail Gorbachev ushered in the policies of *glasnost'* and 'democratization' has been the way in which the nationalities problem in the Soviet Union has not only forced its way into the open but put the Kremlin's entire new course to the test. This has helped to clear up the misconception that the Soviet Union and Russia are the same thing, and has brought home the fact that the USSR is the world's largest multinational state and the last of the great empires.

But just how serious is the Soviet Union's nationalities problem today? Is it simply a case of groups of extremist nationalists jeopardizing Gorbachev's plans for reform? Or is the Soviet Union finally going through a crisis of empire with all that that entails? How long has the nationalities problem actually been there, and how has the Soviet state managed to keep its vast heterogeneous domain intact for so long? What are the implications of the present national unrest and what choices does the Kremlin face? These are the sorts of questions that will be examined in this book.

Today, more than ever, some understanding of the dynamics of the national question in the Soviet Union is crucial for all those who are interested in what the Soviet system represents, what is going on within it, and where it is headed. About 50 per cent of the Soviet Union's 285·7 million inhabitants are non-Russians, and both the non-Russian nations of the USSR and the Russians themselves are currently experiencing vigorous national revivals. Furthermore, as the Kremlin itself now admits, the national problem touches on the other major areas of concern: economic, socio-political and military.

To appreciate what is happening in the Soviet Union today, things have to be seen in some sort of perspective. This is what the authors of this study have sought to do. They also wanted to fill what until now was a gap in the literature on the USSR: although there has been no shortage of works examining specific aspects of the national question in the Soviet Union, no general history of this issue was available in the English language.

One of the reasons for this is the daunting scale and complexity of the subject. After all, apart from the 15 major nationalities in the Soviet Union which have their own fully-fledged republics, there are dozens of other ethnic groups, both large and small. The languages, customs and histories of these peoples vary immensely. Furthermore, apart from the problems facing the non-Russian peoples as a result of Moscow's rule and Russian predominance, some of them also have long-standing 'national problems' with non-Russian neighbours or national minorities.

This book traces the history of the national problem from the inception of the Soviet state up to the era of *glasnost'* and *perestroika*. It concentrates on the relationship between the Russians and the non-Russians, which is what Lenin, Stalin and their successors have always considered to be the essence of the matter.

The age-old problem of Russian imperial ambitions and colonial expansion, something that was obvious enough to Marx and Lenin, has not always been so readily understood in more recent times in the West. Although there has been considerable sympathy for the Czechs and Slovaks, the Poles and the Afghans, the disparate non-Russian peoples within the USSR were for years virtually written off and a deaf ear turned to their protests and appeals. To refer only recently, for instance, to the Balts as 'captive nations' was generally regarded as betraying a Cold War mentality.

Although in some respects the Soviet empire resembles a classic colonial power, it also has its own peculiarities. The 'ruling' Russian nation has itself suffered the ravages of communist rule, and its living standards are not as high as those of some of the subject peoples. But few Russians over the years have questioned the political and economic price of empire. Indeed, the argument has frequently been reversed into complaints about how 'ungrateful' the non-Russians are in view of 'everything that the Russians have done for them'.

The Russians, in sheer numbers, pose problems for their smaller neighbours. To put this in some sort of perspective, a parallel can be drawn with Germany. Many Europeans, both East and West, still fear the prospect of a reunified Germany. But the united German state would have about 77 million inhabitants, while, by contrast, the Russian population in the USSR (145 million in 1989) is almost twice as large as that of the two Germanies combined. Under the tsars, the Russians did not conceal their dominance; nowadays it has to be disguised. All the same, the problem of Russian great-power chauvinism is real enough for the non-Russians. Moreover, some 25 million Russians have flooded into the Ukraine, the Baltic republics, Moldavia and Soviet Central Asia. With relatively few exceptions, they have not bothered to learn the local languages and have tended to regard these 'sovereign' republics as extensions of the Russian Motherland.

In order to bring out the nature of the grievances, demands and aspirations that the non-Russians have voiced over the years, the authors have focused on manifestations of national dissent and cultural assertiveness.

The authors tell the story from the perspective of the non-Russians who were first incorporated into the new Soviet state by force, and then offered promises, concessions and inducements designed to win their loyalty and to dispel their distrust and resentment. They show how the Soviet failure to live up to these proclaimed guarantees, their violation of this implicit 'national contract', and the resulting glaring gap between theory and practice in the Soviet approach to federation and managing national relations, have remained at the heart of the national problem.

The book examines what has gone on all these years behind the Soviet facade of unity and the pretence that the USSR was a harmonious multi-national socialist society based on 'free and equal' partnership in which all forms of national oppression and discrimination were supposedly outlawed. It describes the way in which an empire masquerading as a new model society crushed resistance, imposed alien values and even an alien language on its subject peoples, and left many of them fearing about their very survival as distinct nations.

All this was done in the name of progress, and the Soviet government routinely points to, say, the achievements in Soviet Central Asia where living standards have been raised to a level unmatched in any of the neighbouring Islamic states. Undoubtedly, significant advances have been made, but as this book shows, there is another, less flattering, side to the story. What has been the cost of this imposed progress in terms of human lives and human suffering? In terms of the destruction of traditional life styles; of the assault on national cultures, religions and customs; of the lasting damage done to the environment? Surely what the non-Russians themselves feel on this matter – whether gratitude or colonial ingratitude – is ultimately what counts.

The authors have drawn on a broad range of sources, including the Soviet press, unofficial or *samizdat* writings, interviews with former Soviet dissidents, and the best of the Western literature on the subject. Needless to say, there are still some aspects of the Soviet nationalities problem that are shrouded in secrecy or about which little information is available. Without claiming to have produced an exhaustive study, the authors hope to have sketched the main contours of this tricky subject and to have shed light on a problem that is likely to be around for some time.

Although this book represents a joint effort, the division of labour between the two authors should be mentioned. Victor Swoboda wrote the first eight chapters dealing with developments until the death of Stalin, while Bohdan Nahaylo wrote the remaining ten chapters covering the post-Stalin years.

Bohdan Nahaylo, Munich
and Victor Swoboda, London
1990

A Note on Dates

Under the tsars and the Provisional Government of 1917, the Russian empire followed the Julian calendar, which had been abandoned in much of Europe in 1582, and in England in 1752. In February 1918, the new Bolshevik government changed over to the Gregorian calendar, thus bringing their territories into line with the rest of Europe. As there was a discrepancy of 12 days between the two calendars, 10 February that year was followed by 23 February. In this book, all dates up to and including 10 February 1918 are based on the Julian calendar then in operation (Old Style), and all dates from 23 February on the Gregorian calendar (New Style).

A Note on Names

Proper and geographic names as well as titles of publications in Notes and Bibliography written originally in the Cyrillic alphabet are transliterated following the Library of Congress and the British Library system, with the ligatures and diacritical marks omitted. Byelorussian ў (ŭ) is, however, rendered as *w*. Names of Turkic and Caucasian origin are mostly transliterated from their Russian versions as they occur in the sources, though in some instances Turkic forms are also given. For some well-known names, established or traditional English forms are used. Names from languages written in the Latin alphabet (Estonian, Latvian and Lithuanian) are reproduced in their original spelling, though diacritical marks are mostly omitted.

Some hints as to an approximate pronunciation of words transliterated from Cyrillic may be useful. Vowels: *a* is pronounced as in 'father', *o* as in 'for', *u* as *oo* in 'boot', *y* as in 'myth'; *e* mostly as in 'bed', but after vowels, initially in a word, and in "*e* it is pronounced as *ye* in 'yes'; *i* as *ee* in 'meet', but after another vowel (including another *i*) mostly as *y* in 'boy', and before other vowels as *y* in 'you'. Consonants: on the whole as in English; *g* always as in 'go', *s* as in 'see'. Combined characters: *sh* as in 'shoe', *ch* as in 'cheese', *kh* as *ch* in Scottish 'loch', *zh* as *s* in 'pleasure'. Hence, *dzh* is pronounced as *j* in 'John', e.g. 'Tadzhik', though the same *j* sound is spelt as *j* rather than *dzh* in the traditional English form 'Azerbaijan'. The apostrophe ' represents the Cyrillic sign of 'softness' ('palatalization').

The chief differences between the modern transliteration system adopted here and the older, 'British', system still used in some books and in the press are as follows: *ii* = *iy* or, if final, *-y*; *i* before or after other vowels mostly = *y*; and often *e* = *ye* if thus pronounced.

Abbreviations used in the text and the Notes

AFP	Agence France Press
AP	Associated Press
APN	Novosti Press Agency
AS	Arkhiv samizdata, published by Radio Liberty, Munich
ASSR	Autonomous Soviet Socialist* Republic

*In the early Soviet period, in this and all other names containing these two words, they were in the reverse order: 'Socialist Soviet'.

CC	Central Committee
CDSP	*The Current Digest of the Soviet Press*
CEC	Central Executive Committee (i.e. government)
Cheka	Extraordinary Commission for Struggle with Counter-revolution and Sabotage, *also* ChK, and VChK (All-Russia *etc.*) (1918–22)
CP	Communist Party
CP(B)	Communist Party (Bolsheviks)
CP(B)B	Communist Party (Bolsheviks) of Byelorussia
CP(B)U	Communist Party (Bolsheviks) of the Ukraine, *also* CPU (1918–52)
CPSU	Communist Party of the Soviet Union (1952–)
CPSU(B)	Communist Party of the Soviet Union (Bolsheviks) (1925–52)
CPT	Communist Party of Turkestan
CPU	Communist Party of the Ukraine (1952–)
Gulag	Chief Administration of [Corrective Labour] Camps
KGB	Committee for State Security (security police) (1953–); its previous incarnations were: Cheka, OGPU, NKVD (from 1934) and MGB.
MGB	Ministry for State Security (1946–53)
MVD	Ministry of Internal Affairs (1946–)
NEP	New Economic Policy
NKVD	People's Commissariat of Internal Affairs (1917–46)
OGPU	Joint State Political Directorate (1922–34)
RAD	Radio Free Europe Research and Analysis Department, Munich
RCP(B)	Russian Communist Party (Bolsheviks), *also* RCP (1918–25)
RFER	Radio Free Europe Research, Munich
RL	Radio Liberty Research Bulletin (since January 1989, *Report on the USSR*, Munich)
RSDLP	Russian Social Democratic Labour Party (1898–1912)
RSDLP(B)	Russian Social Democratic Labour Party (Bolsheviks) (1912–18)
RSFSR	Russian Soviet Federative Socialist Republic
SSR	Soviet Socialist Republic
TASS	Telegraph Agency of the Soviet Union
UPI	United Press International
USSR	Union of Soviet Socialist Republics
VSKhSON	All-Russian Social-Christian Union for the Liberation of the People

PART ONE

PART ONE

1

Nations of the Russian Empire

'Russia' and the 'Soviet Union': for many in the West, including journalists, teachers and politicians who should know better, the two terms are still more or less synonymous. Today, even after all the national unrest that has been in the headlines since Mikhail Gorbachev took over and *glasnost'* was inaugurated, ignorance and confusion about the nature of the Soviet multinational state still abounds. Just how 'Russian' is the Soviet Union? What proportion of the Soviet population is composed of non-Russians and how have they fared? Is the Soviet Union an empire or an exemplary experiment in building a harmonious multi-ethnic society on socialist principles? Just what precisely is the 'nationalities question' which the Soviet Union inherited from the Russian empire, and which it still claimed to have solved, but which plagues it to this very day?

The Soviet Union is the world's largest multinational state. It is structured as a federation of 15 Soviet Socialist Republics (SSRs); these are also referred to as Union republics, underlining the fact that they are the constituent entities forming the Soviet Union. Each Union republic has the right to free secession from the USSR, a guarantee that is enshrined both in the USSR Constitution and in those of each Union republic. Two of them, the Ukrainian and the Byelorussian SSRs, are members of the United Nations both in their own right, *and* as constituent parts of the USSR.

The Soviet republics are constituted along ethnic lines. Ethnic differences among the major nations comprising the Soviet Union are considerable. At one end of the scale, there are the three members of the East Slavonic group, Russians, Ukrainians and Byelorussians, whose languages originate from Common Slavonic and are related in much the same way as the three Romance languages of the Iberian peninsula, Castilian Spanish, Portuguese and Catalan. In Moldavia, to the south-west of the Ukraine, the Moldavian language differs less from the neighbouring Romanian, which is a descendant of Latin, than does, say, the Yorkshire dialect from the English spoken in the south of England. Then there are the two Baltic languages, Lithuanian and Latvian, more different from Russian than Danish is from English. Even more different still is Armenian in Transcaucasia. Although an Indo-European language like all those mentioned so far, it has no close relatives.

Tadzhik, the language of the republic of the same name in Central Asia, is another member of the Indo-European family and first cousin to Persian in Iran to the west across the border. There are also languages belonging to other families – the Altaic family, which includes closely related members of the Turkic group: Azeri Turkish or Azerbaijani of Transcaucasia and Uzbek, Kazakh, Turkmen and Kirghiz of Central Asia; Estonian, which belongs to the Finnic branch of the Uralic family and is mutually intelligible with Finnish to the north across the water; and Georgian, another Transcaucasian language, forming, together with some neighbouring minor languages, the Caucasian family, to which Basque may well be related.

The Soviet ethnic mosaic is not limited to the 15 national groups just mentioned: there are several dozen other nationalities which either possess no territorial unit or have one whose status is below that of a Union republic. Half a dozen of these nationalities have populations of between one and two million, and one, the Tatars, number over six million. Despite this, the Tatars have not been granted the status of a Union republic, even though the smallest of the nationalities with their own Union republic, the Estonians, have barely one million.

Since World War II, the population of the USSR has been rising steadily, from 209 million in 1959 to 242 million in 1970, 262 million in 1979, and 286 million in 1989; extrapolations to the year 2000 show figures around the 300 million mark. But the rates of growth vary among nationalities; thus, between 1979 and 1989 the average annual growth among the Russians was 0·55 per cent, while the Moslem nationalities averaged 2·83 per cent, so that the percentage of Russians in the Soviet Union declined from 54·65 per cent in 1959 to 50·8 per cent in 1989, and is likely to drop below 47 per cent by the year 2000. (See p. 206 below.) The USSR's dominant Russian nation, therefore, is only barely a majority nation at present.

The Eastern Slavs

The Russians, Ukrainians and Byelorussians, who now comprise about 70 per cent of the USSR's total population, constitute the eastern branch of the Slavs. From the first century AD, they went through a series of migrations and tribal and quasi-state formations, as well as invasions and subjugations by more powerful neighbours. By the early ninth century, the Varangians had arrived from Scandinavia. They were the same Viking Norsemen familiar as the Normans, who established the Scandinavian Duchy of Normandy around the same time.

The Varangian Prince Riurik settled in Novgorod, or Novgorod the Great, south of the Gulf of Finland, which became the first Varangian-Russian centre in 862. Its area included both Slavonic tribes, the Russian Slovenians, the Byelorussian Krivichians, and Finnic ones, the Ves' and the Vod'. Varangian colonists from Novgorod, Askol'd and Dir, founded the Kiev

Principality, halfway along the trading waterway between the Gulf of Finland and the Bosphorus. This principality, whose main population was the Ukrainian Slavonic tribe, Polianians, became the centre of a whole group of principalities extending over a large area of eastern Europe, controlled from Kiev by the Riurik dynasty. In the earliest chronicle, this vast collection of principalities and ethnic groups was called 'Rus''. While the origin of this word is still controversial, it was distinguished both in Arabic and Greek sources from 'Slav', and, although both terms are often mentioned together, 'Rus' ' was identified with the Nordic Germanic 'Varangian' both by outside observers and by the local chronicler. Like their brethren in Normandy, whose Norse succumbed to Old French, the Varangian rulers soon began to speak the language of their Slavonic subjects.

Although Varangian Rus' offered a semblance of unity over a vast area, it was of a rather loose nature. In the ninth century, the Russian and Byelorussian principalities of the north were in the Scandinavian orbit and had originally paid tribute to the Varangians. The Ukrainian principalities of the south, meanwhile, were closer to Kiev and paid tribute to the Khazars. There was already then also a linguistic divide between the two areas.[1] As a result of its proximity to the Byzantine empire, however, Kiev was steadily permeated by Christian culture. In 988 it officially adopted Christianity, along with Old Bulgarian – or Old Macedonian – writing and religious literature, and went on to flourish as a centre of East Slavonic culture for several centuries.

Early Russian conquests
Moscow, 'Moskva', is first mentioned in a chronicle under 1147. Its name is of Finnic origin, and it was a fortified Russian outpost in a Finnic country. Its environs were still densely populated by Finnic peoples in prehistoric times, when the first Russian conquests took place; three tribes, the Ves', Meria and Muroma, are known to have been the victims, as pointed out by the eminent Soviet Marxist historian, M. Pokrovskii (1868–1932).[2]

Another major city of the future Muscovite state was Nizhnii ('Lower') Novgorod, now Gor'kii, on the Volga. It was originally the capital of the Mordvin people, who were also Finnic, and was destroyed by the joint forces of three Russian principalities – Suzdal', Riazan' and Murom – in 1172; this was followed by a two-century war against the Mordvins, in the final stages of which the forces of the growing Moscow principality also took part.[3] The conquest and assimilation of a considerable number of Finnic peoples (only some of which have been mentioned here) over the course of half a millennium was an important element in the formation of the Russian people.

With the invasion of the Mongols under Batu Khan (grandson of Genghis Khan) in 1237–40, Kiev ceased to be a renowned centre of Christian culture, an emporium of trade, and a city resplendent with ecclesiastical art and architecture. The lands of the Eastern Slavs remained without a focus of authority for a long period, as the power of Novgorod the Great was weakened by internal dissensions. Gradually, three principalities in the Russian north-east, Vladimir, Suzdal' and Rostov, emerged as a new centre of political power in the region. For two centuries, however, its princes had to pay tribute to the Khan of the Golden Horde and to receive their titles from him; and it was in this period that a succession of astute princes in Moscow won for themselves the favour of the Khan and set about annexing piecemeal the towns and territories of neighbouring principalities. The process began with the incorporation of the town of Kolomna and ended with the establishment of the Muscovite state.

Moscow first came into prominence in the fourteenth century, and in 1380 it was able to defeat the Mongols; from then onwards the political prestige of Muscovy increased as rapidly as that of the Golden Horde declined. Moscow grew in importance as a trade centre on a west–east route; its population is estimated to have reached several tens of thousands by the end of the century, at a time when there were perhaps only three cities in Europe numbering a hundred thousand. Within the Russian ethnic area, only the city-republics of Novgorod the Great and Pskov were larger than Moscow. Novgorod's far-flung colonial area extended north-east to the Arctic Ocean and beyond the Urals, roughly to the River Ob'. Moscow's first serious clash with Novgorod occurred in 1397–98, when Moscow seized from Novgorod the Dvina and Zavoloch'ie regions, which had been the chief source of furs in which Novgorod had held virtual monopoly for the whole of Europe. M. Pokrovskii characterized it as 'a colonial war in great style, in which Moscow acted with considerable circumspection, apparently intending to secure firmly her possession of the seized lands'.[4] Although this war ended with Novgorod recovering them, Moscow finally took possession of the Dvina region in 1471, and in 1494 conquered Novgorod itself and abolished its *Veche*, or popular assembly.

The city of Pskov, originally Novgorod's dependency, soon outgrew its metropolis and became an independent republic in 1348. From the end of the century, however, it grew more and more dependent on Moscow to maintain its economic independence from the neighbouring Baltic German colonies. The process was a gradual one, and while the Pskov *Veche* and citizenry were often indignant at Moscow's refusal to honour their ancient rights and privileges, they were powerless to do anything about it. By the early seventeenth century its absorption was complete.

Two significant independent principalities in the Russian ethnic area remained: Tver', which was conquered in 1486 for refusing to submit into vassalage; and Riazan', which was annexed piecemeal between 1456 and 1520. Muscovite gains in the later sixteenth century were chiefly in the east. The Tatar khanates of Kazan' and Astrakhan' fell in the 1550s, after which Cossacks under Ermak penetrated into western Siberia, following the route of the Russian conquerors of Iugria in the fifteenth century, and took possession of the Nogai khanate of Sibir', which was to give its name to almost the whole of Asiatic Russia – Siberia.

The Russians' southern and western neighbours

After the disintegration of Kievan Rus', which was the first historical Ukrainian state,[5] the Ukrainian principalities of Galicia and Volhynia survived as independent states until the fourteenth century. Galicia was annexed by Poland in 1387, and Volhynia as well as Kiev, by Lithuania; in 1569, most Ukrainian lands came under Poland. From the beginning of the sixteenth century, Kiev revived as a major spiritual and cultural centre. For the next two centuries the Ukraine, which had benefited from its ties with the West, supplied many cultural and religious figures to Muscovy, long isolated from the rest of the Christian world.[6]

In 1648, Zaporozhian Cossacks, a Ukrainian martial brotherhood, described by Marx as a 'Christian Cossack republic', rebelled against Poland and sought help from Muscovy with which the Ukrainians shared the Greek Orthodox rite. In 1654 an agreement was concluded between the Zaporozhian Host and Moscow. The Ukraine's rights under the treaty were gradually reduced, and an attempt by Hetman Ivan Mazepa to break free was savagely crushed by Peter the Great in 1709 at Poltava. Its autonomy within the Russian empire was finally abolished in 1783. The 1793–96 partitions of Poland brought the remaining parts of the Ukraine under Russian rule. The nineteenth century was marked by strenuous efforts of the tsarist administration to Russify the non-Russian Slavs – Ukrainians, Byelorussians and Poles – in order to project an image of an imperial all-encompassing 'Russianness', which in the end proved unsuccessful. Galicia was the only major Ukrainian land never to have been under Russian imperial rule: it came under Austrian control in 1772 and, after the fall of Austria-Hungary in 1918, it proclaimed independence as a West Ukrainian Republic, but was seized by Poland after an armed struggle in June 1919.

Baltic tribes, the forbears of today's Lithuanians and Latvians, arrived in the region of modern Byelorussia during the last two millennia BC, pushing out or absorbing the indigenous Finno-Ugric tribes of Estonians and Livs. Until the fourth century AD, Lithuanians occupied much of the territory, but in the course of the fifth and sixth centuries they were pushed northwards or assimilated by the Byelorussians.

The Principality of Polotsk was the first Byelorussian state formation, ruled by one of Prince Riurik's men and inhabited by a tribe called the Krivichians. It was first mentioned in the chronicles under 980. In the second half of the eleventh and the first half of the twelfth century it struggled for political separation from Kiev. A feudal social order began to emerge in Lithuania in the early thirteenth century, and led to the establishment of the Grand Duchy

LATVIA ESTONIA

LITHUANIA

BYELO-
RUSSIA

UKRAINE

MOLDAVIA

⊞ Moscow

RUSSIAN SOVIET FEDERA

Ural Mts

GEORGIA

ARMENIA

AZERBAIJAN

KAZAKHSTAN

TURKMEN-
ISTAN

UZBEK-
ISTAN

KIRGHIZIA

TADZHIKISTAN

0 500 0

THE GROWTH OF RUSSIA/USSR

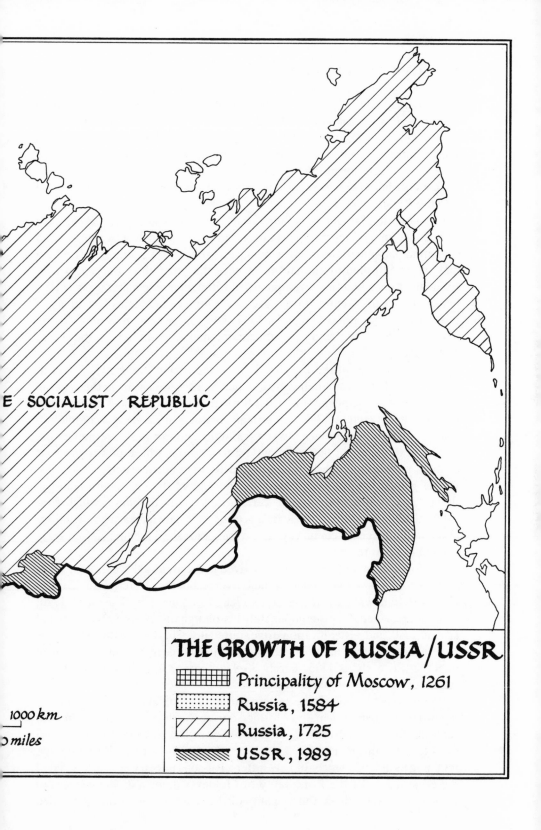

E SOCIALIST REPUBLIC

1000 km

0 miles

THE GROWTH OF RUSSIA/USSR

Principality of Moscow, 1261
Russia, 1584
Russia, 1725
USSR, 1989

of Lithuania and the founding of the capital Vilnius in 1323. Over these two centuries, Byelorussia and the Central Ukraine were incorporated into the Grand Duchy, whose official language became Byelorussian. The Grand Duchy entered into dynastic union with Poland in 1385, which was followed by political federation in 1569. In 1697, Polish became the official language. In the course of the 1772–96 partitions of Poland, Byelorussia was incorporated into the Russian empire.

In 1796, the Lithuanian ethnic lands were also absorbed, except for Lithuania Minor (comprising certain western areas taken over by Prussia) and the Lithuanian-inhabited areas around Königsberg (now Kaliningrad), which had been controlled by the Germans since the fifteenth century. It was in Lithuania Minor that the development of Lithuanian into a literary language began in the early eighteenth century and continued at Vilnius University in the early nineteenth century. The Russian administration countered the national revival by banning Lithuanian-language printing in the Latin alphabet.

After the arrival of the Eastern Slavs in the region, the Latvians had to protect their lands from their constant incursions as well as from those of the Vikings. But at the beginning of the thirteenth century, a new threat arose from Germany, and by 1290 the German conquest of Latvia was completed. The population were reduced to serfs, and the country was governed by the newly created class of land-owning German barons whose power survived through subsequent Polish, Swedish and Russian conquests until 1917–18. Russia gained control over Latvia by the end of the eighteenth century, though the local nobility kept a certain degree of autonomy, which contributed to the survival of non-Russian culture. Despite increasing restrictions in the late nineteenth century, the Latvian national awakening started early enough to resist them.

The forbears of today's Estonians arrived in the area 5,000 years ago. Their early history was similar to that of the Latvians, but they were subdued by the Germans somewhat earlier, around 1220. Conquered by Russia in 1720, Estonia preserved its autonomous status, although this began to be restricted around 1840, and a Russification drive started in 1880. Despite this, Estonians were a fully literate nation by 1900 (the first book in Estonian had been published as early as 1535, barely 80 years after Gutenberg's invention), conscious of their national identity.

Present-day Moldavia is the eastern part of old Moldavia, which was one of the two Romanian principalities formed during the thirteenth and fourteenth centuries and originally the Roman province of Dacia. In the sixteenth and seventeenth centuries it entered into a vassalage treaty with the Porte, though retaining its independence. In 1812, after a Russo–Turkish war, Turkey ceded the eastern part of the Principality of Moldavia, known as Bessarabia, to Russia. Karl Marx denied the legality of the cession, noting that the ceded territory was not actually within the Ottoman empire,[7] while in 1890, Engels wrote:

> Finland is Finnish, Poland is Polish, Bessarabia is Romanian. There is no question of bringing together various populations, dispersed and related, who could be called Russian. This is brutal and undisguised conquest of foreign territories, this is purely and simply a theft.[8]

The Transcaucasus

Georgians have lived in the Caucasus since at least the second millennium B C. Their first state was the kingdom of Colchis on the Black Sea in the sixth century B C, and in the third century B C, the kingdom of Kartli (or Iberia) united most of Georgia. In the late first century A D both kingdoms were conquered by the Romans. Christianity came to eastern Georgia about 330, and to western Georgia about 520. From 523 till the end of the ninth century, Georgia was under Persian and then Arab domination. During a period of independence which lasted until invasion by Genghis Khan's lieutenants in 1235, Georgia enjoyed economic advance and a cultural flowering. Mongol hegemony lasted until the fourteenth century, and after a short respite and recovery the country was reduced to ruins by Tamerlane's eight invasions between 1386 and 1403.

After a low ebb in its fortunes, which included being a battlefield between Turkey and Iran early in the sixteenth century, Georgia re-established its independence in the middle of the eighteenth century. In 1782, to secure its position against Turkey and Iran, Irakli II asked Catherine II to place the kingdom of Kartli-Kakhetia under Russian protection, and a treaty of friendship was signed the following year. However, when Georgia suffered yet another disastrous invasion by Iran, in which the capital Tbilisi was burnt down, no Russian help was forthcoming. Instead, on 12 December 1801, Alexander II unilaterally issued a decree annexing Kartli-Kakhetia to the Russian empire. The remaining Georgian lands were incorporated as a result of Russo–Turkish wars in 1811, 1828–29 and 1878.

Armenians arrived in the Caucasus before the fifth century B C. A united Armenian state existed between 190 B C and 428 A D; its power reached its height in the first half of the first century B C, when it extended as far as today's Syria and Lebanon. Later, however, it became a client state of the Romans. Christianity was adopted in 301. After a long period in which the country was disputed between Byzantium and, in turn, Persians, Arabs and Turks, an autonomous Armenia was re-established in the tenth century. It prospered only until the mid-eleventh century, however, when it fell to the Turks. Before long Armenia became the scene of struggle between Ottoman Turks and Persians, who finally divided it between themselves in 1639. The Russians conquered Persian Armenia in 1828.

Turkic tribes migrated into Azerbaijan in the tenth to twelfth centuries AD, and by the fifteenth century it was inhabited by a people of Irano-Turkish origin. Its inhabitants being Shiite, the Azerbaijani khanate was more closely linked with Persia than with their Turkish kin. Peter the Great defeated Persia and annexed the Derbent and Baku regions of Azerbaijan in 1724. Though later regained by Persia for a dozen years, the khanate was finally ceded to Russia in 1813. In the nineteenth century, there was no Russian interference in the traditional Islamic way of life in the countryside. The last three decades were marked by the rise of national consciousness and the emergence of the Moslem Left. In the early twentieth century, political organizations arose; the most important of these was Musavat, with its programme of Moslem unity and independence of Moslem states.

Kazakhstan and Central Asia

In Kazakhstan, Turkic tribes appeared in the eighth century, and Mongols settled there from the thirteenth; the Kazakhs emerged in the fifteenth century as a mixture of the two peoples. Around 1456, having broken off from the declining Golden Horde, they formed three Hordes, Great, Middle and Little. In 1731 the Little Horde submitted itself to the advancing Russians, but from 1783 to 1797 it rose against them. In 1835 the Kazakhs rebelled again, and in 1916 there was a major revolt against conscription.

The varied population of Turkestan (Central Asia) was formed by successive waves of Turkic and Mongolian peoples, while Iranian ancestors of the Tadzhiks are known from historical record to have lived there as early as the sixth to fourth centuries BC. In the eighth and ninth centuries AD the area fell under the influence of Islam. Arabic civilization flowered there in the Middle Ages; Samarkand, a city now two and a half millennia old, became the capital of Tamerlane's empire, and Bukhara the centre of learning and the religious focus of the region. With a shift in trade routes in the fifteenth and sixteenth centuries, this Central Asian Islamic civilization entered a long period of decline, disintegrating into feuding principalities until the Bukharan emirate and the Khivan and Kokand khanates emerged as the major political units. Russia conquered Turkestan between 1865 and 1884. No policy of Russification was pursued in the area, but resentment was caused by large-scale Slav immigration into the region. As in Kazakhstan, there were revolts against conscription in various parts of Turkestan in 1916.

The nineteenth century and the fall of the empire

By the nineteenth century, Russia had amassed a vast colonial empire, chiefly by means of armed conquest. In Europe, meanwhile, national liberation movements were flourishing as the Ottoman empire crumbled. They were echoed in various ways among the subject nations of the Russian empire. Here, the tsarist regime's increasingly oppressive policies, aimed at

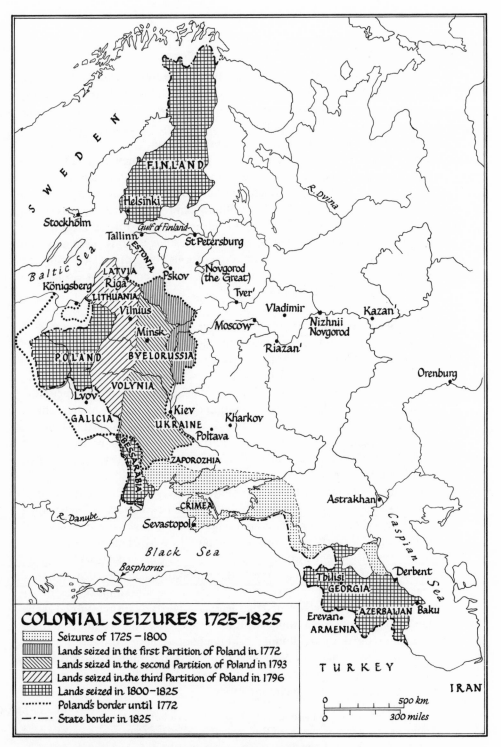

COLONIAL SEIZURES 1725–1825

Seizures of 1725 – 1800

Lands seized in the first Partition of Poland in 1772

Lands seized in the second Partition of Poland in 1793

Lands seized in the third Partition of Poland in 1796

Lands seized in 1800 – 1825

.... Poland's border until 1772

—·— State border in 1825

0   500 km

0   300 miles

COLONIAL SEIZURES 1725–1825

destroying national cultures, provoked ever greater resentment and the growth of national consciousness and resistance. This ultimately led to the formation of political parties and other patriotic organizations among the non-Russian nations. The 1905 revolution briefly removed the worst national oppression but within two years reaction set in again.[9]

The fall of tsarism in February 1917 offered exciting new opportunities to Russia's oppressed nations. Seeking national emancipation, they were sufficiently encouraged by the democratic transformation of Russia to entertain hopes for the emergence of a free multinational republic. Russia was still at war, however, and the Provisional Government used this as a pretext to prevaricate. Although unable to resist the restive nations' demands and forced to placate them with partial concessions, it kept on deferring the question of Russia's new structure to the decision of a constituent assembly to be convoked after the end of the war.

The Bolsheviks and the nations of the empire

Such was the situation at the time of the Bolshevik seizure of power under Lenin's leadership on 25 October 1917, after the Russian democratic interlude which lasted all of eight months. Every Soviet leader, from Stalin to Gorbachev, has derived his, and his Party and government's, legitimacy from Lenin. The same holds for the legitimation of the nationalities policy which, invoking the founder of the Soviet state, is usually described as the 'Leninist nationalities policy'. Lenin's Bolshevik Party and its antecedent, the Russian Social Democratic Labour Party (RSDLP), being Marxist, derived their tenets from the writings of Marx and Engels.

The domain of Marx and Engels's teaching was economics, and its mode of action was class struggle. The proletariat was seen as the revolutionary force uniting for common action across national borders; hence the International and its slogan, 'Workers of the world, unite!' With their preference for nations with an advanced working class, Marx and Engels did not produce an exhaustive or systematic treatment of the nationalities problem, though they frequently expressed their opinions on Russia's imperialist annexations of her neighbours. Thus, Engels opined that Russia 'could only be mentioned as the detainer of an immense amount of stolen property, which would have to be disgorged on the day of reckoning'.[10] Lenin quoted these words approvingly, spelling out that 'stolen property' meant oppressed nations.[11] In 1864, in his inaugural address to the International Working Men's Association (the First International) in London, Marx mentioned

> the shameless approval, demonstrative sympathy or idiotic indifference with which Europe's upper classes observed Russia's conquest of the Caucasian fastnesses and her murder of heroic Poland.[12]

The First Congress of Lenin's RSDLP in 1898 adopted a resolution proclaiming 'the right of nations to self-determination' in accordance with a resolution of the 1898 Congress of the Second International,[13] and at the Second Congress of the RSDLP in 1903 this right was included in the Party statutes. While defending the right to self-determination, however, Lenin advocated working-class unity of all nationalities and opposed the Polish socialists' demand for Poland's secession from Russia.[14] In 1903 Lenin narrowed his support for self-determination:

> As the party of the proletariat, the Social-Democratic Party considers it to be its positive and principal task to further the self-determination of the proletariat in each nationality rather than that of peoples or nations.[15]

Ten years later, still advocating the unity of proletarians of all nationalities in their revolutionary struggle for the overthrow of the monarchy, Lenin insisted in his *Theses on the National Question* that the Social Democrats should 'demand the settlement of the question of such secession only on the basis of a universal, direct and equal vote of the population of the given territory by secret ballot'.[16] This advocacy of a referendum on a secession proposal may have been inspired by the referendum on the secession of Norway from Sweden in 1905 where 99·5 per cent of the votes cast were for secession.[17] Lenin referred to Norway's secession by referendum as an example of a truly civilized and democratic way of implementing the self-determination of a nation on at least ten occasions between May 1913 and May 1917,[18] pointing out that

> it did away with the stupid and destructive friction, it strengthened the economic and political, the cultural and social *gravitation* of the two nations to each other, and strengthened the fraternal alliance between the workers of the two countries.[19]

A mere few months before the revolution, he repeated this view in his article *The Socialist Revolution and the Right of Nations to Self-determination*. Moreover, having been a resolute opponent of any federation (he used to view the choice as being merely between full separation or complete integration), he now had to admit that federation might turn out to be the only option, a half-way house on the way to 'full democratic centralism':

> The right of nations to self-determination implies exclusively the right to independence in the political sense, the right to free political separation from the oppressor nation. Specifically, this demand for political democracy implies complete freedom to agitate for secession and for a referendum on secession by the seceding nation. This demand, therefore, is not the equivalent of a demand for separation, fragmentation and the formation of small states. It implies only a consistent expression of struggle against all national oppression. The closer a democratic state system is to complete freedom to secede the less frequent and less ardent will the desire for separation be in practice, because big states afford indisputable advantages, both from the standpoint of economic progress and from

that of the interests of the masses and, furthermore, these advantages increase with the growth of capitalism. Recognition of self-determination is not synonymous with recognition of federation as a principle. One may be a determined opponent of that principle and a champion of democratic centralism but still prefer federation to national inequality as the only way to full democratic centralism. It was from this standpoint that Marx, who was a centralist, preferred even the federation of Ireland and England to the forcible subordination of Ireland to the English.[20]

Another European state which Lenin held up as an instance of an exemplary solution of the nationalities problem was Switzerland. He was enthusiastic about Switzerland's three official languages, the fact that referendum bills were printed in five languages, two of which (the Romansh dialects) were spoken by one per cent of the total population, and that Italian deputies often spoke French in the Swiss federal parliament. Hence Lenin concluded that if Russian ceased to be the sole official language the majority of the population would soon, for economic reasons, voluntarily adopt the language most advantageous for general communication[21] (obviously meaning Russian).

Lenin was consistent in his demand that the Social Democrats must proclaim the nationalities' right to self-determination while advising the workers against the use of that right, thus causing disagreements with many of his party comrades who found this formula misleading. Writing about the 'Revision of the Party programme' only 18 days before the start of the October Revolution, he spelt out his view:

Instead of the word self-determination, which has given rise to numerous misinterpretations, I propose the perfectly precise concept: 'the right to free secession'. After six months' experience of the 1917 Revolution, it is hardly possible to dispute that the party of the revolutionary proletariat of Russia, the party which uses the Great-Russian language, is obliged to recognize the right to secede. When we win power, we shall immediately and unconditionally recognize the right for Finland, the Ukraine, Armenia and any other nationality oppressed by tsarism (and the Great-Russian bourgeoisie). On the other hand, we do not at all favour secession. We want as vast a state, as close an alliance of the greatest possible number of nations who are neighbours of the Great Russians; we desire this in the interests of democracy and socialism, to attract into the struggle of the proletariat the greatest possible number of the working people of different nations . . . We want *free* unification; this is why we must recognize the right to secede (without freedom to secede, unification cannot be called free). The more so must we recognize the right of secession, because tsarism and the Great-Russian bourgeoisie have by their oppression left great bitterness and distrust of the Great Russians generally in the hearts of the neighbouring nations, and these must be eradicated *by deeds* and not by words . . .[22]

Lenin knew that even after a socialist revolution

National antipathies will not disappear so quickly: the hatred – and perfectly legitimate hatred – of an oppressed nation for its oppressor *will* last for a while; it will evaporate only *after* the victory of socialism and *after* the final establishment of completely democratic relations between nations.[23]

Lenin's early principles regarding the nations of the empire were thus not without their ambiguities; their practical application after the Bolsheviks' seizure of power will be seen in the subsequent chapters.

2

1917 Revolutions: The Empire Breaks Up

The fall of tsarism and the democratic revolution of February 1917 brought an upsurge of the spirit of freedom throughout the Russian empire, and in many of the non-Russian lands national councils, parliaments and autonomous national governments were soon set up. This was a process parallel to the creation of soviets (councils) in Russia, at first multi-party bodies, but in later months often dominated by Bolsheviks. Russians in non-Russian lands also organized soviets there. As early as March, an All-Ukrainian National Congress took place in Kiev with the prominent participation of Ukrainian Socialist Revolutionaries and Social Democrats. It created the Ukrainian Central Rada (Council) and demanded from the Provisional Government in Petrograd far-reaching autonomy for the Ukraine, but the latter insisted that all such demands were to be decided by the Constituent Assembly, which was to be elected only after the end of the war.

In Byelorussia a similar Rada was established in July 1917; National Councils were set up in Estonia, Latvia, Lithuania, Georgia, Armenia and Azerbaijan; Kurultais (Moslem councils) in the Crimea, where Tatars comprised a considerable part of the population, and Bashkiria, west of the Urals; Alash-Orda in Kazakhstan; Shuro-i-Islam in Turkestan; the Alliance of United Mountaineers of the Caucasus (a collective designation for a number of ethnic groups in the region); and the Cossack councils, with their umbrella organization, the Council of the Alliance of the Cossack Hosts. In their majority, these bodies demanded greater freedom for their nations to manage their own affairs and the transformation of the unitary Russian state into a federation of nations possessing equal rights.

The promise of sovereignty

Within a week of the October Revolution, Lenin's government issued the 'Declaration of the Rights of the Peoples of Russia' proclaiming 'the policy of a voluntary and honest alliance/union of the peoples of Russia' and enunciating the following four principles:

1. The equality and sovereignty of the peoples of Russia.
2. The right of the peoples of Russia to free self-determination including secession and formation of independent states.

3. The abolition of all national and national-religious privileges and restrictions of any kind.
4. The free development of national minorities and ethnic groups populating the territory of Russia.[1]

It is unfortunate or convenient, depending on one's point of view, that the original Russian word used here, *soiuz*, has two very different meanings: 'union', as in *Sovetskii Soiuz*, 'The Soviet Union', and 'alliance', as in *Sviashchennyi Soiuz*, 'The Holy Alliance'.

In a speech delivered on 22 November, Lenin's reaction to the rapid dissolution of the Russian empire foreshadowed future policy:

> We now see a national movement in the Ukraine and we say that we stand unconditionally for the Ukrainian people's complete and unlimited freedom . . . We are going to tell the Ukrainians that as Ukrainians they can go ahead and arrange their life as they see fit. But we are going to stretch out a fraternal hand to the Ukrainian workers and tell them that together with them we are going to fight against their bourgeoisie and ours. Only a socialist alliance of the working people of all countries can remove all ground for national persecution and strife.[2]

This last paragraph encapsulates the strategy pursued in the following few years in order to instal Bolshevik rule in most of the newly independent non-Russian republics. In the eyes of the Russian Bolsheviks, the only genuine spokesmen for the Ukrainian (Byelorussian, Latvian, Finnish, Armenian etc.) workers were the local Bolsheviks, who belonged to regional organizations of the Russian Bolshevik Party. Their common fight against the local 'bourgeoisie', i.e. the non-Bolshevik government which had been set up as the local people 'arranged their life as they saw fit', would necessitate military aid from the Moscow Bolsheviks and result in its overthrow and the installation of a Soviet Bolshevik government in its place.

The leaders of Bolshevik organizations in non-Russian lands were often (though by no means always) ready to follow Lenin's line. In December 1917, while Lithuania was under German occupation and struggling for independence, the Lithuanian Bolshevik V. Mickevičus-Kapsukas declared from Russia that

> we recognize the right of self-determination for all nations, but this does not mean independence . . . We have in mind the needs of nations and of the Lithuanian proletariat. Since in an independent Lithuania these needs may suffer, we reject independence and fight against it.[3]

An independent Ukraine

Two days after the October Revolution, the Kiev Russian Bolshevik-dominated soviets in Kiev had resolved to recognize the Soviet government in Petrograd, and attempted to seize power from the deposed Provisional

Government's local agencies. They were thwarted by the troops of the Central Rada, which numbered some 18,000, and on 7 November the Rada declared its non-recognition of the Petrograd government as 'central', and proclaimed the Ukrainian People's Republic with itself as the sole state power. Its declared intention was not to secede from the Russian Republic, but to strive toward transforming it into a federation of equal nations.[4]

On 16 December the Petrograd government adopted a manifesto to the Ukrainian people, written by Lenin, in which

> . . . the Council of People's Commissars – the Socialist government of Russia – reaffirms that the right to self-determination belongs to all nations oppressed by tsarism and the Great-Russian bourgeoisie, up to and including the right of these nations to secede from Russia. Accordingly we, the Council of People's Commissars, recognize the People's Ukrainian Republic, and its right to secede from Russia or enter into a treaty with the Russian Republic on federal or similar relations between them.

But the same manifesto also expressed displeasure with the Ukrainian Central Rada's policies, particularly its non-cooperation with the Petrograd government's campaign against the Don Cossacks, whose council and government had refused to recognize the new Soviet government's power over the Don Lands. The Cossacks regarded themselves as ethnically different from the Russians and demanded their right to national self-determination; their elected leader, *Ataman*, General Kaledin, declared that 'the establishment of order in the Don is a matter for the Don Cossacks', and 'As regards the relation of the Don to Russia at large, we recognize the necessity for ties with her, with the broadest autonomy or even more – independence for the Don.'[5]

The Ukrainian Rada refused to permit free passage of Russian Red Guards through Ukrainian territory, and disarmed those who were found there. This was deemed to be sufficient reason for issuing a 48-hour ultimatum and then invading the Ukraine in order to instal a Bolshevik government there, in clear contradiction to the first part of the manifesto quoted above.[6] The Central Rada was in fact much more representative of the Ukrainian people's wishes than the Bolshevik government in Russia, but this fact did not seem to have been taken into account by Petrograd when deciding to invade. Nor was Lenin ignorant of the Rada's standing in the Ukraine; he himself admitted several months later that in the elections to the Constituent Assembly in November 1917 a two-to-one majority in the Ukraine voted for the Ukrainian socialist candidates as against the Russian ones,[7] while the Bolsheviks themselves failed to get a majority in those elections.

The invasion started from the north-east. In Kharkov and in a number of cities and towns of the industrial Donbass where the Russian minority was stronger, Russian Bolshevik Soviets seized power. On 30 December 1917 they established a rival government of the Ukrainian People's Republic in Kharkov. The Ukraine was to be in a federal relationship with the Russian Soviet Republic, and subject to all decrees and laws of the latter. A massive two-month offensive by Soviet Russian troops together with local Bolshevik Red Guards, composed almost exclusively of ethnic Russian workers, ended in February 1918 with nearly the whole Ukraine occupied by the Bolshevik forces and the Soviet regime 'established by means of bayonets' in the Ukrainian capital, as the commander of the Bolshevik forces reported to Lenin.[8]

In Byelorussia, the national Rada convoked a Byelorussian National Congress on 28 December 1917 which proclaimed the autonomy of Byelorussia. The Russian Bolshevik troops dispersed the Congress, but the delegates gathered again to finish their work under the protection of the Minsk railway workers, and elected an Executive Committee; the leadership then went underground. Supported by Russian troops, Soviet rule was set up in Minsk.[9] An uprising against it in January 1918 was unsuccessful, but Soviet rule was swept away on 8 February by the advancing Germans. The Rada proclaimed the independence of the Byelorussian People's Republic.

A voluntary federation of nations

Having re-annexed most European non-Russian lands (with the notable exception of Finland, whose independence it was judged to be expedient to recognize) on 12 January the Third All-Russia Congress of Soviets adopted a 'Declaration of the Rights of the Working and Exploited People' drafted by Lenin. It had this to say on Soviet Russia's national structure:

> 1. Russia is hereby proclaimed a Republic of Soviets of Workers', Soldiers' and Peasants' Deputies. All power, centrally and locally, is vested in these Soviets.
> 2. The Russian Soviet Republic is established on the principle of a free union of free nations, as a federation of Soviet national republics . . . [it is left] to the workers and peasants of each nation to decide independently at their own authoritative Congress of Soviets whether they wish to participate in the federal government and in the other federal Soviet institutions, and on what terms.[10]

The admirable principle of voluntariness did indeed work in the case of Finland, though in other cases bayonets facilitated the right decision.

In March 1918, the Bolshevik government signed the Treaty of Brest-Litovsk with the Central Powers. In order to extricate itself from World War I, it was forced to give up most of its outlying lands, and the first Soviet Constitution adopted by the Fifth All-Russia Congress of Soviets on 10 July incorporated the Declaration adopted by the Third Congress in January including the paragraphs on national structure just quoted above,[11] without elaborating them in any way.

Communist Parties from the borderland nations now found themselves in exile. The CP(B) of the Ukraine was formed at the Taganrog Conference, at the first stopover on the way into exile, in April. It was created by the Bolshevik government and Party functionaries from the Ukraine and was meant to be a section of the International in its own right. It was thus to be a party fully independent from the Russian CP(B) to appeal to the Ukrainian masses repelled by the hardly disguised Russian chauvinism of the latter. The CP(B)U soon incurred the disapproval of the Russian CP(B), its independence was revoked, and at its First Congress in Moscow that July, it resolved to struggle for the revolutionary unification of the Ukraine with Russia on the basis of proletarian centralism within the boundaries of the RSFSR.[12]

In October, a conference of communist organizations from the territories occupied by the Central Powers was held in Moscow, and Mickevičus-Kapsukas, referring to his advocacy of incorporating non-Russian lands into the RSFSR, declared:

> My thesis on federation with the RSFSR has met with objections from some comrades who drew attention to the fact that we stood on the threshold of a World Federation. I remain with my original opinion about the need of a federation with Soviet Russia since it is the only country which has liberated itself from capitalism while a World Federation is only being expected . . . For us communists there must be only one slogan: 'Long live the Communist Federative Soviet Republic!'

The conference passed a resolution declaring that 'the right of nations to self-determination is now becoming not only a Utopia but simply fiction since the class struggle between the proletariat and bourgeoisie splits all nations in a most implacable way'.[13]

The following month, as the Latvians, like the Lithuanians, still struggled for independence, the Communist Party of Latvia declared that the proletariat demanded that Latvia be joined to Russia. Latvia, it claimed, was linked to Russia by cultural and economic ties; the proletariat did not recognize any right of nations to self-determination since this merely strengthened bourgeois dictatorship. In consequence, the slogan of the Latvian proletariat was and had to be, the Soviet Republic of Latvia as an integral part of the RSFSR.[14]

'Independent' Soviet governments in re-occupied lands

The November Revolution in Germany allowed the Soviet Government to annul the Brest-Litovsk Treaty; as the German withdrawal started late in 1918, the Red Army re-occupied Byelorussia and liquidated the Byelorussian People's Republic. The Minsk District Revolutionary Committee submitted plans for the creation of a Byelorussian Commune to the North-Western Regional Committee of the RCP(B) (Byelorussia being within that region). Not surprisingly, they were rejected for reasons which V. Knorin, the then secretary of the latter, had expounded in a typically Bolshevik view of Byelorussia a few weeks previously:

> We consider that Byelorussians are not a nation, and that those ethnographic peculiarities which separate them from other Russians must be got rid of. Our task is not the creation of new nations but the destruction of old national partitions. But the Byelorussian movement represents indeed just such an erection of new national partitions which have hitherto not existed, and therefore Communists may on no account whatsoever take part in this movement.[15]

However, it was at this very juncture that the Central Committee of the RCP(B), while gratified by the eagerness of the non-Russian Bolsheviks to get their nations absorbed by Russia, nevertheless decided to turn them into sovereign Soviet Republics. This change of tactics was due to the need for a chain of buffer states for defence purposes, as was explained by A. Ioffe, a member and emissary of the Central Committee of the RCP(B), at a meeting of the Central Bureau of the Communist Party of Byelorussia in Minsk:

> In order not to repeat former mistakes when it was necessary for us [that is, Soviet Russia] to fight directly against German imperialism, we in the Central Committee decided to separate Soviet Russia from Europe with buffers, but in such a way that they should not become a barrier separating us. They will have [to contain] the coming imperialist thrust so that it would meet an obstacle and lose impetus.[16]

This change of tactics also reflected the experience of the previous year, which had shown how strong the idea of political independence among the non-Russian nations was. The Central Committee of the RCP(B) believed that the proclamation of national freedom for the non-Russians on the basis of their state sovereignty would cut the ground from under the feet of the independentist non-Russian parties who had accused the RCP(B) of simply continuing the ways of tsarist imperialism. It was no longer acceptable blatantly to get the Soviet regime 'established by means of bayonets'; from now on the Red Army's bayonets were to be used merely *pour encourager les autres* to establish 'their own' local Soviet governments. Lenin and Stalin spelt it out in their telegram to the Red Army's Commander-in-Chief I. Vacetis:

> 29/11 [1918]
>
> As our troops push on westwards and into the Ukraine, provisional regional Soviet governments are being formed to back up the Soviets in the localities. This has the advantage of depriving the Ukrainian, Lithuanian, Latvian and Estonian chauvinists of a chance to regard our troop movements as occupation and of creating a favourable situation for further advance. Otherwise our troops would have been in an impossible situation on occupied territory and the local population would not have met them as liberators. In view of the situation, please issue an order to the commanders of the corresponding units so that they render all possible support to

the provisional Soviet governments in Latvia, Estonia, the Ukraine and Lithuania, but, of course, only to the Soviet governments.

Lenin[17]

The non-Russian Bolshevik leaders, who a mere month or two earlier were ordered to condemn, and eagerly did condemn, the right of nations to self-determination, were now nonplussed by yet another sudden U-turn, as the chief of the CP of Lithuania, Mickevičus-Kapsukas, admitted 17 years later:

> Over many years we struggled against social-patriotism, separatism and Lithuania's independence; we rejected the slogan about the self-determination of nations up to secession as 'unacceptable'. Therefore for us it was not easy to adopt the decision about proclaiming a revolutionary government of an independent Lithuania . . . Soon a letter was received from Comrade Stalin on behalf of the CC RCP(B) in which he even more sharply stressed the idea that a workers' and peasants' government of Lithuania had to be created without delay. This had a decisive importance for us, although even then in our ranks there was no clear notion about the need immediately to create a revolutionary government of Lithuania.[18]

Thanks to this U-turn, the Minsk Revolutionary Committee, having been rebuffed by the district Russian Party comrades, was able to take its case to Moscow where the Central Committee of the RCP(B) was persuaded of the strength of Byelorussian national feeling. The demand for a Byelorussian government fitted in with the buffer zone plan, and on 25 December the committee informed Knorin's colleague in the administration of the North-Western Region, A. Miasnikov:

> The Central Committee of the Party for numerous reasons, which cannot be discussed now, has decided to agree with the Byelorussian comrades regarding establishing a Byelorussian Soviet government.[19]

Thus an independent Byelorussian Soviet Republic was born. Was the infant going to survive for long?

3

1919: Sovereign Soviet Republics

In November 1918, in the wake of the Red Army's westward and southward thrust, the creation of a series of sovereign Soviet republics began, a process which was to stretch over many months. One of them, the Byelorussian Soviet Republic, was born in Moscow on Christmas Day, 1918. Its independent existence was barely three weeks old, when its parents, the Central Committee of the RCP(B), decided that this was long enough, and on 16 January 1919 resolved that

> At the Congress of Soviets of Byelorussia of 2 February a proposal be adopted about the start of negotiations concerning joining up with the Soviet Russian Republic, for which a commission be elected at the Congress. The Congress must also take the initiative regarding the start of similar negotiations with the Soviet Russian Republic about joining up with the recently created Soviet Republics (Latvia, Estland, Lithuania etc.). The Congress must turn with such a proposal to the republics mentioned.[1]

This 'proxy' method, whereby non-Russians were made to initiate measures devised by the Russian centre, was used more than once. The plan was, however, a medium-term one: an immediate merger would destroy the still needed buffer effect, as the Central Committee's emissary, A. Ioffe, explained to the Byelorussians. At the same time, the Central Committee decided 'temporarily' (*sic*) to reduce Byelorussia's territory under the specious pretext of reducing territorial loss to Poland in case it claimed Byelorussia, but the members of the Central Bureau of the CP of Byelorussia defended their republic's sovereignty and opposed Moscow's decision. Ioffe demanded compliance, and in the end the Byelorussians had to give in, 'at the same time reserving the right to appeal to the Central Committee with a request to reconsider the decision'.[2]

The buffer function of the republics necessitated the creation of their own armed forces. These were subordinate to the Supreme Command of the RSFSR's Red Army; communists employed in the military establishments of the republics carried out instructions received directly from the Central Committee of the RCP(B) rather than from the corresponding Committee of the Communist Party of the republic itself.[3]

Changing fortunes at the Civil War fronts, chiefly the threat from the rallying anti-Bolshevik Russian forces, made a Soviet military union/alliance a matter of urgency. On 23 April Lenin ordered:

> It is necessary **urgently** *immediately*:
> 1. to draw up the *text* of a directive from the Central Committee to all 'nationals' about military *unity* (merger);
> 2. to give it *also* to the press for a series of articles . . .[4]

(The English word 'nationals' does not fully convey the patronizing flavour of Lenin's original Russian expression *natsionaly*; the closest equivalent is perhaps the North American 'ethnics'.) The directives, signed by Lenin and Stalin in May, specified that all military supplies and rail transport were to be strictly centralized and totally controlled from the RSFSR; but all this was to be only 'for the duration of the socialist war of defence'.[5]

A paradoxical situation arose: the republics were still deemed to be separate, while at the same time they were already regarded as parts of the RSFSR (a close military alliance surely did not have automatically to mean political merger). These two conflicting descriptions could occur in the same document, as, for instance, in the section on national Party organizations in the resolution on organizational issues passed at the Eighth Party Congress held in late March:

> At present, the Ukraine, Latvia, Lithuania and Byelorussia exist as separate (*osobye*) Soviet Republics. Thus, at the given moment, has the question of the forms of *statehood* been solved. But this does not mean at all that the RCP must, in its turn, organize itself on the basis of a federation of independent Communist Parties.
>
> The Eighth Congress of the RCP resolves: The existence of a *unitary* centralized Communist Party with a single Central Committee directing all the work of the Party in all parts of the RSFSR is imperative. All decisions of the RCP and its leading authorities are unconditionally binding on all parts of the Party, irrespective of their national composition. The Central Committees of the Ukrainian, Latvian and Lithuanian Communists have the rights of regional committees of the Party and are completely subordinate to the Central Committee of the RCP.[6]

The second inconsistency in this section (the whole resolution was passed *nem con* with one abstention) was stressed at the Congress by the rapporteur on organizational issues, Zinoviev, who thought that it would be impossible to uphold for long the contradiction of 'one single centralized Party alongside a federation of states'. He predicted that of the two principles it would be the federative principle that would yield to the centralism of the Party.[7]

The conspicuous absence of any mention of Estonia – 'Estland' – in this resolution betrays the signal failure of all attempts to Sovietize the country as Estonians resolutely resisted, and ultimately repelled, repeated Russian invasions.

The beginnings of a 'National Contract'

The Eighth Congress crystallized certain facets of the inchoate 'national contract' between the state which the Bolsheviks were creating and the nations which they were drawing into that state. The dispute at the congress was chiefly between Lenin and the Left, represented, on this question, by Bukharin and Piatakov. Lenin insisted that the recognition of the right of nations to self-determination was vital for the Communist Revolution,[8] while his opponents proposed replacing 'nations' with 'the working classes of each nationality'. Bukharin objected to Lenin's formula because it would give that right to all classes, the bourgeoisie as well as the proletariat, and the Bolsheviks would have to recognize 'the fictitious so-called "will of the nation" which is usually embodied in nothing other than a referendum of the so-called "whole population", including also the ruling classes'. Bukharin also disparaged 'universal, equal and secret ballot' in this connection, which Lenin had insisted on back in 1913. He accepted self-determination, though, for those nations 'where the proletariat has not formed itself into a class', by which he meant colonial nations, although European colonies were apparently excluded:

> If we proclaim the slogan 'the right of nations to self-determination' for colonies, for the Hottentots and Bushmen, Negroes, Hindus, etc., – we shall not lose anything by it. On the contrary, we shall win, because the whole national complex will be harmful to foreign imperialism, and its struggle will enter the common system of struggle against the imperialist regime.[9]

Here Lenin chided Bukharin for forgetting, nearer home, Russia's Bashkirs, Kirghiz and others, 'and to these we cannot deny recognition', and faulted his simplistic wishful thinking about class differentiation in European-type nations; for instance, even in such an advanced country as Germany the proletariat had not differentiated from the bourgeoisie, while, on the other hand, thanks to Finland's self-determination its proletariat was (in Lenin's view) breaking with its bourgeoisie.[10] The awkward question about how to deal with a proletariat which itself insisted on self-determination was answered by Piatakov:

> An international party, the party of the proletariat, can in no way permit that a question [of secession] affecting the interests not only of the proletariat of those regions [which attempt secession] but also to a considerable extent the interests of the proletariat of the whole capitalistically developed world were to be solved exclusively by the working class of that country [or regions].
>
> Let me give you a concrete example. Now a struggle for the establishment of the dictatorship of the proletariat is in progress in the Ukraine, and you know perfectly that the fate of the Ukraine is of immense interest not only to the working masses of that country but also to the working masses of Russia, Latvia, Byelorussia and the other Soviet republics . . . Can we permit that the form of existence of the

proletarian-peasant Ukraine were to be determined exclusively and independently by the working masses of the Ukraine? Of course not!

He also stressed the inconsistency of pursuing an economic merger of all the Soviet republics while proclaiming self-determination:

> Since we merge economically, create one administrative machinery, one Supreme Council for National Economy, one railway adminstration, one bank, etc., then this whole notorious 'self-determination' is not worth a farthing. This is either simply a diplomatic game which has to be played in some cases, or it is worse than a game if we take it seriously . . . Where the proletariat has been victorious there an immediate merger must take place, and we must pursue one line.[11]

So as not to offend non-Russian representatives among the Congress delegates, Lenin diplomatically advised that 'one has to be particularly cautious towards various nations, for there is nothing worse than the mistrust of a nation'. In the end, the compromise resolution of the Congress on the national question had, instead of 'self-determination', 'the recognition of the right to state secession for colonial nations and those not having equal rights' (obviously to apply outside the former Russian empire). The merger of nations was put off to an unspecified future: the Party proposed 'the federative union of states organized according to the Soviet type as one of the transitional forms on the way to complete unity'.[12]

Military alliance (or union) formalized

The next step was taken on 1 June 1919 with the decree adopted by the All-Russia Central Executive Committee at a joint meeting with the representatives of the non-Russian republics on their military alliance:

> A military alliance of all the mentioned Soviet Socialist Republics must be the first answer to an attack from the common enemies. Therefore, standing fully on the basis of recognizing the independence, freedom and self-determination of the toiling masses of the Ukraine, Latvia, Lithuania, Byelorussia, and the Crimea . . . the All-Russia Central Executive Committee considers it necessary to carry out a close amalgamation of:
>
> (1) Military organization and the military command, (2) Councils of National Economy, (3) Railway administration and management, (4) Finance, (5) The Commissariats for Labour, of the Soviet Socialist Republics of Russia, the Ukraine, Latvia, Lithuania, Byelorussia, and the Crimea, so that the direction of the mentioned branches of national life be concentrated in the hands of single boards . . .[13]

It was just a formal step, since Lenin had already ordered the amalgamation of the armed forces on 23 April, while the merger of other agencies of state had been proceeding in practice for some time even if not yet formalized; a progress that was noted by Piatakov at the Eighth Congress in March.

Ukrainian communists v. Bolsheviks

The detailed formalization of the alliance, however, was effectively stopped by the reversal of Soviet fortunes in the Civil War. Most of the Ukraine was overrun by the White armies under General Denikin, who was hostile to Russian Bolsheviks and Ukrainians alike. Both the Bolsheviks and the independentists of the Directory – the successor government to the Ukrainian Central Rada – fought against Denikin; among those who found themselves fighting on the Bolshevik side were a number of non-Bolshevik Communist Parties, the most significant of which was the Ukrainian Communist Party (Borot'bists), thus called after their newspaper, *Borot'ba*. They enjoyed considerably greater support among the Ukrainian masses than did the Bolsheviks. Their aim was an independent Soviet Ukraine, and their immediate demand – which remained unfulfilled – was the formation of an independent Ukrainian Red Army.

On 28 August, the Borot'bists, while still fighting Denikin, applied to the Executive Committee of the Communist (Third) International for recognition as the Ukraine's one and only Communist Party and as an independent section of the International.[14] The day before their application was, after a long delay, due to be discussed they sent a letter to Lenin:

SUCH ARE THE FACTS

The Soviet troops reached Kiev and took the whole Left-Bank Ukraine [the half of the Ukraine east of the Dnieper]. Then 'Soviet' construction started. At first those who had been awaiting Soviet power were observing the deeds of Soviet power and were forgiving it many things; the dictatorship of ignorant adventurer strangers repelled the local Communist forces and itself did not give anything positive. Then uprisings. Then Soviet power was burning down whole villages and shooting Red Army men of the Tarashcha Division and poor peasants . . . Soviet power in the Ukraine fell . . . But Soviet power lives in the Ukraine. It also will live there if the Russian Communist Party shows real internationalism and does not pursue a policy of spreading 'red' imperialism (Russian nationalism) in the Ukraine.

Comrade Petrovs'kyi declared in the press that the Ukrainian cause (*ukrainstvo*) was supported by kulaks and rogues; Comrade Rakovskii while being the Chairman of the Council of People's Commissars [of the Ukraine] demanded the dictatorship of Russian culture in the Ukraine. This is too far removed from an internationalist understanding of communism. This is too near to the tsarist dictum, 'There has not been, there is not, and there cannot be a Ukrainian language.' [A quotation from an edict of 1863 banning publications in Ukrainian.]

And if the leaders look at the matter in this way then no wonder that a gang of chance-comers from Russia shoot members of their own Party (the CPU); a tried revolutionary, respected by the poor peasants of the district, merely for having declared his Ukrainian sympathies (H. Zen'kov, of Poltava Region); Comrade Rudenko, a member of a local group of the CPU, was shot, or rather tortured to death, by the decision of the group's general meeting without any trial or investigation after a simple show of hands . . .

It was not clear what [they] wanted: if Soviet power, then we are for it, but why the struggle against the poor peasants . . . why the boorish treatment of toilers, insults, humiliations – did [they] want to make the Ukraine a colony, but then this does not square with the idea of Soviet power as an historical phenomenon . . . How then can one explain such an attitude toward local revolutionary forces, the one and only basis of Soviet power . . .

Let me tell you that, seeing the outrages done in the name of Soviet power in the Ukraine, many were convinced that it was a mistake, that the 'centre' did not know the real state of affairs. In particular, many believe in the power of your authority.

Give a reply. Much depends on your reply. The voice of a true revolutionary is now essential.

5 November 1919, Moscow.

[Signature illegible][15]

Negotiations in the Communist International in Moscow were conducted between the representatives of the CP(B)U, S. Kossior and Kh. Rakovskii, and the Borot'bist representative H. Hryn'ko from 6 November to 26 December 1919 and again, after yet one more Borot'bist application, from 5 February to 22 April 1920. Zinoviev, the President of the International, chairing the negotiations, recommended that the two parties should amalgamate. Rakovskii accused the Borot'bists of involuntarily becoming a nucleus round which petty-bourgeois counter-revolution was gathering. He based this on a letter from the Secretary of the CP(B)U Manuil's'kyi who denounced the Borot'bists for trying to organize a Ukrainian Red Army and ominously added that surveillance of their activity was handed over to the Cheka, the political police.[16] Commenting on the resolution of the International, Lenin wrote on 22 February: 'I strongly urge that the Borot'bists be accused *not* of nationalism, *but* of counter-revolutionary and petty-bourgeois tendencies.'[17] He chose this formula to avoid appearing tainted with Russian chauvinism. In the end, the Borot'bists decided to abide by the International's decision, and many of them joined the CP(B)U. Lenin was convinced that, had the Borot'bists not been 'neutralized' by their merger with the Bolsheviks, their uprising would have been inevitable, as he confessed to the Ninth Congress of the RCP(B).[18]

All the same, Lenin had implicitly to admit that the Borot'bists were right in their protests at the way the RCP(B) was treating the Ukraine. In his 'Draft Resolution of the CC RCP(B) on Soviet Rule in the Ukraine' which he prepared for the Eighth RCP(B) Conference in November 1919, he started by reiterating the mainstay of the 'national contract':

The CC RCP, while unswervingly implementing the principle of the self-determination of nations, considers it necessary to affirm once again that the RCP stands unswervingly on the point of view of recognizing the independence of the Ukrainian SSR.

But then he went on to express his apprehension that the rough methods of the RCP members in the Ukraine – particularly grain requisitioning and the forcible herding of peasants into communes – would dangerously alienate peasants from the RCP. He went on to propose that

> RCP members on Ukrainian territory must put into practice the right of the working people to study in the Ukrainian language and to speak their native language in all Soviet institutions; they must in every way counteract attempts at Russification that push the Ukrainian language into the background.[19]

Lenin's draft resolution went to the Politburo's 'Resolutions Commission' to be edited before being put to the conference's vote. The commission edited out Lenin's phrase 'attempts at Russification', substituting the vague 'attempts by artificial means' before the resolution was passed by the CC RCP(B) and approved by the full conference.[20]

Some Russifiers in the Politburo obviously did not appreciate Lenin's candour, but the stark facts which Lenin himself confirms are that the independent and sovereign Ukrainian Soviet Republic was *de facto* run not by the CP(B)U but in an overbearing way by the RCP. Among other things, the RCP had made the use and study of Ukrainian illegal; and this was done after the use of Ukrainian in teaching in the Kiev school district had been authorized by the Petrograd Provisional Government as early as 14 March 1917.[21] Even if economic measures, however high-handed, could find a modicum of justification in the 1 June decree, not an iota of justification could conceivably be found there or elsewhere for the agents of one of the sovereign states, present *en masse* in the territory of another state, actually banning that other state's language and imposing their own. (It was only in February 1920 that Ukrainian schools were restored.[22]) All this was regrettably typical of the way the 'national contract' had been constantly breached by the stronger side; nor, as Lenin obviously feared, was this the best way to win friends and influence people.

4

The Moslem Nations

Within weeks of the October Revolution, on 20 November 1917 (3 December NS), the Russian Bolshevik government, the Council of People's Commissars, addressed an appeal, signed by Lenin and Stalin, specifically to the Moslems:

> Moslems of Russia, Tatars of the Volga and the Crimea, Kirghiz and Sarts of Siberia and of Turkestan, Turks and Tatars of Transcaucasia, Chechens and Mountaineers of the Caucasus, all you whose mosques and prayer houses used to be destroyed and whose beliefs and customs were trodden underfoot by the Tsars and oppressors of Russia!
>
> From today, your beliefs and customs and your national and cultural institutions are declared free and inviolate. Order your national life freely and without hindrance. You are entitled to this. Know that your rights, like the rights of all the peoples of Russia, are protected by the whole might of the Revolution and its agencies, the Soviets of the Workers', Soldiers' and Peasants' Deputies.
>
> Support, then, this Revolution and its sovereign Government![1]

From 5 to 13 December 1917 the Third All-Kazakh National Congress took place in Orenburg, organized by Alash-Orda, the Kazakh National Party. It proclaimed the autonomy of the Kazakh-Kirghiz Regions and set up its government, the Provisional People's Council of Alash-Orda. Also in Orenburg, on 29 November the Second Bashkir Congress proclaimed autonomy. On 20 December 1917 its Constituent Council, Kurultai, created a government. However, the Russian Bolshevik Red Guards took Orenburg in late January 1918 and disbanded both governments, while the Kazakh and Bashkir forces went over to the Whites. In February 1918, in Kazan', a commission appointed by the Tatar Medzhilis ('Majlis', or National Assembly) decided in favour of an autonomous Idel-Ural (Volga-Ural) state to extend from the present-day Mari ASSR in the north-west to the Caspian Sea in the south. Soon the Bolsheviks intervened, and in April arrested the commission.

The People's Commissariat for Nationality Affairs, chaired by Stalin, was created in the Bolshevik government in November 1917. In April 1918, the Commissariat issued an appeal to the Soviets of the Moslem lands of Kazan',

Ufa, Orenburg, Ekaterinburg and Turkestan. Faced with the fact that a number of autonomous non-Soviet (therefore 'bourgeois', according to Soviet terminology) Moslem governments had arisen in several areas, the appeal laid down:

> It is necessary to take their autonomy from them . . . and transform it from a bourgeois one into a Soviet one . . . Some local Soviets have decided . . . to reject altogether any autonomy, preferring to solve the national question by the force of arms. But this way is completely unsuitable for Soviet power; this way is capable only of rallying the masses around the bourgeois-national leadership and of representing this leadership as saviours of their motherland and defenders of their nation, which on no account is acceptable to Soviet power. But the granting of autonomy, not its denial, is the next task of Soviet power. Only it is necessary to construct this autonomy on the basis of local Soviets. Only thus can the power become popular with the masses and their own.[2]

Tatar national communists

The beginnings of Moslem national communism date from April 1917, when the Moslem Socialist Committee of Kazan', pan-Islamic and Marxist in its tendency, was formed by Sultan-Galiev and Mulla-Nur Vakhitov (Vahitov). On 1 February 1918 Stalin set up within the Commissariat for Nationalities the Central Moslem Commissariat, offering its chairmanship to Vakhitov. It was to control the Kazan' Committee, which became a Provincial Moslem Commissariat, as well as similar commissariats or bureaux then created by Vakhitov in other cities of the Volga and the Urals area. In May, Vakhitov convened a conference of communists and sympathizers from the Kazan' area to discuss the possibility of creating an autonomous Soviet socialist Tatar-Bashkir republic similar in area to the Idel-Ural state proposed by the Medzhilis commission. The autonomy of the Tatar-Bashkir territory had already been proclaimed in the April appeal of the Commissariat for Nationalities,[3] although its extent was not defined. Vakhitov's plan was enthusiastically approved despite the Russian delegates' opposition. He concluded: 'We perceive the Tatar-Bashkir Republic as the revolutionary hearth whence the rebellious sparks of the socialist revolution shall penetrate the heart of the East!'[4]

In June, Vakhitov convened in Kazan' a conference of provincial branches of the Moslem Commissariat at which a Russian Party of Moslem Communists (Bolsheviks) was established, with a separate Central Committee. However, before the plans for a new republic could be implemented the rebellion of the Czech legions (which consisted of former prisoners of war in Russia) overthrew Bolshevik rule in the region, and Vakhitov, together with some prominent local Bolsheviks, was executed.

Sultan-Galiev took over as head of the Central Moslem Commissariat, and set about starting afresh. In November 1918, at the First Congress of Moslem

Communists in Moscow, he proposed a federal party system with autonomy for the Party of Moslem Communists.[5] He argued that Moslems themselves were better placed than the central Party to propagate communism in the East. Stalin concurred: 'Nobody could bridge the gap between the West and the East as easily and as quickly as you can, since the doors of Persia and India, Afghanistan and China are open to you.'[6] Nevertheless, he rejected Sultan-Galiev's proposal, forced the congress to dissolve the Russian Party of Moslem Communists (Bolsheviks) and subordinate local branches of the Moslem Commissariat to the local offices of the RCP(B). The Central Committee of the dissolved party was reconstituted as the Central Bureau of Moslem Organizations of the RCP(B), directly subordinate to the Central Committee of the RCP(B), with Stalin as its permanent representative to the Central Bureau.[7]

In March 1919, Stalin further thwarted the pan-Islamic and pan-Turkic tendencies of Moslem national communists by removing 'Moslem' from its name; it now became the Central Bureau of the Communist Organizations of the Peoples of the East. Soon afterwards the Central Moslem Commissariat was split into regional ones, the chief of them being the Tatar-Bashkir Commissariat and the Turkestan and Transcaucasian ones. In this way the Moslem communist movement was deprived of its legitimacy.

Bashkiria

At the same time the plan to create a Soviet Tatar-Bashkir Republic was also abandoned. After the suppression of Bashkir autonomy back in January 1918, considerable Bashkir forces went over to the Whites. In March 1919, however, dissatisfied with the way they were treated by the Whites, and enticed by a concession of unusually extensive self-rule, the Bashkir leader Zeki Validov and his troops went over to the Soviet side. The soviets in the area were, however, ethnically Russian and hostile to Bashkir autonomy, distributing most of the land confiscated from large estates to Russian settlers. Once the Civil War was over, on 19 May 1920 the Soviet government withdrew most of the rights granted to the Bashkirs.[8] Bitterly deceived in their hopes, their Revolutionary Committee resolved:

> In view of the imperialistic tendencies of the Russians which hinder in every way the development of the national minorities; in view of the lack of good faith from the centre towards Bashkir Communists, Bashkir officials are leaving Bashkiria and departing for Turkestan, for the purpose of creating there an independent Eastern Communist Party . . . The aim of this exodus is by no means to rouse the national masses against the Soviet government but rather . . . to protest against Russian chauvinism.[9]

After the departure of nearly all the Bashkir government officials and the Revolutionary Committee into the Urals, a Bashkir uprising broke out.

Punitive detachments of Russian peasants and workers, while 'suppressing a counter-revolutionary uprising', instituted a reign of terror, carried out indiscriminate looting and murder of the Bashkir population, and seized their land and cattle.[10] More and more Bashkirs joined the rebels in the mountains.

During the summer of 1920, Bashkirs were removed from Bashkiria's Party and state agencies. All Bashkir delegates sent to the First Congress of Soviets of Bashskiria held in the autumn were arrested as 'nationalists', and the government of the reconstituted Bashkir A S S R elected at the Congress was devoid of Bashkirs.[11] Within several months the uprising was suppressed.

In the summer of 1920, the Tatar A S S R was established, although most Tatars remained outside their republic. The rest of the Volga-Ural Moslem/ Turkic area was broken up into small units. Sultan-Galiev and his fellow national communists, dissatisfied with this solution, allegedly began discussing the idea of forming a Soviet Socialist Republic of Turan which was to comprise the Tatars, Bashkirs, Central Asia, the Moslem parts of the North Caucasus, and Azerbaijan.[12] Charged with 'national deviation', Sultan-Galiev was arrested in May 1923. This marked the beginning of Stalin's liquidation of all national communists, who were often, if they were Tatars or other Moslems, accused of the specific crime of 'Sultangalievism'. Sultan-Galiev himself was released after a short while, only to be arrested again in 1928, tried and sentenced to ten years in the infamous Solovki Islands camp. He was released in 1938, but his subsequent fate is unknown.

The North Caucasus

In the North Caucasus, the lands of the indigenous Moslem population had been seized by the Russians after a lengthy war less than a century earlier. In the aftermath of the February Revolution, their leaders set up the Alliance of United Mountaineers of the Caucasus. In December 1917, they declared the alliance 'an autonomous State of the Russian Federative Republic' with the stated aim of defending the national and religious interests of the Moslems. Its authority extended over the Terek Region, Daghestan and some other Moslem areas. On 23 January 1918, the All-Daghestan Congress of Mountaineers elected Nadzhmuddin of Gotso (Gotsinskii), an Arabic scholar, as the Chief Mufti (Imam) of the North Caucasus. Another of their leaders, Sheikh Uzun Hadzhi, appealed to the mountaineers to rise against Russia and create a Moslem *shari'at* monarchy in the Caucasus. He soon became the Imam of the Chechens and of Daghestan, and, following his appeal, the mountaineers razed many Russian and other European colonists' settlements to the ground. But in March 1918 the Russian Bolshevik armies abolished the Imamate in Chechenia and in May also took control of Daghestan. That same month in Batumi, Georgia, at a conference of the exiled Alliance of United Mountaineers of the Caucasus, the independence of the North Caucasus was proclaimed, and a government of the Mountaineers' Republic was elected.

After Turkey's defeat in World War I, some British troops arrived in Daghestan, and soon the Mountaineers' Republic was occupied by Denikin's anti-Bolshevik Russian Volunteer Army. His treatment of non-Russians was high-handed, to say the least. On 10 September 1919, the Allied Majlis of the Mountaineers of the Caucasus complained to the British that the Volunteer Army had burned down dozens of villages and was committing murder, robbery, rape, and desecrating mosques. It appears that the British, being committed to aiding Denikin, were unable to help them. By March 1920, the Russian Red Army had defeated the Volunteer Army in the North Caucasus, and by mid-1921 quelled the uprising led by Nadzhmuddin and Uzun Hadzhi.

The Crimea

In November 1917, an All-Crimean Tatar Constituent Assembly, the Kurultai, was elected by the vote of all adult male and female Tatars, and on 26 November it was convened in Bakhchisarai. It assumed authority in the internal administration of the Crimean Tatars, adopted a constitution of a Western democratic type and formed a national government, the Directory. It achieved the relocation of Tatar military units from the front home to the Crimea. Meanwhile, in November and December of 1917, the Sevastopol' Soviet was taken over by armed Baltic sailors sent there by the Petrograd Bolshevik government. In order to forestall a clash, the Kurultai decided to offer the Sevastopol' Bolsheviks participation in an All-Crimean government. They accepted the offer subject to the Kurultai's recognition of the Petrograd government, which the Kurultai voted against. Conflict became inevitable, and on 12–16 January 1918 the Bolsheviks took the Tatar-held cities of Bakhchisarai and Simferopol' and disbanded the Kurultai. In early March the Bolsheviks convened the First Regional Congress of Soviets in Simferopol' in order to form an Executive Committee to govern the Crimea. Among its delegates were 91 Tatars, mostly from the left wing of the disbanded Kurultai, who demanded some seats on the Committee. In the event, out of the total of 21 portfolios, only one, that of Crimean Moslem Affairs, was given to a Tatar. Thus, the Committee failed to represent the fact that Tatars still constituted a quarter of the population, despite a steady stream of emigration to Turkey since the Russian seizure of the Crimea in 1783.

After the Treaty of Brest-Litovsk, the Bolsheviks abandoned the Crimea to German occupation in May 1918. The left wing of the socialist-inclined Crimean Tatar National Party, Milli Firka, established cooperation with the communist underground, and when Soviet troops returned in April 1919 several left-wing members of Milli Firka were given important posts in the government. In June, this government fell under the onslaught of the Whites, and Milli Firka joined forces with the communists in the underground. When Soviet rule was finally re-established in October 1920, however, Milli Firka's offer of continued cooperation was rejected and it was branded as counter-revolutionary.

This amounted to the rejection of a major part of the Tatar intelligentsia, while the hostility of the Tatar peasantry was provoked by the Soviets' failure to distribute large landowners' confiscated estates to landless peasants; instead, these were turned into state farms, run by ex-tsarist and colonial officials. Early in 1921, the Commissariat for Nationalities and the Central Committee sent Sultan-Galiev to the Crimea on a fact-finding mission. In his report he was very critical of Soviet rule there, including Russificatory attitudes towards Tatars in the Department of Education, and recommended that a Crimean Soviet Socialist Republic be created, that more Tatars be admitted to the Party, and that landless peasants be given land.[13] The Moscow authorities followed his recommendations and despite the local communists' objections established the Crimean ASSR in November 1921.

Turkestan: the rise and fall of Kokand autonomy

In Tashkent, the administrative centre of Turkestan, Russian workers overthrew the Provisional Government's administration on 31 October 1917 and established Soviet rule in that city. This was soon extended to Samarkand and other cities of the territory. The Third Territorial Congress of Soviets of Workers', Peasants' and Soldiers' Deputies which met in Tashkent in late November proclaimed Soviet rule in the territory and elected the Turkestan Central Executive Committee and Council of People's Commissars. According to Mustafa Chokayev, who in January 1918 was to become head of the Autonomous (Moslem) Government of Turkestan,

> One of the strangest peculiarities of this Congress was the fact that no representatives of the native population of Turkestan took part in its deliberations. The soldiers sent thither from the interior provinces of Russia; the peasants settled therein by the old (tsarist) regime on the lands confiscated from our people, and the workers accustomed to regard us haughtily, from above – these were the people who were to decide at this moment the fate of Turkestan.[14]

The Moslem Congress was held in Tashkent at the same time as the Congress of Soviets. It proposed to the Congress of Soviets the establishment of a broadly-based government by giving the representatives of the indigenous population one half of the seats in the governmental bodies of the territory – a modest enough request indeed, considering that the indigenous Moslem population of Turkestan comprised over 90 per cent of the total. The Congress of Soviets was, predictably, unwilling to face any dilution of the European supremacy in the government, and rejected the Moslems' proposal outright. On 19 November, the joint Bolshevik and Maximalist faction tabled at the Soviets' Congress a palpably racist and colonialist declaration, which was carried *nem con* and laid down among other things that

> The inclusion of Moslems in the higher agencies of the territorial revolutionary government is unacceptable both in view of the complete uncertainty as regards the attitude of the indigenous population toward the power of Soviets of Soldiers', Workers' and Peasants' Deputies and in view of the absence among the native population of class proletarian organizations whose representatives in the agencies of the higher territorial government the faction would have welcomed.[15]

The refusal of the Congress of Soviets to allow Moslems to participate in the Tashkent Soviet led the Turkestan Moslem Central Council to convene the Fourth Extraordinary Moslem Congress in Kokand, which on 11 December passed this resolution:

> The Fourth Extraordinary Regional Congress, expressing the will of the peoples of Turkestan to self-determination in accordance with the principles proclaimed by the Great Russian Revolution, proclaims Turkestan territorially autonomous in union with the Federal Democratic Republic of Russia. The elaboration of the form of autonomy is entrusted to the Constituent Assembly of Turkestan, which must be convened as soon as possible. The Congress solemnly declares herewith that the rights of the national minorities settled in Turkestan will be fully safeguarded.[16]

A People's Council was elected, with 36 seats apportioned to Moslems and 18 to Russians. It was to act as a provisional parliament until the Constituent Assembly met on 20 March 1918. On 13 December (the anniversary of the birth of the prophet Mahomet), the Provisional Autonomous Government of Turkestan was solemnly proclaimed.

Thus a system of dual authority came into existence. The authority of the Tashkent Soviet extended over a number of cities including Kokand's new quarter and its fortress, while the jurisdiction of the Autonomous Government was confined to Kokand's native old city and the Ferghana valley. Of the two rival governments, the Kokand government was the weaker, having neither arms nor funds. Unable to dislodge its rival, it summoned a 'Turkestan Workers' and Peasants' Congress' in January 1918, which made an appeal to the central Soviet government to dissolve the Tashkent Soviet since it 'leaned on the foreign elements [i.e. Russians and other Europeans] hostile to the native population of the country contrary to the principles proclaimed by the October Revolution of the self-determination of peoples'.[17] The central government was unable to intervene, however, because Central Russia was then cut off from Siberia and Central Asia; the People's Commissar for Nationality Affairs, Stalin, limited himself to a rather disingenuous reply:

> The Soviets are autonomous in their internal affairs and discharge their duties by leaning upon their own actual forces. The native proletarians of Turkestan, therefore, should not appeal to the Central Soviet power with the request to dissolve the Turkestan *Sovnarkom* [Soviet of People's Commissars], which in their opinion is leaning upon the army units foreign to Turkestan, but should themselves dissolve it by force, if such force is available to the native proletarians and peasants.[18]

In the meantime, the Fourth Territorial Congress of Soviets of Workers' and Soldiers' Deputies in Tashkent adopted a resolution that 'the self-determination of a people means only the self-determination of the labouring strata'[19] (paraphrasing Lenin's well-known 1903 slogan, 'self-determination of the proletariat'), and declared that the Soviets alone should be the undisputed masters of Turkestan.[20] Since there was practically no native proletariat, this was a recipe for the continued dominance of the Russian workers over the indigenous population.[21] Moreover, it signalled action against the Autonomous Government of Turkestan.

On 29 January, some members of the Autonomous Government's forces tried to take over the Kokand fortress but were repelled. Its Russian garrison sent for reinforcements to the garrisons of Tashkent and other towns. On 5 February, a strong detachment of Russian soldiers, augmented by German and Austrian POWs taken on as mercenaries, arrived from Tashkent, led by the Military Commissar of the Tashkent Soviet government. He ordered truce negotiations to be broken off and the Moslem Old City to be stormed the next morning. Heavily outnumbered, the Moslem defenders were dispersed. After three days of looting and slaughtering all the Moslems who had not escaped, numbering over 14,000, when there was nothing left worth stealing, the soldiers poured petrol on the houses and turned old Kokand into a continuous sea of conflagration.[22]

Basmachi: the Mujahedin of Central Asia

After the fall of the Kokand autonomy, the chief of its armed forces, Irgash Bey, established his base near Kokand in a village turned into a fortress. Moslem clergy elevated him to the status of a religious leader; he was styled a fighter for Islam, a defender of the oppressed, and *Amir al Musulmin*, 'leader of the true believer', declaring a Holy War against the Soviets. Men gathered from everywhere to join him, as all through 1918 and most of 1919 the native population continued to suffer unabated persecution, expulsions from the land, and looting by the Red Guards, the settlers, and the Soviet Russian administrators, who were largely old tsarist colonial officials.[23]

Moscow's April 1918 appeal belatedly admonished the Turkestan Soviet against the use of arms in solving the national question, and advised 'granting' autonomy. Seemingly complying with this directive, in April 1918 the Fifth Territorial Congress of Soviets, to which some Moslems were admitted for the first time, decreed the establishment of an Autonomous Republic of Turkestan within the RSFSR. In reality, very little changed in the Russian colonialist monopoly of power. A year later, on 10 July 1919, the basic principles of a new Soviet policy toward the native population were spelled out in a radio telegram from the Central Committee of the RCP(B) to the CEC (i.e. the government) of the Turkestan Republic and the Territorial Committee of the RCP(B):

A broad proportional involvement of the Turkestan native population in state activity is essential, without obligatory Party membership, it being sufficient for the candidatures to be proposed by Moslem worker organizations.

The requisitioning of Moslem property without the agreement of territorial Moslem organizations is to stop, and all friction creating antagonism is to be avoided.

Most local Communist Party organizations in the territory resisted this directive, however.[24]

Irgash Bey soon extended his sway in the rural areas around Kokand, and attacked Russian settlements and Red Army detachments. In 1918 and 1919, some 40 other Basmachi guerilla detachments were active as well. By late 1919 there were over 20,000 Basmachi fighters. The most prominent among these detachments was that of Madamin (Muhammad Amin) Bek. His support extended beyond the Moslem population to include Russian White officers, some of whom were even appointed to commanding posts. In November 1918 he led his detachment of around 600 men in a raid on Russian settlements. Peasant settlers, installed there by the tsarist government on land seized from the native population, set up self-defence detachments. These were soon legalized by the Turkestan Soviet authorities, themselves short of armed forces. This 'Peasant Army of Ferghana' often harassed and marauded the native population; this increased the latter's antagonism towards the Soviets, since they identified the Russian Peasant Army with the Russian Red Army.

The declaration of War Communism in Turkestan in summer 1919 aroused the settlers' discontent; the Peasant Army became hostile to the Soviets, and concluded a truce with Madamin Bek. On 22 August, the Military Council of the Peasant Army passed a resolution demanding new elections to all soviets and administrative bodies in the Turkestan Republic 'on the basis of a general, equal, direct, and secret ballot while allocating one half of the seats to the Moslems', economic freedoms and the abolition of the Cheka and political commissars.[25]

The Peasant Army joined forces with Madamin Bek, and the combined army of 20,000 seized the towns of Dzhalal-Abad, Osh and Andizhan. However, the alliance did not prove to be very firm: the natives refused to fight side by side with the Russian settlers who had been their oppressors, while the Russian peasants wavered and did not want to fight their own kin, the Russian workers in the Red Army. During the last week of September, the Soviet forces recaptured the three towns, and the Russian peasants started deserting from the army and returning to their homes.

Madamin Bek and the Peasant Army's commander-in-chief, Monstrov, formed a Provisional Government of Ferghana in the rural territories they still controlled, with Madamin Bek as president; he did everything he could to strengthen his army and the whole movement, which was riven by discord, as well as carrying out reforms in the territory controlled by his government. In December, an Afghan delegation came to him and, promising funds and arms, tried to reconcile him with other Basmachi leaders who had refused to submit to him, but its mission was unsuccessful. Relations between the Moslems and the Russian settlers in Madamin Bek's army were getting more and more strained, and in late January 1920 Monstrov and the settlers surrendered to the Soviets. He and a number of their leaders were executed by the Revolutionary Tribunal, while most settlers were amnestied.

In the summer of 1919, an amnesty had been declared for those Basmachi who voluntarily stopped resistance; this now began to produce results as three detachments of Basmachi, some 5,600 men in all, went over to the Soviets together with their leaders on 31 January and 2 February 1920. Madamin Bek's forces continued fierce resistance, but, having suffered a major set-back, he declared that he recognized Soviet rule. The Revolutionary Military Council of the Ferghana Front promised him that in the case of surrender his detachment would enter Soviet service as an independent military unit within the Turkic Brigade, and on 6 March 1920 an agreement was signed to this effect.

Among the leaders of the Basmachi who continued resistance in Ferghana, the most prominent was Kurshirmat (Kurbashi Shir Muhammad). He united them and declared himself the Commander of the Islam Host. The Basmachi who had gone over to the Soviets, meanwhile, used the respite thus gained to refurbish their detachments with the Red Army's weapons and ammunition. Some of their leaders, now Red Army commanders, refused to obey higher orders, whereupon it was ordered that regiments consisting of former Basmachi be disarmed. This resulted in most Basmachi leaders fleeing with their detachments into the steppe and joining Kurshirmat, or the chief leader of the Kirghiz Basmachi, Khal Khodzha. At the beginning of 1921, some 6,000 Basmachi were active in Ferghana.

Link with Russia restored
The restoration of land communication between Soviet Russia and Central Asia in the autumn of 1919 allowed the central Soviet Government to intervene more actively in Turkestan. It was clear to it that the *de facto* continuation of old colonial rule antagonized the native population which was, not surprisingly, solidly on the side of the Basmachi. In order to deal with all the problems there, a high-powered governmental Commission on Turkestan Affairs was created, arriving in Turkestan from Moscow in November. The area's importance was stressed by the fact that in the same month Lenin himself found it necessary to address the Bolsheviks in Turkestan:

It is no exaggeration to say that the establishment of proper relations with the peoples of Turkestan is now of immense, epochal importance for the Russian Socialist Federative Soviet Republic.

The attitude of the Soviet Workers' and Peasants' Republic to the weak and hitherto oppressed nations is of very practical significance for the whole of Asia and for all the colonies of the world, for thousands and millions of people.

I earnestly urge you to devote the closest attention to this question, to exert every effort to set an effective example of comradely relations with the peoples of Turkestan, to demonstrate to them by your actions that we are sincere in our desire to wipe out all traces of Great-Russian imperialism and wage an implacable struggle against world imperialism, headed by British imperialism. You should show the greatest confidence in our Turkestan Commission and adhere strictly to its directives, which have been framed precisely in this spirit by the All-Russia Central Executive Committee.[26]

Turkestan's national communists

Even Moslem members of the RCP itself, however, could not be relied upon to obey the Party unquestioningly. Moslem intellectuals, many of whom were admitted to the RCP and the Government of Turkestan following Lenin's message, soon formed a national communist group led by the chairman of the Turkestan CEC, T. Ryskulov. The Fifth Turkestan Territorial Conference of the Communist Party of January 1920 promised to be guided by the CC RCP(B)'s directives, but went on to adopt the Ryskulov group's resolution that the Communist Party of Turkestan be named the Turkic Communist Party, and the country itself the Turkic Republic with the aim of including both Central Asian Moslems and those elsewhere in the RSFSR, and eventually those outside the RSFSR as well. However, the Commission on Turkestan Affairs vetoed this proposal.[27] The Ryskulov group's demands also included full independence for the territorial Military Commissariat, the creation of a separate Moslem army independent from the central command, and the withdrawal from Turkestan of all non-Moslem units.

In May, a delegation from Turkestan's Communist Party Committee and government headed by Ryskulov arrived in Moscow to negotiate with the Central Committee of the RCP, the government, the Third International and Lenin himself. The delegation submitted their proposals as above, demanded the liquidation of the Turkestan Commission, which it regarded as 'the chief obstacle on the road to our autonomy', and raised the question of independent relations with contiguous countries.[28]

Bearing in mind the 'very practical significance' of Turkestan, as Lenin put it in his November appeal, for the national liberation of 'the whole of Asia and for all the colonies of the world', the delegation insisted in their submission that

All action in rousing the East must proceed *exclusively* by means of the organized revolutionary forces of Moslem countries, both those forming part of the RSFSR and those not doing so. *Only by leaning on their political and armed forces and by the use of them* is it possible to move to the East.[29]

Lenin reasserts direct rule

The Politburo of the RCP studied the delegation's submission, and, as proposed by Lenin, rejected it. Instead, the Central Committee drew up its own decisions, which it passed on 29 June 1920 and published under the title 'On Our Tasks in Turkestan'. Recognizing that Soviet power had been 'in the hands of a thin stratum of Russian workers infected by colonialist psychology', and that this had exacerbated the situation, the Central Committee aimed to do away with the old colonialist heritage while maintaining firm central rule. It proposed:

(a) To take away from settlers in the Kirghiz districts all land allocated by the [pre-revolutionary] Migration Office or seized from the Kirghiz without authority, leaving for the settlers land parcels of the size of a working allotment . . . To have as the basis for the allocation of native agricultural holdings the principle of equalization with Russian peasants . . .

(b) To provide landless *dekhkans* [native Turkestani peasants] with land.

(c) To smash all *kulak* [i.e. well-to-do Russian settler] organizations, to disarm the *kulaks* and, by employing the most resolute measures, to deprive them of any possibility not only of directing but even of influencing the organization of local rule . . .

(d) To deport from Turkestan into Russian concentration camps (*kontsentratsionnye lageri*) all former officers of the police, gendarmerie and political police, and those from among the tsarist officials whose employment in Turkestan is politically unacceptable . . .

(e) By way of redistribution of Party personnel, to transfer and place at the disposal of the Central Committee all those Turkestan communists who are infected with the colonialist spirit and Great-Russian nationalism, and at the same time to conduct in the centre the mobilization of several hundred Communists for work in Turkestan . . .[30]

On the delegation's return from Moscow, Ryskulov reported on the Central Committee's decision to a meeting on 19 July of the Territorial Committee of the CP of Turkestan, the majority of whose members opposed the Central Committee's decisions. The Turkestan Commission, Moscow's agency *de facto* ruling the country, meted out swift retribution for this act of insubordination: on the same day it dissolved the Territorial Committee of the CPT, later appointing a provisional Central Committee of the CPT apparently comprising nine Moslems and five Europeans.[31] Similarly at governmental level the Presidium of the Turkestan CEC was reshuffled. In both bodies, Moslem intellectuals of the Ryskulov trend were replaced by Moslem representatives from the lower classes, relied upon to serve faithfully in the role of 'Communists-internationalists'.[32]

5

National Contracts with the Non-Russians

External national contracts: the Balts

By the autumn of 1919 Lenin had at last decided to abandon the Red Army's attempts to annex Estonia. An armistice was signed on 31 December, and by the last months of 1919 both the German and Russian troops were removed from Estonia. A peace conference met in Tartu on 5 December, and on 2 February 1920 the peace treaty between Estonia and Soviet Russia was signed, in which it was declared that.

> In consequence of the right of all peoples to self-determination, to the point of seceding completely from the State of which they form a part, a right proclaimed by the Russian Soviet Federative Socialist Republic, Russia unreservedly recognizes the independence and autonomy of the State of Estonia, and renounces voluntarily and for ever all rights of sovereignty possessed by Russia over Estonian people and territory.[1]

This enabled the Bolsheviks to claim over the next two decades that it was their generosity at the Peace of Tartu which had established the new republic.

The Lithuanians drove the Bolsheviks out on 30 August 1919. The RSFSR recognized Lithuania's independence by a peace treaty, signed at Moscow on 12 July 1920, similar to that with Estonia.[2] Within three days of signing it, the Bolsheviks had crossed into Lithuania and occupied Vilnius, the traditional capital. But, weakened by their defeat at Warsaw, they soon withdrew from the country. In October 1920, Polish troops seized Vilnius. The Lithuanian advance to recover it was halted by the League of Nations, which promised a peaceful settlement; in the end, however, the Poles were not forced to withdraw, and held Vilnius for the next two decades.

When the German forces left Latvia in mid-December 1919, the Red Army still maintained a Latvian Soviet Republic in Latgale in the south-east. The Latvians, therefore, delayed signing an armistice with the Soviet Russians (negotiated at the same time as the Russian–Estonian one) until the latter evacuated Latgale in January 1920. The peace treaty between the RSFSR and Latvia was signed in Riga on 11 August; the former renounced voluntarily and for ever Russia's rights over independent Latvia 'in view of the desire definitely expressed by the Latvian people to possess an independent state existence' in terms similar to the treaty with Estonia.[3]

The gathering of the Caucasus
In Transcaucasia, the three national parties, the Georgian Mensheviks, the Armenian Dashnak and the Azerbaijani Musavat, united in a coalition, and on 15 November 1917, with the participation of the local Russian Mensheviks and Social Revolutionaries, they formed in Tiflis (now Tbilisi) the Transcaucasian Commissariat. This became the area's government, independent from Soviet Russia. The only Soviet enclave there was Azerbaijan's industrial centre, the city of Baku, where the Russian-dominated Soviet, supported by workers, soldiers and sailors, seized power on 2 November and declared allegiance to the central Russian Bolshevik government. It was strongly opposed by the Musavat party, whose leader Mamed Emin Rasul-Zade had declared at its First Congress in October 1916 that 'the aim of the Turkic people is progress and striving so that in the blossoming garden of mankind a fragrant Turkic flower should grow. And this flower will join a common bouquet together with the other groups comprising the Moslem International' – in other words, a united Turkic state together with other Moslem nations.[4] On the morning of 30 March 1918, Musavat armed detachments based in Baku's old quarter attacked the Baku Soviet's forces. This engagement, which involved some 20,000 fighters and cost over 3,000 lives, resulted in Soviet victory in Baku.

On 22 April 1918, a Transcaucasian Seim in Tiflis proclaimed Transcaucasia an independent federative republic. The three national parties were equally represented in the government of the Transcaucasian Federation, but it soon dissolved. On 26 May, the National Council of Georgia proclaimed the creation of an independent Republic of Georgia; two days later the Central National Armenian Council declared Armenia an independent republic; and on 17 June an Azerbaijani government was created. Cut off from its central Russian power base after the Treaty of Brest-Litovsk, Soviet rule in Baku collapsed on 31 July.

After the Armistice, the Red Army was more successful in the Caucasus than in the Baltic. Lenin was anxious to secure the all-important Baku oil fields, and on 17 March 1920 he sent a coded telegram to S. Ordzhonikidze and I. Smilga, who were in charge of the Caucasus Front Revolutionary Committee, urgently ordering them to take Baku,[5] the capital of independent Azerbaijan. Their 70,000-strong Eleventh Red Army crossed Azerbaijan's border at midnight on 25 April and occupied Baku on 28 April. In accordance with Lenin's instructions of November 1918 (see pp. 23–4), a Provisional Military-Revolutionary Committee of the Azerbaijani Soviet Independent Republic was set up the same day. The committee immediately sent a telegram to Lenin asking him, rather redundantly, for fraternal aid in the shape of Red Army detachments.[6]

Contract with Georgia

Ordzhonikidze believed that a few weeks would be enough to overrun next the two independent republics, Georgia and Armenia. When his advance units attempted to cross the Georgian border, however, they met with vigorous counter-attacks. Lenin was unwilling to get involved in a protracted campaign while his hands were full with the Polish war, and ordered Ordzhonikidze to stop the hostilities. On 7 May 1920 the RSFSR signed a peace treaty with Georgia unconditionally recognizing its independence and renouncing all interference in its affairs.[7] The treaty was thus broadly similar to the one signed with Estonia earlier that year.[8] It had, however, a secret supplement in which Georgia undertook to guarantee local communists (i.e. pro-RSFSR Bolsheviks) freedom of activity.[9] Armenia was not so lucky: Ordzhonikidze's Eleventh Army managed to conquer it in December 1920.

Meanwhile on the European scene, Britain and France recognized Estonia, Latvia and Georgia *de jure* at the Paris Conference of the Great Powers on 26–27 January 1921. Georgia was recognized as an independent state by twenty-two countries. Lithuania became a member of the League of Nations on 21 September 1921 and was recognized by the United States *de jure* on 27 July 1922; due to its conflict with Poland, Britain and France withheld *de jure* recognition until 22 December 1922.

Having annexed Armenia, Ordzhonikidze was eager to invade Georgia, Transcaucasia's last independent state. From Baku, he asked Lenin's permission, which was refused. Despite this, and apparently without Moscow's knowledge, his army invaded Georgia from Azerbaijan on 16 February 1921, just as the Georgian ambassador A. Chkhenkeli reached Paris, charged with the task of establishing diplomatic representations in European capitals. On 25 February, accompanied by the Master of Ceremonies, the ambassador solemnly proceeded in the state coach of the Élysée Palace with a cavalry escort from the Georgian Mission to the residence of the President of the French Republic in order to present his credentials to M. Millerand; on the very same day, Soviet troops entered Georgia's capital, led by a Georgian Bolshevik Commissar on a white charger and holding a red flag.[10]

There were similarities in the histories of the six Baltic and Transcaucasian nations: incorporated into the Russian empire comparatively recently, they are culturally and ethnically different from the Russians. They showed their will for independent statehood, and fought for it with determination. The *de facto* independence of all six was recognized by the great powers, though *de jure* recognition came too late for two of the Caucasian nations. Soviet Russia recognized the independence of the three Baltic states and Georgia by peace treaties. The national contracts with the Baltic states were honoured for 20 years (disregarding the small matter of the brief invasion of Lithuania within a couple of days of the signing of the treaty), and for a little less than ten months with Georgia. Even this latter breach was 'accidental', the result of a local commander's initiative, ostensibly undertaken without Moscow's approval; but unlike in the Lithuanian case, different circumstances made it possible to 'stay put' rather than rectify the 'mistake'.

There were also important differences. The Baltic states were on Western Europe's doorstep, and the great powers were prepared to support them. When it came to creating an 'ensemble' of Caucasian states similar to the Baltic one, Transcaucasia's remoteness was its undoing. As a Georgian participant in the international negotiations, Zourab Avalishvili, wryly remarked:

> There were many difficulties; local forces were insufficient to overcome them, and 'the Supreme Council of Allied Powers' had neither the power nor the desire to create anything – or seriously help to create anything – to the east of a definite meridian.[11]

In the League of Nations, too, while the Baltic states were admitted to full membership, and Georgia's application was regarded *avec faveur*, it was clear that the obstacle to its full membership was Article 10, which imposed a duty to come to the aid of a fellow member being attacked. 'The political moral', according to Avalishvili,

> amounted to the following: *if Georgia were attacked from without, neither the League of Nations, nor the powers behind the League of Nations could or would defend it.* France had made its declaration, and so had England . . .[12]

Contracts with independent – or federated? – Soviet Republics

These years also saw another series of treaties, described as 'Workers' and Peasants' Treaties', between the RSFSR and the remaining sovereign Soviet republics. The first, of 30 September 1920, was between the RSFSR and the Azerbaijani SSR proclaiming 'a close military and financial-economic alliance/union'. It was very brief and omitted the mutual recognition of the sovereignty of the parties to the treaty, apart from references to the two (separate) governments. The detailed agreements on the merger of individual commissariats and other agencies spelt out the massive subordination of those of Azerbaijan to those of the RSFSR.[13]

The treaty of 28 December 1920 with the Ukrainian SSR, on the other hand, did acknowledge 'independence and sovereignty' and stressed that 'no obligations for the Ukrainian SSR towards anyone follow from the fact itself of the territory of the Ukrainian SSR having previously belonged to the former Russian empire'.[14] This treaty served as a model for those concluded with Byelorussia and Georgia on 16 January and 21 May 1921 respectively.[15]

Despite all the formal declarations of 'self-determination', 'independence', and 'sovereignty', by 1920 Lenin regarded the Soviet republics as already linked in a *de facto* federation, and demanded that 'In recognizing that federation is a transitional form to complete unity, it is necessary to strive for ever closer federal unity.'[16] This was elaborated at the Tenth Congress of the RCP(B) held 8–16 March 1921, where Stalin, the Party's chief spokesman on nationality affairs, presented his 'Theses to a report . . . on the immediate tasks of the Party in the national question endorsed by the Central Committee of the Party'. The theses contained a virtual re-statement of the 'national contract' and had this to say on the subject of federation:

> Russia's experience in employing different forms of federation, ranging from federation based on Soviet autonomy (Kirghizia, Bashkiria, Tataria, the Highlands, Daghestan) to federation based on treaty relations with independent Soviet republics (the Ukraine, Azerbaijan), and permitting intermediate stages (Turkestan, Byelorussia), has fully proved the expediency and flexibility of federation as the general form of state union of the Soviet republics.
>
> 6. But a federation can be stable . . . only if it is based on mutual confidence and the voluntary consent of the federating countries . . . the RSFSR is the only country in the world where the experiment in the peaceful coexistence and fraternal cooperation of a number of nations and nationalities has been successful . . . there are here neither dominant nor subject nations, neither metropolises nor colonies, neither imperialism nor national oppression . . . This voluntary character of the federation must be preserved without fail, for only such a federation can serve as a transitional stage to that higher unity of the toilers of all countries in a single world economic system, the necessity for which is becoming increasingly apparent.[17]

In the following discussion, one of the leading Ukrainian Bolsheviks, V. Zatons'kyi, stressed that not all was well in the sphere of national problems, and that Russian chauvinism was ubiquitous. He demanded that mutual relations between the members of the federation be defined more precisely, arguing that

> We must extirpate the idea of the Soviet federation as necessarily a Russian federation from our comrades' heads, for the point is not that it is Russian but that it is Soviet.[18]

Another leading Ukrainian, M. Skrypnyk, an Old Bolshevik (Party member since 1897) and Stalin's senior, was also dissatisfied with the treatment of the topic and, objecting to the motion that the discussion should be terminated, remarked tersely:

> The national question is important and urgent (*nabolevshii*); in Comrade Stalin's report this morning this question has not been solved to the slightest extent . . .

Skrypnyk's motion to continue the discussion was rejected by a show of cards

(72 per cent of the delegates were Russians).[19] Stalin was not going to forget Skrypnyk's words in a hurry . . .

Stalin's autonomization scheme

Indeed, not all was well in the treaty relationships; some republics began to protest against Russian governmental agencies assuming the role of central agencies of the treaty federation. On 9 May 1922 the Central Executive Committee and the Council of People's Commissars of the Ukrainian SSR passed a resolution protesting against the extension of the RSFSR tax collecting machinery to the Ukraine, pointing out that this contravened the Constitution of the Ukrainian SSR.[20]

The situation obviously needed clarifying, and in August the Politburo of the Central Committee of the RCP(B) requested its Organizational Bureau – the caucus of the Party – to create a commission 'for preparing the question about relations of the RSFSR with independent republics' in order to have it considered at the Central Committee's plenum on 6 October.[21] Stalin, who had been in charge of the Organizational Bureau since 1921, was the chief member of this commission. He accordingly compiled a 'Draft of a Resolution Concerning the Relations between the RSFSR and the Independent Republics' at the end of August and circularized it to the republics' Central Committees for discussion and approval. The Azerbaijani Central Committee, firmly under Ordzhonikidze's Stalinist heel, promptly approved it, but the Georgians flatly rejected it, as did the Ukrainian leadership, after a month's delay, and the Byelorussians.

On 4 September, however, Manuil's'kyi, the pro-Stalin Secretary of the Central Committee of the Ukraine, without waiting for his colleagues' decision on the draft, sent Stalin a very revealing private letter:

> The past year's experience has shown that the situation which has arisen in the borderlands and in particular in the Ukraine and which has led to a series of conflicts between the central and local departments cannot continue any longer. This situation . . . must be radically revised, for it also no longer corresponds to objective circumstances . . . I believe that [it must be revised] in the direction of the liquidation of the republics' independence and its replacement by a broad real autonomy . . .
>
> The creation in the borderlands of independent republics . . . was an unavoidable concession to elemental national forces set in motion by the Revolution; they, drawing on the discontent of the peasant masses, could have turned into a very dangerous Vendée. The change in the economic situation [i.e. NEP] brought calm to the countryside having cut the ground from under political separatism . . . The introduction of autonomy . . . will not provoke any serious national movement in the sense of opposition to this move . . .

Manuil's'kyi was aware that the abolition of the non-Russian republics' independence by Moscow would look too much like blatant imperialism, so he suggested the well-tried stratagem of making the 'nationals' themselves beg to be relieved of their independence:

> But I believe it is necessary to put this measure into practice in such a way that the initiative should come from the national congresses of Soviets, receiving its legislative completion at the All-Russia Congress of Soviets in December.[22]

Despite the fact that most of the republics had failed to approve his draft, Stalin pressed ahead with it. On 23 September he reconvened his commission which finalized the draft and adopted it as their resolution. Its aim was the 'formal entry into the RSFSR' of the republics of the Ukraine, Byelorussia, Azerbaijan, Georgia and Armenia, the operative clause being in the opening clause of the first section:

> 1. To consider as expedient the conclusion of a treaty between the Soviet Republics of the Ukraine, Byelorussia, Azerbaijan, Georgia, Armenia and the RSFSR about the formal entry of the former into the RSFSR . . .

This 'entry into the RSFSR' meant transforming these republics into autonomous republics of the RSFSR, like for instance the Bashkir ASSR which has never been a sovereign Soviet republic and whose status differs little from that of a Russian province. Curiously, the designation 'autonomous', though manifestly implied, does not occur in the resolution; Manuil's'kyi in his above letter was not beating about the bush when he referred to the same process as the 'liquidation of the republics' independence and its replacement by . . . autonomy'. This proposal of Stalin's to absorb the hitherto formally sovereign non-Russian republics into the Russian Republic by turning them into 'autonomous' units was known as Stalin's autonomization scheme.

The resolution specified that the people's commissariats dealing with foreign affairs and foreign trade – specific attributes of sovereignty – should, among others, be amalgamated with those of the RSFSR, while those that were of merely local significance should be left alone. 'The present decision', it concluded in a paragraph which was kept confidential,

> is not to be published but to be passed to national Central Committees as a circular directive for its implementation at the level of Soviets through the Central Executive Committees or the Congresses of Soviets of the above republics until the convocation of the All-Russia Congress of Soviets at which it [this decision] is to be declared as the desire of these republics.[23]

Lenin's compromise: the USSR
Lenin strongly disagreed with this resolution, summoned Stalin and severely criticized it. In his memorandum of 26 September to his deputy Kamenev and all Politburo members, Lenin suggested, as a concession to the non-Russians, replacing 'formal entry . . .' by 'formal joining up together with the RSFSR

into a Union of Soviet Republics of Europe and Asia'. This Union was to be governed by its own federal government and not by that of the RSFSR. 'The spirit of this concession,' he explained,

> is, I trust, clear . . . It is important that we should not provide arguments for the 'independentists', should not destroy their *independence*, but create another *new tier*, a federation of republics *possessing equal rights*.[24]

Between August and the end of September Lenin saw nine representatives from all the Soviet republics; among them was Mdivani, described by Lenin as 'a Georgian Communist suspected of "independentism"', whom he saw the day after writing the above letter.[25] It is possible that it was Mdivani or one of the other eight who persuaded Lenin to include the right to free secession and alter the name of the proposed Union from the 'Union of Soviet Republics of Europe and Asia' to the 'Union of Socialist Soviet Republics'.

These and other changes were introduced into the final draft of the resolution of Stalin's commission as presented to the Central Committee's plenum on 6 October.[26] On the day when the plenum was meeting, Lenin, unable to attend due to ill-health, sent Kamenev a note declaring 'war to the death on Great-Russian chauvinism' and adding that

> It must be *absolutely* insisted that the Union's Central Executive Committee should be *presided over* in turn by a Russian, Ukrainian, Georgian, etc. *Absolutely!*[27]

The plenum approved the final draft, adopting it as its own resolution, and created yet another commission of the Central Committee to draft the necessary legislation and prepare appropriate resolutions to be put through the CECs of the independent republics.[28] The latter procedure accorded with Stalin's original recommendation that the proposal should appear to come from the republics, and it seems to have been put into action without delay. Having obviously received Moscow's instructions through Party channels, the Ukraine's CEC resolved on 16 October to instruct its government to start negotiations with other republics concerning the creation of Union legislative and executive bodies while 'stressing the complete equality of rights of all the contracting Soviet republics and the full voluntariness of their workers-and-peasants union'. On 3 December, the Second Congress of Soviets of the Armenian SSR passed a resolution which followed Moscow's instructions practically verbatim.[29] The Georgian Old Bolshevik Central Committee, on the other hand, seem to have tried to preserve their country's independence by taking the voluntariness principle at its face value. However, they were soon out of the way.[30]

On 21 November, the new commission resolved to draft the Fundamentals of the Constitution of the USSR, and to instruct the Party Central Committees in the republics to get the Fundamentals adopted at their respective Congresses of Soviets. These Fundamentals were then to be used as directives for special delegations to be sent to Moscow to a Congress of Soviets furnished with mandates ready for the signing of the Union Treaty.[31] The Fundamentals were duly drafted, approved by the Politburo of the Central Committee on 30 November,[32] and sent out to the non-Russian republics in order to be rubber-stamped by them as 'their own proposals'.

The Ukraine's Seventh Congress of Soviets replied first, on 13 December, and in greater detail than the others. While largely following the offered text, the Congress added a preamble which stressed that the Union was created by the free will of the contracting parties, which had equal rights, and it must safeguard the republics' cultural and certain economic independence. In the body of the text, two 'notes' were inserted. The object of these was to prevent the same person holding the office of chairman or of commissar of the Union at the same time as a corresponding office in an individual republic, and to ensure that 'Decrees and enactments of the USSR shall be published in all languages recognized as official in its constituent republics.'[33]

The first of these notes was obviously aimed against the government of the RSFSR attempting to become, by sharing its personnel, the actual government of the Union, effectively reverting to Stalin's original plan with Lenin's cosmetics. Ukrainian apprehensions about this were by no means unfounded: even before the 6 October plenum, M. Kalinin, President of the All-Russia CEC (i.e. President of the RSFSR), had written to Stalin proposing that 'Pending the creation of an independent CEC of the RSFSR, all prerogatives of the All-Russia CEC of the RSFSR shall pass to the "Union CEC".' This seems a puzzling suggestion to come from a Head of State: that his own CEC (i.e. the legislature) be liquidated, a *new*, supranational, 'Union CEC' be created, and his CEC be created anew at some unspecified future date. His ostensible motive for this was 'reducing expenditure for new *apparats* of power without which we can manage for some time'.[34] The real purpose of his suggested addendum was simply to rename the CEC of the RSFSR the Union CEC, which would then govern all the republics.

Kalinin, as a member of the Central Committee, happened to have been appointed a member of its commission set up on 6 October to prepare resolutions requesting the creation of a union of Soviet republics, which were to be sent to the independent republics to be passed 'as their own'. As the Tenth Congress of Soviets of the RSFSR, at which these resolutions were to be presented, approached, Kalinin made strenuous efforts to uphold this fiction. The question of the proposed union, he wrote in *Izvestia*,

has been raised by the republics allied with us. It is there that it is debated and discussed at their congresses of Soviets; it is from them that the initiative comes. It seems to me it will meet a lively response in the RSFSR, and the Congress of Soviets, most probably, will receive this proposal with enthusiasm, but for quite understandable reasons the Government of the RSFSR is not making any official pronouncement until the decisive moment, until a concrete proposal is received from the republics allied with us.[35]

The next day, 18 December, the Central Committee plenum met again. The agenda consisted of Stalin's draft 'Treaty with Union Soviet Republics', and the decisions adopted by the plenum prescribed in detail the steps to be taken. First, the Tenth Congress of Soviets of the RSFSR was to be directly followed by the Union Congress; its agenda was specified, and included adopting a declaration on the formation of the USSR and working out the text of the treaty. Then, the latter had to be passed to the republics' CECs to be approved, and finally confirmed by the future Second Congress of Soviets of the USSR.[36]

The scenario was played out as Kalinin had predicted. At the Tenth Congress of Soviets of the RSFSR, the representatives of the non-Russian republics recited one by one 'their initiative' to create the USSR, after which, on 27 December, the Congress recognized 'as timely' the joining up of the republics into the USSR. (Natural modesty seems to have prevented the predicted Russian 'enthusiasm' from being recorded in the lengthy resolution on the subject.)[37] On 30 December, plenipotentiary delegates from the republics signed the Declaration and the Union Treaty, the latter being an expanded version of the Fundamentals.[38]

On the same morning, the Tenth Congress of Soviets of the RSFSR was transmogrified into the First Congress of Soviets of the USSR. Chaired by Kalinin, with Lenin, still absent through illness, elected Honorary Chairman, the Congress's first action was to confirm the two documents in general. Following the proposal of the Ukraine's delegate M. Frunze, 'in view of the extraordinary importance of the adopted Declaration and the concluded Treaty' they were referred to the CECs of the Union Republics for additional examination.[39]

Lenin's Testament

Meanwhile Lenin, the architect of the USSR, was having second thoughts about his creation as he followed its progress, now largely out of his hands. As the First Congress was finishing he dictated, bedridden, a series of extensive notes that became known as his 'Testament'. The Presidium of the Twelfth Party Congress the following year decided not to publish this document; it was read only at the official delegations' meetings and not at the Congress itself, where non-delegates were present. It was published 'only for members of the RCP(B)' in the Fifteenth Congress bulletins (December 1927). Suppressed in the 1930s, it was made accessible to the general public only in 1956, three years after Stalin's death.

The larger part of this document was devoted to the 'autonomization' issue,[40] and expressed Lenin's growing apprehensions about Great-Russian chauvinism. He was particularly appalled at Stalin's henchman, Ord-zhonikidze, using physical violence against a leading member of the Central Committee of the Georgian Bolshevik Party. The bulk of that committee had strongly disagreed with Stalin's plan for a Transcaucasian Federation, and ultimately the whole committee had resigned in protest. He considered Stalin, Ordzhonikidze and Dzerzhinskii to be specifically guilty in this instance of Russian chauvinism. The pre-revolutionary Russian bureaucracy that had been taken over by Soviet institutions was also imbued with chauvinism. Its ugly face confronted him both in the Party and in Soviet bureaucracy. After decades of his Party's fight against non-Russian (but never Russian) 'nationalism', he had to admit that a Russian Bolshevik was nearly always a chauvinist, and warned that

> A distinction must necessarily be made between the nationalism of an oppressor nation and that of an oppressed nation, the nationalism of a big nation and that of a small nation. In respect of the second kind of nationalism we, nationals of a big nation, have nearly always been guilty, in historic practice, of an infinite number of cases of violence; furthermore, we commit violence and insult an infinite number of times without noticing it . . .
>
> Nothing holds up the development and strengthening of proletarian class solidarity so much as national injustice; 'offended' nationals are not sensitive to anything so much as to the feeling of equality and the violation of this equality, if only through negligence or jest – to the violation of that equality by their proletarian comrades. That is why in this case it is better to overdo rather than underdo the concessions and leniency towards the national minorities.

Singling out the language issue, he instructed:

> The strictest rules must be introduced on the use of the national language in the non-Russian republics of our union, and these rules must be checked with special care . . . A detailed code will be required, and only the nationals living in the republic in question can draw it up at all successfully.

Significantly, Lenin seems to have been the only Soviet leader to admit the existence of the phenomenon of Russian communist imperialism:

> The need to rally against the imperialists of the West . . . is one thing . . . It is another thing when we ourselves lapse, even if only in trifles, into imperialist attitudes towards oppressed nationalities, thus undermining all our principled sincerity, all our principled defence of the struggle against imperialism.

Russian chauvinism being rampant, Lenin was afraid that

> It is quite natural that in such circumstances the 'freedom to secede from the union' by which we justify ourselves will be a mere scrap of paper, unable to defend the non-Russians from the onslaught of that really Russian man, the Great-Russian chauvinist, in substance a rascal and a tyrant, such as the typical Russian bureaucrat is.[41]

Indeed, it is axiomatic that the ultimate sanction against an irremediable breach of the 'national contract' must be the right to secede, which Lenin was afraid would be worthless if the law of the fist prevailed. Alas, how infinitely less than even the proverbial scrap of paper was this right going to be worth when the fist was replaced by the prison camp and the firing squad.

But in practice, Lenin insisted that the Union had to be preserved and strengthened, while non-Russians were to be granted concessions and favoured with positive discrimination. The Union Treaty provided for the merger of all more or less important People's Commissariats, leaving to the republics only a few independent commissariats of purely local significance. But if the merged commissariats proved to be incapable of equitable and fair dealing as regards the interests of non-Russian republics, Lenin envisaged the possibility of all of them splitting, except the two which were vital for the preservation of the Union:

> We cannot be sure in advance that . . . we shall not take a step backward at our next Congress of Soviets, i.e., retain the union of Soviet socialist republics only for military and diplomatic affairs, and in all other respects restore full independence to the individual People's Commissariats.

At the same time, to pacify those of his colleagues who would be horrified by this 'retrograde' suggestion, he reminded them that the centralized Party would still be in ultimate control.[42]

Non-Russians strive to safeguard their rights

As the Declaration and the Treaty of the Union were referred to the individual republics for additional examination, a new concept surfaced, that of a bicameral organization of the Union government. It was advocated by the government of the Ukraine;[43] and, although in common with the majority Bolshevik opinion, including Lenin, Stalin originally opposed the idea, he adopted it at the 12–14 February 1923 plenum of the Central Committee, having decided that this device could be used as a further means for the unification of peoples. His blueprint for the second, national, chamber, which he made public on 23 April at the Twelfth Party Congress in his report on the national question, was for it to be elected by the national republics and regions, each being represented equally,[44] thus assuring a safe absolute majority for the RSFSR with its 15 autonomous republics and national regions. (The RSFSR majority of some three-quarters was also assured in the first chamber, where representation was to be based on population numbers.)

During the ensuing debate, Ryskulov, a delegate from Turkestan, advocated that the proposed second, national, chamber should possess certain well-defined real rights,[45] while Ia. A. Iakovlev (from the Central Committee *apparat*) pointed out that a bicameral arrangement could not guarantee the solution of the national question, just as the first chamber did not decide independently on any matters of principle (i.e. being controlled by the Party); only the Congress could give such a guarantee, which could be achieved by a wide circulation of Lenin's letter on the national issue.[46] The plan was subsequently discussed on 24 April in a special section on the national question. Out of the 100 individuals in the section, only 24 were from non-Russian republics,[47] and Stalin's plan was adopted.

The debates on the main body of Stalin's report at the Congress were revealing. H. Hryn'ko, from the Central Committee of the CP(B)U, and Rakovskii, representing the Ukraine's government, protested that even before the creation of Union agencies, RSFSR commissariats in Moscow had started taking charge of the Ukraine's and other republics' economies and were, moreover, doing this in a wrong-headed and harmful way; to counteract this, they advocated wider budgetary and economic rights for the republics. Rakovskii warned that the Party was 'committing fatal errors in the national question', and, unless this was dealt with sensitively and with understanding, 'it promises a civil war'.

Ryskulov pointed out that Russian *kulaks* were again on the offensive against Turkestani peasants, and that Russian chauvinism was growing among the old tsarist officials serving in the Soviet bodies as well as among the new Soviet functionaries. The Georgian F. Makharadze, deciding to call a spade a spade, remarked that the republics' 'independence' so much talked about at the congress was a fiction, as everyone knew, since it was the one and only Central Authority of the Party which alone determined for each republic absolutely everything down to appointing functionaries for them.[48] He also quoted a remarkable, though very typical, dialogue which could not but reinforce doubts as to whether the stronger party might be expected to observe a national contract:

> Comrade Bukharin said that he had met someone arriving from the provinces and asked him: how are things there in your parts?
> Well then, says he, there is no news. We just bash nationalists.[49]

The rich, idiomatic fragrance of the reply is lost in translation; the original word *dushim* evokes a whole bouquet of associations – strangle, stifle, throttle, suffocate, smother, oppress, repress, suppress . . .

In his reply to the discussion on his report, Stalin alluded to Lenin's Testament:

> We are told that we must not offend the non-Russian nationalities. That is perfectly true; I agree that we must not offend them. But to evolve out of this a new theory to the effect that the Great-Russian proletariat must be placed in a position of inequality in relation to the formerly oppressed nations is absurd. What was merely a figure of speech in Comrade Lenin's well-known article, Bukharin has converted into a regular slogan. Nevertheless, it is clear that the political basis of the

dictatorship of the proletariat is primarily and chiefly the central, industrial regions, and not the border regions, which are peasant countries. If we exaggerate the importance of the peasant border regions, to the detriment of the proletarian districts, it may result in a crack in the system of the dictatorship of the proletariat. That is dangerous, Comrades . . .

There are cases when the right to self-determination conflicts with another, a higher right – the right of the working class that has come to power to consolidate its power. In such cases – this must be said bluntly – the right of self-determination cannot and must not serve as an obstacle to the working class in exercising its right to dictatorship.[50]

The next task after the conclusion of the Treaty of the Union was to draft the USSR Constitution, which would be the fundamental document of the 'national contract'. For this task, a Special Commission of the CEC of the USSR, as well as constitutional commissions in the republics, were set up, and a number of drafts were produced, which were in essence elaborations of the treaty. All of them contained the formula referring to the Soviet republics uniting into 'a single union state'[51] except the one from the Ukrainian SSR which said that the Soviet republics 'conclude the present Treaty on the formation of the Union of Soviet Socialist Republics . . .' Another very important difference was in the Ukrainian draft proposing only seven Union commissariats and as many as 16 republican ones as against the ten Union and ten republican commissariats in the Moscow draft.[52]

The effect of the Ukrainian proposal was to remove the commissariats for labour, food and the inspectorate from Union jurisdiction, and to have all the seven remaining Union commissariats paralleled in each republic, as opposed to the Moscow draft which deprived the republics of commissariats for foreign affairs, military and naval affairs, foreign trade, transport and post and telegraph. The Ukrainian proposal was to give some substance to the 'sovereignty of individual republics comprising the Union'. With regard to the two chambers of the CEC, the Ukrainian proposal was for each to have its independent presidium, while the Moscow version allowed no rights to these, all rights being vested in the CEC's common presidium.[53]

None of these proposals from the Ukrainian SSR was accepted by a Commission of the Plenum of the Central Committee. At the Fourth Conference of the Central Committee with Responsible Workers of the National Republics and Regions on 9–12 June, Skrypnyk and Rakovskii, supported by Mdivani, argued again in favour of the Ukrainian decentralizing proposals and pressed for their acceptance by the conference. Stalin heavily inveighed against his opponents:

Was it accidental that, when examining the well-known draft Constitution adopted at the Congress of the Union of Republics, the Ukrainian comrades deleted from it the phrase which said that the republics 'are uniting into a single union state'? Was that accidental? Did they not do that? Why did they delete that phrase? Was it accidental that the Ukrainian comrades proposed in their counter-draft that the People's Commissariat of Foreign Trade and the People's Commissariat of Foreign Affairs should not be merged but be transferred to the directive category? What becomes of the single union state if each republic retains its own People's Commissariat of Foreign Affairs and People's Commissariat of Foreign Trade? Was it accidental that in their counter-draft the Ukrainians reduced the power of the Presidium of the Central Executive Committee to nil by splitting up between two presidiums of the two chambers? All these amendments of Rakovskii's were registered and examined by the Commission of the Plenum of the Central Committee, and rejected. Why, then, repeat them here? I regard this persistence on the part of some Ukrainian comrades as evidence of *a desire to obtain in the definition of the character of the Union something midway between a confederation and a federation, with a leaning towards confederation*. It is obvious, however, that we are creating not a confederation, but a federation of republics, a single union state, uniting military, foreign, foreign trade and other affairs, a state which in no way diminishes the sovereignty of the individual republics.[54]

When, in the course of discussion, he was charged that his insistence on a *single* union state smacked of the old tsarist concept of 'Russia, one and indivisible', Stalin pointed out that he himself had denounced it in the resolution on the national question he had tabled at the Twelfth Congress, and reiterated that he was for federation, 'whereas the Ukrainians are trying to force confederation upon us'.[55]

The National Contract finalized

On 6 July 1923, the Second Session of the CEC of the USSR accepted the USSR Constitution as elaborated by the Moscow Constitutional Commission, which after April had been expanded to include the republics' representatives. The original commission of 13 members was augmented by four representatives of the RSFSR and two each from the Ukraine, Byelorussia, and the Transcaucasian Federation; a Russian absolute majority was still assured.[56]

On 13 July, the Presidium of the CEC of the USSR internationally publicized the newly concluded 'national contract' in an address 'To All Peoples and Governments of the World'. This address surveyed the governmental structure of the new 'single union state', reiterated the fiction that 'the peoples' of the Soviet republics had 'unanimously' decided to form the USSR, and assured the world that

This union (*ob"edinenie*) of peoples with equal rights remains voluntary, precluding national oppression and compulsion on any people to remain within the borders of this state, while granting the right of free secession from the Union and at the same time opening voluntary access to it to all socialist soviet republics, also to those which will arise in future.[57]

The definitive version of the Constitution, the basic document of a 'contract' among the nations of the new state, was confirmed by the Second Congress of Soviets of the USSR on 31 January 1924.[58] Lenin, the founder of that state, died two days before the opening of the Congress, on 24 January 1924.

The national contract did not reflect Bolshevik magnanimity; rather it was the product of harsh political exigencies. Lenin had come to realize that force alone was not enough to weld together the fragmented Russian empire and that the non-Russians would have to be won over by concessions designed to dispel their mistrust and hostility. He had also recognized the precarious nature of Soviet rule even though the Civil War had been won by the Bolsheviks and how essential it was to conciliate the peasantry. The New Economic Policy (NEP) which he had introduced in the spring of 1921 was aimed at placating the peasantry and consolidating Soviet rule. Because the non-Russian nations were largely composed of peasants, the inauguration of the NEP inevitably had implications for Soviet nationalities policy. The non-Russian peasant masses would have to be wooed through the medium of their native languages and cultures. The more liberal approach in the economic sphere was therefore translated into the area of nationality policy. This was why the later Lenin and his 'principles' in nationality policy were to become a standard and a shield for the non-Russians.

6

The National Contract Torn Up

In late March 1922 at the Eleventh Party Congress it was decided, in order to improve the efficiency of the secretariat of the Central Committee, to name a Politburo member General Secretary of the Central Committee. To choose one was to be the Committee's task; this body, in turn, had first to be elected on the last day of the Congress. During this election, some delegates wrote 'General Secretary' after Stalin's name. This angered Skrypnyk, chairman of the Elections Committee, who demanded that these ballots be declared invalid. All the same, when the new Central Committee met straight after the Congress on 3 April, Kamenev successfully proposed, from the chair, that Stalin be elected to the newly created post.[1]

At that time the General Secretary was not considered the main official in the Party, and 'no one ascribed any special significance' to Stalin's appointment.[2] By skilful manipulation, however, he gathered ever more reins of power. Observing this, and having increasingly graver doubts about Stalin's personal qualities, in late December 1922 Lenin dictated from his sick-bed his 'Letter to the Congress' on Party organizational matters, among other things warning the Party:

> Comrade Stalin, having become Secretary-General, has unlimited authority concentrated in his hands, and I am not sure whether he will always be capable of using that authority with sufficient caution.[3]

Eleven days later, on 4 January 1923, he was much more definite in his addendum to that letter: '. . . I suggest that the comrades think about a way of removing Stalin from that post and appointing another man in his stead . . .'[4]

In accordance with Lenin's wish, this part of his 'Testament' – as, along with his notes on 'autonomization', it came to be called – was held back until after his death, when it had to be handed in to the next Party Congress. This was the Thirteenth Congress, held 23–31 May 1924. The Central Committee Plenum of 21 May decided that the Testament be read out at the meetings of individual delegations, and this was where the question of removing Stalin from his post was discussed. In the event,

The delegations to the Congress were in favour of leaving J. V. Stalin in the post of

General Secretary, meaning that he would take V. I. Lenin's critical remarks into account and would be able to correct his defects.[5]

Lenin in his lifetime was the most venerated Bolshevik leader, he was of course *the* Leader, and was virtually deified immediately after his death. And yet his Testament was disregarded: he definitely did not suggest that Stalin could be given a chance to improve his character traits. The Congress delegates were not to know that their failure to remove him was going to cost most of them their lives, as well as the lives of tens of millions of others, within the next two decades.

Ironically, it was Stalin who was now to elaborate the terms of the 'national contract'.

The National Contract observed?
The June 1923 Fourth Conference of the Central Committee with Responsible Workers of the National Republics and Regions also produced something that was advantageous to the non-Russians. Speaking at the conference, Stalin declared that

> the more literate and cultured a country, a republic, or a region is, the closer is the Party and Soviet apparatus to the people, to its language, to its manner of life . . . Nine-tenths of the misunderstandings are due to the shortage of responsible workers from among the local people. Only one conclusion can be drawn from this: the Party must be set the urgent task of accelerating the formation of cadres of Soviet and Party workers from among local people.[6]

Stalin also prepared a 'Draft Platform on the National Question' for the conference and had it endorsed by the Politburo;[7] with minor alterations, it was adopted as a resolution entitled 'Practical Measures for Implementing the Resolution on the National Question Adopted by the Twelfth Party Congress'.[8] These guidelines proved important in years to come. The section on measures for involving local working people in Party, trade union and Soviet activity, however, began with an ominous paragraph prescribing

> A purge of the state and Party apparatuses of nationalist elements (this refers primarily to the Russian nationalists, as well as to the anti-Russian and other nationalists). The purge must be carried out with caution, on the basis of proved data, under the control of the Central Committee of the Party.

This prescription could, and in the event did, lead to immense abuses. While Russian chauvinists remained practically immune, the Central Committee could brand any free-thinking among non-Russians in the cultural, economic, or political spheres as 'nationalism', which could lead, especially in later years, to judicial prosecution with dire consequences.

Other measures included

> making the state and Party institutions in the republics and regions national in

character, i.e., gradually introducing the local languages in the conduct of affairs, and making it obligatory for responsible workers to learn the local languages . . . selecting and enlisting for the Soviet institutions the more or less loyal elements among the local intelligentsia . . . training cadres of Soviet and Party officials from among the [local] members of the Party.

These prescribed measures were the basis for the policy of involving indigenous non-Russian populations in the work of the Party and local Soviet government (all under strict central control, of course), so that the hitherto largely Russian ruling agencies would provide a semblance of indigenous self-government. This policy became known as 'indigenization' (*korenizatsiia*), and in individual republics it was also known under specific names, such as Ukrainization, Byelorussianization or Tatarization.

The section on 'Measures to Raise the Cultural Level of the Local Population' envisaged the encouragement of literacy in national languages through clubs, societies, schools and the promotion of publishing. Literacy and education in non-Russian languages were seen basically as means of winning the allegiance of the non-Russian masses to the Party and raising the efficiency of the Soviet administrative machinery among them.

Soviet policy on national military units has been inconsistent, except in one respect: individual republics have never had the right to have their own complete armed forces. The resolution's section on national military units noted that in Tataria and Bashkiria national militia regiments could be organized straight away using local old military cadres; 'Georgia, Armenia and Azerbaijan seem already to have a division each'; and one militia division each could be formed in the Ukraine and Belorussia for 'defence against possible attacks by Turkey, Afghanistan, Poland etc.'. (Nevertheless, the vast majority of non-Russian recruits would still serve under Russian commanders in ethnic Russia, in the Red Army, a prime tool of Russification, as was pointed out at the Twelfth Party Congress by Skrypnyk and Iakovlev.)[9]

Finally, regarding Party education, the resolution proposed:

(a) To create schools for elementary political education in the native languages;
(b) to create a Marxist literature in the native languages;
(c) to have a well organized periodical press in the native languages.

These directives (besides their political aims) could well contribute to the cultural development of non-Russian nations and hence to the observance of the national contract. The latter found its authoritative and succinct expression in the preamble ('Declaration') to the USSR Constitution which promised that the 'single union state' would be 'able to ensure both the external security and the internal economic prosperity and the freedom of national development of peoples', while in Article 3 'the Union of Soviet Socialist Republics safeguards sovereign rights of Union Republics'.[10]

The role of a governmental agency having the task of promoting national development was to be played by a Commissariat for Enlightenment. Each republic (Union as well as Autonomous) was to have its own Commissariat for Enlightenment (or Education), with cultural matters coming under it, while the USSR had no such common commissariat, though 'the establishment of general principles in the area of people's enlightenment' was within the purview of the Union. The republics' constitutions, safeguarded by the Union, were the extensions of the national contract.[11] For example, Article 13 of the Ukrainian SSR Constitution proclaimed:

> In the area of cultural construction, the Ukrainian Socialist Soviet Republic sets itself the task of ensuring by all means the development along proletarian paths of Ukrainian national culture and the culture of national minorities and of resolutely struggling against nationalist prejudices.[12]

National cultural matters appeared also in other republics' constitutions: those of the RSFSR and the Uzbek SSR guaranteed national minorities their right to be taught in their native language in school;[13] so did the Byelorussian SSR Constitution, but this reinforced the 'right' by adding 'and real possibility'. It also guaranteed free economic and cultural development and rising prosperity for working people of all nationalities; Byelorussian was chosen as the predominant language for official business, though Byelorussian, Yiddish, Russian and Polish were equal in all offices and organizations, and major legislation was to be published in these languages.[14] In the Turkmen SSR Constitution, Turkmen and Russian were declared to be official ('state') languages.[15]

In the second half of the 1920s much was achieved in the development of their republics by national communists in cooperation with active national elements. Significant facts and figures illustrating such achievements in the largest non-Russian republic, the Ukraine, can be gleaned from a publication put out in 1929 by the All-Ukrainian Society for Cultural Relations with Foreign Countries.[16] On the problem of the dichotomy of the Russified town and the Ukrainian countryside, it notes:

> Only 3 to 4 years passed since the Ukrainization of the towns was begun, but today we have already unmistakable practical results. The whole of the Government work is effected now in the Ukrainian language. All of the official negotiations are transacted in the same [Ukrainian] language unless with a person of other nationality. The employees of the State are furthering their knowledge of the Ukrainian language, literature and culture by constant studies at various courses and groups. At present the urban population has already got a firm grip of the language.[17]

In the educational field, 81·6 per cent of schools are said to have used Ukrainian as the language of instruction in 1927–8. The total number of pupils in all schools was 2,383,000, which included 393,750 pupils in schools with other languages of instruction,[18] whence it appears that the percentage of pupils in Ukrainian schools was 83·48 per cent, as compared with 80·02 per cent of Ukrainians in the Ukraine's total population. In technical and tertiary education, the report admits that 'we have not been in the position to do as much'. In professional schools only 55·1 per cent of teaching was in Ukrainian, and in technical schools only 54 per cent, while 'the institutes [viz. universities, including technical ones] have not yet begun teaching in Ukrainian to any satisfaction'.[19]

National minorities were catered for: they had their own schools, professional schools (among them 39 Jewish) and others; in Mariupol' there was a Greek section in the teacher training college. The Ukrainian Academy of Sciences had a section of Jewish Culture with a branch in Odessa; there was a Mendele-Moikher-Sforim Museum, and special minorities' sections (Jewish in Poltava, Greek in Mariupol', and some others) were attached to some museums. There was a Jewish theatre at Kharkov, and a Polish studio theatre in Kiev.[20] The Ukrainian Government, through Skrypnyk's efforts, pressed for similar satisfaction of the national needs of the seven-million Ukrainian minority in the RSFSR, and demanded – in the event, unsuccessfully – the transfer to the Ukrainian SSR of those adjacent RSFSR districts with an ethnic Ukrainian majority.

Progress was also made, with local variations, in other republics. The national language and cultural situation in Georgia was much more favourable to start with: even in 1923 it was possible to say that 'the Georgian language prevails [in Georgia] wherever it is necessary to contact the Georgian masses'. In Armenia, the policy of 'indigenization' was pursued systematically, so that the personnel at all levels of all institutions were Armenians. In all Moslem republics, the secularization of education was accompanied by the abolition of Arabic script and the creation of Latin-based alphabets (as was also done in Turkey) for each ethnic group, according to the repartition into national republics and regions. This was conducive to the consolidation of national identities and languages, while at the same time counteracting pan-Islamic feeling.

Very significant advances in culture are illustrated in the steep rise of publishing in non-Russian languages. Taking just one indicator, the number of book titles published in these languages per annum rose to nearly a quarter of the Soviet total in 1927 and to one-third in 1930, more than doubling in absolute figures between 1926 and 1930. Progress among individual nations was uneven; in order to take account of their differing populations, the numbers of book titles in each language published per 100,000 of the respective nation provide a useful gauge. Thus, in 1928 the Armenians and Azerbaijani equalled the Russians with around 30 titles each, the Georgians were ahead of them with 42, the Ukrainians, Byelorussians, Uzbeks and Turkmens had around only ten each, while the Tadzhiks and the Kazakhs with the Kirghiz lagged behind with six each. In 1930, the Armenians, Azerbaijanis and Georgians, with 50 to 65 titles, overtook the Russians with about 40, the others ranging around the 20–5 mark, except for the Kirghiz and Turkmens with 10 and 15 titles respectively. National literatures and arts flourished, writers' organizations proliferated.

Ominous breaches of the National Contract

In political life, the Party and administration were becoming relatively more 'national' through the policy of 'indigenization' adopted in 1923; thus, all in all, it seemed that the National Contract, in the sense of ensuring 'the freedom of national development of peoples', was being observed. However, even in that 'golden age' in the life of non-Russian nations of the USSR, breaches of the contract were frequent and blatant.

Among the first targets of 'purges' (at that time amounting to transfers elsewhere and/or demotions of varying severity) were those prominent communists who were former members of other, socialist or national communist, parties, as well as those who had started as Bolsheviks but paid too much attention to their nations' interests. An early example was Sultan-Galiev and his real or alleged followers in Moslem lands. These included the former members of the Azerbaijani Hümmet (Social Democrats allied with the RSDLP, who after Sovietization became the CP[B] of Azerbaijan), headed by Khanbudagov, who had formed a faction demanding the expulsion of the Russian and 'European' colonists and workers settled in Moslem Transcaucasia and their replacement by Turkic nationals.[21] He and his followers were swept away in an early purge.

There were numerous other cases of this sort. The Ukraine's Commissar of Education O. Shums'kyi had to leave the Ukraine and move to Moscow in 1927 for allegedly overdoing Ukrainization and other 'sins' (the major one being that he was a former Borot'bist communist). H. Hryn'ko, another ex-Borot'bist, was Commissar of Education from 1920 until his transfer in 1924 to chair the nationally neutral State Planning Commission of the Ukrainian SSR; he, too, was banished from the Ukraine and eventually shot in 1937.

Among top Kazakh Bolshevik leaders, Baitursun (Baitursunov) was removed in 1925, and other leaders of the early period – even opponents of the independentist Alash Orda, among them Seifullin, Mendeshev and Sadvakasov – disappeared in 1927–8. In 1925, in what is today the Kirghiz SSR and was then the Kirghiz Autonomous Region, a group of Party leaders known as 'The Thirty' submitted a memorandum to the CC RCP(B) in which they criticized the conducting of official business in Russian, complained that native education was neglected, and insufficient native cadres were being trained under indigenization, advocated bringing educated natives into the government, demanded a halt to repression, and requested the removal of Russian communists from leading posts; whereupon The

Thirty were removed from their posts, expelled from the Party, and put on trial. Their leader, Abdukarim Sidik-uulu (Sydykov), was exiled from Kirghizia.[22] Another Kirghiz group, 'Ur-tokmok', led by K. Khudaikulov, head of the Soviet-organized Kirghiz Poor Peasants' Union, and the Second Secretary of the region's Party, D. Babakhanov, apparently supported traditional native leaders; in February–March 1926 the Ur-tokmok leadership was expelled from the Party; in February 1927, the two leaders as well as several others were tried and imprisoned.[23] In Azerbaijan, a second purge removed most of the old Hümmet members, in fact, the local Old Bolsheviks. In Tadzhikistan, the state apparatus was purged in 1927–8.

By the end of the 1920s Soviet rule had been consolidated and there was no longer such a need to conciliate the peasantry. Stalin, amassing ever more power, began to abandon the NEP. The breaking of the truce with the peasantry was accompanied by the abrogation of the national contract.

Initial blows against the national cadres

In the non-Russian lands the Terror started on a massive scale as early as 1928–9, aimed against the wide circles of national, chiefly non-Party, intelligentsia. This marked the unequivocal and brutal tearing up of the national contract which had been meant to ensure 'the freedom of national development of peoples'. Between 1929 and 1934, the political police, OGPU, arrested several thousand individuals in the Ukraine and Byelorussia who were tried on charges of belonging to a number of alleged organizations such as the Union for the Liberation of the Ukraine (which 'consisted exclusively of intellectuals: scholars, writers, artists . . .'[24]) and the Union of Ukrainian Youth, both 'uncovered' in July 1929; the Union for the Liberation of Byelorussia (June 1930); the Ukrainian National Centre (February 1931); the Byelorussian National Centre (summer 1933); and several other, chiefly Ukrainian, organizations, apparently all fictitious. The similarity between the names of the two pairs of Ukrainian and Byelorussian organizations gives further support to the usual assumption that they were figments of an OGPU chief's imagination and that he did not even bother to introduce variety into his fiction.

National forces in other non-Russian lands were also subject to mass persecution. In the Tatar ASSR in 1929 the Society for Tatar Studies was denounced as a 'centre of nationalism' and closed. Between 1930 and 1933, after similar allegations, sweeping purges hit the Pedagogical Institute of the East and Tatar schools for the preparation of national cadres. In January 1928, in the Crimean ASSR, the Chairman of the CEC, the Crimean Tatar national communist Veli Ibrahimov (Ibraimov, Ibragimov) was charged with supporting the underground Tatar national party, Milli Firka, and abetting its struggle against Soviet activists. He was executed in May, and in the following year some 3,500 of his followers, mainly Party and government officials and intellectuals, were shot, imprisoned or exiled.[25] The Commissariat of Education was singled out for a thorough purge, and two Tatar literary journals were liquidated. In the same year, a heavy blow was struck against the native elite in Kazakhstan, and a major purge began to gather momentum in Azerbaijan.

Collectivization: the rural Terror

'The peasant question is the basis, the quintessence,' Stalin emphasized in 1925, 'of the national question. That explains the fact that the peasantry constitutes the main army of the national movement.'[26] In his onslaught on non-Russian nations, therefore, the peasantry became another prime target. Among the peasants, the *kulaks* were viewed by the rulers as the main enemy; in James Mace's very apt comparison, they were for the Soviet regime 'an omnipresent foe whose role in the Bolshevik world view was comparable to that of the Jews in Nazi ideology: evil incarnate'.[27] The *kulaks*, who were in fact strong, industrious, intelligent farmers[28] as well as bearers of national consciousness, were to be 'liquidated as a class'; this, as well as the sudden campaign of forced total collectivization, was announced by Stalin on 27 December 1929 and formulated in the CPSU(B) Central Committee resolution of 5 January 1930.[29] The qualifier 'total' was to distinguish it from the slow and partial collectivization of the preceding year or two, which had met with widespread resistance from the peasantry.

All *kulaks*, as well as those 'middle' and poor peasants who opposed collective farms, were 'dispossessed' and exiled, some 10 million people, according to the Soviet historian Roy Medvedev; 2 or 3 million died during 'dispossession' and exile. Whole villages – for instance, in the Kuban' area, a block of 16 villages – were exiled; similarly in Byelorussia.[30] Another Soviet authority, V. Tikhonov, calculates that in the course of collectivization some 3 million households, with not fewer than 15 million individuals, were liquidated.[31]

But in Kazakhstan, collectivization began in earnest as early as 1929. Some top Kazakh communist leaders opposed it, along with the growing centralization of power and were purged by Moscow for 'bourgeois nationalism'. Collectivization involved the forcible settlement of Kazakh herdsmen on the land, causing large-scale slaughter of cattle. Revolts in 1930 and 1931 were crushed by Budennyi's cavalry army.[32] Those who resisted were killed or deported, and hundreds of thousands died in the ensuing famine which broke the resistance of the survivors. Altogether, it is thought that over 1·5 million Kazakhs, or roughly one in three of the population perished during the 1930s, and that 80 per cent of the herds were destroyed. Some 15–20 per cent of the Kazakhs left their republic at this time, in addition to a large number who had managed to migrate to China with their herds at the end of the 1920s. Relative to the size of their population, the Kazakh holocaust exceeded that of any other nation in the Soviet Union at the time.[33] Collectivization was completed by 1937.

The main targets were the Ukraine and the North Caucasus where the famine was particularly severe. The main population in the North Caucasus were the Don Cossacks in the north and the ethnically Ukrainian Kuban' Cossacks in the south. During the Civil War they had defended their own independence, at times in alliance with the anti-Soviet Russian White forces. After their defeat by the Soviet armies many Cossacks left the country rather than surrender. Those who remained were one of the population groups specifically discriminated against: they were not allowed to serve in the Red Army until 1936,[34] and have never been recognized as a nation. Being 'enemies', they experienced the full fury of the liquidation of the *kulaks*, forced collectivization and total grain extraction, and were left to starve to death in their millions. Stalin took his final revenge on the Cossacks who had left the country when, at the end of World War II, Britain handed them over to him for slaughter, although they had never been Soviet subjects.[35]

Roy Medvedev estimates that 'hardest hit was the southern Ukraine. Less affected were the North Caucasus, the Volga area, Kazakhstan and Soviet Central Asia', and his conservative guess is that 'altogether 6 million people died during the famine'.[36] (The affected Volga area comprised the Volga German ASSR and some nominally Russian regions with large Tatar populations.)

The Ukrainians, the USSR's largest nation after the Russians, were the major object of Stalin's hatred. The fact that they had had an independent government and resisted Russian reconquest for three years, with pockets of guerilla activity for a few more, made their loyalty suspect. Their Bolsheviks were also suspect: an influential Ukrainian writer, Mykola Khvyl'ovyi, could urge, 'Away from Moscow!', and as for the veteran Bolshevik Skrypnyk, Stalin could not forgive the former's sharp rebuff to his high-handed April 1918 telegram to the Soviet Ukrainian government ('Enough playing at a government and a republic. It's time to drop that game; enough is enough');[37] nor could Stalin forgive Skrypnyk's barbed remarks at Party congresses, blocking his election by the Eleventh Congress to the post of General Secretary and, together with other non-Russians' leaders, successful resistance to Stalin's plan of absorption by Russia of non-Russian republics. Nor would Skrypnyk acknowledge Stalin's seniority, while commanding the allegiance and respect of his Ukrainian Bolshevik colleagues and the Ukrainian people at large. Thus Stalin saw potential disloyalty in all Ukrainian communists as well as the Ukrainian masses.

The collectivization in the Ukraine was directed in the villages chiefly by Party emissaries from Russia, most of whom were industrial workers whose lack of any knowledge of agriculture was compensated by the power of the gun. The first stage was the removal – deportation or sometimes murder – of the *kulaks* in early 1930. The loss of some 200,000 of the most efficient and industrious farming families was in itself a severe blow to agriculture. The remaining smaller farmers were driven into collectives, which simply meant that all livestock and implements were put together (there was no additional equipment available for large-scale cultivation). Party emissaries put in charge of these so-called collective 'farms' were not qualified to manage them, and the results were disastrous.[38]

There were numerous armed risings by peasants, chiefly in the Ukraine, the North Caucasus, the Middle Volga area, Transcaucasia, Central Asia and in Krasnoiarsk Region in Western Siberia, next to Kazakhstan. Between January and March 1930 alone, there were more than 2,000 such cases.[39] Against them security police troops, and sometimes, notably in the Don and Kuban' areas and in some regions of the Ukraine, tanks and military aircraft were deployed. A three-day battle in August 1930 in the Dnepropetrovsk region resulted in thousands of peasants being killed, while the survivors were deported to labour camps; in two villages, mass executions were carried out on the edges of ravines, after which these villages were set on fire.[40] Sometimes the Red Army units (mostly peasants' sons, after all) refused to fight the rebelling peasants and even joined them.

By March 1930 Stalin had accepted defeat, blaming the excesses committed on local Party men and condemning the application of compulsion. Most peasants left the collective farms. Not for long, though: within months, Stalin started an all-out drive with increased ruthlessness, but this time round he applied the hunger weapon.

Stalin's chief aim was the liquidation of free peasantry, the only economically independent major force in the land,[41] and 'the main army of the national movement' among the non-Russians, and hence a potential obstacle to his absolute power. Stalin's method was shatteringly simple: to demand grain deliveries far in excess of actual production and starve the peasants into total submission. Thus, when the original delivery quotas were mostly fulfilled in August 1932, another two levies were imposed in October and in early 1933, and everything edible was seized at gunpoint leaving neither food nor seed. On 7 August 1932, a decree was passed 'On Protection of the Property of State Enterprises, Collective Farms . . .', the effect of which was that a starving peasant who gleaned a few ears of corn, even if they were left in the field after harvest, could be shot, or under 'extenuating circumstances' imprisoned for a minimum of ten years, with confiscation of all property.[42] With famine conditions ever worsening, by the end of 1932 the bulk of the peasantry had been herded back into the collective farms. Skrypnyk and certain other Ukrainian Bolshevik leaders appealed to Moscow to reduce delivery quotas, but to this Stalin turned a deaf ear. By the summer of 1933, some six million had died of starvation in the famine he deliberately engineered.

The neighbouring Russian districts along the north-eastern boundary of the Ukraine were hardly affected by the famine, but the border was closed by the security troops to stop starving Ukrainian peasants getting bread from the Russian side, though some succeeded in doing so by night.[43] In Byelorussia, which lagged behind the rest of the USSR in the speed of collectivization, famine was much less severe than in the Ukraine, and a large number of Ukrainians who were able to move to Byelorussia managed to save their lives.[44] This border seems not to have been closed.

About one million *kulaks* and their 'henchmen' were deported with their families to Siberia, and towards the end of 1932 all pretence of a 'class' approach was dropped. New mass repressions were carried out under the direction of Lazar Kaganovich (the former Ukraine Party boss) and Molotov in the Ukraine, Byelorussia and especially the North Caucasus, where entire villages are known to have been deported.[45] Any official or communist or member of the security police at any level in the hierarchy, from local to central, who showed compassion for the starving, or was not confiscating absolutely all foodstuffs, or was arresting a smaller number of people for deportation or execution than the quota ordered from above, risked being liquidated himself as a saboteur and helper of the *kulaks*. To insure against this and to get into the higher authorities' good books, many of them would greatly overfulfil their quotas. Some tens of thousands were shot during collectivization, either in the course of resistance or by a summary court procedure. The security police greatly reduced the numbers of homeless orphans left by the famine by rounding up and shooting them between 1932 and 1934.[46]

In Central Asia, denomadization and collectivization, started in 1927–8, met with widespread opposition and open rebellion between 1928 and 1932. Many Kirghiz slaughtered livestock or drove their herds into China. The Basmachi rebel movement, which had seemed a spent force, reappeared.[47] In March 1929 Ibrahim Bek returned from Afghanistan with a 600-strong force to head the resistance in Tadzhikistan,[48] while three months later Dzhunaid Khan crossed from Persia into Turkmenistan, where he directed a force of some 1,500 men.[49] Pacification was carried out by the Red Army and Russian-dominated political police and militia units; collectivization, largely by Russian officials, workers and brigades. The last two major Central Asian uprisings against collectivization took place in 1931 in the Kara Kum Desert, and in 1932 near the Iangi-Tuar Oasis where a considerable number of Red Army men, led by Pavlo Dybenko, a former member of Lenin's first government, fell in action against the Basmachi. For faithful service, Stalin was to reward Dybenko with a bullet in 1938.[50] After the 1932 battle, intermittent raids from across the border by small Basmachi bands continued for another year or so.[51]

In Transcaucasia, there was armed resistance against collectivization, particularly in Armenia and Georgia, and Red Army units suffered serious losses from guerilla attacks. In 1929, there was a major peasant uprising in Adzharia in the south-west of Georgia.[52] The hatred towards the invading collectivizers was so overwhelming that in the summer of 1930 Armenians and Azeri Turks are reported to have joined forces against them. The climax of the resistance came in the summer of 1931, and it was broken by Russian troops early in 1932. Armenian rebel forces retreated to the mountains and, by late 1934, had fled into Persia.[53] Famine conditions prevailed, notably in Armenia, from 1931 to 1934.

The most detailed study so far of Stalin's rural Terror is Robert Conquest's book *The Harvest of Sorrow*. He considers the following figures to be 'reasonably sound estimates' of the numbers who died: peasant dead as a result of collectivization and dekulakization, 6·5 million; died in the Kazakhstan catastrophe, 1 million; total deaths in the 1932–3 famine, 7 million (therefrom 5 million in the Ukraine, 1 million in the North Caucasus, and 1 million elsewhere); the total peasant dead between 1930 and 1937, 11 million, with a further 3·5 million who were arrested during this period and died later in the camps.[54] The total number of those deported has been calculated by Moshe Lewin, a leading specialist on Soviet policy towards the peasantry, to have been 10 million or more, 'of whom a great many must have perished'.[55] Some deportees were put into prison camps, and it was in 1930 that this enormous increase of prisoner numbers led to the establishment of a vast complex of forced labour camps known by the name of its headquarters, Gulag, which is the Russian acronym for the Chief Administration of [Corrective Labour] Camps. In 1928 there were probably fewer than 40,000 inmates of labour camps; by the mid-1930s their numbers had increased more than a hundredfold to about 5 million. Other deportees were placed in 'special settlements' (*spetsposelenie*). These 'settlements' were in most cases simply open spaces, with no shelter, in harsh climatic conditions. Mortality was very high in both types of deportation, and the labour camps often resembled the extermination camps of the Nazis. According to a conservative Soviet calculation, no fewer than 5 million died in the famine from starvation and epidemics caused by it, and 1 million *kulaks* were shot.[56] According to another authority, as many as 5 million families were branded as *kulaks* and deported.[57]

Assault on the nations

The national contract having been torn up, the annihilation of its shreds proceeded apace. Since the 1920s, national elites had been subjected to selective persecution: first, former members of independent non-Soviet governments, then former members of parties other than communist, then old non-Party intelligentsia, then those non-Bolshevik communists who had joined the Bolshevik Party, then members of any factions within the

Bolshevik Party, and finally those Bolsheviks not guilty of any such 'sins'. Charges against non-Bolsheviks were usually 'criminal', such as membership of an anti-Soviet 'nationalist' organization; against Bolsheviks, they could also be 'political', such as 'national deviation'. The security police and the Party would usually make those still in good standing join in the hounding of the next victim or group of victims. During the collectivization campaign and the famine, Bolsheviks trying to avert the disasters being inflicted on their nations could also be accused of sabotaging the campaign and aiding the 'enemy'.

In Central Asia the Uzbek national communists were accused of charging Moscow with making Uzbekistan a 'cotton colony'.[58] In Kirghizia, the former leader of 'The Thirty', Abdukarim Sidik-uulu, who had returned from exile and was director of the Kirghiz State Planning Commission, was alleged to have created a conspiratorial organization to oppose collectivization and overthrow the communist regime in Kirghizia with arms obtained from China and elsewhere.[59] Two members of the Turkmenian government, the Commissar of Education, Boriev, and the Commissar of Supply, Ak Murad Orazov, were charged with aiming at the establishment of an independent Turkmenian state under British protection; they were allegedly connected with a nationalist organization particularly active between 1927 and 1931 aiming at Turkmenistan's secession from the USSR.[60] In Tadzhikistan, the national communists' resistance led to several purges between 1927 and 1931. The collectivization campaign, completed in 1934, ended with a major purge of 'bourgeois-nationalist elements' in the political apparatus. The 1934 purge affected 66 per cent of total party membership, including the top leaders, as it dropped from 14,329 in January 1933 to 4,791 in January 1935.[61]

In January 1933 Stalin's new lieutenant in the Ukraine, Postyshev, appointed to the all-powerful post of the Second Secretary of the CP(B)U, arrived from Moscow with a large staff of Russian officials and security police. Blaming the CP(B)U for the breakdown of agriculture and non-fulfilment of delivery quotas, he instituted, amid a raging famine, a major wave of terror in the Party. Between June 1932 and October 1933, 75 per cent of Soviet officials and 80 per cent of Party committee secretaries were replaced by Postyshev's men, and most were either deported to labour camps or shot. In early 1933 the security police fabricated another fictitious case, that of a 'Ukrainian Military Organization' (UVO). Those arrested included Shums'kyi, the former Commissar for Education, although he was in Moscow where he had worked for the preceding six years; a number of former functionaries of the Communist Party of the Polish-occupied Western Ukraine who had emigrated from there and mostly worked in Skrypnyk's Commissariat of Education; and many former non-Bolshevik communists. On 1 March Postyshev demoted Skrypnyk from the post of Commissar for Education to that of Chairman of the State Planning Commission. In March–May the security police stepped up its arrests of those associated with Ukrainization. On 13 May, the leading writer Khvyl'ovyi was driven to suicide.

In early June, at the Central Committee of the CP(B)U, Postyshev attacked Skrypnyk for 'nationalist deviation', and demanded an admission of his 'errors'. Stalin probably planned to use Skrypnyk's 'admission' to dispose of him in a trial. Skrypnyk made no admission; the Ukrainian Politburo met five times that month to discuss the matter. When Skrypnyk did eventually submit a letter, it was rumoured to be more of an accusation than a confession.[62] On 7 July, the Politburo decided that Skrypnyk's 'document does not meet the Central Committee's demands and ignores a series of directions given to Comrade Skrypnyk by the Central Committee'.

The next item on the agenda was Skrypnyk's continued membership of the Politburo, and he retired from the meeting at the beginning of this item's discussion and went to his office in the same building. In his absence, the Politburo decided to remove him from its membership. Unbeknown to them, this was not necessary, as he was no longer alive. Having reached his office, he shot himself.[63]

Shums'kyi was sentenced in the UVO case to 'only' ten years' labour camps; in 1943, when he was due for release, he, who had fought against the German occupation of the Ukraine in 1918, offered his services in the current struggle for communism's survival. He was neither rehabilitated nor released, and in protest committed suicide on 18 September 1946.[64]

After Skrypnyk's death, the Terror was increased. By 15 October, 27,500 Party members had been expelled and arrested. By the end of 1933, 29 per cent of all members (47,000 at 1 October) were purged, and during 1934 an additional 15 per cent were expelled. Some 2,000 school teachers and 1,650 teachers in higher education were dismissed in late 1933, chiefly for 'nationalism'.

Similar havoc was wrought in Byelorussia, where in the summer and autumn of 1933, 6,002 members and 3,767 candidates were expelled from the Party, constituting 15 and 28 per cent respectively. The Commissariat of Education, and school and higher education teachers were among the chief purge targets, charges of 'nationalism' abounded, and the national and cultural leadership were almost completely liquidated.

The Great Terror

Having engineered the assassination of the Leningrad Party chief Kirov on 1 December 1934,[65] Stalin intensified the Terror. The 'Great Terror' in its main phase lasted for four years, till late 1938, with the frenzied climax in 1937 and 1938. By the middle of 1989, no detailed Soviet figures were available, though Roy Medvedev, while admitting that his figures were very conservative, calculated that Stalin's rule had inflicted terrible suffering on perhaps 38 million people – roughly a fifth of the Soviet population of the time – and had taken the lives of at least 12 million;[66] at the same time, another source has estimated the number of those killed by Stalin as being not less than 20 million.[67] Robert Conquest, in his unsurpassed work on the subject, offers his conservative estimate that from 1930 to 1953 the Stalin Terror against the nations of the Soviet Union was responsible for 20 to 30 million dead, both through execution and very high camp mortality rates. This estimate excludes deaths from starvation in the countryside, but includes peasants executed or dying in labour camps in consequence of collectivization.[68]

In 1936, on the eve of the worst year of the Terror, Stalin offered his surviving subjects a bigger and better Constitution. While it reiterated the promises of the original Union Constitution, however, Stalin's actions made a mockery of them. The original Constitution promised to ensure 'the external security of the peoples', but Stalin's execution of 40,000 Red Army officers – three-quarters of its officer corps – handed Hitler a massive strategic advantage. It promised to ensure the economic development of the peoples, but their crippled agriculture, basic to their economies, was to be kept stunted for the next half century. It offered the freedom of national development of peoples, but their teachers, academics, writers, actors and other cultural figures were exterminated and their languages excluded from official use. And, while it claimed to safeguard the sovereign rights of the Union republics, those same rights were in practice totally stripped away.

Practically all of the leaders of the non-Russian republics – both those who had signed the original Union treaty and their successors – were even deprived of their right to life. Successive heads of the Soviet Ukrainian government were liquidated, among them Iurii Kotsiubyns'kyi who had held this office in 1917–18 and was executed in 1936, and Vlas Chubar, who had held office since 1923, was forced to resign in 1934, and killed in 1939 or 1941.[69]

At the February–March 1937 Central Committee Plenum, Stalin succeeded, with the Security Police guards waiting in the wings, in crushing the attempt by the committee's moderates, who were in the majority, to halt the purge. Now he was free to prepare the Great Trial, considerably larger than the two preceding show trials, in order to dispose of Bukharin, Rykov and many other top oppositionists, as well as to step up monstrously the Terror against the population at large.

While in Russia he was selective in his destruction; in the Ukraine, where the leadership showed solidarity in opposing the extension of the purge, their destruction was total. Stalin planned a mammoth show trial with over 200 defendants, who, according to his scenario, were members of a 'National-Fascist Organization' headed by Liberberg, Postyshev's former assistant, who was allegedly acting on the instructions of Hitler himself. The ideological leader of this 'brutal gang of nationalist terrorists' was supposedly none other than Panas Liubchenko, Chairman of the Council of People's Commissars (that is, Premier) of the Ukraine.

In August 1937 a Moscow Politburo commission consisting of Molotov, Khrushchev and Ezhov arrived in Kiev with a large force of 'special troops' of the security police. At a session of the Central Committee of the C P(B)U, Molotov proposed the dismissal of Petrovs'kyi, Kossior, Liubchenko and others from their posts. The Ukrainian Central Committee refused to vote as instructed, in spite of Molotov's ringing Stalin for instructions. Finally, Molotov suggested that the Ukrainian Politburo should go to Moscow for a combined session with the central Politburo. Rather than walk into this obvious trap, on 30 August 1937 Liubchenko shot himself and his wife. Having lost the principal actor, Stalin decided to abandon the show trial already carefully scripted by the security police. The arrests and executions or deportation to camps of all the others nevertheless followed, and the charge of belonging to the 'National-Fascist Organization' was levelled at most of them. Among its 'members', Hryn'ko, at that time People's Commissar of Finance in Moscow, was ultimately sentenced to death in the Great Trial of March 1938, and Iakir, the Commander of the Kiev Military District, arrested on 31 May 1937, was court-marshalled in the 'Tukhachevskii conspiracy' case on 11 June. The phantom 'organization' also included numerous cultural, educational and academic figures, among them director of the Ukrainian State Opera Ianovs'kyi, director of the Shevchenko Institute of Literature Academician Ievhen Shabliovs'kyi and a researcher at that institute Anatol' Kostenko. The latter two were among the small minority to survive their two decades in the Gulag.[70] Of the 102 members of the Ukrainian Central Committee, only three survived to take part in the Fourteenth Congress of the C P(B)U in June 1938.

In Byelorussia in 1935 and 1936, more than half of the Party membership was expelled. The Chairman of the Council of People's Commissars, Mikola Haladzed, was shot for 'bourgeois nationalism' in June 1937, and so was the First Secretary of the C P(B)B, Hikala (himself a purger of others). At the same time, the Chairman of the Central Executive Committee (that is, the President) Aleksandr Charviakow, one of the oldest Byelorussian communists and the founder of Soviet Byelorussia, was charged with being 'the inspirer and the leader of the Byelorussian nationalist deviation on the C P(B) of Byelorussia', and committed suicide on 16 June. This was followed by the arrests or executions of almost the entire leadership, including the People's Commissars, and of many thousands of high and middle government and Party officials. Vasil' Sharanhovich, installed by Stalin in March 1937 as First Secretary in place of Hikala, was denounced in August by Moscow's emissary, who also liquidated, among others, Charviakow's successor Natalevich. Sharanhovich ended up among the defendants with Bukharin in the Great Trial, and was shot in March 1938, while the Central Committee of the C P(B)B was purged.

The First Secretary of the Armenian Party Aghasi Khandzhian was secretly shot by Beria in his own office in 1936, whereupon many Armenian Party and government officials were rounded up and charged with complicity in that murder.[71] Ter-Gabrelian, who had been chairman of the Council of People's Commissars in 1935, was killed while being interrogated by the security police in mid-1937. The new First Secretary Amatouni, and almost the whole leadership of the Central Committee and Council of People's Commissars with its chairman, were arrested in September. Mass arrests spread throughout the republic. That year, there were more than 3,500 among leading officials alone, many of whom were shot without the formality of a trial. Most of those appointed as replacements to the leading Party bodies were in turn liquidated within a few months.

In Georgia and Azerbaijan, the Terror of 1937–8 was probably worse than in the other republics, barring the Ukraine.[72] The chief Georgian victim among the many to perish in July 1937 was the Old Bolshevik Budu Mdivani, former Premier of Soviet Georgia, whom Lenin had defended against Stalin and whose case had been Lenin's final reason for wishing to remove Stalin from the General Secretaryship. Another prominent victim was the Old Bolshevik M. Okudzhava (the poet Bulat Okudzhava's father). In September, thousands in the Party, government and economic leadership were destroyed. In Azerbaijan, the 1937–8 purge, directed by Bagirov, swept away many top officials including G. M. Musabekov, former chairman of the Council of People's Commissars of Transcaucasia, and Husein Rakhmanov, secretary of the Central Committee and chairman of the Council of People's Commissars of Azerbaijan.[73]

In other non-Russian republics, too, Party leaderships and governments were found, virtually simultaneously, around September 1937, to consist everywhere of traitors and 'bourgeois nationalists', and their destruction, directed by emissaries from Moscow, followed a similar pattern. In 1937–9, 18 Kazakh leaders were executed, including the veteran national communist and former chairman of the Turkestan CEC, T. Ryskulov,[74] the chairman of the Central Executive Committee, Kulumbetov, the deputy chairman of the Council of People's Commissars, Eskarev and the secretary of the Party organization in the capital, Alma-Ata, Dasvokezov. In 1933–8, three successive chairmen of the Kirghiz Council of People's Commissars, Abdrakhamanov, Irakaev and Salikhov, perished, as well as three successive first secretaries of the Kirghiz Communist Party (not ethnic Kirghiz), Shakhrai, Belotskii, Ammosov, and the chairman of the Kirghiz CEC, Urazbekov. Kirghizia's new intelligentsia was decimated, and Party membership declined by nearly 51 per cent between 1934 and 1939.[75] A large number of Turkmen Party and government leaders and creative intelligentsia were accused of nationalism, 'Pan-Turkism' or of assisting the Basmachi and national resistance movements, and purged.[76] In Tadzhikistan, successive leaders were removed, and by the end of the 1930s the Tadzhik political apparatus, virtually denuded of local cadres, was run outright by Russians sent out by the centre. The entire government of the Tatar ASSR was under arrest by the midsummer of 1937. The Tatars and Bashkirs lost virtually their entire intelligentsia and almost all their political leaders.

Destruction of the cultural elite

Having liquidated the non-Russian republics' political leaders, Stalin installed in their place his obedient servants, well trained in the art of denunciation. The policy of indigenization having been abandoned in the early 1930s, many, or often most, of those replacing the liquidated officials were no longer of the indigenous nationality but Russian.

But this was only the tip of the iceberg: the Great Terror disposed of countless other non-Russian victims, the majority of them being members of the new Soviet intelligentsia: writers, school teachers, engineers, professors, lecturers in establishments of higher education, scholars, agronomists, technicians and others. The cultural intelligentsia, especially writers and literary scholars, who were the leading bearers of national consciousness, was a prime target. In all of the republics, numerous writers perished. Most were charged with 'nationalism', or, among the Moslem nations, with dzhadidism.

Of the 259 Ukrainian writers who were being published in 1930, only 36 continued to be so after 1938.[77] From among Ukrainian men of letters active in the 1920s and 1930s, about 500 were 'repressed': of these, a manifestly incomplete list names some 150 known to have perished.[78]

In Georgia the highly talented poet Titsian Tabidze was shot, and Paolo Iashvili, his friend and equal, killed himself as the result of the execution of Tabidze and other Georgian literary figures. In Uzbekistan, the writers Fitrat (formerly a Bukharan political leader) and Cholpan, both of whom were originally dzhadidists, were purged in 1937–8, as was the dzhadidist reformer Bekbudi. In Kirghizia in the late 1930s, Qasim Tinistan-uulu, a dominant figure in cultural and intellectual life regarded as the founder of Kirghiz Soviet literature, was arrested; his early poem 'To the Alash', addressed to the independentist Kazakh-Kirghiz party Alash Orda, was obviously remembered by his prosecutors. The writers Sidik Qarach-uulu – another former adherent of Alash Orda – Kenesarin, Namatov and Dzhamgirchinov were also arrested. The Tatars and Bashkirs lost practically all their pre-Revolutionary writers.

Of the 700 writers representing all the Soviet nations, including Russia, who attended the First Congress of Soviet Writers in 1934 as delegates, only 50 or so survived until the Second Congress in 1954.[79] Eduard Beltov, a Russian journalist on the staff of the Moscow monthly *Druzhba narodov* ('Friendship of the Peoples') who in the 1970s and 1980s spent 15 years collecting material about 'repressed' writers, was surprised to discover that

Russian writers were in the minority among them. Out of 1,000 writers who perished in the Terror and whose names he was able to gather by June 1988, about 700 were from non-Russian Union and autonomous republics. He concluded that

> National [non-Russian] literatures were dealt such a devastating blow that some of them have not yet recovered from it, and will hardly recover in the near future . . . That which was inflicted on Ukrainian literature defies description. This is due to the fact that the struggle with 'bourgeois nationalism' began with the Ukraine and Byelorussia.

By November 1988 Beltov's total had crept up from 1,000 to nearly 1,300, a figure which he still considered incomplete.[80]

Russification

The destruction of non-Russian writers was appalling in percentage terms, although in absolute figures the victims numbered in the hundreds. The losses of the rest of the intelligentsia, from scholars and professors to engineers, agronomists and school teachers, were in the many hundred thousands. This beheading of the non-Russian nations was accompanied, throughout the 1930s, by advancing Russification in all spheres. Indigenization having been abandoned, all official business was now conducted in Russian; technical secondary education as well as higher education in technical, and often other, subjects was switched to Russian; the percentage of primary and general secondary schools with Russian as the language of instruction was growing, albeit as yet slowly but steadily; while in schools with an indigenous language of instruction, Russian became an obligatory subject. The Red Army became more than ever a tool of Russification, the few separate national units having all been abolished. The number of books published in non-Russian languages dropped to a fraction of their figures for 1931–2, and their quality was for the most part abysmal; the cultural renaissance of the 1920s had to give way to virulent attacks on 'bourgeois nationalism', treacly paeans to Stalin, and expressions of servile gratitude for the happiness he was bestowing on the Soviet peoples.

Among teachers and academics, those specializing in non-Russian languages and literature suffered most in the Terror, as did the institutions with which they were connected. Practically all lexicographic work in these languages that had been done in the 1920s was declared 'nationalist' and banned. Their vocabularies were purged of 'archaisms', which harked back dangerously to national history, and 'alien' elements: in Ukrainian and Byelorussian, for example, vocabulary of Polish origin was dubbed 'fascist', while in Moslem languages, it was Arabisms that were condemned. These were replaced by 'internationalist' elements – Russian-derived modern scientific-technical and socio-political vocabulary – and grammatical constructions borrowed from Russian. Between 1927 and 1930, Arabic script was replaced by the Latin alphabet in Moslem languages (as was also done in Turkey); at that time it was not thought politic to replace it by the Russian alphabet instead, as this would have smacked of Russification. By the late 1930s, such compunctions had gone by the board, and the Russian alphabet supplanted the Latin between 1938 and 1940. Moldavian underwent the same change at this time; in 1933, it had been given the Romanian (Latin) alphabet[81] (Moldavian and Romanian are actually the same language).

Nevertheless, Russification did not progress uniformly: some nations were again more equal than others. Thus, the Georgian and Armenian SSRs were the only republics whose 1938 constitutions declared their respective languages the official ('state') languages of their republics. In Armenia, the study of Russian became obligatory in secondary schools and establishments of higher education only in 1938. At the other extreme were the Jewish schools. In 1931 there were 1,100 of them, from primary schools to teachers' training colleges and technical secondary schools, with 130,000 pupils; in the course of the 1930s their number fell swiftly until few remained.

Genocide

Destruction by deportation of several million Ukrainian peasants and intelligentsia, as well as hundreds of thousands of members of other nations, does indeed fall within the definition of genocide, even though the destruction of these nations was not complete. One could argue, however, that the reasons for such destruction were political or economic, however monstrously perverted. But at the same time Stalin embarked upon the course of a 'purer', more thorough and complete variety of genocide: the extermination by deportation of *complete* nations and national groups identical in principle to Hitler's extermination of the Jews and Gypsies. The better known wartime and post-war deportations of whole nations were preceded by the deportations of virtually complete national groups, all of them Soviet citizens, belonging to nations whose main body lived, in most cases, outside the Soviet Union.

As far back as the early 1930s, Chinese and Koreans, many accused of being Japanese agents, were deported from the Far East as well as from the European Soviet Union to penal 'special settlements'.[82] The Armenians in the Ukraine were rounded up in September 1937, 600 of them in Kharkov alone.[83] In the same month, the Latvians in the European part of the Soviet Union were arrested. It was preposterously alleged that a Latvian secret organization had worked for a Greater Latvia stretching over a large part of European Russia, including Moscow.[84] From December of that year, the Greeks were arrested everywhere on the equally fantastic charge of plotting to create a Greater Greek Republic over a large part of the Ukraine.[85] In 1941, a great number of Kurds, possibly over 60,000, practically the whole

Kurdish population of the Kurdistan District in Azerbaijan, were removed, and their district abolished. They were deported to Kazakhstan, Kirghizia and other areas, and many must have perished during transportation.[86]

All these national groups, with the exception of the Kurds, had been domiciled over relatively wide areas. At the same time, however, a different scenario was being rehearsed for massive and 'instant' deportations among the compactly settled nations of the North Caucasus. On 28 July 1937, Stalin's notorious henchman E. G. Evdokimov, the Security Police representative in the Caucasus, gave instructions to the assembled Party leadership of the North Caucasus for a long-planned 'super-purge'. The first phase of this 'general operation' in the Chechen-Ingush ASSR consisted of the arrests and executions, or mostly deportation, of 14,000 people, or one in every 30 of the republic's population; they were all rounded up in the small hours of 1 August. The total toll in the North Caucasus was 80,000. By 10 August, some 100,000 people had been arrested in the area, or between 3 and 4 per cent of the population. Another similar mass operation was supervised by the Security Police Chief Ezhov's right-hand man, Shkiriatov. This time all Chechen and Ingush Party and government leaders from the highest down to the village level, as well as leading intellectuals, were rounded up, starting on 7 October, and charged with 'bourgeois nationalism', among other things. Arrests went on till November 1938.[87] After a lull, the deportation activities shifted to the west, where the instant removal technique practised on the Chechens and Ingush was applied to tens of thousands in the Baltic states (see Chapter 7). Once the technique had been perfected, it was applied once again, with a vengeance, to the North Caucasus and elsewhere, to deport, instantly and totally, all the remaining Chechens and Ingush and several other nations: populations running into millions (see Chapter 8).

This, then, was Stalin's version of 'the freedom of national development of peoples'.

7

Between Hitler and Stalin

During World War I and the Civil War, large parts of the non-Russian lands were occupied by the Germans, and there was also the sporadic presence of Allied expeditionary forces, chiefly in support of the anti-Bolshevik Whites and sometimes of independent non-Russian governments. From then on, the Bolsheviks were conscious of the possibility of an external threat: thus, in 1923 a resolution adopted at the Twelfth Congress of the RCP(B) pointed out

> the danger of possible new [military] intervention attempts on the part of the most implacable elements of the imperialist camp . . . the more the international bourgeois reaction (fascism) grows the more chances there are that at a given moment a new attempt at military pressure will be made against the USSR.[1]

The Bolsheviks watched Hitler's rise to power with apprehension. As early as June 1933, the Soviet Government protested against German *lebensraum* claims, which were transparently intended to be satisfied at the expense of Soviet territory.[2] The threat to the Soviet Union was aggravated by Germany's Anti-Comintern Pact with Japan (1936) and Italy (1937). The Soviet Commissar for Foreign Affairs Litvinov branded Hitler's 1938 *anschluss* of Austria as 'the forcible deprivation of the Austrian people of their political, economic and cultural independence'.[3] and in March 1939 protested to the German ambassador in Moscow against the dismemberment of Czechoslovakia.

In April, Neville Chamberlain reversed Britain's policy of appeasement, offered guarantees to Poland, Romania, Greece and Turkey, and invited the USSR to join Britain and France in the guarantee system. The Soviet Union replied by proposing that Finland and the two Baltic states bordering on the USSR, Estonia and Latvia, also be included in the system. The Baltic states, however, did not desire such guarantees,[4] since they would involve the USSR demanding bases on their territories, leading unavoidably to loss of sovereignty. As R. A. B. Butler said in the House of Commons, 'the main question has been whether we should encroach on the independence of the Baltic states. We are in agreement . . . that we should not do so.'[5] By early August the 'negotiations . . . broke down on this very question of the Baltic countries and Finland', as Stalin put it to Anthony Eden some two years later.[6]

The unholy alliance

Although no love seemed to be lost between Hitler and Stalin, a major trade and credit agreement between Germany and the USSR was concluded in 1935, and negotiations for further agreements were started in the same year[7] as well as in 1938 (twice) and in early 1939, all of them on the German initiative.[8] And when on 15 August 1939 the German Government intimated its desire for a serious improvement in relations with the USSR,[9] the government of the latter proposed the conclusion of a trade and credit agreement as a prelude to a non-aggression pact.[10] The agreement was speedily concluded on 19 August.[11]

Stalin's alliance with Hitler, in view of the latter's virulent anti-communism (though Britain and France were not enthusiastically pro-communist either), may seem surprising, and indeed it was a profound shock to the European communist movements. However, there is an undeniable affinity between the two dictators and the systems over which they presided. After the war, some scholars described both regimes as totalitarian; but the Bolsheviks themselves recognized in the fascists (including the Nazis) their ablest pupils at least as early as 1923. Thus, at the Twelfth Party Congress the Party theoretician Bukharin said in his report on behalf of the Russian representation at the Central Committee of the Comintern:

> Characteristic of the methods of fascist struggle is the fact that they, more than any other party whatsoever, have adopted, and apply in practice, the experience of the Russian revolution. If they are considered from the *formal* point of view, i.e. from the point of view of the technique of their political methods, then it is a full application of Bolshevik tactics and especially of Russian Bolshevism . . .[12]

Bukharin was not challenged on this at the congress or in the first, 1923, edition of the proceedings; but the commentators of the second, 1968, edition decried Bukharin's comparison as 'absurd', 'groundless and antiscientific'.[13] For another chilling parallel between the two systems, M. Voslensky quotes Stalin's 'jovial' remark, when in 1939 he introduced his Security Police Chief, Beria, to Ribbentrop with the words, 'This man is our Himmler.'[14]

Hitler's Foreign Minister Ribbentrop arrived in Moscow on 23 August 1939, and on the same day together with his opposite number Molotov (who supplanted Litvinov in April or May) signed the non-aggression pact. Its infamous Secret Additional Protocol on 'the delimitation of their respective spheres of interest in Eastern Europe' specified that Finland, Estonia and Latvia were to be in the Soviet, and Lithuania in the German, sphere of interest, and that the ethnically largely Ukrainian lands in the south and the Byelorussian ones in the north, flanked by a strip of ethnic Polish territory, were to be in the Soviet sphere. The protocol also emphasized the Soviet interest in Bessarabia.

The pact enabled the Germans to attack Poland on 1 September, within a week of signing it, thereby unleashing World War II.[15] The USSR, in turn, invaded Poland on 17 September. On 28 September, a Soviet–German friendship and frontier treaty was concluded in Moscow, with another two Secret Additional Protocols. The first of these amended the Secret Protocol of 23 August 'to the effect that the territory of the Lithuanian State falls to the sphere of interest of the USSR', while the ethnic Polish strip fell to Germany. The second contained an agreement to suppress in their respective territories 'any Polish agitation which has repercussions on the territories of the other party'.[16]

On 28 June 1940 the USSR issued an ultimatum to Romania to surrender Bessarabia and northern Bucovina, and invaded them immediately without even waiting for a reply.

Sovietization of the new acquisitions

The partition of Poland liberated Ukrainians and Byelorussians living in former eastern Poland from Polish oppression (which was relatively mild compared with that of the Stalin regime) and united them with their brethren in the two respective Soviet republics in the east. The peasants looked forward to receiving the lands of the Polish landlords. In Western Byelorussia, the people greeted the Red Army with enthusiasm, and 'the liberators, in accordance with an old custom, were offered bread and salt in the street'.[17] The west Ukrainians, on the other hand, knew a great deal about the regime's egregious ruthlessness in the Ukrainian SSR in the 1930s, and their reception of the Red Army was muted.

The conquerors deemed it necessary to provide a semblance of 'voluntariness' and 'the people's will' in the annexations of all these territories to the USSR. For this purpose, the Soviet Military Command announced on 6 October that elections to the People's Assemblies of the Western Ukraine and Western Byelorussia would be held on 22 October. Although the people were supposed to have received 'genuinely democratic rights' and the elections 'were held on the basis of a democratic electoral law',[18] there was only one list of communist or communist-sponsored candidates, prepared under the supervision of the Red Army commanders and high Party officials from the USSR. According to the official figures, 92·8 per cent of voters voted in the Western Ukraine and 96·7 per cent in Western Byelorussia, of whom 90·9 per cent and 90·7 per cent respectively voted for the sole lists of 'national candidates'.

On 26 and 28 October respectively, each of the two People's Assemblies unanimously voted for their lands to join the USSR, and sent plenipotentiary commissions of 50 and 66 persons respectively to Moscow to submit their requests. In accordance with these, on 1 and 2 November respectively the USSR Supreme Soviet passed two laws granting their requests and incorporating their lands into the Ukrainian SSR and Byelorussian SSR respectively, and requesting the Supreme Soviets of the two republics to submit for consideration their own drafts of boundary delimitation between the two republics.[19]

In the north, the first Soviet move was to demand mutual assistance pacts with each of the three Baltic states and Finland which would allow the maintenance on their territories of Soviet land and air bases with garrisons of 20–30,000 in each while guaranteeing non-interference in their domestic affairs. Finland refused a pact on such conditions, but the three Baltic states knuckled under and signed theirs in September–October.[20] Rumours began to spread about their impending annexation, which Molotov denied in a speech to the Supreme Soviet declaring that 'all the spreading of nonsense about Sovietizing the Baltic countries is only to the interest of our common enemies, and of all anti-Soviet provocateurs'.[21] As for recalcitrant Finland, the USSR attacked it and after incurring considerable losses in the 'Winter War' of 28 November 1939 to 12 March 1940, annexed strips of its territory.

At the end of March, all seemed to be still as well with the Baltic states as could be expected. But by mid-May a new and ominous note had entered Soviet discourse, inspired by Hitler's conquest of Belgium, the Netherlands and Luxembourg:

> The recent war events have once more proved that the neutrality of small states which do not have the power to support it is a mere fantasy. Therefore, there are very few chances for small countries to survive and to maintain their independence. All considerations of small countries on the question of justice and injustice in relations with the Great Powers which are at war for their 'to be or not to be' are, at the very least, naïve.[22]

Practical consequences were not slow to follow. At the time of the fall of Paris, on 14 and 16 June Molotov issued ultimata to each of the three Baltic states that new governments be formed 'immediately' and that they give free access for much larger numbers of Soviet troops. Without waiting for the formation of suitable puppet governments to give formal assent, several hundred thousand Soviet troops poured into the three states.

In each state, a Soviet government emissary then took charge of the formation of governments that would be fully subservient to Moscow. In Lithuania, it was Dekanozov, 'one of the most active members of the Beria gang';[23] in Latvia, Vyshinskii, the notorious prosecutor at the Moscow show trials of the 1930s specializing in sending people to their deaths after false 'confessions' extracted under torture; and in Estonia, Zhdanov, who was later to lend his name to the bleak days of mature Stalinism. Each of them had a list of a new cabinet for the 'people's government' of each state, consisting of reliable stooges.

There were a few cases of misjudgement, quickly rectified. One, in Lithuania, proved an embarrassment: a famous and popular writer, V. Krėvė-Mickevičius, reputed to be strongly leftist and Russophile, was on Dekanozov's list as Vice-Premier and Foreign Minister: in his simplicity, Krėvė-Mickevičius believed the new government to be a legitimate one, but soon discovered that the country was ruled not by his premier and himself but by Dekanozov. Thinking that this was happening without Moscow's know-ledge, on 2 July he took his complaint to Molotov. Unable to understand the latter's equivocations, he inadvertently goaded Molotov into plain speaking:

> You provoke my candour, Mr Minister . . . You force me to say something which I had no wish to say at this time. Therefore we shall speak openly . . . You must take a good look at reality and understand that in the future small nations will have to disappear. Your Lithuania along with the other Baltic nations, including Finland, will have to join the glorious family of the Soviet Union. Therefore you should begin now to initiate your people into the Soviet system, which in the future shall reign everywhere, throughout all Europe; put into practice earlier in some places, as in the Baltic nations, later in others.[24]

On 5 July, the next step was taken: elections (Soviet-style, of course: one seat, one candidate) to new parliaments were announced and scheduled for 14 July. In each country, a Union of the Working People was set up as a quasi-coalition, although it was in fact an overwhelmingly communist grouping. Electoral committee were made up of communists, and proposal papers of 'bourgeois' (i.e. non-communist) candidates were annulled,[25] while the heavy presence of the Soviet Army made it impossible to protest about this. Political opponents were rounded up before the election; in Lithuania some 2,000 were seized, starting on the night of 11–12 July. It is significant that, although the platforms of the three communist fronts included such demands as the confiscation of large landholdings and their distribution to poor peasants, or the arrest of 'enemies of the people', they did not call for the Baltic states' incorporation into the Soviet Union. Rather, they denied any such intention; this issue was not meant to be at stake in these elections. In Estonia, some local communists even talked about an 'Outer Mongolian status' for the country. The turn-out was very low: in Lithuania, for instance, it was an estimated 20 per cent on 14 July, after which the next day was added for voting, and on 17 July the manifestly fictitious results were announced: 95·1 per cent of all voters had cast their votes, 99·19 per cent of whom voted for the candidates. The figure concocted by the Estonian electoral commission, 93 per cent for the communist front, looked somewhat less absurd. With the Soviet Army in charge, it would have been unthinkable to demand recounts.

On 21 July, only 16 days after the original announcement of elections, the new 'parliaments' met and voted to petition for admission to the USSR. Each parliament sent a plenipotentiary commission to the USSR Supreme

Soviet, which passed three laws on 3, 5 and 6 August, admitting Lithuania, Latvia and Estonia respectively as SSRs.[26] Just 15 months earlier, the Soviet Commissar for Foreign Affairs Litvinov had argued that

> It is difficult to admit that any people would voluntarily agree to the destruction of their independence and to their inclusion in another State, still less a people that . . . have already for twenty years maintained their independent existence.[27]

This invective against Hitler's annexation of Czechoslovakia is no less applicable to Stalin's annexation of the Baltic states, and gives the lie to the sorry charade of their 'voluntary' abdication of independence.

Meanwhile, with regard to the southernmost acquisition, on 2 August the USSR Supreme Soviet decreed the division of Bessarabia and northern Bucovina, whereby the latter plus the extreme north and south of Bessarabia, all three areas ethnically largely Ukrainian, were given to the Ukrainian SSR, while the ethnic Romanian bulk of Bessarabia was turned into the Moldavian SSR. Since Soviet Russia had never recognized the validity of Bessarabia's voluntary merger with Romania, the charade of 'elections', 'national assemblies' and 'petitions' was dispensed with, and the new SSR was created within five weeks of the ultimatum to Romania.[28]

Counting the loot

On 1 August, a few days before the Supreme Soviet of the USSR was due to examine the Baltic states' application to join the USSR, Molotov offered a 'national contract' to the three new entrants:

> the affiliation of these Republics to the Soviet Union will assure their rapid economic development and the flourishing of their national culture in every way; their entry into the Soviet Union will, moreover, greatly enhance their strength and ensure their security,

but then, continuing, he mentioned the really important factor: 'and at the same time still further increase the might of the Soviet Union'. More precisely,

> The fact that the frontier of the Soviet Union will now be shifted to the Baltic coast is of first-rate importance for our country. At the same time we shall now have ice-free ports in the Baltic of which we stand so much in need.

Likewise, as a result of the annexation of Bessarabia,

> the frontiers of the Soviet Union have shifted to the west and now reach the Danube which, next to the Volga, is the biggest river in Europe and one of the most important commercial routes for a number of European countries.

Counting all acquisitions, 'the increase in the population of the Soviet Union during the past year will exceed 23 million . . . the USSR will now be able to speak with the powerful voice of a population of 193 million'. In order to justify the annexations, Molotov added:

> It should be noted that nineteen-twentieths of this [newly acquired] population previously formed part of the population of the USSR, who had been forcibly separated by the western imperialist powers when Soviet Russia was militarily weak.[29]

In fact, not a single one of these populations belonged to the USSR when it was formed in December 1922 and until August 1939; due to a Freudian slip, Molotov identified the USSR with the Russian empire, with regard to which his figure would have been true; another similar slip was identifying the post-1922 USSR, a whole, with the pre-1922 Soviet Russia, which was to become the USSR's constituent part. What is more, Molotov chose to forget the peace treaties with the Baltic states in which their independence was recognized 'in consequence of the right of all peoples to self-determination', and not as a result of their separation by imperialists. But then all this was history, and Molotov was busy rewriting it.

Breaking in the new members of the Soviet family
After the annexations, the USSR Government proceeded, in Molotov's words, towards 'the political and economic reconstruction of the new Soviet Republics'.[30] The Soviet-style uniformization proceeded apace throughout all the annexed territories, though with certain variations. Thus, the nationalization of banks, industry and trade affected Ukrainians and Byelorussians less since these institutions had been mostly out of their hands. Similarly, the confiscation and distribution of large estates to poor and landless peasants which proceeded everywhere was particularly welcomed by these two national groups among whom land hunger was particularly acute, and where all large landowners had been Poles.

In the Baltic republics, where the countryside was nationally homogeneous, a 'class struggle' of poor peasants against more efficient and prosperous indigenous farmers, analogous to the *kulaks* of the Soviet 1930s campaigns, was engineered, in the course of which all landowners and farmers with over 75 acres had their property confiscated. If they were judged politically reliable, they might be allowed to retain up to 75 acres, while those *kulak* farmers with 62·5 to 75 acres were ruined by extortionate taxation and delivery quotas. This was followed by collectivization; at first it was voluntary, but when this had infinitesimal results, it became compulsory. Its progress was very uneven; by January 1941, only two or three collective farms had been set up in Estonia, and only one in Lithuania. The compulsory stage was foreshadowed in early 1941 by a spate of propaganda articles in the press. At the other extreme, in neighbouring Western Byelorussia, communist propagandists started their work immediately after annexation. The voluntary period resulted in a mere 40 collective farms by spring 1940; the threat of exile in Siberia was then used, and by spring 1941 there were hardly any individual farms left.

In the cultural sphere, Sovietization took different forms. In the Western Ukraine, where under Poland the state educational system had been Polish throughout, it was now fully Ukrainized (though Polish schools were provided for the Polish minority); in contrast, the Romanian ('Moldavian') population of the Moldavian SSR were deprived of their Romanian literary language (which is written in the Latin alphabet) and were ordered to use 'Moldavian', that is, Romanian written in Russian script and into which many archaic words, chiefly of Slavonic origin, were reintroduced in order to remove it as far as possible from mainstream Romanian.

Although the main wave of the frenzied mass Terror in the Soviet Union had subsided by the end of 1938, the population of the annexed territories were made to live through a similar process. In all of them, thousands of non-communist activists were rounded up and imprisoned before the 'elections', and the arrests continued afterwards, gathering ever greater momentum. Some were shot, others deported to prison camps. In the Western Ukraine and Western Byelorussia, Polish officials, settlers and prisoners of war were deported to Siberia and Central Asia, and 14,111 Polish officers were shot in the Katyn Forest and elsewhere.[31]

In the Baltic republics, the deportations reached their climax on the first anniversary of the Soviet invasion and eight to nine days before the German one. The operation, the experience for which was gained in the North Caucasus in 1937, was directed by the notorious Serov, the Security Police Chief Merkulov's deputy. In every republic a 'deportation staff' was set up which received lists, compiled by the Security Police in the early spring of 1941, of 'counter-revolutionary elements' to be deported. According to Serov's 'Instructions' of early 1941, the arrests and removal of all deportees had to be performed quietly and quickly in a single night, within not more than three hours, and in the case of families the father was to be separated from his wife and children. All this was done with extreme cruelty. They were transported in goods trucks, given no food or water, and taken mostly to prison camps beyond the Urals. Nearly 10,000 people were deported from the whole of Estonia, 15,000 from Latvia and 25,000 from Lithuania on the night of 13–14 June 1941. On that night, all major Latvian political leaders, among them President Ulmanis and the commander of the Latvian forces, J. Balodis, disappeared. In all, within the 12 months of Soviet rule in 1940–1 59,700 people disappeared in Estonia, of whom around 1,000 were executed. In Latvia, 34,250 died or disappeared. In Lithuania 30,500. Most of those deported from the Baltic states in that year and after the war perished, and less than 20 per cent returned after Stalin's death.

In Western Byelorussia, deportations and executions began in September 1939. By late June 1941, about 300,000 people had been deported, at least 50,000 of them after the German attack of 22 June 1941; thousands were killed in these few days. In the Western Ukraine, some 10,000 political prisoners were killed in several prisons both before and after that date. The total number of individuals who were Polish citizens in September 1939 and who were deported from these two areas is estimated to have exceeded a million: among them 52 per cent were ethnic Poles, 30 per cent were Jews and 18 per cent were Ukrainians and Byelorussians.[32]

Hitler invades: one people deported – another abandoned

Having exterminated most of his own high and middle command in 1937–8, and having an army whose soldiers were to a large extent drawn from a peasantry routed in his deadly war against it in 1930–3, Stalin could hardly have expected much enthusiasm or efficiency from the army that was supposed to defend the Soviet Union. He sought comfort in the misguided belief that Hitler would not break their mutual pact. The Nazi attack at dawn on 22 June 1941 was followed by a rapid German advance. As the Soviet armies retreated, they abandoned nations whose safety had been guaranteed under the national contract.

Among the abandoned peoples, two were special cases: the Jews and the Gypsies. There are only sketchy data about the plight of the latter, of whom a particularly great number were killed in Bessarabia in the last stage of the war. As regards the Jewish population, the Soviet rulers knew full well the fate that awaited them if they were abandoned to the Nazis, but there was no evacuation plan specifically for this nation. There are grim testimonies about the attempts, chiefly by Jews, to flee from the newly acquired Soviet territories before the advancing Germans. Unless they had Party membership cards, they were abandoned to their fate.[33] A sizeable though small minority from all areas sought salvation in the forests, and some were able to join the partisans, though survival was difficult. However, the Soviets saved several thousand Jews from Hitler's executioners completely unintentionally, by deporting them as 'counter-revolutionary elements'. These included prominent figures in Jewish national life such as leaders of Zionist organizations, those active in the Zionist press, Bund activists, writers and leaders of Jewish military formations in the Baltic states.

When the Germans had attacked Poland on 1 September 1939, some 200,000 Jews fled east, but they were all rounded up by the Soviets and deported beyond the Urals. Before Hitler's attack on the USSR, some 10,000 Jews were deported from Lvov as 'counter-revolutionaries', while in Bessarabia and Northern Bucovina such deportations had barely started on the eve of the German and Romanian invasion and even continued for some days after the beginning of the invasion.[34]

In the old Soviet territories at least, no Jews fleeing from the Germans were condemned to death by being turned back. Several tens of thousands of those serving in the Red Army survived the war. In the industrial east of the Ukraine it was possible to evacuate many establishments and industrial enterprises together with their personnel and workers, and many Jews, often with families, were able to make use of this. However, here again there were no schemes for the evacuation of Jews as such and those who had no place of work to be evacuated with usually had no access to transport, and few were able to flee. The situation was worst in smaller towns and rural areas.

Moreover, some Jewish artisans, misled by the Soviet media's silence (for obvious political reasons) on the Nazis' racist policy, and having no access to independent information, did not expect much harm from 'a cultured people'. Those among them who remembered the German occupation of 23 years earlier when 'things were not so bad' might well have compared it favourably with Stalin's reign of terror.[35] They were in part the victims of Stalin's misinformation, and he bears some measure of responsibility for their deaths at the hands of his former ally. Of the 3,100,000 Jews in these territories, not less than 900,000 perished in the Ukraine, not less than 300,000 in Byelorussia, and not less than 100,000 in the occupied parts of the RSFSR, a total of not less than 1,300,000. From the total number of old and new Soviet Jews, some five million, not less than three million perished in the Holocaust.

Ironically, it was the ethnic Germans for whom contingency plans had been made. They were descendants of peasant settlers invited by Stalin's tsarist predecessors in the eighteenth and nineteenth centuries. In August 1941, they were 'evacuated' from the Ukraine and the Crimea, ostensibly as a pre-cautionary measure, and within days a decree was issued announcing the 'transfer' of some 400,000 Volga Germans to Siberia and Kazakhstan. At the same time, Stalin abolished their republic, the Volga-German ASSR. Altogether, about 800,000 ethnic Germans were deported.

For all the internationalist rhetoric of the preceding decades, it was obvious that Stalin no longer believed – or never had done – in the new 'Soviet man' whose loyalty was to the 'supra-national' USSR rather than to his ethnic nation. Stalin presumably feared that the Soviet Germans' loyalty would be to the practically unknown country of their distant forbears, now ruled by an abominable regime, and not to their adopted country in which they had lived for many generations; though as a realist he was no doubt aware how abominable his own regime was, after the collectivization holocaust, to a nation of hard-working farmers. The Volga Germans were therefore regarded as a 'fifth column' of 'spies and saboteurs' (though there is no evidence of any having ever been discovered) and exiled to remote areas beyond the Urals, where the local inhabitants, suitably 'prepared' by the authorities, treated the deportees as traitors.[36]

The response of the non-Russians

After a year of Soviet Terror, the Balts' reaction to the news of the German attack was instant and, predictably, not favourable to the Russians. On 23 June 1941, 100,000 Lithuanians rose up against the Soviets, in bitter fighting drove the Red Army out of the country at the cost of thousands of casualties and proclaimed the restoration of independence and the formation in Kaunas of a Provisional Government.[37] Two days later the Germans entered the city. Though there was no place in the Nazis' plans for the independence of the Baltic states in any form, they refrained from immediately using brute force against the Provisional Government, as it would have been embarrassing internationally. It functioned for six weeks in the face of mounting German obstruction, repeatedly protesting to the Germans against, among other things, the mass executions of Lithuanian Jews,[38] but in the end, under protest, it declared itself involuntarily suspended.

In Latvia, Soviet troops at first succeeded in overwhelming insurgents who rose up in Riga on 28 June, but within three days the city was in Latvian hands as the German units reached Riga on 1 July. In Estonia, the insurgent 'Forest Brethren' cleared areas of the country of Soviet forces and succeeded in gaining control of Tartu before the Germans broke through.[39] Also in the Ukraine, once Lvov had been taken by the Germans, on 30 June the Bandera faction of the Organization of Ukrainian Nationalists (active in the Western Ukraine) hastily convened a 'national assembly' and proclaimed the restoration of an independent Ukrainian state and the formation of a government. Unlike in Lithuania, the Germans soon arrested its leaders and interned them in concentration camps.

Stalin appeals to the Russians

Ten days after Hitler's attack, on 3 July, Stalin appealed to those of his subjects he had not yet butchered, addressing them in quite a novel way as 'Comrades! Citizens! Brothers and Sisters! . . . I turn to you, my friends!' Calling for a 'scorched earth' policy and the formation of a partisan movement, Stalin proceeded to appeal directly to Russian patriotism by comparing Hitler's onslaught to Napoleon's invasion repulsed by Russia in 1812, and described the current war as 'our patriotic war' (*otechestvennaia voina*, literally also 'fatherland war'), 'the great war of the whole Soviet people'.[40] The 'Fatherland' was, first and foremost, Russia. Stalin went further in his address in Red Square on 7 November 1941, the anniversary of the Bolshevik October Revolution. He concluded his speech by invoking the military heroes and saints of Russia's tsarist, and earlier, past.[41] Soon after that, various items of tsarist military symbolism, rejected as far back as in the February 1917 Revolution, were resurrected, such as officer titles and ranks, the wearing of epaulettes, and privates saluting officers.

Extolling the Russians and appealing to their patriotism and historical memory, such as the victory over Napoleon, began as early as 1938 when the threat of war had become manifest with Hitler's *anschluss* of Austria. Among a number of articles of this type appearing in the Party's journal *Bol'shevik*, one entitled 'The Great Russian People'[42] was particularly noteworthy. After Hitler's invasion, the Russians were placed as 'the first among the equal peoples of the USSR' in a *Pravda* editorial of 29 July 1941. After this, the old tsarist colonial idea that the Russians were 'the elder brother' to the other nations, which had been rejected by the early Bolsheviks, was resurrected, and over the following months the term began to appear with growing frequency in the Soviet press. It became a mandatory phrase to be used by non-Russians for obsequiously expressing their love, gratitude, etc. for all the blessings 'the great Russian people' conferred on them.[43]

Even the Russian Orthodox Church, ruthlessly persecuted during the whole preceding Soviet period, was now employed to mobilize patriotic fervour. This led to an informal concordat between church and state which was given expression in September 1943 when Stalin demonstratively received the church leaders and permitted them to elect a new patriarch and synod. In return, they saw to it that the church became a servant of the state in all political matters.

Stalin invokes 'national contracts'

In mid-December 1941, as the Germans were approaching the gates of Moscow, Stalin was negotiating with Anthony Eden, Britain's Foreign Secretary, for an agreement on cooperation in their war against Hitler. He was apprehensive that Britain might not allow him to keep the Baltic states given to him by his former ally:

> We are fighting our hardest and losing hundreds of thousands of men in the common cause with Great Britain as our ally and I should have thought that such a question as the position of the Baltic states ought to be axiomatic . . .

In fact, the whole lengthy midnight session of 17 December 1941 consisted of Stalin repeatedly asking the question whether Britain was prepared to recognize Soviet ownership of the Baltic states and Eden each time patiently explaining, 'I cannot commit the country [Britain] to your propositions without consulting my own government, the Dominions and the USA.' Stalin argued that

> According to our Constitution the three states form part of the USSR. This is the result of a plebiscite in which the great majority of all the inhabitants voted in favour of coming into the USSR. If the USSR retained these three republics in their Constitution does the British Government have any objection?

Eden replied, 'Of course, we cannot take objection to what the Soviet

Government do or do not put into their Constitution,' but then added:

> under the Atlantic Charter we have pledged ourselves to take into account the wishes of the inhabitants. It may be that in this case they have been taken into account but that is a matter that we must check up on before we arrive at a decision.[44]

As has been shown above, there was in fact no plebiscite. The vote in each of the three states was that of a small diet, e.g. 79 members in Lithuania, all from the communist fronts, and in no way representing the great majorities of the respective populations. And even those votes, by show of hands, were not free but taken under duress, watched by the Russian military and Security Police. However, what is important is Stalin's recognition that a plebiscite (advocated also by Lenin in his time) was a vital pre-condition for legitimating the annexation of territory.

From near-defeat towards victory

By the end of 1941, the Germans had occupied all the western non-Russian republics, reached the outskirts of Moscow and taken three million prisoners of war. Their forces' technical superiority was no doubt important, but arguably even more important was the fact that Stalin's army was to a great extent already a defeated army before the German attack; defeated, that is, by Stalin himself. In particular, the non-Russians, the less equal 'younger brothers' – who probably formed the majority among the three million – could hardly have been expected to be enthusiastic about defending the regime which had gone out of its way to prove itself their implacable enemy. This became clear to the Soviet leadership and, in late 1941, they issued top-secret directives acknowledging that most Soviet nationalities had proved unreliable and warned against using them in large concentrations.[45]

The advancing German troops were, hardly surprisingly, at first welcomed as liberators from Stalin's murderous regime, but the Nazi racial doctrine made any concessions to the 'inferior' Slavs unthinkable. Once the conquered nations were placed under civilian jurisdiction, such as that headed by the fanatical Nazi Erich Koch in the Ukraine, terror and brutality became the methods of government, with merciless political subjugation and economic plunder as its chief aims. This was Stalin's salvation: the Nazi regime was seen as being worse even than Stalin's, and this stiffened the Red Army's combat morale and determination to smash the Germans.

Stalin's fortunes improved within a year, thanks to the political ineptitude of Hitler and his henchmen, and massive aid from the Western Allies. But the price was millions of human lives. By May 1944, according to incomplete figures, more than two million Soviet POWs of all nationalities had died, several hundred thousand Soviet soldiers were unaccounted for,[46] and millions fell in the field. Among the civilian population, the victims included three million Jews, some 200,000 Byelorussians, some two million Ukrainians and tens of thousands of others. But this was not the full price; when, in May 1944, Stalin regained virtually the whole of his old 1938 possessions, further punishments were in store for the Soviet nations.

8

Stalin's Last Years: The Terror Against Nations

═══

After Hitler's defeat in a war in which, among all Soviet peoples, the Jews, Byelorussians and Ukrainians suffered the greatest losses, Stalin, in an imperial chauvinist mood, abandoned all pretence of 'a union of equal nations'. He explicitly ascribed a leadership role to the Russian people and glorified their superiority over all the other peoples of the USSR in terms not unlike those used by Nazi propagandists to glorify the racial superiority of the German nation. His notorious toast at a Kremlin reception for Red Army commanders on 24 May 1945 ran as follows:

> I should like to propose a toast to the health of our Soviet people and above all of the Russian people.
>
> I drink above all to the health of the Russian people because it is the most outstanding nation of all the nations comprising the Soviet Union.
>
> I propose a toast to the health of the Russian people because it earned in this war general recognition as the guiding force of the Soviet Union among all the peoples of our country.
>
> I propose a toast to the health of the Russian people not only because it is the leading people but also because it has a clear mind, a firm character and patience.
>
> Our government made quite a few mistakes and there were moments in 1941–2 when our situation was desperate, when our army had retreated, had abandoned our villages and towns of the Ukraine, Byelorussia, Moldavia, Leningrad Region, the Baltic area, the Karelo-Finnish Republic, had abandoned them because there was no other way out. Another people might have said to its government: you have not fulfilled our expectations, away with you, we shall set up another government which will conclude peace with Germany and bring us rest. However, the Russian people did not do so, because it believed in the correctness of the policy of its government, and it made sacrifices in order to ensure the defeat of Germany. *And this faith of the Russian people in the Soviet Government became the decisive force which ensured our historic victory over the enemy of mankind, over Fascism.*
>
> Thanks be to it, the Russian people, for its faith!
>
> To the health of the Russian people![1]

This was the culmination of the wartime progress of extolling the Russians. What is significant is Stalin's frank admission that the Soviet Government had not fulfilled its national contract, and that therefore there was enough reason for the non-Russians to abrogate it ('away with you!'). What saved Stalin was the fact that 'another people' – the other peoples? – were not allowed by 'the leading nation' to have any say in the matter; had it not been for that, Stalin's guilty conscience (if it is not too offensive to associate the concept of 'conscience' with him) would have made him fear the worst.

Deportation of nations; the 'Tatarenrein' Crimea

As has been seen above, Stalin started deportations of whole national groups or considerable parts of nations before the war, obviously regarded non-Russian troops as unreliable in the war, and very shortly after its outbreak deported all ethnic Germans. The same fate awaited seven more entire nationalities which were accused of treason during the war. At the end of 1943, the Kalmyks, Karachai and Balkars were deported *en masse* from their homelands by Security Police troops. Whole villages were surrounded and their inhabitants rounded up and taken to the nearest railhead. Crammed into goods wagons, the deportees died in their thousands during the long tortuous winter journey into exile.

In February 1944 the same fate befell the Chechens and Ingushi, already partially deported in 1937. According to eyewitness accounts, the Security Police units entered the Chechen-Ingush A S S R disguised as ordinary troops. On 23 February, when people were assembled in villages to mark Red Army Day, they were suddenly surrounded by security forces and informed of the deportation decree. The sheer absurdity of the accusations of their wholesale collaboration and treason is obvious: their territory had never been occupied by the Germans. Next it was the turn of the Crimean Tatars. On 16 May 1944, less than a week after the last Germans had been driven out of the Crimea, the almost a quarter-of-a-million-strong population was awoken in the early hours by armed Security Police units and within hours all of them, including women, children and old people, were herded into goods wagons or dropped into railway oil tankers.[2] The murderous rail journey to Central Asia and the punitive regime imposed on the deportees in the places of exile took an enormous toll. Crimean Tatar estimates place total losses as high as 46 per cent of their number.

Although some collaboration with the Germans had undoubtedly taken place among these small peoples, it had not been a case of wholesale disloyalty. Many Crimean Tatars, Kalmyks and members of the other nationalities had fought in the Red Army. The Crimea having been occupied by the Germans for as long as two and a half years, an extensive anti-German underground partisan resistance developed there, in which Tatars took part together with the members of the Crimea's other national groups. None of this was taken into account, and the entire peoples, including those individuals who were not even in the German-occupied territories such as Soviet army officers and men (including decorated war heroes), members of the governments of the respective national republics and leading Communist Party members, were branded as traitors. In the case of the Crimean Tatars, existing documentary evidence of their participation in the partisan movement was suppressed by local Communist Party functionaries (Russians) in their wartime reports to their superiors in Moscow, creating an impression of the Tatars' total treachery. As for the 20,000 Crimean Tatars who undoubtedly did serve in Hitler's 'East Legions', most of them faced a stark choice between donning a German uniform or dying in a German camp. (In any case, for instance, an estimated 150,000 to 200,000 Central Asians and Volga Tatars similarly served in the same 'East Legions', yet Stalin did not punish the respective nations.) Gross anti-Tatar falsifications of the historical record continued unabated not only during the rest of the Stalin period but also later.

In the case of the Meskhetians (Georgians who were Turkicized and Islamicized in the seventeenth century) and several smaller Turkicized groups living in the same area, no accusation of disloyalty was ever made, as the Germans never reached the Transcaucasus. It appears that the deportation in November 1944 of about 200,000, and in 1947 another 80,000, Moslem people from districts in Georgia along the Soviet–Turkish border was connected with Stalin's designs on north-eastern Turkey. In order to forestall possible problems with the Meskhetians and the smaller Moslem groups in the event of Soviet–Turkish hostilities, they were simply expelled from their homeland. It is likely that a similar consideration applied to the other deported Moslem nationalities, all of them from the North Caucasus and still quite near to Turkey, and from the Crimea which faces Turkey across the Black Sea. In this way a total of some two million people belonging to eight small nationalities were effectively condemned to national extinction.[3]

The deportation of Soviet citizens belonging to national groups whose main body resided outside the USSR, begun before the war, was resumed when the war reached its final phase. In 1944, the remaining Soviet Greeks were deported from the Crimea and the Ukraine's Black Sea coastal region where they had lived for two centuries or more; Greece's friendly relations with Britain seem to have been enough for them to be deemed 'imperialist agents'. At the same time, Bulgarians, too, were removed from these areas.[4]

The restoration of Soviet 'Ordnung'
Mass deportations of sections of larger Soviet nations continued, too. Deportation on a huge scale was used to break the strong resistance to the reimposition of Soviet rule in the Western Ukraine and the Baltic countries. Here the war against nationalist guerilla movements was to continue into the early 1950s and to cost many thousands of lives. The pacification and collectivization of these recalcitrant regions resulted in the deportation of about half a million Ukrainians[5] and 600,000 Balts.[6] In Estonia, for instance, this resulted, by 1949, in a loss of about 10 per cent of the population, in

addition to the 6 per cent who had left Estonia for the West before the return of Soviet rule in 1944. According to Khrushchev's report at the Twentieth Party Congress, Stalin would have liked to deport the whole Ukrainian nation, but there were too many of them.[7] In the place of the deported Ukrainians and Balts, several hundred thousand Russians were brought in to fill positions in government, the police, education and industry. There were also mass deportations from Moldavia, which reached their peak in 1949; also in that year, thousands of Armenian families were exiled to the Altai region.[8]

There were other groups that were punished. Soviet soldiers – about half of them non-Russian – captured by the Germans, as well as the *Ostarbeiter* ('eastern workers', Ukrainians and Byelorussians forcibly taken as slave labour to Germany), were regarded by the Soviet regime as traitors or as politically suspect. It was not that most of these unfortunate millions had actually been disloyal in some way, but rather that they were considered to have become ideologically contaminated through contact with the non-socialist world. The Western Allies honoured their promise to repatriate Soviet citizens from Germany and elsewhere, and handed over two million people to the Soviet authorities, many of them against their will. The story of these 'victims of Yalta' has been well documented in recent years.[9] What is generally less known though is that over three million Soviet nationals, mostly non-Russians from the western Soviet republics, returned home from areas of Eastern and Central Europe which had come under Soviet control. Altogether then there were more than five million Soviet repatriates. It seems that at least 50 per cent of them ended up in the Gulag or were exiled to Siberia and other remote areas.[10]

There is no telling how many collaborators (including Russians) were punished by the Soviet authorities once the Germans had been driven out. One estimate puts the total at not less than three million.[11] What is certain though is that the Soviet authorities, and especially the Red partisans, had made it quite clear that, on the re-establishment of Soviet rule, vengeance and even death awaited all those and their families who had worked with the Germans.[12]

Very soon after their return to the Western Ukraine, the Soviet authorities initiated the liquidation of the four-million-strong Ukrainian Catholic Church of the Eastern Rite; in inter-war Poland, as well as in the previous age, it had been a bulwark of Ukrainian national consciousness there. This joint enterprise by the Security Police and the Russian Orthodox Church was greatly reminiscent of a similar onslaught in nineteenth-century tsarist Russia by the same joint forces against the same target in Volhynia. In April 1945, the entire Ukrainian Catholic hierarchy was arrested, and soon afterwards hundreds of the clergy who refused to be converted to Russian Orthodoxy were also rounded up. Most of them were imprisoned or exiled. The following year, at a specially convened and stage-managed synod in Lvov, some of the remaining

Ukrainian Catholic clergy were forced to proclaim their church's 'voluntary reunion' with the Russian Orthodox Church. The decapitated and officially proscribed Ukrainian Catholic Church was not destroyed, however, but continued to exist as a catacomb church.[13]

The post-war armed resistance of the Ukrainians and the Balts

The largest of the nationalist resistance forces was the Ukrainian Insurgent Army (UPA) which operated mainly in the Western Ukraine. In the latter half of 1943, both the Polish underground and the Germans estimated its strength at between 40,000 and 50,000.[14] Taking on both the Germans and the Soviets, in May 1943 the UPA killed the German SA chief Viktor Lutze and the following spring ambushed and fatally wounded the leading Red Army general Nikolai Vatutin. After the Red Army had swept through the Western Ukraine, the UPA remained a formidable force which enjoyed the support of much of the local population.[15]

Between the end of 1944 and spring 1946 three major campaigns were launched against the UPA in which Soviet forces 'lost thousands of men'.[16] Entire villages were deported, forests burned down and young men drafted *en masse* into the Red Army. Punitive detachments often consisting of criminal elements, as well as Security Police units disguised as UPA fighters, were let loose on the population. From the Soviet side, Lieutenant-General A. P. Kozlov of the security forces, among others, describes how difficult and costly it was for the Soviet authorities to crush the armed resistance of the Ukrainians years after World War II had ended, and how the insurgents would strike against representatives of the Soviet regime and those who cooperated with them.[17] The last vestiges of armed resistance in the Western Ukraine were not effectively extinguished until 1952.

In the Baltic republics, too, resistance to Soviet rule drove thousands into the forests. In view of how the Soviet authorities had behaved in 1940 and 1941, for many the perilous life of a guerilla seemed preferable to deportation, imprisonment or execution. Moreover, as was the case with the UPA, expectations persisted that sooner or later a war would break out between the Soviet Union and the West. Such hopes made the outlook appear less gloomy than it really was. In all three Baltic republics the national guerillas were known as the 'Forest Brethren' and enjoyed considerable popular support.

The strongest Baltic resistance movement was in Lithuania, where as many as 30,000 guerillas may have been involved all told. The Lithuanian guerillas avoided direct engagements with Red Army detachments. Instead, they attempted to disrupt the Soviet administration, harassed the security forces, and hit out at compatriots suspected of assisting the regime.[18] The pacification of Lithuania after its reoccupation by the Red Army was directed by Mikhail Suslov, whose chief qualification for this job was a major role he played in the brutal deportation of the Karachai, Chechens and Ingushi in 1943–4. The command of the security troops in the republic was entrusted to Beria's deputy and eventual successor, Sergei Kruglov. Mass repression against the population was initially counterproductive, but gradually began to achieve its purpose. Armed resistance was, however, temporarily boosted in 1948 and 1949 by the intensification of collectivization and the increase in deportations. By the end of the following year the number of Lithuanian guerrillas is thought to have fallen to about 5,000. But it was only at the end of 1952, after eight years of desperate struggle against Soviet rule, that they abandoned the forests in order to continue resistance by peaceful means.[19]

Soviet sources estimated that 20,000 on each side died in the fighting, while Lithuanian nationalist sources put the figure at 30,000 for the guerrillas alone.[20] Officials of the KGB were quoted[21] confirming that, including those guerrillas who died in the labour camps, 50,000 of them perished. The chairman of the KGB of the Lithuanian SSR, E. Eismuntas, set for the period of Soviet rule in Lithuania until 1954 a total figure of those who were deported, convicted of 'state crimes', or who perished as members of the guerrilla forces at about 200,000 individuals.[22] The duration and scope of Ukrainian and Lithuanian armed resistance to Soviet power was unequalled among Soviet nations since the Basmachi movement in Central Asia during the 1920s and early 1930s.

In Latvia and Estonia, the Forest Brethren may have had at their peak as many as 15,000 and 10,000 men respectively. Latvian armed resistance lasted until the end of 1949, while in Estonia it did not peter out until 1953. There is reported to have been some cooperation between Lithuanian and Latvian guerrillas.[23]

Apart from the armed insurgency in the Western Ukraine and the Baltic republics, there was considerable ferment inside the Gulag. Uprisings and strikes in the labour camps began not after Stalin's death, as is generally thought, but were already happening in the first post-war years. For the period from 1946 to the end of 1952 more than a dozen separate strikes or insurrections have been recorded.[24] After the war, the camps received many thousands of those who had actually taken up arms against the Soviet system: Ukrainian and Baltic insurgents, supporters of Vlasov and others who had fought alongside the Germans or collaborated with them in other ways, and those who had spent time beyond the Soviet borders and who knew that there was another world outside. The influx of these anti-Soviet militants acted like leaven on the political prisoner population, in which non-Russians formed a majority. In many cases the leading role in the organization of self-defence in the camps was played by Ukrainians from the UPA and the OUN. Retaining their *esprit de corps* as strongly motivated and disciplined freedom fighters, they quickly organized themselves in the camps and took the lead in waging a ruthless struggle against informers and criminal gangs.[25] Their successes inspired others and helped create a sense of solidarity and confidence among political prisoners.

Witch-hunt for 'nationalists'

The armed insurgency in the western borderlands notwithstanding, the Soviet Union emerged from the war more powerful than ever, with Stalin's personal authority at its zenith. In the course of its life-and-death struggle with Nazi Germany, the Soviet regime had managed to bolster its legitimacy through its identification with the salvation and aggrandizement of Russia. It had made substantial gains beyond the USSR's borders and, after Tehran and Yalta, had been given virtually a free hand to extend its influence, and inevitably its control, over Eastern and Central Europe.

After the enormous efforts and sacrifices that had gone into defeating Hitler, it was widely hoped among those who had backed the Soviet regime that the worst was now behind them and that there would be no regression to the climate of the 1930s. But, victory or no victory, the Stalinist leopard was not about to change his spots. There was no amnesty for political prisoners; political controls were soon tightened and mass Terror renewed. Apart from the cruel treatment of former POWs and *Ostarbeiter* already mentioned, the first major indication of what was to come was provided by Stalin in his famous toast of 24 May 1945 quoted above. It became clear that Stalin was determined to continue to harness Russian nationalism for the regime's ends, regardless of the formal equality and rights of the non-Russians; the national contract had been torn up long since, and Stalin showed no inclination to resurrect it.

Even more openly than before the war, the predominance of the Russians was everywhere emphasized and, in blatant contradiction of Lenin's warnings, Russian chauvinism was officially fostered in a Soviet guise. Campaigns against 'bourgeois nationalism', 'localism' and 'survivals of the past' in the non-Russian republics once again became commonplace. In the Ukraine, the Party leadership passed no fewer than eight resolutions between 1946 and 1948 in this spirit,[26] and Ukrainian writers and historians were accused of nationalist deviations in 1946–7 and 1950–1. In Kirghizia, the campaign started even during the war: at the Eighth Plenum of the Kirghiz CP on 7–8 September 1942, it was revealed that anti-Soviet nationalist activity had been uncovered and that Party members and some former state and Party officials were involved.[27] In 1952 the leading Kirghiz poet and writer Aaly Tokombaev was criticized for incorporating 'pan-Islamic, pan-Turkic nationalist and anti-Russian ideas' in his novel in verse *The Blood-stained Years* on the Kirghiz struggle against tsarism.[28] The Turkmen historian G. Nepesov was charged with admiring the anti-Bolshevik Basmachi guerrillas in his 1950 work already mentioned.[29] The witch-hunt intensified, especially after the October 1952 Nineteenth Party Congress, and in 1951 and 1952, purges were carried out, notably in Central Asia and the Caucasus.[30]

Russification: blotting out non-Russian histories

The non-Russians' national and cultural development was trammelled, and Russification was stepped up. Even in a republic such as Armenia, where the dominance of the native language in all spheres of life including education used to be unchallenged, in 1946 Russian became a mandatory subject from the second year (form, or grade) onwards. In order to project Russian supremacy into the past and to belittle the national identities of the non-Russian peoples, their histories were distorted still further.

The concept of 'lesser evil' was abandoned after the war, when all Russian conquests and annexations came to be treated as progressive and an absolute good, and the non-Russians' resistance to Russian conquest and their national liberation movements as reactionary. M. D. Bagirov, the First Secretary of the Central Committee of the CP of Azerbaijan, for instance, equated the role of the Russians in the Soviet Union with that in the historic (tsarist) past:

> The leading, unifying, cementing and directing force in the family of peoples of our land is their elder brother, the great Russian people. This position and role of the Russian people in the family of peoples of the Soviet Union has deep historical roots.

Turning to the history of Azerbaijan, he quoted an early-eighteenth-century Jesuit procurator observing that 'the people living near the Caspian Sea pray for nothing so much as for the coming of the Muscovites as quickly as possible to free them from the yoke of the Persian monarchy'. Bagirov added that 'the entry of Russian troops into Derbent in 1722 and into Baku in 1723 was greeted with joy, and everywhere they were given a warm welcome by the local people'.[31]

The internationally famous nineteenth-century resistance leader and statesman Shamil, the national hero of Daghestan and the North Caucasus, greatly honoured in the pre-war Soviet Union for his long and valiant struggle against the tsarist invaders, was attacked by the Party in 1950 as a reactionary, and the intensive anti-Shamil campaign (which cost at least one historian his life) culminated in a book-length denunciatory selection of documents entitled *Shamil, Henchman of the Sultans' Turkey and the British Colonizers*.[32] Similarly, the Kazakh anti-colonial national liberation movement of 1836–47, led by Sultan Kenesary Kasymov, was condemned as reactionary in 1945 and repeatedly after that. Analogous re-evaluations were undertaken with regard to a number of other nineteenth-century Central Asian revolts, as well as the major one of 1916.

What all this boiled down to was that the Party's post-war requirement for the rewriting of the histories of all the non-Russian nations was that the chief content of their early existence, be it independent or in some other state's vassalage, had to be represented exclusively as a longing for the ultimate joyous fulfilment of their destiny, to be annexed by the Russian empire; and that this annexation was always deeply progressive. No nation was to be credited with a desire to preserve its independence, or to regain it once annexed by the tsarist empire, and any independence movement had to be shown as not rooted in popular support, reactionary and instigated from outside (preferably by Britain). In short, non-Russian nations were no longer allowed to have their own distinct histories.

This was to apply not only to academic histories (including, very importantly, school books) but also to the history of centuries gone by held in the collective memory of the peoples. Such are the great oral national epics: the Kirghiz *Manas*, 'the Iliad of the steppe', which comprises all the Kirghiz legends and folk tales centred around Manas, the hero of countless battles against the Kirghiz' enemies, especially the Chinese, and is supposed to be the longest epic work in world literature;[33] the Uzbek *Alpamysh*; and the Turkmen *Korkut Ata*, which in Azeri appears as *Dede Korkud*, and has been ranked with the renowned twelfth-century Kievan Rus' epic, *The Lay of Igor's Campaign*. Until the end of the war, they were considered to be among the most honoured works in the literary heritage of these peoples. But soon the folk character and historicity of *Manas* was questioned;[34] *Alpamysh*, according to a Party spokesman, was 'impregnated with a reactionary and feudal sentiment, exhales Moslem fanaticism and preaches hatred of the foreigner and the unbeliever';[35] and from April 1951 onwards the Party denounced *Dede Korkud* as 'anti-popular' and 'reactionary'.[36] These epics disappeared from libraries and exhibits on their heroes were removed from the museums.

The reason for the condemnation of the epics was not only that they 'idealized the feudal reactionary past', but also because the celebration of any national hero, no matter how far removed in the past, had to be stopped unless he could be shown to have striven towards his nation being annexed by the Russians. And there was even more reason to condemn a work such as the Siberian Vogul epic poem *Iangaal-Maa* which, instead of rejoicing, laments the disastrous consequences of Russian conquest and oppression since the sixteenth century, and chronicles the insurrections against it.[37]

Anti-Semitism: official
On the all-Union cultural front, a drive to restore ideological discipline was launched in August 1946 under the direction of Stalin's ideological watchdog, Zhdanov. The bleak years that followed until Stalin's death were marked by Russian chauvinism, xenophobia, anti-Semitism and renewed attempts to force literature and the arts into the strait-jacket of crude socialist realism. In particular, the regime sought to isolate the Soviet population from the outside world, and especially to block supposedly pernicious ideological influences

from the West. Even captured anti-Western Nazi films were dubbed into Russian and shown in cinemas.[38]

On 13 January 1948 Shlomo Mikhoels, the eminent Jewish actor and the chairman of the Jewish Anti-Fascist Committee, was killed in Minsk, reportedly in a traffic 'accident' staged by the Security Police. Late in 1948, the committee itself (which was set up at the beginning of the war in order to generate support for the Soviet war effort chiefly among American and British Jewry), its organ *Einigkeit*, printing shop and book store were all closed down, and over 400 Jewish intellectuals were arrested, including those connected with the committee, among them the writers Leib Kvitko, Perets Markish, Itsik Fefer, Der Nistor, David Bergelson and David Hofshtein. The Jewish schools that had been re-established after the war were already very few compared with the 1920s and 1930s, and now these too were abolished, as were Yiddish publications and theatres. Thus, the limited post-war revival of Jewish cultural activity was extinguished.[39]

On 28 January 1949, a campaign against 'rootless cosmopolitans' was officially launched by *Pravda*,[40] ostensibly directed against those writers, literary and theatrical critics, and other intellectuals allegedly kowtowing to the West. Its victims were virtually exclusively Jewish intellectuals, who were subjected to what was in effect an officially generated wave of rabid anti-Semitism, which also took the shape of a witch-hunt for 'Zionists'. Many victims of the campaign were imprisoned and died in camps.

In the last years of his life, Stalin stepped up the Terror in a series of unpublicized major purges. It started with the 'Leningrad Case' in which, between 1949 and 1951, about 3,000 senior Party members in Leningrad were arrested and treated with particular brutality. Many of them were shot, including Nikolai Voznesenskii, a leading Soviet economist and a member of the Politburo, A. A. Kuznetsov, Secretary of the Central Committee, and other leaders.[41] Similar purges were carried out elsewhere, and more were planned but for some reason abandoned or deferred. There were dozens of 'national cases' in Union and autonomous republics, in all of which 'brutal gangs of bourgeois nationalists' were alleged to be active 'preparing the secession of their republics from the fraternal family'.[42] There are indications that Stalin was planning a show trial of Ukrainian 'nationalists', in which the leading part was to be played by the internationally renowned film producer Oleksandr Dovzhenko. In view of Dovzhenko's prestige, Stalin must have been reluctant to fabricate charges against him in the usual way; and so for three years, a General S. of the security police kept on visiting Dovzhenko as an 'acquaintance' and used to tell him 'many dreadful things about his service and his boss Beria', in an obvious attempt to provoke Dovzhenko to self-incriminating anti-Soviet and/or nationalist talk. In the end, Beria demanded from S. 'an annihilating report on Dovzhenko', and S. enraged Beria by replying that 'conscience does not permit me to write anything except good about him'.[43]

From 11 to 18 July 1952, a secret trial of 25 Jewish intellectuals, later known as the 'Crimean Case', was held in Moscow. The defendants had been arrested in 1948, and included the writers mentioned above as well as some members of the liquidated Jewish Anti-Fascist Committee. They were accused of 'serving foreign powers and attempting to make the Crimea Jewish and sever it from the USSR', and were shot on 12 August. For four years the fact of Stalin's murder of the main Jewish writers was kept secret, and both Ehrenburg and the Western communist press affirmed that Bergelson, Markish and the others were alive and continued to write.[44] While the writers were imprisoned and not yet tried some Western visitors enquired after one of them. The Security Police speedily groomed him, put him in a new suit and produced him to the visitors, successfully convincing them that he was a free man. Some time before mid-October there was another wave of mass arrests of Jewish intellectuals both in Moscow and in Kiev, where, ominously, professors of the faculty of medicine and some 25 doctors were arrested as 'followers of Academician Bernshtein', who had been charged with anti-Marxism.

The 'Doctors' Plot'
There were also unmistakable signs that Stalin was preparing to launch a massive new purge of the Soviet leadership. According to Khrushchev, 'Stalin evidently had plans to finish off the old members of the Politburo,' including Molotov and Mikoian, against whom, speaking at the Central Committee plenum after the Nineteenth Congress, he laid 'some baseless charges'. A pretext was soon found: at the end of 1952 a woman doctor (who was, according to Khrushchev, put up to it) levelled accusations of incompetence against her colleagues in the Kremlin hospital. Stalin personally ordered that a conspiracy be concocted from her accusations, and nine eminent physicians, seven of them Jews, were duly arrested. Khrushchev later revealed that Stalin had warned the Minister for State Security, S. D. Ignat'ev: 'If you do not obtain confessions from the doctors we will shorten you by a head,' and instructed the investigating judge to 'beat, beat, and once again, beat'. The confessions were extracted, but only after two of the doctors had died under torture.

On 13 January 1953, TASS announced the arrest of the group of 'doctor-murderers'. On the basis of 'documentary evidence' and their confessions, it asserted that they had killed two Politburo members, Zhdanov (who had died in 1948) and A. S. Shcherbakov (a notorious purger who had died in 1945), had been 'striving to undermine the health' of several marshals and generals, and were agents of foreign intelligence. TASS stressed the doctors' alleged connection with the 'international Jewish bourgeois nationalist organization

Joint' which 'under the guidance of American Intelligence conducts extensive spying, terrorist and other subversive activity'.[45] Yet back in 1924, the Soviet Government had asked Jewish organizations abroad, including the American Joint, for financial assistance in its campaign of Jewish agricultural settlement. They had responded generously, and, among other things, in July 1924 founded Agro-Joint specifically to support this project.[46]

In the following weeks, a blatantly anti-Semitic governmental campaign raged throughout the Soviet Union: Jews were arrested in Leningrad; already imprisoned Jewish officials were shot in some Ukrainian towns; in Byelorussia, articles on the crimes of Jews, chiefly doctors, were published; and in Lithuania, Jewish spies were 'unmasked'.[47] A gratified Stalin told the Politburo, 'You are blind like young kittens; what will happen without me? The country will perish because you do not know how to recognize enemies.'[48]

Among other things, this fabricated affair, the discovery of ever more Jewish 'enemies' everywhere, and the blind anti-Semitic rage whipped up by the whole of the centrally-directed Soviet press was going to be used to justify the deportation of the Jews. According to A. Antonov-Ovseyenko, a million copies of a pamphlet entitled 'Why Jews Must be Resettled from the Industrial Regions of the Country' had already been prepared and all that was necessary was the signal for distribution to begin.[49] Il'ia Ehrenburg told Roy Medvedev that it was also intended to publish an appeal which was to be signed by leading Jewish intellectuals calling on all Soviet Jews to submit to the deportation decision.[50]

Fortunately, on 5 March 1953, just as the new nightmare was about to unfold, Stalin died.

PART TWO

9

Towards a Partial Restoration of the National Contract

At the time of Stalin's death the nationalities problem seemed to be well under control. Nationalist resistance in the western borderlands had been crushed and the non-Russian elites terrorized into submission. Russian predominance in the Soviet system, symbolized in the notion of the Russian 'elder brother', had been made an inviolable principle, and history had been rewritten accordingly.

Beneath the surface, though, the situation was rather more complex. Western Ukraine and the Baltic republics had been pacified but hardly won over. Within the Gulag, Ukrainians, Balts and other non-Russians not only formed a majority of the huge political prisoner population, but were also setting an example of political recalcitrance and organized self-defence. The small deported nations still struggled to survive under punitive regimes in hostile surroundings. Like the countless thousands of Balts, Ukrainians, Poles and others who had also been exiled to Siberia and Central Asia, they clung to the slender hope that someday the injustice would end. As for the non-Russian elites, they may have been cowed, but only at the price of increasing their resentment of the Russian 'elder brother'. Furthermore, as was subsequently revealed, the broad masses of the peoples of the Soviet Union, whose level of education was steadily rising, had by no means lost their sense of national identity.

Beria attempts to play the nationalities card

What was also not apparent at the time and is still largely unacknowledged to this day is that the nationalities problem was one of the main spheres in which the struggle for power both just before and immediately after Stalin's death was played out. Even now it is not known precisely what happened behind the scenes in those desperate months at the end of 1952 and at the beginning of 1953. One thing is certain though: Lavrentii Beria, the chief of the secret police, made a move that was interpreted by his colleagues in the post-Stalin 'collective leadership' as an all-out bid for power, and the promotion of bold changes in nationalities policy was one of its key elements.

In 1952 Beria saw his power slipping and must have realized that he was in danger of becoming a victim of Stalin's next major purge. Interestingly, as

Charles H. Fairbanks, Jr, has noted, as early as October of that year Beria sounded a discordant note on nationalities policy: at the Nineteenth Party Congress his speech was almost exclusively concerned with the nationalities question and was at variance with the official line of the day. Scarcely mentioning 'bourgeois nationalism', Beria was the only speaker to refer to 'great-power chauvinism' and 'national oppression'. He also avoided the standard phrase 'great Russian people', alluded to the sovereignty of the Soviet republics, and emphasized the importance of safeguarding the native languages and relying on native cadres in the non-Russian republics.[1] Beria, although head of the repressive agencies, was sticking his neck out by projecting himself as a champion of the non-Russians. Was this some sort of calculated gamble from an official whose fiefdom in Georgia had recently been purged by Stalin?

Whatever the explanation, Beria outlived Stalin. Once death removed the dictator from the scene, it became apparent almost immediately that there would be some softening of policy towards the non-Russians. At Stalin's funeral, none of his three leading heirs – Georgii Malenkov, Nikita Khrushchev and Beria – raised the issue of bourgeois nationalism or Zionism. With the shock announcement at the beginning of April that the Doctors' Plot had been a fabrication based on confessions extracted under torture, it became clear that the new campaign against the Jews had been abandoned. Soon, too, articles began to appear in the press suggesting a more conciliatory approach towards the nationalities.

At first Beria, who now took charge of the Ministry of Internal Affairs (MVD), carried out a counter-purge in Georgia in order to re-establish his authority in the Transcaucasus. He also began appointing his own men to run the MVD in the republics, starting with the Ukraine and the Baltic states. Then, suddenly, strange things began happening. In early May, the Ukrainian Old Bolshevik and former President of the Ukrainian SSR, Hryhorii Petrovs'kyi, was belatedly decorated in connection with his 75th birthday: this was the first public rehabilitation of a disgraced communist after Stalin's death.[2] Just over two months later, the Party leader in the Ukraine, Leonid Mel'nikov, was abruptly dismissed and accused of distorting 'Leninist-Stalinist nationalities policy' by, among other things, Russifying institutions of higher education in the Western Ukraine. He was replaced by Oleksii Kyrychenko, who became the first Ukrainian ever to head the Ukrainian Party organization.[3] By the end of the month similar admissions about 'serious mistakes' in the implementation of nationalities policy were also made at sessions of the Central Committees of the Lithuanian and Latvian Parties.[4]

While these astonishing developments were taking place, the Soviet press published a number of articles that also signalled a change of course in nationalities policy. As early as 21 April, *Literaturnaia gazeta* declared that 'national deviation' is 'all the same, whether it is a deviation towards Great Russian nationalism or a deviation towards local nationalism'. In June, *Kommunist* published a remarkable article by the journal's former editor, P. Fedoseev, in which the author attacked all forms of chauvinism and racism, and emphasized the importance of respecting national feelings and the equal rights of all citizens irrespective of their nationality. What was also striking about his article was its omission of any mention of the special role that had been assigned to the Russian language under Stalin, as well as the author's reference to attempts by some historians to 'whitewash the reactionary policies of tsarism'.

Sometime towards the end of June, Beria was secretly liquidated by his rivals in the Soviet leadership. On 10 July *Pravda* announced his removal and declared him a 'vicious enemy of the Party and the Soviet people'. It portrayed him as a 'hireling of foreign imperialist forces' (and a British spy at that) who was planning to seize power and introduce 'a policy of capitulation which in the final analysis would have led to the restoration of capitalism'. Significantly, among the more specific accusations was the following:

> In various treacherous ways Beria tried to undermine the friendship of the peoples of the USSR, the very basis of the multinational Soviet state and the main condition for all the successes of the fraternal Soviet republics, tried to sow discord among the peoples of the USSR, to intensify the activity of bourgeois nationalist elements in the Union republics . . .

Fortunately, there is more evidence than just the official denunciations that Beria did indeed attempt to strengthen his position by pursuing policies designed to win over non-Russian cadres. Khrushchev claims in his memoirs that Beria

> fabricated some sort of document about the state of affairs in the Ukrainian Party leadership . . . The Presidium [of the USSR Supreme Soviet] began to discuss a memorandum by Beria about the ethnic composition of governing bodies in the Ukraine . . . Then a memorandum appeared concerning the Baltic states, followed by another concerning Byelorussia. Both stressed the principle of drawing the republican leadership from the local population. We passed a decision that the post of First Secretary in every Republic had to be held by a local person and not by a Russian sent from Moscow.[5]

Of course, Khrushchev was out to vindicate himself and to discredit Beria; therefore, in his account of the latter's manoeuvring, he ascribes the familiar sinister motives to his political adversary. Beria, he insists,

> was preaching that the predominance of Russians in the leadership of the non-Russian republics had to be reversed. Everyone knew that this was right and that it was consistent with the Party Line, but at first people didn't realize that Beria was pushing this idea in order to aggravate national tensions between Russians and non-

Russians, as well as tensions between the central leadership in Moscow and the local leadership in the Republics.[6]

Khrushchev, however, evidently did not tell the whole story. A *samizdat* appeal to the Party leadership issued in the summer of 1971 by 17 Latvian communists indicates that Beria had been set on something far more radical than Khrushchev cared to admit. The document confirms that on 12 June 1953 the Presidium reached a major decision on the future course of Soviet nationalities policy, which, had it been implemented, would have meant a virtual return to the practices of the 1920s, or, in other words, the restoration of a good portion of the national contract. On 22 June 1953, a plenum of the Latvian Central Committee was given the details of this decree by the Latvian Party leader Janis Kalberzins. According to the *samizdat* account, he announced that:

The Presidium of the CPSU CC resolved:
1. To charge all Party and state organs with the task of correcting thoroughly the situation in the national republics – to put an end to the mutilation of Soviet national policy.
2. To organize the preparation, education and wide selection for leadership positions of the members of local nationalities, to abandon the present practice of selecting leaders who are not of the local nationality, and to relieve individuals who do not have the command of the native language, and have them recalled by the CPSU CC.
3. All official business in the national republics should be conducted in native languages.[7]

Even in this abbreviated form, the instructions appear almost revolutionary in comparison to the policies that had been followed under Stalin.

With the advent of *glasnost'* under Mikhail Gorbachev, this *samizdat* account has been substantiated by the testimony of Vilis Krumins, who was second secretary of the Latvian Communist Party in the 1950s. In an interview published in the Soviet press in September 1988, Krumins confirmed that in June 1953 the Latvian Party leadership received instructions from Beria to proceed promptly with the Latvianization of the cadres in accordance with 'a special resolution'. Furthermore, Beria himself paid a secret visit to the republic.[8]

There is also some circumstantial evidence that points to the bold nature of Beria's moves in the sphere of national relations. Oleksandr Korniichuk, a Ukrainian dramatist known to have been a friend of Beria's,[9] was elevated to the Presidium of the Central Committee of the Ukrainian Communist Party, and the Ukrainian film-maker Oleksandr Dovzhenko – whom Beria had attempted to frame just a few years earlier – recorded in his notebooks that an attempt to woo him was made at this time by one of Beria's associates.[10]

There is a further intriguing case. Shortly after Stalin's death, the imprisoned primate of the officially 'self-liquidated' Ukrainian Catholic Church, Metropolitan Iosyf Slipyi, was reportedly taken to Moscow and offered his freedom and a high-ranking position in the Russian Orthodox hierarchy if he would repudiate his church's loyalty to Rome.[11] A former Ukrainian Catholic prisoner in the Gulag who was close to Slipyi has recorded that he and others were questioned in May 1953 by a special commission about the Metropolitan's attitudes and their views on how the situation in Western Ukraine could be improved.[12] In the event, the Ukrainian Catholic leader refused the offer made to him and was punished for his fortitude by a further prolongation of his captivity.

How did the non-Russians react to Beria's machinations in the area of nationalities policy? The Ukrainian author Mykola Rudenko, who was then a high-ranking official in the Ukrainian Writers' Union, has told the authors about his feelings when he heard the details of the Presidium's decision read out. He recalled that he and his colleagues were pleased by the good news but added that it was clear enough to everyone that the security chief's main goal was power.[13] One can only imagine how Beria's efforts were perceived by those members of the Soviet leadership and apparatus who upheld Russian supremacy and who had been in the ascendant for so long. It is hardly surprising that they would have felt threatened by Beria's attempt to embark on a comparatively liberal nationalities policy, and that his 'meddling' with national relations figured so prominently in the official indictment against him.

Most of Beria's daring scheme died with him. After his removal, the Soviet leadership quickly backtracked. Although it did not revert to the Stalinist nationalities policy in its crudest form, it retreated to a position that fell far short of what the Presidium had committed itself to only a fortnight or so before Beria was disposed of. In the press, the theme of Russian pre-eminence soon reappeared, and the nationalities question was relegated to the background.[14]

A special deal for the Ukrainians?

All the same, the events of May and June 1953 were a boon to the non-Russians. Local leaderships sought to reassert their prerogatives and to nativize their republic's Party personnel.[15] Shielding themselves behind references to the 'friendship of peoples', the creative intelligentsias in the non-Russian republics began to tend the injuries done to their national cultures. Some non-Russians began cautiously airing grievances and demands. This was particularly evident in the Ukraine, where the changes engineered by Beria seem to have had the greatest impact.

The Ukrainian SSR was closely connected with Khrushchev's political career, and after Beria's removal he was careful not to do anything that might lose the goodwill of the Ukrainian cadres. Khrushchev was a Russian who was born in the Ukraine; he once told the British journalist Iverach McDonald that he knew Ukrainian 'rather well' but had difficulty understanding it when it was spoken quickly.[16] His former aide, Fedor Burlatskii, has also pointed out that Khrushchev retained a sense of guilt about his unsavoury role as Stalin's henchman in the Ukraine in the late 1930s.[17] Certainly, there were further personnel changes in the Ukrainian Party and state organs along the lines proposed by Beria. Letters began appearing in the Soviet Ukrainian press complaining about the Russification of education in the republic and the shortage of films and records in the Ukrainian language. A group of Ukrainian teachers even raised the issue of teaching in the native language in the all-Union press.[18] In August, a Ukrainian deputy to the USSR Supreme Soviet, the poet Pavlo Tychyna, proposed that a Ukrainian Academy of Pedagogical Sciences and a Ukrainian Academy of Arts be established.[19]

What is also rather intriguing about the Ukraine at this time is the vehemence with which leading representatives of the Ukrainian Party organization and intelligentsia began denouncing Beria, and the way in which they also reaffirmed their loyalty to Moscow and the bond between the Ukrainians and the 'great Russian people'. Was then some sort of implicit *modus vivendi* worked out at this time between Kiev and Moscow, or was the Soviet Ukrainian establishment worried, in view of what Beria had attempted, about a possible Russian chauvinist backlash, and simply responding very cautiously to an uncertain situation?

That Moscow recognized the importance of the Ukraine and was intent on wooing its population, or at any rate the Ukrainian cadres, became evident at the end of 1953 with the announcement that during the forthcoming year there would be country-wide celebrations of the 300th anniversary of the Treaty of Pereiaslav.[20] Under the terms of this agreement, the fledgling Ukrainian Cossack state led by Bohdan Khmel'nyts'kyi had placed itself under the protection of the Muscovite tsar. In the 1920s and early 1930s, Russian historians had openly acknowledged that this arrangement had had dire consequences for the Ukrainians. As late as 1935, the *Large Soviet Encyclopaedia* had stated that the Treaty of Pereiaslav had 'juridically formalized the beginning of colonial domination of Russia over the Ukraine'.[21] None the less, the Kremlin decided to play up the tercentenary of the accord, in order, it seems, both to offer the Ukrainians a new deal as junior partners of the Russians, and to set out the Party's view of how the 'special' Russo–Ukrainian relationship was to be understood.

The announcement of the jubilee was followed in January 1954 by the publication of special 'Theses' drawn up for the occasion by the Central Committee of the CPSU. Among other things they announced that there were now two 'great' peoples in the USSR – the Russians and the Ukrainians.[22] During subsequent months the Ukrainians were lauded as 'the first after their Russian brothers' to have embarked 'on the road to socialism'.

In February, as a token of 'the strengthening of the unity and indissoluble friendship of the Russian and Ukrainian people', the Russian Federation handed the Ukrainian SSR 'a gift from the Russian people' – the Crimea. The issue of the deported Crimean Tatars was simply ignored.[23]

These concessions to the Ukrainians did not, however, represent some new Russian magnanimity, for they had their price. In return for an improved status within the Soviet system, the Ukrainians were asked to accept a highly distorted version of their history as defined by the Kremlin. Going beyond even tsarist and Stalinist schemes, the new interpretation reduced their history to an age-old longing for 'reunion' with the Russian nation and redefined Ukrainian patriotism in terms of a commitment to inseparability from, and dependence on, Russia.

The Central Committee's Theses also indicated the Soviet leadership's position on the nationalities question as a whole. While reaffirming the pre-eminence of the 'great Russian people' in a way reminiscent of the Stalin era, the document reiterated the familiar claim that the Soviet Union 'is an inspiring example of a country which has solved, for the first time in the history of mankind, the national problem'.[24]

The practical consequences of this new arrangement were soon in evidence. During 1954, as attacks against Ukrainian 'bourgeois nationalism' were renewed, leading Ukrainian writers eulogized the 'great' Russian people and stressed the 'indissoluble' ties between the two Slavic nations. Moreover, some Ukrainian cadres took advantage of the opportunities for career advancement offered by the new emphasis placed on their republic.[25]

Kazakhstan and the 'Virgin Lands Scheme'

After Beria's removal a struggle for power took place between Malenkov and Khrushchev. While it was going on, the nationalities policy (apart from the Ukrainian aspect) did not figure very prominently. Economic issues were brought to the fore and Malenkov initially made the running by giving more attention to improving living standards and developing the light and food industries. Khrushchev, however, soon staked his political future on a highly ambitious scheme that was to have dire consequences for the Kazakh nation. The treatment of the Kazakhs was to demonstrate that the post-Stalin leadership was quite prepared to ride roughshod over a non-Russian nation in the name of economic exigencies.

The Kazakhs had already been decimated by Stalin's brutal collectivization drive. Their second major trial within a quarter of a century took the form of the innocuously sounding 'Virgin Lands Scheme'. In February 1954 Khrushchev launched a campaign to transform vast areas of untilled steppe in Kazakhstan and south-western Siberia into new grain-producing regions. Warnings that the Virgin Lands would be turned into a dust-bowl were ignored and hundreds of thousands of 'volunteers' sent in from the European parts of the USSR to settle and cultivate the supposedly 'idle' areas of Kazakhstan, where in fact the Kazakhs had for centuries bred livestock. For the European migrants Kazakhstan was to become the new frontier and land of opportunity; for the Kazakhs, though, the Virgin Lands Scheme represented a colonization that threatened their very survival.

Although the full story of what befell the Kazakhs has yet to be told from their perspective – there is no shortage of Western works on the Virgin Lands project that completely ignore this aspect – it is clear from a few clues provided in Soviet publications that the nation's elite resisted as best it could. Just before the announcement of the scheme, a purge of the Kazakh Party leadership was launched. It began with the replacement of the republic's Party leader, Zhumabai Shaiakhmetov, a Kazakh, and his deputy, by two Russians – P. Ponomarenko and Leonid Brezhnev. At the time Moscow Radio accused Shaiakhmetov of nepotism and 'local favouritism' in his cadres policy.[26] Only later, in 1955, did *Kommunist* hint that some Kazakh officials had opposed the Virgin Lands Scheme.[27] Four years later the same journal acknowledged that there had been what it called instances of 'national narrow-mindedness' in Kazakhstan during the period when Khrushchev's project was being implemented and that calls had been made for a return to the 'indigenization' policies of the 1920s.[28] The resistance of the Kazakhs was overridden, and by 1959 their share in the population of their own republic had dropped to under a third.

A leading role in forcing through the Virgin Lands Scheme in the face of Kazakh opposition was played by Khrushchev's lieutenant, Leonid Brezhnev, who in 1955 assumed for a short time the Party leadership in Kazakhstan. Like the Ukraine, this republic became a power base for Khrushchev. Despite considerable difficulties and setbacks, Khrushchev's gamble paid off and within a few years Kazakhstan was transformed into a grain producer rivalling the Ukraine.

A state of flux
The first years after Stalin's death were ones of hope and uncertainty. Towards the end of 1953 the beginnings of a thaw in the literary sphere seemed to presage better days ahead. Yet this was also the time when another important process was unfolding, for in the labour camps the prisoners had mounted a campaign for more humane conditions and for a review of their sentences. While non-Russians may not have been so prominent in calling for greater truthfulness and creative freedom in literature, in the camps, Ukrainians and Balts played leading roles in organizing the wave of strikes and protests, such as at Vorkuta, Noril'sk and Kengir, that shook the Gulag during the first 15 months after Stalin's death and forced his heirs to decide what to do about the vast labour camp system. Although the authorities quelled some of the risings with great cruelty, sending in soldiers and tanks

against defenceless prisoners, gradually reforms were instituted and the Gulag began to disgorge its inmates.[29]

There was pressure, too, from the deported peoples. In 1954 and 1955 the restrictive 'special settlement' regime that had been imposed on them was moderated, and in some cases lifted altogether. Straight away, undeterred by the threat of arrest and punishment, increasing numbers of North Caucasians, especially Chechens and Ingushi, attempted to make their way home. A small number apparently succeeded. In the case of the ethnic Germans, Moscow also had to reckon with outside intervention from Bonn. Eventually, after Konrad Adenauer's visit to Moscow in September 1955 and the establishment of diplomatic relations between West Germany and the Soviet Union, Soviet Germans were freed from 'special settlement' restrictions, though they were still forbidden to return home.[30] The alleviation in the situation of the deported peoples inevitably raised the question of their political rehabilitation and return to their homelands.

Behind the scenes, representatives of other national groups also sought redress of their grievances. The Armenian E. G. Ovannisian, for example, is known to have written to Khrushchev on the eve of the Twentieth Party Congress asking the Soviet leadership to unite with the Armenian SSR territories which they claimed and which had been placed under Azerbaijani administration in the early 1920s, namely the Nagornyi Karabakh Autonomous Region and Nakhichevan. He received the reply 'that the Central Committee cannot at present take up this question'.[31]

In many areas religion was closely linked with national feeling. After Stalin's death the portents for religious believers were rather contradictory. At first there was a lull in anti-religious activity, but in July 1954 the Central Committee issued a decree calling for a stepping up of the campaign against religion. Four months later, though, a further decree warned officials not to get carried away and to refrain from resorting to 'administrative measures' and 'insulting attacks' on believers. After this, although anti-religious propaganda continued, more tolerance was shown for a time towards religion.

In 1955 most of the imprisoned religious believers appear to have been released. In Lithuania, where the Roman Catholic Church was legally recognized but had in reality been under siege, the return from exile of 130 priests and two bishops brought some relief.[32] In the Western Ukraine also, the return home of remnants of the Ukrainian Catholic clergy is known to have stimulated clandestine Uniate activity and raised expectations that the ban on the Ukrainian Catholic Church might be lifted.[33]

Soon there were signs of dissatisfaction with the way that the history of the non-Russians was being written, particularly that of the Daghestani hero Shamil. The first challenge to the standard line on the Shamil movement appeared in print in the summer of 1955. The following January, two weeks before the Twentieth Party Congress took place, the issue was singled out at a conference of the readers of *Voprosy istorii* as an example of the falsification of history by Soviet historians. At this meeting, calls were heard for a reappraisal of tsarist conquests.[34]

As far as the republican leaderships and bureaucracies were concerned, the most promising development was the Kremlin's recognition of the need to decentralize the economy and to devolve certain rights to the republics. Khrushchev acknowledged as much in March 1954, and the first changes were not long in coming. At first several Union ministries were transformed into joint republican-Union ministries: ferrous metallurgy, coal, oil, and subsequently higher education (the Ukrainians were also given their own republican ministry of higher education). Later the republics were given local control over justice, automotive transport and highways, urban and rural construction and building materials industries. In the Ukraine, support for decentralization was apparent from the numerous letters that appeared in the republic's press. Moreover, in February 1955, at a session of the Supreme Soviet of the USSR, a Ukrainian deputy, M. Hrechukha, requested outright that 'the financial rights of the Council of Ministers of the Ukrainian SSR be enhanced'.[35]

The Twentieth Party Congress and the new course

It was against this background that Khrushchev delivered his sensational secret speech at the Twentieth Party Congress in February 1956, condemning some of Stalin's crimes. Among other things, Khrushchev admitted that under Stalin there had been 'monstrous' and 'gross violations of the basic Leninist principles of the nationalities policy of the Soviet state', namely that entire nations had been deported on spurious grounds. He mentioned by name five of the peoples deported by Stalin: the Karachai, Chechens, Ingushi, Balkars and Kalmyks. The Soviet leader also described how Stalin had killed thousands of his Georgian countrymen, ostensibly because of their nationalism.[36] Although Khrushchev left a great deal unsaid, his secret speech was nevertheless a bombshell.

The statements which he made about nationalities policy in his public report to the congress were also important. Khrushchev seemed to go out of his way to reassure the non-Russians. Signalling a more accommodating attitude, he declared that 'far from erasing national differences and peculiarities', socialism, on the contrary, assures the 'flourishing' (*rastsvet*) of the cultures of the non-Russian peoples. At no stage did he stress the importance of the Russian language or extol the Russians as the USSR's leading nation. Instead, he emphasized the supposed equality of the peoples of the Soviet Union. So as to leave no doubt that a new line was being introduced, he rejected the notion 'that love of one's motherland contradicts . . . socialist internationalism. Such an interpretation,' he added, 'insults the national sentiments of people, and certainly does not contribute towards the strengthening . . . of international solidarity' and cooperation.

Khrushchev stressed that new conditions required a 'substantial revision' of the 'old methods of managing the economy'. 'Petty tutelage of the Union republics is impermissible,' he declared. Better use would have to be made of national cadres, and the powers of the republican ministries would be enlarged. It was also necessary to give 'serious thought' to allowing the republics some say in the way budget funds were distributed among them. 'Within the framework of fixed all-Union economic plans,' Khrushchev continued, the republics ought 'to decide for themselves concrete questions of development of particular branches of their economy'.[37]

The new conciliatory attitude towards the non-Russians was also demonstrated by two other speakers at the congress, Anastas Mikoian, a member of the Soviet leadership and an Armenian, and the Russian historian Pankratova. Both of them raised the delicate question of how the history of the non-Russians was being distorted. Among other things, Mikoian cited the example of a recent piece of 'historical nonsense', as he called it, that had been written by a Moscow historian about the establishment of Soviet rule in the Ukraine. 'I believe that Ukrainian historians will be found who will write a better history of the emergence and development of the Ukrainian socialist state,' he added.[38]

Pankratova, probably the Soviet Union's most senior historian at the time, acknowledged that

> Our textbooks and books on the history of individual peoples pay almost no attention to exposing the national colonial oppression of the tsarist autocracy . . . It is essential to study more thoroughly the history of national movements in Russia . . . We . . . must continue the struggle on two fronts – against great-power chauvinism and local nationalism, for these are two sides of the same coin.[39]

Khrushchev's statements at the congress and its resolutions made it clear that, in its nationalities policy, the Party intended to emphasize the pragmatic position that Lenin had adopted in the last years of his life when he had stressed the need for tact and concessions in order to win over the non-Russians. This change in direction was further underlined in June 1956 when the Party's main theoretical organ, *Kommunist*, published the full text of Lenin's 'Testament'. After more than 30 years, the Soviet public was finally allowed to read the candid instructions that the founder of the Soviet state had left on the need to keep 'Great Russian chauvinism' in check and to recognize that 'it is better to overdo rather than underdo the concessions and leniency towards the national minorities'.[40]

De-Stalinization and the nationalities

The Twentieth Party Congress was barely over when the Georgians, in a bizarre sort of way, became the first of the national groups to react to the repudiation of Stalin. Here, however, it is necessary to set the record straight. The famous riots in Tbilisi in the early part of March 1956 were not simply an outburst of hurt Georgian pride, as the popular version has it, because the 'great son' of their nation had been denigrated. According to witnesses and participants in the protests, what actually happened was that the initial pro-Stalin demonstrations that occurred not only in the Georgian capital but also in Sukhumi, Gori and Batumi, rapidly developed into nationalist protests. By 9 March, when troops were sent into Tbilisi to quell the disturbances, demonstrators were no longer concerned about Stalin, but the question of Georgian self-determination and civil liberties. Some apparently openly called for Georgian independence, while others attempted to transmit appeals to the outside world. The soldiers opened fire and 'many' demonstrators were killed or wounded before order was restored.[41] As late as May of that year, the KGB was reported to be carrying out arrests in Tbilisi after the appearance of nationalistic posters.[42] Although there were hints in the local press that nationalism was to blame for the upheaval, Moscow never acknowledged this; it remained secretive about the entire matter and, when pressed, ascribed the trouble to Georgian pro-Stalin sentiment.

Ironically, the first direct beneficiaries of the change in nationalities policy after the Twentieth Congress were the Russians. Because the entire Soviet state had been identified with them, their own Russian Federation had lacked some of the trappings of statehood possessed by the non-Russian republics. Shortly after the congress this anomaly was rectified. At the end of February 1956 a special Bureau of the Party Central Committee was set up to oversee the RSFSR. Then, on 1 July 1956, a new daily called *Sovetskaia Rossiia* (Soviet Russia) began appearing. Gradually, separate RSFSR organizations were established in a variety of fields: by the end of the decade writers, artists and composers of the RSFSR had begun holding their own congresses.

It was not long, however, before republican powers were increased as had been promised at the Twentieth Congress. In May 1956 economic decentralization was taken a step further by a decree placing a substantial number of industrial enterprises under the control of the republics. By the end of the year the republics had taken charge of enterprises accounting for some 55 per cent of the USSR's industrial production, as compared with 31 per cent in 1953.[43] The following February, an Economic Commission of the Council of Nationalities of the USSR Supreme Soviet was established to provide the republics with some say in the formulation of the state's economic plans. That same month, the republics were also given responsibility for judicial administration within their borders. The high-point of Khrushchev's economic decentralization came in May 1957 with the introduction of the *sovnarkhozy*, or regional economic councils. These new economic agencies supplanted the central industrial and building ministries. Although under the general authority of the central planning authorities, for all practical purposes supervision of them was left to the republican governments.

Not surprisingly, the non-Russians responded enthusiastically to the broadening of the rights of their republics. The Ukrainian Party daily *Radians'ka Ukraina* declared in its editorial of 10 May 1957 that the new decentralization was proof of 'the reinstatement of the Leninist nationalities policy'.

Cultural revivals and renewed national assertiveness

For a time after the Twentieth Party Congress, a form of what would now be called *glasnost'*, or openness, was tolerated in the area of national relations. What was truly extraordinary was the degree of vitality and assertiveness which the non-Russian nations began to show so soon after the ravages of the Stalin era. The Soviet press began to air some of the grievances and demands of the non-Russians. In articles by intellectuals and letters from workers and peasants, the non-Russians spoke out in defence of their native languages and cultures and implicitly attacked Russification and Russian cultural hegemony. They also sought the rehabilitation of cultural and political figures who had been purged or proscribed under Stalin, and called for more truthful accounts of their history. Basing themselves on Lenin's teachings and the terms of the unfulfilled national contract, the non-Russians insisted that their national rights be respected.

This surge of national assertiveness was not restricted to the European part of the Soviet Union. On 26 June 1956, *Literaturnaia gazeta* published an article signed by a Kirghiz and two Slavs. It contained an outspoken condemnation of the hostile attitude shown towards Central Asia's cultural and religious heritage by officials whom they described as ignorant 'nihilists'. Urging that Central Asia's cultural distinctiveness be respected, the authors cited the example of how Russian folklore epics, even if they had religious themes or praised the Russian monarchy, were admired, yet Kirghiz and other Central Asian epics were denounced as reactionary. They pointed out that it was acceptable to read works by Lermontov or Pushkin which contained derogatory references to the Moslem peoples under tsarist Russian rule, yet the writings of the Central Asian literati of the last century that contained 'disrespectful' references to the Russians were disapproved of. The authors also stressed sardonically that evidently 'the vulgarizers did not want to remember' that the peoples of Central Asia had 'sampled not only leading Russian culture, but above all, subjugation by Russian imperialism'.[44]

In October 1956 there was a particularly impressive display of the new national assertiveness in Uzbekistan. The local Party leadership convened a 'Congress of the Intelligentsia of Uzbekistan', which was attended by 1,200 delegates. At the gathering, the Uzbek Party leader Nuritdin Mukhitdinov sought to placate the republic's intellectuals by appealing to national pride and announcing the rehabilitation of various Uzbek writers and communist officials who had perished during the Stalin era. Describing Central Asia – a region that had until now been depicted by many Soviet writers as backward – as 'one of the most ancient centres of the development of human culture', he appealed to the Uzbek intelligentsia to take responsibility for the development of the nation's culture, the preservation of its historical monuments, and the training of national cadres. The past mistakes in nationalities policy, he assured his compatriots, would not be repeated.[45]

The language question

As Russification was eased, the non-Russian nations sought the restoration of their native languages in the educational and public life of their republics. The role of the Russian language as the USSR's lingua franca was not questioned, but it was made clear that this function should not mean the perpetuation of privileges for it at the expense of the non-Russian languages.

In the Ukraine a campaign in the defence of the Ukrainian language soon got under way in the pages of the republic's press. Writers, engineers, workers, students, as well as Ukrainians living in other republics of the Soviet Union wrote in to express concern about the situation of their national language and culture. One of the best examples of the public mood was an article by the writer Mykyta Shumylo entitled 'Love for the Native Language' that appeared in the July 1956 issue of the youth magazine *Zmina*.

Shumylo argued that a person's mother tongue is a repository of the cultural and historical values accumulated over the ages by his or her people. Only a 'savage' could be indifferent to it. Far from being a vestige of nationalism, he continued, love for one's native language was 'an organic element of internationalism'. 'If you do not love your people and show disrespect for its language,' he asked, 'who is going to believe that you love and respect neighbouring peoples?' Tact, not Russification, was what Lenin had demanded.[46]

In Byelorussia, numerous voices were also raised in defence of the nation's language and cultural heritage. Here, Russification had made greater inroads than in the Ukraine, and even the republic's writers had begun using Russian at their conferences. In the spring of 1957, the Byelorussian Party Central Committee acknowledged some of the consequences stemming from this.

> In many seven-year and secondary schools, all subjects except Byelorussian language and literature are taught in Russian. This adversely affects the students' level of knowledge and impedes their mastery of the Byelorussian language . . . Many teachers teach in a mixture of Byelorussian and Russian and fail to impose on themselves sufficiently high standards in the matter of cultivating language. Consequently, students also speak a bastard language and express their thoughts illiterately both verbally and in writing.[47]

A desperate campaign in defence of the national language was waged by the Kazakh intelligentsia. In the summer of 1957 *Kommunist Kazakhstana* carried an article that acknowledged that nationally-minded Kazakh intellectuals were opposing Russification on the grounds that it was a 'deviation from the Communist Party line regarding nationalities policy' and because of its 'negation of the national individuality of the Kazakh people'. The author of the article, N. Dzhandil'din, agreed that it 'would be good for Russian comrades working in Kazakhstan to know Kazakh', but warned that 'under present conditions the study of the Kazakh language must be voluntary'.[48]

Not all the traditionally Moslem peoples were confronted with such an unaccommodating attitude. In August 1956 an amendment was added to the constitution of the Azerbaijani SSR proclaiming Azerbaijani as the official language of the republic.[49] Concessions were also made to the Uzbeks[50] and Kirghiz, enhancing the status of their national languages. In 1958 Kirghiz was made a compulsory subject in Kirghizia's Russian-language schools; a quota was established for Kirghiz in the republic's higher educational institutions; and the history of Kirghizia was introduced in schools.[51] Of the other peoples, the Ukrainians had some success in increasing the level of Ukrainian-language teaching in the higher educational institutions of their republic.[52]

These improvements did not mean, however, that the promotion of the Russian language was neglected. On the contrary, after the Twentieth Party Congress more attention began to be paid to improving the quality and effectiveness of the teaching of Russian. In August 1956 the first general inter-republican conference devoted to this question was held in Tashkent. Although it was attended by delegates from all over the Soviet Union, it seems to have been primarily concerned with the unsatisfactory situation in the Central Asian republics. Among the problems that were acknowledged by some of the participants was that many of the teachers of Russian in these republics did not have a sufficient knowledge of the native language of their students.[53]

There also appear to have been cases where, behind the scenes, Russification was pursued just as doggedly as before. In December 1986, for example, a Byelorussian newspaper quoted from a letter that it had received from a senior teacher of Byelorussian and Byelorussian literature. The letter writer revealed that in 1956, when she had been a member of an education commission in the Byelorussian capital, she and her colleagues had been told categorically 'that the Byelorussian language would not be taught in Minsk'. When she had complained to the Byelorussian Minister of Education, she had been shocked by his indifference.[54] In the second half of the 1950s, this sort of insensitive and unforthcoming attitude was denounced by the more nationally minded non-Russian spokesmen as 'national nihilism'.

Literature and history
The non-Russians also showed considerable assertiveness in the literary and historical spheres. A bolder, more candid spirit pervaded their literature, and

the new elements of social criticism which it contained often alluded to aspects of the nationalities problem. This, together with the rehabilitation of some of the writers who were liquidated or silenced during the Stalin era – survivors were still returning from labour camps and places of exile – and the general rejuvenation of cultural life at this time, stimulated literary revivals. One Uzbek literary scholar, who, in May 1987, compared this period with what was taking place under Mikhail Gorbachev, wrote: 'It felt as if the warm rays of the sparkling springtime sun had illuminated those many creations in life that had grown dim.'[55]

A number of non-Russian authors produced significant anti-Stalinist works which unfortunately never achieved the fame of similar novels or poems by Russian authors. In December 1956, the Latvian Harijs Heislers became one of the first to describe Siberian exile in a Soviet publication. His autobiographical poem 'The Unfinished Song' evoked the tragic experience of many tens of thousands of Balts who had been deported after the Soviet occupation of their countries.[56] That same month in Armenia, Gevork Emin published a poem entitled 'Conversation with a Pharisee' which was addressed to Stalinist Party functionaries. The following two excerpts give some idea of its outspokenness:

> Halt, what are you doing?
> In whose face are you bolting the door? . . .
> Shut up, you frighten me.
> For God's sake leave off with your slogans
> and your lying sermons all in the name of our age.
> Stop! I have been awaiting this moment
> for a very long time.

> Unlike you, Pharisee,
> I cannot make empty speeches.
> The ground under my feet is thickly strewn with offal.
> I should sweep it away with a steel broom
> And not with speeches . . .
> We own no share of the capital
> Invested in your shop, trading in refuse,
> And we want no share in your bankruptcy.[57]

The Stalin era was not the only period about which the Soviet population sought fuller and more truthful information. The non-Russians wanted to retrieve their entire national histories from the distortions and omissions of Stalinist historiography. One of their central tasks was to set the record straight about Russian imperial expansion under the tsars. In their newspaper *Radians'ka osvita* of 14 August 1956, Ukrainian teachers asserted that

> it is necessary to describe correctly the national-liberation movements and the policies of Russian tsarism that oppressed Russia's numerous peoples and turned

Russia into a 'prison of peoples' . . . The teacher must emphasize that the Caucasian peoples' struggle under the leadership of Shamil against colonialist oppression occurred at the time when Russia was the gendarme of Europe. The Mountaineers' struggle was progressive because it weakened the forces of tsarism.[58]

The Shamil case had by now become a touchstone of official policy towards the histories of the non-Russian peoples. In July 1956 *Voprosy Istorii* published an article by G. D. Daniialov, a historian from Shamil's homeland of Daghestan, which for the first time since 1950 depicted Shamil's movement as progressive. None the less, the controversy continued and eventually developed into an open tug of war between Moscow and Daghestani historians.[59]

Several other concessions that were made to the non-Russians at this time should also be mentioned. Some of the small non-Russian nationalities living in the RSFSR were given their own institutions of higher learning: universities were opened in Kabarda (Nal'chik), Daghestan (Makhachkala), Morvdvinia (Saransk) and Iakutia (Iakutsk).[60] Furthermore, the Ukrainians were allowed two important new publications. In 1957 Ukrainian historians obtained their own historical monthly periodical, *Ukrains'kyi istorychnyi zhurnal* (The Ukrainian Historical Journal). The following year, Ukrainian writers were permitted to resume publishing their own monthly equivalent of the Russian journal *Inostrannaia literatura* devoted to foreign literature called *Vsesvit* (Universe).[61]

Deported peoples

Of all the non-Russian peoples, the ones who were probably most immediately affected by the Twentieth Party Congress were the nationalities that had been deported under Stalin and whose 'punishment' had been condemned by Khrushchev. When the details of Khrushchev's secret speech reached them, they interpreted this as a signal that they could finally return home. Without waiting for their formal rehabilitation, some 25,000 Chechens and Ingushi followed their compatriots who had already returned without authorization to their native lands.[62] Eventually, at the end of 1956 and the beginning of 1957, the Chechens, Ingushi, Kalmyks, Karachai and Balkars were rehabilitated and their autonomous territories restored.

But their problems did not end there. Often, as in Kalmykia, the returning deportees encountered a hostile reception from the settlers who had moved in after the indigenous inhabitants had been evicted. Racial tensions in Checheno-Ingushetia became so acute that violent clashes broke out. The worst of these occurred in the summer of 1958 in Groznyi when the Russian inhabitants went on a three-day rampage and massacred an undisclosed number of Chechens. Among the slogans they are reported to have used were: 'Long live the Stalinist nationalities policy!' and 'Keep the Chechens and Ingushi out of the Caucasus!' In the case of the Ingushi, an additional source of grievance was created: the Ingush Prigorodnyi district was handed to Northern Ossetia.[63]

For the three deported peoples who had not been mentioned by Khrushchev and who were not rehabilitated along with the others – the Soviet Germans, Crimean Tatars and Meskhetians – there was disappointment and resentment. In the case of the Germans, many of whom apparently hoped that they would be allowed to emigrate to West Germany, the blow was cushioned somewhat by a number of cultural concessions. They were provided with two newspapers in their mother tongue, and German-language radio broadcasts. Also, in 1957 teaching in the German language was made available in areas where they were concentrated.[64]

The other two peoples, however, did not have a foreign state interested in their welfare and were left to fend for themselves. After the 'special settlement' restrictions were lifted from them in the spring of 1956, they quickly began campaigning for their rehabilitation and the right to return home. In June 1957 the Crimean Tatars sent their first collective petition, containing 6,000 signatures, to Moscow.[65] The Meskhetians, too, began lobbying in Moscow and Tbilisi.[66]

National dissent and unrest

The ferment in Soviet society brought about by Khrushchev's secret speech was most evident among students and the creative intelligentsia, especially the writers. In the summer and autumn of 1956, attention, especially in the USSR's western borderlands, focused on Poland and Hungary, where de-Stalinization gave rise to movements of national emancipation. The Hungarian Revolution had a resonance within the borders of the Soviet Union and its brutal suppression by Soviet troops sent shock waves eastwards as well as westwards.

On 2 November 1956, traditional observances of All-Saints Day in the Lithuanian cities of Vilnius and Kaunas turned into mass public protests during which Lithuanian patriotic slogans were reported to have been interspersed with shouts of 'Long Live the Hungarian Heroes!'[67] Three weeks later there was a similar display of Latvian national feeling in Riga when, on the occasion of independent Latvia's Remembrance Day, thousands of candles were lit in front of the city's statue of Latvia.[68] Not long afterwards, the Party leaders in both Lithuania and Latvia acknowledged that the Hungarian uprising had encouraged 'bourgeois nationalist' elements in the republics.[69]

According to a Soviet Ukrainian study, the events in Hungary also reactivated 'the remnants of nationalist elements' in the Western Ukraine.[70] This is confirmed by the veteran Ukrainian activist Danylo Shumuk who in the second half of 1956 was enjoying a brief spell of freedom. He recalls what occurred in his native district:

In the Volhynia region, for example, workers on the collective farms, especially the women, became so hostile to the authorities that the brigade leaders and heads of the collective farms were afraid to approach them. The collective farmers began warning officials: 'Soon the same will happen in the Ukraine as in Hungary. We'll drive you from our land too . . .' The rising in Hungary and developments in Poland, together with the transportation of Soviet troops to the USSR's western borders, led many people to believe that a revolt inside the Soviet Union would also erupt and that the Soviet system would be toppled. The authorities began to show their nervousness and began expelling newly returned former political prisoners from the Western Ukraine.[71]

It is hard to know just how widespread such feeling was. It is worth adding, though, that Hungarian deportees who were briefly held in prisons in the Western Ukraine later told a United Nations Committee that the local inhabitants had been sympathetically disposed towards them and had informed them of student demonstrations in Kiev and Leningrad.[72]

In some of the republics there were also indications of trouble with the writers. On 4 December 1956 *Pravda* reported that two respected members of the Writers' Union of the Ukraine, V. Shvets' and A. Malyshko, both of whom were Party members, had been censured for making 'utterances of an anti-Party, hooliganish nature aimed at undermining the friendship of the peoples'. The newspaper added that a third writer, the above-cited Shumylo, acknowledged having made 'mistakes' in some of his previous statements. Elsewhere, in the early part of 1957, Heislers, Emin and other outspoken authors are known to have come under attack.[73]

In Kazakhstan the mood of the national intelligentsia was causing such concern that the republic's Party theoretical organ *Kommunist Kazakhstana* devoted a candid article to the problem in its issue for July 1957. It admitted:

> There are individuals in our midst who spread provocative rumours and slander and send anonymous letters, full of bitter invective against the Communist Party, its nationality policy, and honest workers of the Party. It is true that such monsters are rare. Unfortunately, their mischievous ideas are shared by a part of our intelligentsia.[74]

Even at this time of relative liberalization, dissenters who were deemed to have overstepped the mark ended up as political prisoners. Among non-Russians known to have been imprisoned at this time for political reasons were the Ukrainian student, Anatolii Lupynis, who was arrested in October 1956 in Kiev for writing poems in which he compared Khrushchev to Stalin,[75] and the Estonian Enn Tarto and seven of his student friends, who were rounded up on Christmas Day of that year.[76]

Russian students who ended up in the Gulag at this time have reported that they found the camps to contain relatively few of their own compatriots and a disproportionately high number of Ukrainians and Balts. Most of the latter were former participants in the post-war anti-Soviet guerrilla movements who had been given 25-year terms, and quite a few of whom had been further punished for organizing the recent strikes and risings in the Gulag.[77] During the next few years the flow of new political prisoners from the non-Russian republics was to increase.

10

Khrushchev Changes Course Again

The events in Poland and Hungary and the ferment in the Soviet Union frightened the Kremlin, and from the end of 1956 ideological controls were gradually tightened. Because of Khrushchev's struggle with the 'anti-Party group', however, the climate remained unsettled. Thus, in March 1957, *Kommunist* attacked the editorial board of *Voprosy Istorii* for, among other things, its lenient position on the Shamil question, and shortly afterwards the editors were purged.[1] Yet a few months later, when Khrushchev was anxious to discredit his rivals within the collective leadership, Lazar Kaganovich was accused of persecuting leading Ukrainian cultural figures in the second half of the 1940s. This had the effect of encouraging Ukrainian intellectuals to continue speaking out about the injustices of the Stalin era.[2] Later still, the 'anti-Party group' was accused of 'chauvinism' and opposing decentralization.[3]

Although the more candid approach to the discussion of nationality problems in the press was to last for a while longer, new themes, or rather dangers, were increasingly highlighted. The most important of these were 'revisionism', 'national communism' and, particularly, 'localism', that is, autarkic tendencies. The Soviet authorities were clearly uneasy about the possible spillover effect of 'revisionist' ideas from Eastern Europe. They were also determined not to allow the rehabilitation of 'national communists' from the 1920s, such as the Ukrainian Old Bolshevik Mykola Skrypnyk, to go too far in case embarrassing questions were raised about why the concessions to the non-Russians after the Twentieth Party Congress fell well short of the rights they had enjoyed 30 years earlier. The message, in short, was that while there may have been 'different roads to socialism' for East Europeans – a principle conceded by Khrushchev during his visit to Belgrade in May 1955 – the nations of the USSR were not to deviate from the course determined by Moscow.

Still, there was no getting away from the fact that in the non-Russian republics de-Stalinization had stimulated revivals in national culture and the growth of national assertiveness. On top of this, the local leaderships were tending, where possible, to promote local cadres and to take advantage of economic decentralization to promote republican interests, thereby appearing to place these 'local' interests over the all-Union ones as defined by Moscow. These trends in themselves hardly constituted a threat to the cohesion of the Soviet polity; rather, they demonstrated that, after a long period of excessive centralization, the non-Russians were taking the declarations of the Khrushchev leadership about changes in nationalities policy at face value.

From about the second half of 1958 it became increasingly evident that the Kremlin was not only having second thoughts about the more liberal course in nationalities policy, but actually beginning to backtrack. It is still not clear what exactly caused this retreat. Was it fear that the non-Russians would somehow get out of hand, or Khrushchev's utopian belief that communism was achievable within the near future and that, therefore, national distinctions should be reduced not perpetuated?

Both of these reasons probably played a part. At any rate, Khrushchev now adopted a more militant policy against 'vestiges of capitalism', among which he included nationalism, religion and an improper attitude towards socially useful labour. While toughening nationalities policy, he proceeded to launch a major campaign against religion that was to last for as long as he remained in power and to introduce the notorious 'anti-parasite' laws that were aimed at citizens 'avoiding socially useful work', but were frequently used as a weapon against nonconformists.

Fusion instead of diversity

In August 1958 *Kommunist* published what proved to be an important programmatic article advocating a shift of emphasis in the nationalities policy away from the promotion of the 'flourishing' of the cultures of the peoples of the USSR, to the acceleration of their eventual 'fusion' or 'merger' (*sliianie*). The author, conveniently enough, was a non-Russian – the Tadzhik scholar and director of the Oriental Institute of the USSR Academy of Sciences, Bobodzhan Gafurov. 'It can hardly be doubted,' he wrote, 'that on the higher levels of communist society the disappearance of national differences and the fusion of nations will be inevitable.'

Although Gafurov sought to create the impression that his approach was fair-minded and not in any way prejudicial to the non-Russians, his emphasis on the 'expressions of national narrow-mindedness' which he claimed were hindering the drawing together of nations, as well as his extolling of the Russian language as a 'mighty medium of communication' gave an unmistakable assimilationist thrust to his article. Among the faults that Gafurov ascribed to the non-Russians were the assertion of national interests in economic and cadres policy, 'the idealization of the historical past' and a disregard for the principle of 'Party-mindedness' (*partiinost'*) in dealing with culture, literature and the arts. What this amounted to was condemnation of just about any activity by the non-Russians that affirmed their national distinctiveness. On the other hand, everything that facilitated their absorption of 'the very great achievements of Russian culture' and assimilation was to be encouraged.[4]

Khrushchev's education law and its imposition

It was not long before pressure on the national languages was stepped up again. In November 1958 the draft of a proposed new education law was published.[5] Among its provisions was a clause – 'Thesis 19' – which immediately aroused the sensibilities of the non-Russians and generated intense debate throughout most of the Union republics. Since 1938 teaching in Soviet schools had been conducted in the native language but Russian had been a compulsory subject. Now it was claimed that children were 'overloaded' with having to study these two languages and a foreign one as well. Instead, it was proposed to give parents the right to choose whether to send their children to schools teaching in the native language or the Russian language, and to rescind the obligatory study of the native language in Russian schools in the non-Russian republics, and, in theory only, vice versa.

The non-Russians immediately saw through the camouflage and grasped that what was disguised as 'the most democratic presentation of the [language] problem' was in fact designed to enhance the role and status of Russian at the expense of the national languages. The terms on which parents were supposedly being offered a free and genuine choice between Russian or native language teaching for their children were hardly equal. In a society where the Russians were predominant and their language was hailed as the gateway to science, learning and culture, non-Russian parents were under strong pressure to acknowledge the advantages for their children in studying Russian. Furthermore, because the study of the native language was being made optional in Russian schools, Russians living in non-Russian republics would no longer have to learn the language of the people around them.

The opposition to Thesis 19 has been analysed by the American scholar Yaroslav Bilinsky and the Canadian author John Kolasky.[6] What emerges from their studies is both the remarkable degree of resistance to this change from representatives of the national elites, and the heavy-handed manner in which, after first appearing to give way, Moscow forced through the controversial clause. It is clear that the non-Russians recognized the cogent reasons for learning Russian as a lingua franca and sought to preserve the status quo whereby both the native language and Russian were compulsory subjects in the schools. In other words, unlike Moscow, the non-Russians defended the idea of genuine bilingualism.

Among the first to speak out against Thesis 19 were Azerbaijani scholars and the Chairman of the Council of Ministers of the Latvian SSR, the writer V. T. Lacis. The latter was reported by *Pravda* on 29 November 1958 as declaring:

To work effectively in a republic a man needs a knowledge of the national language. Abolition of the compulsory study of the Russian and Latvian languages in the schools will hardly promote the strengthening of the friendship of peoples.

A few days later, in the same newspaper, the Georgian Party leader V. Mzhavanadze stressed the importance of learning Russian but added: 'At the same time opinion is being expressed for making obligatory the study of the language of the republic in which the young boy or girl is living or working.' A similar view was expressed by the Director of the School Administration of the Armenian SSR. In the Ukraine, a meeting of the Writers' Union passed a resolution condemning Thesis 19 and urging that the Ukrainian Ministry of Education be given control over all schools in the republic.[7]

When the Supreme Soviet of the USSR debated the proposed new educational law on 22–5 December, Ukrainian, Byelorussian, Latvian, Lithuanian, Estonian, Georgian, Armenian, Azerbaijani and Kirghiz deputies opposed Thesis 19. The Georgian representative I. V. Abashidze warned: 'We must not set up the Russian and local languages against each other by allowing people to choose between them.' Also, while the Supreme Soviet was in session, two of the Ukraine's leading literati, Maksym Ryl's'kyi and Mykola Bazhan, published a joint article in *Pravda* arguing that only the compulsory teaching of both the national language and Russian in the non-Russian republics, on a basis of equality, would 'correspond to the principles of Leninist nationalities policy' and be 'really democratic'.

The deputies who opposed Thesis 19 included Stepan Chervonenko, the Ukrainian Central Committee Secretary responsible for ideology, and Mykhailo Hrechukha, the First Deputy Chairman of the Council of Ministers of the Ukrainian SSR. The Latvian spokesman was Arvid Pelshe, the Second Secretary of the Latvian Communist Party, who was to become the Latvian Party leader in 1959. Similarly, the Byelorussian spokesman was P. Masherov who was to take over the Party leadership in his republic in 1965.

Faced with this opposition from the cultural and political elites of the different republics, the Kremlin appeared to retreat. Thesis 19 was not incorporated into the all-Union education law that was passed at the end of the debate in the Supreme Soviet, and formally it was left up to the republics to decide whether or not they wanted to include its provisions in their legislation. In fact, this concession turned out to be nothing more than a ploy. Although it remained abundantly clear that in most republics Thesis 19 was not wanted, one by one the republics were brought into line.

A new offensive against 'local' nationalism
At the end of 1958 and the early part of 1959 there were other signs that Moscow wanted to reassert its control over the non-Russian republics. Part of

the problem seems to have been that the republican leaderships had been reacting to mixed signals from the centre. On the one hand they were being encouraged to take more responsibility for local policies, which the local elites interpreted as a chance to give some meaning to the nominal sovereignty of their republics. On the other hand, the Kremlin soon began to intimate that the relaxation of controls was not actually supposed to lead to any real change in the existing order of things. Decentralization, it was made clear, was prompted by the need for greater economic rationality: its purpose was to increase efficiency by reducing the size of the bureaucracy, not to stimulate autarkic and centrifugal trends. Likewise, it was emphasized that the more lenient attitude to the non-Russian cultures did not mean that Stalin's old formula 'socialist in content, national in form' was going to be stood on its head.

One of the first trouble spots was Turkmenistan where the local Party leader Suhan Babaev and his supporters clashed with the republic's deputy Party leader Grishaenkov and other Russian officials over cadres policy. The Turkmen communists argued that preference should be given to local cadres in appointments to the top posts. Grishaenkov and his colleagues opposed this demand and were backed by Moscow. In December 1958 Babaev and his supporters were purged and expelled from the Party. The following month the former Turkmen First Party Secretary was denounced at the Twenty-first Party Congress for having 'grossly ignored Leninist standards of Party life, distorted the Party's sacrosanct principle of internationalism' and for having been 'disdainful of personnel of other nationalities'.[8]

At the Twenty-first Party Congress itself, Khrushchev did not devote much attention to the nationalities question. He was primarily concerned with spelling out that the Soviet Union was entering 'the period of the extensive building of communist society'. Although he reiterated that 'The Soviet Union is a multinational socialist state based on the friendship of peoples enjoying equal rights', and spoke of the Party's 'consistent application of Leninist nationalities policy', he hinted that the new phase would entail new tasks. 'One cannot wait calmly,' he told the delegates, for the 'survivals [of capitalism] to vanish of themselves; it is necessary to wage a determined struggle against them, to direct public opinion against any manifestations of bourgeois views and ways, against anti-social elements.'[9]

Khrushchev was more direct when it came to identifying emerging problems in the economic sphere. Singling out localism, he stated that:

> The establishment of economic administrative regions has made economic ties more rational both within the regions and among them and has yielded substantial economic benefit to the country. But there is also a wrong, localist conception of an integrated economic region as autarky. It is necessary energetically to combat such anti-state tendencies.

The other difficulty he mentioned was that of attracting sufficient numbers of workers to move to remote areas of Siberia and Kazakhstan. Clearly, the many tens of thousands of 'volunteers', many of them young people, who in recent years had left the European part of the Soviet Union to work in what Khrushchev himself described as 'desolate localities', was insufficient.[10]

Two of the speeches made at the congress by non-Russians stand in contrast to one another and are indicative of the ambiguous atmosphere. One was delivered by the Lithuanian Party leader A. Snieckus, who was mainly concerned with reassuring the delegates that the Lithuanian Party was doing its utmost to keep local nationalism in check and to thwart 'those who seek to disrupt friendship with the great Russian people and the other Soviet peoples'.[11] This was not all that surprising because as early as February 1958 the authorities in Lithuania had been criticized in *Voprosy filosofii* (Questions of Philosophy) for being too lax in 'overcoming survivals of bourgeois nationalism'.[12] The second speech, though, by Mukhitdinov – the first official from a Moslem republic to be promoted to the Presidium – invoked the terms of the 'national contract' and in parts sounded like a caveat on behalf of all the non-Russian leaderships. Under Lenin's nationalities policy, he asserted:

> A broad programme was laid down for abolishing the inequality of peoples that was inherited from the old order. This programme provided for the creation and development of industry, including heavy industry, in the national republics, the transformation of agriculture on a socialist basis, the carrying out of a cultural revolution and the training on a broad scale of cadres from the working class and the national intelligentsia . . . The great Lenin cautioned that 'nothing so retards the development and consolidation of proletarian class solidarity as national injustice, and to nothing are "offended" nationals so sensitive as to the sense of equality and to the violation of that equality even out of carelessness or as a joke . . .' All peoples are proud of their history and culture, of their contribution to world civilization. We must do everything possible to encourage this noble feeling without forgetting, at the same time, that national culture is constantly being enriched by the values created by all humanity.

Mukhitdinov also voiced his opposition to Thesis 19, stressing that 'the nationwide discussion' of the new education law 'rightly emphasized the need to study both the local language and Russian' in schools. From the way in which he underlined the fact that the Bolsheviks had promised to bring equal economic development, 'including heavy industry', to all the national republics, he appears to have been alluding to the complaints of Central Asian officials that their republics were treated primarily as a vast cotton plantation, that there was insufficient economic diversification in them, and that most of the skilled jobs, in whatever local industry there, were going to Europeans.[13]

Purges in the non-Russian republics

For a time the non-Russians continued to hold out against the toughening of the nationalities policy. The resistance took both explicit forms, as in the opposition to the imposition of Thesis 19 and the continuing efforts by Daghestani historians to rehabilitate Shamil,[14] and implicit ones, as occurred in May 1959 at the Third Soviet Writers' Congress in Moscow. At this gathering, some of the non-Russian writers carefully made the point that not enough attention was being paid to their literatures and that in practice contacts with Russian writers were not what they were supposed to be. For instance, the Ukrainian writer Oles' Honchar complained that the organ of the Soviet Writers' Union, *Literaturnaia gazeta*, tended to overlook the literatures of the non-Russians and was 'unfair' towards that of his own people.[15] His colleague Andrii Malyshko expressed concern that some young poets in the Ukraine were now reluctant to give their works any national content whatsoever.[16] A Tatar representative protested about the small print runs of Russian translations of important Tatar works,[17] while a Turkmen writer urged that a publishing house for the non-Russian literatures be established in Moscow.[18]

In the summer of 1959 Moscow moved against the Party leaderships in the two remaining republics that had not incorporated the provisions of Thesis 19 into their legislation and were considered to be showing nationalist tendencies. In Azerbaijan most of the leading native communists were removed and the deposed First Secretary, I. Mustafeev, was accused, among other things, of having 'caused bewilderment on the completely clear language question'.[19]

In July, a major purge of 'national communists' began in Latvia where the republican authorities had recently increased the number of compulsory hours devoted to the study of the native language and Latvian history.[20] One by one the top Latvian officials were removed and finally in November the republic's Party leader Kalberzins was replaced. As the Latvian writer Janis Peters was to confirm in 1986, even the Russian Aleksandr Nikonov, who was Latvia's Minister of Agriculture at the time, was denounced for alleged 'Latvian nationalism'.[21]

Altogether over 2,000 Party and government officials were removed. Their 'sin' was that they had sought to establish a modicum of autonomy for the Latvian SSR. Specifically, they had demanded:

> a halt to immigration into Latvia; the promotion of only those industries in Latvia for which there was an adequate local supply of raw materials and labour; the integration of Latvia's cultural heritage into the contemporary cultural life of the republic; and upgrading the status of the Latvian language in relation to Russian in the republic.[22]

In January 1960 the new Latvian First Party Secretary Pelshe accused his former colleagues of having deviated from 'the right path in carrying out

Leninist nationality policy'. Stressing that Lenin had taught that 'the aim of socialism is not only to eliminate any isolation of nations, not only to bring nations together, but to merge them', he claimed that some of the republic's officials had 'become like the snail in their ambition to preserve the ethnographic and linguistic features of Latvia's antiquity. They have drawn into their shells and do not want to hear the mighty roar of the sea or see the blinding rays of the sun.'[23]

Shortly after the purges in Azerbaijan and Latvia were launched, *Kommunist* carried an article by the Kazakh Party Secretary N. Dzandil'din devoted to the issue of local nationalism. The author sought to clarify what Gafurov had written the previous year by placing even greater emphasis on the inevitability of the fusion of nations, which

> cannot be envisaged as a process that can begin only after communism has triumphed in all countries of the world. The formation in the future of a single language for all mankind and the fusion of national cultures into a single culture for all mankind is a complex and lengthy process which, it seems to us, is already beginning in our reality and will continue for a very long time, even after the victory of communism on a worldwide scale . . .

Dzandil'din went on to explain that any attempt to hinder this 'natural process' would mean the revival of reactionary nationalism. He assailed the efforts of some Kazakh officials and intellectuals to protect the status and purity of their language, and suggested that some of the non-Russian communists were making appointments on the basis of nationality rather than political qualities.[24]

In January 1960 the Central Committee of the CPSU issued a decree defining the 'Tasks of Party Propaganda Under Present-day Conditions'. Party organizations were instructed to 'campaign relentlessly against any sign of bourgeois nationalism', idealization of the past and manifestations of national narrow-mindedness.[25]

Next it was the turn of Kirghizia. At the beginning of 1960 nationally minded Kirghiz intellectuals who had been seeking the rehabilitation of various writers and cultural figures were attacked. After this the Kirghiz Party even reversed some of the decisions about rehabilitations that it had taken in 1956–7. At the First Congress of the Kirghiz Intelligentsia held in Frunze in May 1960, the need for Russian to be taught in all the schools of the republic was stressed and the customary warnings sounded about national narrow-mindedness, localism and the idealization of the past.[26] At around this time, two of the three concessions that had been made to the Kirghiz only two years earlier – the Kirghiz language being made a compulsory subject in schools, and the establishment of a quota in higher educational establishments for the indigenous population – were condemned as 'an infringement upon the rights of other nationalities' and withdrawn.[27]

The campaign against local nationalism made itself felt in other Union republics as well. In Armenia, for instance, in July 1960, the Party leadership expressed concern about nationalist trends in the republic's cultural life.[28] Between 1959 and 1961 the Party First Secretaries of Uzbekistan, Moldavia, Armenia and Kirghizia were replaced, although it is not clear to what extent their removal was connected with the nationalities policy.[29] In 1962, the Tadzhik Party leader was also purged after being accused of tolerating corruption and nepotism.[30]

By the second half of 1961 one Soviet scholar was already advancing the idea that 'a new historical community' – a single 'Soviet people' – had come into being. Writing in *Voprosy filosofii*, M.D. Kammari, a corresponding member of the Academy of Sciences of the USSR, argued:

> The development of the socialist division of labour among the national republics and regions has woven all the nations of the USSR into a single monolithic whole, into a single and at the same time *multinational Soviet people*, sharing a common territory and economic life, [and] common psychological traits manifesting themselves in the community of a single culture that is socialist in content.[31]

From all this it can be seen how complete an about-turn Khrushchev had made in such a relatively short space of time. He had spent barely a year or two placating the non-Russians and assuring them that the restoration of Leninist principles meant not just a respite for them, but the promising new start of a more tolerant and equitable nationalities policy. For the next three or four years, however, he concentrated on tightening the reins again and shifted the emphasis to integration and homogenization. No doubt then, it was with some apprehension that the non-Russians now awaited the Twenty-second Party Congress and the unveiling of the New Party Programme.

National dissent and opposition

Before discussing developments at the Twenty-second Party Congress some other aspects of Khrushchev's policy towards the non-Russians need to be mentioned. What is particularly striking is how severely prototype dissidents and members of underground nationalist groups were dealt with at this time. After the Hungarian uprising and the tightening of ideological controls, quite a few former Ukrainian and Baltic political prisoners were rearrested.[32] Towards the end of the 1950s, numerous Ukrainians and Balts who had not been involved in the post-war nationalist movements in their republics also ended up in the camps. As one former political prisoner – Boris Weil, a Russian Jew – notes in his memoirs, from 1959 onwards most of the new arrivals in the camps were young people from the Ukraine and the Baltic republics.[33] That very year at the Twenty-first Party Congress Khrushchev claimed that 'there are now no cases in the Soviet Union of people being tried for political crimes'.[34]

Information about the clandestine nationalist groups that were uncovered in the late 1950s and early 1960s by the Soviet security forces is scanty. What does emerge, however, is that in many, if not most, of the cases, the KGB seems to have fabricated evidence to make the views of those arrested seem extreme and their activities highly dangerous, and therefore deserving the heaviest penalties, including the death sentence. The existence of four Baltic nationalist groups has been recorded, three of them Latvian, and the other Estonian.[35] Typically, one of the Latvian groups, which was led by Gunnars Rode and broken up in 1962, was accused of having planned to overthrow the Soviet Government by violent means. In fact, Rode and his seven co-defendants had set up a discussion group called the 'Baltic Federation'. Rode was given a 15-year sentence and his colleagues received terms of from six years upwards.[36]

More information is available about the numerous political arrests and trials – all of them secret – that took place in the Ukraine. At least a dozen clandestine groups are known to have been uncovered in the republic between 1958 and 1962. The largest of them was the United National Committee, 20 of whose members were tried in Lvov in December 1961, and the United Party for the Liberation of the Ukraine, which was broken up at the end of 1959 in Ivano-Frankovsk. Although none of these groups is known to have used violence, the state prosecutors depicted their members as terrorists and frequently demanded the death penalty. Some of the death sentences that were passed were commuted to 15-year terms of imprisonment, but two leaders of the Ukrainian National Committee, Bohdan Hrytsyna and Ivan Koval', as well as a member of a group uncovered in Khodoriv in 1962, Mykola Protsiv, were shot.[37]

The best documented of these cases is that of the group of nationally minded Ukrainians led by the lawyers Levko Lukianenko and Ivan Kandyba and it amply illustrates how the Soviet authorities responded to national dissent. As Kandyba later explained in a document smuggled out of a labour camp:

> We were a number of individuals who saw around them many different outrages – mass violations of socialist legality and of the political rights of citizens, national oppression, great-power Russian chauvinism on the rampage, the ill-treatment of peasants, and many, many other abnormalities.[38]

In 1959 and 1960, the seven colleagues, all of them based in the Western Ukraine and most of them Party members, discussed setting up an organiza-tion – provisionally called the Ukrainian Workers' and Peasants' Union – that would campaign openly for the Ukraine's withdrawal from the USSR on the basis of Article 17 of the Soviet Constitution that guaranteed Union republics the right to free secession from the Soviet Union. Although at the time of their arrest – they were turned in by an informer – the members of this 'Jurists'

Group' had decided instead to concentrate on 'the formation of a lawful organization, the purpose of which would have been to remove illegal limitations on citizens' rights',[39] they were charged with treason. At their trial, in May 1961, Lukianenko was sentenced to death but his sentence was later commuted to 15 years' imprisonment. The other six defendants received terms ranging from ten to 15 years.[40]

Lukianenko was later to point out that at the time when he and his colleagues were arrested, the Soviet Ukrainian Government was signing the Declaration on the Granting of Independence to Colonial Countries and Peoples. If he still harboured any illusions, it was soon made very clear to him that the Soviet Government was not about to practise at home what it preached about decolonization and national liberation abroad. During the pre-trial investigation, the senior investigator – a certain Denisov – cynically told Lukianenko: 'You are a literate man, so why pretend to be a simple-minded dolt? You understand perfectly well that Article 17 of the Soviet Constitution only exists for [the delusion of] the outside world.'[41]

There were political arrests in other areas of the Soviet Union. The first Crimean Tatar activists were apparently arrested in 1959, and in 1961 two of them are known to have been given sentences of seven and five years respectively for 'anti-Soviet agitation and propaganda'.[42] That same year in Georgia, several young intellectuals were detained and falsely accused of conspiring to assassinate Khrushchev. One of them was also sentenced to death but had his sentence commuted to 15 years' imprisonment.[43]

Apart from these cases involving small groups of national dissenters, there was at least one nationalistic demonstration by non-Russians on a mass scale during this period. It occurred in July 1960 in Lithuania when Mikhail Suslov, then a member of the Party's Presidium and who, after the war, had directed the pacification of this republic, visited Kaunas. Protests and disturbances broke out, troops were called in, and several youths are reported to have been killed by the soldiers.[44]

Khrushchev's attitude towards the Jews also has to be mentioned. Although Stalin's successors dissociated themselves from the Doctors' Plot, at no stage did they acknowledge its anti-Jewish nature or begin to combat anti-Semitism. Moreover, they also turned a deaf ear to pleas for the restoration of the Jewish cultural institutions destroyed under Stalin. In several interviews given to foreign visitors between 1958 and 1959, Khrushchev denied that there was any 'Jewish problem' in the USSR and, while betraying his own prejudices against the Jews, made it clear that he favoured their rapid assimilation. A Canadian Jewish communist, J.B. Salzberg, who had the opportunity to discuss the Jewish question with Khrushchev in August 1956, came away with the impression that the Soviet leader's 'words are of the order of Great Russian chauvinism, which Lenin fought all his life'.[45]

In the late 1950s and early 1960s, official anti-Zionist and anti-Judaic propaganda was stepped up, stimulating anti-Semitic sentiment. Furthermore, in 1958 and 1959 a number of reports filtered out of the USSR about the persecution and imprisonment of Zionists, mostly young people.[46] Eventually, on the eve of the Twenty-second Party Congress, the issue of anti-Semitism was raised by Evgenii Evtushenko in his celebrated poem 'Babii Iar'. Although the poem was published by *Literaturnaia gazeta*, it incensed the Party leadership, and Evtushenko was forced to make alterations. Khrushchev himself later commented that the poem had revealed that its author 'did not show political maturity'.[47]

The Twenty-second Congress and the New Party Programme
The Khrushchev leadership's assimilationist policy that had been taking shape for four years crystallized at the Twenty-second Party Congress in October 1961. Although it saw further dramatic attacks on Stalin by Khrushchev and his supporters, as far as nationalities policy was concerned, this gathering confirmed the abandonment of the more conciliatory line that had been proclaimed at the Twentieth Party Congress. This time, there was not even the semblance of any compromise with the non-Russians: the Party had decided on a melting-pot scheme and that was that.

The draft of the new Party programme was published at the end of July 1961, and it says something about the political impotence of the non-Russians that they were unable to challenge, never mind amend, any of the details in the section dealing with nationalities policy.[48] While the programme did mention the flourishing of nations under socialism, it specified that it was the development of 'the socialist content of the cultures of the peoples of the USSR' that the Party would be encouraging; that is, those elements which facilitated the development of an 'international culture common to all the Soviet nations'.

Although the Party's new theoretical blueprint did not mention 'fusion', it declared that 'full-scale communist construction signifies a new stage in the development of national relations in the USSR in which the nations will draw still closer together until their complete unity (*polnoe edinstvo*) is achieved'. Ominously, the programme even stated that 'the boundaries between the Union republics within the USSR are increasingly losing their former significance . . .' It also warned against any lapses into 'national narrow-mindedness'. Here, it called for a 'continuous exchange of cadres among the nations' and cautioned against tolerating any 'manifestations of national insularity in the rearing and employment of workers of different nationalities in the republics'. The entire thrust of the section dealing with national relations was directed against the national assertiveness of the non-Russians and nowhere in the document was there any reference to Russian nationalism or 'great-power' chauvinism.

The programme reaffirmed the proclaimed equality and right to free development of the languages of all the peoples of the Soviet Union, but stressed the special role and importance assigned to Russian. It described the Russian language as having 'in effect, become the common medium of intercourse and cooperation among all the peoples of the Soviet Union', and a bridge to world culture. For these reasons, the document emphasized, the 'voluntary study of Russian in addition to the indigenous language has a favourable significance'.

Khrushchev, too, in his report to the Congress, repeated assurances that the Party 'will continue to make sure that the languages of the peoples of the USSR develop freely and will prevent any restriction, privilege or compulsion in the use of a particular language'. He qualified this, however, by underlining that 'the development of national languages . . . must tend not to reinforce barriers between peoples but to draw nations together'. In response to those 'who complain about the effacement of national distinctions', Khrushchev stated quite bluntly that the Party was 'not going to freeze and perpetuate national distinctions'. On the contrary, its task was to display 'uncompromising Bolshevist implacability' in eradicating 'even the slightest manifestation of nationalist survivals'.[49]

Khrushchev's report also contained a hint that economic controls over the republics would be tightened. 'Life already indicates,' he argued, 'the need for setting up several inter-republic zonal agencies to improve the coordination of the republics' efforts in carrying out the plans for communist construction.'[50] What this would mean in practice became clearer a year later when in November 1962 the four Central Asian republics were merged into one *sovnarkhoz* headed by a Russian, and bureaux were established for Central Asia and the Transcaucasus within the Central Committee apparatus. As A. Avtorkhanov pointed out at the time, in essence this represented 'a return to the early system of direct on-the-spot rule over the national Union republics by plenipotentiaries of the all-Union Central Committee in Moscow'.[51] The following year, the trend towards economic recentralization continued with the reduction of the number of *sovnarkhozy* from 100 to 47.[52]

After the Congress, a debate about the future of the nations of the USSR and the Soviet federal structure began in the scholarly journals. This was particularly worrying for the non-Russians as Khrushchev was soon talking about the need to draft a new Soviet Constitution. Encouraged by the Party's new commitment to hastening the fusion of nations, the proponents of assimilation and the dismantling of the federal system appeared to have the wind in their sails. Defenders of national statehood, however, opposed the prospect of denationalization by stressing the importance of the flourishing of nations as an essential prerequisite for their eventual fusion in the remote future. This debate about the fate of nations under socialism, or rather the Soviet form of it, has continued ever since.[53]

One particular example of the exchanges stands out. On 5 December 1961, a Daghestani poet, Akhmed Agaev, published an article in *Izvestia* effectively calling on non-Russian writers to switch to writing in Russian. He was firmly rebuked by the poet Vladimir Soloukhin, who was one of the few Russian patriotic writers who went out of their way during this period to defend the cultural rights of the non-Russians as well. The latter ridiculed the idea of 'internationalizing' literature and gradually doing away with the non-Russian languages. 'Everyone writes in the language in which he wishes to write,' Soloukhin opined in *Literaturnaia gazeta* on 6 February 1962. 'But to advise writers to discard their own languages,' he continued, 'and to go about "declaring" and "decreeing" a rejection of their own language, I would consider, to put it mildly, simply absurd.'[54]

The Khrushchev leadership also continued to stress the importance of the inter-republican 'exchange of cadres' and to pursue a policy of migration and settlement that led to the intermixing of the peoples of the USSR and was instrumental in promoting Russification. The many thousands of non-Russians, especially Ukrainians and Byelorussians, who either volunteered to work in other parts of the Soviet Union, or, as was often the case with graduates and young skilled workers, were assigned to work outside their own republics, were not provided with any cultural facilities in their own language. In essence they were condemned to Russification themselves, and at the same time served as agents of Russification in the regions where they settled. In his incisive discussion of this policy, the Ukrainian dissenter Ivan Dzyuba charged that it entailed 'the spiritually ravaging displacement of large masses of the population, often without any economic justification'.[55] Meanwhile, large numbers of Russians moved into Latvia, Estonia and the Ukraine, where, needless to say, their cultural needs were provided for. The continuing influx of Russians invariably increased competition for the better jobs in these republics and exacerbated national tensions.[56]

Ferment and the affirmation of national identity

During Khrushchev's last three years in power there was a visible reaction among the non-Russians, and some Russian patriots too, to the new emphasis on accelerating integration and homogenization. Resistance was probably most pronounced in the Ukraine where the inchoate campaign in defence of the Ukrainian language and culture began to assume the form of a cultural self-defence movement. It was reinvigorated at the beginning of the 1960s by the appearance of a bold new generation of literati known as the *shestydesiatnyky* (Sixtiers), whose representatives were to spearhead the revival in the Ukraine's cultural and public life.

The defiant mood of the Ukrainian cultural intelligentsia was graphically expressed at a conference dealing with the culture of the Ukrainian language that was held in Kiev in February 1963 and attended by over a thousand scholars and specialists. The gathering turned into an impressive demonstration of national assertiveness. Participants 'unanimously condemned the absurd theory that a nation has two languages' and passed a series of resolutions calling for the Ukrainization of all aspects of public, educational and cultural life in the Ukraine. These were submitted to the Central Committee of the Communist Party of the Ukraine. The republican press, however, played down the significance of the conference and failed to publish the resolutions. Fortunately, *Nashe slovo*, the newspaper of the Ukrainian minority in Poland, informed the outside world about what was probably the most important event in Ukrainian national-cultural life since Stalin's death.[57]

The negative official attitude of the authorities only inflamed the national resentment felt by increasing numbers of Ukrainian students and young intellectuals and between 1962 and 1965 unofficial patriotic activity was on the rise. The volume of Ukrainian *samizdat* literature expanded and began to include not only uncensored literary works, but also works of a political nature. Protests against Russification became frequent. The symbol of the patriotically minded younger Ukrainian generation was Vasyl' Symonenko, whose powerful publicistic poems were widely circulated. 'My people exists! My people will always exist!' he declared in one of his verses. 'No one can blot out my people!'[58]

In neighbouring Byelorussia, intellectuals also spoke out in defence of their national language and culture. In January 1963 a Byelorussian Komsomol journal published a poem called 'My Language' by the young writer Ryhor Baradulin. 'Historians and philologists,' he wrote, 'claim that the boundaries between nations are gradually disappearing' and that 'as a remnant from the past, my language, Byelorussian, will inevitably disappear'. This will never happen, Baradulin asserted: Byelorussian will never become a 'dead Latin', for it is 'immortal'.[59] Other Byelorussians complained about the lack of plays being performed in Byelorussian, the neglected situation of Byelorussian music, and the destruction of Byelorussian architectural monuments.[60]

The authorities frequently made their disapproval of such attitudes known. For example, in June 1962, the Uzbek Party leader Sharaf Rashidov referred to a letter that had been sent to the authorities by a student at a pedagogical institute which allegedly contained 'base and dirty slander against the nationality policy of our Party'.[61] The following January, Tatar intellectuals were taken to task for resisting 'internationalization' by showing too much concern for the preservation of their national culture and the purity of their language. 'Some individuals, even ones holding responsible positions', the Tatar Party leader charged, were trying 'in an artificial way' to remove Russianisms from their language and to reintroduce 'archaic' words of 'Arabic and Persian origin'. He condemned this tendency as being at odds with the Party's goal of 'instilling the people of the USSR with internationalism'.[62]

There was a similar response the following year in Georgia, where some inhabitants of Batumi founded an informal 'Society for the Struggle for the Preservation of the Purity of the Georgian Language'. The members of this group fined one another for the use of non-Georgian words in Georgian speech. Even this activity was considered too nationalistic. On 24 September 1964 *Izvestia* endorsed the attacks on the society by local officials, pointing out that the 'zealous' way in which the Georgian patriots were 'driving all "non-Georgian" words out of their vocabulary . . . was interfering with the enrichment of the Georgian language'.[63]

All this time Khrushchev's drive against all forms of religion was continuing, and hundreds of churches and mosques were being closed or pulled down. This extirpative campaign only added to the fears and resentment felt by growing numbers of Soviet citizens, including Russians, who concluded that the Khrushchev leadership was vandalizing their cultural and historical heritages. Between 1959 and 1965 some 10,000 – around half – of all the working Russian Orthodox churches were locked up or destroyed.[64] A Soviet sociological journal revealed in 1987 that the hardest hit areas were the eastern parts of the Ukraine and Byelorussia,[65] where national autocephalous Orthodox churches, tolerated in Georgia, had earlier been banned during the Stalin era. The number of mosques and synagogues was also drastically reduced: the total of working mosques fell from about 1,500 in 1958 to under 500 in 1968;[66] during the Khrushchev period the number of synagogues declined from 500 to 97.[67]

Catholics in the Baltic republics and the Western Ukraine were also affected. In Lithuania, between 1958 and 1961, three Roman Catholic bishops were banished to rural areas for refusing to comply with the state's more restrictive controls over religious life.[68] In Latvia, Julijans Vajvods, a leading Roman Catholic cleric (who was later to become a cardinal), was imprisoned in 1958 for two years for circulating his religious writings.[69] Needless to say, in such a climate the situation of the outlawed Ukrainian Catholic Church of the Eastern rite did not improve. Although the Ukrainian Catholic primate Metropolitan Slipyi was finally freed in February 1962 and flown to Rome after the personal intervention on his behalf by Pope John XXIII, his co-religionists in the Western Ukraine had to continue their existence as a beleaguered catacomb church.[70]

Paradoxically, the Kremlin's efforts to blur national distinctions and build a socially homogeneous communist society led to a 'surge of interest in their past among Soviet peoples and ethnic groups', as one Soviet scholar described it in 1987.[71] This was plainly evident in Georgia, and was soon to be seen in Russia too. Clearly inspired by what he witnessed during a visit to Georgia, Soloukhin informed his Russian compatriots in an essay published in 1965 that 'more than 300,000 volunteer members' had joined the Georgian Society for the Preservation of Cultural Monuments. He went on to call for the formation of such societies in other republics, especially the RSFSR.[72] By the time his article appeared, some Russians, like the *Rodina* (Homeland) club founded in Moscow in 1964, had already made a start.[73]

But in some quarters there was also a more radical reaction to Khrushchev's policies. Three of the largest nationalist organizations opposed to Soviet rule to emerge in the post-Stalin period were formed between 1964 and 1966. In Armenia, the Union of Armenian Youth was active from 1963 until 1966 when it was superseded by the clandestine National Unification Party, whose members advocated Armenian independence.[74] In the Ukraine, the Ukrainian National Front was formed in the Ivano-Frankovsk region in the second half of 1964 and managed to operate underground until 1967.[75]

Interestingly, the third of the groups was a Russian one. Formed in Leningrad in February 1964 by Igor Ogurtsov, it sought the armed overthrow of the Soviet Government. Calling itself the All-Russian Social-Christian Union for the Liberation of the People (VSKhSON), this clandestine Russian nationalist organization had a neo-Slavophile orientation and stood for the replacement of the Soviet system with a theocratic and corporatist state. Its strong commitment to Russian Orthodoxy and Russian imperial nationalism strictly limited the organization's appeal. None the less, this group, which before it was smashed in early 1967 attracted some 60 members and sympathizers, was significant as it reflected a Russian nationalist backlash against Khrushchev as well as an attempt to formulate a Russian nationalist anti-Soviet programme.[76]

It was during this period, too, that the Crimean Tatars and Meskhetians improved their organizational infrastructures and campaigning strategies. Between 1962 and 1964 the Crimean Tatars developed a network of local committees which sent delegations in rotating order to lobby the authorities in Moscow.[77] Meanwhile the Meskhetians set up a Turkish Society for the Defence of the National Rights of the Turkish People in Exile and a Provisional Organizing Committee for the Return of the People to the Homeland. They also sent frequent delegations to the Soviet capital.[78] In this way, both groups, together with the dissenting Baptists who had been galvanized by Khrushchev's anti-religious offensive, became pioneers of legalistic campaigns in defence of basic civil rights.

Although the Khrushchev leadership refused to budge in the case of the Crimean Tatars and Meskhetians, it once again showed somewhat more flexibility as regards the Soviet Germans. In August 1964 the ethnic Germans were formally rehabilitated. Curiously though, for some reason the decree was not announced in the Soviet press for several months. This, and the fact that there was still no mention of the restoration of the Volga German republic, disappointed the Germans and led them to redouble their petitioning activity.[79]

The Soviet Germans were not the only group whose situation was a source of concern outside the USSR. The degeneration of Khrushchev's final years in power into scarcely concealed anti-Semitism aroused considerable criticism in the West. What made matters even more sinister was that between 1962 and 1963 the Soviet authorities were known to have executed over 250 people for 'economic crimes', of whom over 60 per cent were Jews and that most of these cases were exploited for anti-Semitic propaganda.[80] As before, Khrushchev continued to deny that there was any problem. In a reply to Bertrand Russell, written in February 1963, the Soviet leader assured the British philosopher that the Soviet Constitution 'proclaims equality regardless of nationality and race' and bans 'advocacy of racial or national discrimination . . . There is not, and never has been, an anti-Semitic policy in the USSR,' he declared.[81]

The USSR also had to face the embarrassment of being challenged on the Moldavian, or rather Bessarabian, issue by two socialist states. In July 1964, China, already estranged from the USSR, backed up its support for Romania's independent foreign policy by including Bessarabia among the territories that it claimed the Soviet Union had seized illegally. The Soviet–Romanian dispute over Moldavia was to continue festering; at the same time, the national question was to become another bone of contention between Moscow and Peking.[82]

At the time of Khrushchev's removal in October 1964 then, there was mounting dissatisfaction at home with the Party's nationalities policy, as well as its new war against religion, and its stop-go approach towards de-Stalinization generally. Abandoning the pledges made at the Twentieth Party Congress to show greater respect for the rights of the nations of the Soviet Union, and those given at the end of 1954 by the Party leadership about showing restraint and moderation in its policy towards religious groups, Khrushchev had ended up not only disappointing and antagonizing the non-Russians but also alienating Russian patriots and nationalists. Furthermore, he and his colleagues had come to power denouncing the Doctors' Plot, yet within a decade even some Western communist parties were expressing concern about the rise of anti-Semitism in the Soviet Union. The Chinese, too, had begun criticizing the USSR about a nationality issue. The big question now was how would Khrushchev's successors proceed?

11

Brezhnev and Kosygin Make Their Mark

After Khrushchev was deposed by his colleagues in a palace coup, he was accused of 'subjectivism' and 'voluntarism'[1] and many of his reforms were rescinded. His handling of the nationalities policy was not questioned, though; while the new collective leadership headed by Leonid Brezhnev and Aleksei Kosygin did soften the language used to discuss Kremlin policy towards the non-Russians, its initial actions showed a readiness to be even tougher than Khrushchev had been. In fact, fears that Khrushchev's successors wanted to abandon, and even reverse, de-Stalinization, soon led to the growth of a spontaneous public protest campaign. In Moscow, this was to develop into a civil rights movement, while in the Ukraine, where the protests strongly accented national rights, an inchoate Ukrainian human and national rights movement emerged.

Within months of Khrushchev's removal from office, the Central Asian *sovnarkhoz* and Central Committee bureaux for Central Asia and the Transcaucasus were abolished. But the trend towards recentralization was soon in evidence again. In September 1965 the regional economic councils were liquidated and the industrial ministries restored. There were rumblings of disapproval from some of the republican leaders and the Chairman of the USSR Council of Ministers, Kosygin, sought to placate them with vague hints that an extension of the republics' rights was in the offing. In the event, the republics were not compensated for this further reduction of their limited economic autonomy.[2]

The first real test of the Brezhnev–Kosygin leadership's approach to national relations came on 24 April 1965 when 100,000 Armenians took part in mass demonstrations in Erevan to commemorate the 50th anniversary of the 'Turkish genocide'. The Armenians had been permitted to organize official meetings on this day, but the crowds turned out to be far larger than anticipated and the gathering in the city's Lenin Square turned into a spontaneous manifestation of Armenian nationalism. Throughout the day the demonstrators shouted the slogan 'Territories', alluding to Armenian claims to lands held by Turkey and the Nagornyi Karabakh and Nakhichevan regions under Azerbaijani administration.[3] In the evening, as the protests threatened to get completely out of hand, firemen were ordered to douse the demonstrators with their hoses, and militia volunteers were sent in to clear the streets. Clashes then broke out.

The Armenian Party leadership later described the demonstrations in Erevan as 'unfortunate' and blamed them on a 'misinterpretation' of the Turkish massacres by young people who had allegedly been 'moved more by passion than political sense'.[4]

The protests in Erevan were an unexpected reminder of the strength of national feeling after almost 50 years of Soviet rule. Soviet specialists on national relations were themselves divided not only on the future prospects of the nations of the USSR, but also on more basic questions about the nature of nations and nationality dynamics. In May 1965, therefore, the editors of *Voprosy istorii* (Questions of History) announced that the journal would conduct a symposium to clarify some of these issues. A Western scholar who studied the ensuing discussion concluded, however, that although the symposium was presented as

> a disinterested search for truth through a comradely and scholarly exchange of ideas, several considerations suggest that it may well have been a politically-inspired move supported by those elements in the elite who fear non-Russian nationalism and favour a faster assimilation of the national minorities.[5]

The new leadership also seems to have been well aware of the potential difficulties of resurgent Russian national feeling, and wanted to avoid exposing its flank. According to John Dunlop, a leading writer on Russian nationalism,

> the regime . . . moved immediately after taking power to placate Russian nationalist and religious elements. It also seems to have been the case that at least some of the members of the new Politburo – the names of D. Polianskii, Deputy Chairman of the Council of Ministers, and A.N. Shelepin, Secretary of the Central Committee and Deputy Chairman of the Council of Ministers, might be cited here – sympathized with certain aims of the more conservative nationalists. As a result of the regime's retreat from Khrushchevian socialist militancy, the years 1965–1966 saw a mushrooming of the influence of Russian nationalism.[6]

In July 1965, official approval was given for the founding of an All-Russian Society for the Preservation of Historical and Cultural Monuments. At first there were complaints from patriotically minded Russian intellectuals about the extent of the bureaucratic control, but once the organization was officially inaugurated the following June, its membership began to soar.[7] The anti-religious campaign was also wound down[8] – as it turned out, not a moment too soon. In the summer of 1965 there were signs of dissent within the Russian Orthodox hierarchy, and later that year, two priests, Nikolai Eshilman and Gleb Iakunin, sent letters to the Moscow Patriarchate and to the Soviet Government protesting about the state's 'illegal' interference in church life.[9]

As far as some of the more immediate problems with the non-Russian nationalities were concerned, the Brezhnev–Kosygin leadership seems to have wanted to create the impression that it was more amenable to the ethnic German and Crimean Tatar movements. Nevertheless, although representatives of both of these communities were received in Moscow, it soon became clear that Khrushchev's successors were no readier to yield on the fundamental issues. In June 1965, the Chairman of the Presidium of the USSR Supreme Soviet, Mikoian, met with a delegation of Soviet Germans. He agreed with them that the restoration of the autonomous Volga German republic 'would be the best solution' to their problem but informed them that economic considerations (he told them that the Germans were indispensable to the economies of the Virgin Lands of Kazakhstan and Karaganda) ruled out this solution. Instead, he promised the representatives further cultural concessions and better representation for their people.[10]

In August 1965 Mikoian received a delegation of Crimean Tatars. Their movement was still growing and attempts by the authorities to contain it by harassing and arresting its leading activists were proving futile. The meeting did not produce any tangible results, and so the Crimean Tatars kept up their campaign.[11]

Ferment in the Ukraine

It was in the late summer of 1965, though, that the Brezhnev–Kosygin leadership demonstrated a new firmness by launching an extensive crackdown on nationally minded Ukrainian intellectuals, and arresting two Russian writers, Andrei Siniavskii and Yulii Daniel', who had been publishing their uncensored writings abroad pseudonymously. Beginning on 24 August 1965, that is, about two weeks before Siniavskii and Daniel' were detained, at least 26 people were arrested throughout the Ukraine, dozens of homes were searched, and scores of individuals were interrogated. It was the first major KGB operation of this sort since Stalin's death, and its purpose appears to have been to intimidate the defiant elements within the Ukrainian intelligentsia and silence Ukrainian dissent.[12]

To the surprise of the authorities, their repressive actions in the Ukraine backfired. Not only did most of the 18 'dissenters' who were eventually brought to trial the following spring refuse to plead guilty to charges of 'anti-Soviet agitation and propaganda', but the arrests also triggered off numerous public protests and focused attention on the nationalities problem within the republic. Thus, at precisely the same time that a human rights movement was being born in the Soviet capital, Ukrainian activists began developing their own 'legalistic' campaign in defence of human and national rights.

The first public protest against the arrests in the Ukraine took place on 4 September 1965 at the Kiev premiere of Sergei Paradzhanov's internationally acclaimed film *Shadows of Forgotten Ancestors*. It preceded by a full three months the demonstration in Moscow's Pushkin Square in defence of Siniavskii and Daniel'. Furthermore, whereas in the case of the latter two, protests from prominent 'establishment' figures appear to have been forthcoming only after the trial of the two writers had taken place the following February, in the Ukraine, several prominent personalities, including high-ranking officials, made their disquiet known within weeks of the clampdown in their republic. Early in 1966, moreover, 78 writers, scholars, students and workers sent a petition to the Soviet Ukrainian authorities in which they expressed their concern about what had happened.[13]

Something else that occurred in the Ukraine at around this time and which did not become known in the West until 1972 also sheds light on the Brezhnev–Kosygin leadership's approach to the nationalities policy. In August 1965 the Minister of Higher and Secondary Specialized Education in the Ukraine, Iurii Dadenkov, unsuccessfully attempted to introduce measures aimed at the gradual Ukrainization of higher education in the republic. This move by 'national communist' elements within the Ukrainian Communist Party, which since 1963 had been led by Petro Shelest, was blocked.[14] Some eight months earlier, a group of Ukrainian communists had issued an appeal to communists in the outside world in which they had protested against 'the Russification and colonialist policies of Moscow'. As an example of the fictional character of the Ukraine's supposed sovereignty, they claimed that Shelest was unable to authorize even the building of an underpass for pedestrians in Kiev without Moscow's approval. The Ukraine, like all the other 'sovereign' Union republics, they argued, had been transformed into 'a colonial administrative-territorial region of the Russian empire'.[15]

Ivan Dziuba and his *Internationalism or Russification?*
The most powerful indictment of what happened in the Ukraine came from the young literary critic and prominent dissenter Ivan Dziuba. In response to the arrests he wrote a penetrating critique of the Soviet nationalities policy entitled *Internationalism or Russification?* in which he set forth Ukrainian grievances and aspirations. Presented at the end of 1965 as a memorandum to the Party and state leaders of the Ukrainian SSR, Dziuba's detailed book-length study urged the authorities to replace a nationalities policy that the author claimed was characterized by 'chauvinism, great-power ideology, national liquidationalism, national boorishness and bureaucratic standardization' with 'freedom for the honest, public discussion of national matters, freedom of national choice, freedom for national self-knowledge, self-awareness and self-development'.[16]

Written from a Marxist-Leninist perspective, Dziuba's study was concerned with what he argued was the betrayal of Leninist ideals, first as a result of Stalin's 'great-power policy', and then of Khrushchev's 'pragmatism'. He maintained that the Ukrainian nation was 'not experiencing a "flowering"', as was being officially claimed, 'but a crisis' in all the aspects by which 'Marxism-Leninism defines a nation'.

> *Territorial unity and sovereignty* are being gradually and progressively lost through mass resettlement . . . and through the doubtful sovereignty of the government of the Ukrainian SSR over the territory of the Ukraine. This latter reason, coupled with excessive centralization and a total subordination to all-Union authorities in Moscow, makes it equally difficult to speak about the *integrity and sovereignty of the economic life* of the Ukrainian nation . . . Ukrainian national *culture* is being kept in a rather provincial position and is practically treated as 'second-rate'; its great past achievements are poorly disseminated in society. The Ukrainian *language* has also been pushed into the background and is not really used in the cities of the Ukraine. Finally, during the last decades the Ukrainian nation has virtually been deprived of the natural increase in population which characterizes all present-day nations.[17]

More and more people were expressing their alarm. What had emerged, he explained, was a 'spontaneous, multiform self-originating process of a nation's "self-defence" in the face of a clear prospect of disappearing from the human family'.[18] The official response, though, had been repression. Listing numerous examples of the extra-judicial persecution that had preceded the arrests of the summer of 1965, he declared:

> If all the facts of this kind were to be amassed, the resultant picture of an indefatigable, pitiless and absurd persecution of national cultural life would frighten the very stage managers of this campaign themselves, and would force a great many people to do some thinking.[19]

Dziuba's critique of Soviet nationalities policy circulated in *samizdat* and eventually found its way to the West where it was published as a book. It remains a remarkable example of independent political thinking and represents one of the earliest calls for *glasnost'* – the author even used this very term – to be extended to nationalities policy. Dziuba, it should also be pointed out, was no narrow-minded nationalist. *Internationalism or Russification?* was written in a democratic spirit and the author made clear his opposition to all forms of chauvinism, oppression or discrimination. A year or so after he completed this work, Dziuba made an impassioned speech at Babii Iar in which he condemned anti-Semitism and called for Ukrainian–Jewish understanding and cooperation. On that occasion, too, he deplored 'the lack of openness and publicity given to the nationalities question' in the Soviet Union.[20]

Silva Kaputikian's Warning
In February 1966 the heavy sentences given to Siniavskii and Daniel' shocked liberal opinion in the Soviet Union and brought a wave of protests from

abroad. There were even fears that the Party leadership intended to rehabilitate Stalin at the forthcoming Twenty-third Party Congress. In the Ukraine, the trials of dissenters began in January and continued into April. They were conducted in such a way that they made a mockery of 'socialist legality'. Arrests of Crimean Tatar activists continued unabated, but this did not deter their movement.

On the eve of the congress, the irrepressible Crimean Tatar campaigners stepped up their pressure. They bombarded the Party and government bodies with over 14,000 letters and numerous telegrams, and submitted a petition to the congress containing 120,000 signatures. The latter document attested to the fact that almost the entire adult Crimean Tatar population had been mobilized. In Moscow itself, the Crimean Tatars deployed about 125 representatives. Finally, a day before the congress opened, ten of the Crimean Tatar lobbyists were received by M. Georgadze, Secretary of the Presidium of the USSR Supreme Soviet. It turned out, however, that he had nothing new to tell them.[21]

Shortly before the Party congress was to meet, Armenia's best-known poet, and a member of the Communist Party, Silva Kaputikian, made a sensational speech in Erevan defending the national rights and aspirations of her people in particular, and of the USSR's non-Russians in general. Her address, delivered on 2 March, was so forthright that it was not published in the Soviet Union; it circulated in *samizdat* and eventually appeared in Armenian emigré publications. Kaputikian forcefully rebutted those who had denounced the demonstrations in Erevan the previous April and had accused Armenian intellectuals of 'incitement'. The poet argued that the real reason why the Armenians had taken to the streets had been the half-hearted manner in which the authorities had organized the commemoration of the genocide. She also criticized Moscow for showing great insensitivity by improving Soviet–Turkish relations while at the same time ignoring numerous letters, some of them collective ones, that were being sent to the Kremlin from Armenia expressing grievances and calling for their redress.

Stressing the 'fidelity of the Armenians to Russia', she warned that this devotion should not be taken for granted or allowed to give way to 'fear, hypocrisy [and] blind subordination'.

Kaputikian pointed out that thanks to the Soviet policies of industrialization and modernization – and, in fact, contrary to Soviet expectations – everywhere national awareness was growing and the peoples of the USSR were experiencing vigorous revivals. Each nation, she declared, from the largest to the smallest, had a right to preserve and develop its national existence, culture and language, and to assert fully its unique individuality 'within the Soviet multinational family'. Like Dziuba, she rejected the view that healthy national pride was incompatible with building communism, implicitly criticized the Party's assimilationist course, and made clear her opposition to the predominance of any one nation in the USSR.

The Armenian poet stressed that there were nationality problems in the USSR that had long awaited resolution, and that other new ones were appearing. She argued that this was in no small measure due to the fact that the principles of nationalities policy laid down in the early 1920s had 'remained on paper'. To top it all, she issued the following blunt warning about the dangers inherent in such a situation:

> Comrades, the nationalities question is a complex one. History is replete with examples where, having failed to manage nationality problems, multinational states disintegrated.[22]

It was at this time, too, that the Soviet–Romanian dispute began to escalate. The Moldavian authorities were clearly troubled by the way in which Romania was continuing to challenge the Soviet line on Bessarabia. In early March 1966 at the Twelfth Congress of the Moldavian Communist Party, the Moldavian Party leader I. Boidul accused Romania of beaming nationalist propaganda into Moldavia in its radio and television broadcasts and of seeking a revision of the post-war territorial status quo. This only led the Romanian leader Nicolae Ceausescu to raise the issue of the Molotov–Ribbentrop Pact and denounce the way in which this act of Nazi–Soviet collusion had decided the fate of Bessarabia and Northern Bucovina.[23]

The Twenty-third Party Congress
It was against this troubled background that the Twenty-third Party Congress opened on 29 March 1966. In the style that was to become a hallmark of his period of rule, the new Soviet Party leader Brezhnev ignored in his report the various social and national tensions that had made themselves felt.[24] It was left to the writer Mikhail Sholokhov to reveal the attitudes of the neo-Stalinist elements that had gained ground since Khrushchev's fall. Castigating those who had been appalled by the treatment of Siniavskii and Daniel', he reminded the delegates that in earlier times such 'traitors' would probably have been shot.[25]

All the same, Brezhnev was rather more tactful in his references to nationalities policy than Khrushchev had been at the previous congress. While stressing the need to continue promoting the integration and homogenization of the Soviet population, he asserted that 'the Party will continue to show solicitude for the interests and the national characteristics of each people', and avoided the charged subject of fusion. The nearest he came to it was when he stated: 'We are proud that all the national detachments of our Party merge, as the waters of rivers merge in a mighty ocean, in the Communist Party of the Soviet Union – a union of like-minded Leninists, with one will, one aim, one ideology.'[26]

Subsequently, although the concept of fusion continued to be discussed in the specialist journals, Brezhnev preferred not to use this term and refrained from reiterating that the disappearance of nations was the Party's long-term goal. Moreover, the *Voprosy istorii* symposium on the 'nation' also failed to set out a clear line. 'The most serious attempt undertaken since the adoption of the Party programme to lay respectable theoretical foundations for rapid "internationalization"', it only confirmed once again the division between advocates and opponents of fusion.[27] The result of this new vagueness was an uneasy compromise. The Kremlin continued to emphasize the drawing together of the nations, while some of the local elites, particularly in the Ukraine and the Central Asian republics, highlighted the 'flourishing' and formal sovereignty of their republics.

In practice, though, the Brezhnev leadership adhered to the assimilationist policies that Khrushchev had launched. During 1966, for instance, the Brezhnev–Kosygin leadership went a step further than their predecessor in restricting the rights of the republics in the area of education. The American historian Roman Szporluk has pointed out the consequences:

> a decree of the Supreme Soviet's presidium established a federal Ministry of education to which the secondary and elementary school network was subordinated. Republic Ministries of education were placed under the Moscow body, and such matters as school curricula in the non-Russian schools, the hours of Russian language to be taught, the length of the school term, choice of examination requirements, etc., were placed under central regulation. This gave them the same status as colleges and specialized secondary schools, which, with some exceptions, had been put under central control in the 1930s.[28]

Towards the 50th anniversary of Soviet rule

As the 50th anniversary of the Bolshevik Revolution approached, there were further unmistakable indications that national tensions persisted, and that despite the Party's efforts to eliminate nationalism, national awareness, pride and assertiveness were on the rise.

Dziuba was not the only one at this time to draw attention to the total lack of cultural facilities for millions of Ukrainians and Byelorussians living outside their republics. In October 1965, Ivan Kavalionak, a Byelorussian living in the Siberian city of Tomsk, protested about this 'cultural terrorism' in a letter addressed to the authorities.[29] The following year, a Ukrainian *samizdat* document reported that Iu. Dolishnyi and 'a group of Ukrainian intellectuals from the city of Karaganda' in Kazakhstan had been imprisoned 'for their attempt to open a Ukrainian school for their children, which is a right guaranteed by the constitution'.[30]

Less than three months after the trial of Siniavskii and Daniel', Byelorussian writers rallied to the defence of their colleague Vasil' Bykaw (Bykov) after he was sharply criticized in the press for writing a very frank and, by Soviet standards, heterodox war novel. Sixty-five of them sent a protest to the Byelorussian Party leadership. Bykaw himself made a defiant speech on 13 May 1966 at the Fifth Congress of the Byelorussian Writers' Union. He ended with the words: 'So long as writers are united on such vital matters and are prepared to declare ourselves openly, the Byelorussian people may rest assured about the future destiny of their literature.'[31]

Similarly, in November of that year, bold patriotic statements were made at the Fifth Congresses of the Writers' Unions of Armenia and the Ukraine. At the meeting in Erevan, two prominent authors, Paruir Sevak and Gevork Emin, 'lashed out against the prevalence of attitudes that distorted legitimate national sentiments, and complained of informers within their midst'. Both 'asserted the right to national self-respect and pride'. Emin, who had been censured for his outspokenness a decade earlier, attacked those who 'by attaching political stigma to our national sentiments are in vain trying to restore the grim era of the cult of personality'.[32]

In the Ukraine, the writers' congress took place against the background of continuing protests against the recent political trials in the republic. It turned into another demonstration of national assertiveness by the Ukraine's cultural elite which, this time, was personally endorsed by the Ukrainian Party First Secretary Shelest. Quite a few of the writers spoke forthrightly about the pressures that the Ukrainian language and culture were facing. The head of the Ukrainian Writers' Union Oles' Honchar, for example, deplored the fact that in both higher and secondary education in the republic, 'through force of certain circumstances, the native language in school sometimes finds itself in a worse position than a foreign one'. He argued that it was a duty to protect the native language, if need be, even 'with authoritative state measures'.[33]

Another speaker, the literary scholar and critic Leonid Novychenko, attacked proponents of assimilation, particularly Agaev, and the journal *Voprosy iazykoznaniia* (Questions of Linguistics), which in 1962 had implied that both Ukrainian and Byelorussian were languages 'without a future'.[34] Alluding to Khrushchev's role in the nationality sphere, he asserted that the reason why Agaev's 'odious' publications had 'generated such a widespread and anxious response' was that they had been backed by 'very influential . . . voluntaristic' and 'subjectivist' tendencies. Novychenko also praised Soloukhin for having at the time defended 'the genuine equality of national cultures and their languages'.[35]

A Russian guest at the Ukrainian writers' congress followed the example that Soloukhin had set. Sergei Baruzdin, the editor of *Druzhba narodov*, declared that he and his colleagues had come to the conclusion that it was time to raise 'more frequently and candidly' questions related to nationality issues that 'agitated' the literary community. He agreed that until Khrushchev had been removed, 'there had been considerable confusion' about such matters. He added:

> For me as a Russian, the haste with which we started speaking about the fusion of cultures was not always understandable. Furthermore, while apparently interpreting Lenin in different ways, we forget Lenin's words on this matter. Lenin said that this question was delicate, that . . . one should not rush here.

Baruzdin also supported the efforts that Ukrainian writers were making to preserve the purity of their native language and assured them that his editorial board was also concerned about 'national culture' and cultivating 'a thoughtful attitude' towards tradition and language.[36]

The highlight of the congress, though, was the speech by Shelest in which he urged Ukrainian writers to 'cherish and respect our beautiful Ukrainian language' and to work towards 'the further enrichment and development of the national culture and language'. He assured the Ukrainian cultural elite that their efforts in this direction 'have been and always will be supported by the Communist Party'. Although Shelest added a warning that 'Ukrainian bourgeois nationalists abroad' were seeking politically to exploit 'vague or ambiguous' works by Soviet Ukrainian writers and called for increased ideological vigilance,[37] his identification with Ukrainian cultural values laid the basis for the establishment of a *modus vivendi* between his 'Ukrainian' faction in the Communist Party of the Ukraine and some of the republic's nationally minded intellectuals.

The following May, the Fourth Soviet Writers' Congress was held in Moscow. Surprisingly, despite the salience of the national question at some of the writers' congresses that had preceded it in the Union republics, this issue was effectively suppressed at the meeting. Still, the non-Russian delegates did manage to come away with at least one modest improvement. Until then the Secretariat of the Board of the Soviet Writers' Union had been a Russian preserve. At the congress, a proposal to include 'representatives of the Writers' Unions of the fraternal Union republics', as *Pravda* put it, was accepted.[38]

National dissent

During the jubilee year of 1967, the authorities rounded up members of the two relatively large underground opposition groups that had been formed back in 1964: the Russian VSKhSON organization and the Ukrainian National Front. Four of the leaders of the first group were tried in November and were sentenced to terms ranging from eight to 15 years. The following spring a further 17 of their colleagues stood trial. The second group had issued its own *samizdat* journal and had sent a memorandum to the Twenty-third Party Congress calling for Ukrainian independence. Nine of its activists were tried and given sentences of eight to 15 years' imprisonment.

Ukrainian national dissent saw a number of other important developments during this period. In August 1966, the young journalist Viacheslav Chornovil was arrested. He had protested against the political arrests and trials in the Ukraine in 1965–6, and compiled a dossier on the numerous infractions of justice that had occurred. His detailed exposé of the 'wanton disregard of socialist legality' was one of the first *samizdat* works employing the 'legalistic' approach that was to be adopted and developed by Soviet human rights campaigners. It also earned him the Nicholas Tomalin Award for Investigative Journalism awarded by the *Sunday Times*.[39]

At his trial on 15 November, Chornovil declared:

> I must remind the state prosecutor that it was in Soviet times, when the USSR already existed, that V. I. Lenin untiringly stressed that local nationalism did not vanish of its own accord, that it was always a reaction against great-power chauvinism, and that the best method of combating nationalism was to eradicate its source – chauvinism.[40]

Throughout 1966 and 1967 Ukrainian *samizdat* was also enriched by numerous protest writings by Ukrainian political prisoners who were among the first to expose the nature and scale of political imprisonment in the Soviet Union in the post-Stalin period. These documents also highlighted the national problem and denounced the official nationalities policy. For instance, Mykhailo Masiutko, who was one of those who had recently been imprisoned, stressed that the Ukrainians formed a majority of the inmates in the Mordovian camps and asked sardonically: 'Why did one so seldom hear Ukrainian spoken in Ukrainian cities and why did one hear it so often in the camps for political prisoners?'[41] Another of the documents to emerge from these camps was a brilliant essay written in April 1967 by the young historian Valentyn Moroz. Entitled 'A Report from the Beria Reservation', it dealt with the Gulag, the KGB, and lawlessness and dehumanization as methods of political control and oppression. It was to be hailed both inside and outside of the Soviet Union as one of the early masterpieces produced by the diverse Soviet human rights movement.[42]

One Ukrainian political prisoner in particular distinguished himself with his broad approach to the nationalities question. Sviatoslav Karavans'kyi, a translator and writer from Odessa, and a former political prisoner under Stalin, had been arrested in November 1965 for sending letters to the authorities complaining about Russification in the Ukraine and made to complete the eight and a half years of his sentence that remained when he was amnestied. In his various protests and petitions, apart from commenting on the situation in the Ukraine, he raised issues such as 'discrimination against the Jewish population', the 'outrageous' injustices suffered by the Crimean Tatars, Volga Germans and other deported peoples, 'the practice of settling Russians in the towns of the other republics', the internal passport system as a way of restricting freedom of movement, the lack of adequate cultural facilities for national minorities, and the need to rectify various unsatisfactory border arrangements between some of the Union republics. He urged the Council of Nationalities of the USSR Supreme Soviet to get over its 'inertia of inactivity' left over from the Stalin period, and appealed for 'a broad discussion in the press' of nationality problems.[43]

The year 1967 was also an important one for the Crimean Tatars and Soviet Jews. In September 1966 the Soviet authorities had introduced new legislation aimed at preventing the sort of public activities, such as the organization of meetings and demonstrations, on which the Crimean Tatars had been relying. This only exacerbated the situation and in July the Crimean Tatars planned to demonstrate in Red Square. On the 21st of that month, however, a delegation of 20 activists was received in the Kremlin by Georgadze; Yurii Andropov, Chairman of the KGB; Roman Rudenko, the USSR Procurator General and Nikolai Shchelokov, the Minister of Internal Affairs. This time, the Crimean Tatars were promised that their people would soon be politically rehabilitated, though the question of repatriation was left unresolved. Andropov, according to one of the Crimean Tatars who participated in the meeting, revealed that the Politburo's decision about rehabilitation had been 'unanimous', but the Soviet leadership was still divided on the question of allowing the Crimean Tatars to return to the Crimea.[44]

An unexplained delay in announcing the rehabilitation of the Crimean Tatars led to two large-scale protests in Tashkent on 27 August and 2 September at which over 130 people were arrested. Finally, on 9 September, the decree rehabilitating the Crimean Tatars was published in the Central Asian press. The fine print revealed, however, that the Crimean Tatars had won only half of their battle. The document referred to their nation as 'citizens of Tatar nationality formerly resident in the Crimea' and contained several provisions designed to prevent them from leaving the areas to which they had been deported. After such a long and determined struggle, the Crimean Tatars were not about to give up. In the last months of 1967 their movement entered a new phase as thousands of Crimean Tatars attempted to take up residence in the Crimea.[45]

For Soviet Jewry, 1967 also became a watershed. The Israeli victory in the summer Six Day War rekindled national consciousness and pride among Soviet Jews, and directed their attention towards Israel. It also brought another virulent anti-Zionist campaign in the Soviet press and further restrictions on the Jews' opportunities for professional advancement. From this time onwards, more and more Soviet Jews were to consider leaving the Soviet Union. It soon became clear to them, however, that this was a right for which they would have to organize and campaign.[46]

By no means all the movements campaigning for the redress of national grievances at this time were known to the outside world. The Soviet human rights movement and its *samizdat* network were still in an embryonic stage and it was almost impossible for Western correspondents restricted to

Moscow to know what was happening in the Soviet peripheries. Indeed, even in the case of the Ukraine, it was seven months before the wave of arrests there during the summer of 1965 was first reported in the Western press.[47]

One campaign that became known about in the West only much later was the one that had been conducted intermittently ever since Stalin's death by the Georgian inhabitants of the Saingilo district in Azerbaijan. In numerous protests over the years, they had complained to Moscow that they were denied Georgian language schools and other cultural facilities and were facing discrimination and forced assimilation. Moscow's failure to intervene led to concern and expressions of solidarity within the Georgian intelligentsia. In 1967, 160 Georgian intellectuals are reported to have sent a petition to Brezhnev about the case of their fellow-countrymen in Saingilo, but without result.[48]

What little information there is suggests that there were problems in Central Asia and the North Caucasus, too. On 19 September 1965, a Secretary of the Central Committee of the Uzbek Communist Party, R. Nishanov, referred to 'individual elements . . . who write anonymous declarations in which they try to blacken, slander and distort the great friendship of peoples'.[49] The press in these regions also indicated that unofficial Islam was still very much alive in spite of, or perhaps because of, Khrushchev's anti-religious offensive. In 1966, L. Klimovich, a leading anti-religious propagandist, acknowledged that 'at present, the clergy of the "out-of-the-mosque" (unofficial) trend are everywhere much stronger than that of the "mosque" trend. In certain regions, for instance in the North Caucasus, practically all members of the clergy belong to the *murid* [clandestine Sufi] communities.'[50]

Meanwhile, Russian nationalism was welling to the surface through the outlets provided by the authorities. On 9 June 1967, TASS reported that the All-Russian Society for the Preservation of Historical and Cultural Monuments had attracted three million members during the first year of its official existence.[51] The mid-1960s also saw the emergence of important new *derevenshchiki*, or 'village prose' writers, especially Vasilii Belov and Valentin Rasputin. This atavistic current, with its explicit Russian nationalism, muted religious themes and at times frank social criticism represented a search for the uncontaminated sources of Russian culture. Its consternation at the erosion of traditional values in the face of industrialization and urbanization was at times to come dangerously close to condemning the consequences of Sovietization.[52]

Soon, however, a darker side to this broad 'Russian' movement was revealed. The Russian associations concerned with the preservation of cultural and historical monuments became strongholds of chauvinistic and anti-Semitic elements, whose ideology was based on 'an interest in Russianness, a belief in the messianic role of Russia and an extreme scorn and hostility towards everything non-Russian'.[53] Two tendencies emerged: the neo-Slavophile, and the National Bolshevik. The latter, which had quasi-fascist features, seems to have started taking hold within the Party and Komsomol in the mid-1960s. In 1965, for example, a Komsomol functionary in Moscow called Valerii Skurlatov is reported to have distributed 'A Code of Morals' which, among other things, stressed the importance of preserving racial purity, advocated the branding and sterilization of Russian women who gave themselves to foreigners, and propagated a cult of the strong.[54] Two or so years later, also in Moscow, an economist and Party member named Fetisov, along with three others, began espousing fascistoid views based both on Stalinism and Nazism, and which, incidentally, foreshadowed the Pol Pot regime's programme of de-urbanization and a return to the agricultural commune. In May 1968, shortly after he had resigned from the Party, Fetisov and his colleagues were arrested and placed in a prison mental hospital.[55] Ironically then, 50 years after the Bolshevik revolution, neo-fascism was stirring not in the western non-Russian republics whose inhabitants were still being reminded in the official press about 'collaboration' with the Germans, but in the very heart of Soviet Russia.

Challenges from without and within

During 1968 the Kremlin was faced with trouble in Eastern Europe and the further growth of dissidence within the Soviet Union itself. Its alarm about these developments was evident at the April Central Committee plenum at which the perceived danger from attempts to 'undermine socialist society from within' was highlighted and Party members exhorted to go on the offensive against inimical ideological influences.[56] Other signs included the attacks in the press on Alexander Solzhenitsyn, and on writers who had protested against the arrests of dissenters,[57] as well as the disgraceful treatment of the Crimean Tatars.

After their rehabilitation, thousands of Crimean Tatars attempted to settle in the Crimea but were forcibly expelled. Their protests were left unanswered. On 21 April 1968, when a large group of Crimean Tatars gathered in the Uzbek town of Chirchik to celebrate the 95th anniversary of Lenin's birth, they were forcibly dispersed by soldiers and the police, and 300 of them were detained. In May, 800 Crimean Tatar representatives travelled to Moscow to deliver a new petition but were detained and sent home. In desperation, the following month the Crimean Tatar movement issued an appeal addressed to international public opinion in which they described their struggle and pointed out that over the years they had submitted petitions and protests containing more than three million signatures.[58]

By this time the Crimean Tatar movement was beginning to attract support from individuals who were to form the core of the Soviet human rights movement. One remarkable opponent of tyranny and injustice, the Russian writer, communist and political prisoner under Stalin, Aleksei Kosterin, had defended the rights of the Crimean Tatars and other deported peoples since the late 1950s.[59] In the spring of 1968, when Kosterin was ailing, his place as the champion of the Crimean Tatar movement was taken by the Ukrainian former Red Army Major-General turned dissident, Petr Grigorenko (Petro Hryhorenko). He urged the Crimean Tatars 'to use all the means' available to them under the Soviet Constitution to continue their struggle.[60]

Both Kosterin and Grigorenko realized that the Crimean Tatar problem went beyond the question of the fate of a small nation of some 300,000 people. They emphasized that it symbolized the unresolved national problem in the Soviet Union and the persistence of neo-Stalinist attitudes. As dissident communists they were also well aware that the treatment of the Crimean Tatars belied the image that the USSR projected of itself as the champion of oppressed peoples. In February 1968, Kosterin wrote in an appeal to a consultative conference of Communist parties in Budapest: 'The national question in our country . . . looks particularly vile against the background of our "defence" of all those oppressed and persecuted in Greece, Spain . . . America and Africa . . .'[61]

The other significance of the Crimean Tatar problem was that for many Russian human rights activists, it was to be the issue that first sensitized them to the national question. In the first half of 1968 there were two notable developments that attested to the crystallization of a civil (or human) rights movement. At the end of April a group of activists in Moscow began publishing a regular bulletin which they named the *Khronika tekushchikh sobytii* (Chronicle of Current Events). Its editors were soon to establish links with human rights activists in various parts of the Soviet Union, thereby creating a rudimentary unofficial information network.[62] Furthermore, in June, the distinguished Russian nuclear physicist and academician Andrei Sakharov made his debut as a dissident with his stimulating essay 'Thoughts on Progress, Peaceful Coexistence and Intellectual Freedom'. Interestingly, although the author did not dwell on the national problem, he mentioned the plight of the Crimean Tatars, and referred to Stalin's 'Ukrainophobia', as well as the 'zoological kind of anti-Semitism that was characteristic of Stalin's bureaucracy'. Nationality problems, he also warned, 'will continue to be a reason for unrest and dissatisfaction until all departures from Leninist principles are acknowledged and analysed and firm steps taken to correct mistakes'.[63]

The increasing assertiveness and militancy of some of the non-Russian dissenters at this time can be seen from the prompt response that Sakharov's treatise drew from a group signing itself 'Numerous Representatives from the Estonian Technical Intelligentsia'. Their reply, which was circulated in *samizdat* later that year, was entitled 'To Hope or to Act'. In it, they took issue with Sakharov for, among other things, his omission of the question of the right of peoples to sovereign and independent state existence.[64]

The Prague Spring, though, dominated 1968. Moscow was fortunate that while the Czechoslovak reform movement was developing, the nationally assertive Ukrainian Party leader Shelest acted as a leading critic of what was happening on the western border of his republic. Some Ukrainian intellectuals followed the process of liberalization in Czechoslovakia with considerable interest and sympathy. Valentyn Moroz, for example, wrote to Shelest from a labour camp in praise of the Czech 'national rebirth' and urged Ukrainian communists to learn from their example.[65] The sizeable Ukrainian minority in the Presov region of eastern Czechoslovakia not only provided information about what was going on, but acted as a window to the outside world. This seems to have made Shelest uneasy about the possibility of ideological contagion from the Ukraine's Eastern European neighbour. Since Shelest was something of a national communist himself, he could not afford to be tainted with 'revisionism', and in this situation acted almost more Catholic than the Pope.[66]

The invasion of Czechoslovakia came as a shock to the more liberally inclined Soviet public and triggered off more protests, such as the celebrated one in Red Square on 25 August 1968.[67] The fourth issue of the *Chronicle of Current Events* reported that in the Baltic republics 'leaflets condemning the invasion of Czechoslovakia have come to circulate widely'. It also provided information about an Estonian student who had been 'savagely beaten up while in detention' for writing 'CZECHS, WE ARE YOUR BROTHERS' on a cinema wall in Tartu.[68]

The Soviet military intervention in Czechoslovakia was followed by an intensification of repression against dissenters, including many national rights campaigners. In Armenia, for example, members of the National Unification Party, who had started putting out their own *samizdat* journal, were imprisoned in 1968 and 1969.[69] In the summer of 1969, ten leading Crimean Tatar campaigners were tried in Moscow.[70] The following April, the Ukrainian dissident Valentyn Moroz was rearrested shortly after emerging from the camps. In November he was given a draconian 14-year sentence for his protest writings.[71]

These blows, however, failed to stop the development of dissent and opposition; in some cases they had the opposite effect and merely radicalized disaffected groups. The Meskhetians, for instance, were treated just as shabbily as the Crimean Tatars. In May 1968 the Presidium of the USSR Supreme Soviet issued an order affirming that they had the right to settle anywhere they wanted, but at the same time made it clear that they were officially regarded as having 'taken root' in the areas to which they had been deported. Meskhetians who attempted to return home were prevented or expelled. In July 1968, 7,000 Meskhetians gathered in Tbilisi to protest. In August 1969, after the 33rd attempt to persuade the authorities in Moscow to change their attitude failed, some of the Meskhetian representatives demonstratively renounced their Soviet citizenship. The following year the Meskhetians began appealing to Turkey, and later also the United Nations, for support.[72]

In Lithuania, the harsh official response to a burgeoning Roman Catholic protest campaign turned the latter into a mass movement in which religious and national aspects became intertwined. Lithuanian religious dissent surfaced in 1968 in the form of a petitions campaign headed by some of the clergy. At the beginning of the 1970s, the authorities exacerbated the situation by arresting and trying three priests and an elderly woman teacher. By the end of 1971 thousands of signatures were being collected for appeals addressed to Brezhnev and the United Nations. That same year, a Lithuanian sailor, Simas Kudirka, who had attempted to escape to the United States, became a harbinger of a more defiant Lithuanian spirit. At his trial in June he asserted his Roman Catholic faith, condemned Soviet policies towards his nation, and declared himself in favour of an independent Lithuanian state.[73]

In neighbouring Latvia, in the summer of 1971, an anonymous group of 17 veteran communists issued a *samizdat* appeal addressed to foreign communist leaders in which they accused the Soviet Communist Party of violating Marxist-Leninist nationalities policy, and of having 'deliberately adopted a policy of Great Russian chauvinism'. Contrasting the attempts that were made immediately after Stalin's death to remedy the situation with the 'determined policy of coercive assimilation' that they claimed had been pursued both under Khrushchev and Brezhnev, they urged the leaders of foreign communist parties to intervene because Moscow's nationalities policy was damaging to the world communist movement.[74]

Some individuals turned to extreme forms of protest. On 5 December 1968 a Ukrainian teacher, Vasyl' Makukh, set fire to himself in Kiev's main street and died shouting: 'Long Live Free Ukraine!'[75] The following January a Russian army engineer lieutenant, Anatolii Ilyin, opened fire on Brezhnev's motorcade in an unsuccessful attempt to assassinate the Soviet leader.[76] In February 1969 another Ukrainian, Mykola Breslavs'kyi, attempted to burn himself in Kiev in protest against Russification.[77] Three months later, Ilia Rips set fire to himself in Riga in protest against the invasion of Czechoslovakia, but passers-by managed to put out the flames in time.[78]

There were also indications of trouble in Central Asia and the North Caucasus. In April and May of 1969 ethnic disturbances were reported to have broken out in several places in Uzbekistan with rioters demanding: 'Russians, get out of Uzbekistan!' Troops had to be sent to Tashkent to restore order. Simultaneously, there was also trouble among the republic's large Tadzhik population after attempts were made to change the designation of their nationality in their identity cards to 'Uzbek'. Several 'Russian administrators' were reported to have been murdered.[79]

In May and July of the same year in Groznyi, bombs were placed under the statue of the Russian tsarist general Ermolov who had distinguished himself during the conquest of the Caucasus.[80] A resident of the same city, Elim Makhaev, was arrested during 1969 and placed in a mental hospital for attempting to found a 'United Party for the Liberation of the Caucasus'. It is not clear whether this Moslem fundamentalist was responsible for the explosions.[81] On 29 March 1969, *Pravda* carried a report from Groznyi complaining that leaders of local clandestine Moslem groups had held a secret council the previous summer and issued a set of regulations for their members. During 1968, there was also an outbreak of unrest in neighbouring Daghestan.[82]

One particular act of political extremism that was planned but never carried out was to become a milestone in the development of the Jewish emigration movement. In June 1970, ten Jews, a Russian and a Ukrainian, who were preparing to hijack an aeroplane in order to get around the ban on emigration from the Soviet Union, were arrested in Leningrad. Two of the Jews, Eduard Kuznetsov and Mark Dymshits, were sentenced to be shot (the sentences were later commuted), while their colleagues received lengthy terms of imprisonment. The case caused an outcry both at home and abroad, highlighted the situation of Soviet Jewry, and gave an impetus to the rapidly growing Jewish emigration campaign. By the beginning of the 1970s, this large, well-organized and militant movement, which enjoyed the support of the Jewish diaspora, had managed to force open the gates to emigration.[83]

At the end of the 1960s there were also signs of growing cooperation between activists of different nationalities on the basis of a shared commitment to the defence of human rights. In May 1969, an Initiative (Action) Group for the Defence of Civil Rights in the Soviet Union was formed which united campaigners for civil, national and religious rights. The 15 founding members included Russians, Jews, a Ukrainian, a Crimean Tatar and an Armenian.[84] That same year, a new underground opposition group issued a lengthy document entitled 'Programme of the Democrats of Russia, the Ukraine and the Baltic Lands' which advocated democracy and national self-determination for the non-Russian peoples.[85] Much later it became known that the authors were in fact the same circle of people in Estonia who had replied to Sakharov's *samizdat* essay. Apart from Estonians, the group included a Russian, Sergei Soldatov, and a Ukrainian, Artem Iuskevych.[86] Two years later, a number of Ukrainian and Russian dissidents formed a 'Citizens' Committee' to defend the arrested Ukrainian human rights activist Nina Strokata-Karavans'kyi; it was one of the first organizations of this type to be founded in the Soviet Union.[87]

Cooperation between representatives of different nationalities did not always function so smoothly. Positions first had to be clarified and mutual suspicion and distrust overcome. Russian civil rights campaigners seem to have had no problems about supporting the Crimean Tatars, but when it came to dealing with representatives of the larger non-Russian nations whose grievances were directed at Russian domination, matters were not quite so simple. For Ukrainian and Baltic activists, however, the idea of human rights was inseparable from that of national rights. For them, the test of whether a Russian civil rights activist was a genuine democrat who could be cooperated with depended on his or her attitude towards the national question. At this stage, though, most of the Russian activists had not been exposed to this issue and a good many of them seem to have been suspicious of non-Russian 'separatists'.

The Russian Orthodox writer and dissenter Anatolii Levitin-Krasnov has recorded very candidly in his memoirs the sort of 'grilling' that he and other Russian activists gave to one of the leading Ukrainian dissidents, Chornovil, when he came to Moscow in May 1969.[88] For their part, the Ukrainians soon showed their distrust of Russian human rights campaigners. The new *samizdat* organ of the Ukrainian patriotic movement, the *Ukrainian Herald*, which made its appearance at the beginning of 1970, emphasized that Ukrainian dissenters were not seeking just 'freedom of speech and belief', and even criticized the Moscow-based Committee for Human Rights founded by Sakharov and others, also in 1970, for not defining its position on the national question. The editors of the *Ukrainian Herald* also complained that the *Chronicle of Current Events* concentrated too heavily on events in Russia, 'principally in Moscow', and did not adequately reflect the 'situation in the USSR'.[89] Gradually, though, these sorts of problems were mainly overcome and the links forged at this time between the core of Moscow's human rights activists and the various democratic national movements were to stand the various tests that lay ahead. As for the *Chronicle of Current Events*, in a remarkably short time it was providing quite comprehensive coverage of the many forms of dissent and opposition.

The Sino–Soviet conflict and the national question

At this time of trouble at home and in Eastern Europe, the Soviet Union's strained relations with China deteriorated still further, culminating in border skirmishes between the two sides in March 1969. During the second half of the 1960s, fear of 'the yellow peril' was on the rise in the Soviet Union, and for some Soviet citizens the conflict with China brought home the vulnerability of the multinational Soviet state in the event of war. Aishe Seitmuratova, one of the Crimean Tatar representatives who were received in the Kremlin in July 1967 by high-ranking Soviet officials, recalls that Andropov, the KGB chief, did not disguise his concern about the Chinese threat, but acknowledged that 'in the East, the USSR was sitting on a powder-keg'.[90]

What is of particular interest here is that it was Soviet citizens, not Western analysts, who at this time first began to envisage the possible disintegration of the Soviet empire. In the first half of 1979, for example, the Russian dissident Andrei Amalrik wrote his provocative essay entitled 'Will the Soviet Union Survive Until 1984?' in which he anticipated that in the event of a Sino–Soviet war, 'nationalist tendencies of the USSR's non-Russian peoples will sharply intensify', and might lead to 'unavoidable "de-imperialization"' of the USSR.[91] At about the same time as Amalrik was writing his prognostic study, Anatole Shub, the Moscow correspondent of the *Washington Post*, reported the following views that he had encountered among Soviet citizens about what might happen if the Soviet Union and China went to war:

> What will happen in our border areas, where there are dissatisfied non-Russian nationalities? Do you know that more than half the prisoners in our camps these days are so-called bourgeois nationalists – Latvians, Lithuanians, Georgians, Ukrainians and the rest? I am afraid that – unless there is a radical change of policy, and we go back to Lenin's principles (permitting independence for the Finns, the Balts, etc.) – all these people will see the war with China as a signal to rise against what they consider Russian colonialism, although we Russians know that what it really is is Stalinism . . .[92]

Of course, it is hard to gauge the extent to which the Kremlin shared these fears. What is known, though, is that Peking evidently considered the national question in the USSR to be an important issue and exploited it in its propaganda war with Moscow. From the spring of 1969, the Chinese news media began to carry frequent reports on the 'oppression' of the non-Russian peoples of the USSR and the 'acuteness' of the nationalities problem in the USSR. On 4 July 1969, for example, *Peking Review* made the following comment about the situation in the Soviet Union:

> What they call 'nationalism' actually means the legitimate demands of the oppressed nationalities in the Soviet Union and their struggle against the Soviet revisionist new tsars. What they mean by 'irreconcilable struggle' against 'nationalism' is in fact the stepping up of the suppression of the Soviet peoples of all nationalities . . . To drape their fascist bourgeois rule with 'Leninist' trappings, the Soviet revisionist new tsars allege that they are 'true to the Leninist national policy'. This is a shameless lie.

These sorts of accusations emanating from another leading socialist state must have been quite embarrassing for Moscow. Soviet newspapers, particularly in the traditionally Moslem republics, countered with articles criticizing China's treatment of her own national minorities. Peking's leaders were accused of 'great-power chauvinism' and the 'repression, persecution and murder of national cadres'. In 1969 the USSR began radio broadcasts aimed at the Uighurs – a Central Asian Moslem people estimated to be over five-million strong – the majority of whom live on the Chinese side of the Sino–Soviet border in Sinkiang. These transmissions were increased and strengthened at the end of 1971. The Sino–Soviet propaganda exchanges on the national question is a fascinating subject which unfortunately still remains under-researched.[93]

Moderation or a holding action?

Apart from all these problems at home and abroad, during the late 1960s the Brezhnev leadership found itself in something of a quandary for another reason. It was becoming increasingly apparent that Khrushchev's timetable for building communism in the Soviet Union by the 1980s had been utopian. This also meant that the prospect of the fusion of the nations of the USSR receded into the very far distant future. In the meantime, national awareness was growing not only among the non-Russians, but in the Russian nation too. How was the Party to recognize the 'postponement' of fusion, and yet maintain the momentum of its drive towards ever greater unity? This uncertainty about the way forward seems to have put those responsible in Moscow for nationalities policy on the defensive and to have introduced an element of fluidity which was capitalized on by some of the non-Russian elites, as well as emerging Russian nationalist forces.

One other factor made itself felt more and more during this period – demographic trends. As an article in *Literaturnaia gazeta* put it in January 1967: 'The rate of growth of the country's population is now clearly unsatisfactory. This is clear to many people now.' Part of the problem was that the birth rate in the European part of the USSR was declining, while the traditionally Moslem republics were experiencing a population explosion. Apart from the unwelcome implications for nationalities policy generally, this trend was compounding economic difficulties connected with the distribution of the USSR's manpower resources. The newspaper explained:

> The population of the USSR is not distributed over its territory in the best possible way. While there is insufficient manpower in some places, there is more than enough in others. Migration ought to remove these shortcomings. Often however, it makes them worse (the ebb of the population away from Siberia and the tide of people into Central Asia, for example). To put it frankly, we have no valid, scientific system of regulating migration.[94]

Realizing the growing seriousness of the demographic problem and heeding warnings from specialists about the need both to avoid some of the 'mistakes' that were made in organizing the 1959 All-Union census, and to broaden the questions for the forthcoming one in 1969, the Soviet government decided to postpone the next census for a year in order to provide time for more thorough preparation. In March 1968, it was announced that changes would be made to the questionnaire so as to 'determine not only the native languages of all the country's inhabitants, but also what second languages are spoken fluently by those questioned'. During this time, there were also calls in the press for 'a scientifically substantiated state policy . . . in the sphere of the birth rate'.[95]

As early as November 1967, Brezhnev alluded to the problem that the Party leadership faced in reconciling in some dialectical manner centrifugal tendencies with centripetal ones. In a speech given on the 50th anniversary of Soviet rule in the Ukraine, he declared:

> the drawing together of nations is a complex historical process, and neither ill-considered haste, artificial restraint nor aimless drifting can be allowed.[96]

Two years later, an editorial in *Kommunist* indicated drift in the Party's nationalities policy. Rather curiously, at a time when ideological controls were otherwise being tightened, it seemed to be aimed at reassuring the non-Russians. 'The drawing together of Soviet nations and their internationalist unity', the editorial, which appeared in September 1969, stated,

> should not be regarded as fusion. The removal of all national differences is a long process, which cannot be achieved except after the complete victory of communism in the world and its consolidation.

Also, in something of a new departure, the Party's main theoretical organ added the following warning:

> national relations belong to the most complex social phenomena which require, in the solution of this or that task, utmost tact and sensitivity, and ability to take into account the national characteristics of peoples. Indifference and nihilism as regards national problems cannot be tolerated.[97]

Perhaps, however, this editorial, published in connection with the 100th anniversary of Lenin's birth, was meant to be read in the context of the Sino–Soviet conflict. Towards the end, it denounced 'the anti-people group of Mao-tse Tung', accusing it of pursuing 'a great-power nationalistic policy which has nothing in common with Marxism-Leninism and the principles of proletarian internationalism'.[98]

Shelest and the Ukraine

In the late 1960s not only was national dissent on the upsurge, but also, some of the non-Russian elites were once again demonstrating considerable national pride and assertiveness. The case of Shelest and the Ukraine has already been referred to. He seems to have actively encouraged the development of a 'Soviet' Ukrainian patriotism and afforded some protection to dissenters like Dziuba who were prepared to work 'within the system'. Although efforts to de-Russify higher education in the Ukraine had failed, Shelest persisted in his defence of the Ukrainian language and urged the republic's scientists to use it in their work. One noteworthy success was the fact that the USSR's first encyclopaedia of cybernetics, which appeared in Kiev in 1973 in two volumes, was published in the Ukrainian language.[99]

Under Shelest there was a revival of Ukrainian historical studies; he himself did not conceal his admiration for the Ukrainian Cossacks and their state in his book *Ukraino nasha radians'ka* (Ukraine, Our Soviet Land).[100] This later led him to be accused of 'idealizing' the Ukrainian past. In 1968 his friend Oles' Honchar, who was head of the Ukrainian Writers' Union, published a novel *Sobor* (The Cathedral) that defended Ukrainian culture and raised environmental issues. A rival faction in the Ukrainian bureaucracy launched a vicious attack on the book, and Moscow became concerned about the degree of Ukrainian national consciousness that was being permitted under Shelest. In April 1988, the Ukrainian literary journal *Dnipro* revealed that the Kremlin had been involved in the *Sobor* case. When Sholokhov had attempted to intervene on Honchar's behalf, Brezhnev sent him to Andrei Kirilenko, a member of the Politburo and a Central Committee Secretary. The latter informed him that the problem with *Sobor* was its 'Cossackophilism'.[101]

Significantly, one of the outstanding works of Ukrainian *samizdat* in the second half of the 1960s was a Marxist critique by the historian Mykhailo Braichevs'kyi of the interpretation of the Treaty of Pereiaslav as formulated by the Soviet leadership in 1954.[102] Ukrainian historians also sought to renew study of the Kievan Rus' period, a subject which in the late 1940s had effectively been made the preserve of Russian specialists, and to rehabilitate Ukrainian political figures from the nineteenth and early twentieth centuries. Perhaps the major achievement in the historical sphere, though, was the initiation of a project to publish a multi-volume history of the Ukrainian SSR, which ultimately resulted in a monumental 26-volume history of the cities and villages of the Ukraine.[103]

The Ukrainians were also assertive in two other important areas. Shelest and his supporters opposed the diversion of funds away from the Ukraine for the development of Siberian regions, favoured a measure of economic self-sufficiency for the republic, and even proposed that the Ukraine be allowed to experiment with a computerized system of planning and economic management.[104] Furthermore, lawyers in the republic devoted considerable attention to the question of the Ukraine's 'sovereignty' and frequently alluded to the terms of the 'national contract'. In the October 1967 issue of the Ukrainian legal journal *Radians'ke pravo* (Soviet Law), for example, two specialists stressed that the creation of the USSR 'was an act of the sovereign will' of nations 'with equal rights', and that it 'did not signify abdication from independent existence and sovereignty'.[105]

'Mirasism' in the Moslem republics

A similar cultural resurgence, emphasis on sovereign rights and 'quest for autonomy' were also apparent at this time in the Central Asian republics. In some respects, the elites here went further than the Ukrainians. On

5 November 1969, in an unmistakable display of solidarity and assertiveness, the main Russian-language dailies in five Central Asian republics published a 'joint issue' commemorating the 50th anniversary of Lenin's letter to the Bolsheviks in Turkestan in which he had called for the elimination of vestiges of 'Great Russian imperialism' in the region.[106] Only a few months before, the Chairman of the Presidium of the Supreme Soviet of Uzbekistan had published an article in the Uzbek Party journal recalling the Soviet government's appeal of 20 November 1917, which assured the Moslems of the former Russian empire that they were free to order their national life as they saw fit.[107]

The main feature of the vigorous cultural revivals in the traditionally Moslem regions was *mirasism*, a rediscovery and affirmation of the Islamic heritage which was especially evident in literature and historiography. This movement strengthened the growing pride and confidence of the Soviet-educated elites in Central Asia and Kazakhstan, who in the second half of the 1960s had begun to come into their own. It manifested itself in efforts to upgrade the status of the native languages and provide preferential treatment for native cadres, as well as a tendency to turn a deaf ear to warnings about 'idealizing the past' and 'local nationalism'.[108] By the end of the 1960s, this led to a backlash as Russians and other Slavs in these 'Moslem' republics – as well as in the Tatar and Bashkir ASSRs – had started complaining about discrimination at the hands of the indigenous peoples.[109]

This does not mean that Central Asia and Kazakhstan were beginning to seethe with political disaffection. What there was was a strong sense of being different to the Europeans – an incipient cultural 'nationalism', not developed political dissent. Even the Crimean Tatar and Meskhetian movements, which were based in Central Asia, do not seem to have had much of a resonance among fellow-Moslems in these republics. There was also apparently little or no indigenous political *samizdat*, which is one reason why so very few cases of dissidence have been recorded. One intriguing case that is known, though, involved the young Turkmen poet Annasoltan Kekilova, who in August 1971 was locked up in a mental hospital for 'criticizing shortcomings' in her native republic in letters addressed to the Twenty-fourth Party Congress. Despite her mother's protests, Kekilova was not freed and later died in a lunatic asylum.[110]

There was, of course, also the problem of unofficial Islam, but this phenomenon does not appear to have been quite so strong and anti-Russian in Central Asia as in the North Caucasus. In September 1970, a Tadzhik newspaper reported that a group of Moslem religious dissenters had been tried after a certain Rakhman Nurov had 'gathered a group of bad people around him' in the region of Navabad and:

worked out a plan to destroy the social order and to diminish the reputation of a group of activists. According to these plans, Sh. Sharapov continuously sent libellous and accusatory letters, complaints and petitions to state and Party organizations.[111]

The Russites

All this time Russian nationalism was flourishing. In 1968 *Molodaia gvardiia* (Young Guard), the monthly organ of the Komsomol, was effectively taken over by advocates of a neo-Slavophile orientation and began publishing articles that were highly ethnocentric and vehemently anti-Western. That it managed to do this for several years with the backing of other publications – *Ogonek*, *Literaturnaia Rossiia* (Literary Russia), *Moskva* (Moscow) and *Nash sovremennik* (Our Contemporary) – indicates that there was support in high places for the chauvinist views that it was propagating.[112] Another example was the continuing growth of the All-Russian Society for the Preservation of Historical and Cultural Monuments: by 1972 its membership had reached seven million and was still rising.

Visitors to the Soviet Union at the end of the 1960s and beginning of the 1970s were struck, as one of them – Michael Scammell – put it, by the 'rapidly growing phenomenon of Great Russian nationalism and the appearance of a rather amorphous group known as the *rusity*, or "Russites"'. He reported that at one end of the spectrum, the Russites linked up

> with those numerous intellectuals who advocate taking a greater interest in the national Russian past and seek to rehabilitate pure Russian culture in all its forms . . . But it is the other extreme that gives cause for alarm, for it expresses a powerful revulsion away from the token internationalism (however attenuated and distorted) of official Soviet policy and a flight into isolationism, chauvinism and reaction.[113]

Another traveller to the USSR, Jonathan Harris, noted that the most extreme Russites espoused an ideology that has since come to be labelled as National Bolshevism: they considered the Soviet state as 'the heir and defender' of such 'worthy' pre-revolutionary traditions as authoritarian government, the 'one and indivisible' Russian empire and anti-Westernism. They also had a special reverence for Stalin as the leader who had made Soviet Russia strong and mighty.

Why was such a current tolerated? Harris recorded the explanations that were being offered at the time in Moscow's liberal circles:

> Many members of the intelligentsia fear that the current regime encourages the growth of Russian chauvinism as an emotional alternative to the discredited and lack-lustre slogans of contemporary Soviet ideology, and in order to counter those dissidents who demand the introduction of Western political practices. Others claim that the military leaders, who are regarded with great intellectual contempt, seek to foster these views to bolster their own growing role in the system.[114]

Peter Reddaway offered a slightly different explanation. Although the Kremlin's motives in tolerating the Russites were 'doubtless mixed', he suggested that

> The major purposes were probably to test how effectively a sanitized Russian nationalism could be used against the generally West-oriented liberal intelligentsia, and, more broadly, whether such nationalism could be adequately synthesized with Marxism-Leninism, thus producing a modified official ideology with wider popular appeal.[115]

Eventually, *Molodaia gvardiia* overstepped the mark by publishing a quintessential National Bolshevik article by Sergei Semanov, entitled 'On Relative and Eternal Values', in its August 1970 issue. Semanov described the Bolshevik revolution as the 'Great Russian Revolution', heaped praise on the 1930s – the decade in which the Stalinist state was erected – and depicted the USSR in imperial terms as a 'united and monolithic whole'. In November *Kommunist* thundered its disapproval and a move was made to bring *Molodaia gvardiia* into line by replacing its editor, Anatolii Nikonov. At least, this seems to have been the intention. In actual fact, as Alexander Yanov points out, 'nothing changed': the journal did not abandon its Russite positions, Nikonov was given a job running another magazine, and a new monthly publication, *Nash sovremennik*, which had sympathies similar to those of *Molodaia gvardiia*, appeared.[116]

The most outspoken Russian nationalist writing was now channelled into *samizdat*. At the beginning of 1971, an important Russian nationalist *samizdat* journal called *Veche* was founded by the Slavophile Vladimir Osipov. Within a short space of time it had become the organ of what Yanov dubbed 'the Russian New Right'.[117] The first half of 1971 also saw the appearance of a *samizdat* manifesto ambiguously entitled *Slovo natsii*, which in Russian can mean either 'The Word of the Nation', or 'A Word to the Nation'. Its anonymous authors signed themselves simply 'Russian Patriots'. Racist in tone, it upheld the idea of Russian supremacy, ridiculed the national aspirations of the non-Russian nations, and ended with the slogan: 'Long live a great, single and indivisible Russia! May God be with us!' What was particularly noteworthy about this document, though, was its claim that the Russians were the most underprivileged nation in the Soviet Union.[118] This theme was to be taken up over the years by a variety of representatives of the Russian cause, ranging from patriots to chauvinists.

The Twenty-fourth Party Congress enunciates a 'new' formula

At the Twenty-fourth Party Congress in March 1971, the Brezhnev leadership clarified its nationalities policy. In his report, Brezhnev announced that after more than 50 years of Soviet rule, a 'new historical community of people – the Soviet people (*sovetskii narod*)' – had emerged which was united in 'monolithic solidarity' by ideology and shared experience. Although the Soviet leader was careful to emphasize that the Party remained opposed to all forms of nationalism and chauvinism, and intended to foster 'a spirit of profound respect for all nations and nationalities', he stressed that it would 'continue to do everything' to strengthen the unity of the country, and to promote the further drawing-together of nations.[119]

The concept of the 'Soviet people' was hardly a new one: it had been advanced by proponents of fusion in the early 1960s, and Khrushchev had used the term at the Twenty-second Party Congress. The Brezhnev leadership, however, adapted it to the requirements of a period in which tacit recognition was being given to the realization that communism was not just around the corner and that a protracted interim stage of 'developed' or 'mature' socialism would first have to be traversed. With 'fusion' deferred indefinitely, the idea of the Soviet people provided the Kremlin with an expedient formula to acknowledge the enduring multinational nature of the Soviet state while emphasizing a supposedly higher unity transcending national distinctions.

Brezhnev did not even allude to the various problems in the nationalities sphere that had been building up in recent years. What he did do, though, was implicitly acknowledge the surge of Russian national feeling by delivering the sort of paean to the 'Great Russian People' that had been familiar before the Twentieth Party Congress:

> All the nations and nationalities of our country, above all the Great Russian people, played a role in the formation, strengthening and development of this mighty union of equal peoples that have taken the path of socialism. The revolutionary energy, selflessness, diligence and profound internationalism of the Great Russian people have rightfully won them the sincere respect of all the peoples of our socialist homeland.[120]

Although Brezhnev showed a little more tact by staying off the subject of the role of the Russian language, his tribute to the Russian nation made it plain enough that in what was supposedly a model new internationalist community there would continue to be a first among 'equals'.

12

Forging the Soviet People

Shortly after the Twenty-fourth Party Congress the long-awaited results of the 1970 All-Union census began to appear.[1] The figures indicated that despite the assimilationist nature of Soviet nationalities policy, the Russians' share of the USSR's population was falling and that their position as a majority nation was being eroded. In 1959 they had accounted for 54.65 per cent of the population; in 1970, 53.37 per cent. Although this was only a small drop, the Moslem populations were increasing at about three and a half times the rate of the Russians. Moreover, three-quarters of the indigenous population of Soviet Central Asia still did not know Russian.

In all the non-Russian republics except the Ukraine and Byelorussia, more than 90 per cent of the titular population continued to regard their national language as their native language, and the percentage of pupils attending native-language schools was growing.[2] At the same time, the non-Russian press was also steadily expanding.[3] As Kaputikian had pointed out five years earlier, under the impact of modernization, far from atrophying, the major non-Russian nations were consolidating and showing increasing vitality.

It was not long before more concern about demographic trends was being shown in the press and specialized literature. In February 1971, *Voprosy ekonomiki* (Questions of Economics) expressed alarm that the birthrate in the USSR as a whole was 'lower than in a number of developed capitalist countries (the Netherlands, Japan)'. It went on to emphasize that there were 'large regional variations in the birthrate'. In Russia, the Ukraine and the Baltic republics, 'the reproduction index' was 'less than one'. In parts of Russia the population was even 'beginning to decline'.[4]

A few weeks later, *Literaturnaia gazeta* presented the other side of the coin. Between 1959 and 1970, the Central Asians and Azerbaijanis had increased their numbers by 50 per cent. Their annual increase of about 4 per cent was among the highest in the world. As a result, the share of the Central Asian nationalities in the Soviet population had risen from 6 per cent in 1959 to 8 per cent, that is, to almost 20 million.[5] Indeed, the 1970 census revealed that one Moslem people, the Uzbeks, had overtaken the Byelorussians and, with a population of 9.2 million, was now the USSR's third largest nation after the Russians and Ukrainians. If other traditionally Moslem groups such as the

5.9 million Tatars, 1.2 million Bashkirs, and the various Moslem nationalities of Transcaucasia and the North Caucasus were also added, the total 'Moslem' proportion of the population became higher still.

This is not to say that there were no encouraging results in the census for the Kremlin. As one specialist, Eduard Bagramov, noted in *Pravda* on 16 July 1971, almost half of the USSR's non-Russian inhabitants could communicate in Russian. Bagramov argued that this was proof of the voluntary and 'progressive' nature of bilingualism and 'the democratic nature of Soviet nationalities policy'.[6]

Bagramov passed over in silence the question of what percentage of the 21,760,000 Russians living in the non-Russian republics (up from 16,251,000 in 1959) had mastered the language of the people among whom they lived. According to one estimate based on the 1970 census, 'only 3.0 per cent of the Russians living in non-Russian units' had 'acquired knowledge of some non-Russian Soviet language'.[7] Bagramov also avoided the issue of the different social functions being assigned to Russian as compared with the non-Russian languages and the practical implications of this 'division of labour'. As one Western scholar observed, the major non-Russian languages were being gradually relegated to spheres of social activity 'relating to home-life, leisure-time activity, and *belles lettres*'.[8]

The data from the census and Brezhnev's proclamation of the formation of the 'Soviet people' encouraged advocates of assimilation. 'Marxists have never doubted that assimilation is a natural and progressive process, reflecting the economic and cultural proximity between the nations, their friendship, equality of rights and consolidation,' A. Boiarskii, the Director of the Scientific Research Institute of the USSR's Central Statistical Administration wrote in *Izvestia* on 9 May 1971. The following month, E. Mordionov, a philosopher from Iakutsk, argued in *Voprosy filosofii* that 'the drawing together of the socialist nations cannot be separated from the process of their fusion, nor from their reaching full unity'.[9]

Bagramov, too, introduced themes into his article that reflected this trend and which were to become more and more prominent during the 1970s. Until now the standard formulation on the economic aspects of nationalities policy had been that 'the interests of the republics' had to be combined with all-Union ones. A shift to a new position was now signalled. The Party, Bagramov wrote:

> proceeds from the premise that the economy of the USSR is not the arithmetical sum of national economies but an *integral national-economic complex* that is developing according to a single plan through the unified efforts of our country . . . Needless to say, the republics cannot individually achieve a mighty new economic upsurge; this will be the result of the unified activity of the working people of all nations and nationalities . . .

The other subtle difference apparent in Bagramov's article was his assertion that 'Every Soviet republic has now become multinational, a place where dozens of various nationalities live and work. All of them enjoy equal rights.' Thus, even the national character of the Union republics was now being placed in some doubt.[10]

As before, this tendency towards accelerating integration and assimilation did not go unchallenged. Mordionov's article drew strong criticism from a historian writing the following June in the journal *Istoriia SSSR* (History of the USSR). The author of the rebuttal, V. P. Sherstobitov, attacked writers who 'rush ahead to propose conceptions of the "mutual assimilation of nations in the USSR", "the dying away" of certain features of the socialist nations and the "denationalization" of the Union republics'. Sherstobitov cautioned those 'who feel that the Soviet federal structure has outlived its usefulness', adding that it was 'wrong to underestimate the significance of national statehood and the great role it plays in promoting national development and stimulating each people to contribute to the common cause'.[11]

In the very same issue of this journal, however, an Armenian author of a book on *Lenin and the Solution of the National Question*, V. N. Mnatsakanian, was taken to task for glossing over 'the objective tendency of peoples towards unity'. Among other things, he was accused of treating Lenin's writings in a one-sided manner, 'with an overemphasis on his call for self-determination' and his struggle against 'great-power chauvinism'.[12] Perhaps the most forthright defence of the republics' rights, though, was made in articles written during 1971 and 1972 by the Kirghiz legal expert K. Nurbekov. He went as far as to assert in print that the state did not have the right to prosecute individuals who advocated the secession of Union republics from the USSR, nor to change the borders of Union republics without the consent of their inhabitants.[13]

Meanwhile, events continued to belie the official declarations about the satisfactory state of national relations. The imprisonment of Odabashev and other Meskhetian leaders in the summer of 1971 was hardly a demonstration of the 'friendship of peoples';[14] in fact, while the approaching 50th anniversary of the formation of the Soviet Union was being hailed in the Soviet press, thousands of Lithuanian Catholics were signing protests about the persecution of priests, Ukrainian dissidents were publishing further issues of their *samizdat* journal and continuing to protest against the violation of human and national rights in their republic, and the Jewish emigration campaign was continuing to gather force.

At the end of 1971, in a more sober assessment of the situation, the Kremlin's chief ideologist, Suslov, acknowledged that 'problems left over from the past in the sphere of national relations' were not about 'to disappear of their own accord'. Nevertheless, Suslov claimed that there was no social basis for national tensions in the Soviet Union and that if there were difficulties here and there in the area of national relations, it was only because of 'vestiges' from the centuries-long nationalities problem as it had existed under the tsars. The best he could propose was a redoubling of efforts aimed at combating 'all forms of nationalism' and educating 'the masses in the spirit of socialist internationalism in a persistent and systematic manner'.

Suslov also emphasized that 1972 would be an important jubilee year as it marked the 50th anniversary of the creation of the USSR. He predicted that it would be 'a shining celebration of the friendship of the brotherhood of the peoples of our great country'.[15] As it turned out, the jubilee year was certainly memorable, though not for the reasons that Suslov had had in mind.

The political and cultural purge in the Ukraine

During 1971 Moscow and Washington had laid the groundwork for the period of East–West accommodation that became known as 'detente'. But greater flexibility in external affairs was not accompanied by any loosening of controls at home. Quite the contrary. At the end of that year the Soviet leadership decided to strike a crippling blow against dissent by suppressing the two most irritating *samizdat* publications – the *Chronicle of Current Events* and the *Ukrainian Herald*. Arrests, searches and interrogations commenced the following month in Moscow, Leningrad, Kiev, Lvov and other cities.[16] In the Ukraine, however, what began as a large-scale police operation against dissidents soon developed into a broad political and cultural purge that affected even the republic's top Party leadership.

As it was, the scale of the crackdown on Ukrainian dissent made it the 'heaviest single KGB assault' on any dissenting group since Stalin's death.[17] Beginning on 12 January 1972 and continuing intermittently well into the following year, the KGB rounded up scores of Ukrainians who had prepared or circulated *samizdat*, signed protests, or who had associated with dissenters. A much larger number of people were searched, questioned, or subjected to extra-judicial forms of pressure. Initially, while the authorities were lamely attempting to justify the arrests by linking them with the detention and 'confession' of a Ukrainian emigré 'courier', there were quite a few protests from the Ukrainian public. In May, however, shortly after the historian Braichevs'kyi had been compelled to issue a statement condemning the 'misuse' of his study 'Annexation or Reunification?' abroad, and Dziuba was expelled from the Writers' Union of the Ukraine and arrested, one of the latter's colleagues was received by a deputy of Shelest's and told that the Ukrainian Party leadership 'was unable to intervene in KGB matters'. A few days later Shelest himself was replaced by his rival Vladimir Shcherbitsky and transferred to a post in Moscow as one of the deputy chairmen of the USSR Council of Ministers.[18]

At this stage it was not clear why Shelest had been removed. This led to speculation in the West – fuelled by Soviet spokesmen[19] – that he was a hawk on foreign policy issues who had had his wings clipped. While his views on foreign policy may indeed have been a source of friction with Brezhnev and other members of the Soviet leadership, it was subsequently confirmed that it was his approach to nationalities policy that was the real reason for his downfall.

During the remainder of 1972 and throughout 1973, extensive sackings, demotions and other personnel changes took place in the Ukraine's academic and cultural institutions, media and Party and government bodies. At the same time, ideological campaigns were launched against 'deviations' in the social sciences and humanities, and controls tightened markedly, particularly in the fields of history, literature and philosophy.[20] The peak of this ideological offensive in the Ukraine was reached in April 1973 when Shelest, though still formally a member of the Politburo, was denounced in public for having idealized the Ukrainian past and been too lax in dealing with nationalism. As Tillett points out, 'Not since Trotsky's day had a sitting member of the Politburo suffered such humiliation by official Party sources.'[21]

Later that same month, Shelest was finally dropped from the Politburo. Like Khrushchev, he became a non-person and vanished into obscurity. According to an account that appeared in the spring of 1974 in a Ukrainian *samizdat* journal, Shelest was 'retired', put under house arrest, and a close KGB watch placed on his family. It was only in the first half of 1988 that questions about the reasons for Shelest's removal and his subsequent fate began to appear in the Ukrainian press and that he finally surfaced again.[22]

In early 1989, Shelest gave an interview to the weekly liberal publication, which of late has acquired, due to its outspokenness, a circulation of tens of millions, *Argumenty i fakty*, in which, among other things, he explained why he had been removed. He depicted Brezhnev as a 'cowardly, mistrustful and dull-witted man' who had surrounded himself with sycophants. Mikhail Suslov was an exception though, and Brezhnev relied on him to make up for 'his own incompetence on many issues'. A withdrawn, 'inward-looking' type in a Stalinist mould, Suslov took a hard line on nationalities policy. This led to 'repeated clashes' with the Ukrainian Party leader 'over questions of ideology and culture'. Eventually, Suslov organized an attack on Shelest for his book *O Ukraine, Our Soviet Land* 'for extolling the Cossacks' and the latter was 'accused of nationalism'. Brezhnev duly informed Shelest that the action had been taken 'on Suslov's orders'.[23]

From the summer of 1972 onwards many of those who had been arrested, including Dziuba and Chornovil, were tried for 'anti-Soviet agitation and propaganda' and given heavy sentences of up to 12 and 15 years. Some, like the mathematician Leonid Pliushch, were locked up in mental hospitals.[24] One of the victims, the poet Vasyl' Stus, argued in a protest written in a labour camp and entitled 'I Accuse' that the purges of 1972–3 in the Ukraine had transformed the young generation of nationally minded intelligentsia into 'a generation of political prisoners' and inflicted 'irreparable damage to the Ukrainian nation and its culture'.[25] Issue No. 7–8 of the *Ukrainian Herald*, which appeared in the spring of 1974 after a hiatus of two years, labelled what had happened in the republic as the 'General Pogrom' and accused the Kremlin of attempting 'to carry out spiritual ethnocide through the liquidation of the nationally conscious intelligentsia'.[26]

All this raises another important question. Although, as we shall see, during 1972, the Kremlin also tightened political controls in Georgia, the purge there was aimed at reducing corruption and economic crime. It did not develop into an assault on Georgian national-cultural life. Why was it that the Ukraine was singled out for such a devastating blow against its cultural and political elite that left the nation virtually decapitated?

The explanation seems to be that from the early 1970s onwards Soviet nationalities policy became more purposeful but less uniform in the way that it was applied to different groups of republics. For instance, in the case of the Central Asian republics, an implicit *modus vivendi* came into being. In return for their political loyalty, the local elites were permitted considerable latitude in the cultural sphere and to bolster the role of native cadres through the operation of implicit affirmative action policies.[27] On the other hand, a determined effort was made to stop and reverse the trends in the Ukraine that had brought about the revival in the nation's public and cultural life and led the Shelest faction to assert the republic's individuality and importance. Blatant Russification was restored, and restrictions on the development of Ukrainian culture and scholarship, particularly historical research and writing, were drastically tightened.[28]

The abrupt hardening of policy towards the Ukraine in 1972–3 suggests that it had already been decided to concentrate assimilationist efforts on the Ukrainians, who as Slavs, together with the less problematic Byelorussians, were particularly vulnerable to Russification. The thinking seems to have been that while the Soviet people was being forged, the Ukrainians and Byelorussians would be moulded to form part of the Russian-speaking Slavic core of this entity. Not only would this neutralize any potential danger from the USSR's largest non-Russian nation, but also ensure that the 'Russian' nucleus of the Soviet people would remain numerically unassailable. This was a variation on the scheme that had been implicit in the 1954 designation of the Ukrainians as junior partners of the Russians, only this time the conditions were even less appealing. To ensure the Ukrainians knew their place and did not stray from it, the Kremlin prescribed a course of social engineering entailing a two-pronged attack aimed at the Ukrainian language and national memory.

Georgia and the question of corruption

Another republic where there were serious problems at this time was Georgia. Here, however, the difficulties were of a rather different sort and involved corruption and the excessive toleration of the 'second economy', particularly forms of private enterprise. The Kremlin began clamping down in the spring of 1972 and before long a major shake-up of the republican Party leadership was under way. In September the head of the Georgian MVD Eduard Shevardnadze replaced Vasilii Mzhavanadze as First Secretary of the Georgian Communist Party and stepped up the anti-corruption campaign. During the next 18 months, some 25,000 arrests are reported to have been made in an all-out effort to break up local mafias and eliminate 'capitalistic' tendencies. There was fierce opposition to this purge. It took the form of arson and bombings, including the destruction of the Tbilisi Opera House in May 1973, and, apparently, assassination attempts against Shevardnadze.[29]

Perhaps this is the right place to touch on some of the broader questions associated with the issue of 'corruption' in the non-Russian republics. On one level, corruption has been endemic to the highly centralized and bureaucratized Soviet system. Some of the revelations that were to be made under Gorbachev about what went on at the highest levels while Brezhnev was in power, and indeed among Brezhnev's own relatives, aptly bore this out. On another level, what Moscow has periodically branded as corruption in the non-Russian republics has sometimes been simply the local way of doing things and of circumventing the centre's stifling economic controls. Some Western observers, however, have uncritically taken the Kremlin's viewpoint on these matters and overlooked the fact that for many of the indigenous inhabitants of, for example, the Caucasus or Central Asia, the economic and social policy dictated by Moscow has been an alien system imposed from a distant imperial metropolis.

While the Kremlin may have been dissatisfied with the self-centred Georgian approach to economic matters, the fact is that the economic latitude tolerated by Mzhavanadze and his supporters enabled the republic's population to achieve standards of living that were higher than in most other parts of the USSR.[30] In the case of the Central Asian republics, the Kremlin has frequently expressed concern about the preference that local cadres have shown for 'their own' in the allocation of jobs and opportunities. Yet anthropologists point out that 'nepotism' is 'the natural order of things' in a traditionally kinship-based society:

> Asiatic man normally goes to his kinsmen if he wishes to start any kind of enterprise. And if he is secretary of a Party cell, he will see to it that his various sons, cousins, nephews, uncles work side by side with him in other key posts. If they get better pay for this, it is only natural because their kinsman is the local chief.[31]

The Soviet Government's affirmative action policies, as Nancy Lubin observes, 'only tended to reaffirm, if not intensify, this process'.[32]

While the crackdown in Georgia was not aimed primarily at local nationalism, there were, nevertheless, signs that Georgian national feeling remained strong and was a source of concern. In April 1972 the Tbilisi City Party authorities passed a resolution condemning a book by U.I. Sidamonidze, a senior staff member of the Institute of History, Archaeology and Ethnography of the Georgian SSR Academy of Sciences. The author was accused of having made 'serious theoretical and ideological blunders' by depicting Georgia's declaration of independence as a 'progressive act', and of 'whitewashing' the Georgian Mensheviks and other Georgian 'petit-bourgeois parties'. All the same, Sidamonidze and those who had authorized the publication of his study were dealt with rather leniently, indicating that there was considerable support for the national-minded scholars.[33]

During 1972, a number of Georgian patriots were outraged by corruption and theft within the Georgian Orthodox Church and what seemed to be collusion on the part of the authorities. Individuals like Valentina Pailodze, a choirmaster, and David Koridze, a procurator, sought to expose what was going on. In this particular case, however, the authorities did their best to keep the truth suppressed. The official reluctance to clean up corruption in one of Georgia's most important national institutions was eventually to precipitate the emergence of open Georgian national dissent.[34]

Other developments during the jubilee year

While purges were taking place in the Ukraine and Georgia there were also a number of other telling developments. In March 1972 the religious petitions campaign in Lithuania entered a new stage with the appearance of the first issue of the *samizdat* publication *The Chronicle of the Catholic Church in Lithuania*. This important new underground bulletin set itself the task of reporting regularly on the situation of Lithuanian Catholic believers generally, and on those subjected to persecution in particular.[35] At around the same time a petition signed by 17,054 Lithuanians was received in the West. It was addressed to UN Secretary General Kurt Waldheim who was asked to pass it on to Brezhnev. This protest against the denial of religious freedom indicated the scale of popular discontent in Lithuania.[36]

Shortly afterwards, in mid-May, the unrest in Lithuania erupted. A 19-year-old student named Romas Kalanta set fire to himself in a city square in Kaunas in protest against Soviet oppression. On the day of Kalanta's funeral mass rioting broke out in the city and it was not until the following day that troops were able to quell the nationalistic disorders. During the next few months, three more self-immolations were reported by human rights activists in Moscow, although a Lithuanian dissenter claimed that the number of protest suicides was as high as ten.[37] The authorities responded by imprisoning eight of the alleged organizers of the Kaunas demonstrations and tightening ideological controls.[38] In this way, a republic that had until recently been relatively tranquil was transformed into a new trouble spot.

To the north in Estonia, at least two attempts to form underground nationalist groups are known to have been foiled by the KGB in 1969 and 1970. In the early 1970s, however, a new underground publication, *Eesti demokrat* (Estonian Democrat) made its appearance. It was published by a group calling itself the Estonian National Front (or Democratic Movement) but which, it later transpired, consisted of the same activists that had founded the Democratic Movement of the Soviet Union. Their programme advocated Estonian independence and called for a referendum on the issue of national self-determination. In October 1972 the Estonian activists sent a memorandum to Waldheim protesting against the Soviet occupation and Russification of their country and seeking help for the restoration of Estonia's independence and its admission to the United Nations.[39]

Also at this time, in traditionally Buddhist Buriatia, there was a particularly distasteful case of political repression. The victim was the renowned Buddhist scholar and expert on the Tibetan language, Bidia Dandaron, who had been imprisoned under Stalin. He was arrested in August 1972 in Ulan-Ude as part of what seems to have been a determined effort by the authorities to stop the growth of interest in Buddhism spreading from Buriatia to intellectual circles in the European part of the Soviet Union. Dandaron and his colleagues were shamelessly accused of having conducted religious rites involving 'blood sacrifices' and sexual perversion. Despite numerous protests, including one from the Chief Lama of Buriatia, in December 1972 the 58-year-old scholar was given five years in labour camps. He did not survive the ordeal and died within two years.[40]

The Iakovlev affair

On the very eve of the 50th jubilee of the formation of the USSR there was a curious development. In November 1972 the Party again signalled that the Russite writers had gone too far. This time the Party's acting chief of agitation and propaganda, Alexandr Iakovlev, delivered a lengthy attack in the pages of *Literaturnaia gazeta* against those whom he saw as deviating from the prescribed 'class' approach to history and flirting with 'the reactionary-conservative traditions of the past'.

'We will not idolize every church's onion dome or every minaret,' he declared, 'and we do not intend to moan over "holy relics" and "wailing walls".' Iakovlev also intimated that unbridled Russian nationalism was a threat to the cohesion of the USSR. 'We must talk about these manifestations,' he concluded, 'if certain "zealots of the national spirit" are not to *make a complete mess of things.*'[41] The warning was echoed a few days later by *Pravda.*[42]

What was intriguing about this case was both the history of Iakovlev's article and the author's subsequent fate. According to the American journalist Robert G. Kaiser, 'informed sources' notified him that Iakovlev's '10,000-word article was written ten months ago and published only after a long dispute inside the Party bureaucracy'. The American journalist noted that Iakovlev's article had generated a lively discussion among Moscow's intellectuals about 'a basic question of Soviet life: can Russian nationalism endure in the multinational Soviet state, in which Russians are soon to become a numerical minority?'[43]

The following April, after Iakovlev was denounced in the seventh issue of *Veche* (19 February 1973)[44] as a traitor to Russia's interests, he was suddenly given an ambassadorial post in Canada, where he remained until after Brezhnev's death. Clearly, behind the Kremlin walls, there were sharp differences on the issues of what constituted palatable Russian nationalism and how the phenomenon should be handled.

Veche's rejoinder to Iakovlev sheds light on the mindset of Russian imperial nationalists. On the one hand Iakovlev was taken to task for allegedly negating Russia's history and cultural values; on the other, he was berated for failing to realize that his opposition to 'Russophilism' logically envisioned the 'suicide' of the Russian-led Soviet multinational state.

The article also revealed how the Russian ultra-nationalists were becoming acutely aware of anti-Russian sentiment in the non-Russian republics:

> We advise Comrade Iakovlev to experience for himself the low, barbaric chauvinism, the zoological hatred of Russians which has emerged precisely on a non-national basis. Present-day chauvinism in the borderlands is a reaction against the falsely internationalist propaganda which calls for unity among renegades, for a union of all who have renounced their nation.[45]

Instead of attempting to analyse soberly the reasons for this problem, they put the blame on the Kremlin's 'misguided' policies – and as often as not the Jews[46] – and sought to portray the Russian nation as an injured and at the same time wrongly maligned party. What this approach failed to face up to, though, was that the nationalities problem had not been created by the Bolsheviks but inherited by them from the former Russian 'prison of nations'. The idea of Russian supremacy and cultural tutelage over the non-Russians was no less distasteful to the latter coming from chauvinistic Slavophiles than it was from communists.

Brezhnev's 50th anniversary speech and its implications

Despite the salience of the national problem 50 years after the USSR had been established, Brezhnev's jubilee speech delivered on 21 December 1972 contained no real surprises. The Soviet leader claimed that 'we have every reason to say that the nationalities question, in the form in which it came down to us from the past, has been resolved completely, resolved definitively and irrevocably'. A little further on, however, he acknowledged that although there were no longer any 'objective preconditions' to sustain national antagonisms, he explained that 'nationalistic prejudices and exaggerated or distorted manifestations of national feeling', were 'extremely tenacious phenomena'. Moreover, the USSR's 'class adversaries' were losing no opportunity to encourage and exploit these 'nationalistic survivals'.

Essentially, the address elaborated the themes that had figured in Brezhnev's report to the Twenty-fourth Party Congress. Once again the Soviet leader singled out the Russian people and the RSFSR for special praise as 'the first among equals', who by their help to 'backward outlying national areas' had made 'glorious' contributions to internationalism. He also hailed the emergence of a Soviet people, stressing that it provided a stronger basis for the further drawing together of the nations of the USSR 'in both the spiritual and material spheres'. Here, however, Brezhnev hinted that this process was not proceeding quite as smoothly as was officially made out. He admitted that:

> there are also objective problems in our federal state – such as finding the best paths for the development of the individual nations and nationalities and the most correct combination of the interests of each of them with the common interests of the Soviet people as a whole.[47]

At the heart of the matter seems to have been the perennial question of the pace and manner in which the 'drawing together' of the peoples of the Soviet Union should be pursued. A few weeks before Brezhnev delivered his jubilee address, a new call had appeared in print advocating a speeding up of this process. *Pravda*, however, countered with two pieces on 12 and 18 December supporting 'gradual' (*postepennoe*) drawing together.[48] The Soviet leader appeared to take the middle position. In his anniversary speech, he declared that 'the further drawing together of the nations' of the USSR was 'an objective process' and that the Party was 'against forcing' matters in this respect. None the less, he followed this with a warning that seemed to echo Khrushchev's words at the Twenty-second Party Congress:

> the Party regards as impermissible any attempt whatsoever to hold back the process of the drawing together of nations, to obstruct it on any pretext or artificially to reinforce national isolation, because it would be at variance with the general direction of the development of our society, the Communists' internationalist ideals and ideology and the interests of communist construction.

In addition to this qualification, Brezhnev's comments about the economic side of nationalities policy made it clear that despite his assurances to the non-Russians the Kremlin was not going simply to allow the supposedly 'objective' process of the drawing together of the nations to take its own course. The

Soviet leader declared that the past 50 years had confirmed Lenin's ideas about 'the advantages that are offered by a large-scale centralized economy as compared to a fragmented economy' and indicated that more, not less, centralization could be expected.[49]

It could hardly have been a coincidence then that during the jubilee month *Voprosy ekonomiki* carried an article by Viktor Kistanov of the State Planning Board (GOSPLAN) which argued that the boundaries of the Soviet republics needed to be adjusted to reflect existing economic realities.[50] This, too, sounded reminiscent of what Khrushchev had said in 1961 about republican boundaries losing their significance. For the non-Russians it had just as ominous a ring to it as before. At the Twenty-second Party Congress Khrushchev had called for the preparation of a new Soviet Constitution; Brezhnev, in his jubilee speech, said that it was time to complete work on this document and announced that a draft was expected to be ready by the next Party Congress. That same month, Nurbekov, the Kirghiz doctor of juridical sciences who had argued that any 'forcible' change in republican borders was 'a violation of the principle of the self-determination of nations', was sharply criticized.[51] Once again the future of the republics looked uncertain.

Artificial forcing in all but name
Brezhnev's emphasis on the all-round drawing together (*vsestoronnee sblizhenie*) of the nations of the USSR left little doubt that in practice he wanted to see this process proceed faster rather than slower. Yet from the speeches made by most of the non-Russian representatives at the celebrations of the 50th anniversary of the formation of the USSR it was evident that they preferred a more gradual tempo. It was quite telling, for instance, that the majority of them referred far more often to the Soviet 'peoples' rather than to the Soviet 'people'.[52]

During the next few years there were more signs that behind the facade of official unanimity on the general direction of nationalities policy there existed divergent views. Kistanov's recommendation about changing republican borders on the basis of economic criteria was promptly challenged by a Soviet government official of Lithuanian origin working in Moscow.[53] Almost a year later, Kirill Mazurov, the First Deputy Chairman of the USSR Council of Ministers and a Byelorussian, also implicitly rejected Kistanov's arguments even though they had recently been publicly endorsed by Suslov.[54]

Brezhnev himself, in a speech given in Alma-Ata in August 1973, seemed to go out of his way to allay fears about the direction in which nationalities policy was being steered:

We absolutely do not have in mind that national differences have already vanished, and even less that the fusion of nationalities has already occurred. All nations and nationalities that live in the Soviet Union preserve their national peculiarities, traits of national character, language and their best traditions. They have available all the necessities to achieve still greater flourishing of their national culture.[55]

Moreover, the following month, *Kommunist* stressed in an editorial that 'the Soviet people' did not mean a Soviet 'nation' and that 'the new historical community' retained a multinational character.[56]

Despite the cautious public pronouncements of the Brezhnev leadership on the national question, in reality it continued to do what it had proclaimed to be impermissible, namely artificially to force the process of the drawing together of nations. Much later under Gorbachev, when Brezhnev's rule during the 1970s was discredited and euphemistically labelled 'the period of stagnation', non-Russian writers would point out that in nationalities policy there was anything but inertia during this period. Far from simply muddling through in this area, during the 1970s the Kremlin stepped up Russification and increased pressure on many of the national cultures. Moreover, the attitude that it fostered had the effect of encouraging the growth of a cynical 'national nihilism' among bureaucratic careerists in the non-Russian republics. These 'super-internationalists', as they were subsequently dubbed in the second half of the 1980s,[57] took it upon themselves to display the sort of hostility towards the non-Russian languages and cultures that officials in Moscow could never have permitted themselves to sanction openly.

Apart from the massive promotion of the concept of the Soviet people, the 50th anniversary of the USSR was followed by more thoroughgoing efforts to improve the study and teaching of Russian in the non-Russian republics. Attention was increasingly focused on the pre-school institutions. In the early part of 1973, Soviet newspapers and pedagogical journals began to praise the experimental 'preparatory classes' in Russian that had recently been set up for six-year-olds in the Central Asian republics. As well as providing immersion in the Russian language, the classes were also designed to instil 'internationalism' through the cultivation of love for things Russian. The pedagogical publications recommended that such classes be introduced in other republics as well. As *Sovetskaia pedagogika* put it:

> A well-thought out activity on the part of the teacher in the Union republic schools develops among the youth a sincere love for the Russian language, as their second mother tongue, and as a necessary means not only of international understanding but of recognition of the heights of the artistic achievements of Russia's writers, whose works have found world-wide recognition.[58]

That same year the Council on Questions of Secondary School Education of the USSR Ministry of Education adopted a decree providing for the further improvement of 'the Teaching of the Russian Language and Literature in the National Schools of the Union Republics'. During the next two years, additional Party and government resolutions along the same lines were passed. The importance of the language issue was underlined again in October 1975 when no less a body than the Central Committee of the CPSU convened a major conference in Tashkent to discuss ways of spreading and improving Russian-language teaching for non-Russians. At this meeting, the Soviet Minister of Education, Mikhail Prokof'ev, called for the broadening of teaching in the Russian language in the non-Russian republics. Among other things, he advocated the introduction of Russian-language education (alongside instruction in the native language) in kindergartens and nurseries in the national republics, as well as in the first year of elementary education.[59]

While these changes were being followed up, emphasis was also placed on the ideological importance of promoting the study of the Russian language. As one book on the subject published in 1977 put it:

> The study of Russian promotes the formation of the scientific world view, aids the formation of the communist ideology, and broadens general culture and outlook. In the epoch of the extensive construction of communism the Russian language promotes further drawing together of nations and achieving by them of their complete unity – the unity of statehood, economy, ideology and culture.[60]

According to another Soviet author, also writing in 1977, the Russian language served 'to cement the unity of Soviet culture' and acted as 'an effective accelerator of the drawing together of nations'.[61]

How did this renewed emphasis on the Russian language translate into practice? Although this was a Union-wide development its purpose and effects were not uniform. As far as the Central Asian republics were concerned, the problem facing the Kremlin was essentially a practical one of getting more of the indigenous population to acquire a knowledge of Russian. Here, it was not a case of Russification pure and simple, and the campaign to promote the study of Russian does not seem to have been quite as much at the expense of the local languages as in other parts of the Soviet Union. On the other end of the scale, however, the Ukraine and Byelorussia, where proficiency in Russian was hardly a major problem, were subjected to a new wave of blatant Russification. Clearly, the rationale behind language policy in these republics went beyond purely practical considerations. As we shall see, the primary object in this case seems to have been to modify psychological attitudes in order to facilitate the forging of a Russianized Slavic core for 'the Soviet people'.

A Soviet ethnographer writing in the spring of 1987 alluded to what occurred in the sphere of language policy during the 1970s as follows:

> Unfortunately, in the 1970s something of an extreme became noticeable: although we spoke of the need to safeguard national languages, we mainly propagandized the successes in the mastering of the language of inter-nationality discourse [that is, Russian]. And we not only propagandized them, but also at times transposed the solution of this question into the realm of organizational measures.[62]

One concrete example of what this involved is that between about 1973 and 1975 it became a requirement that all candidate and doctoral dissertations be submitted in Russian.[63]

But the measures went far beyond this. An explicit description of what happened in the Ukraine was provided by Oles' Honchar in an article published, also in 1987, both in *Literaturna Ukraina* and *Literaturnaia gazeta*:

> The most blatant violation of Leninist norms was that, because of artificially – I repeat, artificially – created conditions, especially in the 1970s, Ukrainian national schools were closed in their dozens and hundreds, and all this was done in order to flaunt 'loyalty', zeal and orthodoxy in one's capacity as an official.[64]

Pressure was also put on the national languages in another way. In the mid-1970s, the Soviet Government adopted a policy of promoting unrestricted growth of the Russian-language press and of gradually restricting the circulation of non-Russian periodicals. This seems to have been a response to the rapid growth of the non-Russian press before 1975–6. Between 1975 and 1982, 81 new titles were added to the 929 Russian-language journals already in existence. Most of the larger non-Russian nationalities obtained only one or two more titles during this period. The Ukrainians were the exception: they lost 13 titles, bringing the number of journals in the national language of the second largest nation of the USSR down to 50.[65] Significantly, most of the Ukrainian journals that stopped appearing or were converted into Russian were scholarly, particularly scientific and technical, ones such as *Ukrains'kyi fizychnyi zhurnal* (The Ukrainian Physical Journal) and *Ukrains'kyi matematychnyi zhurnal* (The Ukrainian Mathematical Journal).[66]

Another indication of the direction in which things were moving was provided by the way in which some of the Party leaders in the non-Russian republics took their cue from Brezhnev and began once again to eulogize the Russian 'elder brother', to stress the indebtedness of their nations to the Russians, and in some cases, even switched to speaking Russian at meetings of the republican Party organization. In September 1973, for instance, during Brezhnev's visit to Tashkent, the Uzbek First Party Secretary Sharaf Rashidov expressed the Uzbeks' 'feelings of special gratitude to their elder brother and true friend – the great Russian people . . . who bear on their shoulders the greatest share of the burden of the struggle for the progress of society and for the happiness of peoples of all nationalities . . .'[67]

The following month, the Ukrainian Party leader Shcherbitsky offered the following explanation at a meeting of Kiev University's Party members of how internationalism should be understood:

> To be an internationalist means to express feelings of friendship and brotherhood towards all peoples of our country and, first of all, toward the great Russian people,

their culture, their language – the language of the Revolution, of Lenin, the language of international intercourse and unity. To be an internationalist means to lead an uncompromising struggle against nationalism, and in particular against the worst enemy of the Ukrainian people – Ukrainian bourgeois nationalism – and also against international Zionism; it means to be intolerant of any manifestations of national narrow-mindedness [and] national conceit.[68]

'National conceit', it would appear, was permitted only to representatives of one particular nation.

In the spring of 1976, on the eve of the Twenty-fifth Party Congress, the Georgian Party leader Shevardnadze caused quite a stir among his compatriots when he delivered his report to the Georgian Party Congress in Russian.[69] At the Twenty-fifth Party Congress itself, the national question hardly figured. According to one Western observer, the Ukrainian and Byelorussian Party leaders 'spoke like some Russian regional secretaries, as if unconcerned by the whole matter'.[70] In fact, some of the other republican leaders spoke almost as if they were vassals come to pay homage to their feudal lord, Brezhnev. Two, however, outdid all the others. The Armenian First Secretary, Karen Demirchian, declared that his nation's motto had become: 'Blessed be the sacred hour when Russians set foot on our soil!'[71] Shevardnadze told the congress: 'Georgia is called the country of the sun. But for us the true sun rose not in the East but in the North, in Russia – the sun of Lenin's ideas.'[72]

In defence of national rights
Among the unmistakable signs that national problems were becoming more rather than less acute was the further growth of national dissent and the fact that prominent Russian dissidents began to express their concern about the situation. Moreover, it was also clear from the growing number of protests and petitions being smuggled out of the labour camps and prisons that not only did non-Russian national rights campaigners form a majority of the USSR's political prisoners, but also that they were becoming more radicalized.

A new militancy was particularly evident among Ukrainian political prisoners and dissidents. The KGB offensive of 1972–3 in the Ukraine transformed what had largely been a movement of cultural self-defence into an uncompromising political nationalism opposed to Moscow's rule. Quite a few of the new Ukrainian political prisoners renounced their Soviet citizenship and played leading roles in organizing protests within the camps and prisons. This radicalization was also attested to by the strident tone of issue number 7–8 of the *Ukrainian Herald* which appeared in the spring of 1974. Its editors saw their journal as the organ of 'all democratic, anti-colonial groups in the Ukraine' seeking to 'broaden the national-liberation struggle' and to resist 'the colonial policy of Moscow's occupation forces'.[73]

Political nationalism was becoming more of a problem in the Transcaucasian and Baltic republics. During 1973–4, in Armenia alone, there were nine political trials resulting in the imprisonment of 18 members of the National Unification Party for periods of up to ten years.[74] One of its leaders, Paruir Airikian, declared in his final statement: 'I am being condemned for my patriotic convictions . . . You fear me greatly, and this shows that you are very weak . . . Only the very weak fear words, and answer words with brute force . . . Long live a free and independent Armenia.'[75] In neighbouring Georgia, the dissenter Valentina Pailodze was arrested in March 1974 and imprisoned for one and a half years. Her case was taken up by an Initiative Group for the Defence of Human Rights which was founded in Tbilisi at this time by the literary scholar Zviad Gamsakhurdia and the musicologist Merab Kostava.

In 1975 Gamsakhurdia began to publish a *samizdat* journal called *Okros satsmisi* (The Golden Fleece). The first issue carried the text of a speech criticizing Russification in Georgia that had been delivered at a Party meeting of the Georgian Writers' Union in 1973 by the author Nodar Tsuleiskiri.[76] Although Gamsakhurdia was harassed and threatened by the authorities, he managed to put out four issues of *The Golden Fleece* containing information on some of the obstacles facing the development of Georgian culture. In 1976, together with Kostava, he brought out a new *samizdat* journal called *Sakartvelos moambe* (The Georgian Herald), the aim of which was to publicize 'urgent national and social problems'.[77] That same year, another Georgian writer, Revaz Dzhaparidze, delivered a further outspoken attack against the growing Russification of the republic's educational establishments. Speaking at the Eighth Congress of Georgian Writers, he warned his colleagues: 'My friends, evil resides in doing nothing, in keeping silent and suppressing our disquiet.'[78]

There were also more radical forms of opposition in the Transcaucasian republics. During the mid-1970s there were more bombings and acts of arson in Georgia, most of which were apparently a response to the continuing drive against corruption. Three explosions set off by a certain Vladimir Zhvania, however, appear to have been politically motivated. In January 1977 he was convicted and executed by a firing squad.[79] That very same month a bomb went off in the Moscow Metro killing seven and injuring over 40 people. In connection with this crime, the authorities arrested three Armenians, one of whom, Stepan Zatikian, was a former member of the National Unification Party. At the beginning of 1979 they were tried in camera, found guilty and executed. Because the entire case was shrouded in secrecy there was some doubt that the three had genuinely been responsible for the explosion and there was suspicion that the KGB had exploited the incident in an attempt to discredit the Armenian national movement.[80]

These were not the only problems in Transcaucasia and the Caucasus. The mixture of peoples in this region and the sometimes arbitrary way in which borders had been drawn up between them continued to be a source of ethnic antagonisms. In April 1973 Shevardnadze alluded to difficulties with the 83,000-strong Abkhaz minority, who had their own autonomous republic within Georgia, but who resented Georgian domination. He complained that 'In Abkhazia a half-baked "theory" according to which responsible posts should be filled only by representatives of the indigenous nationality has gained a certain currency.'[81] Three years later, however, at the Twenty-fifth Georgian Party Congress, Shevardnadze conceded that 'insufficient attention' had been paid to the cultural and educational needs of the republic's national minorities.[82]

To the north in the Chechen-Ingush ASSR, resentment of the discrimination against Ingushi living in the Prigorodnyi district that had been made part of North Ossetia finally resulted in large public protests. For several days in February 1973 there were demonstrations in Groznyi in support of demands for the return of the Prigorodnyi district to Checheno-Ingushetia. Even though the chairman of the RSFSR Council of Ministers, Solomentsev, went to Groznyi to defuse the situation, the central press failed to report the unrest. Once the protests subsided, a new campaign was launched against nationalism and the hold of unofficial Islam over the local population.[83]

In the Baltic republics, despite numerous arrests, national dissent was on the upsurge. In 1974 and 1975, a major effort by the authorities to suppress the *Chronicle of the Lithuanian Catholic Church* failed. In fact, in the mid-1970s, new Lithuanian *samizdat* journals appeared such as *Ausra* (The Dawn), *Varpas* (The Bell) and *Dievui ir Tevynei* (For God and the Fatherland). In Estonia, the arrest of Sergei Soldatov and four of his colleagues at the end of 1974 was a serious blow, but it did not destroy the Estonian democratic national movement. Soon new Estonian *samizdat* documents began reaching the West, including one signed by the 'Estonian Patriotic and Democratic Front'. In Latvia, too, new groups sprang up with names like 'Latvia's Independence Movement', 'Latvia's Democratic Youth Committee', and 'Latvia's Christian-Democratic Association'.

By 1975 there were also signs of cooperation and coordination between some of the dissenters in the Baltic republics. Among the joint appeals known to have been issued at this time was the Memorandum of the Representatives of Estonian and Latvian Democrats, and a letter from six dissident Baltic organizations addressed to the World Baltic Conference.[84]

There was no shortage, either, of evidence of solidarity between imprisoned representatives of the various non-Russian nations. As early as the end of 1973, 17 political prisoners being held in the Mordovian labour camps – including nine Ukrainians, four Balts and two Armenians – sent a joint programmatic statement to the Council of Nationalities of the USSR Supreme Soviet denouncing the nature and goals of Soviet nationalities policy and proposing instead a series of measures that would safeguard the political, economic and cultural rights of the non-Russians.[85] Another noteworthy example of such cooperation was the message sent in 1976 by 14 political prisoners of different nationalities 'To the American People on Independence Day'. It read:

> Two hundred years ago the people of the English colonies in America proclaimed the two fundamental principles of contemporary civilization: every individual's right to liberty and every nation's right to independence.
>
> Neither barbed wire nor machine guns on watchtowers nor guard dogs can prevent us, Soviet political prisoners, from being with you in spirit on this historic occasion.
>
> We wish for the American people the realization of the founding-fathers' goal – the creation of a brotherhood of free nations, a family of free peoples.[86]

The movement that attracted the most attention and support in the West during the first half of the 1970s, though, was undoubtedly that of the Soviet Jews. The determination and resourcefulness of the leaders of the Jewish emigration campaign on the one hand, and the resonance which their movement found in the West, particularly the United States, on the other, brought spectacular successes. By 1974, the 100,000th Jew had been allowed to leave the USSR. None the less, for the many who wanted to emigrate but were refused permission – the so-called 'refuseniks' – conditions were tough. They faced loss of employment, harassment and in some cases, even arrest and imprisonment. Some could only sit it out in the hope that eventually they would receive their exit visas. Others, however, became involved in unofficial study groups for learning Hebrew and Judaism. From 1972 onwards, activists even regularly organized unofficial seminars for Jewish scientists who had lost their jobs.[87]

The example set by the Jewish emigration movement inspired other groups within the Soviet Union, especially the Germans. Despairing of ever achieving the restoration of their autonomous republic, and conscious of how Moscow was prepared to exploit the question of Soviet German emigration in its dealings with West Germany, more and more Soviet Germans sought to leave the USSR. In 1974, 6,445 Soviet Germans were allowed to leave, 5,752 in 1975, and 9,626 in 1976. As in the case of the Jewish emigration campaign, Soviet policy remained ambivalent: while thousands of Soviet Germans were allowed to emigrate, the authorities attempted to suppress the German emigration movement and did not hesitate to harass and even arrest some of those seeking to leave.[88]

The Crimean Tatar movement also kept up its campaign. The sense of frustration and indignation felt by its activists was reflected in the more radical tone which they injected into some of their documents in the early 1970s. For example, the 'All-Nation Demand for Answers from the Crimean Tatar

People to the Politburo of the Party Central Committee' which was signed by almost 7,000 people and submitted to the authorities in December 1973, no longer explained the plight of the Crimean Tatar nation simply in terms of Stalinist injustices. The document blamed 'the seizure of the national home-land' and 'suffocation of the national existence of the Crimean Tatars' on the forces of 'imperialism and chauvinism'. The Uzbek Party leadership was also criticized for allowing its republic to be turned into a 'reservation for entire peoples'. Commenting on the broader implications of Soviet policy towards the Crimean Tatars, the document asserted:

> The urge to single out 'great' nations, which, as instruments for implementing nationalities policy, possess the right to dispose of the fate of other peoples, categorized as 'small', is tantamount to the reduction of national relations to a system of national hierarchies in every republic, every zone, every group of states and throughout the whole world, which substitutes for equal rights, and results in the suppression of small peoples. It is clear to these peoples that such a position on the national question is indivisible and cannot be applied differently in the internal and international arenas.[89]

The authorities were not swayed by such arguments. They continued to deny the Crimean Tatars the right to return to their homeland and to imprison Crimean Tatar activists. The best known of the leaders of the Crimean Tatar movement, Mustafa Dzhemilev, was kept in labour camps or in exile throughout most of the 1970s.

Soviet policies with respect to human rights were now drawing considerable criticism from the West. Occasionally there was censure of Soviet practices in the nationalities sphere from socialist countries as well. The Soviet–Romanian differences over Bessarabia had, of course, not disappeared. Furthermore, in December 1974, a group of 15 Polish intellectuals, including such distinguished figures as the economist Edward Lipinski, the writer Tadeusz Konwicki and the poet Antoni Slonimski, embarrassed the authorities in Warsaw and Moscow by issuing an appeal on behalf of the 1.2 million Poles living in the USSR. They declared: 'We wish our countrymen in the Soviet Union to have the unhindered possibility to express themselves on their needs, particularly in matters of culture, education and religion.'[90]

The renewed emphasis on the Russian 'elder brother' also did not pass unnoticed. In February 1977 the organ of the Croatian Communist Party *Vjesnik* attacked Shevardnadze for his extolment of the Russians. It expressed its astonishment at the way in which in the Soviet Union one nation was being depicted as superior to all the others, adding that 'we in multinational Yugoslavia are for a genuine equality of nations and nationalities as the basis of our society'.[91]

Russian responses

By the mid-1970s prominent Russian dissidents had begun acknowledging the seriousness of the national question. On being forced to leave Russia, Alexander Solzhenitsyn declared at a press conference in Zurich on 16 November 1974:

> The national problems in the Soviet Union of today are far more acute than in old Russia. If you used a twelve-point seismic scale to register the degree of national differences, in old Russia it could be put at about the second point; in the USSR today it is about force ten.[92]

Whether Solzhenitsyn understated the acuteness of the national question in tsarist Russia is open to discussion. The point, though, is his appraisal of the severity of this problem more than 50 years after the formation of the USSR.

The physicist and, with Sakharov, founder of the Moscow Human Rights Committee, Valerii Chalidze, also ended up in the West. In his book *To Defend These Rights*, published in the United States in 1974, he explained:

> The special place of the Russians in the [Soviet] power system is due to the fact that for the Russians the Soviet regime is largely their own regime. For other nationalities in the Union it is a Russian, alien regime. [. . .] The special position of the Russian national group in the USSR leads to internal conflicts of a purely national character, especially in connection with the fact that the Russification of the culture of national minorities is gradually being accomplished.[93]

Sakharov, too, in his book *My Country and My World*, which appeared in 1975, called on representatives of the Western intelligentsia to defend, among other human rights in the USSR, 'the rights of the national minorities – the Crimean Tatars, the Germans, the Lithuanians, the Estonians, the Latvians, the Ukrainians, and many others'.[94] What is indicative here is how Chalidze and Sakharov, for all their goodwill, referred to the non-Russian peoples as 'minorities', something that Western writers still often do. The larger non-Russian peoples rarely, if ever, describe themselves as minorities. The Ukrainians, Balts, Georgians and Armenians, for example, stress their nation-statehood and desire to be in control of their own affairs.

The Russian dissident who showed the greatest courage and honesty in speaking out at this time on the national problem was, however, Vladimir Bukovsky. In the summer of 1975, while a political prisoner in the notorious Vladimir Prison, he sent a statement to the Chairman of the Council of Ministers of the USSR, Aleksei Kosygin, entitled 'Once More About Russification and Nationalism'. Expressing his solidarity with the non-Russian 'nationalists' who, he pointed out, made up the majority of the political prisoners imprisoned alongside him, Bukovsky wrote:

> I am a Russian. And it pains me for my country, where official representatives

preach chauvinism, where Russification is elevated to the level of state policy.

It pains me that [today] Russia is a prison of nations on a greater scale than was the case 60 years ago; and in prisons the inmates are not there by choice.

I, a Russian by nationality, culture and language, affirm: in the USSR there exists national discrimination and forcible Russification; years spent in camps and prisons have convinced me of this.

The one place in the Soviet Union where there was genuine internationalism, he continued, was in the camps and prisons among the political prisoners of the various nationalities. Bukovsky ended by asserting that if those who were imprisoned for defending the rights of their nations were 'nationalists', then he too was one, 'for democracy means freedom both for individuals and for separate nations'.[95]

What of Russian nationalism? In 1973 the authorities unsuccessfully attempted, as Reddaway put it, to 'co-opt' the *samizdat* journal *Veche* and steer it away from Russian Orthodoxy. When this failed, pressure was applied against the editorial board, causing a split in its ranks. Even then, the object seems to have been, 'by neutralizing the most independent figures, to bring the dissenting nationalists as closely into line as possible, but by largely avoiding arrests, to keep their alienation to a minimum'.[96] At the end of November 1974, however, after Osipov had begun publishing a new *samizdat* journal called *Zemlia* (The Earth), he was arrested and the following September given an eight-year sentence for 'anti-Soviet agitation and propaganda'.[97] His case was exceptional, for he was the only well-known Russian nationalist to be imprisoned during the 1970s.

Another Russian nationalist, Leonid Borodin, managed to publish two issues of a journal called *Moskovskii sbornik* (Moscow Compendium) between September 1974 and January 1975 before being stopped by the KGB. What seemed to be a more serious blow to the Russian nationalist cause was struck in the spring of 1976 when Dmitrii Polianskii, who was regarded as its spokesman in the Politburo, was suddenly sent off to be Soviet ambassador in Japan. The reasons for his demotion, though, do not seem to have been connected with his Russian nationalism. In any case, Russian nationalism continued to flourish. The journal of the RSFSR Writers' Union *Nash sovremennik* and individual publicists as, for example, Sergei Semanov, continued openly to promote National Bolshevik views. At the same time, dissidents such as the Russian Orthodox priest Father Dmitrii Dudko, on the one hand, and the more extreme Gennadii Shimanov on the other, propagated neo-Slavophile and Russite ideas respectively.[98]

A good example of the strength of the Russian nationalist sensibilities was offered by the response to Olzhas Suleimanov's highly controversial book of essays entitled *Az i ia* which was published in Alma-Ata in 1975. In it, the celebrated Kazakh poet sought to retell the history of the medieval period from a Turkic perspective as opposed to a Russian point of view, thereby challenging the dominance of the Russocentrist line in Soviet historiography. He was immediately subjected to harsh criticism for 'pitting himself against Slavonic and Russian history and culture', and even accused of 'barbarous incursions'. The book was withdrawn from circulation and the author forced to publish a recantation. The affair indicated how little some things had changed since the 1950s.[99]

The Helsinki monitoring groups

The signing in August 1975 in Helsinki of the 'Final Act' of the 35-nation European Conference on Security and Cooperation provided Soviet dissidents with new opportunities for open activity. By the terms of the accords, in return for the recognition of its post-war political and territorial gains, the USSR undertook to observe certain basic human rights at home and agreed to its compliance with these provisions being reviewed. In May 1976 human rights activists in the Soviet capital set up a group to monitor the Soviet Government's record in the sphere of human rights. This 'Public Group to Promote the Implementation of the Helsinki Accords in the USSR', better known as the Moscow Helsinki monitoring group, soon became the new hub of the Soviet human rights movement. Its members documented and publicized a broad variety of human rights violations, including the plight of some of the non-Russian peoples.

Within a few months, similar groups began to spring up in the non-Russian republics. What was particularly encouraging for the non-Russian dissidents was that the Helsinki Final Act upheld the equal rights of peoples and their right to self-determination. 'All peoples,' the document read, 'always have the right, in full freedom, to determine, when and as they wish, their internal and external political status, without external interference, and to pursue as they wish their political, economic, social and cultural development.' The signatory states also pledged to respect the 'human rights and fundamental freedoms' of persons belonging to national minorities.[100]

The first non-Russian Helsinki monitoring group to be formed was in the Ukraine in early November 1976. Its ten founding members included two well-known writers, Mykola Rudenko and Oles' Berdnyk, former Major-General Petr Grigorenko, who represented the group in Moscow, and several former political prisoners, including two of the defendants in the 'Jurists' Case' of 1962, Levko Lukianenko and Ivan Kandyba. With the formation of the group, Ukrainian national dissent, driven underground by the KGB offensive of 1972–3, resurfaced. In a statement issued by the Moscow Helsinki group greeting the inaugural declaration of the Ukrainian Helsinki monitors, the Russian dissidents noted that:

> Ignoring the fact that the Ukraine is formally a member of the United Nations with full rights, it was not invited to the [Helsinki review] conference in Belgrade; there

are no Western correspondents based in its capital; in fact, there are also no diplomatic representatives there, that could be given information . . . Considering the conditions existing in the Ukraine, the creation of the Ukrainian Public Group is an act of great courage.

In the very first documents which the Ukrainian Helsinki monitoring group issued it made it clear that it considered human rights to be inseparable from national rights, and that in the Ukraine the violation of these rights was especially pronounced. The group's members set themselves the twin goals of highlighting the situation in their republic and reducing its international isolation. Typically, one of their documents, *Memorandum No. 5*, addressed to the countries participating in the Belgrade 'Helsinki' review conference, declared:

Let us stop playing at blindman's bluff: this statehood of ours is nothing but a paper mirage. And the time has come to dot all the 'i's, to end with the incessant and insidious game with our sovereignty, as well as with the sovereignty of all other Union republics . . . why should Moscow be making the decisions for us at international forums . . .? Why should the Ukraine's cultural, creative, scientific, agricultural and international problems be defined and planned in the capital of the neighbouring (even if allied) state? We are not naive simpletons. We understand that at work here is [the] spirit of imperialism and chauvinism . . .

Although the Ukrainian Helsinki monitoring group was greatly handicapped by the incessant harassment and arrest of its members, it managed to issue numerous documents that exposed the violation of human and national rights in the Ukraine and clarified the programmatic aspect of Ukrainian national dissent. The group's members took up a broad range of issues affecting all of the republic's citizens, regardless of their nationality or religion. At the same time, they did not conceal their commitment to the idea of Ukrainian independence. During the four-year existence of the Ukrainian Helsinki monitoring group, over 20 of its members were arrested, half of them receiving sentences of ten years or more.[101]

Just over two weeks after the formation of the Ukrainian Helsinki monitoring group, five Lithuanian dissenters established a similar body. Not surprisingly, their first documents reminded the states that had signed the Helsinki Final Act that Lithuania had been occupied by Soviet troops in 1940 and focused on the situation of the Lithuanian Catholic Church. Subsequent documents drew attention to the persecution of Baltic campaigners for national rights, discrimination against Germans living in Lithuania, and the question of the reunification of families. The group's membership was soon depleted by the departure to the West of the prominent writer and poet Tomas Venclova, and the arrest in August 1977 of Viktoras Petkus, a former political prisoner who had been active in furthering cooperation between the Baltic national movements.[102]

At the beginning of 1977 a Georgian Helsinki monitoring group was formed. Almost immediately, however, two of its leaders, Viktor Rtskiladze and Zviad Gamsakhurdia, were arrested, as well as their associate, Merab Kostava. Rtskiladze, an historian, was a champion of the Meskhetian cause and before his arrest had done his best to publicize their case. The authorities eventually succeeded in forcing him and Gamsakhurdia to recant.[103]

The Armenian Helsinki monitoring group founded in April 1977 by Eduard Arutiunian, an economist, Robert Nazarian, a physicist and deacon in the Armenian Apostolic Church, and Samuel Osian, a student, laid as much stress on the national question as did its Ukrainian counterpart. In a 13-point statement of aims, the Armenian Helsinki monitors sought respect for the civil, religious and cultural rights of their compatriots, curbs on Russification in 'state, economic and cultural life', the reunification with Armenia of 'ethnic Armenian territory' in Azerbaijan, and proposed that Armenia become a member of the United Nations.[104] A later document published in June 1976 accused the Soviet authorities not only of depriving Armenians of their civil rights but also of encroaching on their national rights by pursuing a 'great-power' assimilationist policy towards the Soviet Union's non-Russians. As elsewhere, the authorities responded by arresting the group's leaders.[105]

The formation of Helsinki monitoring groups in four of the non-Russian republics marked an important new stage in the development of national dissent. At great personal risk, non-Russian dissenters attempted to link their struggle for national rights to the international 'Helsinki process' and to act openly in accordance with the provisions of the Helsinki accords. Forced to clarify their demands and grievances, they contributed to the crystallization of dissenting thought in their republics and drew international attention to national problems in the Soviet Union. Although democratic in orientation and moderate in their activity, the Helsinki monitoring groups were harshly suppressed, leaving no outlets for pent-up national discontent.

13

Acceleration Amid 'Stagnation'

All this time, work on the new Soviet Constitution was proceeding and Soviet social scientists were continuing to discuss and research aspects of the nationalities question, albeit within the limits imposed on the one hand by the general thrust of Soviet nationalities policy under Brezhnev and, on the other, by the lack of candour about this issue. Between 1971 and 1976, some 200 'scholarly' works appeared on this subject[1] and numerous conferences were held. Although some experts were beginning to call for more sophisticated approaches to studying nationality questions such as taking 'ethnopsychological' factors and public opinion into account, the political climate did not encourage bold departures nor the presentation of results that conflicted with the official line.

In 1969 a Scientific Council for Nationality Problems had been established within the Social Sciences Section of the USSR Academy of Sciences, but for the first seven years it seems to have existed mainly on paper. In October 1975 it met to outline a five-year plan for research on nationality problems. Its chairman, Academician Evgenii Zhukov, a known 'hard-liner' on nationalities policy, accentuated the 'ideological' nature of the issue. A Western scholar who read the report of the meeting concluded:

> The Council, as it is now constituted and defines its duties, is a deliberate and willing political instrument of the regime and for that reason cannot be expected to produce dispassionate or innovative scientific analyses of ethnic developments in the Soviet Union.[2]

During 1977 the Soviet authorities stepped up arrests of non-Russians protesting against the official nationalities policy and continued to disregard the numerous complaints and appeals that bore testimony to the acuteness of the national problem. Such cries of anguish and despair or defiance became more and more frequent in the second half of the 1970s. They came even from areas which were not noted for strong national feeling. In the spring of 1977, for example, an anonymous Byelorussian patriot completed a lengthy 'Letter to a Russian Friend' in which he depicted the beleaguered state of his nation's language and culture. In this moving *samizdat* document, the author declared: 'It is difficult for me to conceal my annoyance that stereotyped opinions of my native language can be held by educated Russian minds, including those who are today anguishing about the fate of the Russian idea.'

This is how he went on to portray the situation of his nation:

We are now witnessing in Byelorussia a process of wide-scale assimilation. Those responsible for this process of national spiritual castration are acting under the banners of 'internationalism' and 'inevitable fusion of nations'. They ignore the elementary truth that the future united family of man will not be formed out of tongueless nations of *castrati* which have forgotten their names and true worth; each nation will bring its own unique understanding of truth and beauty. Why should Byelorussians have to concede to anyone the right to express for them their purpose on this planet? This question needs to be asked in view of repeated attempts of the Byelorussian nation's powerful neighbours to express their will for them, attempts which have frequently resulted in harm to the Byelorussian nation and have created in this corner of civilized Europe something of a 'cultural' parallel to colonial Africa.[3]

Equally indicative of the situation are three appeals issued by a group of Tatars and Bashkirs in April 1977. One of the documents was addressed to the US representative at the UN and to Western media. It consisted of the text of an appeal which had been sent to the authorities in Moscow in February 1976 by 26 Tatars and Bashkirs. In it they described the 'national oppression' and Russification of their peoples and called for a special commission to investigate the situation. Their plea was ignored and so, over a year later, they turned to the outside world for support.[4] The two other documents were also requests for help and were addressed to 'representatives of other non-Russian nationalities',[5] and to the Turkic peoples of the USSR,[6] respectively. The latter appeal was written in a Pan-Turkic spirit and was strongly anti-Russian. Among other things it referred to the suppression of Islam and destruction of ancient mosques, expressed support for 'the struggle of the Crimean Tatars', and stressed the need for unity among the Turkic peoples of the Soviet Union. It also alluded to ethnic friction between Russian youths and Tatars and Bashkirs, mentioning a specific incident in which a gang of Russians armed with sticks and knives had broken up an informal Tatar-Bashkir social evening.

Another national problem to which the Brezhnev leadership was continuing to turn a blind eye was that of the Armenian majority in Azerbaijan-administered Nagornyi Karabakh. This issue was still simmering, and in the summer of 1977 the Armenian writer Sero Khanzadian sent an open letter to Brezhnev pointing out how tense the situation had become. He reminded the Soviet leader that recent appeals 'from a great number of representatives of Soviet Armenia' had gone unanswered, and implored him to intervene and 'settle a question which, for half a century already, has been an embodiment of injustice'.[7] His appeal, too, fell on deaf ears.

The Brezhnev Constitution

In June 1977, the long-awaited draft of the revised Soviet Constitution was published. It allayed the worst fears of the non-Russians about the possible dismantling of the federal structure, but on closer examination turned out to be a mixed blessing.

Introducing the new document, Brezhnev gave the following assurance:

> Comrades! *The Soviet Union is a multinational state*. Experience has shown that the basic features of the USSR's federal structure have fully proved their worth. Therefore, there is no need to make any fundamental changes in the forms of Soviet socialist federalism.[8]

But the Soviet leader also made it clear that the new Constitution had been drawn up in the spirit of greater centralization. Indicating what could be expected, he announced that

> The draft, like the 1936 Constitution, points out that the sovereign rights of the Union republics are protected by the USSR. The guarantees of these rights remain . . . On the other hand, the progressive drawing together of the USSR's nations and nationalities has prompted a need for strengthening the state's federal principles. This has been reflected in the definition of the USSR as a unitary, federal and multinational state (Art. 69). The strengthening of the all-Union principle has also been reflected in certain other provisions of the draft.[9]

The new Constitution broadened Moscow's jurisdiction over the governments of the Union republics (Art. 73). The latter were also deprived of the nominal right to maintain their own military formations, and to pardon or grant amnesties to citizens sentenced by a Union republic's judicial organs. Furthermore, although the Union republics retained the right to secede from the USSR (Art. 72), this guarantee was in effect neutralized by the new definition of the USSR as a 'unitary' state whose 'sovereignty . . . extends to all its territories' (Art. 75).[10] Brezhnev did make the claim that the republics were being given certain additional rights, but in practice this was to have no real meaning.

Public discussion of the draft's provisions concerning national relations was quite muted. Nevertheless, from the various proposals that did appear in the press, it was apparent that, on the one hand, there were those who favoured extending republican rights and affirming more emphatically the sovereignty of the Union republics, and, on the other, that there were also those who wished to see republican rights curtailed and Russian declared the state language.[11] On 4 October 1977, on the eve of the promulgation of the new Constitution, Brezhnev openly acknowledged that 'some comrades' would have preferred to have seen federalism abolished but had been overruled.[12]

The reassurance offered little comfort, for, of course, it did not correspond to the real state of things. The republican rights which Brezhnev claimed to be upholding – that of secession and the independent conduct of foreign relations – had long been a legal fiction. Lip service was still paid to Lenin's instructions regarding national relations and the 'national contract', but in practice they were disregarded. The facade of federalism was being maintained, and important though this was for the non-Russians, politically and economically the USSR would continue to be run like a centralized unitary state. And had it not been for the national assertiveness of the non-Russians, perhaps the pretence of federalism would have been dispensed with after all.

There was far less discretion, for instance, when it came to adopting a new national anthem for the Soviet Union. Approved by the USSR Supreme Soviet in May 1977 on the very eve of the publication of the draft of the new Constitution, it gave a clearer indication of how the Brezhnev leadership viewed the 'Soviet People'. The first verse of what in fact was simply a modified version of the old Stalinist anthem with references to Stalin removed declared:

> An unbreakable union of free republics
> Great Rus' [here meant as Great Russia] has
> welded forever to stand.
> Long live the united, mighty Soviet Union
> Created by the will of the peoples![13]

In precisely this spirit, in open contradiction of Brezhnev's repeated assurances and in the face of growing non-Russian resentment, the Kremlin was to continue 'artificially forcing' along all that went under the euphemism of 'the drawing together of nations'.

Another turn of the screw

It was not long before the pressure on the non-Russian nations was intensified, though not without initial difficulties. In the spring of 1978, when it came to adopting new constitutions in the Union republics based on the 1977 Soviet Constitution, an attempt was made to remove the anomaly of the three Transcaucasian republics, where Georgian, Armenian and Azerbaijani had the status of the state language. The omission from the drafts of the new constitutions of the articles stipulating the official languages caused an outcry. In Georgia demonstrations broke out and on 14 April thousands protested on the streets of Tbilisi until Shevardnadze gave them an assurance that the official status of the Georgian language would be retained. In Armenia, the national intelligentsia is reported to have made its indignation felt and, according to *samizdat* sources, the Armenian Party leader Demirchian warned Moscow how delicate the situation was. Faced with such unexpectedly strong resistance, the authorities retreated and restored the articles that had come to mean so much to the three largest peoples of Transcaucasia.[14]

What made the situation even more complex in Georgia was the Abkhaz question. In December 1977, 130 Abkhaz intellectuals sent a letter to the Supreme Soviet of the USSR protesting against Georgian encroachments on the national rights of their small people, which accounted for less than 2 per cent of the population of Georgia. This seems to have triggered off a campaign for the secession of the autonomous Abkhaz republic from Georgia and its incorporation into the Russian Federation. The Abkhaz case highlighted another aspect of the nationalities problem in the Soviet Union, where the problem was not that of Russian control and Russification but of the domination by one large national group of a smaller one.

Matters reached a head in April 1978, the same month that the Georgians were protesting against Russification. By the end of that month, according to the *New York Times*, mass meetings involving up to 12,000 people were held. In order to defuse the crisis Moscow dispatched Central Committee Secretary Ivan Kapitonov to Georgia with the terms of a compromise. The Abkhaz request to be transferred from Georgia to the RSFSR was rejected, but their basic grievances were recognized and they were granted considerable cultural and economic concessions.[15] In this way, Moscow was forced by public pressure to face up to one of the numerous national problems which it had preferred not to acknowledge.

The fact that the Soviet authorities unexpectedly brought the 'non-existent' Abkhaz issue into the open was an exception, though, and did not herald a more candid approach to the national problem. In May 1978 an anti-Russian race riot involving as many as 13,000 people was reported to have occurred in Dushanbe, the capital of Tadzhikistan.[16] The Soviet press, however, made no mention of any difficulties in the republic. Only in December, after the Chinese News Agency Xinhua claimed that there had been an 'ethnic uprising' in Tadzhikistan, was there a Soviet response: TASS angrily dismissed the report as a 'slanderous' provocation.[17]

In the spring of 1978 a brutal new campaign was launched against the 700 or so Crimean Tatar families that had moved to Crimea but had not been granted residence permits by the local authorities. On 23 June, Musa Mamut, a 46-year-old father of three, set fire to himself in protest against the evictions and confiscation or destruction of Crimean Tatar homes. In November, another Crimean Tatar, Izzet Memudallaev, also committed suicide because of unbearable harassment.[18] Meanwhile, like the Crimean Tatars, Jews, ethnic Germans and Meskhetians continued to brave arrest and imprisonment to keep their respective movements going.

In the case of the ethnic Germans the Soviet leadership apparently planned a move to defuse their problem but mishandled the whole affair. In June 1979, word got out that a part of Kazakhstan where Kazakhs had lived from ancient times was to be given to the Germans as an autonomous territory. Angry Kazakh students, apparently secretly encouraged by the Kazakh authorities, staged protests in Tselinograd in defence of the territorial integrity of their republic. The project was abandoned and it later transpired that neither the Kazakhs nor the Germans had been consulted about it.[19]

Not surprisingly, it was the political prisoners who were the most outspoken and radical as regards the national problem. The Russian dissident and founder of the Moscow Helsinki monitoring group, Yurii Orlov, observed in the second half of 1978 in a report smuggled out of a labour camp:

> The nationality policy being conducted within the country is reflected in the national composition of the political camps. Of the prisoners in the Mordovian and Ural [Perm] camps, 30 to 40 per cent, and in some cases a higher percentage, are Ukrainian, about 30 per cent are from the Baltic area and fewer than 30 per cent are Russians and representatives of the other peoples of the USSR. It was the Ukrainians who suffered most from the arbitrariness of the camps in Stalin's times, and they are still suffering most today.[20]

In the summer of 1978 a group of about 20 political prisoners in Perm Camp 36 conducted a series of protests under the heading: 'Ten Days of Solidarity among the Peoples Struggling against Russo-Soviet Imperialism and Colonialism'. The participants included Ukrainians, Armenians, Jews, Estonians, Tatars and a Russian.[21] The following April, six prisoners in Chistopol Prison, including the Jewish human rights activist Anatoly Shcharansky, declared that they intended to continue this tradition.[22] A number of Russian political prisoners, namely Sergei Soldatov,[23] Vladimir Balakhonov and Mikhail Kazachkov, joined their non-Russian colleagues in calling for the dissolution of the 'Soviet Russian' empire.

Despite the sensitivity of the language issue, in 1978 and 1979 the Soviet authorities introduced major new legislation to increase the already substantial level of Russian-language teaching in the non-Russian republics. Interestingly, the first of the new provisions – the decree of the USSR Council of Ministers dated 13 October 1978 – was not published in the Soviet press. Its substance, however, became known in the West through *samizdat* channels. The new measures covered every aspect and stage of the Soviet educational system, and, for the first time, made the teaching of Russian compulsory in every non-Russian kindergarten and nursery.

In December 1978 the Soviet Minister of Higher and Secondary Specialized Education followed up this decree with a directive of his own. The following May a second major conference devoted to the improvement and extension of the teaching of the Russian language was held in Tashkent under the heading: 'The Russian Language – the Language of Friendship and Cooperation of the Peoples of the USSR'. Its recommendations were incorporated into further instructions issued by the USSR Ministry of Education in June and July 1979.[24]

Aimed ostensibly at the attainment of complete bilingualism in the Soviet Union, the one-sided character of the changes was evident enough to the non-

Russians. No provision was made to encourage the 23.9 million Russians who, according to the all-Union census of 1979, were living in the non-Russian republics, to learn the national language of the people around them. Moreover, the promotion of Russian was conducted in an insensitive manner which reduced the attention devoted to the non-Russian languages and cultures in the schools and further diminished their relative status.

In April 1979 Lithuanian dissenters were the first to sound the alarm after obtaining confidential details about the draft recommendations prepared for the conference in Tashkent. They warned that the proposals signalled yet another wave of 'Russification' that was more subtle, yet potentially more damaging than similar tsarist measures. Describing what was going on as 'denationalization imposed with an iron fist', they appealed in desperation for help from the outside world.[25] In the autumn of 1979 more than 5,000 Lithuanians signed a statement addressed to authorities in Vilnius and Moscow in which they demanded that Lithuanian children not be taught in Russian in nurseries and that citizens of the Lithuanian SSR be allowed to exercise their constitutional right to education in their own language.[26]

The titles of two dissident works on the national problem which were confiscated by the authorities in 1979 reflected the charged atmosphere. In the Ukraine, the philologist Iurii Badz'o had worked for several years on a huge work examining Soviet policy towards his nation, entitled *The Right to Live*. In 1977 his 1,400-page typescript mysteriously vanished from his home. Badz'o started to write a second variant but at the beginning of 1979, when he had completed about 400 pages, the KGB raided his home and seized the new material.[27] The other work, *Spiritual Genocide in Lithuania*, was written by Vytautas Skuodis, a Lithuanian national and religious rights campaigner. It was confiscated in November 1979 during a search of his home. Both authors were arrested and imprisoned.[28]

Protests against Russification continued. In 1980, 365 members of the Georgian intelligentsia, including some of Georgia's most respected academicians, sent a letter to Brezhnev and Shevardnadze protesting against the increased pressure on the Georgian language in the republic's educational institutions, 'the exclusion of the Georgian language from science', the limitations imposed on the teaching of Georgian history, and the manner in which bilingualism was being promoted. They called for the reversal of a policy which they claimed was leading 'to a gradual loss of the national rights of the Georgian people that were won in the struggle against tsarism, is at variance with Leninist nationality policy, and constitutes a violation of the constitutional status of the Georgian people'.[29]

In October 1980 there were mass student demonstrations in Tallinn and other Estonian cities. The rough treatment of the protesters led 40 Estonian intellectuals to issue an open letter addressed to *Pravda* and various newspapers in Estonia. Seeking to highlight the reasons for the fact that 'dissatisfaction' had 'deepened in recent years', the authors stressed the 'national aspect of social conflicts' in their republic and complained that neither the authorities nor the press had been willing to acknowledge this. They argued that the demonstrations had been an expression of the insecurity and fear which Estonians felt about their future as a nation because of Russification, the influx of 'aliens' into Estonia, and disregard for the ecological balance in the republic – all of which was 'rationalized as being economically necessary'.

The Estonian intellectuals called for public discussion of all important issues affecting the life of the republic and a 'guarantee that the native inhabitants of Estonia will always have the final word on the destiny of their land and people'. Specifically, they demanded that:

> Every Estonian within the boundaries of the Estonian SSR possesses the self-evident right to an Estonian-language secondary and higher education and to use Estonian in spoken or written form in the conduct of business . . . We wish for Estonia to become and remain a land where not a single person will suffer insults and handicaps because of his or her mother tongue or ethnic origin . . . where no one feels any injury to his national pride or endangerment to his national culture.[30]

The Kremlin's race against time

The demographic trends that had appeared in the 1970 census were continuing to give the Kremlin all manner of headaches. Because of the declining Russian birthrate and the continuing very high growth rates of the Central Asian peoples, it became clear that by the end of the century, on the one hand, the Russians would no longer be a majority nation, while on the other hand, between one in four and one in five of all Soviet citizens would probably be from a 'Moslem' background. Preliminary forecasts based on the 1979 census data, both in the West and in the Soviet Union, estimated that by the year 2000 the Russians would be reduced to a plurality of between 44 to 47 per cent.[31]

The unease caused by these trends was evident from the debate that had started up among Soviet demographers about whether or not to stimulate the birthrate in regions where it was low (for example, by introducing special allowances for children), and encouraging smaller families in areas where it was high. As one Soviet specialist put it at the beginning of 1978:

> The state is interested not only in the quantity of its citizens, but also in their quality. The state is not indifferent to which segment of the population, of the labour force, is at issue when it comes to population increase – whether it is a group with high or low qualifications, with a high degree of mobility or, by dint of various circumstances (including large families or a language barrier), one that is bound to a certain region.[32]

In private, some Russians were even more blunt. Robert Kaiser, who was the

Washington Post's correspondent in Moscow, wrote in 1976 in his book about the Soviet Union:

> There has been a suggestion for increasing the 'Russian' population in other ways. Lawyers working on a new Soviet constitution, I was told, have proposed allowing citizens of other-than-Russian parents to designate themselves as ethnic Russians if Russian is their principal tongue and 'culture'.[33]

Apart from whatever psychological and political fears these demographic patterns may have raised, there were also serious ramifications for the economy and the armed forces. In 1979 almost 40 per cent of the non-Russians still had little or no Russian.[34] Moreover, rural areas of Central Asia and parts of the Caucasus had large and growing labour 'surpluses'. Yet the unassimilated Central Asians remained highly reluctant to migrate to labour-deficit regions, such as the underdeveloped areas of Siberia and the Far North. They also constituted a rapidly increasing proportion of draftees: at the beginning of the 1980s 28 per cent of the draftees were drawn from Central Asia and the Transcaucasus. Together with other non-Russians, they had to be integrated into multinational units in which Russian is the sole language of command and instruction.[35]

These problems were compounded by the tenacity and complexity of national consciousness, something that was increasingly recognized in the more sophisticated specialist literature which began appearing in the second half of the 1970s. All these factors inevitably had implications for cadres policy, economic development policies and possible economic reform. This predicament seems to have spurred the Brezhnev leadership to take the sort of decisive action in the sphere of nationalities policy that it was loath to do in other areas where there were mounting difficulties. Hence, in what appears to have been perceived as a race against time, it stepped up its efforts to integrate the Soviet state and to bolster the position of the Russian language.

Put on the defensive by unfavourable demographic trends, the Russians took steps to safeguard their dominance. The 'Russian' element at the highest levels of power was strengthened: the percentage of Russians in the Central Committee rose from around 57 per cent in 1966 to 68 per cent in 1981; the highly important Central Committee Secretariat remained virtually a Russian preserve; and Russian representation in the Politburo increased from six out of 11 full members in 1966, to ten out of 14 in 1981.[36]

Even more attention was devoted to stressing the 'oneness', both in the past and in the present, of the Ukrainians and Byelorussians with the Russians. The message was spelt out by Ukrainian Party leader Shcherbitsky in January 1979 on the occasion of the 325th anniversary of the Treaty of Pereiaslav. 'Indissoluble union' with Russia, he declared: 'that is how it has been, how it is, and how it will be for ever!' The means to promote the unity of the Ukrainians and Byelorussians with the Russians included stressing common blood links and 'genetic affinity', and depicting the ancient state of Kievan Rus' as a forerunner of the USSR.[37]

Shortly before he was arrested in April 1979, the Ukrainian philologist Iurii Badz'o wrote an open letter to the Soviet authorities in which he provided a synopsis of his mammoth study *The Right to Live*. This long letter became the most important critique of Soviet nationalities policy in Ukraine since Dziuba's *Internationalism or Russification?*. Badz'o concluded it with this assessment:

> There is enough evidence to see that my description of the present national predicament of the Ukrainian people as a state of siege possesses not only a metaphorical and ideological import, but also a practical one. The official ideology of the 'internationalization', 'drawing together', and fusion of nations and the historiographic concept of Ukraine leave the Ukrainian people virtually no room for free movement either forward or backward. They block our access to the future and to the past; and the practical creators of this predicament beat over the head anyone who rises above the level of planned national extinction, anyone who tries to tell the truth about the reality of the Ukrainian nation, or, God forbid, tries to evaluate the overall picture on an all-national, historical scale according to political criteria.[38]

For doing precisely this, Badz'o was given a 12-year sentence of imprisonment and internal exile.

There was another side to this 'acceleration' of the forging of the 'Soviet people'. In his final years, Brezhnev and those around him seemed to go out of their way to praise the virtues of the 'great Russian people' and to provide the rising tide of Russian nationalism with officially sanctioned outlets. During the 1970s a major new element came to figure in the thought of many Russian patriots: the argument that Russians have suffered more than anyone else from communist rule, coupled with the rejection of any notion of the Russians as a 'ruling' nation in the USSR. To back up this claim, they pointed to the higher standards of living enjoyed by many non-Russians as conclusive evidence that the Russians were not the exploiters but the exploited. Alexander Solzhenitsyn became the best-known champion of this position in which all the blame was placed on communism and the problem of Russian imperialism, both in the tsarist and Soviet periods, evaded.[39]

Not all Russian patriots, however, took such a blinkered view. That other great contemporary Russian man of letters, Andrei Siniavskii, for example, warned in an interview published on 22 November 1979 in the *New York Review of Books* about what was taking place in the Soviet Union:

> The Russian nationality is the dominant one within the Soviet Union, and as it did at times before the revolution, the Russian sense of self is becoming very assertive, very insistent. It takes on a chauvinistic cast. There is a lot of hostility toward the rest of the world – toward other Soviet nationalities.

(*Top left*) The Ukrainian 'National Communist' Mykola Skrypnyk, 1931

(*Above*) The Tatar 'National Communist' Mirza Sultan-Galiev, 1922

(*Left*) One of the most prominent Basmachi leaders, Kurbashi Shir Muhammad Bek (Kurshirmat), 1920s

Session of Estonian 'Parliament' voting to petition for admission to the USSR, 21 July 1940; the man at the rostrum is believed to be Arnold Veimer, chairman of the assembly

Ukrainian Insurgent Army (UPA) fighters celebrating Easter Sunday, 1946

(*Above*) Latvian demonstration in Riga on the 48th anniversary of the Molotov–Ribbentrop Pact, 23 August 1987

(*Left*) Estonian national rights campaigner Mart Niklus receiving a hero's welcome after his release from a labour camp, July 1988

Armenians demonstrating in Nagornyi Karabakh, July 1988

A rally organized by the Azerbaijani Popular Front in Baku,
September 1989

(*Left*) A 10,000-strong demonstration in Kiev demanding greater national rights on 24 September 1989, five days before Gorbachev's visit. The central banner says, in Ukrainian and Yiddish: 'Rehabilitate the languages!'

(*Right*) A young girl waving the yellow, green and red Lithuanian national flag shortly before riot police were sent in against peaceful demonstrators in Vilnius, 28 September 1988

A demonstration of the Uzbek Popular Front 'Birlik', Tashkent, 21 May 1989

(*Left*) Police breaking up a Byelorussian patriotic demonstration in Minsk, 24 March 1989

(*Below*) Georgian demonstrators in Tbilisi just before the massacre of 9 April 1989

(*Right*) A Moldavian rally in Kishinev, summer 1989

(*Below*) During the inaugural Congress of the Popular Movement of the Ukraine for Restructuring, or *Rukh*, Kiev, 8–10 September 1989

Posters from a Kirghiz ecological demonstration in Frunze, 7 October 1989; one of them demands: 'Stop genocide by toxic chemicals!'

A protest in Alma-Ata against the testing of nuclear weapons in Kazakhstan, 21 October 1989

At the end of the 1970s the Brezhnev leadership permitted Russian patriotism to become overshadowed by Russian ethnocentrism. Suslov, the Kremlin's chief ideologist, appears to have acted as a patron of the nebulous so-called 'Russian party' – Russian nationalists who were prepared to work within the system.[40] For example, in 1978 and 1979, the controversial Russian ultra-nationalist painter, Il'ia Glazunov, was allowed to exhibit his works in Moscow and Leningrad. The two exhibitions attracted 600,000 and up to one million visitors respectively.[41] The Brezhnev leadership also permitted other open manifestations of Russian nationalism, such as occurred during the celebrations in 1980 of the 600th anniversary of the defeat of the Tatars by the Muscovites at Kulikovo Pole, and in 1981 in connection with the centenary of Dostoevsky's birth.[42] Gennadii Shimanov was able to put out two large issues of a new *samizdat* miscellany called *Mnogaia leta* (Many Years) which was strongly anti-Western and hailed the Bolshevik revolution as having saved Russia from a 'Jewish – Masonic – Plutocrat' plot.[43]

The non-Russians refuse to be silenced
The end of the 1970s saw a turn for the worse in other respects as well. Towards the end of 1979 the Soviet authorities launched a major drive against all forms of dissent that was to continue into the 1980s and result in the arrest of hundreds. Clearly disturbed by the upsurge and variety of open dissent since the mid-1970s, the Kremlin had to contain this 'epidemic'. To what extent this crackdown was linked to the Soviet invasion of Afghanistan in December 1979, or the approach of the Olympic Games in Moscow in 1980 is difficult to say. What was evident, though, is that the Soviet occupation of Afghanistan effectively destroyed what was left of 'detente' with the West and, as a result, the Soviet authorities became even less concerned about their 'human rights' image. This was especially evident from the fact that the emigration of Jews, Germans and others from the Soviet Union was now drastically reduced.[44] What did worry Moscow, however, was the fear of possible 'contagion' from Iran, Afghanistan and Poland. This, and the deterioration of relations with the West, led to a return of the 'siege mentality'.

Despite the toughening of policy towards dissent – national rights campaigners usually ended up receiving maximum 12-year sentences for a first offence and 15-year ones for a second – the non-Russians refused to be muzzled. If anything, their resistance became more radical and militant. In August 1979, 45 Baltic activists issued a declaration in connection with the 40th anniversary of the Molotov–Ribbentrop Pact in which they called for restoration of the independence of the Baltic states.[45] The following month 20 Baltic activists sent a message of support to Lech Walesa who was then emerging as a leader of Poland's 'peaceful revolution'.[46] Baltic dissidents were also among the first to condemn the invasion of Afghanistan. In January

1980, 21 of them addressed an appeal to the UN Secretary General comparing the occupation of Afghanistan to the fate that had befallen Lithuania, Latvia and Estonia.[47]

There were further joint Baltic actions in the early 1980s. In 1981, for example, 35 Lithuanians and one Latvian sent Walesa a greeting on the first anniversary of the formation of the Polish free trade union movement Solidarity,[48] and 38 Baltic activists signed an appeal for the creation of a 'Baltic nuclear-free zone'.[49] National dissent was conspicuous in all three of the Baltic republics but especially in Lithuania, where it assumed mass proportions and in some ways resembled the situation in Poland. The Lithuanian Roman Catholic Church provided a rallying point in the struggle for human and national rights, and since November 1978 an unofficial Catholic Committee for the Defence of Believers' Rights had played a prominent role.[50] *Samizdat* publications proliferated, with over ten *samizdat* journals appearing regularly. There was even a striking parallel to the Polish workers' celebrated struggle to build a church in Nowa Huta: in 1979 148,149 Lithuanians signed a protest against the closure of their church in Klaipeda.[51]

The election of a Polish pope was also beginning to have a significant impact on the Catholics in the USSR's western borderlands, especially in Lithuania and the Western Ukraine. Unlike his predecessor, Pope John Paul II went out of his way to demonstrate his support for the Catholics in the USSR, whether of the Latin or Eastern rite, and he made it clear that these communities would no longer be effectively written off by the Vatican as 'churches of silence'. His stance clearly irritated the Kremlin but inspired millions of members of his church.[52]

In the Ukraine the situation was especially difficult. Here the republican KGB under the control of Vitalii Fedorchuk distinguished itself by its harsh and cynical treatment of dissenters. During the second half of the 1970s numerous Ukrainian activists were arrested on the basis of trumped-up criminal charges ostensibly unrelated to their political or religious views. Quite a few dissenters were also attacked and savagely beaten up by 'unknown assailants'. Furthermore, in most cases, Ukrainian activists were not released on the expiry of their sentences because new charges were brought against them to prolong their imprisonment.[53] In 1980, for example, Chornovil was given a further five years in the camps on a fabricated charge of attempted rape. While in internal exile in Iakutia he had joined the Ukrainian Helsinki monitoring group and, among other things, had reported on ethnic clashes that had taken place in Iakutsk in June 1979 between Iakut and Russian students.[54]

Nevertheless, Ukrainian voices of protest continued to be heard. In early 1980 an anonymous group calling itself the Ukrainian Patriotic Movement issued two appeals, one calling for the 'decolonization' of the USSR, and the other urging Ukrainian workers to form independent trade unions.[55] The following year, five students were arrested in Kiev for pasting up leaflets in support of Ukrainian political prisoners.[56] There was also a resurgence of activity by Ukrainian Catholics. In October 1982, five activists of the outlawed Ukrainian Catholic Church, led by former political prisoner Iosyf Terelia, announced the formation of a body to campaign for the legalization of their church – the Initiative Group for the Defence of Believers' Rights and the Church.[57]

In Georgia and Armenia the early 1980s brought further manifestations of nationalism which was becoming directed more and more against Moscow. In 1980, several Georgian nationalists, including Nikolai Samkharadze, were arrested. Later, leaflets calling for the release of 'fighters for Georgian independence' were circulated. By now, Georgians living in Abkhazia, where they outnumbered the Abkhaz, had begun protesting about discrimination at the hands of the latter. In January 1981 hundreds of Georgian intellectuals are reported to have expressed their concern about the situation in Abkhazia in a petition addressed to Shevardnadze and Brezhnev. During 1981 at least five demonstrations are known to have taken place in Georgia at which the Abkhaz question figured alongside broader issues connected with the defence of the Georgian language, history and culture.

On 23 March 1981, some 1,000 students protested at the University of Tbilisi against the dismissal of Akaki Bakradze, a popular 'patriotic' professor who taught a course on Georgian literature. At the end of the month a large group of students and intellectuals demonstrated in defence of Georgian national rights outside the building in Tbilisi where the Ninth Congress of Georgian Writers was taking place. Shevardnadze came out to meet the protesters and agreed to receive their representatives. The following month the Georgian activist Gamsakhurdia, who for a time had stopped his dissident activity after partly recanting at his trial in 1978, handed a document entitled 'The Demands of the Georgian People' to the Georgian Party leader.[58] It included proposals to safeguard the status of the Georgian language, improve the teaching of Georgian history and the preservation of Georgian historical monuments, and protect the Georgians in Abkhazia and Saingilo.

Other Georgian protests took place in the ancient city of Mtskheta. Here, in October 1981, some 2,000 people demonstrated in defence of the Georgian language. The unrest in Georgia continued into the following year when numerous intellectuals protested against the arrest of dissenters on trumped-up charges.[59]

In Armenia, although there were no mass protests as in Georgia, there were other signs of trouble. At the end of 1978 and the beginning of 1979 several thousand anti-Soviet leaflets are reported to have been distributed in Erevan. In 1980, Aleksandr Manucharian, a medievalist at the Armenian Academy of Sciences, and two others were arrested. They were accused of forming an underground nationalist organization. Manucharian, it seems, had also written two 'anti-Soviet' articles: 'All About the National Question' and 'Imperialism'. At around the same time the Armenian authorities rounded up five members of a nationalist group calling itself the Union of Armenian Youth. Led by Mrzpet Arutiunian and Ishkhan Mkrtchian, its aim was to promote the idea of Armenia's secession from the USSR.[60]

Russification was also causing anxiety in Armenia. In May, Silva Kaputikian delivered an impassioned speech at the Congress of the Writers' Union of Armenia in defence of the Armenian language. The assignment of Russian as the sole gateway to social advancement, she argued, was already giving rise to concern: Armenian parents, who in the past 'would have been prepared to die rather than sacrifice their native tongue', were now sending their children to Russian schools. Moreover, outside Armenia, in other Soviet republics, 'tens of thousands of Armenians' no longer had the basic cultural facilities which they had enjoyed before the war. Kaputikian stressed that she was not the first to raise these issues and that 'a large number of letters' expressing concern about the position of the Armenian language had been sent to the Armenian Party leadership.[61]

As before, information about the situation in the traditionally Moslem areas of the Soviet Union was less accessible. Nevertheless, despite the lack of *samizdat* from Central Asia and the Caucasus, it was occasionally possible to detect signs of ferment. In 1979, for example, a Turkmenistan official revealed in a brochure that some of the Turkmen population had not only been listening regularly to religious broadcasts from Iran in their native language, but that cassette tape recordings had been made by mullahs and played to groups of Moslems throughout the republic.[62] In December 1980, in neighbouring Azerbaijan, where the population is Shi'ite, as in Iran, rather than Sunni, the KGB chief warned that the USSR's enemies were carrying out 'ideological sabotage' in the republic. The Azerbaijani authorities, he said, were engaged in 'rebuffing manifestations of nationalism and chauvinism' and were working to 'curb anti-social actions by the sectarian underground and the reactionary Moslem clergy'. He also disclosed that 'crimes against the state' were being committed by 'politically immature' elements of the population, 'especially young people'.[63]

In Checheno-Ingushetia, Moslem fundamentalists were evidently as troublesome as ever. This is how the editor of a Groznyi newspaper described the situation in an article published in January 1981:

> An important part of the population is still under the strong influence of the Moslem religion. Certain clerics and sectarians, playing on the confusion between religious and national feelings, inflame fanaticism and xenophobia . . . Under the influence of the so-called 'religious authorities', fanatics bully and persecute Russian teachers and other representatives of our intelligentsia.[64]

The same author also revealed that, only 'a few years ago', a political 'bandit', Khasaki Magomedov, had been killed in the mountains by security forces. He had been active since the war, 'sowing death and terror', and had 'killed 40 Communists, Soviet activists and members of the Komsomol'.[65]

The tensions between the Ingushi and the Ossetians also continued. In October 1981 serious disturbances were reported to have broken out in the North Ossetian capital of Ordzhonikidze after an Ossetian taxi driver was murdered. A crowd numbering several thousand took to the streets and fought with the police. Only after troops with tanks were called in and the chairman of the RSFSR Council of Ministers Mikhail Solomentsev had addressed the protesters was order restored.[66]

Mystery also surrounded an incident which took place in Kirghizia at the end of 1980. This republic has a border with China and is only 60 miles away from Afghanistan. On 4 December the Kirghiz premier Sultan Ibraimov was assassinated. Rather surprisingly, Western correspondents in Moscow were told by officials that he had been killed for political reasons, allegedly by 'Moslem nationalists'. This was the first known political assassination of a senior Soviet official since the Stalin period.[67]

Several other 'Moslem' acts of protest or opposition can be mentioned. In 1982, on the eve of the 1 May holiday, the building of the Central Committee of the Turkmen Party in Ashkhabad is reported to have been set on fire.[68] That summer the authorities in Uzbekistan uncovered a profitable unofficial religious publishing operation in Tashkent. Thirteen people were eventually tried for printing and distributing a booklet called *About the Islamic Faith*.[69] To the south-east in Tadzikistan, in the second half of 1982, five people were arrested in Dushanbe for circulating leaflets against the Soviet occupation of Afghanistan.[70]

On the cultural level, the Central Asians continued to demonstrate their assertiveness. At the end of 1980, the Kirghiz writer Chingiz Aitmatov who, like Suleimanov, wrote in Russian, published his celebrated novel *I dol'she veka dlitsia den'* in *Novyi mir*. Permeated with a deep attachment to the cultural heritage of the USSR's Turkic peoples, it showed how modernity in a Soviet form, with its emphasis on political uniformity and cultural homogenization, was depriving man of his individuality. Some of the most memorable passages dealt with the ancient Kazakh legend about the 'mankurts', slaves whose memories were erased by torture so that they would not remember their past life and who they were. 'A man without a sense of history, without memory of the past,' Aitmatov stressed, 'lacks any perspective and lives only for the present, for the day.'[71]

The problem of preserving national memory also figured in the works of less well-known Central Asian writers. But while Aitmatov's novel was generally well received, the works of some of the bolder authors came under fire. In Uzbekistan, for example, Mamadali Mahmudov's nationalistic novel *Olmas qaialar* (Immortal Cliffs), which was published in November 1981 in the chief Uzbek literary monthly and took a negative view of the Russian conquest of Central Asia, was attacked for its ideological lapses.[72]

Difficulties begin to be admitted

For the Soviet Union the early 1980s were a time of international isolation and mounting difficulties at home: economic stagnation, problems with supplying the population with food, corruption, bureaucratic petrification and growing political apathy and cynicism, not to mention national tensions, resistance to Russification and latent social unrest. Moreover, the events in Poland and Afghanistan reverberated in different ways throughout the domain, causing the Soviet authorities further discomfort and unease. By withstanding these challenges, the system appeared to demonstrate that its stability and strength were not to be underestimated. Only later would it be acknowledged that matters had actually been drawing to a crisis.

In what appears to have been a tacit recognition that the situation required some adjustments, during the final two years of Brezhnev's rule the Party began to display a more sober and somewhat franker attitude towards some of the pressing domestic issues, including the national problem. Poland, where Moscow had just seen the Polish Communist Party virtually disintegrate, undoubtedly had something to do with this. At the Twenty-sixth Party Congress in February 1981, Brezhnev warned that 'events in Poland confirm anew how important it is for the Party and for the strengthening of its leading role that it pay close attention to the voice of the masses'.[73] He also conceded that 'the dynamics of the development of such a large multinational state as ours give rise to a good many problems requiring the Party's sympathetic attention'. What was also apparent from his and other speeches made at the congress was that the nationalities question was being viewed more and more from an economic angle and also that the situation in the Central Asian republics was becoming worrisome.

Brezhnev singled out two issues which were to assume considerable importance during the 1980s. First, he mentioned the problem of utilizing the manpower surplus in Central Asia and the Caucasus, emphasizing that 'the population of those areas must be drawn more actively into the development of the country's new territories'. In what seemed to be an implicit acknowledgement of the difficulty of persuading members of the traditionally Moslem peoples to move to labour-deficit regions, he called on Party organizations to pay closer attention to the 'specific needs in the fields of language, culture and everyday life' of individuals living outside their own republics. The provision of basic cultural facilities, he seemed to be suggesting, would make the idea of migration more attractive. In retrospect, it appears that the only real follow-up to these instructions was the announcement in July 1982 that the non-Russian periodical press would be made available on subscription throughout the Soviet Union.[74]

Brezhnev also spoke of the need for 'due' or 'appropriate' representation of all nationalities living in a given republic in Party and government organs. He was not, of course, referring to the predominance of Russians in the Politburo and the Secretariat. What he was getting at was that the Kremlin was having second thoughts about its policy of recruiting regional officials from 'locals', and particularly about the affirmative action programmes which in some republics gave preferential treatment to representatives of the indigenous population as regards access to higher education and top-level job opportunities. The result in some republics was an over-representation of the titular nationality in the top Party and government bodies. At a time of growing national assertiveness on the part of some of the local elites, especially in the Central Asian republics, Russians and members of other non-indigenous nationalities had come to see themselves as the victims of exclusionary practices. In fact, in the late 1970s more Europeans had begun moving out of the Central Asian republics than were moving in.[75]

By bringing up this question, Brezhnev indicated that in some republics affirmative action programmes had gone too far and that the situation needed to be rectified. As if to underline the message, he also praised the 'unselfish assistance of the Russian people' to the non-Russian nationalities.[76]

Moscow's Central Asian predicament

A year later it became clearer what was bothering the Kremlin about Central Asia. During a visit to Uzbekistan in March 1982, Brezhnev criticized both the economic performance of the most populous of the traditionally Moslem republics and the reluctance of Uzbeks to seek employment outside their republics. Suggesting that at a time of economic difficulties, Uzbekistan was not pulling its weight, the Soviet leader indicated that the republic would be expected to make a greater contribution to food production, improve the quality of its cotton, and reduce inefficiency in the industrial sector. 'Internationalism' in the early 1980s, he declared, meant 'above all, honest, conscientious and fully effective labour by all the country's peoples for the common good'.[77]

Part of the problem was connected with cotton production. The Soviet Union is one of the world's leading exporters of cotton, and 'white gold', as cotton was sometimes referred to in the Soviet press, has been an important source of much-needed hard currency. In the early 1980s, however, not only was the quantity and quality of cotton produced in Central Asia declining, but also the USSR was facing tough competition from China in the world cotton market. At the heart of the malaise was Moscow's economic policy towards the region: at a time of scarce resources, Moscow was reluctant to pump new investments into the region in order to improve the technology of production and provide material incentives. Instead, the Central Asians were being told to make do with what there was when clearly it was no longer enough. Matters were also not helped by Moscow's deafness to pleas from Central Asian representatives that more of the cotton grown in Central Asia be manufactured locally instead of being shipped to textile centres in the European part of the USSR. In the early 1980s under 5 per cent of the cotton produced in Central Asia was manufactured in the region.[78]

Another important aspect of internationalism, Brezhnev told his hosts in Tashkent, was strict adherence to the correct cadres policy. Not only had attention to be paid to providing due representation for all the nationalities living in the republic, but also 'proper use' had to be made of local specialists. Brezhnev complained that the educational system in Uzbekistan was turning out far more specialists than the economy required in some fields, and not enough in others. This problem was compounded by 'parochialism – the desire to place all specialists in jobs in their own republics, even if the jobs aren't in their specialities, when there may even be major shortages in their fields in other regions'. This tendency would have to be overcome, he said, and greater efforts made generally to induce surplus manpower from Central Asia to migrate to areas of the USSR where there was a shortage of labour.

It is worth noting that while he was in Tashkent Brezhnev did not raise the problem of corruption or attack the local Party leadership directly. While praising Uzbekistan's achievements, he did, however, imply that the republic was becoming too preoccupied with its cultural heritage and that some Uzbek communists were becoming 'conceited'.[79]

In addition to these issues there was also the crucial question of Central Asia's dwindling water resources. With the prospect of acute water shortages in their republics by the end of the century arising from economic development and the population explosion, the elites in Kazakhstan, Turkmenistan, and especially Uzbekistan, had for years been lobbying for an ambitious and controversial project known as 'Sibaral' to be approved. This involved the diversion of some of the waters of Siberian rivers southward to the arid areas in Central Asia and Kazakhstan. At the Twenty-sixth Party Congress the Uzbek Party leader Sharaf Rashidov had even argued that the scheme would enable Central Asia to 'make an enormous contribution' to easing the USSR's difficulties with food supply.[80] The project, however, was left hanging in the air and in 1982 there were new exchanges in the press between its proponents and opponents. Brezhnev did not help matters by remaining silent about the issue when he spoke in Tashkent.[81]

From about the beginning of the 1980s the Soviet authorities also significantly stepped up their attacks on Islam at home, though abroad they posed as a true friend of Islamic states. They also betrayed their unease about a potential domestic 'Moslem problem' by repeatedly denying that there was any such danger and by blaming the West for seeking to stir up trouble in the traditionally Moslem republics. Brezhnev himself had indicated at the Twenty-sixth Party Congress that the USSR felt itself somewhat vulnerable in Central Asia. Alluding to the danger of a spillover of Islamic fundamental-ism to the USSR's 'Moslem' peoples, he had warned that Islamic slogans could be used for reactionary as well as progressive ends and had explained that the Soviet Union had been 'compelled' to intervene militarily in Afghanistan because it had perceived 'a direct threat to the security of . . . [the USSR's] southern border'.[82]

Typically, the first deputy-head of the KGB, S. Tsvigun, warned in October 1981 in *Kommunist* that 'reactionary Islamic organizations abroad' had intensified their anti-Soviet propaganda, 'trying to capitalize on events in Iran and around Afghanistan'. His important article reflected the official Soviet view of the world and of the internal situation in the USSR in the final years of Brezhnev's rule. The Soviet Union was portrayed as being under siege from the 'imperialists' led by the United States, who were accused of having launched a massive campaign of ideological subversion against the USSR. A prime target was said to be Soviet youth. What was also revealing were Tsvigun's claims that the USSR's enemies were relying on nationalism as one of their main weapons and were seeking 'to find anti-Soviet, nationalist turncoats and persuade them to engage in actions against the state'. It was therefore essential, he concluded, that the Soviet population show 'heightened political vigilance'.[83]

A policy in need of reappraisal

During these generally bleak years, there were, however, a few modestly encouraging developments. A number of moderates among the Soviet experts on the national question, such as Mikhail Kulichenko, head of the Section for the Theory of Nations and National Relations of the Party's Institute of Marxism-Leninism, and Petr Fedoseev, a vice-president of the USSR Academy of Sciences, began to advocate a more balanced approach to language policy. They argued that the promotion of Russian should not mean the displacement of the native languages. Kulichenko, for instance, wrote in 1981:

It is totally inadmissible to place any kind of restrictions on the possibilities for the genuinely free utilization of their native language by the toilers of all nationalities. A model for taking into consideration the real needs in the lives of the peoples takes shape when simultaneous measures are adopted in the republics for improving the study of the Russian language as well as the language (languages) of the indigenous population.[84]

More importantly, here and there the authorities began to display a more responsive and conciliatory attitude. At the end of the 1970s in the Ukraine, for example, the Shcherbitsky leadership seemed to indicate that the 'nor-malization' of the republic after Shelest's removal had gone far enough and started easing up a little in the cultural sphere.[85] In 1979 in Georgia a number of measures were introduced to improve the teaching of the Georgian language.[86] Two years later in Estonia, it was acknowledged that more attention should be devoted to teaching the Estonian language, particularly in Russian schools, for unless Russian pupils made some effort to learn the language of the indigenous population, the two communities would tend to remain apart.[87]

It is not clear whether such moves were local initiatives or whether, after the strong opposition to intensified Russification, they reflected a measured moderation by the centre of its policies. What is interesting, though, is that in both Georgia and Estonia, this semblance of increased sensitivity by the authorities did not prevent further protests against Russification. The demonstrations in Georgia in 1981 have already been mentioned. In March 1982, 15 Estonian intellectuals signed an open letter, subsequently published in a Finnish newspaper, describing in detail the Russification of their republic and resistance to it. The situation was such, they claimed, that in their own homeland Estonians constantly had to ask themselves: 'Where am I? Is this really my home town? My country?' They also noted that after the beatings of students who had taken part in the demonstrations in Tallinn in the autumn of 1980, slogans had appeared on the walls saying: 'Fascists out of Estonia.'[88]

That there was a little more realism and fluidity than before was attested by the major all-Union conference to discuss national relations in the USSR which was held in Riga in June 1982. At first only the speeches by the Latvian Party leader Avgust Voss and candidate Politburo member Boris Ponomarev were published in the press. But even from Voss's statements, it was apparent that it had been an unusual meeting. The Latvian first Party secretary revealed that in his republic the authorities were striving towards a more genuine form of bilingualism: while improving the study and teaching of Russian, they did not want to neglect the local language. Voss also stressed how important it was for Russians and other non-indigenous nationalities in the republics to learn the language of the given republic through the school system.[89]

Surprisingly, the proceedings of the conference were promptly published in 12 volumes. According to their American reviewer, Paul Goble, 'Their breadth, detail and wide distribution represented a major departure from the way in which earlier conferences of this kind had been handled . . . But the most impressive trait of the proceedings was the breadth and frankness of the discussions and the specificity of policy proposals.' One of the main refrains was the need 'for more study of nationality issues and better utilization of academic expertise in the formulation of policy'. Goble notes: 'This wish was most clearly expressed in a call for the creation of special councils – within all republic, krai, and oblast Party committees – for the study of nationality relations.'[90]

The Riga conference also witnessed a sharpening of the debate on nationality issues between the 'moderates' and the 'hardliners'. Kulichenko had recently been pointing out that the idea of the fusion of nations was disturbing to many.[91] At the conference, the chief editor of *Kommunist*, R. Kosolapov, attacked Kulichenko and other specialists for attempting 'to ignore the Leninist idea of fusion of nations, or worse still . . . to portray it as if it were an echo of great power chauvinism'. But even here there was a new twist. In criticizing Kulichenko and his colleagues, Kosolapov came out with a watered-down interpretation of fusion. 'Of course,' he declared, 'the Lenin-ist idea of the fusion of nations has nothing in common with the vulgar-utopian usages according to which fusion is treated as the destruction of national features, and the effacing of all linguistic and ethnic differences.'[92]

What may have helped clear the air a little was Suslov's death in January 1982. By this time Brezhnev himself was clearly ailing, and the removal of the ideological supremo led to a hotting up of the Kremlin succession struggle. In May 1982, Andropov relinquished his post as chairman of the KGB and moved to the Central Committee Secretariat where he took over Suslov's responsibilities for ideology. Yet the prospect of a former KGB chief – who for almost a decade and a half had overseen the suppression of national dissent – eventually taking over as the new Party leader could scarcely have been attractive to the non-Russians. Moreover, the fact that Vitalii Fedorchuk – the scourge of Ukrainian dissidents – was made the new head of the KGB also seemed to rule out the possibility of any let-up in the Kremlin's policy towards dissent.

The only clue as to what could be expected was the abrupt change in attitude towards Russian nationalism. With Suslov out of the way, the Russian nationalists soon also came under attack. Two dissidents, Anatolii Ivanov-Skuratov and Leonid Borodin were arrested; the prominent National Bolshevik Sergei Semanov was removed from his position as editor of *Chelovek i zakon* (Man and Law); and, in July 1982, the 'village prose' writers were implicitly ordered into line by a Central Committee decree directed at literary-artistic journals.[93]

While this mini-crackdown on Russian nationalism was taking place, a bizarre incident in the Soviet capital confirmed the existence of Russian neo-Nazi groups. On 20 April a group of self-styled young fascists dressed in black shirts and wearing swastikas gathered in Moscow's Pushkin Square and attempted to hold a meeting marking Hitler's birthday. Scuffles broke out before the police finally intervened. Despite other reports about such groups, the Soviet media remained silent about this ugly problem.[94]

In November 1982, on the eve of the 60th anniversary of the formation of the USSR, Brezhnev died and Andropov did indeed emerge as the new Party general secretary. Although a few years later Brezhnev was to be denigrated by his successors and his period of rule denounced as years of 'stagnation', in the sphere of nationalities policy there had been anything but inertia. The

Kremlin had forcefully pursued the integration of the Soviet multinational state, markedly intensified the promotion of the teaching and use of the Russian language, and for all its platitudes about 'internationalism', equality and the need for tact in national relations, had preserved Russian dominance.

14

Andropov and Chernenko Keep up the Pressure

Within weeks of taking over, Andropov had two opportunities to speak about nationalities policy on the occasion of the jubilee marking the 60th anniversary of the formation of the USSR. The most striking thing about the first address, given on 21 December 1982, was that the new Party leader once again publicly endorsed the concept of fusion. He reaffirmed: 'Our final goal is clear. It is, in Lenin's words, "not only the drawing together of nations, but their fusion".' Seen in the context of the rest of his speech, though, this assertion was not quite as threatening as it may have sounded. Andropov added that 'the Party is well aware that the road to this goal is a long one' and that 'on no account must there be any running ahead here, just as there must be no holding back of processes that have already matured'. Furthermore, from the sensitivity he showed in the address to the feelings of the non-Russians, it also seems that he did not mean fusion in the 'vulgar-utopian' sense, but as Kosolapov had recently interpreted it.

Showing rather more frankness and realism than his predecessor, Andropov went on to say that national problems would remain as long as nations and national distinctions existed, adding that the latter 'will survive for a long time to come, much longer than class distinctions'. He acknowledged what Soviet social scientists had been pointing out, namely that modernization and economic development were not weakening but strengthening national self-awareness. Furthermore, like Brezhnev before him, he fully recognized the importance of the economic aspects of the nationalities question. What all this meant, Andropov stated, was that 'problems of relations among nations' were 'still on the agenda' and that they called for 'special concern and constant attention'. It was therefore essential, he stressed, that the Party devise a 'carefully considered, scientifically substantiated nationalities policy'.

The new Soviet leader also broke with tradition by declaring that it would be wrong to blame 'negative phenomena' in the area of national relations 'solely on vestiges of the past'. He elaborated:

Among other things, they are sometimes fostered by the mistakes we make in our own work. Here, comrades, nothing can be dismissed as insignificant. Everything counts – the attitude to language, monuments of the past, the interpretation of historical events, and the way we transform rural and urban areas and influence living and working conditions.[1]

This more sober approach to the nationalities problem, which perhaps reflected Andropov's intimate knowledge of the grievances of non-Russians from his lengthy tenure as head of the KGB, was also apparent in his remarks on the nationalities question made three weeks later before the Presidium of the USSR Supreme Soviet.[2] On both occasions the Soviet leader condemned national conceit and disrespectful attitudes towards other nations. Moreover, in something of an unusual departure, he seemed to want to reassure certain nationalities – 'Germans, Poles, Koreans, Kurds' and others – that they were 'fully-fledged Soviet citizens'.[3] These four nationalities represent groups who have the majority of their co-nationals living outside the Soviet Union; in practice, they have been treated more like 'foreigners' than Soviet citizens, and one Soviet source even lists them separately from other Soviet peoples as 'nationalities whose main body lives outside the USSR'.[4]

In other respects, however, Andropov spoke in the same vein as Brezhnev had before him. He stressed the need for greater economic integration and the 'better distribution of productive forces', raised once again the issue of due representation, and spoke of the positive role of migration and multi-national workers' brigades in fostering the spirit of internationalism. He also made it clear that the Party remained opposed to conserving 'bad' and 'outdated' elements in 'the cultural heritage, traditions and customs of each nation'. This last point was echoed in a resolution adopted by the Supreme Soviet on 13 January 1983 in connection with the jubilee. Among other things, it called for more resolute efforts 'to counter attempts to idealize outdated customs and values [and] to develop new Soviet traditions and ceremonies'.[5]

Under Andropov, the Kremlin's attitude towards Russian nationalism was distinctly cooler. All the same, in his main jubilee address, Andropov did not omit the standard praise of the Russian people for their 'unselfish fraternal assistance' to the non-Russians.[6]

Language, ideology and discipline

Six months later at the Central Committee plenum held on 14–15 June, both Andropov and Konstantin Chernenko, Brezhnev's close associate who delivered a report on ideological work, touched on nationalities policy, but made no reference to 'fusion'. It remains unclear why Andropov revived this concept in the first place, and why it again vanished from the political lexicon of the Soviet leadership. At the plenum Andropov made the important admission that the Party programme introduced under Khrushchev had been utopian and announced that a new one was being prepared. As far as the nationalities policy was concerned, he simply stated that it would 'hold an appropriate place in the new edition of the CPSU programme' and reiterated that the Party was set on a 'steady course' of drawing together the peoples of the USSR.[7]

Chernenko was a bit more candid, though. He also stressed the importance of 'pursuing a well thought-out, scientifically substantiated nationalities policy', adding that ideological work in a multinational state was 'inconceivable without a thorough study . . . of the specific interests and the features peculiar to [the] national psychology and culture' of the peoples of the USSR. Maintaining that the key to success lay in the intensification of 'internationalist and patriotic' education and the struggle against 'alien views' such as religion and nationalism, he singled out two particular problems. The state was 'still not fully able to attract and direct [surplus manpower] reserves' to the areas that were in particular need of them, and the Party, he admitted, was searching for a way out of this quandary. Furthermore, there was still a sizeable number of Soviet citizens who did not know Russian well enough and this state of affairs could not be allowed to continue.[8]

Clearly, Chernenko was not alone in the Soviet leadership in thinking that still too few non-Russians knew the Russian language well enough. A month before the plenum, the Central Committee and the USSR Supreme Soviet adopted a joint resolution on supplementary measures to improve the teaching of Russian in the non-Russian republics.[9]

According to the 1979 all-Union census, 58.6 per cent of the Soviet population gave Russian as their native language and 62 per cent of all non-Russians claimed to be fluent in Russian.[10] A Central Committee resolution published in February 1982 in preparation for the 60th anniversary of the formation of the USSR had even highlighted the fact that 82 per cent of the population was now fluent in Russian and that 'every Soviet citizen has the possibility of learning the great Russian language'.[11] For Moscow, though, the main problem was now undoubtedly the Central Asians. Not only did a large proportion of them still have little or no knowledge of Russian but also they rarely intermarried with 'outsiders' and were reluctant to seek work outside their republics. This was hardly what was envisaged by 'internationalism' and 'internationalization'. There was also the military aspect – the problem of Central Asian conscripts with poor Russian – an issue which was receiving more and more attention in the press and at special meetings and conferences.[12]

But as before, the Ukraine and Byelorussia, where knowledge of Russian was widespread, were subjected to strong pressure. Details of the additional measures to improve the study of Russian that were introduced by the Ministry of Education of the Ukrainian SSR on 29 June 1983 reached the West. According to these documents, educational staff were to be encouraged to bear in mind that:

the fluent use of Russian on a level with the native language constitutes an objective necessity for every citizen, promotes the further consolidation of the friendship and brotherhood of the peoples of the USSR and the development and strengthening of the material and spiritual potential of the Soviet people.

Among the numerous concrete measures introduced to back up the ideological emphasis on the importance of Russian was a 16 per cent pay rise for teachers in the Ukraine of Russian and Russian literature.[13]

As the 'leaking' of this document demonstrated, non-Russians in republics where 'internationalization' had made the most headway were becoming seriously concerned by the ever increasing promotion of Russian at the expense of the national languages. Another example of this can be seen in the following comment published in 1982 in a Kazakh women's journal:

> You can see many Kazakh children who do not speak Kazakh. When you ask their parents why this is so, they say, 'There is no higher educational establishment in Kazakhstan that teaches its students in Kazakh. There is no special kindergarten for Kazakh children. So what is the use of speaking Kazakh?'[14]

Concern about the standing of the Kazakh language seems to have been shared by the leadership of the Kazakh Party headed by Dinmukhamed Kunaev. At the end of 1983, the controversial author Olzhas Suleimanov was placed at the head of the Writers' Union of Kazakhstan and among his first statements was that the language issue needed more attention.[15]

The traditionally Moslem regions were also heavily affected by another development. On coming to power, Andropov launched a campaign to increase labour discipline and reduce corruption. This initiative, which was accompanied by the continuing emphasis on tightening ideological controls, was soon to affect nationalities policy: although the new drive against corruption was pursued on an all-Union basis, the Central Asian republics, especially Uzbekistan, ended up taking the brunt of it. The Azerbaijani Party leader Geidar Aliev, who had for a time headed the KGB in Azerbaijan and had overseen a crackdown on corruption in his own republic, was elevated to full membership of the Politburo and made a first chairman of the USSR Council of Ministers.

The first traditionally Moslem region to undergo an extensive purge of its Party officials, however, was Bashkiria. At the beginning of 1984 *Pravda* revealed that during the last year 160 local communist officials had been dismissed for 'abuse of their position', ineffective ideological work and tolerating 'anti-social manifestations'.[16] Although the nature of the 'anti-social manifestations' was not specified, and it is not clear to what extent it was simply a case of weeding out corrupt officials, it is worth pointing out that during the previous two years concern had been expressed about the survival of Islam among the population of the Tatar ASSR, especially the young, and Tatar intellectuals had voiced their apprehension about a decision to build a nuclear power station in the republic.[17] In Kirghizia, the tougher policy was reflected in a warning given in May 1983 to historians and the cultural intelligentsia by the Party leader Turdakun Usubaliev about nationalistic lapses.[18]

Another ominous development was the creation in April 1983 of a Soviet 'Anti-Zionist' Committee consisting of a number of Soviet Jewish apologists for the Soviet Government's policies towards the Jews. At a press conference convened by this group on 6 June 1983 it was made clear that the days of large-scale Jewish emigration from the Soviet Union had ended. According to Novosti press agency, Western correspondents were told that 'the people who had left were mainly those whose families had been split up during World War II. This process of reuniting families is, for the most part, now complete.'[19] The 12-year sentence given to Jewish activist Iosif Begun in October of that year only reinforced the impression that the Kremlin's attitude towards the Jews was becoming even more unyielding.

During 1983 there were further numerous arrests of non-Russian activists. In Armenia, for instance, three 'nationalists' were tried for *samizdat* activities.[20] In Georgia, where there was considerable opposition to the official celebrations of the 200th anniversary of the Treaty of Georgievsk which had placed part of Georgia under Russian protection, the problem was more serious. Eventually, at least ten Georgians are known to have been arrested in connection with the protests.[21] In the Baltic republics too, there was no let-up in the pressure on the national rights campaigners. In Lithuania, Father Alfonsas Svarinskas was arrested in January and subsequently given a ten-year sentence. A member of the Catholic Committee for the Defence of Believers' Rights, he was the first Lithuanian priest to be detained since the early 1970s. Not long afterwards, a second priest, Father Sigitas Svarinskas, was also arrested.[22] Other Baltic dissidents who were arrested included Enn Tarto, Heiki Ahonen and Lagle Parek in Estonia, and Gunars Astra and Janis Roskalns in Latvia.[23]

Andropov's tenure as Party leader lasted only 15 months. From the summer of 1983 he was increasingly incapacitated by illness, and he died in February 1984. During this short space of time there was no practical follow-up to some of the more realistic comments that he had made at the outset about the national problem. The emphasis remained on improving the teaching of Russian, instilling 'internationalist' values, while at the same time continuing to suppress national dissent and combat 'hostile' foreign influences.

The Chernenko interlude

The new Party leader, Chernenko, did not even last as long as Andropov. Only on one occasion during his 13 months in power did he make noteworthy comments about the national problem. This was in a speech delivered at a Central Committee plenum in April 1984, when he reiterated that the nationalities question 'may not be removed from the agenda' and that it needed to be studied seriously with 'all the fine points of the matter' being taken into account. Rather cryptically, though, considering that a new edition of the Party programme was being drafted, he also added that 'we cannot regard the existing relations between nations in our state as something set in concrete and unalterable, as something that is not subject to the influence of time and new circumstances'.[24]

Taking their cue from Andropov and Chernenko, during 1984 a number of experts on the nationalities question began urging a more open and honest approach to this issue. In January, for instance, the Azerbaijani, Afrand Dashdamirov, called for an end to 'a declarative approach' to nationalities policy,[25] while later on in the year the Lithuanian, Genrikas Zimanas, criticized the 'hushing up of shortcomings and mistakes' in this area.[26] But the most candid article appeared in the autumn and was written by Gamlet Tavadov. He charged that

> In the 1970s and the beginning of the 1980s, in the scholarly and propagandistic literature, a 'facile', oversimplistic idea prevailed about national problems in the period of developed socialism. During those years, the following thesis was promoted in every way possible: the main things have already been done – the national question has been solved, it is no longer on the agenda – and now it is the question of national relations under mature socialism that require management and regulation. The existence of real problems and emergent contradictions was discussed vaguely and superficially, without in-depth analysis.

It was only since the Twenty-sixth Party Congress, Tavadov argued, that a more realistic attitude had become discernible, with the Party shifting the emphasis from highlighting 'successes and achievements' to the 'problems which require constant attention and a prompt solution'. Even so, not all Soviet social scientists had yet 'sufficiently elaborated the meaning and content of the principal Party tenets on the national question'. In fact, he pointed out, there was still no consensus among Soviet experts 'on a number of important aspects of the theory and practice of national relations'. Moreover, in dealing with the officially prescribed formulation of the simultaneous flourishing and drawing together of nations, 'many' specialists 'played down or simply did not notice the complexity of this process and its contradictory nature'.

Tavadov went on to identify four categories of 'contradictions' or tensions still troubling the multinational Soviet state. First, the differences arising between the interests of a particular nation and those of the Soviet people as a whole, especially in the economic sphere. Second, strains in relations between the national republics over the solution of regional economic problems. Third, tensions between different nationalities within the republics. And fourth, difficulties occurring in workplaces, educational and scientific institutions and creative organizations where the personnel was multinational. Although Tavadov was careful to cover himself by denying that these 'contradictions' were 'antagonistic in nature' and led to 'social conflicts', his analysis indicated that national tensions permeated Soviet society and that the national problem was more complex and serious than had hitherto been admitted.[27]

Occasionally, forthright articles defending the non-Russian languages and cultures also appeared. At the beginning of 1984, for example, an Uzbek scholar, H. Pulatov, called on his fellow-countrymen not to be ashamed of national pride and taking an interest in their national culture and identity. The study of the 'rich' past of the Uzbek people, he argued, 'should be used to contribute to the strengthening of socialist self-awareness'. Interestingly, Pulatov also endorsed the revised interpretation of fusion. 'The fusion of nations in the future,' he wrote, 'does not aim to cast aside or ignore the spiritual wealth of nations.'[28]

Another article in the same spirit appeared in May 1984 in a Byelorussian-language Komsomol newspaper. Written by the Byelorussian scholar, U. Konan, it reminded Byelorussians of their obligation 'to remember, preserve [and] cherish' their national language and culture.[29]

The publication of a few franker articles, though, was not accompanied by any noticeable change in nationalities policy or, for that matter, in the general political climate. In fact, there were also outspoken articles and speeches advocating what can only be described as a strict, 'no nonsense', attitude towards the non-Russians. In November 1984, for example, at an all-Union conference of heads of specialized councils in the field of historical studies, one of the Soviet Union's senior historians, Sergei Tikhvinskii, called for a reassertion of the centre's control over the writing of history in the non-Russian republics. Claiming that not all non-Russian historians sufficiently highlighted the role of the Russian people as a benefactor to the non-Russians, and that some of them were prone to 'national conceit' or 'narrow-mindedness', he declared that the choice of areas for study had to be guided 'by the need to reach political upbringing objectives and resolve the tasks of the ideological struggle'.[30]

There was even a call in print for a more aggressive language policy. On 26 February 1985 the ethnographer and secretary of the Scientific Council of the USSR Academy of Sciences for Nationality Problems, Mikhail Guboglo, published an article in the Estonian Party daily, *Sovetskaia Estoniia*, arguing in effect for a further diminution of the role of the non-Russian languages. In view of the fact that educated people are supposed to know Russian, why, he asked, did so much inferior literature continue to be published in the national languages, why were films in Estonia, where there was a large Russian minority, dubbed into Estonian, and so on. The appearance of such a provocative piece in a republic where the language issue was particularly sensitive is unlikely to have occurred without approval 'from above'.[31]

Under Chernenko the anti-corruption campaign continued, and Uzbekistan became the principal target. The death in October 1983 of the Uzbek Party leader Rashidov, who had been a close friend of Brezhnev's, had cleared the way for an extensive purge of corrupt Party and government officials. It now transpired that under Rashidov there had been serious economic mismanagement, massive padding of cotton production figures and embezzlement, not to mention rampant nepotism and bribery. The situation in the republic that produced about two-thirds of the USSR's total cotton crop was considered so alarming by Moscow that Slavs began to be sent in to take over important posts. Thus, in July 1984, for the first time since 1956, a Russian was appointed republican procurator.[32]

By the end of the year it also became more apparent that there were other aspects to the crackdown in Uzbekistan apart from economic considerations. The new Uzbek Party leader, Inamzhon Usmankhodzhaev, acknowledged as much when, at the beginning of November, he answered enquiries from the readers of *Izvestia* about the situation in his republic. He admitted that Islam and 'outdated, and backward views' still posed a problem and that there were Party members, highly educated ones at that, who took part in Moslem religious rituals. It was important, he commented, to combat such negative vestiges wherever they remained, 'but for regions with a rapidly growing population, like Central Asia, where the influence of survivals of the past is more perceptible, it is doubly important'.[33] Furthermore, the following month Uzbek writers were criticized in the press for ideological shortcomings in their works.[34]

Resistance in a neo-Stalinist climate

The tough policies towards national rights campaigners and dissidents in general remained. In fact, new measures were introduced under Andropov and Chernenko which made Soviet laws even more repressive. In the labour camps conditions became harsher, and several prominent non-Russian political prisoners died because of ill-treatment and medical neglect. In 1981 the death behind barbed wire of the Estonian activist Iurii Kukk had been a great shock.[35] In 1984, however, three Ukrainian activists died in the camps: Oleksii Tykhyi, Yurii Lytvyn and Valerii Marchenko.[36] Between 1983 and 1985, the Soviet Ukrainian press published purported recantations from four Ukrainian dissidents who were either still serving sentences or had recently been freed: Vasyl' Romaniuk, Ivan Sokul's'kyi, Oles' Berdnyk and Yurii

Shukhevych-Berezyns'kyi.[37] Sokul's'kyi later managed to get a message out of the labour camp in which he was being held. In it, he denied that he had recanted and described the inhuman conditions in which he was being kept and the pressure aimed at breaking his resistance.[38]

Towards the end of the year, the former head of the Armenian Helsinki monitoring group, Eduard Arutiunian, died. He had been released from confinement only when he was in the last stages of a terminal illness.[39] Another example of the worsening conditions is what occurred in March 1984 when the mother of the leading Estonian dissident Mart Niklus went to visit her son in Chistopol Prison. Niklus was beaten up by the guards in front of his mother for refusing to speak with her in Russian.[40]

Despite the neo-Stalinist climate, opposition to Moscow's nationalities policy, and to Moscow itself, continued to manifest itself in different forms and locations. In the Baltic republics and Western Ukraine, where the authorities still showed signs of unease about 'contagion' from Poland, nationalism remained a potent force.[41] Where it overlapped with religion, in this case Catholicism, it was particularly strong. Although in Moscow the oldest regular Soviet *samizdat* journal, the *Chronicle of Current Events*, had by now been suppressed, in Lithuania *The Chronicle of the Lithuanian Catholic Church* was still appearing and by the beginning of 1985, 65 issues had come out. In the Western Ukraine, in the spring of 1984, Ukrainian Catholic activists began publishing their own *samizdat* journal, *A Chronicle of the Catholic Church in the Ukraine*.[42]

In both the Ukrainian Catholic chronicle and in Lithuanian *samizdat* journals there was strong revulsion against the Soviet occupation of Afghanistan and the fact that non-Russians were being made to fight and sacrifice their lives in what the Lithuanian and Ukrainian dissidents viewed as the latest 'Russian' imperial venture.[43] As before, it was difficult to assess what impact the war in Afghanistan was having on the traditionally Moslem population. The fact that the Soviet media frequently referred to the Afghan insurgents as Basmachi, the name given to the Moslem groups which fought against Soviet rule in Central Asia from 1918 to 1932 with the aim of establishing an independent Islamic state, and in the final years of that period fighting against forced collectivization, could not have helped matters.

The situation on the eve of Gorbachev's accession

In December 1984, when Chernenko was visibly ailing, *Kommunist* published a major article signed by him that evidently represented a consensus in the leadership's thinking about what the Party's long-term strategy and new programme were. It added more gloom to Andropov's sober appraisal of what the future held for the USSR. The leitmotif of the article was that the achievement of communism had been put off indefinitely and that the interim would consist of what Chernenko euphemistically termed 'a historically long period of developed socialism'. Stressing the 'colossal amount of work' that still lay ahead and 'the difficulties and contradictions' that would have to be overcome, the Soviet leader stated that from now on the road to communism would be constructed 'without a shadow of utopianism'. The two crucial tasks for the foreseeable future were, on the one hand, to raise the efficiency of production and accelerate the country's economic development, and on the other, to instil a better work ethic by further inculcation of the population with 'socialist' values.[44]

That same month, Chernenko's heir apparent, Mikhail Gorbachev, elaborated on these priorities in a keynote address to an all-Union conference on ideology. Dwelling primarily on the need to improve and modernize the country's economy, he seemed to emulate Andropov in his stress on the need for order and better organization, discipline and political vigilance. Although Gorbachev mentioned the need to abandon 'obsolete approaches and methods', he had nothing new to say about nationalities policy. He simply described the sphere of national relations as 'the most complex area of social relations' and placed at the top of his list of outstanding problems the 'rational distribution of productive forces and their further integration into the overall national complex'.[45] Thus, at the time of Chernenko's death in March 1985 and Gorbachev's takeover, there did not seem to be any real grounds to expect changes in the nationalities policy.

15

Gorbachev and the Advent of Glasnost'

Gorbachev brought a dynamic and assertive style of leadership that had not been witnessed since Khrushchev had been at the helm. From the very outset, the new leader made it clear that his first priority was to reinvigorate the stagnant economy, and he spoke of the need to 'restructure the economic mechanism'. The new talk of reform remained very vague, though, and initially what it all seemed to amount to in practice was the familiar prescription of stricter labour discipline and firmer action against corruption. Gorbachev and members of his 'team' did call for more *glasnost'*, or openness in public life, as well as for more attention to the 'human factor' in social and economic life; but these, too, appeared to be mere slogans devoid of any real substance.

Although at the Central Committee plenum in April 1985 Gorbachev did acknowledge in passing that it was 'important to enhance the responsibility of republic and local agencies' for economic, cultural and social affairs,[1] this was not a theme that he elaborated or to which he subsequently returned. Indeed, he gave no indication of being at all interested in grappling with the nationalities question: during his first year in power he made no major statements on this issue. His approach appeared to be to avoid tinkering with this thorny problem unless economic exigencies demanded it.

This does not mean that Gorbachev was unaware of the national question. Quite likely, although he had not served in a non-Russian republic, he had had his fair share of exposure to it. After all, he had made his political career in the ethnically mixed Stavropol' Territory in southern Russia where, among others, representatives of some of the smaller traditionally Moslem peoples – including ones that were deported by Stalin – live. Gorbachev himself points out in his book *Perestroika* that he spent 'many years in the North Caucasus, a region inhabited by a host of nationalities', and whose history 'contains several gloomy pages'. He also admits that he knows from his 'own experience' how sensitive the Mountaineers there are 'to any displays of arrogance towards them'.[2]

Although Gorbachev goes on to claim in his book that relations between the different nationalities in the Stavropol' Territory are harmonious enough, the evidence suggests that the situation in this region has not been entirely satisfactory. In January 1985, for example, *Pravda* reported that some local intellectuals had still not freed themselves of 'a compromising attitude towards vestigial practices' and implied that there was complacency about the Party line on nationalism and religion.[3] Three years later, *Sovetskaia Rossiia* was more blunt. It spelt out that 'the problem of national relations . . . is very serious in the Stavropol' Territory' and that its management was one of the 'main tasks' facing the local Party leadership.[4]

A new leadership – but no new nationalities policy

Gorbachev may have had some experience of dealing with aspects of the national question, but did he understand national feelings and was he sensitive to nationality issues? The first indications were not encouraging. On 8 May 1985, in his address on the 40th anniversary of the defeat of Nazi Germany, Gorbachev echoed Stalin's famous toast of 24 May 1945 eulogizing the 'leading' role of the Great Russian people during World War II, which had ushered in a wave of Russian chauvinism.[5] A few weeks later, during a visit to Kiev, the capital of the Ukraine, he twice referred in an extemporaneous street conversation shown on Soviet Television to the Soviet Union as Russia. Referring to the USSR's economic recovery after World War II, Gorbachev exclaimed:

> We coped. They predicted that Russia would never rise again after the war. But we rose again . . . For all people who are striving for good, Russia – the Soviet Union, I mean – that is what we call it now, and what it is in fact, for them it is a bulwark.[6]

There were also some signs that the Gorbachev leadership would be prepared to tolerate a certain amount of Russian nationalism. The Russian nationalist current in literature had been allowed to reassert itself during the second half of 1984 when Chernenko had been fading and Gorbachev had been responsible for ideology. Within weeks of the Gorbachev succession, the controversial painter and ideologue of the "Russian group", Il'ia Glazunov, was appointed director of a new State Museum of Decorative and Applied Art, situated in the Grand Palace of Catherine II's unfinished residence in Tsaritsyno outside Moscow.[7] In June 1985, 'Russian nationalist' forces were allowed to exploit the lavish celebrations of the 80th anniversary of the birth of Mikhail Sholokhov.[8] Later in the year, in November, the army newspaper *Krasnaia zvezda* carried an article recalling Stalin's wartime speech in which he had invoked the spirit of tsarist Russia's military leaders and stressing 'the glory of previous generations of Russian fighting men'.[9]

On the other hand, no corresponding gestures were made to placate the non-Russians. The appointment some time in the summer of 1985 of Aleksandr Iakovlev – the critic of Russian nationalism who had been 'banished' to Canada in 1973 – to head the Propaganda Department of the CPSU Central Committee provided limited comfort. His attack on Russophilism had been delivered from an 'internationalist' position that was hostile to all types of nationalism. Furthermore, there was no evidence to suggest that Iakovlev, whose career had taken off again in 1983 after he had arranged a successful visit by Gorbachev to Canada, owed his new position to his reputation as a foe of Russian nationalism. In fact, the new propaganda chief seemed to keep his distance from nationality issues and his presence certainly did not deter Russian intellectuals from beginning to air their concerns on cultural and environmental issues.

A more powerful figure at this stage was Egor Ligachev, who was elevated to the Politburo in April 1985 and assumed responsibility for ideology. By the summer he had established himself as the apparent second-in-command. A stern, rather puritanical figure who is believed to have been responsible for launching the new campaign against alcoholism, he was also very much a Russian and had a soft spot for Siberia where he had spent most of his political career. According to the *Guardian*'s Moscow correspondent, Martin Walker,

> During his years in Tomsk, Ligachev became something of a hero among Russian conservationists for the drive and money he put into preserving the old heart of the city. He was also the driving force behind the celebrated Tomsk Library, which has built an unrivalled collection of original manuscripts of Soviet literature, usually donated by the authors . . . He personally persuaded Soviet authors to visit Tomsk, to give public lectures and classes, to stay there as the city's guests and to write on Siberian themes.[10]

Whatever Ligachev's role behind the scenes, it was soon evident that cultural figures promoting Russian national values were being given a platform in the press. For instance, Glazunov appeared in *Pravda* on 11 June with a call for a return to the 'school of Russian art'. On 3 November, *Izvestia* published an interview with Valentin Rasputin in which he discussed the environmental damage being done to Siberia by overzealous and uncaring bureaucrats and planners. What was striking about his comments was his central message: that a person's primary duty is to his or her native land. Almost as if he were addressing Gorbachev and his 'team' directly, this leading Russian 'village prose' writer advised:

> Depth and quality of patriotism manifest themselves when a person invested with authority and power – and, similarly, a person who carries out orders – gears his actions to the benefit they bring to his native land – and not just short-term benefit that may turn into disaster tomorrow.[11]

It was Ligachev, rather than Gorbachev, who lost no time in setting a tough tone in the area of nationalities policy. During a visit to Armenia in June 1985, he stressed that it was necessary to 'assert Soviet patriotism and international- ism with diverse practical deeds'. Specifically, he mentioned 'the fulfilment of collaborative deliveries to other republics, the inter-republican exchange of specialists and students, mastery of the Russian language – the language of inter-republican contact'. He also singled out the issue of 'the participation of the working people of the Union republics in the commercial development of the productive forces of Siberia and the Far East'. More had to be done in this area, he stressed. This was 'required by the country, and thus by each republic too'. Ligachev's comments had the ring of a command rather than the customary exhortation.

At the same time, the new ideology chief also avoided alluding to the existence of any national tensions in the Soviet Union and demonstrated the kind of smugness that had been familiar during the Brezhnev years. In the same speech, delivered in Erevan, Ligachev proclaimed:

> The entire history of the Soviet state is essentially a hymn to the great friendship of the peoples and to the great life-giving force of the CPSU's Leninist nationalities policy. We have created a society in which the truly harmonious combination of statewide interests and the interests of each of the republics and the flowering of all nations and ethnic groups are ensured.[12]

Another ominous development was the appearance in *Pravda* on 21 June 1985 of an unusually hard-line article which, though ostensibly directed at the USSR's East European neighbours, also pertained to the non-Russian peoples of the Soviet Union. 'Nationalism', the pseudonymous author, O. Vladimirov, claimed,

> continues to be the chief hope of the class enemy. The West's propaganda services are trying to capitalize on problems that the socialist countries have inherited from the past, to impose pseudo-patriotic, nationalistic sentiments on them, and to exaggerate 'injustices' and 'blank spots' in the history of the Soviet Union's relations with a number of fraternal countries.
>
> The experience of the socialist countries shows that deviations from the Marxist-Leninist line are related, in one way or another, to nationalistic tendencies. On the domestic level, this may lead to a narrowing of the influence of Marxist-Leninist ideology, the appearance of modified theories of 'national communism' and the exacerbation of the nationalities question. On the level of relations with other socialist countries, nationalistic manifestations are undoubtedly capable of weakening internationalist ties. Nationalism, when it takes the form of covert – let alone overt – Russophobia and anti-Sovietism, undermines the unity and solidarity of the socialist peoples and damages socialism as a whole and each country in particular.[13]

It looked then as if the new Soviet leadership was determined to rein in its East European allies and to reassert Moscow's authority within the socialist community. Similarly, at home, the centre continued to strengthen its control over the non-Russian republics under the banner of combating economic inefficiency and corruption. As before, Central Asia, and especially Uzbekistan, was the main target. In what seemed to be a hallmark of the new

Gorbachev leadership, considerations of efficiency took precedence over tact. National sensibilities were disregarded and Russians were brought in to fill strategic posts. As a result of this 'exchange of personnel', by early 1986, the Uzbeks, who in 1979 made up 68.7 per cent of the population of their republic, no longer constituted a majority in either the republican Party Central Committee Secretariat or Bureau (equivalent to a republican Polit-buro). Even the post of first secretary of the Tashkent city Party Committee was taken over by a Slav.[14] In the last two months of 1986 the Party leaders in the Kirghiz, Turkmen and Tadzhik republics were replaced.

What was no doubt also worrying for the Central Asians was the fact that 'Sibaral', the Siberian rivers diversion scheme, was omitted from the draft guidelines of the Twelfth Five-Year Plan (1986–1990) published in November 1985, although the northern rivers (of Northern Russia) diversion project was included. To add to the disappointment, from the end of 1985 an influential lobby of Russians opposed to the latter scheme – and by implication also to 'Sibaral' – on cultural and environmental grounds, began to crystallize and make itself heard.

The only modest improvement in nationalities policy was limited to the Meskhetians. As early as June 1985 their case was raised by Revaz Dzhaparidze during a round table discussion organized by the Writers' Union of Georgia. He revealed that the Georgian intelligentsia had been lobbying on behalf of the Meskhetians for over a quarter of a century. From his statement and an article which appeared in the Georgian press in September of that year, it emerged that during recent years the authorities had been allowing a trickle of Meskhetians to return to their homeland in Georgia. Now, at last, their case was out in the open.[15]

The change of leadership, however, did not bring any relaxation in policy towards dissent and the treatment of political prisoners. During Gorbachev's first year in office, non-Russian activists who were imprisoned (sometimes after being rearrested while completing a previous sentence) included: the Ukrainians, Mykola Horbal' (11 years), Petro Ruban (14 years) and Iosyf Terelia (12 years); the Lithuanian, Vladas Lapeinis (7 years); the Estonian Jaan Korb (8 years); the Georgian Merab Kostava (2 years); the Armenian Paruir Airikian (3 years); and the Jew Roald Zelinichok (3 years). There were also more deaths of non-Russian political prisoners being held in labour camps. In April 1985, the 28-year-old Armenian Ishkhan Mkrtchian was apparently driven to commit suicide.[16] On 4 September that same year, the outstanding Ukrainian poet and national rights campaigner Vasyl' Stus died at the age of 47 in the sixth year of his second term of imprisonment.[17]

Despite the ever more frequent references in the Soviet press to *glasnost'* and 'the human factor', Gorbachev made it clear that he was not contemplat-ing ushering in political liberalization or a new wave of de-Stalinization. In February 1986, barely two weeks before the Twenty-seventh Party Congress was due to be held, Gorbachev gave a candid interview to the French Communist Party daily *L'Humanité*, which was also reproduced in the Soviet press. In it, he denied that there were any political prisoners in the Soviet Union, described Andrei Sakharov as a criminal and dismissed the issue of Soviet Jewry as 'part of a frenzied anti-Soviet campaign, a veritable psychological war against the USSR'. Asked whether 'the vestiges of Stalinism have been overcome in the Soviet Union', Gorbachev replied:

> Stalinism is a concept thought up by the enemies of communism and widely used to discredit the Soviet Union and socialism as a whole.[18]

The new Party programme – more of the same for the non-Russians?

In October 1985 the draft of the new Party programme was published. The section on the nationalities question was only half as long as its 1961 counterpart, and it contained no changes in basic policy. As before, this was formulated as the promotion of the 'further flourishing of nations and ethnic groups and their steady drawing together', leading to their complete unity 'in the remote historical future'. There was no mention of 'fusion'. Also, as was to be expected, the notion of a 'new social and international community – the Soviet people' was enshrined in the revised programme.

The only real surprise was that the new draft did not single out the Russian people and praise them for their fraternal aid to the non-Russians, as was the case in the 1961 document. Nor did it refer to 'formerly backward peoples'. The importance of the Russian language was reiterated, and this time the need for the non-Russians to 'master' Russian in addition to their own language was stressed. References to the possible expansion of the rights of the Union republics in economic management and the creation of inter-republican economic agencies were dropped, suggesting that no substantial decentralization of economic decision-making to the republics was envisaged. There was also no mention of the inter-republican boundaries losing their importance as this issue had been effectively defused in the mid-1970s during the drafting of the new Soviet Constitution.

The Party's 'basic tasks' in the field of national relations were broken down into three groupings: the 'all-round consolidation and development of the multinational Soviet state', entailing intolerance towards all manifestations of localism and national narrow-mindedness; the economic imperatives, with their emphasis on the rational use of resources and the proper contribution of the republics and autonomous units to the good of the 'integral countrywide economic complex'; and the 'development of the Soviet people's single culture – socialist in content, diverse in national forms, and internationalist in spirit'. Included here were the standard statements about the mutual enrichment of cultures, and the equality and free development of languages.[19]

For all the talk of *glasnost'* and the new emphasis on facing up to the complications in the area of national relations, the ensuing 'discussion' in the Soviet press of the relevant section of the draft Party programme was very restricted. In the letters that appeared in *Pravda* between November 1985 and January 1986, for instance, there were calls for even more stress to be placed on the Russian language, for the role of the Russian people to be lauded, and for an end to affirmative action practices in higher education. The subject of federalism, or rather the future of the federal structure, was disposed of in two letters. The few proposed amendments reflecting the concerns of the non-Russians were markedly modest. In the event, none of the suggestions was incorporated into the final version of the programme.

While much of the discussion appeared to be pro forma, there were two notable exceptions. The perennial question of 'fusion' was raised at the beginning of 1986 by two Moscow-based Armenian scholars, Tsolak Stepanian and Eduard Tadevosian, who proposed that the concept be included in the new Party programme.[20] On 21 February, though, Yurii Katcharava, writing in the Georgian daily, *Kommunist*, denounced the 'irresponsible and frivolous attitude towards theory' and 'inclination to run ahead' on the part of 'certain researchers' and 'bad propagandists', which, he claimed, had led to erroneous conclusions about fusion and the solution of the nationalities question.[21]

First glimmers of *glasnost'* – in Moscow

By the end of 1985 it was beginning to look as if Russian writers were being given the opportunity to be more candid and to get things off their chests. Almost as soon as he had taken over, Gorbachev had called for more *glasnost'*. Initially though, the new candour was applied very selectively as a means of exposing and weeding out corruption and inefficiency. There was no mention in the Soviet press of the anti-Soviet protests and clashes between Latvian and Russian youths in Riga in May that were reported in Western newspapers, for example. Gradually, however, the situation began to change. Anxious to get his economic restructuring drive under way, Gorbachev started wooing the Soviet Union's intelligentsia, particularly the opinion-makers – writers and media workers – in the hope that they would not only back him but also use their influence to mobilize popular support for his policies. To win them over, he began loosening controls in the cultural sphere and reducing censorship. At first the main beneficiary was the Russian creative intelligentsia, and as a result, the new cultural thaw was largely restricted to Moscow and Leningrad.

The Russian poet Evgenii Evtushenko played an important role in broadening *glasnost'*. In September *Pravda* published his poem 'Don't-Rock-the-Boaters' in which he touched on such themes as censorship in literature and collectivization.[22] His poem 'Fuku', which appeared in *Novyi mir* in November, dealt, among other things, with Beria, the notorious Kolyma camps of the Stalin period, and even the disturbing phenomenon of young Soviet neo-Nazis.[23]

Evtushenko also made an outspoken speech at the Congress of Writers of the RSFSR which took place in December 1985 and at which *glasnost'* made itself felt. Focusing on a whole series of 'blank spots' in Soviet history and contemporary life, ranging from 'dekulakization' and the Stalin Terror to shortages of food and the privileges enjoyed by the Soviet *nomenklatura*, he stressed that 'articles rhetorically calling for publicity are not the same as publicity itself'. This and quite a few other bold passages from his speech failed, however, to appear in the Soviet press.[24]

The more 'nationalist' Russian writers, such as Yurii Bondarev, Valentin Rasputin and Sergei Zalygin, made use of the opportunity to air their opposition to the northern rivers diversion scheme as well as their concern about the preservation of Russian culture, historical monuments and Russia's environment. Rasputin also indicated that Russian writers felt free again to express their national feeling. He declared: 'There is no life for us, and we have nothing to say, apart from Russia.' He went on to affirm something that many non-Russian writers had been arguing for years: 'A healthy internationalist feeling rests on national feeling – such things hardly need to be explained.'

Non-Russian writers from the Russian Federation also made use of the *glasnost'* at the RSFSR Writers' Congress. Representatives of two of the small minorities living in the Russian Federation voiced some of their complaints. A Mordovian pointed out that for quite a few of the small nationalities dispersed throughout the Russian Republic it was difficult to obtain literature published in their language and that his own people 'badly needed' their own children's magazines. A Iakut delegate, however, raised an issue that affected other non-Russians as well. He complained:

> Iakutia today is the native land not only of Iakuts, Evens, Evenki, Iukagir. It is the homeland of hundreds of thousands of Russians, Ukrainians, Byelorussians and Tatars who were born, study and work in the harsh northern land. But in the schools in which children of the non-indigenous nationalities study, they do not offer courses in the history of Iakutia or its literature. Graduates of these schools, well informed about the history of ancient Rome or Egypt, do not possess even elementary knowledge about their own native republic . . . I am talking about this because it is the situation not only in our republic but in other republics, territories and provinces as well.[25]

For the time being, this was the maximum openness that the non-Russians could expect. For their Russian colleagues, however, this was only the start. In December, the campaign against the northern rivers diversion project began to receive coverage in the Soviet press. *Sovetskaia Rossiia* led the way by publishing criticism of the scheme by the ecologist and UN environmental expert, Mikhail Lemeshev.[26] On 3 January it also carried a letter from a group of distinguished Russian literary figures, including Valentin Rasputin, Vasilii Belov, Sergei Zalygin and Academician Dmitrii Likachev. The following month, the economist Abel Aganbegian and others added their voices in the pages of *Pravda*.[27]

In the early part of 1986 there was very limited *glasnost'* at the republican Party congresses which preceded the Twenty-seventh Party Congress. Nevertheless, some of the problems that had been evaded during the discussion of the new edition of the Party programme were brought up. In Estonia, the Party first secretary, Karl Vaino, devoted considerable attention in his speech to the persistence of nationalism in his republic, the lack of enthusiasm on the part of the Estonians for Russian immigrants and the Russian language and the susceptibility of the population to Western influences. He also revealed that the Collegium of the USSR Ministry of Culture had criticized Estonia's theatres and concert halls for having too much of an 'Estonian' repertoire and not including enough works that promoted 'internationalist upbringing'.[28]

In the case of the Central Asian republics, in Tadzhikistan, Kirghizia and Uzbekistan, concern was expressed about the resilience of religion and its links with nationalism, as well as the survival of 'backward traditions and customs'. Alluding to Iran and Afghanistan, a speaker at the Tadzhik Party Congress stated that, 'doubtless' Islam had been 'activized' to some degree 'by the circumstances surrounding regional events of recent years in certain countries'.[29]

At the Uzbek Party Congress there were extraordinary developments. Here the republican Party leader, Inamzhon Usmankhodzhaev, delivered a scathing attack on his predecessor, Rashidov, who had been the Uzbek Party first secretary for 24 years until his death in 1983. The criticism focused mainly on the abuses and corruption that had gone on under the latter. But there were no less sensational disclosures about Rashidov's approach to nationalities policy. According to Usmankhodzhaev, 'major miscalculations were made in the selection, placement and education of ideological cadres'. Antireligious propaganda had been neglected; 'religious rites' had 'captivated many people', including a significant number of Party and Komsomol members; unofficial Islam had not been combated forcefully enough, and the 'class enemy' was reviving 'long-obsolete ideas of pan-Islamism' and inflaming 'nationalist passions'.[30]

This was not all. Rashidov had claimed enormous successes in increasing proficiency in Russian among Uzbeks. At the congress, however, it transpired that during his tenure 'these ideas were not, however, backed up by concrete organizational work', and that 'the teaching of Russian deteriorated in a number of schools'.[31]

Significantly, Usmankhodzhaev also disclosed that at a time when the authorities were intensifying their efforts to contain religion and nationalism in Central Asia, in Uzbekistan, at any rate, the drive against corruption was being viewed by some Uzbeks as more of a political than an economic action. He acknowledged that 'there have been individual, albeit veiled, attempts to portray the struggle to restore order and justice as an almost anti-national campaign'.[32]

The Twenty-seventh Party Congress
With an unchanged course in nationalities policy already plotted in the new edition of the Party programme, the Twenty-seventh Party Congress in February 1986 produced no real surprises. Although Gorbachev specified that the development of national relations was of 'enormous importance' for the Soviet multinational state, neither he nor Ligachev, who was the only other member of the Soviet leadership to address the nationalities question, devoted much attention to this issue. Nevertheless, from what they said, it was clear where the emphasis lay. Gorbachev again accentuated the economic element, stressing that it was 'especially important' to ensure that all of the republics put the interests of the single national economic complex above their own, and that no manifestations of localism were tolerated. Ligachev, for his part, concentrated on the problem of due representation.

The Soviet leader adhered to what had become the set formula in the 1980s in high-level statements on the nationalities question, with one notable exception: he omitted any reference to the debt of gratitude supposedly owed by the non-Russians to the Russians. After rehearsing the usual 'outstanding' achievements in the area of national relations claimed by the Soviet state, Gorbachev stressed that this did not mean that 'national processes are without their problems'. He went on to acknowledge that the perennial evils of 'national exclusiveness', 'localism' and 'parasitism' had not yet been fully overcome, and that 'reactionary-nationalistic and religious survivals' conflicting with the official ideology were still being encountered 'in certain works of literature, the arts and in scientific works'. The Party, he declared, was well aware of the need to proceed tactfully in its nationalities policy, but it would continue to wage a 'principled struggle against all manifestations of national narrow-mindedness and arrogance, nationalism and chauvinism'.[33]

Ligachev was more direct and to the point. The central theme of his address was the need to improve cadres policy and, in particular, to strengthen the representation of Russians in the Party and state agencies of those non-Russian republics where, as he put it, 'localist, compatriot (*zemliacheskie*) attitudes' had 'taken the upper hand', leading to 'self-isolation, stagnation and other negative phenomena'.[34] Needless to say, he did not talk explicitly about the status and role of Russian personnel in the non-Russian republics, but from the context, from what was happening in the Central Asian republics, and from what various Soviet specialists on the nationalities question had been saying quite openly, it was clear that this is what the problem of the 'correct' selection and placement of cadres boiled down to.

Another indication of the Kremlin's approach to the question of due representation and the exchange of personnel was the fact that there was no significant improvement in representation for the non-Russians at the apex of power. With the exception of the Azerbaijani Aliev, promoted by Andropov to full membership of the Politburo and made first deputy prime minister; Shevardnadze, elevated to full membership of the Politburo and made minister of foreign affairs; and Nikolai Sliunkov, the Byelorussian Party leader, who was made a candidate member of the Politburo under Gorbachev, all the appointments to the Politburo and Party Secretariat since Andropov had been Russians.

Nevertheless, one potentially significant concession was announced at the Congress by Ligachev. He raised an important theme connected with nationalities policy – one which was somewhat out of keeping with the Party's usual warnings about preoccupation with, or idealization of, the past. 'The Party,' he stated, 'highly values and supports the upsurge in patriotic feeling, of which we are all aware and the increased public interest in the homeland and the wealth of our age-old, multinational culture.' He went on to praise efforts to preserve 'all that is dear to the people's memory' and declared that 'the Party must take people strictly to task for neglect of national shrines'.[35]

Central Asia remains the main problem

At first it seemed as if it was mainly the Russians who were to be given more scope to affirm their past. On 13 March 1986 the distinguished Russian literary scholar Academician Likhachev, a representative of the liberal wing of Russian nationalism, was given 90 minutes on Soviet television to air his views. Among other things, he presented the 'Russian' case against the northern rivers diversion scheme. Likhachev asked:

> Why does the population of the Russian North, which has lived there since the twelfth century, and is exceptional in its qualities, including its moral qualities and its work traditions, its folk traditions, its literary traditions, and so on, have to give up its monuments, its work traditions, to lose its native country in order to divert water to the south?

The academician's television appearance highlighted the clash of interests between Russians concerned with the protection of Russia's environment and their national heritage and Central Asians desperate to secure more water for their parched southern republics. At the Party Congress, Usmankhodzhaev, speaking for the pro-Sibaral lobby, had reiterated that the fulfilment of 'national economic tasks' in Uzbekistan was being hindered by the 'shortage of water resources'. Expressing dismay about the continuing 'fruitless' discussions about the Siberian rivers diversion project, he had asked: 'We need an answer at long last: what is to be done?'[36]

An implicit reply was forthcoming. The northern rivers diversion project was deleted from the final text of the Guidelines for the Twelfth Five-Year Plan adopted by the Party Congress. Furthermore, on 4 March, the deputy chief of the state planning organization, GOSPLAN, Leonard Vid, confirmed that both the Siberian and northern rivers diversion schemes had been shelved.[37]

There were several signs after the Party Congress that the Kremlin continued to view the Central Asian republics as a region requiring close attention. In early April 1986 an all-Union scientific conference on improving national relations was held in Tashkent and it seems to have focused largely on the Central Asian nationalities.[38] The following month in the same city a two-day conference on improving the military-patriotic education of young people and their preparation for military service was convened by the Central Committees of the Uzbek and Turkmen Parties.[39]

The problem of integrating Central Asian conscripts into the armed forces was one issue that had been receiving considerable attention in the press. The military was pressing for better Russian-language training and, from time to time, had even emphasized the need for the basic cultural needs of non-Russian soldiers to be respected. Some effort had also been put into encouraging non-Slavs to apply for officer training.[40]

In May *Kommunist* published an article by Academician Bromlei providing an authoritative overview of the Party's approach to nationalities policy in the light of the new Party programme and what had been said at the Party Congress. Once again, what was striking was that most of the problems which he discussed – especially due representation, insufficient migration to labour-deficit areas and inadequate knowledge of Russian – were connected primarily with the Central Asian republics. As before, there were the customary warnings about manifestations of national narrow-mindedness and idealization of the national past. There was, however, one refreshing note in Bromlei's piece. He stressed that 'a major aspect of the language problem' in the non-Russian republics was the need for Russians and other non-indigenous groups to make an effort to learn the language of the indigenous population.[41]

This theme was taken up more forthrightly at the Congress of Latvian Writers in early April 1986 by the Russian author Marina Kostenetskaia. She criticized 'Russian writers who, having lived for many years among Latvians, do not learn their language, and are insufficiently familiar with the history of their national culture'. Readers in other parts of the Soviet Union were able to read a brief summary of what she had said in *Literaturnaia gazeta*.[42] Even more outspokenness was shown later that month by Estonian writers at their congress. They not only strongly criticized censorship, the distortion of history and the proscription of writers deemed politically unacceptable, but also such restrictions as the lack of freedom to travel abroad. Furthermore, as in Latvia, the Estonians devoted considerable attention to the language question and the strained relations with Russians living in their republic. The discussion appears to have placed the authorities in something of a dilemma, for it took about four months before a decent amount of what had been said appeared in the Estonian press.[43]

Environmental issues and the Chernobyl' nuclear disaster

A month before the Estonian Writers' Congress, a group of Estonian scientists had sent a *samizdat* letter to the West reflecting the mounting concern in the republic about the ecological threat from mining and construction projects that had been decided upon in Moscow and the further inflow of Russians into Estonia which these schemes would entail.[44] For the Estonians, at any rate, the environmental issue was already identified with the nationalities problem.

In other republics, too, there were signs of greater interest in environmental questions, including the location and safety of nuclear power plants. As early as March 1983, for instance, a Tatar literary monthly had indicated that there was some local unease about the construction of a nuclear power station on the Kama River in the Tatar ASSR.[45] In March 1986, 365 Armenian intellectuals addressed an open letter to Gorbachev protesting against the alarming level of industrial pollution in their republic and revealing that there was also widespread concern about plans to construct a second nuclear reactor at the Metsamor atomic power station outside Erevan.[46]

The Ukraine, a highly industrialized republic which shared a border with several of the USSR's partners in COMECON, had been designated the major centre of the Soviet nuclear power industry. According to what the Ukrainian writer Mykola Nehoda told the *Christian Science Monitor*, public concern about nuclear energy existed in his republic even before the nuclear disaster at Chernobyl' on 26 April 1986.[47] Indeed, less than a month before the accident, the Ukrainian literary weekly *Literaturna Ukraina* published an article criticizing the poor safety standards and numerous problems at the giant plant near Kiev.[48] Furthermore, a week before the explosion at Chernobyl', the president of the Ukrainian Academy of Sciences, Boris Paton, had proposed that the republic's scientists make a study of safety procedures at nuclear power plants and review how sites for them are selected.[49]

When the 'impossible' happened at Chernobyl' and one of the USSR's biggest and 'safest' nuclear power plants blew its top, it was three days before Moscow acknowledged the world's worst nuclear accident. The main radiation cloud was blown in a north-west direction by the wind from northern Ukraine, through Byelorussia and across the Baltic republics into Scandinavia. Only after the Swedes had expressed their concern and the Polish Government had started issuing warnings about radiation contamination did the Soviet leadership gradually begin providing information. Yet even at the height of the danger and uncertainty, the Soviet authorities attempted to minimize the scale of the disaster and to create the impression that the situation was under control. On 1 May, the May Day celebrations in Kiev were transformed into what one Western author calls 'a surrealistic charade' as thousands of youngsters were paraded before the Ukrainian Party leaders.[50]

The Kremlin's initial response to the Chernobyl' catastrophe exposed the limits of *glasnost'*. Faced with strong criticism from abroad and shock and confusion at home, the Soviet leadership seems to have realized that secrecy was not the way to handle the crisis. After about a fortnight it began to make amends. Details about what had occurred were gradually released and the accident and its implications began to be discussed in the press. The Chernobyl' disaster also appears to have led the Kremlin to review its general policy towards dealing with information and debate. Thus, what had seemed a major setback for the campaign for more openness ended up giving *glasnost'* new impetus.

Inevitably, the Chernobyl' nuclear disaster raised awareness and concern about environmental issues among the Soviet population. In the non-Russian republics it also appears to have sharpened sensitivities about the extent of Moscow's control over them and the power of the central ministries. This was particularly evident in the Ukraine where the accident traumatized the population and goaded the nation's writers, and eventually also scientists, into action.

The non-Russians start taking *glasnost'* at face value

Less than a month and a half after the Chernobyl' disaster, the Writers' Union of the Ukraine held its Ninth Congress. The tone at the meeting was set in the opening speech by Oles' Honchar, the leading Ukrainian literary figure. Chernobyl', he declared, had shaken not only his nation but the entire world. It had concentrated the minds of his colleagues and made them see their tasks and responsibilities to their people in a new light. Now they would have to show more civic courage and live up to the demands of the time.

Drawing on the example being set by Russian writers, Honchar argued that just as it was necessary to protect the environment, it was also important to conserve the nation's cultural and linguistic heritage. He castigated those who destroyed historical monuments or held that the Ukrainian language was 'without a future'. Having survived 'all the tsarist bans', he asserted, 'our beautiful language, in defiance of all those who do not care, had and will have . . . [a] future'. Other speakers at the congress endorsed his message that it was time for Ukrainian writers to begin speaking out in defence of the Ukrainian language and culture and voicing their concern about the damage to their republic's natural environment.[51]

The bolder spirit that had been evident at some of the congresses of the non-Russian Writers' Unions was all the more conspicuous during the Eighth Congress of Soviet Writers, which was held in Moscow in the last week of June 1986. On the very eve of this meeting an important taboo was broken. On 25 June, the first channel of Moscow television showed a discussion during which it emerged that there had recently been racial disturbances between Iakut and Russian students in Iakutsk. Although the programme provided few details, the very fact that the ethnic clashes had been mentioned in the Soviet media was a sign of progress.

It was at the Eighth Soviet Writers' Congress that the non-Russians can be said to have rediscovered their voices. Not only did they match their Russian colleagues in candour and outspokenness, but they also demonstrated that their concerns were rather different from those of their Russian colleagues. Whereas Russian representatives pressed, say, for the easing of censorship and the publication of the works of Boris Pasternak and Anna Akhmatova, one non-Russian after another protested about the displacement of their national languages by Russian and about Moscow's control over the national-cultural life of their nations generally. Pointing implicitly to the gap between theory and practice in nationalities policy, the non-Russians came out with what was probably the most forthright and comprehensive expression of grievances and demands voiced at any official forum since the 1920s.

Perhaps the most outspoken of the non-Russian representatives was the Ukrainian poet, Boris Oliinyk. He denounced 'home-grown' Russifiers, who in their zeal to implement 'political orthodoxy' in the republics 'in the name of the Russian people', act as 'great-power chauvinists'. Deploring the fact that the Ukrainian language was being progressively squeezed out of education and public and cultural life in his republic, he warned that 'the problem of the native language in the school, in the theatre, in the kindergartens – this is already a question of our Leninist nationalities policy, and the violation of its principles is very painful'. Here was a writer presenting the language problem in political terms and saying out loud the sort of thing that many non-Russian dissidents were still imprisoned for.

Oliinyk also emphasized that the Chernobyl' nuclear disaster had 'forced us to rethink a great deal'. Questioning the safety of nuclear energy, and implicitly also the ambitious Soviet nuclear energy programme, he declared:

Chernobyl' demands of us that we convince the scientists that sometimes they are confident to the point of cocksureness, seeming to know everything but in reality [knowing] far from everything.[52]

A Kalmyk writer praised Oliinyk's speech and lamented that his people 'had lost the sense of being masters' on their native land. The Tatar representative warned that 'if a man is deprived of the feeling of having a native land, he

turns into a rolling stone'. Janis Peters from Latvia referred to 'denationalization' and discussed the language question and the worrying demographic
situation in the Baltic republics. The Kazakh representative, Olzhas Suleimanov, brought up the subject of the collectivization that had decimated his
nation. 'Sometime,' he pointed out, 'we will have to fill in the dotted line from
the recent past and explain to the readers why we are not writing about the
1930s, about collectivization, for example.'

An Estonian, Vladimir Beekman, drew attention to the difficulties non-
Russians faced because of Moscow's control over the books which they could
publish, which works they could translate, and which publications they could
sell abroad. Complaining about excessive centralization and the 'absurdities'
arising from it, he challenged the notion 'that all questions are always best
seen from Moscow'.

An Uzbek author criticized the USSR Writers' Union for showing little
interest in Uzbek literature and the situation in his republic. Other speakers,
however, complained that their nations were receiving the wrong kind of
attention from the Russians. According to the *New York Times*, 'some harsh
clashes were reported between right-wing Russian nationalist writers and
writers of non-Russian nationalities, particularly the Georgians, who reportedly walked out of the hall at one point'.[53] Apparently, Georgian authors
protested about what they saw as Russian nationalist slurs on their nation,
while an Armenian representative objected to the stereotyping and caricatur-
ing of non-Russians in Soviet films.

What was also interesting was that several Russian writers went beyond
purely 'Russian' cultural and environmental concerns and indicated that
they, too, wanted to see *glasnost'* encompass the national problem. Valentin
Rasputin, for example, referred to the nationalities question as 'a subject
which is delicate and would seem to be forbidden to a Russian person'. He
maintained that the various peoples of the USSR 'live in a common home . . .
We can see everything, good or bad,' he explained. 'We cannot hide
anything, and any malaise, any shortcoming is not a personal matter nor a
personal attribute – everyone is affected.' Another Russian 'village prose'
writer, Vasilii Belov, seemed to challenge the entire thrust of Soviet nationalities policy. 'As a Russian person,' he declared, 'I am certainly not glad, say,
about the prospect of the slow, gradual disappearance of a nation, of its
complete fusion with other nations.'[54]

Although what occurred at the Soviet Writers' Congress marked a breakthrough, it was still early days for *glasnost'* in the area of national relations.
There was virtually no follow-up in the Soviet press on the sensitive issues that
had been raised. Even the accounts of the speeches delivered by the non-
Russians were toned down in *Literaturnaia gazeta*. Nevertheless, a more
defiant mood now gripped some non-Russian authors. On 30 July, for
example, the Latvian poet and translator Lavs Egelsberg, writing in the

Latvian Komsomol newspaper *Padomju Jaunatne*, asked why so little was still being written about national problems. 'Ostriches,' he pointed out, 'are not, and cannot be good internationalists.'

Moscow rules out real change

The following month, the Gorbachev leadership seemed to signal that economic 'restructuring' and a measure of *glasnost'* did not mean any basic change in nationalities policy. On 13 August, Radio Moscow broadcast an interview with the specialist on national relations, Eduard Bagramov. Apart from repeating what had already been said about nationalities policy during and after the Twenty-seventh Party Congress, he went on to make one thing quite clear: a return to the policies of the 1920s was out of the question. As he put it:

> The principle of indigenization of the apparatus as the basis for cadres policy, which was valid for the 1920s and 1930s, would be one-sided today given the growth of the multi-national nature of the republics.

The following day *Pravda* published quite a tough editorial on its front page stressing the need to 'cultivate in all citizens loyalty to our fraternity and friendship, a sense of inseparably belonging to the great Soviet motherland'. The newspaper stated that the purpose of 'improving national relations and developing collaboration among our peoples' was to channel 'their creative energy toward the further strengthening of the economic and defence might of the USSR – the unitary Union state'.

Pravda said that the Party was doing all it could 'to rid the thinking of certain categories of Soviet citizens of nationalistic delusions and to direct it into the channel of socialist patriotism and internationalism'. It added:

> We cannot tolerate the fact that in certain republican publications there is a lack of a class and Party approach in the evaluation of the events of the past in the life of a particular nation, [and] in particular, that the undoubted role of religion in inflaming nationalistic prejudices is suppressed and outmoded national customs are idealized.

In a departure from previous practice, the editorial acknowledged that *Pravda* had been receiving letters about 'conflict situations' arising among national groups. It also confirmed that the development of the USSR's eastern regions, especially the Far East, would remain a priority under the Gorbachev leadership.[55] In other words, the Central Asian republics, despite their problems, could not expect more help from Moscow.[56] The announcement barely a week later that it had been decided to discontinue developmental work on Sibaral and the northern rivers diversion scheme must no doubt have left the Central Asian and Kazakh elites thinking about the long-term prospects for their peoples.

Dmitrii Ziuzin, a senior scientific worker in the Scientific Research Institute of Labour of the USSR State Committee of Labour warned in 1986 that unless 7.1 million able-bodied persons move by the year 2000 from the Central Asian republics to other parts of the country, or, failing that, that at least 3.4 million of those fit for work migrate (that is, 40 per cent of the projected increase in manpower during this period) and subsidies are increased from the centre, national income produced per able-bodied person in the Central Asian republics will drop below the current level of 70 per cent of the all-Union figure.[57]

In the same month that *Pravda* delivered its warning about 'nationalistic delusions', Radio Moscow announced that the works of two leading Russian pre-revolutionary historians, Kliuchevskii and Solov'ev, both of whom had been instrumental in developing the 'imperial' Russian historiography that had been denounced in the 1920s by Pokrovskii and his school, were to be published again.[58] This represented quite a success for Russian patriots who had been pressing for the rehabilitation of the classics of Russian, albeit tsarist, historiography. Even the question of rehabilitating a third such historian, Karamzin, who hitherto had been depicted as a staunch monarchist and reactionary, was now being openly raised. For example, at the Soviet Writers' Congress Academician Likhachev did not hesitate to describe Karamzin's history of the Russian state as 'magnificent'.[59]

Religious double standards
A similar double standard was also evident in the official attitude towards the forthcoming millennium in 1988 of the Christianization of the ancient state of Kievan Rus'. Although the Ukrainians, Byelorussians and Russians are all said to trace their historical and cultural heritage from this proto-national polity, the Russian Orthodox Church had been given a monopoly over the celebrations and been allowed to depict the jubilee as a celebration of a thousand years of 'Russian' history, statehood and culture. At the same time, no specifically Ukrainian or Byelorussian elements were acknowledged in the preparations for the celebrations, Ukrainian and Byelorussian churches remained banned, and the press in the Ukraine remained full of attacks against 'Ukrainian nationalists' who viewed Kievan Rus' as a Ukrainian state.[60]

As early as 1983, when Andropov had been in power, the Soviet atheistic state had returned the Danilovskii Monastery to the Moscow Patriarchate, thereby providing the Russian Orthodox Church with a base of operations for its millennium celebrations. By the summer of 1986 the preparations for the jubilee were in their final stages and both the Moscow Patriarchate and the Kremlin were playing up the public relations aspect of the celebrations. In July, the Russian Orthodox Church held a major international historical conference on the Christianization of Kievan Rus' in Kiev, the Ukrainian capital and the former centre of the Kievan Rus' state. In its English-language dispatches, though, the official Soviet news agency TASS repeatedly referred to the conference as dealing with the 'Christening of Russia'. For the next two years, both TASS and Novosti continued to use the word 'Russia' instead of 'Rus'' in their English-language coverage of the millennium celebrations.

It was not only the Ukrainians and Byelorussians who had grounds for thinking that one set of rules applied to the Russians, and another to them. The Lithuanians were preparing to celebrate in 1987 the 600th anniversary of their nation's conversion to Christianity. During 1986 pressure on Lithuanian Catholics was increased and the local press stepped up its attacks against religion. Moreover, on the eve of the jubilee, Lithuania's believers were warned that unauthorized celebrations would not be tolerated.[61]

The campaign against Islam, and especially against Party members in the Central Asian republics who participated in religious ceremonies, was also intensified during the second half of 1986. In October, at a plenum of the Uzbek Party's Central Committee, several officials spoke of 'the complicated religious situation' in the republic, leading *Pravda* to comment that 'atheistic work to counteract religious influence, especially that of Islam' was still 'being conducted in an unsatisfactory way'.[62] The following month, this message was reinforced by Gorbachev himself. During a brief stopover in Tashkent while en route to India, the Soviet leader demanded 'an uncompromising struggle against religious manifestations and the strengthening of political work among the masses and of atheistic work'. Assailing Party members who 'pay lip service to our morals and ideals', he stressed that 'even the slightest discrepancy between words and deeds in this matter is impermissible'.[63]

The non-Russians begin pressing
Despite the lack of any 'new thinking' by the Soviet authorities in the sphere of nationalities policy, nationally minded non-Russians recognized that while *glasnost'* and 'restructuring' remained the order of the day they had a rare opportunity to press their case in the hope of altering official attitudes. Moreover, seeing that even anti-Soviet Russian writers like Gumilev and Nabokov were being rehabilitated, not to mention monarchist historians, they began campaigning for a more honest account of their own past and for the rehabilitation of proscribed non-Russian historians and political and cultural figures. The language issue, however, became the main battleground.

Quite unexpectedly, it was in Byelorussia that a popular campaign in defence of the national language first got under way. Russification had advanced so far in this republic that in the summer of 1985 an Estonian author had mentioned it as an implicit warning of where 'internationalization' was leading to: the Russification even of literary culture and the drastic narrowing of the use of the native language in education and cultural life.[64] Furthermore, because there had been little overt national dissent in Byelorussia, it was widely assumed that Byelorussian national consciousness was very weak.

In September 1986 the Byelorussian literary weekly *Litaratura i mastatstva* published a letter from a teacher deploring the precarious state of his native language and calling for the introduction of legislation to bolster its status. The teacher also criticized Byelorussian parents who sought exemption for their children from having to study the mother tongue. The scale of the language problem was revealed in a commentary by Kastus' Tarasaw (who had been criticized earlier in the year for supposedly making ideological lapses in his writings on Byelorussian history) which the weekly ran alongside the letter. Tarasaw pointed out that in the entire republic, where, according to the 1979 census, 80 per cent of its 7.6 million Byelorussian inhabitants had given Byelorussian as their native language, there was only one urban school providing some instruction in the mother tongue.[65]

The letter and commentary triggered off a remarkable campaign in defence of the Byelorussian language in the republic's press. During the next few months hundreds of letters poured in, some with as many as 50 signatures. As one letter, signed by 13 teachers in Vitebsk, put it,

> This kind of situation cannot be permitted to go on any longer. It has come to the point that, at meetings of the pedagogical council, individual teachers and pupils who dare to speak Byelorussian in the school have been accused of 'nationalism'(!).

A biochemist from Minsk wrote:

> Decisive measures must be taken to correct the situation. Moreover, these should not be limited to the schools alone. The Byelorussian language should also be in the institutions of higher education and in state organizations. A fundamental improvement in its use is needed in cinematography, television, and book publishing. For the all-round development of a language, it is imperative that it be widely used in all spheres of public life.[66]

At the end of October, P. Sadowski, a lecturer at Minsk State Pedagogical Institute, accused the Byelorussian Ministry of Education of violating Leninist norms by hampering the development of the native language and of contributing to the 'indifferent, Philistine-nihilistic attitude towards the native language, history, culture, monuments, names, and other things'. He also condemned 'as a worn-out scare tactic' the 'nod in the direction of "Moscow" ' relied on by domestic Russifiers. Sadowski's and proposals advanced by the numerous other respondents amounted to a call for a return to the indigenization and Byelorussianization policies of the 1920s.[67]

These protests and demands apparently fell on deaf ears, and in early December Byelorussian writers held a meeting at which their nation's 'painful problems' were discussed. The head of the Writers' Union of Byelorussia, Nil Hilevich, urged his colleagues to make full use of *glasnost'* and to rally to the defence of their nation's language, history and culture. At the meeting a letter to Gorbachev was drafted and it was signed by 28 leading Byelorussian cultural figures, including the prominent writer Vasil' Bykaw. They emphasized that the Byelorussian language was barely used in the republic's official life and in the theatres and cinemas and that in 1984 less than 5 per cent of all the literary works published in Byelorussia had been in the native language. The signatories called upon the Soviet leader to take 'decisive measures' to save the Byelorussian nation from 'spiritual extinction'. They also attached to their appeal a detailed list of proposals amounting to a programme for the de-Russification of their republic.[68]

Next door in the Ukraine, writers also led the way. In September, the literary scholar Mykola Zhulyns'kyi raised the question of the distortion and rewriting of national history. He stressed that the problem of the erasure of national memory had become acute and alarming.[69] One and a half months later, at a plenum of the Board of the Writers' Union of the Ukraine, the language question was again given prominence. One of the participants, Volodymyr Drozd, called for the state to intervene and inaugurate the sort of policies that were in operation in the 1920s. 'Appeals to respect the Ukrainian language alone are not enough,' he said:

> What is needed here are decisions by the state. The Ukrainian language must become fundamentally indispensable in everyday life, in the theatre, in scholarship, and in institutions of higher learning; then there will be no need for appeals, and even the Philistine will draw the appropriate conclusions.[70]

Similarly, in the Baltic republics the discussion about the status of the native language sharpened. In September the Latvians were given a fillip by the US–Soviet conference held in the Latvian seaside resort town of Jurmala. The meeting drew attention to the situation of the Baltic republics and led the United States to clarify its policy towards Latvia, Estonia and Lithuania. Latvians were heartened when an American spokesman delivered his side's opening statement in both Latvian and Russian and forcefully reaffirmed that the United States 'has never and will never recognize the forcible incorporation' of the Baltic states into the Soviet Union. Although domestic coverage of the Jurmala meeting again showed up how far *glasnost'* still had to go, word of the American stance at the conference got out. From the subsequent defensive responses in the Soviet press it appears that the overall effect of Jurmala was to reopen the 'Baltic question'.[71]

As the year wore on, both Estonian and Latvian writers began to point to the privileged position of the Russian language in their republics and expose the hostile or indifferent attitude of Russian immigrants to the languages and culture of the Baltic nations. The mood was captured in a letter published at the end of September in the Latvian Komsomol newspaper *Padomju Jaunatne*:

> Yes, indeed, the Soviet people have voluntarily adopted the Russian language as a means of mutual communication between nations . . . But does it also mean that, for example, a Latvian in his own country is compelled to speak Russian all day long – at work, in the street, on public transport, at the polyclinic, at the shops, and so on? That someone, not a tourist but rather a sales clerk, doctor, cobbler, or housing administration employee who lives and works in Latvia, can say [in Russian], looking him arrogantly in the eye: 'I don't understand Latvian. Speak in Russian!' . . . As long as there is no compulsory requirement for at least workers in the service sector to speak (or at least to understand) both languages, nothing will change.[72]

Similar complaints and demands were voiced in Estonia. In October, the novelist Teet Kallas broadcast a series of talks on Estonian Radio in which, among other things, he attacked the chauvinistic attitude of local Russians towards Estonians. The resulting 'us-and-them' attitude, he explained, was creating a 'tinderbox of social tensions'. The least that ought to be done, in his view, was to recognize that 'there are a whole string of occupations for which bilingualism should be mandatory'.

The following month, another writer, Holger Pukk, also criticized the haughty attitude of Russian immigrants, warning that

> Local political arrogance, hooliganism, and a fundamental lack of political manners often have a greater effect than anti-Soviet propaganda from abroad.[73]

Meanwhile, Latvian authors managed to air some of the worries and problems facing Balts and non-Russians generally in the pages of the important central newspaper, *Literaturnaia gazeta*. First, Janis Peters on 5 November, and then three weeks later, Uldis Berzins and Marina Kostenetskaia, came out with modest proposals aimed at improving the status of the Latvian language and furthering mutual understanding and respect between Latvians and immigrants in their republic. Kostenetskaia was able to elaborate her criticism of Russians who had lived in Latvia for decades and yet had not bothered to learn Latvian. For his part, her interlocutor, Berzins, provided an example of the spirit in which he and his colleagues were approaching the national question. Revealing that he and Kostenetskaia had recently visited the Chernobyl' area and seen the abandoned homes of the people who had been evacuated, he commented:

> Ukrainian and Byelorussian children have found a new home in Latvia as well as in other republics. Well, they must be given the opportunity to continue their education in their native language. This too is our international responsibility – we cannot allow children to lose their cultural roots.[74]

Towards the end of November, however, the authorities in Latvia attempted to apply the brake. The Latvian Party's ideological secretary Anatolijs Gorbunovs (a Latvian despite his Russian-sounding name) delivered a speech in which he gave the following instruction:

In response to the suggestions submitted to Party committees and ideological institutions, it was proposed that the most favourable conditions be created for the voluntary learning of the Latvian language for everyone who desired to do so. Regrettably, this proposal has been misinterpreted in some places. Moreover, speculation has appeared to the effect that it is necessary and even obligatory for members of other nationalities living in the republic to possess a command of the Latvian language. Considering these, albeit sundry, facts, the Party organizations must take a principled stand – they must energetically put an end to such speculation on the part of politically immature people.[75]

The negative response of the Latvian Party leadership did not bode well for the prospects of the other non-Russians who were seeking to improve the position of their native language. The mere fact that *glasnost'* was now bringing certain problems to the surface did not necessarily mean that the authorities were any more receptive to what the non-Russians had to say.

16

Glasnost' *but no* Perestroika

After 20 months in power, the Gorbachev leadership made a move that dramatically exposed the dangers of continuing to ignore 'the human factor' in the sphere of national relations. Acting as economic rationalists and disciplinarians, the Gorbachev team disregarded the national sensitivities of the Kazakhs and replaced the veteran Party chief in Kazakhstan, Kunaev, with Gennadii Kolbin, a Russian from outside the republic. The result was mass protests and disturbances by Kazakh youth – the so-called Alma-Ata riots – which sent tremors throughout the Soviet domain.

The Kazakhs had good reason to feel not only insulted but also threatened by the appointment of a Russian over them. In the history of the Kazakh Communist Party, only two of its 17 leaders had been Kazakhs.[1] The abrupt replacement in February 1954 of the first Kazakh to head the Party organization in his own republic, Shaiakhmetov, by a Slav had been the prelude to the imposition on the Kazakhs of Khrushchev's Virgin Lands Scheme. Kunaev had been Kazakhstan's Party chief for nearly a quarter of a century, and during that time, the Kazakhs had gradually begun to recover their position. By the 1980s, much to the discomfort of Russians and other settlers in the republic, they were showing signs of new national pride and assertiveness. In fact, an undeclared policy of Kazakhization seems to have been in operation. Moreover, by the mid-1980s the number of Kazakhs had drawn level with the number of Russians living in their republic (around 6.2 million, with each group forming about 39 per cent of the republic's population), and demographic trends were working in their favour.[2]

The dismissal of Kunaev, whatever his record as an economic manager, spelled trouble. Having already seen the extent of the purge in Uzbekistan, and being aware of the Gorbachev leadership's tendency to appoint Slavs to positions that Central Asians had come to regard as their own and to abolish positive discrimination programmes, not to mention its tougher ideological policy towards the traditionally Moslem republics, it was hardly surprising that there were Kazakhs who feared the worst.

The Alma-Ata riots and their repercussions

Two days after Kunaev's replacement, on 18 December 1986, TASS issued the following announcement in English:

> A group of students, incited by nationalistic elements, last evening and today took to the streets of Alma-Ata expressing disapproval of the decisions of the recent plenary meeting of the Central Committee of the Communist Party of Kazakhstan. Hooligans, parasites and other anti-social persons made use of this situation and resorted to unlawful acts against representatives of law and order. They set fire to a food store, to private cars and insulted townspeople.

Five days later, Novosti issued an eyewitness report by its correspondent Valerii Novikov which he had filed on 17 December. According to Novikov, the protesters were mainly young people who shouted 'nationalistic slogans' like 'Kazakhstan for the Kazakhs!' Some of them brandished sticks and iron rods. Ignoring pleas for order and calm, they 'started committing outrages' in the city's streets. The rioters, he claimed, were immature youths 'doped by liquors and narcotics' who had been 'provoked to "protest" ' by corrupt and inefficient elements of the discredited Kunaev leadership.[3]

These initial Soviet accounts of the disturbances seemed to represent a victory for *glasnost'*. For once, the Soviet media had promptly announced that ethnic riots had broken out. Within days, however, unofficial reports started reaching Western journalists in Moscow which suggested that the Soviet authorities were attempting to minimize the scale and seriousness of what had occurred. The Kremlin's defensiveness was shown in *Izvestia*'s attack of 7 January 1987 on the *Guardian*'s Moscow correspondent Martin Walker for quoting eyewitnesses who had reported that as many as 10,000 demonstrators had taken part in the protests in Alma-Ata, that at least 20 people, including seven policemen, had been killed and 200 seriously injured, and that over 1,000 rioters had been arrested.[4] Speaking at a press conference in Helsinki on 8 January, the chairman of the USSR Council of Ministers, Nikolai Ryzhkov, was at pains to convey the impression that the trouble had involved only 'a couple of hundred people' who were 'without any solid foundation or outlook in life'.[5]

Gradually more details began to emerge. On 14 January *Literaturnaia gazeta* acknowledged that a public order volunteer had been killed but denied that any of the rioters had lost their lives. A few weeks later, *Kazakhstanskaia pravda* revealed that troops had been involved in suppressing the riots.[6] When, in the second half of February, the first group of Western journalists were allowed to visit Alma-Ata, they were told by the chairman of the Kazakh Council of Ministers, Nursultan Nazarbaev, that the protesters had numbered about 3,000, that two people – a public order volunteer and a demonstrator – had been killed, and that 200 had been injured. He also said that 100 people had been detained.

Interestingly, Nazarbaev gave a rather different picture from the one that the Soviet press had been presenting. He did not depict the student protesters as hooligans and parasites. 'On the first day,' he told the journalists, 'there were no drunks or drug addicts.' The students' protest, he confirmed, had been 'a manifestation of nationalism', though social and economic grievances may also have played a part. Angered by the way in which Kunaev had been replaced, the students 'did not say we are against Kolbin, we're for Kunaev. They said give us a local person.' The Kazakh official also revealed that placards used during the demonstrations 'quoted sayings by Lenin on the nationalities question'.[7]

It took a further 16 months for another crucial piece of information about the 'Alma-Ata riots' to emerge. Only in June 1988, when the unrest in Kazakhstan had been overshadowed by new manifestations of national tensions, was it revealed that the nationalist protests following Kunaev's replacement had not been limited to the Kazakh capital. According to *Izvestia*, Kunaev's removal

> was seen by certain young people as a blow against national self-esteem and pride, as a personal tragedy, as the collapse of their hopes. Apart from the organized excesses in Alma-Ata, attempts were made to provoke anti-social marches in 12 of the republic's regional centres, and hundreds of pamphlets and appeals were disseminated.[8]

The shock caused by the eruption of ethnic riots in Kazakhstan was heightened by a number of factors. First, because of its ethnically mixed population, this republic had long been hailed in the Soviet press as 'a laboratory of the friendship of peoples'. Furthermore, the protests in Alma-Ata came across as the first real 'Moslem' revolt. What was perhaps the most striking thing about them, though, and something which the Soviet press certainly brought out, was their anti-Russian nature. The idea of Soviet-educated youth from a traditionally Moslem background openly rebelling against the Russian 'elder brother' while the Soviet Union was still embroiled in Afghanistan was enough to send shivers down many a spine in Moscow. It also raised questions about the efficacy of the Kremlin's policies in Central Asia.

There was, however, another side to all this. The Soviet press coverage of what had happened remained selective and one-sided. Moreover, a certain amount of Russian nationalism was allowed to show through. One letter-writer to *Izvestia* even demanded special privileges for the 'Slavic peoples in every republic'.[9] The Kazakhs, who were berated for their nationalism, lack of internationalist education, and in some cases, insufficient knowledge of Russian, were not really given a chance to reply. Instead, Kazakhs were frequently used by the press to assail their own fellow-countrymen.

On 11 February *Pravda* went as far as to accuse the Kazakh press of having fostered the atmosphere that led to the Alma-Ata protests. Specifically, it accused Kazakh newspapers of having shown excessive concern for the Kazakh language and culture and berated them for publishing articles that had indicated that the Kazakh share of the population of their republic was steadily rising. It singled out a youth paper for special criticism because it had published a letter calling for the opening of more Kazakh schools and kindergartens and allowed a poet to add his wholehearted support. 'It's not hard to see that the words behind this concern for the development of one's native tongue,' *Pravda*'s correspondent commented, 'reveal national egoism. And this is being propagandized in a newspaper whose readers are for the most part young people.' What he failed to mention, though, was that the Kazakhs had good reason to feel anxious: it later emerged in the Kazakh-language press that in 1987 only about 6 per cent of the one million or so children in pre-school facilities in Kazakhstan were attending Kazakh establishments.[10]

By coincidence, two days earlier, in an interview with Radio Budapest, a senior Hungarian Communist Party official, Matyas Szuros, offered a rather different explanation for what had happened in Kazakhstan. Indirectly criticizing the Kremlin's approach, he suggested that perhaps the trouble had occurred because the Soviet authorities had not taken into account the national and religious sensitivities of the Kazakhs.[11]

The biased manner in which the Soviet press dealt with the national problem in Kazakhstan eventually drew protests from inside the Soviet Union. In April 1987, at a plenum of the USSR Writers' Union, the Russian nationalist poet, Stanislav Kuniaev, took *Pravda* to task for having branded a Kazakh poet's love for his native language as 'national egoism'. He declared:

> I think that any normal Kazakh will be outraged when he reads that in the newspaper. And I would be indignant in his place and would think: there you have it – Russification. Does someone perhaps want such feelings about Russians to appear in the republics? If not, why be so tactless about a healthy concern for one's language?[12]

Even more outspoken criticism was to appear in May 1988. Writing in the all-Union literary monthly *Druzhba narodov*, the Ukrainian literary critic Mykola Riabchuk commented:

> Like everyone else, I closely followed what the press was saying about the tragic events in Alma-Ata. The articles were varied – from angry, to compassionate, to plainly demagogic ones which just about tried to convince us that national kindergartens and schools are harmful. But scarcely a single Russian took the slightest blame for what happened. And yet the blame was, and is, there. It is there because hundreds of thousands of Russians don't know – and don't consider it important to know – the languages of the peoples among whom they live.[13]

What Riabchuk may not have known is that according to the 1979 census, only

0.7 per cent of the Russians living in Kazakhstan had claimed a good knowledge of the local language – the lowest figure for any of the Union republics.

Moscow's reaction: attack followed by a partial retreat

Moscow's initial response to the protests in Kazakhstan was to empower Kolbin to take firm action. Within three weeks of the disturbances, *Kazakh-stanskaia pravda* announced that a woman teacher who had participated in the demonstrations had been sentenced to five years in labour camps. By early February another two sentences imposed on protesters were reported: one of seven years and the other of ten.[14] Some idea of the scale of the retribution can be obtained from a subsequent announcement that a total of 787 people were expelled from the Komsomol for their involvement in the protests, 1,138 Komsomol members were given reprimands, and 271 expelled from academic institutions.[15]

Kolbin also proceeded to denounce the corruption, protectionism and inefficiency that had existed under Kunaev. Within a month of his taking over in Kazakhstan, the local press announced that two senior factory managers found guilty of bribery and theft had been sentenced to death and that another two had been given sentences of 20 and 15 years.[16] It seemed, therefore, as if a major clean-up campaign on the scale of what was happening in Uzbekistan would follow.

A week after the disturbances the Politburo met in Moscow and instructed the Kazakh Party leadership

> to investigate carefully the events that had taken place and to adopt the necessary measures to improve substantially the patriotic and internationalist education of the working people, the training and placement of cadres, and the deepening of fraternal ties with other republics of the Soviet Union.[17]

Two days later, on 27 December, *Pravda* reiterated that it was 'necessary to rebuff resolutely any attempts to place local interests above statewide interests' and to struggle against all forms of nationalism.

The standard line was also re-emphasized by officials in the Union republics. On 24 December the Latvian ideological secretary Gorbunovs warned that the continuing calls to make the learning of Latvian obligatory for all nationalities living in the republic threatened to lead to the sort of nationalism that had been demonstrated in Alma-Ata.[18] A week later, *Izvestia* published an article by an Uzbek Party official in which he defended the appointment of Russians to important posts in the Central Asian republics and reproached his compatriots for their attitude towards Islam, their 'private-property mentality' and their reluctance to migrate to other regions of the USSR.[19]

Even more disturbing for the Central Asians was the announcement on

20 January that the Tadzhik authorities were going to take steps to reduce population growth in their republic. Although the birthrate in Tadzhikistan was the highest in the USSR, the launching of a propaganda campaign to persuade Tadzhik women to have fewer children while population growth was being actively encouraged in other parts of the Soviet Union seemed to be another example of the Gorbachev leadership's disregard for national sensibilities.[20]

Despite these worrying signs, the Alma-Ata protests did not turn out to be a major setback for the non-Russians. On the contrary, after the initial tough responses, Moscow began to make the first modest concessions. Partly, this seems to have been because the Alma-Ata protests brought home the explosive nature of the national problem and the inappropriateness of heavy-handed methods of dealing with it. The more constructive approach probably also stemmed from Gorbachev's new emphasis on 'democratization' as an indispensable component of economic and social 'restructuring'. He made this the main theme of his speech delivered on 27 January at an important Central Committee plenum.

In Kazakhstan itself, Kolbin seems to have realized that the tense situation could be defused only if some official recognition of Kazakh national grievances were made. Having already served as the number two man in Georgia under Shevardnadze, he had experience in dealing with manifestations of national assertiveness. Within weeks of becoming the Party chief in Kazakhstan, he created republican commissions to find ways of improving relations between nationalities and to ensure 'fairer' ethnic representation in republican institutions. He also went out of his way to emphasize that his appointment and the clean-up in Kazakhstan were not aimed against the Kazakhs as such, but corrupt officials, whether Kazakhs or Slavs.[21] A notable new experiment in 'democratization' was also permitted: on 14 January TASS announced that a multi-candidate election for the leadership of the Komsomol organization in Alma-Ata had been held.

At the beginning of March it became clearer that, while continuing to denounce Kunaev and his associates, Kolbin and his aides were seeking to conciliate the Kazakhs. On 5 March TASS reported that the Central Committee of the Kazakh Communist Party had adopted a resolution outlining measures to improve the teaching of both Russian and Kazakh in Kazakhstan. The dispatch noted that *Kazakhstanskaia pravda* had admitted that 'in recent times the trend towards a decline in the prestige of the Kazakh language became apparent'. Significantly, one of the provisions of the new measures was to broaden the 'social functions' of the Kazakh language 'in the life of the republic'.[22]

What is also interesting is that the crackdown in Kazakhstan did not result in the anticipated large-scale purge of republican officials. The clean-up proceeded surprisingly slowly and there was little improvement in the republic's economic performance.[23] Whether this was due solely to obstacles standing in the way of change, or whether perhaps there may have been a certain amount of restraint on the part of Kolbin and the Gorbachev leadership, it is difficult to say. A little over a year after Kolbin took over in Alma-Ata, however, *Pravda* was to acknowledge that he himself was being criticized by his colleagues for holding too many meetings and issuing too many orders.[24]

More openness but no change in policy

By one of those odd coincidences, the authorities in Kazakhstan found themselves arresting and sentencing disaffected Kazakhs at the very moment when the Gorbachev leadership had decided to free Andrei Sakharov from internal exile and to begin releasing political prisoners. This extraordinary shift in policy was never really explained by the Kremlin. It came, however, on the eve of the January Central Committee plenum at which the Soviet leader demonstrated his determination to get the process of 'restructuring' under way. By freeing political prisoners and proclaiming the need for 'democratization', he may have been seeking to outflank conservative opponents of reform and to win the goodwill of the West as well as of sceptical elements at home. Whatever the case, the whiff of liberalization invited the more courageous to probe and act while the chance was there.

At the January plenum Gorbachev devoted quite a bit of attention to nationalities policy. With the events in Alma-Ata only a few weeks behind, he acknowledged for the first time the importance of the nationalities question. 'There is not a single fundamental issue that we could resolve, now or in the past,' he declared, 'without taking into account that we live in a multi-ethnic country.' Indicating that more *glasnost'* about national problems would be permitted, he complained:

> It is a fact, comrades, that instead of conducting objective research into real phenomena in the sphere of national relations and analysis of the actual socio-economic and cultural processes – very complicated and contradictory in their essence – some of our social scientists have for long preferred to create 'upbeat' treatises reminiscent at times of complimentary toasts rather than serious scholarly studies. One should admit that the errors which were allowed to occur in the sphere of national relations and their manifestations remained in the shadow and it was not accepted practice to mention them. This resulted in the negative consequences with which we are now dealing.

But that was as far as he went. From the examples that Gorbachev mentioned, it was clear that he was still ascribing 'negative phenomena' in the area of national relations only to the non-Russians. 'Now and then,' he said, 'there have been manifestations of parochialism, tendencies towards ethnic isolation, sentiments of ethnic arrogance and even incidents similar to those which took place quite recently in Alma-Ata.' There was no indication that the Kremlin was about to recognize that some of the grievances of the non-Russians were legitimate. Indeed, though Gorbachev spoke of the need for more tact he failed even to mention the language question.

Although the Soviet leader did also hint vaguely that there were sometimes 'misunderstandings' and disputes between neighbouring regions and districts, his instructions to the Party organizations consisted of a reiteration of the need to 'enhance internationalist education' so as 'to save the rising generation from the demoralizing effect of nationalism . . . We shall be firm and principled,' he stressed, and added the following warning:

> People's national sentiments deserve respect, they should not be ignored, but they should not be flirted with either. Let those who would like to play on nationalist or chauvinistic prejudices entertain no illusions and expect no loosening up.[25]

While Gorbachev's remarks on the nationalities question were disappointing, the non-Russians could at least take heart from other things he said. The most important of these was that restructuring was only just beginning, that democracy was needed 'as we need air', that elections to Party posts should be conducted by secret ballot with more than one candidate proposed, and that *glasnost'* had to be broadened so as to leave 'no zones closed to criticism'.

Certainly, after the Kazakh protests and the January plenum it suddenly seemed that the authorities would no longer keep silent about the existence of national unrest. The Kirghiz and the Tadzhik press, for instance, acknowledged that clashes had been taking place between local and foreign students. The Tadzhik Komsomol leader also hinted that there had been confrontations between representatives of different Soviet nationalities. Moreover, in January and February the Tadzhik press reported the 'capture' and trial of two underground mullahs, revealing that the detention of one of them – he had advocated the establishment of an Islamic state in Tadzhikistan – had led to disorders in the city of Kurgan-Tiube.[26] In Moldavia, the Party chief, Semen Grossu, warned that some young and 'politically immature' Moldavians were 'slipping into a position of nationalism'. Three months later, his deputy admitted that 'deviations and deformations' in national relations of the sort that had been witnessed in Kazakhstan were also present in Moldavia and could not be ignored.[27]

Buoyed by Gorbachev's extension of restructuring to the social sphere, the non-Russians kept up the pressure. On 10 February a meeting of Ukrainian writers in Kiev reopened the debate about Thesis 19 of the 1958 Education Law and demanded that the study of the Ukrainian language should be made obligatory in all of the republic's schools. Oles' Honchar, for instance, attacked the 'falseness and hypocrisy' which called into question 'the need to learn one's native language . . . To learn or not to learn the native language,' he argued, 'such a question cannot arise in any civilized country.' He emphasized that in Byelorussia, the Baltic republics and Turkmenistan writers were also speaking out in defence of their native language.

Another speaker, the poet Ivan Drach, deplored what was happening in some schools in the Ukraine, where, as he put it,

> the Ukrainian language and Ukrainian literature have become a subject for derision and mockery, where gentrified Philistines with a chauvinistic deviation, hiding behind the shield of pseudo-internationalism, frequently scoff at the roots from whence they came.

His colleague, Dmytro Pavlychko, warned in no uncertain terms that unless the official attitude towards not only Ukrainian, but all the non-Russian languages of the USSR changed, there would soon be no 'friendship of peoples' in the Soviet Union.[28]

Three weeks later, *Literaturna Ukraina* published an article by another Ukrainian writer, Serhii Plachynda, in which he provided a list of far-reaching proposals regarding language policy. Among other things, he argued that in each republic the native language and Russian should be granted the status of state languages, and that in autonomous republics three languages should be designated as state languages.[29]

In the second half of February 1987 Gorbachev visited Latvia and Estonia. He failed, however, to address any of the national problems which bothered the Balts. Instead, while in Latvia, he tactlessly praised the 'Russian soldier-liberator who helps the Baltic farmer and fisherman to defend their native land against desecration and servitude, to protect it against the foreign aggressor'.[30] Nevertheless at a meeting in Tallinn at which the Soviet leader called for better 'internationalist education', the chairman of the Estonian Writers' Union, Vladimir Beekman, made use of the opportunity to point out that 'the incompetent handling' of nationalities policy and reliance on 'simple-minded recipes' can 'strike rather deep wounds'.[31]

Once again, the Soviet leader soon revealed his poor grasp of the nationalities question, as well as his general ignorance of the situation in the United States in this regard. In April, he startled a group of visiting Congressmen by suggesting that the United States solve its race problems by setting up separate states for Blacks, Puerto Ricans, Poles and other minorities. 'We have respect for our nationalities in this country,' he was reported to have told his guests. 'Why don't you have these autonomous areas?'[32]

Glasnost' and 'democratization' in action

As *glasnost'* began to take more of a hold, what developed can best be characterized as a dialogue of the deaf. On the one hand the non-Russians continued speaking out and pretending that they did not hear the warnings from local defenders of orthodoxy and the reiteration of conservative positions on the nationalities question by the centre. On the other hand, the authorities both in Moscow and the republican capitals by and large continued to turn a deaf ear to the demands being made by the non-Russians.

A further indication of the centre's unforthcoming attitude was provided in an article by Bromlei – by no means the most hard-line of the leading specialists on the national problem – published in *Pravda* on 13 February 1987. He dismissed the grievances of the non-Russians with the following remarks:

> At times the regular process of internationalization of culture and the intermixing of the population is painful to accept. Some representatives of individual nationalities perceive this process – especially wherever it is particularly intensive – almost as an impending loss of national distinctiveness, culture, language and so on. Hence the feelings of traditionalism, the underestimation of the Russian language as a means of contact between nations, the temptation to isolate themselves within the narrow framework of national cultures and the deadening of international awareness. Nationalist elements take advantage of such feelings, at times quite successfully.

There was no shortage of other examples of insensitivity to the feelings of the non-Russians. For instance, on 19 February *Pravda Vostoka*, Uzbekistan's Russian-language Party daily, published an insulting reference to the Koran. Discussing the need to improve the teaching of the Russian language, a contributor argued that knowledge of Russian was an important means of reducing the influence of Islam. He asked:

> Can one really compare the ringing words of Pushkin, the pathos and vital force of Gor'kii's words, the sharpness and greatness of Lenin's speeches, with the barely intelligible mutterings and abstruse prayers from the Koran?

Needless to say, *glasnost'* was made use of by a variety of groups, including Russian chauvinists. On two consecutive days at the end of March 1987 *Pravda* carried articles written by Russian imperial nationalists. One of the authors, P. Volobeev, a Corresponding Member of the USSR Academy of Sciences, hailed the Bolshevik Revolution as having 'saved Russia from a national catastrophe' by overcoming the 'danger of it losing its national independence and territorial integrity'. The other author, O. Trubachev, a philologist and also a Corresponding Member of the USSR Academy of Sciences, argued that the Russian nation and its achievements had still not received proper recognition, and upheld the predominance of the Russian language in the Soviet Union because of its 'greater cultural influence'. Furthermore, he sought to 'rehabilitate' Pushkin's poem 'To Russia's Slanderers' that had been addressed to West European critics of the Russian suppression of the Polish uprising of 1830.[33]

The spring of 1987 also saw the rise to notoriety of the Russian ultranationalist 'Pamiat'' (Memory) group. This 'historical and patriotic' association had been founded in the early 1980s. Because of its extreme nationalism and anti-Semitism – Pamiat' propagated the belief that Russia's problems should be blamed on Jews and freemasonry – it was officially disbanded at the beginning of 1986. Its members had nevertheless continued to meet as an 'informal' society, and the group had branches and supporters throughout the Soviet Union. On 6 May some 400 supporters of Pamiat' marched through Moscow and succeeded in meeting with the Moscow Party Chief Boris El'tsin. Although Pamiat' subsequently came under fire in the Soviet press, it continued to hold meetings, stage demonstrations and circulate chauvinistic literature.[34]

The inconsistencies in *glasnost'* were shown by the way in which the appeal of the 28 Byelorussian intellectuals to Gorbachev was handled. No mention of this document was made in the Byelorussian press. News of the existence of this document finally got out three months after it was written when, in March 1987, the Byelorussian writer Ales' Adamovich referred to it at a press conference in West Berlin. He also revealed that Moscow had sent a commission to Byelorussia to look into the matter. Eventually, in May, an Estonian cultural monthly published extracts from the Byelorussians' letter.[35]

As in Latvia, in March 1987, the Party leadership in Byelorussia openly rejected the demands concerning the native language being put forward by the Byelorussian cultural intelligentsia. The republic's new Party leader Efrem Sokolov was quite categorical:

> In recent years, as a result of the free will of the toilers of the republic, there has been a certain contraction in the utilization of the Byelorussian language. From this, some creative and scientific workers have drawn the hasty conclusion about an alleged incorrect attitude towards the cultural and linguistic heritage of the Byelorussian people in general. There are no grounds for such assertions . . . those who have lost their orientation in these questions should be helped to see the light . . . The national question has been, is, and will continue to be viewed by us from internationalist positions.[36]

A similar attitude was displayed by Shcherbitsky and the Ukrainian Party leadership.

Nevertheless, the Byelorussian and Ukrainian writers refused to take no for an answer. At a plenum of the Soviet Writers' Union held in Moscow on 27 and 28 April their representatives continued to press for an improvement in the status of their native languages. Outlining his nation's predicament, the head of the Byelorussian Writers' Union, Nil Hilevich, delivered an impassioned appeal for support from the other nationalities. He described the language issue as 'the question of questions' for his people and denounced nihilistic attitudes towards the non-Russian languages and cultures. The Ukrainians pointed out that there were cities in their republic with almost no Ukrainian schools. The poet Oliinyk, alluding to the uncooperative attitude of the authorities in Kiev, went as far as to call on 'Russian brothers' to help the Ukrainians restore Leninist norms in their republic.

Several Russian participants in the plenum expressed their sympathy for the non-Russians. Stanislav Kuniaev, for instance, criticized both the official policies towards the nationalities and the censorship that shielded them from public criticism:

> The situation regarding the existence and the teaching of native languages in the republics (I share the distress felt by Nil Hilevich and Borys Oliinyk), the vulgar class approach to national cultural assets, the pragmatic pressure of short-term politics which oversimplifies the full complexity of the lives and histories of the nations – all this exists in life, yet scarcely at all in literature, because there has always been a taboo in our literature: do not touch the nationalities question, or if you do, paint it only in the most favourable possible tones.

Another Russian author, Sergei Mikhalkov, the head of the Writers' Union of the RSFSR, pointed out that the situation in some of the autonomous republics was especially alarming. 'If we want to preserve the national literatures,' he stated,

> we must urgently take the most decisive measures for the study in schools of two languages: Russian and the native language . . . In the Bashkir and Mari ASSRs a generation is growing up that does not know its native tongue. How can national cultures develop in these republics? How can national literature develop?[37]

Breakthroughs in *glasnost'*
During the middle months of 1987, *glasnost'* really began to make itself felt in the coverage of the nationalities question. The appearance of a number of candid articles helped to give a fuller picture of what the crucial issues were. Moreover, the greater attention paid to national problems not only in the press, but also, for the first time, on Soviet television, began to bring home their seriousness and complexity.

In April the Soviet media acknowledged something which the Afghan resistance had long been claiming – that the Afghan guerrillas had carried out raids into Soviet territory. After the admission of two recent attacks in an area on the Tadzhik–Afghan border, the Soviet media reported that the KGB chief Viktor Chebrikov made a tour of the exposed frontier areas.[38] Following on this, in May, *Literaturnaia gazeta* carried a long two-part article by the political commentator Igor Beliaev, the thrust of which was that it was time to take the threat of Islam and the 'Moslem opposition' in the Central Asian republics and the North Caucasus seriously. Interestingly, Beliaev claimed that 'the young people in Alma-Ata who took part in the well-known December events were also manipulated by Moslem fanatics – Sufis'.[39]

On 7 May *Pravda* finally allowed a non-Russian representative to present a comprehensive, if still rather circumspect, critique of Soviet nationalities policy. The honour fell to that ardent champion of the rights of the Armenian people, Silva Kaputikian. Alluding to the 'grave' events in Alma-Ata, she argued that the growth of national self-awareness and the rise of the native elites demanded 'a new approach'. Moscow was dealing with modern nations, she intimated, not backward peoples groping for literacy.

The Armenian poet went on to say that it was time to restore Leninist principles in nationalities policy and 'harmonize' proclamations meant for the 'peoples of Africa and Asia' with 'our actions in our own house'. Attacking the one-sided bilingualism being foisted on the USSR's non-Russian peoples, she asked why the teaching of Russian in Armenia, where 90 per cent of the pupils were Armenians, was given preference over the teaching of the native language, and why 'with every passing year the sphere of application' of the Armenian language was being narrowed. In a union of supposedly free and equal peoples, how could close centralized control over education or publishing in the Union republics be justified?

Daring to hint at the root of the trouble, Kaputikian delicately noted that there was still an insufficient 'culture of national relations', something that was particularly 'manifested in individual people representing a large nation, in their attitude towards representatives of small peoples'. It was here, she claimed, that 'national egotism and arrogance' were to be found. 'For a long time,' she concluded,

> it was customary not to talk about all this. Yet keeping quiet and slurring over these errors is a kind of ideological data padding which, like all other data padding, has prevented people from seeing the multilayered, sometimes contradictory picture of reality and drawing realistic and constructive conclusions.[40]

Another notable article which appeared that month was by Leokadiia Drobizheva, the deputy head of the Institute of Ethnography of the USSR Academy of Sciences. Writing in the liberal weekly *Moskovskie novosti* (Moscow News), she not only implicitly acknowledged that Russification had been intensified in the 1970s but also touched upon another sore point, the question of equality in national relations and ethnic rivalry over jobs and access to higher education. Acknowledging that the unrest in Kazakhstan 'had come as a rather rude awakening for all of us', she pointed out that

> in order to eliminate emerging conflicts within the Union republics, mental attitudes – not only of the indigenous people but also of Russians, Ukrainians, Armenians, Tatars and Jews, whose cultural and professional standards were until recently higher – should be restructured. They must get used to the idea of equal partnership.[41]

That same month in Estonia, the Tartu daily *Edasi* published the most outspoken attack yet by a non-Russian on Moscow's language policy. The author, Mati Hint, one of Estonia's leading linguists, left virtually nothing unsaid. He exposed how the official promotion of bilingualism for the non-Russians amounted to poorly camouflaged Russification. This policy, he charged, reflected the same sort of attitude towards smaller nations that had been shown by Russian chauvinists under the tsars and by the Nazis towards peoples they deemed worthy of being called Aryans. Continuing in the same bold tone, Hint explained:

> It is not enough to declare good intentions. Democracy is decided on the basis of deeds and reality. The sovereign existence of the language must be guaranteed; this is the first requirement of linguistic democracy. We must know that the Estonian language is not some slowly atrophying appendage or local variant . . . but rather that [the Estonian language] is the Estonian nation's natural and inalienable right, which is protected by law.[42]

In July, the Kirghiz Chingiz Aitmatov, by now one of the Soviet Union's leading writers, spoke out on the national question in a wide-ranging interview published in *Ogonek*. The Stalinist legacy, he argued, was still making itself felt in this sphere. Instead of approaching matters in a 'normal, tolerant' manner, people continued to fear the stigma of nationalism; many leading workers at the local level were afraid to speak in their mother tongue in case they were accused of it. All this was compounded by the growth of 'national nihilism', the disdainful and cynical attitude towards one's native language and culture which Aitmatov said was 'as reactionary as nationalism itself'. The press, he complained, had still not got around to censuring this phenomenon and national nihilists were continuing, for mercenary reasons, to pass themselves off as 'superinternationalists'.

As for the language issue, Aitmatov stressed the need for a more genuine form of bilingualism. There should be constitutional safeguards, he elaborated, guaranteeing 'the equal worth and the equal importance' in public life of the non-Russian languages with Russian. 'Kindergartens and schools should be organized where the national languages are learned as the main language and Russian is also taught from childhood.' Citizens of the USSR would therefore be ensured a knowledge of Russian, but not at the expense of their native languages.[43]

Environmental issues

Environmental issues were also becoming more prominent and were broadening the discussion about the nationalities question. In the Baltic republics, the Latvians and Lithuanians achieved early successes when, in the last two months of 1986, public opposition forced the authorities to reconsider the ecological and economic feasibility of constructing a hydroelectric power station at Daugavpils on the Daugava River in Latvia and drilling for oil off the Lithuanian coast.[44] In Estonia, widespread concern about the planned large-scale mining of phosphorite in the republic – apart from ecological considerations, the project would have entailed a massive inflow of workers from outside the republic – culminated in demonstrations by students on 1 and 2 May in Tartu and Tallinn.[45] Here, too, the authorities appeared to yield, though it subsequently transpired that work on the scheme had in fact continued.

In the Ukraine, which was still feeling the impact of the Chernobyl' disaster, opposition to the expansion of nuclear energy was beginning to make itself felt. Chernobyl' figured prominently in Ukrainian letters, and in March, at a meeting in Kiev, more than 60 scientists met to discuss whether or not to proceed with the building of the fifth and sixth reactors at the site. Only two voted in favour, and at the end of May it was announced that construction work on the additional units would be abandoned. But this was only the beginning of a public campaign against the building of new atomic power stations and reactors in the Ukraine. By the summer Ukrainian writers were drawing up collective protests against the building of 'another Chernobyl'' at Chigirin, in the middle of an area with special historical significance for Ukrainians.[46]

In Armenia the Party leadership acknowledged that the republic's population was 'concerned about questions of ecology, nature conservation and the environment' and in March 1987 introduced a number of measures designed to improve the situation. In the summer, though, the central press revealed that air pollution remained a problem, and that the Armenian authorities were in fact restricting *glasnost'* on this issue.[47] Meanwhile in neighbouring Georgia, intellectuals came out in opposition to a scheme to construct a new railway through the Caucasus Mountains on the grounds that it threatened to cause damage to the environment and historical monuments, as well as to bring a flood of workers from outside the republic.[48]

Environmental questions were also very important in the Central Asian republics. Here, in addition to the poor quality of health care and sanitation, water pollution and the use of toxic agricultural chemicals had raised the infant mortality rate to between two and three times the national average. In March one serious hazard to health was finally removed when the USSR Ministry of Health banned the manufacture and use of Butifos, a highly toxic defoliant that had been used in Soviet cotton plantations since the mid-1960s. In the summer of 1987 it was announced that 1,470 doctors and nurses had been sent to the Central Asian republics to help lower the level of infant mortality.[49]

For the Central Asians the problem of water remained acute. Dejected by the apparent abandonment of the Siberian rivers diversion scheme, local intellectuals, especially Uzbeks, turned their attention to limiting the scale of a looming major ecological catastrophe: the desiccation of the Aral Sea and the resulting alteration of the region's climate and reduction of the growing season.

The shrinkage of the Aral Sea is a largely man-made disaster, the result of the cotton monoculture imposed on the region and the inept irrigation projects which accompanied it. As the Karakalpak representative at the April Soviet Writers' plenum, Tulepbergen Kaipergenov, put it:

> The hoary Aral endured the onslaught of people for a long time. Until 1960 the water level was relatively stable. But the attack continued and more and more new lands were developed . . . To no small degree, the impending disaster is not a defeat by blind elements, but the fruit of man's criminal negligence and overconfidence.

He brought out the tragedy which was befalling the region's inhabitants by pointing out that the question had become a 'truly Hamlet-like one: are people to live or not to live on the land of their ancestors?'[50]

Limited piecemeal concessions

With the non-Russians stepping up the pressure on a broad front, the Gorbachev leadership was forced to begin offering something more than just platitudes about the need for greater tact in dealing with national relations. Without altering its basic policy towards the non-Russians, it began to employ a more pragmatic and flexible approach. This resulted in a series of varied responses to specific situations. In some cases the object seems to have been to placate a discontented national group by granting minimal concessions; in others, to contain or prevent the growth of nationalism.

The measures adopted by the new Party leadership in Kazakhstan appear to have served as a model. The most important of these were the establishment of a republican commission on national relations and the adoption of resolutions to improve the teaching of both the native language and Russian. The creation of the commission was largely a cosmetic change. What was important for the Kazakhs, though, was that the authorities went some way towards recognizing their concern about the status of the Kazakh language; Kolbin himself set an example for his Russian colleagues by announcing that he would learn Kazakh.[51]

The situation in Latvia and Estonia was becoming more and more charged, and it is therefore not surprising that they were the next republics where modest concessions were granted or, perhaps more accurately in the latter case, extracted. In Estonia, an important new factor was beginning to make a difference: some of the more liberal and nationally minded Estonian communists who were concerned about the prospects for their small nation were starting to side with patriotic Estonian intellectuals. The turning point seems to have come in mid-April 1987 when the Tallinn City Party Committee decided at a plenary meeting to take a stand on controlling the influx of Russians and other outsiders into Estonia's capital. Although the decision to restrict the flow of Russians to the city was not reported in the Estonian press, a visiting American journalist, Antero Pietila, was informed about this by 'official sources'. One official told him that 80 to 90 per cent of the local production industries were under Moscow's control and did their hiring regardless of local regulations. Consequently, an average of 8,000 Russians had moved to the city annually in recent years. At the plenum it was also disclosed that only 16 per cent of the employees of the republic's Ministry of Internal Affairs, which includes the police, were Estonians.[52]

In Latvia the tensions between the indigenous Latvian inhabitants and the immigrants had become so strained that gangs of Latvian and Russian youths were clashing on the streets. In April nationalistic Latvian youths demonstrated in Riga. Later that month, the poet Janis Peters warned that if a recurrence of what had happened in Alma-Ata was to be avoided, remedial measures would have to be taken immediately.[53] In May the Latvian Party created a commission on inter-national relations. One of the first tasks it set itself was to examine ways of improving the teaching of Latvian in the republic.[54]

At the end of May, language concessions similar to those in Kazakhstan were granted in Moldavia. The Moldavian intelligentsia had begun protesting against Russification, and anti-Russian feeling was on the rise. Furthermore, the Gagauz, a small Turkic-speaking nationality, the majority of whom (140,000) lived in Moldavia, were demanding autonomy. Together with Moldavia's much smaller Bulgarian minority, they also managed to secure certain basic cultural concessions.[55]

There were improvements for a number of other small groups. For example, in July 1987, the Buriat poet Nikolai Damdinov pointed out in *Literaturnaia Rossiia* that in the mid-1970s great damage had been done to his people's national-cultural life by the arbitrary 'drastic reduction' of teaching in the Buriat language in primary schools. Now he was able to express satisfaction that in the Buriat ASSR:

> The decision about combining harmoniously teaching in the Buriat and Russian languages, the birth of the children's journal, and the planned opening of a literary museum have been for us, the republic's writers, fine harbingers of restructuring.[56]

Under continuing Western pressure, emigration restrictions on Jews, Germans and Armenians were eased. During 1987, 14,000 Germans were allowed to emigrate, compared with 753 in 1986;[57] and just over 8,000 Jews, eight times more than in the previous year.[58] Conditions for Germans and Jews who did not wish to leave also began to show signs of improvement. In June the Presidium of the Supreme Soviet of the Kazakh SSR adopted a decree providing for the improvement of facilities for studying German in the republic. There were calls in the press for similar measures to be introduced in Kirghizia, which also has a large German population.[59] For the Jews, the amelioration was mainly atmospheric. Attacks against anti-Semitism began appearing in the press (largely as a response to the activities of the Pamiat' group) and the cruder anti-Zionist propaganda started to be called into question. Furthermore, in September, the last imprisoned Jewish activist, Aleksei Magarik, was released. There was no sign, however, that the Gorbachev leadership was prepared to allow the Jews more basic cultural facilities beyond what little there was in the Jewish autonomous region of Birobidzhan, where only about 20,000 of the Soviet Union's 1.8 million or so Jews live.

In some republics, however, the emphasis remained on improving 'internationalization' rather than helping the native language and culture to develop more freely. For example, in February the Ukrainian Ministry of Culture introduced a series of measures to increase 'the patriotic and internationalist upbringing of Ukrainian youth'.[60] Similarly in Lithuania, at the beginning of April the Central Committee of the Lithuanian Communist Party adopted a resolution entitled 'On Measures for Improving National Relations in the Republic and Increasing the Effectiveness of Internationalist and Patriotic Education'.[61]

In the summer of 1987, the Gorbachev leadership began emphasizing that there were definite limits to what the non-Russians could hope to achieve. On 3 June Ligachev delivered a tough speech in Tbilisi which was broadcast on Soviet television and published in *Pravda*. He warned that

> nationalist and religious ideas are being kindled and attempts are being made to exploit the deepening of democracy and openness for spreading irresponsible demagogy hostile to the interests of the working people.

The Kremlin's number two man went on to criticize the Georgians not only for their economic performance but also because, as he put it, 'we have been told that there are still many people in the republic who do not speak Russian'. Native language–Russian bilingualism, he told them, 'has been and remains the key avenue for all our work in nationality relations'. Although he acknowledged that the native language should be respected, he implicitly reaffirmed the higher status of the Russian language. In present Soviet conditions, Ligachev reminded the Georgians, 'the specialist who is not fluent in Russian' is at a considerable disadvantage.[62]

In both the Ukraine and Byelorussia, the cultural intelligentsias were keeping up the pressure, especially on the language front; in response, local officials either issued veiled warnings or called on the literary communities to moderate their demands. On 11 June the Ukrainian Party ideological secretary, Iurii Iel'chenko, acknowledged that 'in recent years' there had indeed been 'a certain restriction' in the use of the Ukrainian language and that this was eliciting 'justifiable complaints'. Indicating that modest improvements would be made, he made it quite clear, though, that the basic official position was not about to change: 'We cannot and will not diverge from the Leninist principle of the purposeful formation of national–Russian bilingualism . . . Whether one likes it or not,' he told the writers, the parental choice of schools was a 'democratic' right 'determined by law', and it was there to stay.[63]

A few days later, however, at a plenum of the Board of the Writers' Union of the Ukraine, it was announced that a commission from within the organization had written to the Ukrainian authorities urging that the republican 'Ministry of Education and not parents determine the language of instruction in schools in accordance with the national composition of the children', and that the Ukrainian language, literature and history be made compulsory subjects in schools where teaching was in Russian.[64]

It was hardly surprising that the Ukrainian writers were determined to continue their campaign. At the same meeting, the distressing consequences of the discriminatory legislation that had been introduced since Thesis 19 was included in the 1958 school reform were revealed. The percentage of Ukrainian-language schools in the major cities had been reduced to around 16 per cent even though in 1979 Ukrainians made up 73.6 per cent of the Ukraine's population. Furthermore, in April, it had also been revealed that approximately 50 per cent of the republic's children were being taught in Russian schools and kindergartens.[65] In other words, the language of the Soviet Union's second largest nation was being relegated to the villages and farms.

Outraged by these figures, the poet Pavlychko reiterated the charge that the existing educational laws that allowed parents to choose the language in which their child was to be taught, though depicted as highly 'democratic', were in practice 'hypocritical and anti-democratic'. He explained:

> The right to choose the school language is only well suited for making sure that that language will not be the native language . . . behind this law are the conditions of life, and these conditions are organized in such a way that the need for this or that national language no longer exists.

Pavlychko argued that unless the state intervened to enable the Ukrainian language 'to breathe deeply and peacefully', in the long term it would survive only in Canada, which has a large Ukrainian population and where several of the provinces have facilities for teaching Ukrainian in state schools. Calling for Ukrainization in accordance with Lenin's instructions about establishing a detailed code to safeguard the rights of the national languages, he added,

> Some might say that the articles of such a code would violate human rights; it is now fashionable to speak about human rights. But I feel that there is no greater right in the world than a people's right to life.[66]

In Byelorussia, where the situation of the native language was even more catastrophic, the mounting frustration with the obstructive attitude of the local Party authorities resulted in a second open letter being sent to Gorbachev. Dated 4 June 1987, it was signed by 134 individuals, including, in addition to representatives of the literary and cultural intelligentsia, workers, technicians, scientists, teachers and journalists. The signatories rejected the rosy picture of their republic as 'a region of developed bilingualism' that was being offered by the Byelorussian Party leadership:

> Today's reality shows that 'developed bilingualism' in the Byelorussian S S R exists only on paper, that the Byelorussian language is infringed upon, and that for a long time now its declared freedom of development has not existed. Suffice it to say that in Byelorussian cities, where in 1979 the proportion of the Byelorussian population still amounted to 71.5 per cent, there is not one Byelorussian school left, that Byelorussian schools in the countryside are, in the majority of cases, [Byelorussian] only in official reports and on signboards.

Accusing the Byelorussian Party leadership of continuing 'arbitrarily to interpret and distort Leninist nationalities policy' and of suppressing *glasnost'* on the national problem, the signatories stated:

> We are confident that the Russification of Byelorussia conducted by the bureaucratic apparatus and the destruction of the Byelorussian language cannot but evoke a feeling of shame and protest among the Russian people. We are not against the Russian language, we are for the thorough learning of the Byelorussian and Russian languages in our republic on the same level, remembering that the Byelorussian language is the native language of our people and our culture.[67]

The reply appears to have been delivered by proxy. At the beginning of July the Byelorussian Party's ideological secretary, A. Pechennikov, met with writers and echoed his Ukrainian counterpart. He too admitted that in the 1950s and 1960s 'the uncontrolled exemption of pupils from studying the Byelorussian language increased, which led to the decrease of Byelorussian-language schools'. The lame excuse that he offered was that: 'The public education authorities did not notice this in time and, in essence, let this process take its course.' All the same, he warned that any attempt to view the language question separately from 'the process of the internationalization of social life . . . could lead to national narrow-mindedness'. He too announced certain minimal concessions in the language sphere but left no doubt that the primacy of the Russian language in Byelorussia would not be challenged.[68]

On 21 July *Pravda* published an editorial on the nationalities question that also ruled out the sort of changes for which the non-Russians were campaigning. It declared that 'genuine concern for the development of the native language has nothing in common with demands to restrict administratively the use of the Russian language'. A month later, the same message was again reiterated in *Pravda* by Bagramov, one of the spokesmen for the Party line on nationalities policy. Although his article called for more realism in dealing with national problems – something that had been urged over and over again ever since Brezhnev died – when it came actually to saying what the state of play was with respect to recognizing the demands being made by the non-Russians, it emerged that, apart from the infusion of *glasnost'*, Moscow's nationalities policy had changed very little. 'The main thing,' Bagramov stressed,

> is not to allow a legitimate love for one's native tongue to turn into linguistic chauvinism, which would be a barrier on the path of internationalization. Bilingualism in the native and Russian languages is the main avenue of linguistic development in the USSR. This does not change the legal status of the languages. *But their equality does not mean that their social functions are identical.*[69]

No doubt disappointed, but still full of fight, the non-Russians continued pressing for the de-Russification of their republics. While they were renewing their efforts, the Soviet leader revealed more about his attitude towards the Russian language and culture. On 8 August, Soviet television carried his speech to a group of Russian-language teachers from the United States. At one point, having stressed how widely English was studied in the Soviet Union, Gorbachev complained to the American visitors:

> With respect to the fact that the Russian language is so little studied in your country, I have wondered whether you in America have not become too haughty and conceited. And it is necessary to rid oneself of this, of any kind of chauvinistic presence in our countries.[70]

This was quite a change from how Lenin had understood these matters. He had considered the imposition of Russian on others as chauvinism. Now it appeared that a less than enthusiastic attitude towards learning Russian was interpreted as a form of chauvinism.

Glasnost' put to the test

During the summer of 1987 events in the sphere of national relations began to move with ever greater speed. On 14 June a large demonstration in Riga marked the opening of a new stage in the campaign being waged by the non-Russians. Now the non-Russians began to put *glasnost'* and 'democratization' to the test in the streets and squares. Newly-released dissidents resumed their political activity, this time in the open; new 'informal' patriotic groups sprang up and *samizdat* activity was revitalized. In the new conditions, it was no longer simply a case of protest and defiance: the non-Russians had good reason to believe that the time had come to make themselves heard, to demand what they felt was rightfully owed them, and to ensure that a review of nationalities policy was placed on the agenda.

In the Baltic republics the painful issues connected with the Soviet destruction of the independence of Latvia, Lithuania and Estonia now came to the fore. The initiative taken by the Latvian human rights group Helsinki 86 in announcing that it intended to honour the victims of the mass deportation of Latvians on the night of 14 June 1941 acted as the catalyst. Although the authorities had plenty of warning from the dissidents, they seem to have been unsure how to respond. On the one hand they harassed members of the unofficial group, yet, on the other hand, they gave permission for the commemoration to take place. On the day of the anniversary, several thousand people took part in a peaceful march and gathering by the Statue of Liberty in Riga, the success of which clearly embarrassed the authorities.

The local press promptly claimed that the demonstration had been instigated by 'Western radio voices', the 'reactionary emigration' and 'irresponsible, nationalistic elements'. Nevertheless, the focusing of attention on the events of 1941 only resulted in demands for a more honest depiction of Latvia's history and the removal of 'blank spots' in the treatment of the Soviet takeover of the Baltic states.[71] Similar pressure also grew in Estonia and Lithuania. In July, for instance, an Estonian literary monthly began publishing a long-suppressed novel about the fate of Estonians who had been deported to Siberia.[72]

While Latvian dissidents were contemplating their next move, the Crimean Tatars forcefully reminded the Gorbachev leadership and the outside world of the continuation of their long-standing struggle in defence of their national rights. It seems that some time in the spring the Crimean Tatar movement had renewed its lobbying of the authorities and begun issuing fresh appeals to prominent Soviet cultural figures. Several Russian writers offered their support, including Evtushenko, Sergei Baruzdin and Bulat Okudzhava. In June, Crimean Tatar representatives were received by Petr Demichev, the first deputy chairman of the USSR Supreme Soviet, but did not come away reassured. To maintain the pressure, on 6 July several dozen Crimean Tatars held a protest demonstration in Red Square. Although the police confiscated some of the banners, no arrests were made.

The authorities responded to this new upsurge of Crimean Tatar activity by setting up a special commission headed by the Soviet head of state, Andrei Gromyko, to consider the Crimean Tatars' demands. After their experiences with the Soviet Government in the 1960s, the Crimean Tatars do not seem to have been too impressed by this decision. On 23 July they held another demonstration in Moscow, this time outside the Party Central Committee building. That same day TASS broke the news about the establishment of the state commission. The tone of the announcement, however, was hardly sympathetic and needlessly dwelt on the question of the supposed collaboration of the Crimean Tatars with the German occupiers, a charge from which they had been officially absolved in 1967. The following day more than 100 Crimean Tatars again demonstrated outside the Party headquarters and unsuccessfully demanded to meet with Gorbachev. The protests in the Soviet capital continued even after Gromyko met with Crimean Tatar representatives on 27 July. A few days later, the authorities ended the demonstrations in Moscow by forcing the Crimean Tatar activists, whose numbers had swelled to over 800, to leave the capital.

Although the Crimean Tatars had been allowed to hold their demonstrations, they now had to contend with a tougher stance by the authorities as well as a press campaign aimed at discrediting their leaders as irresponsible fanatics. During August and September there were unofficial reports of continuing Crimean Tatar protests in Uzbekistan and elsewhere. The Soviet press, though, did not acknowledge these demonstrations until 19 September, when the Uzbek daily *Pravda Vostoka* referred to complaints about 'extremists' who were 'provoking a certain section of the Crimean Tatars, particularly young people, to [attend] various assemblages and egging people on to commit breaches of the peace'.[73]

Meanwhile, attention had shifted again to the Baltic republics. Here, in an impressive display of Baltic solidarity, the Latvian Helsinki 86 group, Lithuanian former political prisoners, and the newly-formed Estonian unofficial Group for the Full Publication of the Molotov–Ribbentrop Pact issued calls for peaceful demonstrations to be held in the capitals of all three republics on 23 August, the 48th anniversary of the signing of the Molotov–Ribbentrop Pact. Although the proclaimed purpose was to commemorate the Baltic victims of Stalinism, the implicit motive was to pressure the Soviet authorities to publish the full text of the Nazi–Soviet agreement which had sealed the fate of the Baltic states and to provide a more truthful picture of how Soviet rule had been imposed on the three countries.

Despite warnings to the organizers and the use made by the authorities of the press to defend the Molotov–Ribbentrop Pact and to depict the planned commemorative meetings as provocations hatched in the West, the peaceful demonstrations were held. In both Latvia and Estonia several thousand people were reported to have taken part while in Lithuania the number was in the hundreds. In all three republics the police were present in force but did not attempt to break up the gatherings. Only in Riga, at the end of the day, were there ugly scenes – shown on local television – when the security forces moved in and started beating and arresting the demonstrators, 86 of whom are known to have been detained.[74]

The Baltic demonstrations of 23 August 1987 were a watershed for all three nations. Central issues that had long been taboo were now spotlighted. Although at first there was a virulent press campaign against the organizers of the protests, it proved counter-productive. The Balts were forced to think things through and to decide where their loyalties lay. This politicization of the situation only generated more pressure in defence of national rights. On 16 September, the head of the Latvian Writers' Union, Janis Peters, set the new tone by complaining in *Pravda*:

I think representatives of the social sciences and journalists do not do enough to emphasize in our civic consciousness the idea that each Union republic is a sovereign state, with its own constitution, parliament, and government, anthem, flag and coat of arms.

An even clearer picture of the level of discontent in the Baltic republics was provided in a remarkable protest letter by the leading officials of the Estonian Writers', Composers', Artists', Film-Makers' and Architects' Unions. Objecting to the crude responses in the Soviet press to the demonstration on 23 August, the hitherto conservative cultural functionaries stressed that:

Calling criticism of the actual state of Soviet [life] slander and calling the expression and defence of the interests of small nationalities a manifestation of nationalism does not help to improve the public's mood and the social atmosphere, [nor does it help] in the renewal of society or in activating people or in raising their awareness.

The representatives of Estonia's official cultural establishment also called for the full publication of the Molotov–Ribbentrop Pact and for an end to the suppression in schools of 'complicated and openly tragic historical periods in the life of the Latvian, Lithuanian, Estonian, and all the Soviet peoples'. The letter, addressed to the director of the Estonian Party's Propaganda and Agitation Department, was considered too outspoken to be reproduced in the official press and was published in a *samizdat* journal.[75]

There was trouble on a less dramatic scale in other republics as well. In both the Ukraine and Moldavia the Writers' Unions expressed their dissatisfaction with the modest measures that had been taken to bolster the status of the native language. The Ukrainian writers responded to a resolution on the national question adopted by the Ukrainian Communist Party in the first part of August by putting forward their own 'counter-resolution' that went a lot further than what the Shcherbitsky leadership was prepared to offer. This development in September again highlighted the gulf between the Ukraine's nationally minded intelligentsia and the authorities in Kiev.[76]

The issue of the outlawed Ukrainian Catholic Church also took on a new aspect in the summer of 1987 when two clandestine Ukrainian Catholic bishops and a number of clergy emerged from the underground in order to strengthen the campaign for the legalization of their Church.[77] Moreover, the vitality of religion in Western Ukraine, the Ukrainian Catholic stronghold, was dramatically highlighted by the intense excitement that was generated by the reported apparitions in April of Our Lady by a locked-up Uniate chapel in Hrushiv, near Lvov. In early September, *Moscow News* acknowledged that 'some half a million people [had] dropped everything and rushed to the place where, as they said, the Virgin Mary had appeared'.[78]

In neighbouring Moldavia the situation was becoming more tense. In July a conflict developed between the Moldavian Writers' Union and the republic's

State Committee for Television and Radio Broadcasting. According to a complaint made later that month at a plenum of the Moldavian Communist Party, the Board of the Writers' Union demanded the lifting of 'controls over the ideational content of programmes, the liquidation of bilingualism in broadcasts, and a complete changeover to the use of Moldavian only in television broadcasts'.[79] Another indication of the strained relations between Moldavia's Party leadership and the republic's nationally minded intelligentsia was revealed in September when the Moldavian Party chief, Grossu, revealed that the editors of the Moldavian literary weekly *Literatura shi arta* had been censured for 'serious lapses and mistakes'. From what he said it seems that they had allowed 'national' elements to overshadow 'internationalist' ones.[80]

In the same speech, Grossu admitted the existence of conflicts in the workplace between members of different nationalities and 'manifestations of apolitical, nationalistic, extremist' attitudes among students at a number of institutes of higher education. It was not until the beginning of 1988, however, that details were to emerge about ethnic brawls that took place in Moldavia during the autumn and about students who had got into trouble for allegedly inciting national enmity.[81]

As the long summer of discontent wore on, the head of the KGB, Viktor Chebrikov, delivered a tough speech accusing Western intelligence services of trying to sow discord among the peoples of the Soviet Union. Showing little of the new realism that was being called for in the press, he claimed on 10 September that

> although these efforts are for the most part hopeless and futile, still they are having a negative effect on a certain segment of Soviet people who have been infected by the virus of nationalism. Evidence of this is provided by the nationalistic manifestations in Alma-Ata late last year, the actions of a group of extremists from among the Crimean Tatars, and the recent provocative sallies by nationalists in the capitals of the Soviet Baltic republics.[82]

A similar message was delivered by *Pravda* in its editorial of 27 September. After all the complaints and demands that the non-Russians had voiced over the last 15 months or so, the Party organ ascribed 'arguments . . . about a mythical infringement of the rights of certain nations in the Soviet Union, about the Russification of outlying areas where other nationalities predominate [sic]' to 'bourgeois propaganda'. The only new element in the editorial was a condemnation 'of all forms of national nihilism'. At least the point that Aitmatov had recently made seemed to have registered.

The question of economic autonomy

Until now, the Gorbachev leadership had evaded discussing the question of whether economic reform would lead to a broadening of republican powers.

It was becoming evident, though, that in practice the new process of decentralization was working to the benefit not of the republican governments but of individual enterprises. In fact, republican ministries were being eliminated and enterprises made accountable directly to all-Union ministries in Moscow. On 7 September, for example, it was announced that the Soviet ministries responsible for the coal industry, ferrous metallurgy and geology had been changed from joint Union-republican bodies to all-Union ones.[83] A month later, non-ferrous metals industries were also subordinated directly to an all-Union ministry in Moscow.[84] The extent of this recentralization in the name of decentralization was revealed at the beginning of November by the weekly *News from Ukraine* which disclosed that in the Ukraine 'the ministries of steel and coal industries, geology as well as oil and gas industries are no more'.[85]

It was perhaps not entirely a coincidence then, that on 26 September an Estonian newspaper published a radical proposal by four Estonian communists, hitherto regarded as conformist figures, to turn their republic into a 'self-managing economic zone'. Drawing on the example of the closed economic zones in China and the free-market reforms that had been introduced both in that country and in Hungary, they argued that this bold step would increase economic efficiency as well as trade with the West.[86] Interestingly, on 9 September 1987 *Sovetskaia Estoniia* reported that Estonia had been selected for an experiment in decentralized customs control, whereby the republic was to be given control over customs control on its territory.

Here again was an example of non-Russians taking a general principle which the Gorbachev leadership was promoting – in this case, *khozraschet*, or cost-accounting – and developing it to suit local, or rather national, interests. Although at the time this concept of economic autonomy for the Baltic republics may have seemed utopian, the idea had been planted and was to germinate.

A large measure of economic autonomy was also one of the demands made in a ten-point programme that was issued by the Latvian activists of Helsinki 86 on 3 October. They also called for a free press, recognition of some form of 'republican' citizenship, curbs on large-scale immigration to Latvia, for all residents of the republic to learn and use Latvian, and for cultural facilities for Latvia's non-Russian and non-Latvian minorities such as the Ukrainians, Poles, Jews and Byelorussians.[87]

'Nationalist epidemics'

The 'virus of nationalism' was proving to be hardy and contagious. In Estonia, further political protests took place on 21 October in Voru and 7 November in Parnu.[88] In Latvia, the authorities attempted to prevent any unofficial gathering in Riga on 18 November, the anniversary of Latvia's declaration of independence, by organizing an anti-American demonstration in the Latvian capital. All the same, thousands of Latvians took part in a spontaneous commemoration of Latvia's freedom.[89]

The Crimean Tatars were also continuing their protests. On 7 October police prevented some 2,000 Crimean Tatars from proceeding with their planned 150-mile march from Taman in southern Russia to Simferopol in the Crimea.[90] A week later, the state commission examining Crimean Tatar demands announced a number of cultural concessions, including new newspapers and more publications and broadcast time in Crimean Tatar.[91] Needless to say, this fell far short of what the Crimean Tatars were seeking.

In Armenia, feelings were running high over the problem of environmental pollution and the issue of the territories held by Azerbaijan but claimed by the Armenians. On 17 October several thousand Armenians held a peaceful demonstration in their capital city to demand the closure of a chemical factory that was a main source of pollution.[92] The following day, however, about 1,000 people turned out to demand the transfer of the autonomous regions of Nagornyi Karabakh and the Nakhichevan ASSR to Armenia.

Since the preparations for the Twenty-seventh Party Congress in the autumn of 1985, the Armenians had bombarded the Party and government offices in Moscow with thousands of individual and collective appeals for the unification of Nagornyi Karabakh with Armenia. In 1986 a small group of Armenian intellectuals had formed a committee to campaign for this end. In May 1987 they stepped up their activities and by the autumn had collected the signatures of 80,000 Armenians, 31,000 of them living in Nagornyi Karabakh. Early in October, however, there was some sort of trouble between Armenians and Azerbaijani authorities in the village of Chardakhy in Nagornyi Karabakh, which sparked the protest in Erevan. Even though the demonstrators are reported to have carried pictures of Gorbachev, they were dispersed by the police. Determined to keep up the pressure, the Nagornyi Karabakh Committee led by Igor Muradian decided to try lobbying in Moscow itself and in November sent the first of several delegations to the capital.[93]

By the end of the year, informal patriotic associations were also assuming prominence in the Ukraine, Byelorussia and Georgia. In Kiev, the Ukrainian Culturological Club, formed at the beginning of the summer, provided a new focus for national dissent in the Ukrainian capital. Its unofficial public meetings generated unprecedented exchanges in the pages of the city's evening newspaper.[94] In Lvov, in the Western Ukraine, Viacheslav Chornovil, Mykhailo Horyn' and other former political prisoners renewed the publication of the samizdat journal, the Ukrainian Herald. The Georgians, for their part, founded the Ilia Chavchavadze Society, named after the nineteenth-century writer and national hero. Together with Armenian dissidents, the Ukrainian and Georgian activists also established an Inter-National Committee in Defence of Political Prisoners, the first meeting of which was held in Erevan in January 1988.[95]

Perhaps the most telling sign of the new dynamics of national assertiveness was what was happening in Byelorussia. Until now the nation's writers had been conducting an uphill struggle against Russification. Towards the end of 1987, however, a Byelorussian patriotic movement began to emerge that was led by new informal associations of nationally minded youth. On 1 November several of these groups organized an open-air public meeting in Minsk that turned into a political demonstration. Among other things, participants referred to the mass repressions against Byelorussians in the 1930s as 'genocide', raised the question of the current situation of the Byelorussian language and culture, and called for the 'full historical truth' about their nation's experiences.[96] The growth of the Byelorussian patriotic movement was confirmed by the attendance at the first conference of unofficial Byelorussian patriotic youth associations, which was convened in late December: some 30 groups were represented.[97]

. . . but still no change in policy

While the republican authorities were doing their best to halt the tide of nationalism, all eyes turned to Moscow to see what lead Gorbachev would give in his address on the 70th anniversary of the Bolshevik Revolution. His speech was expected to define the new line on Stalinism and the Khrushchev and Brezhnev periods. Naturally, it was assumed that he would also have something to say about the national question.

On the eve of the jubilee there were a few signs which suggested that perhaps the Soviet leader would take a more candid view of the national problem and would move in the direction of acknowledging the need to restore Leninist principles, as understood by the non-Russians, in national relations. For instance, on 4 October, *Izvestia* carried a long article entitled 'In the Language of Equality', which summarized these principles as: 'the free and sovereign self-determination of nations and the voluntary character of their uniting together'. Moreover, at a time when reform-minded economists were seeking ideas and parallels for 'restructuring' from the NEP period, the author of the piece, Grigorii Melikiants, also stressed that the success of NEP 'had depended on there being a correct line in nationalities policy'.

Another seemingly encouraging indication was the comment that was made in the introductory statement at a special press conference on the national question held in Moscow on 30 October in connection with the 70th jubilee. According to TASS, Nikolai Shishlin, a senior executive of the Central Committee, told foreign journalists:

As is known, we have encountered over the recent period not only manifestations of lofty socialist patriotism, not only the truly internationalist spirit, but also nationalist sentiments. And the remedy here is Lenin's internationalist policy, whose essence is not the proclamation of some truisms, but practical work for firmly asserting real equality for all: economic, political and cultural equality.[98]

In the event, Gorbachev's eagerly awaited speech, delivered on 2 November, proved a distinct disappointment. Not only was his approach to the Stalin period cautious – he hardly went beyond what Khrushchev had acknowledged in 1956 – but he also devoted minimal attention to the nationalities question. He did, however, dwell on the Molotov–Ribbentrop Pact, but here too he merely reiterated the standard Soviet defence of Moscow's actions and failed to discuss the issues that were of such concern to the Baltic nations.[99]

An important chance had been missed to reassure the non-Russians that their concerns were not being ignored. Nevertheless, behind the scenes, it seems that the seriousness of the nationalities question was finally registering and that the Gorbachev leadership had accepted that it had to be seen to be treating the problem with due sensitivity and attention. In the second half of December, the *Guardian*'s Moscow correspondent reported that it had been decided to devote one of the next Central Committee plenums to the national problem and that working papers and research drafts were already circulating among Central Committee staffers.[100]

For the time being, however, the Gorbachev leadership maintained essentially the same approach as before. An editorial in *Pravda* at the end of the year reiterated that 'economic and social tasks must be resolved from statewide standpoints, and manifestations of parochialism and parasitism not be permitted'. The only thing that had changed over the year in the official formulations was that 'national nihilism and chauvinism' were now acknowledged as equal evils, and that *Pravda* was referring to 'nationalist epidemics'.[101]

17

Crisis in the Empire

═══

Early in 1988, after almost three years in power, Gorbachev squandered another opportunity to inject some new thinking into nationalities policy. On 17 and 18 February, the Central Committee held a plenum on education. It met against the background of rising national tensions. The Estonians, Lithuanians, Crimean Tatars, Jews, Georgians and Armenians were all mounting new protests; the Russian ultra-nationalist Pamiat' association was still generating controversy; and the Ukrainian, Moldavian, Byelorussian and Kirghiz intellectuals were in a defiant mood and pressing for the de-Russification of the education system. Yet, apart from more platitudes about 'true internationalism' and respect for the national cultures, all that Gorbachev offered was a general statement acknowledging that the Party 'ought to devote a Central Committee plenum to the problem of nationalities policy'. For all the urgency – the Soviet leader himself described the national problem as 'a most fundamental and vital issue' – he did not indicate how soon such a meeting could be expected.[1] The only new note at the plenum was Ligachev's admission that, when it came to showing proper respect for the native language, 'Party and state agencies in some regions' – such as Bashkiria – lacked 'realism, flexibility and at times even political understanding'.[2]

In contrast to the Gorbachev leadership's sterile approach, the non-Russian activists were busy drawing up constructive proposals and programmes for reducing national tensions. A joint committee of Ukrainian, Armenian and Georgian dissidents, for example, proposed the following 'minimal' reforms: in all the non-Russian republics, the local language should be made a state language; the cultural facilities of small nations or minorities living within the borders of another republic should be safeguarded; provisions in the education laws promoting Russification should be repealed; national problems left over from the Stalin era should be cleared up; the right of peoples and individuals to be reunited with their nations or compatriots living outside the Soviet Union should be recognized; and the non-Russians should be given a greater say in the way that the USSR's resources are distributed and environmental questions handled.[3]

The newly-formed Estonian National Independence Party took a more 'maximalist' position: in January 1988 it issued a platform advocating broad political, cultural and economic autonomy for Estonia, as well as full respect for internationally recognized human and civil rights.[4]

Despite the fact that this was supposed to be a time of *glasnost'* and 'democratization', and that most of the non-Russian dissidents were modifying their tactics accordingly so as to be able to operate 'within the system', the authorities were still determined to prevent these voices from being heard. In December 1987, several leading Ukrainian and Armenian national rights campaigners were prevented from travelling to Moscow to take part in an unofficial human rights seminar at which they were to have chaired a section dealing with the nationalities problem.[5] In January, the Georgian press attacked the informal Ilia Chavchavadze Society,[6] and on 2 February TASS denounced the founders of the Estonian National Independence Party as virtual criminals. In the Baltic republics generally, the local press responded to the new wave of protests by once again blaming the trouble on 'nationalists' and 'foreign radio voices'. In the case of the growing Armenian agitation over the issue of Nagornyi Karabakh, the Soviet media adhered to its other traditional approach – it maintained silence.

So far, however embarrassing or irritating the national unrest that had forced its way into the open, the Gorbachev leadership had been able to live with it and had gotten away with muddling through. Indeed, there seems to have been a belief that while the central task of *perestroika* was being pursued the national problem could be kept on the back burner. The subsequent extraordinary events in the Transcaucasus, though, were dramatically to expose the perils of prevarication and incomplete *glasnost'* and to force the Kremlin to begin addressing the nationalities question with the attention that this issue demanded.

Turmoil in the Transcaucasus
In mid-February the long-smouldering problem of Nagornyi Karabakh suddenly flared up and within days the Gorbachev leadership was confronted with a crisis of staggering proportions. Apart from the ethnic bloodshed between Armenians and Azerbaijanis, the very scale of the civil disobedience was to make it seem as if nationalist passions had caused the entire Armenian and Azerbaijani nations to forget that they were a part of the Soviet Union. Moreover, the spectacle of first the Nagornyi Karabakh authorities acting as if their region was a sovereign unit, and then, despite the Kremlin's fuming, of two neighbouring Union republics entering into a state of open hostility, was both an unprecedented challenge to Moscow's authority and a stark reminder of just how unsuccessful decades of efforts to create a supra-national 'Soviet Man' had really been.

As far as can be ascertained, the sequence of events leading up to the explosion was as follows. Between November and early February three delegations of Armenians from Nagornyi Karabakh went to Moscow to lobby the Party Central Committee and the USSR Supreme Soviet. They were apparently given reassurances by candidate Politburo member Petr Demichev and other officials that their demands were 'neither anti-Soviet nor nationalistic' and led to believe that the question of Nagornyi Karabakh would be reviewed.

Believing that victory was now within their grasp, the Armenians of Nagornyi Karabakh began organizing meetings to pass resolutions about the 'reunification' of their region with Armenia. On 12 February, however, senior Azerbaijani officials arrived in Nagornyi Karabakh and inflamed the situation by denouncing the local Armenian movement and insisting that there could be no question of changing the status of Nagornyi Karabakh. This triggered off Armenian protests and demonstrations throughout the region. In the midst of these, on 18 February, the latest Armenian delegation to Moscow returned to Stepanakert, the capital of Nagornyi Karabakh, convinced, as one eye-witness put it, that 'they had won'. Defying the Azerbaijani authorities, one local soviet after another promptly voted to rejoin Armenia. On 20 February, the Armenian-dominated regional soviet met and decided to call for the transfer of the enclave to Armenia.[7]

This defiant act put Moscow on the spot. If the Kremlin gave way it risked not only alienating the Azerbaijanis but also inviting other claims for contested boundaries between republics to be redrawn. The issue was further complicated by the fact that at the time of the 1979 census, apart from the 123,000 Armenians living in Nagornyi Karabakh, there were a further 350,000 Armenians in other parts of Azerbaijan, while 161,000 Azerbaijanis lived in Armenia.

The Gorbachev leadership decided to be firm and to act before news of what had happened got out. On 21 February the Politburo rejected the demands for the incorporation of Nagornyi Karabakh into Armenia, condemned the 'extremist' manifestations that had led to the disturbance of public order, and ordered the Party organs in Armenia and Azerbaijan to take measures to 'normalize the situation'.[8] Two Politburo candidate members were dispatched to Nagornyi Karabakh to ensure that this was done, and two more senior officials were sent a few days later. But things were already getting out of control.

Despite the news blackout, reports about what was happening in Nagornyi Karabakh reached Erevan on 20 February just as a demonstration of 40,000 people was taking place against the construction of a chemical factory on the outskirts of the city. Pledging their solidarity with their compatriots in the disputed region, the protesters vowed not to disperse until the Armenian authorities came out in support of the transfer of the Nagornyi Karabakh autonomous region to Armenia. The following day there was an even larger demonstration and news of the protests finally reached the outside world. Only on 23 February, when the number of protesters in Erevan had grown to

100,000, did the central press begin acknowledging the crisis. Even then it sought to minimize the scale of the protests and remained silent about the first of the bloody clashes in Nagornyi Karabakh between Armenians and Azerbaijanis that left two Azerbaijanis dead.

By 26 February, Erevan was paralysed by strikes. Between 700,000 and a million protesters massed in the city's streets and squares; an astonishing figure considering that the number of Armenians living in Armenia in 1979 was 2·7 million. Gorbachev appeared on television, appealing to the Armenian and Azerbaijani nations for calm and a 'reasonable approach' to the Nagornyi Karabakh issue based on 'the Leninist principles of nationalities policy'. On the same day, he received an Armenian delegation consisting of two leading writers, Silva Kaputikian and Zori Balian. He complained to them that the Armenians were 'stabbing *perestroika* in the back', but promised that a 'just solution' would be found.[9]

Early Western reports noted that many of the Armenian protesters carried portraits of the Soviet leader. Evidently, they were prepared to forget about the way in which Moscow had ignored the Nagornyi Karabakh problem and to put their faith in Gorbachev and *perestroika*. Kaputikian subsequently recounted how, on meeting the Soviet leader, she had repeated to herself: 'This is the first time in 67 years that Moscow has set eyes on us.' The following day, on returning to Erevan, she told the protesters: 'Why are we here today? Because someone has at last allowed us to raise our heads, to come down into the streets and to speak out.'[10] On hearing reassuring reports from Kaputikian and Balian, the 'organizing committee' that had emerged in Erevan decided to place the nation's hope in Gorbachev and to suspend the demonstrations for a month.

The very next evening, however, the Azerbaijani city of Sumgait erupted. It seems that on learning from Radio Baku that two Azerbaijanis had recently been killed in the ethnic strife, some Azerbaijanis went on the rampage against local Armenians. Eventually, on 4 March, TASS admitted that a total of 31 people of 'different nationalities' had been killed. The Armenians immediately began claiming that the number of Armenian victims was far higher, and that the authorities were concealing the truth. On 29 March, denying that this was the case, *Izvestia* finally provided the first breakdown of the casualties: 26 Armenians killed and six Azerbaijanis.

Terrified Armenians began fleeing from Azerbaijan to Armenia, and vice versa. In Nagornyi Karabakh protests continued, while in Sumgait troops were deployed to maintain order. On 8 March 300,000 Armenians in Armenia held a funeral demonstration for the victims of the Sumgait killings. In Moscow, too, hundreds of Armenians began gathering at the city's Armenian cemetery to exchange information and to protest against the very incomplete Soviet media coverage – 'criminal silence', some of them called it – of the continuing crisis. All this time, and during the weeks to follow, Western journalists were barred from travelling to Erevan or Nagornyi Karabakh.

During his meeting with Kaputikian and Balian, Gorbachev had conceded: 'I now have a number of major nationality issues to deal with.'[11] Indeed, while the Kremlin's attention was focused on the Armenian-Azerbaijani conflict, there were further instances of national unrest elsewhere in the Soviet domain. On 20 February an ethnic brawl broke out in Moscow involving hundreds of Russian youths and workers from the traditionally Moslem republics.[12] Four days later several thousand Estonians defied a ban on demonstrations and gathered in Tallinn to commemorate Estonian Independence Day.[13] The Crimean Tatars, too, kept up their protests and demonstrated in Moscow, Krasnodar and Uzbekistan.[14]

Confronted with this immense challenge, Gorbachev began to modify his tone. On 4 March he discussed the nationalities question with a foreign guest, Franz Muhri, the leader of the Austrian Communist Party. Although the Soviet media did not report on this particular aspect of their talks, Muhri later informed Western journalists that

> Gorbachev told me that many of the problems the Soviet Union is facing now are the result of a too harsh and insensitive nationalities policy in the past.[15]

Just over a week later Gorbachev visited Yugoslavia, a multinational socialist state with a nationalities problem of its own. The Soviet leader went out of his way to create the impression that he was determined not to evade the USSR's nationalities question. Abandoning Moscow's old claim that Soviet society was a model of good national relations, Gorbachev stressed that no country was without its nationality problems. Asked by journalists if the national ferment in the USSR worried him, he replied:

> We are going through that stage of life in all socialist societies when we are producing first and foremost an interpretation of the entire history which we have experienced, and we are drawing lessons from it. It is never too late to learn.

Gorbachev went on to say that, as in Yugoslavia, the multinational nature of the Soviet Union demanded 'constant attention from the state' and the 'creation of conditions in which all peoples feel comfortable in their common home'. This meant that equality had to be ensured in the 'economic, social, cultural, language and literary spheres', otherwise problems made themselves felt.[16] Speaking on another occasion before the Yugoslav Parliament, the Soviet leader declared:

> We think it essential to ensure [the] democratic solution [of nationality problems] in line with the interests of both each individual ethnic group in the Soviet family and our socialist society as a whole.[17]

Referring specifically to the trouble in the Transcaucasus, Gorbachev stressed that the conflict did not have an anti-Soviet, and by implication, anti-Russian, character.

> What was it about? Nobody there raised the question either of Soviet power, or of withdrawal from the Soviet state, or of socialism, no! Both the role of the Party and the policy that it has pursued in the sphere of national relations since Lenin were recognized. What it was about was that there are issues of a cultural and ethnic character that have recently (*sic*) been overlooked. Problems have accumulated. This, in fact, was what it was about.[18]

The Soviet leadership was not able to draw consolation from this half-truth for long. Within weeks, the trust of the Armenians had been lost, and arguably the most loyal friend the Russians had in the Soviet empire became increasingly alienated. Gradually the Azerbaijanis, too, were given reason by Moscow to feel hard done by.

Smothering the fire

With the end of the moratorium on demonstrations in Erevan fast approaching and the Armenians in Nagornyi Karabakh and Moscow continuing their protests, the Kremlin began to act. First, on 9 March, the government leaders of Armenia and Azerbaijan were summoned to Moscow and told by Gorbachev that a special commission would examine the Nagornyi Karabakh issue. Nine days later representatives from the intellectual elites of the two nations were received in Moscow. So far, so good, it seemed. During the next week, however, developments took an odd turn. In an orchestrated campaign that was reminiscent of pre-*glasnost'* days, the presidiums of the Supreme Soviets of all the Union republics except Armenia and Azerbaijan met in quick succession to express their concern and to call on the two errant republics to uphold the 'friendship of the peoples'.

On 21 March *Pravda* signalled that Moscow was not about to yield to the Armenian demands nor tolerate further demonstrations. In a highly tactless article, it blamed shortcomings in 'internationalist upbringing' for the 'feelings of national egotism' which it claimed had taken hold of the Armenian people. Furthermore, contradicting what Gorbachev had said in Yugoslavia, the newspaper charged that the campaign for the reunification of Nagornyi Karabakh with Armenia had 'a distinct anti-socialist tinge' and that its activists were wittingly or unwittingly serving the cause of 'those trans-Atlantic Sovietologists who state that socialism in the USSR can only be defeated by breaking it down into national components'.

This unexpected volte-face outraged the Armenians and brought protesters out onto the streets of Erevan. The following day, *Izvestia* only made matters worse by attacking one of the leaders of the Karabakh Committee, Igor Muradian. Among other things, it alleged that he had threatened to 'look for support beyond the country's borders' – the example of the International

Court at the Hague was cited – and of having asserted that 'Armenians in Nagornyi Karabakh have faith neither in Moscow, nor the Central Committee, nor supreme justice, nor the Russian people, nor anything else'. TASS joined in and accused another Armenian activist of having advocated that Armenia be declared a 'non-Party' Soviet republic.[19]

On 23 March the Presidium of the Supreme Soviet of the USSR met in Moscow and in effect rejected the Armenian demands that Nagornyi Karabakh be transferred to Armenia. It declared that it was 'intolerable' for 'self-styled formations' to try to pressure the State into changing borders. Invoking the Soviet Constitution, it also emphasized that it was the obligation of the USSR to protect the sovereign rights of Union republics and the inviolability of their borders.[20] The following day, the Politburo announced a broad conciliatory programme designed to improve the cultural, economic and social conditions in Nagornyi Karabakh. The package of spending measures, reminiscent of the concessions used to pacify the situation in the Abkhaz ASSR a decade earlier, ignored Azerbaijani arguments that the Nagornyi Karabakh region was already relatively well off.[21] Thus the compromise solution satisfied neither the Armenians nor their adversaries.

It was at this point that the crisis entered a new and more dangerous stage. In order to prevent the resumption of mass protests, demonstrations in Erevan were banned and on 24 March troops were sent into the city. A number of leading Armenian activists, including the veteran national rights campaigner Paruir Airikian, were arrested. For many Armenians the military occupation of their capital was the final straw. They cynically dubbed the military helicopters patrolling overhead 'the first swallows of *perestroika*'.[22] At the end of March, the prominent Moscow-based dissident, Sergei Grigoriants, who is part Armenian, noted the drastic change in attitudes: 'it used to be that the Armenians vented their nationalist sentiments against Azerbaijanis across the border. Now they are venting them against Soviet power.'[23]

The dejection and disillusionment felt by many Armenians was perhaps most poignantly expressed by Silva Kaputikian in her *samizdat* open letter of 5 April to Russian intellectuals. 'Don't panic,' she reassured them, 'we will not leave the Soviet Union . . . in any case, we have nowhere to go because Turkey is behind our back.' But then she went on to describe how after three generations the Armenian nation's trust and hope in Russia had been rudely shattered:

> We went out with slogans of trust in the country of socialism, in the Russian people, in *perestroika*, with portraits of the General Secretary of the Central Committee of the CPSU, M. S. Gorbachev. But they [the Party and government organs, the Soviet media, and the perpetrators of Sumgait] opened fire on us.

Her people, Kaputikian stressed, had experienced a 'spiritual Sumgait'.[24]

Why did Moscow suddenly resort to strong-arm tactics? In order to preempt the renewal of demonstrations in Erevan after a month's pause? To reassert the centre's authority before the situation got completely out of control – that is, out of panic? Kaputikian suspected that Moscow had let the small Armenian nation down because ultimately it attached more weight to the 50-million strong 'Turkic' element in the Soviet Union. But there is another factor that may perhaps have had a bearing on the Kremlin's actions.[25] On 13 March, when Gorbachev was out of the country, *Sovetskaia Rossiia* published a notorious letter by Nina Andreeva, which was denounced only 20 days later by *Pravda* as 'a manifesto of the anti-*perestroika* forces'. During this period the political opponents of Gorbachev, led almost certainly by Ligachev, may briefly have had the upper hand.[26]

Whatever the explanation, the damage was done. Feelings continued to run high in Erevan and Nagornyi Karabakh. Nevertheless, Armenian resentment was expressed in peaceful forms of civil disobedience, such as a crippling strike in Stepanakert. As for the Azerbaijanis, many of them were growing increasingly angry at the way in which their case and the actions of their compatriots who had clashed with Armenians were being depicted in the central press. Thus, although there was an uneasy lull in the crisis, it seemed only a matter of time before there would be more trouble.

Things begin to be called by their names
While national unrest in the Soviet Union was making the headlines around the world, the discussion of the nationalities question in the Soviet press was becoming franker and more substantial. During the first half of 1988, not only did many non-Russians, and for that matter some Russians also, become bolder in speaking out on this issue, but also more attention was devoted to identifying the roots of the national problem and to proposing remedies. Even the delicate question of the relationship between the Russians and the non-Russians began to be broached. In February, the Russian literary editor Sergei Baruzdin, who had already made a greater contribution than most to extending *glasnost'* to the national question, audaciously raised the issue of the Russian 'elder brother' syndrome. He stated in the pages of *Literaturnaia gazeta* that, in his opinion, 'the division of peoples into the "elder" and the "younger" . . . is insulting to both'.[27]

The following month, the Novosti press agency issued a short article in English on the national question by another Russian, Iurii Poliakov, a corresponding member of the USSR Academy of Science. He argued that what was needed was a fundamental change in mutual perceptions and attitudes, a 'psychological restructuring'. The Russians, he explained, 'who have become used to the role of the benefactor have found themselves on an equal footing with other nationalities'.[28]

This problem was evident enough at a plenum of the Board of the USSR Writers' Union which took place at the beginning of March. Baruzdin again denounced the concept of the 'elder brother', stating that it was a consequence of the Stalinist perversion of Leninist nationalities policy. 'The friendship of the peoples,' he pointed out, 'does not suppose the friendship of all around one nation, but equal respect for all, whether they be large or small.' He also stated that it was time to reject the notion that 'all the nations and peoples' had voluntarily united with Russia. The latter, he stressed, 'was a prison of nations – we shouldn't forget it'.

Some of the other Russian representatives, however, took a distinctly defensive and in some cases chauvinistic attitude; they implied that the Russians had suffered more than the other nations under Stalin, that the Russians as a nation were worse off than the non-Russians, and that some non-Russians were forgetting the debt they supposedly owed the Russian people. Aleksandr Mikhailov, for example, spoke of the 1930s, no less, as 'a time when the cultural revolution raced headlong into the regions of the former tsarist empire' and 'the Russian people promoted this advance with very great generosity'. Another Russian writer, Iurii Prokushev, openly defended the idea of the Russian 'elder brother'. It was not a Stalinist formulation at all, he maintained, but simply a reflection of the fact that the non-Russians have had such a selfless patron.

There was little in the frank speeches delivered by numerous non-Russian representatives at the meeting to support Prokushev's view. Both a Ukrainian and a Georgian writer criticized the 'one-sided', 'tendentious' and 'patronizing' attitude of some of the commentators on national problems in the central press and on Soviet television. Ukrainian and Byelorussian writers once again focused on the language issue; the head of the Ukrainian Writers' Union, Iurii Mushketyk, declared that 'to question the necessity of knowing the indigenous language of the republic's population is simply amoral'. Why had so much attention been devoted to the Russian language in Byelorussia, his Byelorussian counterpart Nil Hilevich asked. There were no problems with learning Russian in the republic, but major ones with learning the native language.

Two of the speeches made by non-Russians stood out. The Tatar representative, Tufan Mignullin, pointed out that nations such as his, which had only been given the status of autonomous republics, did not even enjoy the rights and privileges which the Union republics had. He protested that the Tatars, who with a population in 1979 of 6.3 million are the sixth largest nation in the USSR, do not have their own publishing house, film studios, literary and cultural newspaper in the native language, nor youth journal. A feeling of equality, Mignullin emphasized, fosters a sense of human dignity. 'And, naturally enough, it is very painful when you feel yourself somehow cheated out of your due.'

The most outspoken speech of all at the plenum was delivered by the head of the Uzbek Writers' Union, Adyl Iakubov. It amounted to an impassioned protest against Moscow's policies towards his republic. Challenging the way in which the Soviet media were depicting the campaign against corruption in Uzbekistan, he blamed the malaise afflicting his republic on Moscow's demand for excessive levels of cotton production. 'We are fed up,' he declared, 'with reverting to eternal falsifications of production figures in order to save ourselves from unfeasible plan targets.' He also emphasized the serious ecological damage that had been done to 'our exhausted land' by the insistence on the cotton monoculture.[29]

The premises on which Soviet nationalities policy had been based and the 'experts' who had elaborated and justified them also started to come under attack. As Klara Hallik, an Estonian sociologist, put it:

> For quite some time internationalism was interpreted in the USSR mainly as the drawing closer together of all nationalities. Now we're coming to realize that internationalism is not only that. It also means equal opportunities for all-round development of cultures and traditions of all peoples.[30]

Some of the assessments were blunter still. Academician Tadevosian, writing in the March 1988 issue of *Voprosy istorii KPSS* (Questions of the History of the CPSU) stressed that 'in fostering the new political thinking' it was essential to assume 'not only in words but also in deeds' a correct attitude – in the Leninist sense – to nationality issues. Because in practice this had not been the case, he charged that a misguided and damaging nationalities policy had been pursued, the consequences of which were now becoming evident.[31]

In May the Estonian linguist, Mati Hint, delivered a devastating attack in *Druzhba narodov* against the way in which the concepts of bilingualism and 'internationalization' had been manipulated to the detriment of the non-Russians. He also castigated the 'learned' experts, among whom he included Bromlei and Guboglo, who, he charged, had made academic careers out of advancing assimilationist concepts.[32] Criticism of the specialists on national relations even appeared in *Kommunist*. In May, the Party organ published a discussion in which one of the participants, the philosopher N. V. Motroshilova, declared that 'the people that were (and are!) concerned with studying the national problem have clearly discredited themselves'.[33]

The following issue of the journal broached the touchy question of Russia's imperial legacy. The Russian critic I. Dedkov stressed that it was 'necessary to renounce the "heritage" of earlier times, including "imperial" ones, whose psychology and stereotyped behaviour' were still being felt.[34]

More and more, the problems in the nationality sphere were blamed not simply on the years of 'stagnation', but on the abandonment by Stalin of 'Leninist' nationalities policy and the subsequent failure to restore it. Various authors stressed that what was needed was to make national relations more equitable and to safeguard national rights by laws that would be observed and not simply look good on paper. This amounted to a call for the restoration of the 'national contract' and the recognition of the rule of law, a principle that, ironically, Lenin had himself undermined by treating law as a mere political instrument.

At the writers' plenum in March, Arkadii Vaksberg recalled that Lenin had urged in his Testament that a detailed code be introduced to protect the non-Russians from the violation of their national rights. He argued that it had now become essential to put Lenin's instructions into practice and to avoid 'undemocratic and crude' ways of dealing with national problems. What was needed was a legal framework that would both extend legal protection to the non-Russians and also provide legal mechanisms for resolving national conflicts.[35]

Two months later, on 5 May, the Tadzhik philosopher, Akbar Tursunov, reiterated more or less the same arguments in the pages of *Pravda*. He, too, invoked Lenin's final instructions on nationalities policy, in particular his emphasis on the need to 'enshrine in legislation' the 'rights of the national minorities'. Tursunov concluded:

> Now that the hour has come for sober decisions, it is with a profound sense of civic responsibility that we must all realize that only in a harmonious family of peoples with equal rights rallied on the basis of genuine democratic principles, within the framework of a single socialist state accepting the rule of law, can we ensure the progress of our all-Union fatherland.

The Balts lead the way

After the tough action taken in March to suppress the Armenian protests, the Kremlin seemed to be imposing tighter controls on discussions of the nationalities question. On 12 April, Chebrikov, the KGB chief, warned that 'imperialist secret services and foreign anti-Soviet centres' were encouraging 'extremist nationalist actions'.[36] But by now the processes of *glasnost'* and 'democratization' had made a considerable impact, and could not be tampered with so easily. Public consciousness had been affected: fear had receded, and attitudes were changing. Only six days after Chebrikov delivered his 'old-style' speech, *Pravda* published a selection of excerpts from readers' letters on the national question. One of the authors argued that the only feasible way to proceed in nationalities policy was 'not by means of bureaucratic clampdown, but through the all-round development of democracy'.[37]

There were other factors at work. Because of continuing struggles within the Soviet leadership and the Party, conflicting signals emanated from Moscow. An article in *Pravda* or *Kommunist* was no longer necessarily indicative of the Party line on a given issue. In fact, something of a free-for-all was developing in the press, with non-Russian authors pulling in one direction, and defenders of the status quo and Russian imperial nationalists tugging in the other. And, as we have seen, conditions in individual republics varied, with some local leaderships more conservative and unyielding than others.

While the conflict in the Transcaucasus continued to simmer, the focus shifted to the Baltic republics. What occurred during the first half of 1988, first and foremost in Estonia and then in Lithuania and Latvia, was to transform the campaign for the recognition of non-Russian national rights. The Baltic cultural elites now came out with detailed demands for a fundamental change in the existing relationship between Moscow and the non-Russian nations. Within a remarkably short period, mass movements emerged in the Baltic republics and took up the cause.

In the Baltic republics, 1988 had begun with the Party leaderships in Tallinn, Riga and Vilnius indicating their determination to contain the rise of national assertiveness and defiance. At the same time, however, there were clear indications that elements within the Estonian and Latvian Parties sympathized with some of the demands of the nationally-minded intelligentsia. In both Estonia and Latvia measures had recently been taken to bolster the status of the native languages and to limit immigration. In Estonia, enterprises that brought in workers from outside the republic were being made to pay a penalty of 16,000 roubles per worker, while in Latvia the amount was about 11,000 roubles.[38] The governments of both republics, moreover, had taken up the issue of greater economic autonomy.

On 10 February the Estonian Foreign Minister, Arnold Gren, told a news conference in Moscow that Estonians were asking for 'more independence' in the economic sphere because they saw this as a way of speeding up development in all spheres of life and increasing their republic's contribution to the Soviet economy. He also announced that a commission had been set up to examine proposals on this matter. Gren, nevertheless, went on to accuse 'extremist circles' in Estonia of trying 'to fan nationalistic sentiments, using various dates in history as a pretext'.[39]

Even though Estonia's hard-line ideological secretary had been unexpectedly replaced in mid-January by a more moderate official, on 2 February riot police had been sent in against demonstrators in Tartu who had sought to commemorate the anniversary of the 1920 peace treaty by which the Soviet government had renounced in perpetuity any territorial claims on Estonia. Not surprisingly, there were fears about what might happen on 24 February, the 70th anniversary of the founding of the independent Estonian Republic. On 19 February, 48 people, including prominent writers, film-makers, artists and sportsmen, published a statement in *Sovetskaia Estonia* urging both the police and the public to avoid 'provocative actions'. Their appeal, however, also read as a manifesto of sorts. The signatories stated that Estonia should be made into a 'self-managing' republic, that bureaucratic power should be curbed, and 'free, self-governing authorities' should be strengthened.[40]

Further evidence of the importance which the economic element was assuming in Baltic thinking emerged in early March when the Novosti press agency reported on a round table on national relations that it had sponsored in Tallinn. The Baltic participants came to the conclusion, as Novosti somewhat guardedly summarized it, that 'the system of administration from the centre has lately come to contradict to a certain extent the needs of the social and economic development of the republics making up the USSR'. Novosti cited the Deputy Foreign Minister of Latvia, Nikolai Neilands, as complaining that the Baltic republics were not getting their share of the incomes received by the more important industries located on their territory.[41]

Later that month, the Latvian ideological secretary Gorbunovs told the *Morning Star* that 'the national problem has its roots in the extensive development of the economy, which for years has been causing large-scale immigration into the republic'. This was, of course, a roundabout way of admitting that the heart of the matter was the Latvians' lack of control over their own affairs, and Moscow's power to do more or less as it pleased in this supposedly sovereign republic. Gorbunovs acknowledged that nationalism was on the rise in Latvia and that the Party could no longer rely on the old methods of dealing with this problem. 'The nationalists,' he conceded, 'live off the fact that we keep silent about many things.'[42]

But the failings of the republican Party leaderships did not fully explain why anti-Russian feeling was so strong in the Baltic republics. The answer lay in the fact that many Balts still considered that they lived under foreign occupation. They could remember the inter-war period when their states were independent, and were also aware of what life was like in nearby Finland or Sweden. As a result, they resented the fact that Russians could move into 'their' republic and behave as if Latvia were merely an extension of Russia. An indication of what some people felt was provided in an excerpt from an unsigned letter, addressed to Russians, that was published on 3 March in *Komsomol'skaia pravda*:

Of course, nowadays, Russians are not knifed or shot at, but many people who have not been Russified hardly treat you any better. The reason – your great-power expansionism. In the 70 years since the revolution, the Russians have still not lost their sense of empire.

Representatives of the Baltic intellectual elites, though, were by and large more tactful and enterprising in voicing national grievances and formulating demands. A good example of their approach was the article by the Estonian academician, Viktor Palme, which appeared in *Sovetskaia Estonia* on 23 March. In it, the scholar sought to explain in a non-antagonistic way to Russians living in Estonia the nature of the national problem in the republic and what the Estonians were after. Calling for better understanding and co-operation between what in effect had become two separate communities living side by side in Estonia, Palme identified republican sovereignty as the Estonians' main goal.

> I consider that in the conditions of the ESSR, consistent activity to safeguard and broaden the sovereignty of our (and not only our) republic should be considered the key problem of restructuring. Don't panic! Sovereignty is a term taken from the constitution of the USSR. Moreover, the word reflects the essence of the problem more accurately than 'the self-management of a republic'. The latter meaning has a much narrower applicability.

At the beginning of April, the Estonian cultural intelligentsia took a bold initiative that opened a new stage in the quest for national emancipation. In an impressive display of unity, the Council of Estonian Cultural Unions, consisting of the leaderships of the Writers', Artists', Theatrical Workers', Cinematographic Workers', Composers' and Journalists' Unions, adopted two radical programmatic resolutions that amounted to a virtual political platform, demanding the decentralization of the USSR and broad political, economic and cultural autonomy for the republics. Both resolutions – adopted at a two-day joint plenum – warned of the growth of national tensions in Estonia and strongly criticized the republican leadership.

One of the resolutions was addressed to the forthcoming Nineteenth Party Conference and its thrust was that 'it is essential to re-establish the Leninist principles of the sovereignty and equality of the Union republics'. Calling for a radical change in the relationship between Moscow and the republics that would be consistent with 'the principles of socialist self-management and democracy', it proposed, among other things, that a new law be adopted defining and protecting the rights and sovereignty of the republics; that the principles of cost accounting and self-financing be extended to the republics; and that the nations of the USSR be granted 'full and effective independence in dealing with the issues of the national culture, education, the press, and other problems of intellectual life', as well as the right to use their native language unhindered in all spheres of life.

The other, addressed to the Estonian Party and government leaders, contained 18 proposals for reform in the political, economic, social, cultural, ecological and demographic spheres. One of the proposals called on the 'republic's legislative bodies [to] take the initiative to change the all-Union and republican constitutions in order to guarantee the economic and cultural independence of the ESSR'. Another upheld an important new concept that had been advocated in the March issue of the journal *Looming* by the writer Jaan Isotamm and taken up by the Estonian Independence Party, namely, that the idea of an Estonian SSR citizenship be defined in the republic's constitution and laws. It also emphasized that in Estonia the Estonian language and culture should take priority.[43]

This challenge was followed up by another daring move – the formation on 13 April of an Estonian People's or Popular Front in Support of Restructuring.[44] The idea of setting up new independent organizations that backed Gorbachev's policies had been advanced at the beginning of March in *Moscow News* by Boris Kurashvili of the Institute of State and Law of the USSR Academy of Sciences. It was to be further elaborated by him in the Latvian Komsomol newspaper *Sovetskaia molodezh'* on 27 April, and by the reformist sociologist, Academician Tatiana Zaslavskaia, at a press conference held at the USSR Ministry of Foreign Affairs on 23 May.[45]

The new Estonian informal public group was organized by reformist and nationally-minded communist intellectuals who realized the need for some sort of grass-roots movement in support of the goals that had been espoused by the cultural unions. Careful to avoid calling itself a political party, the Popular Front acted as a loyal opposition: it proclaimed support for restructuring and democratization, but remained critical of, and operated outside, the Estonian Communist Party. Its platform advocated 'socialist democracy and pluralism, political and economic sovereignty of the Union republics, cultural autonomy for all nationalities, the protection of civil rights, and the interests of the working people'. Within two months the new movement was claiming more than 40,000 members and around 800 affiliate groups and organizations throughout Estonia.[46]

According to the *Washington Post*, soon after the Estonian Cultural Unions had issued their resolutions, 'Estonian intellectuals began canvassing all of the ethnic capitals of the Soviet Union'.[47] Certainly, the example set by the Estonians did not pass unnoticed in the other republics. On 8 May the Ukrainian cultural weekly, *Kul'tura i zhyttia*, suggested on its front page that an independent cultural council similar to the one in Estonia be formed in the Ukraine. The proposal seems, however, to have been quashed behind the scenes, for the newspaper did not return to this subject. Just over a month later, activists in Kiev launched a Popular Union to Promote Restructuring, but were stymied by the authorities. In Lvov, though, where the level of political consciousness was higher, the leaders of the city's unofficial groups were able to use interest in the forthcoming Party conference to mobilize the citizens. On 16 June, several thousand people gathered to protest about the undemocratic selection of local delegates to the conference. A second unofficial rally in Lvov on 21 June drew an estimated 50,000 people.[48]

In Moldavia, where the authorities were also distinctly unenthusiastic about restructuring and democratization, the writers followed the Estonian lead. On 28 May a plenum of the Moldavian Writers' Union unanimously approved the text of an 'Appeal to the All-Union Party Conference', which in many ways resembled the resolution that had been addressed to the conference by the Estonian Cultural Council. This document was immediately attacked in the Moldavian press, and Moldavia's ideological secretary blamed it on Estonian influence.[49] As had happened in Estonia, representatives of Moldavia's creative unions met on 3 June to form a group to establish a Moldavian Democratic Movement in Support of Restructuring. Its first rally was held in Kishinev on 27 June and attracted some 5,000 people.[50]

It soon became apparent that the other two Baltic republics were not lagging far behind Estonia. On 28 May the Lithuanian literary weekly *Literatura ir Menas* published a statement addressed to the approaching Party Conference signed by the leaders of all the republic's cultural unions. It, too, repeated quite a few of the demands that the Estonians had made. Less than a week later, on 3 June, some 500 Lithuanian intellectuals met and founded Lithuania's Reconstruction Movement, which soon became known as *Sajudis*, 'the Movement'.[51]

In the meantime, on 2 June, the Latvian cultural unions issued their own broad proposals to the Party conference calling on it 'to ensure the effective sovereignty of the republics in respect of their natural and social resources, whose utilization is permissible only with a republic's consent and on terms agreed with it'. Among other things, they called for 'the return to Lenin's concept of the free union of sovereign Soviet republics; for Latvian to be made the official language of the Latvian SSR; for Latvia to get its own seat in the United Nations; for a separate Latvian team for the Olympics; and for the creation of national military units. Within three weeks, a group of well-known figures had invited the public to support the creation of a Latvian people's front.[52]

Even non-Russian dissidents and former political prisoners who had championed the cause of political independence and were now attempting to form a common front seem to have been impressed by the approach taken by the Baltic 'moderates'. On 11 and 12 June, leading national rights campaigners from the Ukraine, Armenia, Georgia, Lithuania, Latvia and Estonia met in the Western Ukrainian city of Lvov and established a Co-ordinating Committee of the Patriotic Movements of the USSR. The programme they adopted stopped short of demanding full independence, and instead resembled the goal proclaimed by the new Baltic popular fronts: 'the complete political and economic decentralization of the USSR' and its transformation into 'a confederation of separate sovereign states'.[53]

A similar position on the national question was also taken by the Democratic Union. This group had emerged in Moscow during the spring, and consisted mainly of Russians. It openly described itself as an opposition political party, and its draft programme, issued on 24 April, declared that federation as proclaimed in the Soviet Constitution had so far been a legal fiction and that 'Russian predominance' and 'Great Russian chauvinism' were features of the existing system. The programme recognized the right of all nations to self-determination and proposed that the USSR be turned into 'a democratic confederation'.[54]

With only two weeks remaining before the Party conference, the nature and pace of developments in the Baltic republics became breathtaking. A revolution of sorts took place and all three Baltic nations began to experience the sort of uplift, excitement and new hope that the Czechs and Slovaks had lived through during the Prague Spring, and the Poles in the summer of 1980.

On 13 June, there was an important breakthrough in Estonia. A commission of the Estonian Supreme Soviet voted unanimously to recommend that Estonian be made the state language of the Estonian SSR, and, even more remarkably, that the long-banned blue, black and white flag of independent Estonia be restored.[55] The surge of patriotism had grown so strong in the Baltic republics that the authorities in all three no longer dared to deny the crimes committed under Stalin or prevent demonstrations. On 14 June, thousands took to the streets to commemorate the mass deportations of the Stalin era. In Estonia, there was considerable anger at the way in which the authorities had sought to prevent delegates supported by the Popular Front being elected to the Party conference. On 16 June, the pressure finally toppled the republic's Brezhnevite Party leader Karl Vaino. The following day, 150,000 people – one tenth of Estonia's population – took part in a meeting in Tallinn called by the Estonian Popular Front at which the delegates to the Party conference were urged to stand firm on the issue of greater national sovereignty.[56] A similar meeting in Vilnius on 24 June organized by *Sajudis* drew more than 50,000 people.[57]

During the last few days before the Party conference the dynamic new Baltic national movements succeeded in forcing the Parties in all three republics to give way and adopt some of their demands. The change in policy was most evident in Estonia, where Karl Vaino's successor Vaino Valjas, who had been Soviet ambassador to Nicaragua, immediately showed himself to be a more liberal figure and sought to heal the rift between the Estonian Party and the popular forces for national renewal. In Latvia and Lithuania, however, the Party leaderships stubbornly resisted right up until the last moment. On 18 June, the Latvian Central Committee issued a stern warning against 'nationalistic, chauvinistic and anti-Soviet recidivism' and 'the conservation of national isolationism'.[58]

Just as matters came to a head in the Baltic republics, the situation in the Transcaucasus became critical again. There were new ethnic clashes and huge demonstrations, this time in Baku as well as Erevan, and on 21 May the Party leaders of both Armenia and Azerbaijan were replaced. This warning failed to halt the unrest, though, and demonstrations and strikes continued. Faced with enormous public pressure in their respective republics, the new Armenian and Azerbaijani Party chiefs took opposite stands on the Nagornyi Karabakh issue. On 15 June, after half a million Armenians had protested in

Erevan, the Armenian Supreme Soviet defied Moscow and called on the USSR Supreme Soviet to approve the transfer of Nagornyi Karabakh to Armenia. Two days later, the Azerbaijani Supreme Soviet declared this demand as 'unconstitutional' and 'interference in the internal affairs of Azerbaijan'. With the two republics at loggerheads, matters were compounded for Moscow by the Regional Soviet of Nagornyi Karabakh voting on 21 June to call on the USSR Supreme Soviet to take control of the disputed region until a permanent solution had been found.[59]

The question now was how Moscow would react to all this. What was the Gorbachev leadership offering on the eve of the Party conference on which so much hope had been placed?

A certain softening – but few reforms

While these dramatic events in the Baltic republics and the Transcaucasus had been unfolding, there had been no sign of any major change in nationalities policy. Overall, of course, a certain softening was discernible compared with the situation of only two or three years earlier. *Glasnost'* had improved the general climate and piecemeal adjustments continued to be made in the republics. Further republican commissions on national relations had been established, and where they already existed, as in Georgia and Kazakhstan, they were upgraded. A number of new newspapers in non-Russian languages had been launched, and greater recognition was being given to the cultural needs of those nationalities who did not have their own territorial units.

On 27 May *Pravda* published a set of theses that had been adopted by the Party leadership in preparation for the conference. Despite everything that had happened in recent months, the theses paid relatively little attention to the national question, which came seventh in the order of priorities. The only new element was a vague statement that the need for the decentralization of administrative functions 'applies in full measure to all forms of national statehood and autonomy'. It did not seem, though, that this would be allowed to amount to very much. The basis of Soviet nationalities policy was still described as 'a course which combines the satisfaction of the interests of all nations with their drawing together and mutual assistance and an internationalist ideology incompatible with nationalism and chauvinism'.

This failure to take the national question seriously caused widespread disappointment. Within a few days, the Latvian cultural unions issued a resolution complaining that the theses underestimated the seriousness of the problem and the need for bolder initiatives in dealing with it. The very fact that there was no mention of 'such important, constitutional concepts as the republics' sovereignty and statehood', they stressed, 'arouses the alarm of Latvians and of other nations of the USSR'.[60]

Two other developments attested to the limited nature of change. Faced with the prospect of the Crimean Tatars attempting to hold new demonstrations in Moscow, on 9 June the Soviet government announced the decision of the state commission that had been examining their case. It rejected their demand for the restoration of an autonomous Crimean Tatar state in the Crimea and also implicitly ruled out any mass resettlement in their homeland. Furthermore, it accused Crimean Tatar activists of ignoring

> the fact that the present administrative-territorial division of the country, which came to exist many decades ago and has been sealed in the constitution of the USSR, makes it possible to accomplish the tasks of economic and social development of all the ethnic groups in the country.[61]

This categorical claim did not impress either the Crimean Tatars or the Armenians. Indeed, on 26 June thousands of Crimean Tatars attempted to demonstrate in Tashkent, but were dispersed by club-wielding police.[62] But other groups were also voicing their dissatisfaction with the existing territorial arrangements. At the beginning of June, Kazakhstan's minister for foreign affairs issued a cryptic warning against any tampering with the territorial integrity of his republic. It was apparently aimed at Soviet Germans seeking the re-establishment of some form of autonomy.[63] Strains had also recently developed in relations between Tadzhikistan and Uzbekistan. Several months earlier, articles had appeared in the Tadzhik press complaining about the lack of cultural facilities for the Tadzhik minority in neighbouring Uzbekistan, where they made up four per cent of the population. By the second half of June, the central press was confirming that the Tadzhik intelligentsia was 'raising the issue of an unjust national-territorial border line'. The leaderships of both republics sought to defuse the problem, and between March and the second half of June several high-level visits by Party and government officials took place. These resulted in the signing of a number of agreements on improving bilateral co-operation.[64]

The other issue on which the Soviet leadership failed to modify its attitude was that of the Russocentric official approach to the millennium of the baptism of Kievan Rus'. For the Moscow Patriarchate to ignore the Ukrainian and Byelorussian aspects of the jubilee was one thing; but for the Soviet Party and state leaders to play up the Russian angle was another. On 29 April, Gorbachev received Patriarch Pimen, and declared that the Christianization of Kievan Rus' had 'not only religious but also political significance, for this was a very important milestone in the centuries-long path of the development of national history, culture, and Russian statehood'.[65] On 11 June, at the culmination of the official celebrations, the Soviet president Andrei Gromyko was even more blunt. Repeating what Gorbachev had said, he added praise for the role of the Russian Orthodox Church

> in consolidating the people during critical historical periods and furthering the unification of fragmented lands into a single state, which became a major European power.[66]

Despite the euphemistic language, this was tantamount to an acknowledgement by the Soviet head of state of the part played by the Russian Orthodox
Church in the creation and preservation of the Russian empire. Such a
statement hardly corresponded to the Gorbachev leadership's repeated calls
for greater tact and sensitivity in dealing with national relations.

Nevertheless, the issue of the banned Ukrainian national churches dimmed
some of the glitter of the official celebrations. Pope John Paul II was
conspicuous by his absence, for he had made the legalization of the Ukrainian
Catholic Church a precondition of his attendance. Furthermore, on 30 May,
President Reagan, in a brief speech delivered at the Danilovskii Monastery in
Moscow, expressed the hope that religious freedom would be extended to the
Ukrainian Catholic and Orthodox Churches. Four days later, during a
remarkable, officially sponsored conference, Sakharov condemned the
'archaic ban on the Ukrainian Catholic Church', adding that it not only
violated the rights of many Ukrainian believers, but also damaged the
international prestige of the USSR.[67]

Ukrainian resentment of this Russian monopolization of the jubilee was
evident from the unofficial celebrations held in various parts of the Ukraine
and from a number of letters that appeared in the Soviet press.[68] Soviet
Moslems contrasted Moscow's benign attitude towards the Russian Orthodox
Church with its treatment of Islam. At a meeting of Uzbek writers held on the
eve of the Party conference, Emin Usmanov noted that the press was
emphasizing the 'progressive significance of the adoption of Christianity in
Rus'', yet at the same time 'busying itself with condemning and finding fault
with Islam'. Echoing a sentiment that was being voiced by more and more
representatives of the USSR's traditionally Moslem peoples, he asked:

> Why have we not tired of looking in a one-sided manner at the dark aspects in Islam
> in our past culture? . . . Hasn't the time come to speak fairly about both the positive
> and the negative side of religion?![69]

In fact, elements of the Central Asian elites were also becoming distinctly
bolder and more assertive on other issues, too. In Uzbekistan, for instance,
some of the writers were openly resentful of Moscow's policies towards their
republic. The Uzbek Party leader Usmankhodzhaev, who had denounced his
predecessor Rashidov, had been replaced in January 1988 and was to be
accused of corruption. His successor Rafik Nishanov, despite the protests of
Uzbek intellectuals, faithfully defended Moscow's line. Responding to calls
for an end to cotton monoculture, he told *Izvestia*:

> We have considered and still consider the growing of cotton not as a burden but
> genuinely as both our national pride and our internationalist duty.[70]

In June 1988, Nishanov revealed that since the crackdown on corruption in

Uzbekistan began in 1983, 100 officials had been charged with corruption and two of them executed. Furthermore, more than 3,000 officials had been demoted and 18,000 Party members expelled.[71]

The new mood among the Central Asian intelligentsia was perhaps best demonstrated at a meeting held by Kirghiz writers in June in preparation for the Party conference. One of the speakers complained about the one-sided approach to the friendship between peoples, charging that

> in recent times, comrades who do not know the situation in the republic have been excessively disparaging about the customs and beliefs of the Kirghiz people, about their national character, and have been trying to eliminate them all, supposedly because they are 'Islamic', thereby doing harm to the people's honour . . . It would be good if Russian comrades who occupy high places in the Kirghiz Party Central Committee thought about this.

At the same meeting, another Kirghiz writer, Kazat Akhmatov, showed that radical proposals were not only emanating from the Baltic republics. Challenging the very idea of a one-party system, he recommended the following to the Party conference:

> First, the [section] dealing with the leadership role of the Party should be removed from the Constitution. Second, a social force equal to the Party should be formed. Third, the system of obligatory study of Party teachings should be eliminated. Fourth, the principle of democratic centralism should be re-examined; it has not justified itself.[72]

On the eve of the Party conference, even some of the USSR's smallest nationalities made themselves heard. For instance, on 17 June, Alitet Nemtushkin, the delegate to the conference from the Evenki, a native Siberian people, pledged in the pages of *Komsomol'skaia pravda* that he would

> not only protest, but rebel [*buntovat'*], if necessary, against former stereotypical methods of nationality policy. These distorted the humane essence of the socialist order and are leading to the disappearance of languages and of the smallest nationalities themselves.

Perhaps the most telling assessment of the situation on the eve of the Party conference was made by Kazakhstan's Party leader Kolbin. He told *Izvestia* on 24 June:

> We are learning to live in democratic conditions in a multinational state – everywhere people are seeking ways of activating institutions in the political system through which national interests must be more objectively revealed and harmonized.

Warning that the spread of national unrest, or 'extreme attitudes' (as he put it) to other regions could not be ruled out, he maintained that the only way of avoiding this were 'measures to further develop the Soviet federation'.

The Nineteenth Party Conference becomes a watershed

The much-awaited Party conference opened on 28 June. There were 5,000 delegates, and even though many of them, if not the majority, were thought to be 'conservatives', there was an air of expectation. It was known that Gorbachev and his team wanted to use the occasion to carry the fight to the opponents of change and to speed up the process of reform. For the non-Russians, the conference offered a golden opportunity to advance their cause and to emphasize that restructuring and the retention of the old imperial structures did not go together. In the corridors and vestibules, representatives of the non-Russian delegations met and conferred. The Baltic representatives exuded an air of confidence, and their radical position emboldened other non-Russian delegates.

This was just as well, for it turned out that what Gorbachev had to say about the national question in his report went only a little way beyond what had been stated in the Central Committee theses. He acknowledged that 'the rights of the Union republics must be reinterpreted and brought into accordance with the radical economic reform' and defined more precisely, but at the same time he made it quite clear that Moscow was not prepared to allow the degree of economic autonomy being demanded by the Balts. 'Those who think that the course of decentralization,' he told the conference, 'is opening the floodgates for parochialism or regional egoism will be making a gross mistake.' The internationalization of the economy and of social life was unavoidable, he emphasized, and 'any obsession with national isolation' would only lead to 'economic and cultural impoverishment'. Gorbachev admitted that *glasnost'* and democratization had exposed problems in the area of national relations that had hitherto been neglected, but warned that the rise in national self-awareness, though on the whole 'a positive phenomenon', had given 'a nationalist hue' to some issues and made them more complex. Alluding to the conflict over Nagornyi Karabakh, he criticized those who were attempting to use *glasnost'* to redraw frontiers, and who were damaging 'the process of democratization and the cause of restructuring' by sowing 'discord and hatred' between nations. Disputes, he stressed, would have to be solved 'within the framework of the existing structure' of the Soviet state.

In his speech, Gorbachev announced, among other things, a major reorganization of the USSR Supreme Soviet. A new enlarged body – the Congress of People's Deputies – was to be elected and meet once a year. It would elect a smaller full-time standing USSR Supreme Soviet, consisting of two chambers, a Council of the Union and a Council of Nationalities. Although the Soviet leader indicated that the Council of Nationalities would be revamped and become more important, what was not immediately clear was how this overhaul of the legislative system would affect the representation of the non-Russians. From the fact that it was intended to add a further

750 deputies to the Congress of People's Deputies that were elected by organizations rather than on a territorial basis, it appeared though that the proportion of non-Russian deputies would probably be reduced.[73]

During the next three and a half days, the conference, as Gorbachev himself was to point out in his concluding remarks, turned into a freewheeling public debate, the like of which had not been seen for nearly six decades. Not surprisingly, the national question figured as one of the prominent themes. It was not only the Baltic representatives who spoke out on this issue; the Armenian, Azerbaijani, Georgian, Ukrainian, Byelorussian, Uzbek, Moldavian, and Komi delegates all in their own way also called for fundamental changes in the nationalities policy and the restoration of the national rights of the non-Russian nations. What was so impressive was not just the virtually united front of the non-Russians and the forcefulness of their statements, but also the fact that now it was the republican Party leaders who were championing national rights.

Among the first non-Russians to address the conference were the new Party leaders of Azerbaijan and Armenia, who inevitably dwelt on the conflict in the Transcaucasus. The Armenian Party chief, Suren Arutiunian, stated outright that it was imperative 'to elaborate new political thinking on the national question', arguing that 'not a single serious problem' in this sphere could be solved 'without renouncing old-fashioned approaches and stereotypes'. He pointed out that the problem of Nagornyi Karabakh was one of the issues that had existed for a long time, 'but which we, as it were, shut our eyes to'. Implicitly assailing the way in which Moscow had conducted its nationalities policy, he stressed that

It was precisely the anti-democratic practice of suppressing information and showing indifference, the desire to brush aside the acute and complex problems that actually exist, and attempts to drive them underground or to resolve them by authoritarian methods, that have led to such an explosive manifestation of them today.

Arutiunian went on to suggest, though, that even under *glasnost'* some of the old practices remained. He strongly condemned attempts to explain the events in Nagornyi Karabakh and Armenia purely in terms of 'the actions of extremist groups', saying that this hardly helped to defuse the situation and was 'painfully offensive to the national feelings' of Armenians. He concluded by pointing out that the existing Soviet Constitution had been promulgated during the period of 'stagnation', and called for a new edition to be prepared.[74]

The Azerbaijani Party leader, Abdul-Rakhman Vezirov, while implicitly condemning Armenian attempts to alter the status of Nagornyi Karabakh, complained that events had shown quite clearly 'the lack of sophistication in the leadership and administration of the processes of international cooperation'.

Like Arutiunian, he suggested that it was time that the Council of National-ities became something more than a formal institution, and proposed that an executive agency be set up to deal with national problems, either a Union ministry or a state committee for national relations. Vezirov also expressed his republic's wholehearted support for decentralization and the strengthen-ing of 'all forms of national statehood and autonomy'.[75]

This theme was elaborated by the Baltic representatives. The first of them to speak was the Latvian Party leader Boris Pugo. He was a conservative figure, and no doubt anxious to avoid being unceremoniously removed like his Estonian counterpart Vaino had been two weeks earlier. His speech was unexpectedly outspoken, and touched on many of the issues that had been highlighted by the Latvian national movement. For one, he acknowledged that

> during restructuring, not only individual people, but also entire nations, including the Latvian people, have begun to show greater social and political activity. We sense people's great dissatisfaction with what has been achieved.

He went on to condemn the 'limitless diktat' of the central ministries and the 'inordinately large' inflow of migrants into Latvia. It had become essential, he maintained, to 'take urgent measures to develop further the Soviet federation of sovereign socialist republics', making it clear that this meant above all changing the relationship between Moscow and the republics. He explained:

> It is necessary to ensure the genuine sovereignty of each republic. Here we have in mind a substantial increase in the independence of Union republics and the expansion of the local soviet agencies' rights in developing the economy, the social sphere, and culture. I stress that it is a question not of isolation but of the exercise of rights enshrined in the USSR Constitution and the decentralization of administration.

This, he added, would require new legislation and changes to the constitution.[76]

The new Estonian Party chief Valjas was equally direct. The system was so overcentralized, he pointed out, that 'more than 90 per cent of the whole economic potential of the republics is virtually in the hands of dozens of Union and Union-republic ministries and departments'. What was impera-tive, he declared, was 'to restore the Leninist principles of federation as the basis of relations between nations and republics'. The Lithuanian Party chief, Ringaudas Songaila, also called for the expansion of the rights of the republics and for appropriate changes to the constitution. He noted that the language question and ecological problems were especially acute in his republic.[77]

The Baltic Party leaders were not the only ones to have been forced to change their tune. The Uzbek Party chief Nishanov now spoke openly of 'the serious consequences for the economy and the environment' of the cotton monoculture. He pointedly raised the issue of national pride, and indicated that Uzbeks were tired of being criticized in the media and depicted as virtually a parasitic nation.[78]

Georgia's Party leader, Dzhumber Patiashvili, came out strongly against 'undemocratic administration in the sphere of inter-national relations'. He stressed that 'the creation of a multinational legal state must begin with the genuine equality of the rights of nations, as enshrined in the USSR Constitution', and that this had to be guaranteed by new legislation and some sort of new mechanism. He, too, considered that it was essential to improve 'Soviet federalism as understood by Lenin'.

There were two other notable speeches by non-Russian delegates. The Ukrainian poet Boris Oliinyk went considerably further than the official representative of the Ukrainian Party. He not only raised the language question and presented a petition with 6,000 signatures protesting the construction of new atomic reactors in the Ukraine, but also called for the truth to be told about 'the cause of the famine of 1933, which cost the lives of millions of Ukrainians'. For his part, the representative from the Komi ASSR, V. Mel'nikov, spoke about the serious national problems facing the smaller nationalities like his, such as economic exploitation and assimilation.

By no means everyone, though, supported the stand taken by most of the non-Russian delegates. Two Russian speakers argued that what was needed to counteract the growth of 'nationalism' was more emphasis on 'internationalization'. Evgenii Primakov, the Director of the USSR Academy of Sciences Institute of World Economics and International Relations, revived a theme that had been so prominent only a few years ago. He argued that recent developments had shown that the 'horizontal rotation of cadres on a countrywide basis' had become all the more necessary. The television commentator and chairman of the Soviet Peace Committee, Genrikh Borovik, defended the idea of the Soviet people and castigated intellectuals who put 'one-nation patriotism' above 'Soviet patriotism'.[79]

All in all though, it was clear from some of the statements made at press conferences connected with the conference that the non-Russians were pleased with the way things had gone. The sense of satisfaction and achievement was, for instance, evident from an interview given to Radio Moscow on 3 July by the Estonian economist Mikhail Bronshtein. He commented:

> In the past our concept of republican financial autonomy virtually caused reactions of horror, but before our delegation had even spoken, the same platform had been put forward by Byelorussia, Georgia, the Komi ASSR, and a whole number of others. There are common problems and they were highlighted very vividly at the conference.

What did these problems boil down to? This is what the elated Bronshtein told Soviet listeners:

Absolute power has ended up in the hands of the Union ministries, absolute power
. . . They often behave like international transnational corporations: they pillage
the environment with no concern for anything, and they take no account of
demographic factors or the indigenous population and their traditions . . . All this is
being decided somewhere in Moscow by an abstract Ivan Ivanovich.

What was important though, was not only the position taken by most of the
non-Russian speakers, but also what ended up in the conference's resolution
on the national question. On the first day of the conference, the non-Russian
delegates had demanded and obtained better representation on the commission drafting the resolution on international relations. Quite a few champions
of national rights, such as the Latvian Janis Peters, who did not have a chance
to address the conference, were elected to the commission. The document
that it produced, and which was endorsed by the conference, was clearly a
compromise. Indeed, it was only the persistence of the Estonian delegates
that at the last minute forced the chairman of the commission dealing with the
national question, Nikolai Ryzhkov, and Gorbachev himself, to accept an
amendment that at least recognized that 'the idea of the transition of the
republics and regions to the principles of cost-accounting . . . merits
attention'.[80]

Although the resolution repeated some of the standard themes and claims
about the 'successes' of Soviet nationalities policy, it nevertheless went well
beyond what Gorbachev had been prepared to say in his report. The
resolution acknowledged that *glasnost'* had revealed the 'negative
phenomena which had accumulated over the decades' in national relations as
a result of the 'departure from Leninist principles of nationalities policy,
violations of legality in the period of the [Stalin] personality cult, and the
ideology and psychology of stagnation'. The Party conference, it stressed,
considered it a matter of historic importance to adhere to Leninist principles
of nationalities policy and to remove all 'artificial accretions and deformations'. More concretely, the resolution recognized that 'urgent measures' had
to be taken to ensure

the further development and consolidation of the Soviet Federation on the basis of
democratic principles. Above all it is a question of the expansion of the rights of the
Union republics and autonomous formations through the demarcation of the areas
of competence of the USSR and the Soviet republics, decentralization, the transfer
to the localities of a number of managerial functions, and the strengthening of
independence [*samostoiatel'nost'*] and of responsibility in the economic sphere,
social and cultural development, and environmental protection.

Acknowledging, albeit cautiously, the importance of the principles of self-
management and economic accountability, the resolution also called for the
creation of 'a qualitatively new mechanism' to regulate economic relations
between Moscow and the republics, the enhancement of the role of the

Council of Nationalities and the establishment of a special state agency for dealing with national relations, measures to satisfy the 'national-cultural demands' of nationalities residing outside their own republics or not having such territorial units, and for more concern 'for the active use of national languages in the various spheres of state, social and cultural life'. To achieve these improvements, the resolution stated that new legislation would have to be introduced and the Soviet Constitution amended accordingly. Furthermore, despite familiar references to the 'Soviet people' and the need to continue strengthening the unity of the Soviet multinational state, the document declared that

> The socialist ideal is not stultifying unification, but full-blooded and dynamic unity within national diversity.[81]

The adoption of this epoch-making resolution crowned the success achieved by the non-Russians at the conference. Not only had the meeting witnessed the most candid discussion of the national question since the 1920s, but also the non-Russians had in effect secured an important new charter. Although the resolution skirted the issue of republican sovereignty, the Party leadership had finally been forced to acknowledge the need to modify its nationalities policy and broaden the rights of the non-Russian nations.

18

Waiting for Gorbachev

Many of the non-Russian delegates to the 19th Party Conference must have returned home confident that the Soviet leadership had finally been forced to alter its attitude towards the national question. The sense of elation in the Baltic republics was demonstrated at a rally on 9 July 1988 in Vilnius. Organized by the Lithuanian restructuring movement, its purpose was to give people a chance to hear reports from conference delegates. Over 100,000 people attended. Lithuanian national flags abounded and, interestingly, the meeting was addressed by representatives of the Estonian Popular Front and an informal Byelorussian group.[1]

Developments at the Party conference also galvanized elements in the Ukraine and Moldavia. On 7 July in Lvov, some 15,000 people took part in a rally to launch an umbrella organization – the Democratic Front to Promote Restructuring[2] – for the city's unofficial groups. A few days later, at their plenum in Kiev, Ukrainian writers expressed their support for the positions championed by the Baltic delegates at the Party conference, and condemned what they called the 'Brezhnev-Suslov' approach to nationality policy, together with its concept of the Soviet people.[3] In Moldavia, the newly formed Moldavian Democratic Movement in Support of Restructuring and the unofficial patriotic association, the Alexe Mateevici Literary and Musical Group, organized mass meetings in Kishinev on 6 and 29 July.[4]

But not all non-Russians were encouraged by the Party conference. In Armenia there was profound disappointment that the conference had produced nothing new on the issue of Nagornyi Karabakh, and on 3 July activists in Erevan called for a general strike. Some of the demonstrators occupied Erevan airport. Two days later, troops stormed the airport and there were casualties on both sides. The violent military intervention only inflamed the situation and spurred the Nagornyi Karabakh Soviet into voting for secession from Azerbaijan.

On 18 July, the Presidium of the USSR Supreme Soviet rejected the transferral of Nagornyi Karabakh to Armenia. Soviet television aired the proceedings and showed Gorbachev frequently interrupting Armenian representatives and forcefully laying down the law. Academician Sergei Ambartsumian, the president of the Armenian Academy of Sciences, however, won the admiration of many Soviet viewers for courageously standing up to the Soviet leader and reminding him that the Armenian popular movement would not be mollified by 'calls to strengthen internationalism and the friendship of peoples' alone.[5]

More contradictions and contrasts
Gorbachev's and the Kremlin's attitude towards the national problem remained ambiguous. The Soviet leader soon began to qualify the concessions made at the Party conference. At the meeting of the Presidium of the USSR Supreme Soviet he expressed his annoyance about the tendency for non-Russians to conclude that 'Moscow is to blame, the centre is to blame'. He also charged that 'under the banner of democratization, shameless pressure' was being exerted on the authorities by national movements.[6] Gorbachev returned to the national problem in his speech to a plenum of the Party Central Committee on 29 July. Confronted with new challenges in the Transcaucasus, the Baltic republics, the Ukraine and Moldavia, he warned Party leaders that all forms of nationalism and 'undermining of the unity of our union' were impermissible, and called for heavier penalties for inciting national enmity and preaching national exclusivity.

All the same, Gorbachev did acknowledge that Moscow's powers vis-à-vis the republics had to be redefined and that new laws and mechanisms were needed for dealing with national relations. He also conceded for the first time 'the special acuteness of language problems', adding that 'it would clearly be worth preparing and submitting for broad discussion a draft law on the free development and equal utilization of the languages of the peoples of the USSR'.[7]

What was particularly disturbing, though, was the decree surreptitiously issued by the USSR Supreme Soviet on 28 July, giving sweeping powers to the troops of the Ministry of the Interior and empowering them, among other things, to suppress unauthorized political meetings and demonstrations. The lack of publicity accorded to the decree contradicted Gorbachev's calls for proper debate and consultation before new laws were adopted. The authorities did, however, publicize another decree issued on the same day requiring all demonstrations to be registered ten days in advance.[8] The consequences of this effective ban on unauthorized meetings were soon evident. On 2 August, police broke up a demonstration in Leningrad organized by a recently formed opposition group, the Democratic Union.[9] Two days later in Lvov, riot police with dogs attacked participants in a meeting called by the city's fledgling popular front.[10] And in Byelorussia, on 20 August, police raided a gathering of members of various unofficial groups and warned the activists.[11]

It soon became clear that different standards of tolerance were being applied in different republics. Whereas in the Ukraine, Byelorussia and Moldavia, the authorities sought to stifle the new popular forces for genuine restructuring and national renewal, in the Baltic republics more and more victories for *glasnost'* and democratization were achieved. Here, the popular fronts continued their dramatic growth and strengthened the Baltic push for real sovereignty.

The Kremlin's new liberal line towards the Baltic republics was enunciated by one of Gorbachev's closest associates, Aleksandr Iakovlev, during his visit to Latvia and Lithuania in August. Displaying considerable tact and flair, the Politburo member and CPSU Central Committee Secretary, who had recently taken over responsibility for ideology, calmly responded to the questions, complaints and demands that were voiced during his numerous meetings with Party workers, intellectuals and media people. Although he left no doubt that certain limits remained, he did not define them and instead stressed the break with the past. 'We cannot continue in the old way,' he told his Latvian hosts.[12] The 19th Party Conference, he assured them, had taken 'the first major step in providing a theoretical and practical basis' for adapting nationalities policy to the era of restructuring.[13] Without elaborating how far he thought the rights of the republics should be extended, on two occasions he cited Lenin to the effect that Moscow should take charge only of defence and foreign affairs and that everything else should be left to the republican governments.[14]

It was apparent that, whether as an experiment or gamble, the Gorbachev leadership had decided to try and harness the forces which had been released in the small, but economically advanced and strategically located, Baltic republics. Indeed, Iakovlev's general message to the Balts seemed to be, as he himself declared in Vilnius, that 'the national factor can and should become one more motive force of restructuring'.[15] Whatever reservations the Kremlin may have had, the Balts themselves felt that they had been given the green light.

In mid-August the Estonian Party daily *Rahva Haal* published the secret protocols of the Molotov–Ribbentrop Pact, whose existence the Soviet authorities had kept silent about for over 40 years. On 23 August, many tens of thousands of Estonians, Latvians and Lithuanians took part in rallies to mark the 49th anniversary of the infamous Nazi–Soviet agreement. The Estonian authorities made other major concessions. They legalized the Estonian national flag, agreed to give the Estonian language the status of a state language, and expressed approval of the Estonian Popular Front and the newly-formed Estonian 'Green' movement. On 11 September, the new Estonian Party leader Valjas endorsed most of the demands being made by the Estonian Popular Front and called for the USSR to become a 'genuine union of free peoples' in which the Estonians would have their own citizenship and control over their economic, cultural and political affairs. That same day he appeared at a rally organized by the Estonian Popular Front and was cheered by a huge crowd of between 200,000 and 300,000 people.[16] Within a month, in both Latvia and Lithuania, the presidiums of the republican Supreme Soviets recommended that the native languages be granted official status and also permitted the limited use of formerly banned national symbols.

At the end of September, though, there was a brief period of anxiety. In Lithuania, the Party chief Songaila seems to have decided that matters were getting out of hand. On 28 September riot police were sent in against nationalist demonstrators in Vilnius and a bloody confrontation took place.[17] Furthermore, the sudden announcement that a Central Committee plenum had been called in Moscow raised fears about Gorbachev's future and the fate of *glasnost'* and restructuring. Gorbachev, however, came out on top. The Estonians were also encouraged by the fact that shortly before the plenum Valjas met with the Soviet leader and apparently received his tacit support.[18]

At the beginning of October history was made when the Estonian Popular Front held its inaugural congress. The first such gathering to be officially sanctioned in modern Soviet history, it turned into an impressive demonstration of free assembly, free speech and national assertiveness. The Estonian Popular Front adopted a radical programme and although it denied that it was a political party, it announced its intention to field independent candidates in future elections.[19]

The following weekend, the Latvian Popular Front held its inaugural congress in Riga and also adopted a charter advocating broad cultural, economic and political autonomy. On the eve of the meeting, Jan Vagris replaced Boris Pugo as Latvian Party leader and, like his Estonian counterpart Valjas, seemed to go out of his way to stay on the right side of the vigorous new movement.[20]

In Lithuania, just before the convocation of the inaugural congress of the Lithuanian Restructuring Movement, the Party leadership also underwent a shakeup. Songaila, who had discredited himself by returning to old-style methods, was replaced by an official who had lately begun to identify himself with reform, Algirdas Brazauskas. Subsequently, the Party authorities not only permitted the proceedings of the constituent congress to be broadcast live on radio and television, but on the very day of its opening, 22 October, announced the decision to return the Cathedral of Vilnius to the Catholic Church.[21]

Outside their own republics, Baltic activists remained among the most radical and outspoken champions of the rights of the non-Russians. The Estonian economist Bronshtein argued in the pages of *Kommunist* that 'republican cost-accounting' should be considered the 'economic basis of political restructuring'.[22] His colleague, Tiit Made, was even more forthright. He gave the following explanation of his nation's predicament to an Italian newspaper:

> If we want to survive we cannot permit ourselves a theoretical internationalism that on the practical level is expressed only in Russian and is based entirely in Moscow . . . We must free ourselves of Soviet economic colonialism. Now or never.[23]

Basic issues were at stake. The Lithuanian philosopher Bronislavas Kuzmickas pointed out in a discussion published in *Literaturnaia gazeta* on 21 September how limited the proclaimed sovereignty of the Union republics really was. In order to enlarge a journal by a single page or to change the number of hours devoted to learning the native language and literature in schools it was still necessary to go to Moscow and obtain approval. On the other hand, as he noted implicitly, Moscow was free, for instance, to continue propagating pseudo-bilingualism. His co-discussant, the Georgian philologist Tengiz Buachidze, went so far as to suggest that the old Stalinist formula of 'national in form and socialist in content' should be stood on its head.

After the 19th Party Conference several Russians came out with very radical statements on the national question. At the beginning of August the ethnographer Drobizheva told a Yugoslav newspaper that after many decades of silence, 'questions were now being raised about Russian domination' and the rights of the republics 'that were increasingly resisting the central administration in Moscow'.[24] Shortly afterwards, stressing the 'flourishing', as opposed to the 'drawing together of nations', she told *Moskovskie novosti*:

> Society needs a well-reasoned, substantiated, and literate concept of national construction. The return to Lenin's norms in relations between different nationalities in our multinational state is no less necessary than economic reform.[25]

The historian Iurii Afanas'ev went further still. In an interview that appeared in *La Stampa* on 1 September, he maintained that 'the model [of national relations] that preceded restructuring must be destroyed' and replaced with 'Lenin's conception of a union of equal socialist countries, all with the same rights'. The root of the problem, he argued, lay in the fact that

> In the conflict between his ideas and Stalin's . . . Lenin lost; the result was a strongly centralized state with very weak [local] autonomies. We do not have autonomous republics but rather provinces subject to the centre.

Rejecting the idea of any forcible unification or centralization, Afanas'ev broke new ground by suggesting that Moscow need not necessarily even remain the centre of things.

But radical views such as these were espoused only by a small group of Russians. In fact, during the last months of 1988 what was far more in evidence were the beginnings of a Russian nationalist backlash. In the Baltic republics, Moldavia and elsewhere, the large Russian communities suddenly began to feel threatened. Having made themselves at home in the non-Russian republics, the Russian settlers were now being made increasingly aware of how unwelcome they were. Some of them started organizing and raised the banner of 'internationalism' against the 'nationalism' and 'separatism' of the non-Russian nations. In Estonia and Latvia 'Inter(national)-fronts' sprang up in October, and the following month a similar movement calling itself *Edinstvo* (Unity) was formed in Lithuania. At the beginning of 1989 an Inter-front also appeared in Moldavia, where the national movement had rapidly come into its own.

Constitutional crisis

Far from wanting to relinquish its control, Moscow was in fact working out a way of shoring up its authority. In October, the Gorbachev leadership suddenly came out with a draft law on amendments and additions to the Soviet constitution that contained provisions which, contrary to the resolutions of the 19th Party Conference, would have limited the rights of the non-Russian republics. The revamped USSR Supreme Soviet was to be accorded the power to overrule the right of the Union republics to secede from the USSR, and to annul decisions of republican governments if these were thought to conflict with the interests of the Union as a whole. Moreover, in such a case, it was to be empowered to proclaim a state of emergency 'in specific localities . . . with the introduction where necessary of special forms of administration'. On top of this, the changes would also have had the effect of increasing the influence of the Russian Federation in the new Council of Nationalities.[26]

This unexpected attempt by the Gorbachev leadership to backtrack from the positions adopted by the 19th Party Conference was interpreted by many non-Russians as a breach of trust. It provoked strong opposition and wide popular protest in several republics and precipitated a major constitutional crisis. On 16 November the Estonian Supreme Soviet defiantly adopted a 'Declaration of Sovereignty' and voted itself the right to veto laws issued from Moscow.[27] This action was immediately condemned by the central media and declared unconstitutional by a commission of the USSR Supreme Soviet.

During the tense fortnight that followed, the Supreme Soviets in Lithuania and Latvia also voiced their objections, though they did not go as far as their Estonian counterpart in asserting their sovereignty. In Lithuania, close to two million people – two-thirds of those eligible to vote – signed petitions expressing their dissent. The Supreme Soviet used the occasion to proclaim Lithuanian the state language of the republic and to designate the flag and hymn of independent Lithuania as the official flag and anthem of the Lithuanian SSR.[28]

Opposition to the proposed constitutional changes was not limited to the Baltic republics. There were mass protests in Georgia and on 24 November the Georgian Supreme Soviet also voiced its reservations.[29] In the Ukraine, there were no protests on the streets; in this republic and in Byelorussia the authorities were still sending out riot police to break up unauthorized meetings. But a group of legal experts implicitly defied the Kiev Party leadership by condemning the proposed changes in the pages of the writers' weekly as a 'step backwards' that went against 'the spirit and letter of the 19th Party Conference'.[30]

Another unmistakable sign of the growing radicalization of the non-Russians during these stormy weeks were the initiatives taken by leading cultural figures in the Ukraine, Byelorussia, Georgia, Tadzikhistan, Azerbaijan, and Uzbekistan to establish Baltic-type popular fronts. By now, ferment was also growing in the Central Asian republics. During 1988 Moscow had begun to moderate its policy towards this region and towards Islam, and in September the Politburo had announced measures aimed at saving what was left of the Aral Sea; but national movements were burgeoning and the Central Asian intelligentsias were becoming more and more outspoken about their native language and culture, their historic past, and ecological problems.

While the constitutional crisis was unfolding, the Armenian-Azerbaijani conflict flared up again. This time the victims of the ethnic clashes included three soldiers. There were new mass protests in Erevan and Baku (where the protesters were reported to have carried Islamic flags and portraits of the Ayatollah Khomeini) and curfews were imposed on the two capitals as well as three other Azerbaijani cities.[31] Armenia's Supreme Soviet also expressed its reservations about the proposed constitutional changes and called for the USSR Supreme Soviet to allow Nagornyi Karabakh to decide its own future.

On 26 November Gorbachev delivered a tough speech at a session of the Presidium of the USSR Supreme Soviet in which he sought to bring the recalcitrant republics into line. In his address, which was later shown on Soviet television, he denounced the position taken by the Estonians as 'political adventurism nudging Estonia on a fatal path of economic isolationism and destroying the country's [i.e. the USSR's] unitary economy. Our future,' he stressed, 'is not in weakening ties among the republics but on the contrary, in strengthening them and expanding co-operation.' Alluding to the conflict in the Transcaucasus, he warned that national discord could be disastrous and 'place in jeopardy our restructuring'. It was necessary, he added, to 'stop demagogues, those who embark on political speculation by taking advantage of the processes of democratization and *glasnost*'.[32]

Nevertheless, Moscow did indicate that it was prepared to make some concessions to defuse what even Gorbachev described as a crisis. For all his bluster, he injected a conciliatory element into his speech. He emphasized that some of the proposed amendments to the constitution had been modified and acknowledged 'the legitimacy of the many real questions which Estonia has come to face'. On 29 November, at a plenary meeting of the USSR Supreme Soviet, Gorbachev's tone was more placatory; he even admitted that some of the problems could have been avoided if Moscow had acted more tactfully.[33]

The crisis was not really resolved, and ended in an uneasy compromise. The decision adopted by Estonia's Supreme Soviet was declared null and void but the Estonians continued to uphold it. The entire experience soured the atmosphere: although Moscow did water down some of the proposed constitutional changes, this could not help alter the impression that the Gorbachev leadership had acted rashly, insensitively and, most important of all, not in good faith.

Inharmonious 'harmonization'

After miscalculating with the proposed constitutional changes, the Gorbachev leadership evidently wanted to avoid creating further problems with the republics. On 12 November *Pravda* had announced that the long-awaited special Central Committee plenum devoted to the national question would not take place until the following summer, and so decisions about the future of Soviet nationalities policy could be put off for a while longer.

The one exception was the continuing crisis in the Transcaucasus. In December, a major earthquake devastated Armenia. The Kremlin appeared to exploit the disaster to round up the leaders of the Armenian 'Karabakh Committee' and the main instigators of the Azerbaijani demonstrations. When Gorbachev visited Erevan he was greeted by scarcely concealed suspicion. The crackdown also drew protests from liberals in Moscow. In January, the Soviet government decided to impose 'a special form of administration' on Nagornyi Karabakh, whereby the disputed enclave remained formally under Azerbaijani control but in practice was to be ruled directly by Moscow.[34]

The republics were now a force to be reckoned with. At the beginning of 1989, just as the latest Union census was about to be carried out, the Party leadership adopted a conciliatory posture and offered the non-Russians fresh reassurances. On 6 January, speaking before a gathering of the USSR's cultural and scientific elite, Gorbachev explicitly disavowed the concept of the fusion of nations and stated that the Party 'cannot permit even the smallest nation to disappear' or 'the language of even the smallest nation to be lost'. It was only now that he suddenly chose to reveal that there had been those who had wanted to enshrine the concept of fusion in the new Party Programme and that he himself had struggled behind the scenes against the proponents of this 'dangerous' formulation.[35] Four days later, the Party Central Committee issued an appeal to the 'Party and to the Soviet people [not peoples]' in which, among other things, it pledged that at the forthcoming Central Committee plenum on nationalities policy it would 'adopt a broad programme' that would result in 'a considerable expansion of the rights of the republics'.[36]

Nevertheless, much of what Gorbachev and the Party leadership said about nationalities policy remained ambiguous or evasive. Gorbachev himself stayed clear of the crucial question of the relationship between the Russians and the non-Russians, the issue of Russification, and the question of the extent to which Moscow was prepared to restore the sovereignty of the Union republics. Significantly, the Central Committee's appeal put forward the slogan of a 'strong centre and strong republics', which, despite the inherent contradiction, was intended to serve as the new underlying principle for reform in the nationality sphere. Furthermore, instead of 'restructuring', or some other term denoting the need for fundamental changes in this area, the new phrase 'harmonization of inter-ethnic relations' was increasingly used.

More forthright language was employed in the wide-ranging debate that had continued in Soviet periodicals and on television since the 19th Party Conference. The discussion had confirmed that there was a great deal of division about what constituted the essence of the national problem and what needed to be done. Estonian and Ukrainian writers, for instance, were now openly condemning Russification. Yet a group of Russian scholars and cultural figures who took part in a conference on the nationality question in Moscow in December 1988 and issued an appeal addressed to their non-Russian counterparts – the first of its kind – clearly had a totally different view of the nationalities problem. They expressed concern about the spread of 'anti-Russian attitudes' and urged that the 'myth of forcible Russification' be combated.[37]

All this time the notorious *Pamiat'* organization had remained active. The alarm caused by the upsurge of national unrest among the non-Russian nations now resulted in the appearance of a number of new Russian nationalist (and in some cases, almost blatantly supremacist) organizations. In November 1988, a group of leading Russian nationalist cultural figures, such as Valentin Rasputin, Vasilii Belov and Viktor Astaf'ev, formed an Association of Russian Artists, one of the chief aims of which was to combat centrifugal forces threatening 'the once-powerful union of the peoples of Russia'.[38] This aim was even more pronounced in the case of the Moscow Russian Patriotic Society, *Otechestvo* (Fatherland), which became a focus for chauvinistic, anti-reform conservatives and pro-military elements.[39]

A minority of Russians, however, continued to take a critical view of the imperial ethos. Perhaps the most forthright was an economist from Akademgorodok, A. I. Prigozhin. In his contribution to a stimulating discussion organized by the liberal monthly of the Soviet Peace Committee, *Vek XX i mir* (The 20th Century and Peace), he pointed to the question of the Russian nation as the 'primary' problem in the sphere of nationality relations. 'The leadership is drawn from the Russians,' he stressed, and 'they predominate among the heads of the main agencies of power.' Because of this, Prigozhin argued, the grievances of the non-Russians were directed at the Russians. In the same discussion, M. Chlenov, a candidate of historical sciences, accused the Soviet government of having pursued an 'ethnocidal' policy towards certain peoples.

That same month, the non-Russians were provided with an unexpected fillip when, at the all-Union congress of educational workers, the chairman of the USSR State Committee for Public Education G. A. Iagodin admitted that 'the textbooks on the history of the USSR to a considerable extent still remain the history of the Russian people and the Russian state system'.[40] Nevertheless, at the same congress, the central authorities strongly opposed the campaign led by the Lithuanian representatives to transfer maximum control over education to the republics.[41]

The major surprise in the last weeks of 1988, though, came on 29 November, when Moscow stopped jamming the broadcasts of the Munich-based Radio Liberty. Financed by the US Congress, this unique radio station seeks to provide a surrogate democratic domestic service for the major peoples of the USSR. After more than three decades of jamming, Soviet listeners from the Baltic republics to Tadzhikistan were finally able for the first time to listen unimpeded to political, cultural and religious programmes broadcast in their native languages.

The crisis deepens

In the Baltic republics the push for genuine sovereignty continued. During the first months of 1989, the polarization between non-Russians wanting to throw off Russian tutelage and Russians determined to preserve the status quo became acute. In Lithuania and Estonia, the Inter-fronts began to organize strikes and demonstrations to protest against measures to make Lithuanian and Estonian the official languages and effectively force non-indigenous residents to learn them. A similar situation also began to develop in Moldavia where the national movement frequently organized mass rallies demanding, among other things, that Moldavian be made the official language of the republic, the restoration of Latin script (which had been replaced by Cyrillic after the territory had come under the control of Moscow), and curbs on the inflow of immigrants. As in the Baltic states, in the Ukraine and in Byelorussia, the Moldavian national movement was democratic in character and, while vehemently opposed to all forms of Russification, upheld the cultural rights of national minorities living in Moldavia.[42]

The situation was more complex in Georgia where relations between the majority Georgian nation, which was also demanding greater 'sovereignty' from Moscow, and the small Abkhaz minority, which had renewed its campaign for secession from Georgia, remained strained. This time it was the Georgians who demonstrated in their thousands in Tbilisi on 18 February 1989 against the discrimination allegedly suffered by Georgians in the Abkhaz ASSR.[43]

There were also louder rumblings of discontent in Soviet Central Asia, especially in Uzbekistan. Some of the demands focused on the language issue. In December 1988 students at Tashkent University held a demonstration in support of calls to make Uzbek the official language of the republic.[44] There was also growing pressure among the Moslem peoples for the reintroduction of Arabic script.

In January, strong domestic opposition to the continuing dominance of cotton in the republic's economy forced the Uzbek authorities to request further reductions in the cotton quota set by Moscow. As the Uzbek poet Muhammad Salih succinctly put it, in tsarist times

> we exported to Russia all the cotton in the form of raw material, and this structure of the economy was called colonial. Today we export ten times as much of this raw material, and we do not know what to call this structure.[45]

The religious aspect was also becoming more pronounced. On 3 February 1989 hundreds of Moslems took to the streets of Tashkent to demand the removal of the head of official Islam in Central Asia, Mufti Babakhan.[46] This manifestation of a more confident and assertive Islamic consciousness had the required effect: Babakhan was soon replaced.

But it was to the Ukraine that the Kremlin now turned its attention, and in February 1989 Gorbachev made an unexpected visit. Although over-shadowed by more dramatic developments in other republics, the Ukraine was far from tranquil. National ferment was growing, unofficial groups proliferated, and a new national revival was making headway. The Ukrainian cultural intelligentsia had become radicalized and had lost patience with the Brezhnevite Shcherbitsky and his conservative team. The writers had come into open conflict with the local Party authorities by renewing attempts to form a Baltic-type popular movement to promote restructuring and national renewal in the Ukraine.

Gorbachev seemed to want to play it both ways. He urged the Ukrainians to remove those who were blocking restructuring but did not openly criticize Shcherbitsky, who accompanied him throughout the visit. Gorbachev also stressed on several occasions that the Soviet government was not 'indifferent' to the fate of the Ukrainian language and culture and went out of his way to meet some of the writers who were heading the process of national regenera-tion. Yet at the same time, he adhered to the standard Soviet line on Ukrainian-Russian relations and stressed the need for unity among the USSR's Slavic nations. Gorbachev delivered his most telling comments in the heavily Russified Donbass coalmining region, where he openly admitted Moscow's concern about the potential consequences of unrest in the Ukraine. The effects of the Nagornyi Karabakh crisis, he said, had been felt throughout the Soviet Union. If disorder broke out in the 51-million-strong Ukrainian republic, restructuring would fail and the whole fabric of the USSR would come apart.[47]

During his visit, Gorbachev told the citizens of Lvov that there could be 'no excessive haste in resolving problems of national relations' but admitted that 'time was slipping away'.[48] Behind the scenes, the apparatus of the Central Committee had been put to work on preparing materials for the Central Committee plenum on the national question. The fact that such a delicate matter had been entrusted to a relatively small group of bureaucrats clearly angered some of the specialists who had long been associated with nationality issues. This, at any rate, was the impression that the authors obtained when, in early April 1989 at a conference at London University, they interviewed Academician Bromlei and his successor as director of the Institute of Ethnography of the USSR Academy of Sciences, Dr Valerii Tishkov.

Bromlei maintained that the Soviet leadership had only just begun to realize that the national question was 'the key issue' of restructuring and was now 'rushing things through'. He complained that the Central Committee apparatus, particularly the recently formed Sub-Section for Inter-Ethnic Relations headed by Dr Viacheslav Mikhailov, as well as the Institute of Marxism-Leninism, had been allowed to monopolize the preparations for the plenum and that they were keeping the ethnographers and other experts out. Tishkov echoed this view, adding that the bureaucrats who were 'defining the new theoretical approaches' to the national problem 'lacked the human touch'. What was needed, he suggested, was a system of public hearings so that everybody could have their say and be heard. Both specialists seemed to doubt that the review of Soviet nationalities policy would go far enough.

Some indication of what was in store was provided on 14 March when *Pravda* published a draft programme for republican economic autonomy. The extent of decentralization that Moscow was prepared to tolerate was quite limited. The scheme envisaged that Moscow would retain control over most heavy industry and leave the republics with restricted control over their own budgets. Baltic representatives promptly expressed their disappointment.

The following month brought another blow to the hopes of the non-Russians. On 8 April, Radio Moscow reported that a special working commission of the USSR Supreme Soviet had rejected calls led by the Balts for a new union treaty that would provide a fresh basis for relations between Moscow and the republics.

Gorbachev proclaims a state of 'tremendous danger'

Despite these setbacks, during the spring the non-Russians made important headway. On 26 March and in subsequent run-off elections, the forces for genuine democratization and radical change scored impressive victories in the elections to the new Congress of People's Deputies. In the Baltic republics, reformist candidates, many of them members of the popular fronts, won in the majority of electoral districts. In Lithuania, for instance, *Sajudis* won 31 out of 39 seats. In the Ukraine, the Party suffered a number of humiliating defeats. No less than five regional Party secretaries did not get in. In Kiev for example, both the mayor and the regional first Party secretary failed to win more than 50 per cent of the votes even though they ran unopposed. In Moldavia and Byelorussia, too, a number of reformist and nationally minded candidates defeated the Party's candidates.

Although some features of these elections could hardly be described as democratic, and the majority of the 2,250 deputies were conservatives, the event marked a psychological turning-point. Not only was a massive protest vote registered, but more importantly, in republics like the Ukraine, Moldavia and Byelorussia, the population saw what could be achieved if it was united against the old order. The results of the elections also brought another crucial breakthrough. The champions of national interests who had been elected had secured greater authority and a measure of immunity in their own republics; and they could now act as spokesmen for their respective constituencies in Moscow. In the Soviet capital they could also form coalitions with other democratically minded deputies, both Russian and non-Russian.

While preparations for the meeting of the Congress of People's Deputies were taking place, another tragedy shook the Soviet Union. On 9 April troops armed with sharpened spades and toxic gas were sent in against peaceful nationalist demonstrators in Tbilisi. Twenty protesters (unofficial accounts claimed a higher figure), the majority of them women, were killed and dozens injured. The authorities also arrested a number of prominent Georgian dissidents and imposed a curfew. The following day, Soviet foreign minister Shevardnadze, himself a Georgian, was sent to placate his outraged nation. Soon afterwards Gorbachev appealed for calm, but issued a strong warning that nationalist troublemakers would not be tolerated. On 14 April the Georgian Party leader Patiashvili resigned and was replaced by the republic's KGB chief Givi Gumbaridze. This was not enough to improve the atmosphere, though. Five days later, six deputies to the new Congress of People's Deputies charged that the authorities had censored and distorted accounts of what had happened. They also stressed that 'Bloody Sunday' in Tbilisi was a warning of how suddenly reform could be shut off.[49]

This lesson was not lost on others and there were manifestations of sympathy and support for the Georgians in the Baltic republics, the Ukraine, Moscow and elsewhere. The general attitude among the non-Russians was one of growing disillusionment with Gorbachev, and the realization that there was no point in waiting for the Soviet leader and his team to 'restructure' nationalities policy of their own accord.

The Balts continued to lead the way. In mid-May in Tallinn, the Baltic popular fronts held their first council. They stopped just short of demanding full independence from Moscow. The 'Baltic Council' rejected the economic autonomy scheme that had been proposed by the Kremlin and instead called for the Baltic republics to be given virtually total control of their economies by early 1990.[50] On 18 May, the Estonian Supreme Soviet defiantly passed a series of resolutions giving the republic control over its own economy and allowing for, among other things, private ownership of land. That same day, the Lithuanian Supreme Soviet voted to declare the republic's sovereignty and its right to veto laws passed in Moscow that concerned Lithuania.

The new Congress of People's Deputies opened on 25 May against a background of protests in Georgia, Moldavia and Uzbekistan, new mass demonstrations in Erevan and Nagornyi Karabakh, and mounting pressure from the Balts. From the very outset, the national problem figured prominently in the debates and also in the central media's coverage of the proceedings. Apart from the now familiar calls to broaden the sovereignty of the republics and to create a genuine federation, there was also strong condemnation of what had occurred in Tbilisi; criticism of the practice of appointing republican second Party secretaries – Moscow's 'satraps', as one Georgian deputy described them – from outside the republics; and demands for the resolution of the Crimean Tatar problem, the restoration of an autonomous republic for Soviet Germans, and the alleviation of the plight of the small Siberian native peoples. A temporary walkout by the Lithuanian deputies underscored that, however small some of the non-Russian delegations, they were not about to be ridden over roughshod by what Iurii Afanas'ev labelled the 'aggressively obedient majority'.

Apart from achieving a great deal of publicity for nationality issues, the non-Russians secured two things: a commission to look into the issue of the secret protocols of the Molotov–Ribbentrop Pact, and another one to investigate the events in the Georgian capital on 9 April. The conservative majority, however, also made its mark. It elected former chairman of the Presidium of the Byelorussian Supreme Soviet Georgii Tarazevich, a known conservative, to head the revamped Council of Nationalities.

For his part, Gorbachev at least acknowledged that 'at the beginning of restructuring' the Party leadership had 'not fully appreciated the necessity of reviewing nationalities policy' and that this had led to a 'delay in solving a number of urgent matters'. But then, as before, he failed to get to the root of the problem and instead blamed what had occurred on others. 'Natural dissatisfaction with economic and social matters had accumulated,' the Soviet leader claimed, and 'certain elements' had sought to make matters worse by 'speculating on the general difficulties'.[51]

The congress had barely ended when there were fresh outbreaks of ethnic violence, this time in Central Asia. Here the bitter fruits of Moscow's policies towards the region were making themselves felt. In the first half of May riots had taken place in Turkmenistan, largely because of the high level of unemployment among local youths.[52] Now far more serious instances of unrest occurred in Uzbekistan and Kazakhstan. During the first two weeks of June at least 99 people were killed and more than 1,000 injured in the fertile Ferghana Valley of Uzbekistan. Here, deteriorating economic conditions fuelled ethnic hostility and resulted in organized attacks by Uzbeks on Meskhetians who had been deported there by Stalin.[53] Gorbachev, evading the real reasons for the unrest, rather tactlessly told journalists while on a visit to West Germany that Islamic fundamentalism 'had bared its teeth'.[54] As troops were bringing the situation in the Ferghana region under control, ethnic disorders erupted in western Kazakhstan between Kazakhs and immigrants from the Caucasus.[55] Once again there was loss of life, and economic and social conditions, particularly unemployment among the local youths, were a major factor. To add to this bleak picture, on 1 July *Izvestia* reported that forces had been sent to defuse rising tensions between Georgians and Azerbaijanis in parts of Georgia.

What was also worrying for Moscow was the escalation of national demands in several non-Russian republics. In Georgia, on 15 June, the Writers' Union presented the Georgian Supreme Soviet with an ultimatum. It demanded that the Supreme Soviet: acknowledge that in 1921 Soviet Russia had violated its treaty with independent Georgia; implement genuine Georgian sovereignty; introduce republican citizenship; and restore Georgian national military formations. In the event of the Georgian Supreme Soviet failing to resolve these issues satisfactorily, the Georgian Writers' Union proposed a referendum on Georgia's secession from the USSR.[56]

Ten days later, a huge rally in Kishinev 'mourned' the annexation of the territory of the Moldavian SSR in June 1940. Banners at the meeting read: 'Let us Stop Colonization and Russification', 'Down with Neocolonialism' and 'We Demand a Sovereign Republic'. On June 28, the actual anniversary of the Soviet takeover, demonstrators in the Moldavian capital forced the cancellation of a gala concert organized by the authorities.[57]

A serious new type of challenge emerged in Lithuania. After the success of *Sajudis* in the elections, the Communist Party leadership realized that it would have to get in step with national aspirations if it were to survive as a credible political force. In June, the Lithuanian Komsomol declared its independence from the all-Union Komsomol and adopted a series of radical reforms.[58] Then, at a plenum held on 1 July, the Lithuanian Party leadership also decided to embark on the road towards independence. Not since Lenin's days had the unitary nature of the Russian-dominated Communist Party been questioned in this way.[59]

For other non-Russians, the Baltic republics continued to be a source of inspiration and, in some cases, also of practical help. The difference in climate between the Baltic republics and those with hard-line Party leaderships was aptly demonstrated when the Byelorussian Popular Front was unable to hold its inaugural congress in Minsk and instead, on 1 July, convened its assembly in the relative haven of Vilnius.[60]

The situation was fast becoming alarming for the Kremlin. On the evening of 1 July Gorbachev delivered a special address on Soviet Television. Appealing for calm, restraint, and confidence in the Party's willingness and ability to improve matters, he warned of the 'tremendous danger' posed by the growing ethnic unrest and stressed that the 'very unity' of the state was at stake. As on previous occasions, however, the Soviet leader spoke in very general terms. He pledged an uncompromising position towards 'nationalist manifestations in any form', yet acknowledged the need for 'a package of measures to improve inter-ethnic relations and remove the causes that underlie the complications that have arisen'. On the one hand he was prepared to acknowledge various distortions and acts of 'lawlessness' in the past, but on the other made it quite clear that Moscow was still not ready to grant genuine self-determination to the nations of the USSR. His speech was both a warning to those whom he accused of 'deliberately fanning inter-ethnic strife' and an implicit rejection of demands for greater autonomy and independence. 'Calls for economic autarky and spiritual isolation must be deemed profoundly alien to the interests of any people and of the whole of society,' he declared. 'The Soviet peoples have a single destiny.'[61]

The centre attempts to draw the line

Gorbachev's warnings were ineffective. Within two weeks there were reports of clashes between Tadzhik and Kirghiz villagers on the Tadzhik-Kirghiz border and of a flare-up in Abkhazia between Abkhazians and Georgians, which claimed at least 18 lives. Faced with these further complications, as well as a major strike by coalminers in Siberia and in the Ukraine, on 18 July the Soviet leader announced that the Central Committee plenum on the national question that had been expected to take place at the end of the month had been postponed. He also categorically rejected the idea of any federalization of the Communist Party.[62]

Remarkably, later that month, the Baltic deputies in the new Supreme Soviet that had been elected by the Congress of People's Deputies won an important victory. After a heated debate in which they faced stiff opposition from the central planners, the Balts secured approval for their plan to gain a degree of economic autonomy. Only weeks before, it had been decried as unacceptable. They were helped by the fact that one of the demands that had emerged during the miners' strike was for greater local control of economic decision-making. Hoping that the Baltic experiment represented a promising model in an otherwise bleak economic environment, representatives of the Donbass miners hailed the Baltic economic autonomy plan as 'a revolutionary step in restructuring the country's economic mechanism'.[63]

At the end of July around 250 radical members of the Congress of People's Deputies joined forces and formed an 'Inter-Regional Group'. This new 'loyal opposition' included numerous non-Russian deputies and was led by, among others, Andrei Sakharov and Boris El'tsin. In a lengthy interview with the liberal weekly *Ogonek*, edited by the Ukrainian poet Vitalii Korotych, Sakharov called for the 'dismantling' of the Soviet Union's 'imperial' structure and its replacement by a voluntary confederation based on a new Union treaty. The non-Russians, he maintained, should be given 'independence to the maximum degree' and their sovereignty limited only by considerations of 'common defence, foreign policy, transport and communications'. This, he emphasized, was not only his own view, but a position that was supported in the Baltic and various other national republics.[64]

Encouraged by their success in Moscow, the Balts kept at it. On 29 July the Latvian Supreme Soviet declared Latvia sovereign and set up a commission to assess the consequences of the Molotov–Ribbentrop Pact. Just over a week later the Estonian Supreme Soviet took the bold step of approving a new election law setting a minimum residence requirement of two years to vote in the republic's elections and five years to run for office. Thousands of Russian workers in Estonia responded by going on strike to protest against what they denounced as political and linguistic discrimination. On 16 August the Presidium of the USSR Supreme Soviet issued a decree signed by its chairman, Gorbachev, declaring that the new Estonian law was contrary to the Soviet Constitution. That same day, *Pravda* attacked the Baltic popular fronts, accusing them of fomenting 'nationalist hysteria'.

As this latest crisis was unfolding, the Party leadership finally unveiled its proposals 'for improving inter-ethnic relations in the USSR and renewing nationalities policy'. The lengthy document was published in *Pravda* on 17 August and entitled 'The Party's Nationalities Policy Under Present Conditions (Platform of the CPSU)'. It seems to have been prepared with a view to placating as many different groups as possible. Much of it was rhetorical, and merely listed general principles without offering any concrete solutions. In essence, the 'Platform' made it clear that the Party leadership was prepared to go some way in making adjustments in nationalities policy, but that it was not about to permit any real 'radical transformation' of the structure of the USSR. The Soviet Union was treated throughout as a 'voluntary association' of 'independent' partners, the idea of confederation was resolutely rejected, Moscow's predominance over the republics was reasserted, and the Russian nation was described as remaining 'the consolidating basis of our entire Union'. Camouflaged as it was, the 'Platform' was in fact a recipe for the preservation, rather than the gradual dismantling, of the empire.

The document euphemistically acknowledged that because of 'deformations' and extreme centralization, the 'republics' sovereignty became largely formal', and that the existing 'ossified forms of national-state structure' did not permit 'consideration of new needs and exploitation of new possibilities'. For all this, the centre reserved for itself the following key powers:

establishing the fundamentals of the political system and developing it, ensuring the country's defence and security, pursuing foreign policy, co-ordinating and resolving common tasks in the spheres of the economy, science and culture, the position of the individual, effective utilization of integrative processes, and the organization of mutual assistance . . . ensuring the dynamic and stable development of the country's national economic complex.

Moreover, the 'Platform' stated that republics had 'the right to raise the question' of revoking all-Union legislation, but that the centre could revoke republican laws if they were deemed to go beyond the limits of the republic's competence.

The idea of renegotiating the national contract was also rejected. Acknowledging that there were calls for the signing of a new union treaty to replace the 1922 Treaty on the Formation of the USSR, the 'Platform' stated:

the Constitution of the Soviet federative state is a treaty document, since it enshrines the basic rights and reciprocal commitments of the union and its constituent republics. As is well known, the 1922 treaty is open and still retains its legal force.

The 'Platform' did, however, contain some encouraging elements as regards the smaller national minorities. It emphasized their needs and rights, and endorsed the idea of restoring national districts and national soviets. All the same, the general formula 'Soviet citizens must feel at home anywhere in the country', described as the 'ultimate goal of all work to harmonize inter-ethnic relations', was just too facile. Now, even the Russians who until relatively recently had felt quite comfortable and secure in the western non-Russian republics had begun to sense what it meant to be unwelcome and to be regarded as a second-class citizen. And as far as groups such as the Crimean Tatars were concerned, they were still unwelcome in their homeland, and were continuing their campaign for the right to return there.

Reacting to the assertiveness of the non-Russians, more and more Russian representatives from the RSFSR, including its president, Vitalii Vorotnikov, had started speaking out in defence of Russia's national interests and the sovereign rights of the RSFSR. At the Congress of People's Deputies, for instance, the writer Vasilii Belov had raised the problem of 'Russophobia'. His colleague Valentin Rasputin had suggested that in view of all the criticism of Russia and the Russians it was perhaps time for Russia to consider seceding from the Soviet Union.[65] The 'Platform' seemed to go out of its way both to reassure and placate the Russians. Not only did it single them out as the unifying force of the USSR and hail the Russian language once again as the Soviet Union's 'language of inter-ethnic communication', it also recognized the need to create Russian political, economic, scientific and other institutions of the sort that the non-Russian republics had but the RSFSR did not.

Thus, while the 'Platform' may have been welcomed by some of the smaller nationalities and quite a few Russians, it was disappointing as far as the larger non-Russian nations were concerned. Although the document stressed that it was 'important to free theoretical thought from a dogmatic approach to the national question' it nevertheless adhered to the largely discredited formula of 'the Soviet people', in which, in some miraculous fashion, the national and the international were supposedly harmoniously reconciled. Yet what the Party was really concerned with was 'augmenting and increasing' the 'international unity' of the Soviet Union. In other words, preserving as much of the status quo as possible even if it meant continuing to talk of unity when in fact there was disunity. Cutting through the dialectical obfuscation, the chief editor of *Pravda*, Viktor Afanas'ev, aptly commented: 'We now have a formula: a strong centre and strong republics. But who has explained what this is?'[66]

No holding back the non-Russians

The publication of the 'Platform' made little difference. In Azerbaijan, the Popular Front had grown so strong that it was able to force the Azerbaijani Party leadership to begin negotiating with it. Some of its economic, social and political demands resembled those of the Baltic popular fronts, but the Azerbaijani movement's leaders also sought the release of imprisoned Azerbaijani activists, new elections, official recognition of their organization, and the reassertion of Azerbaijan's control over Nagornyi Karabakh. In order to extract concessions, the Popular Front of Azerbaijan began organizing demonstrations and strikes. On 19 August half a million or more people attended one of the front's numerous demonstrations in Baku.[67]

A few days later, the 50th anniversary of the Molotov–Ribbentrop Pact was marked by major protests in the Baltic republics and Moldavia. First, however, on 22 August, a commission of the Lithuanian Supreme Soviet declared the Nazi–Soviet agreement illegal and invalid. The following day, almost two million Balts formed a human chain stretching 600 kilometres from Tallinn to Riga and Vilnius. It was a vivid display of the longing of the Estonians, Latvians and Lithuanians for independence and of their solidarity and determination. In Kishinev, too, at least 10,000 protesters gathered to denounce the pact and its consequences.

The Soviet central media had long been under fire from Baltic activists for their generally sparse and one-sided coverage of developments in the Baltic republics. They responded to the new Baltic demonstrations with a barrage of criticism and warnings about the 'dangerous' mood in the Baltic republics. On 26 August, tensions were suddenly escalated. The CPSU Central Committee issued a long, stinging statement, which was read that evening on Soviet Television, denouncing 'extremist, nationalist groups' in the Baltic republics and warning ominously of 'impending disaster'. It also accused the local Party and state authorities of 'losing heart' and giving in to 'nationalist' and 'separatist' sentiments. 'Things have gone far,' the statement declared;

> The fate of the Baltic peoples is in serious danger. The people should know the abyss that they are being pushed towards by their nationalist leaders. If they succeeded in achieving their goals, the possible consequences could be catastrophic for these nations. The very viability of the Baltic nations could be called into question.

Describing the situation as a 'crisis' that was affecting the 'vital interests of the entire Soviet population [and] our entire Socialist motherland', the statement ended with an appeal to the Balts to 'preserve the unitary family of Soviet peoples and the unity of the Communist Party of the Soviet Union'.[68]

Baltic activists interpreted this as a virtual ultimatum. Their reaction, in the words of Aleksei Grigor'ev, deputy editor of the Latvian Popular Front newspaper, was one of 'surprise, insult and indignation'.[69] Although startled by Moscow's menacing tone, the Balts demonstrated that they would not be intimidated. Baltic deputies defiantly fired off telegrams to Gorbachev expressing their disgust and on 31 August the Baltic popular fronts jointly denounced the Central Committee's statement and appealed for support to the other nations of the USSR. 'Probably not since the Stalin era and the events in Czechoslovakia in 1968,' their appeal 'To the Peoples of the Soviet Union' read, 'has a document appeared in our country that is more threatening and dangerous for democracy.' Questioning the very nature of the Soviet multinational state, the document declared:

> If the union is not voluntary, if nations are kept under constraint, if relations between nations are not based on equality, if the centre issues commands and unquestioning compliance is expected of the federated states, then that is no longer a union; there are other terms for it: superpower, empire, prison of nations.[70]

The Balts were not alone in condemning the statement. In an interview given to the French TV presenter Patrick Poivre d'Arvor on 16 September, Andrei Sakharov described it as 'complete madness', adding that 'it aggravates the situation in a totally unnecessary manner'.[71]

During the final days of August, the Soviet central press was also highly critical of the Moldavian national movement. The Moldavian Popular Front had mobilized mass support for demands to make Moldavian the official language of the Moldavian SSR, for the restoration of Latin script, and for republican sovereignty. Russian-speaking residents in Moldavia felt threatened. They insisted that the Russian language be granted parity with Moldavian. As the next session of the Moldavian Supreme Soviet drew nearer, the conflict intensified. Beginning in mid-August, tens of thousands of Russian and other non-Moldavian workers took part in protest strikes. On 27 August, though, more than a quarter of a million Moldavians rallied in Kishinev to press home Moldavian national demands. The following day *Pravda* accused the Moldavian Popular Front of 'national blindness' and of wanting 'to take power on a muddy wave of chauvinism and separatism'.

On 1 September, the Moldavian Supreme Soviet adopted a language law making Moldavian the republic's official language, reinstituting Latin script, and designating both Moldavian and Russian as languages of inter-ethnic communication. This compromise – which was proposed by Gorbachev himself in a telephone call to the Moldavian Party leader Grossu – failed to appease Moldavia's Russian-speaking residents. Demanding the suspension of the new law and that Russian also be made an official state language, they continued with their protest strikes.[72] On 2 September the USSR Supreme Soviet, at the urging of the Russian-speaking protesters, set up a commission to study the situation in Moldavia. Five days later, however, Radio Vilnius reported that a group of Lithuanian members of the USSR Supreme Soviet had complained to Gorbachev about the secretive way in which the commission had been formed.

The situation in the Transcaucasus was also very tense. During August Azerbaijani militants had gradually imposed a virtual blockade of transport routes to Armenia and Nagornyi Karabakh, preventing the delivery of fuel, food and construction supplies. On 29 August the Soviet interior minister Vadim Bakatin announced another death in clashes between Armenians and Azerbaijanis and that he was sending more troops to Nagornyi Karabakh. Two days later, Party leaders from Armenia and Azerbaijan were summoned to Moscow to discuss the 'dangerous character' of Armenian–Azerbaijani relations.[73]

Meanwhile, the Popular Front of Azerbaijan had called a general strike in Baku. It began on 4 September and forced the Azerbaijani Party chief, Abdul-Rakhman Vezirov, to differ with Moscow by calling for the end of its direct rule over Nagornyi Karabakh. The strike continued until 11 September when the Azerbaijani authorities finally agreed to register the Azerbaijani Popular Front and to convene a special session of the Azerbaijani Supreme Soviet to discuss the situation in the republic and in Nagornyi Karabakh. The Azerbaijani Supreme Soviet met on 15–16 September and adopted a resolution proposed by the Azerbaijani Popular Front calling for the restoration of Azerbaijani control over Nagornyi Karabakh. The concessions made by the Azerbaijani authorities were hailed at rallies in Baku in which hundreds of thousands of people took part. It was not simply the issue of Nagornyi Karabakh that fired the Azerbaijani masses. There was also a growing demand for economic sovereignty based on the belief that Azerbaijan was 'being short-changed by Moscow for the oil, industrial and economic wealth' that it contributed.[74]

The victories of the Azerbaijani Popular Front, of course, did not help the Armenian cause. On 14 September *Pravda* painted a grim picture of a blockaded Armenia and warned that the situation was 'pregnant with unforeseeable consequences'. That same day, Arkadii Vol'skii, the Kremlin's plenipotentiary in Nagornyi Karabakh, conceded on Soviet television that the situation in the enclave had never been 'as explosive as today'. Shortly afterwards the Armenian Supreme Soviet met and reiterated Armenians' claims to Nagornyi Karabakh and debated whether to appeal for Moscow's help in breaking the Azerbaijani economic blockade.

There were also important developments in the Ukraine. In early September there were numerous large demonstrations in the republic calling for the democratization of a proposed new electoral law that seemed designed to preserve the advantages held by conservative forces. By now, the Popular Movement of the Ukraine for Restructuring, or *Rukh* (Movement) as it was called in short, could not be held back any longer. Between 8 and 10 September it finally held its inaugural congress in Kiev. Prominent Ukrainian writers, economists, lawyers and liberal People's Deputies and Party members formed a common front with former political prisoners, religious rights activists, and members of the republic's many new unofficial organizations. The latter included the largest of the dissident political associations, the Ukrainian Helsinki Union, the ecological Green World Association, the republican Memorial Society (devoted to commemorating the victims of Soviet repression in the Ukraine), and the Ukrainian Language Society. Ukrainians living outside the Ukraine in other parts of the Soviet Union, Eastern Europe and the West, as well as the Ukraine's national minorities, were well represented. Among the guests was one of Poland's leading Solidarity activists, the historian Adam Michnik. Although there were calls for independence, the majority of speakers called for the broadest economic and political sovereignty for the Ukraine and for the USSR to be transformed from a 'state union' into 'a union of states', or confederation.

The poet Ivan Drach was elected to lead this vigorous new Ukrainian national democratic movement, which was already claiming a membership of a quarter of a million.[75] Although the response of the Soviet Ukrainian press remained mostly very hostile, *Rukh* confidently took on the Shcherbitsky regime. It was assisted by a sizeable group of democratic Ukrainian deputies who had formed their own Republican Deputies' Club that was aligned with the Inter-regional Group of Deputies.

Rukh's mission was complicated, though, by the fact that Ukrainian national feeling remained very strong in the Western Ukraine and much weaker in the more Russified southern and eastern parts of the republic. Indeed, the population in the Western Ukraine had become almost as politically active as in the Baltic republics. In the Western Ukrainian centre of Lvov, large-scale nationalist demonstrations had become almost weekly occurrences and the city had become known as *Vil'na Ukraina* (Free Ukraine). In this region, too, Ukrainian Catholics were campaigning hard for the legalization of their outlawed church. On 17 September over 150,000 of them marched through Lvov and defiantly held a mass in the city. Later that night, many thousands of people in Lvov and elsewhere in the Western

Ukraine held silent vigils with lighted candles as a sign of mourning on the 50th anniversary of the Molotov–Ribbentrop Pact and the ensuing replacement, as they saw it, of the 'Polish occupation' of the region by a far harsher Soviet one.[76]

On 12 September, just as the final link in the chain of independent organizations stretching from the Baltic to the Central Asian republics was being forged, the long-awaited Central Committee plenum on the national question was announced for 19 September.

The plenum on the national question – an anticlimax

The announcement of the special plenum was made against the background of continuing polarization. On one side were the non-Russians and their liberal Russian allies who were seeking an end to the empire and, on the other, imperially-minded Russians and their reactionary non-Russian allies. On 14 September *Sovetskaia Rossiia* revealed that a 'United Council of Russia' had been formed to represent Russian and Russian-speaking workers in the Soviet Union and to strengthen Russia as the consolidating basis of the USSR. Its members included the Inter-front movements from the Baltic republics and Moldavia. The aims of a second Russian group founded in early September in Sverdlovsk, the 'United Front of Workers of Russia', were to oppose market-oriented economic reforms and to combat nationalism in the non-Russian republics.[77] Sakharov publicly condemned the latter organization on Soviet television as 'very dangerous for restructuring and the harmonious development of our country'.[78]

It is also worth noting what the pre-eminent Russian democrat had to say on the eve of the Central Committee plenum on the national question. The large scale of the problems, he told a French interviewer, 'is linked to indecisive, inconsequential and unreasonable policies at the centre of power, which is systematically late in making correct and necessary decisions'. Changes in national and constitutional structures, he added, were indispensable.[79]

The Soviet leadership continued to think otherwise. Gorbachev again made it clear that the Kremlin was prepared to be more flexible up to a point but would not budge on the fundamental issues. On 13 September the Soviet Party leader met with the Party chiefs of the Baltic republics. Although Gorbachev took quite a conciliatory tone and called for a 'search for reasonable compromises', he nevertheless set out three inviolable principles:

> First, all our problems should be solved by all of us only in the framework of the Federation.
> Second, unity of our Party. It is the main guarantor of *perestroika* and the process of national revival. . .
> Third, equality of the citizens of all nationalities.

Once again rebuffing the idea of secession, the Soviet leader warned that if the ties between the Soviet republics were allowed 'to break up', it would 'cast us back decades'. He also declared that the federalization of the Party would be a 'grave political mistake' that would be 'ruinous to its unity'.[80] As for his insistence on the equal rights of citizens of all nationalities – another tacit acknowledgement of the gap that had remained between theory and practice – this principle had a somewhat different ring to it now that Moscow had taken up the defence of the Russians who had settled in non-Russian republics and become used to acting as if they still lived in Russia.

There were some surprises when the Central Committee plenum on the national question finally opened on 19 September, but not all of them were connected with the nationalities policy. After all the expectation, discussion of the national question was actually placed second on the agenda, being overshadowed by Gorbachev's unexpected announcement that the 28th Party Congress would be held in October 1990, five months earlier than planned. Perhaps the major encouraging feature of the plenum was that it brought the 'retirement' from the Politburo of three conservatives, including Shcherbitsky, the Ukrainian Party leader, and Chebrikov, the former head of the KGB. All the same, the plenum provided a good picture of the nature and scale of the national problem in the USSR at the end of the 1980s, the extent to which the Gorbachev leadership's attitude towards it had changed, and just how much progress *glasnost'* and 'democratization' had made in four years.

One key ingredient was missing, though. Despite the importance of the plenum, the central press did not provide data from the all-Union census taken at the beginning of the year on the national composition of the USSR. This important information could easily have been made available, for, on the very day that the plenum was convened, the Estonian-language republican daily *Rahva Haal* published preliminary data on the ethnic composition of the USSR. This showed that the Russians only barely still constituted a majority, for their share of the population had fallen from 52.4 per cent in 1979 to 50.8 per cent; that over 25 million of them lived outside the Russian Federation; and that the outflow of Russians from the eight Central Asian and Transcaucasian republics had accelerated. The Russians had grown by 5.6 per cent and now numbered 145 million; the second largest nation, the Ukrainians, by 4.2 per cent and now numbered 44.1 million; but the third largest nation, the Uzbeks, had grown by 34 per cent and reached 16.6 million.[81]

Gorbachev, too, did not allude to what the census had revealed. His report on the Party's nationalities policy closely reflected the Party's 'Platform' on the national question.[82] He did, however, admit that recognition of the need for change had come rather late in the day and that the situation was now 'extremely complex'. Having acknowledged this, he nevertheless avoided discussing the real nature of the Soviet imperial system and instead attempted to whitewash it. There was plenty in his speech about the supposed enormous advantages which the Soviet Union had brought to its constituent nations, but no attempt to weigh up the costs. 'Any attempts to distort and belittle the true achievements in the sphere of national relations,' he insisted, 'is an outrage against the memory of several generations of Soviet people.'

What was particularly revealing was how the Soviet leader dealt with the historical background to the current predicament. In 1917, 'the country' (as he referred to the Russian empire) had been torn apart by 'inter-ethnic contradictions'. Consequently, 'the problem of a state arrangement' had acquired 'vital significance'. Gorbachev failed to mention the attempts by the non-Russian peoples to achieve national independence and how most of them were subdued by military conquest. Passing straight on to the formation of the USSR, he praised Lenin for devising an 'optimum Party strategy on the national question' and advocating the 'idea of a state federation of an historically new type'. He neglected, however, to mention Lenin's strictures against Russian great-power chauvinism and Russification. Sticking to the standard line, Gorbachev went on to blame all the 'deformities' in the nationalities policy on Stalin, 'excessive centralization' and 'bureaucratic administration'.

If this was disappointing enough, worse was to follow. After proclaiming that 'not a single blank spot must be left in the Soviet state's history' and that 'untruths and half-truths' could not be tolerated, the Soviet leader proceeded as if this did not apply to him. His cursory treatment of the histories of the non-Russian nations under Soviet rule was exemplified by his declaration that 'there are no grounds to question the decision by the Baltic republics to join the USSR and the choice made by their peoples'. Later, avoiding the word Russification altogether, he sought to blame the reduction of 'the usage of national languages' on such 'objective' factors as 'economic, social and demographic forces'.

The object, as Gorbachev put it, was 'to update the nationalities policy', but not 'to reject what has been done so far'. What the Party was after, he explained obliquely, was to determine 'optimum correlations between the international and national'. His explanation of this seemed to echo Khrushchev's formula of 1956: *rastsvet*, or the flourishing of the non-Russian cultures, and simultaneously, in Gorbachev's words, 'the consolidation of our Union'. The Soviet leader was much clearer, though, on a number of specific issues. He branded advocates of secession as 'adventurers', ruled out for the foreseeable future the recarving of borders or the upgrading of autonomous republics to the level of union republics, and suggested that it was time to ban and disband 'nationalist, chauvinist and other extremist organizations'. Predictably, he again inveighed against the idea of federalizing the Party or impinging on the rights of the more than 60 million Soviet citizens who, he said, now lived 'outside their national republics, as a result of economic, social and demographic processes and inter-ethnic migration'.

One new note introduced by the Soviet leader was blatantly at odds with

Lenin's categorical rejection of the idea of Russian as a state language for all the peoples of the USSR. Omitting to recall Lenin's position on this issue, Gorbachev simply announced that because all the peoples of the USSR were supposedly 'vitally interested' in having Russian as a means of communication, 'it is expedient to give the Russian language the status of a common state language across the USSR'. Coming at a time when in so many republics the pressure was for de-Russifying public, cultural and educational life, this move was clearly calculated to preserve the privileged status of the Russian language and to reassure Russians living in the non-Russian republics.

There was also one other new twist. Gorbachev reduced the idea of national self-determination to a bizarre notion of limited self-management. Gorbachev argued that 'in present-day conditions the principle [of national self-determination] is best reflected in self-management'. The Soviet leader qualified this by adding:

> At the same time self-management presupposes the voluntary association of republics and national entities in the name of grappling with needs common to all, and their organic involvement in the advance of the whole country.

This view of national self-determination had little in common with Lenin's proposal that this concept be taken to mean, first and foremost, 'the right to free secession'.

On the whole, Gorbachev's speech was rather defensive, and contained a mixture of warnings and appeals to reason. Throughout the speech he used the collective forms 'we' and 'our': 'everything must be done,' he said characteristically, 'to make *our* plenum a turning point.' He also did not hesitate to state that 'our Party favours a major and strong federal state as it is convinced that this meets the interests of all ethnic groups united in the Soviet Union'.

But just how representative was this important plenum and to what extent did it really reflect the wishes of the peoples of the USSR? Ann Sheehy, who examined the composition of the Central Committee at the time of the plenum, concluded that the non-Russian republics were 'less well-represented among the full, that is voting, members of the Central Committee than at any time in the recent past'. The Baltic republics, Azerbaijan and Armenia, for instance, had no representatives at all among the voting members, and Georgia and Uzbekistan had barely one or two each.[83]

In addition to this imbalance, which made a mockery of Gorbachev's frequent platitudes about the equality of the nationalities and the need for their due representation at all levels, it should also be borne in mind that the majority of the Central Committee still consisted of conservatives. This was evident enough from the discussion that followed Gorbachev's report. The Ukrainian Party's ideological secretary Iurii Iel'chenko, for example, warned that 'the future of our common home' had been put under threat by 'anti-

Soviet forces, nationalists, and extremists', and that it was time to face up to the danger from 'counter-revolution'. Moldavia's Party leader Grossu voiced his dissatisfaction with the 'vagueness and wait-and-see attitude' of the central Party leadership and called for a more resolute policy. For his part, Politburo member and chairman of the presidium of the RSFSR Supreme Soviet Vitalii Vorotnikov, while on the one hand calling for the formation of new Russian 'socio-political structures' such as distinctly Russian organizations within the framework of the CPSU, Komsomol and the All-Union Central Council of Trade Unions, warned that 'the negative aspects in relation to Russians arising in some republics are giving rise to resentment and indignation among the Russian public'.[84]

Not surprisingly, the heads of the Soviet Interior Ministry and the military also expressed their concern. The former, Vadim Bakatin, revealed that since the beginning of 1988, 292 people had been killed in inter-ethnic clashes, 5,520 injured and 360,000 forced to flee their homes. He went on to accuse the authorities in Georgia, Azerbaijan and Armenia of 'bowing to the pressure of extremists' because they had released detained leaders of unofficial groups. Defence Minister Dmitrii Iazov protested that 'nationalistic, separatist and extremist forces' had not been 'duly rebuffed' and were now even coming out with demands, 'accompanied by cynical insults, for the withdrawal of large units . . . to the territory of the Russian Federation'. In several republics, he added, there were more and more 'calls resembling ultimatums for the creation of national troop formations'. Urging more emphasis on military-patriotic education, Iazov also stressed the importance from the military point of view of 'the study of the Russian language in the republics'. During 1988, he disclosed,

> the number of draftees without Russian . . . exceeded 125,000 men. This is 12 times more than 20 years ago. An alarming trend.[85]

What General Iazov did not discuss were the reasons why the Balts, Moldavians, Georgians and others wanted 'Russian' troops out of their republics, why calls by the non-Russians for the formation of national military units were becoming more widespread, and why, for that matter, in the aftermath of the withdrawal of Soviet troops from Afghanistan, anti-military and pacifistic tendencies were on the rise among Soviet youth generally. Nor did he address the problem of the concern and anger that had been expressed in the Baltic republics, Georgia, Armenia and most recently in Uzbekistan, about the victimization, torture and, in some cases, alleged murder of conscripts, on account of their national identity.[86] Iazov's calls to strengthen the 'internationalism' of the Soviet armed forces also rang hollow; the following month, the Soviet military daily revealed that the Soviet General Staff consisted of 85 per cent Russians, 10 per cent Ukrainians and 3 per cent Byelorussians.[87]

For all this, there were also quite a few bold and noteworthy speeches. For example, the chairman of the USSR State Committee for Television and Radio Broadcasting, M. Nenashev, argued that after the 'landmark' 19th Party Conference the 'old inertia' had set in again and that the Party's agitation and propaganda was still 'in many instances based on dogmatism and drum-beating methods'.[88]

One Daghestani representative spoke of the 'second-class status' of the autonomous republics compared to that of the Union republics. The Tatar and Bashkir representatives criticized the Party's 'Platform' on the national question because, as the latter put it, it contained 'no breakthrough from established views, preserving inviolate the hierarchical structure' of the different types of national-state structures.[89] The Tatar speaker, G. Usmanov, reminded the plenum that many autonomous republics were 'in no way inferior to certain Union republics'. He also stressed that sociological research carried out in the Tatar ASSR had shown that 67 per cent of respondents considered that elevating the Tatar autonomous republic to the level of a Union republic would improve the situation.[90] What was left unsaid, however, was that the Russian Federation stood to lose if autonomous republics were transformed into Union republics. Sixteen of the 20 autonomous republics were located in the RSFSR. Even if only some of them were to become full-fledged Union republics, 'Russia' would lose territory and take on a rather different shape.

Representatives of the Soviet Germans and Jews expressed their concern about the high rate of emigration of their peoples from the Soviet Union. Indeed, by the end of October 1989, 51,080 Jews had emigrated from the USSR; more than in any previous year.[91] The German speaker appealed for the prompt restoration of an autonomous German state, saying that this was 'the last chance' for the Soviet Germans 'to survive as a people'. The Party leader from the Jewish autonomous region, B. Korsunskii, complained that Jewish 'national-cultural' needs were still not being met, and attacked the chauvinism and anti-Semitism propagated by Russian ultra-nationalist organizations such as *Pamiat'* and the journals *Molodaia gvardiia* and *Nash sovremmenik*. The Bashkir representative, too, spoke out against chauvinistic slurs against his people in a Russian publication. He also repeated a charge made by the Georgian Party leader, G. Gumbavidze, that the central news media 'demonstrated a total lack of objectivity' in their coverage of developments in the national republics.

The Party leaders from the Central Asian republics were more circumspect, but nevertheless got certain points across. The new Uzbek Party chief, Islam Karimov, brought up the issue of cotton monoculture, and stressed that 45 per cent of the population of Uzbekistan earned less than the subsistence wage of 75 roubles a month, and that there were already one million unemployed in his republic. His Kirghiz counterpart criticized the 'distortions in specialization' which meant that less than 30 per cent of the republic's industrial force were indigenous people. The Kazakh Party chief, N. Nazarbaev, protested against the way in which his republic had been used as a testing ground for nuclear weapons, while the Tadzhik Party leader, apart from confirming that there were 200,000 unemployed in his republic, delicately expressed his disagreement with the Kremlin's reluctance to revise disputed borders.[92]

All in all though, the long-awaited plenum on the national question was historic only in the sense that it was the first of its kind. Gorbachev claimed in his closing speech that there had been a 'frank and direct discussion' that had made it possible to see the real picture. '*We* have reached agreement on the main key issues of the nationalities policy,' he declared.[93] But what was actually offered was a series of compromises on Moscow's terms. The republics and autonomous formations were being offered broader rights and prerogatives; but the nature of those rights remained vague. Gorbachev's proposals rested on what he called a new, 'enriched' concept of self-determination; a concept that in fact distorted the very meaning of this principle. If the non-Russians can be said to have finally broken through at the 19th Party Conference, then the plenum was a belated attempt to repair the breach in the imperial edifice.

This was obvious not only to the non-Russians, but to some of the democratic Russians as well. Sakharov told the French daily *Le Progrès* that Gorbachev's speech at the plenum was a step backward.[94] The Soviet leader, in advocating the formal recognition of Russian as the state language of the USSR, had not hesitated to claim in his closing speech that this 'expressed the prevailing sentiment, the dominant sentiment in our society'. Academician Iurii Ryzhov, a Russian member of the Inter-regional group of People's Deputies and chairman of the Supreme Soviet Committee on Science and Culture, was among those who questioned this. Appearing on Soviet television on 15 October, he argued that the Soviet multinational state could not survive in its present form and that there was therefore no point in making Russian its official language. 'The time of empires has passed,' he warned. 'We will not be able to enter the 21st century with an empire.'

No going back?
It was soon apparent that the plenum did not make much of an impact. Hardly had it ended when the Lithuanian Party published the outline of a draft programme insisting that 'in order to become a political force in the building of an independent Lithuanian state based on the rule of law', the Party would have to become independent itself. Two days later, on 22 September, a special commission of the Lithuanian Supreme Soviet declared the 1940 vote to join the USSR invalid.[95] By now, the commission set up by the Congress of People's Deputies to evaluate the Molotov–Ribbentrop Pact had decided that the agreement and its secret protocols should be denounced. Their findings,

however, had effectively been suppressed, and at the end of the month members of the commission held a press conference in Moscow. They accused Politburo member Aleksandr Iakovlev of having given in to pressure from the Party apparatus to block the publication of the commission's report.[96]

In the Transcaucasus the situation remained highly strained and it took two direct ultimatums from Gorbachev before the Azerbaijanis began to ease their blockade of Armenia. The Uzbek popular front, named *Birlik* (Unity), was by now claiming over half a million members; it organized mass demonstrations in Tashkent on 24 September and again on 19 and 20 October as part of the campaign to press for Uzbek to be made the state language in Uzbekistan. And in Moldavia where, after a month of protests, Russian-speaking workers had only now begun to suspend their strikes, tension remained high.

On 28 September Gorbachev again flew to the Ukraine, this time to oversee the removal of moribund Shcherbitsky, whose position as the Ukraine's Party leader had become even more untenable now that *Rukh* was in the ascendant. Three days later, though, the Ukrainian public was shocked by the news that riot police had been sent in against peaceful demonstrators in Lvov and that people had been injured. This was hardly a good start for the new Ukrainian Party chief, Volodymyr Ivashko. During the next few weeks, however, he made some attempt to project himself as a more reasonable figure than his predecessor. This was particularly evident from his attitude when the Ukrainian Supreme Soviet met between 25 and 28 October and passed two important laws: one on elections that had been made more democratic as a result of strong pressure from below; and the other making Ukrainian the official state language of the Ukrainian SSR and Russian the republic's language of inter-ethnic communication.

The issue of the banned Ukrainian national churches became even more prominent. In Moscow, liberal publications like *Moscow News* and *Ogonek* took up the cause of the Ukrainian Catholics. Moreover, the announcement that Gorbachev would be meeting with the Pope at the beginning of December during his visit to Rome raised hopes that, despite the continuing opposition from the Moscow Patriarchate, the injustices done to the Ukrainian Catholics would cease. Several 'Russian Orthodox' parishes in the Western Ukraine even tested the climate by announcing that they were going over to the Ukrainian Catholic Church. Meanwhile, during 1989, a movement for the restoration of the Ukrainian Autocephalous Orthodox Church also got underway and several Ukrainian priests and a bishop, Ioan (Vasyl' Bodnarchuk) of Zhitomir joined it, having broken with the Russian Orthodox Church.

In Azerbaijan, the powerful Azerbaijani Popular Front continued to score impressive successes. On 5 October a new radical constitutional law was published asserting greater Azerbaijani sovereignty within the USSR, and reaffirming that Azerbaijan viewed Nagornyi Karabakh as an integral part of its territory. The law also emphasized Azerbaijan's right to secede from the USSR if this were decided by a referendum.[97] Meanwhile, the mood in neighbouring Georgia was dramatically illustrated in mid-October by the attendance of some half a million mourners at the funeral of Merab Kostava, a veteran campaigner for Georgian independence, who had died in a road accident.[98] Towards the end of the month thousands of Georgians, including 200 draft-resisters, began a continuous protest outside the government headquarters in Tbilisi demanding a referendum on the issue of Georgian independence.[99]

The non-Russians also kept up their pressure in the USSR Supreme Soviet. On 16 October it rejected the government's draft law for giving the republics more economic autonomy on the grounds that it did not go far enough. Understandably, the approach of elections to the republican legislatures and to local councils was an important issue. On 23 October, Gorbachev voiced his strong opposition to the idea of the national republics directly electing their own presidents. Having himself amassed enormous power in the dual role of Party leader and head of state, he warned that this would result in the concentration of too much power.[100]

Threats or no threats, there was still no stopping the Balts. At the beginning of October a 'Baltic Parliamentary Group' was formed, and attracted the support of 90 Baltic deputies. Later in the month, the prime ministers of Latvia, Lithuania and Estonia met in Riga and agreed to discuss the formation of a Baltic common market to withstand pressure from the central ministries, as well as to plan a gradual transition towards local currencies. In all three Baltic republics anti-draft movements were growing. The strongest was in Lithuania where, by the beginning of November, more than 1,000 young men were reported to have refused to serve in what they, along with *Sajudis*, considered to be an 'army of occupation'.[101]

New Russian organizations also continued to appear. In the second half of October, Soviet television announced that a new club called *Rossiia* had been founded to bring Russian deputies and voters closer together. It was sponsored by four leading conservative and nationalist Russian newspapers and journals.[102] A new umbrella organization uniting some of the more democratic Russian groups also came into being. On 22 October 150 delegates from more than 40 cities met in Iaroslavl' and formed a new 'United Popular Front'. Among their demands was that the Communist Party renounce its monopoly on power.[103]

In the early part of November it became apparent that the non-Russians were ignoring Gorbachev's warnings that Moscow would not countenance moves towards secession from the Soviet Union. Challenges were delivered in three republics almost simultaneously. First, on 4 November, the Lithuanian Supreme Soviet approved a law paving the way for a referendum on secession and another establishing a separate Lithuanian citizenship. The former stated that referendums could be called at the request of half the members of the republic's legislature, or if a petition were signed by 300,000 Lithuanian residents. The Lithuanian Supreme Soviet also approved a constitutional amendment guaranteeing full religious freedom.[104]

In Georgia, on 5 November, after days of mass demonstrations in Tbilisi, it was announced by the jubilant leaders of a newly formed 'Committee for National Salvation' that the authorities had agreed to a major concession that also opened the door to a possible referendum on the republic's secession from the Soviet Union. The local media then confirmed that the republic's Party and state leadership had given in to demands that a right of referendum be introduced into the Georgian constitution.[105] At the same time in Armenia, a founding congress of the All-Armenian National Movement was held at which Armenian patriots from Soviet Armenia, other republics of the USSR, and from the Armenian diaspora adopted a political programme calling for sweeping changes. Although it stopped short of demanding independence, the programme demanded a new treaty between Armenia and the Soviet Union, free elections and a right of referendum, national military units, the establishment of a market economy and the right to join international organizations. UPI cited one of the participants, the Karabakh Committee activist Ambartsum Galtsian, as saying that Armenia was not yet ready for independence because its economy 'is that of a colonial country . . . We are following the Hungarian example', he added.[106]

Interviewed atop the Lenin mausoleum by Soviet television during the annual official parade on 7 November to mark the anniversary of the Bolshevik Revolution, Gorbachev declared: 'To go back would be a colossal mistake. We have to advance forward faster and faster towards the new way of thinking.'[107] The problem was that official thinking on the nationalities policy had not been changing anywhere near fast enough for the non-Russians.

The events that occurred during the anniversary celebrations showed how little the Party plenum had done to ease national tensions. Apart from a remarkable counter-demonstration in Moscow itself by several thousand 'democrats', the official parades in both the Georgian and Armenian capitals were cancelled. In Kishinev, thousands of protesters blocked the military parade and there were clashes with the police.[108] The following day, two Armenians were killed trying to blow up a monument to the friendship of the peoples on the border between Armenia, Azerbaijan and Georgia.[109]

There was another mass protest in Kishinev on 10 November and it turned violent. Angered by the use of force against peaceful demonstrators, a large crowd attacked the headquarters of the republic's Ministry of Internal Affairs and set it on fire. Official figures, disputed by the Moldavian Popular Front, put the number of injured at 215. A 'state of emergency' was imposed on the

Moldavian capital and several thousand troops dispatched to restore order. The Moldavian Popular Front condemned the violence, but continued to call for the removal of Moldavia's conservative leaders and urged the public not to give in to provocations. Some nationalist elements also threatened to call a general strike.[110] On 16 November, the 'inactive arch-conservative' Moldavian Party leader Grossu, as Moldavian Popular Front activists described him, was replaced by Petru Luchinskii.[111]

Back to basics
The 1980s drew to a close with communist regimes falling like dominoes in Eastern Europe, and the republics of the USSR, themselves infected with the democratic virus, seeking to exercise self-determination. But while Moscow put on a brave face about accepting the revolutionary changes in Eastern Europe, at home it stepped up its efforts to control and limit the process of democratization and to halt the imperial dissolution that accompanied it.

On 10 November the Presidium of the USSR Supreme Soviet ordered Lithuania, Latvia, Estonia and Azerbaijan to amend laws that it said contravened the Soviet Constitution.[112] That same day, however, the Latvian Supreme Soviet voted itself the right to veto laws passed in Moscow. It also stuck to its plan to introduce residence requirements for candidates wishing to stand for election and voted to allow alternative service to conscientious objectors.[113] On 13 November, the Estonian legislature declared that the joining of Estonia to the USSR in 1940 was an act of aggression, military occupation and annexation. The following day, Estonian television announced that the republican government had agreed in principle to introduce a national currency.[114]

There was also strong criticism from the Baltic Council, the umbrella organization of the three Baltic popular fronts, of procedures in the USSR Supreme Soviet. At its meeting in the Latvian city of Cesis on 11 November, it called for a new voting rule under which the delegation from each republic would have an equal vote on essential laws concerning the sovereignty of the national republics. The Baltic Council also urged that each republic form legislative commissions which would decide the judicial status of the Soviet army and would discuss the possibility of recreating national territorial army units.

The Lithuanian Party was due to hold its congress in the second half of December, and the Kremlin's alarm about the possibility of the Lithuanian Party splitting off from the CPSU was all too obvious. On 16 November the leadership of the Lithuanian Communist Party was summoned to meet with the Politburo in Moscow. After the unprecedented meeting, Juras Požela, a member of the Lithuanian Party bureau, told reporters that 'the Lithuanian leadership sticks to its previous position'.[115] The Lithuanian Party leader Brazauskas confirmed this and let it be known that he had told the Gorbachev leadership that 'democratization has gone so deep in Lithuania that not everything depends on the Communist Party'.[116]

The perennial language problem had been exacerbated by the Kremlin's intention to make Russian the official language of the Soviet Union. Many of the non-Russians were already very disappointed by the formula that Moscow had devised to 'regulate the social functions' of the languages of the peoples of the USSR, whereby the native language in the Union republics was recognized as the official language of the given republic but the privileged status of Russian was protected by ascribing to it the role of 'the language of inter-ethnic communication'. At the first reading in the USSR Supreme Soviet on 16 November of the bill of the new language law, the Baltic and Georgian deputies strongly opposed its provisions. 'No state other than a colonial one has the right to regulate language,' Latvia's Janis Peters protested.[117]

As an example of the pace and intensity of developments, it is worth looking at what occurred on just one day, Saturday 18 November. In Latvia, hundreds of thousands of Peters' countrymen rallied in Riga to celebrate the 71st anniversary of Latvia's declaration of independence. It was the first time that the Soviet authorities had permitted this anniversary to be celebrated as a state holiday. The Latvian president Gorbunovs addressed the rally and supported the idea 'that Latvia should become independent once again'.[118] In Tbilisi, the Georgian Supreme Soviet reasserted Georgia's sovereignty, including the republic's right to secede from the Soviet Union and to veto laws passed by Moscow that ran 'contrary to Georgian interests'. Furthermore, it approved a report by a special commission concluding that Georgia's incorporation into the Soviet state had been 'for all intents and purposes, an annexation' carried out by military intervention and occupation.[119] Meanwhile in Baku 300,000 people attended a rally called by the Azerbaijani Popular Front, and in Kiev a large crowd gathered at the airport to greet the plane bringing back for reburial in their native soil the remains of three leading Ukrainian political prisoners – Stus, Lytvyn and Tykhyi – who had died in the Perm camps in 1984–85.

During 1989 five national republics had asserted their sovereignty in ways that openly defied Moscow; four of them had also denounced the 'illegal' way in which they had been forcibly incorporated into the USSR; and three had opened the way for referendums on the question of secession. It was no longer only in the Baltic republics that mass national movements had become so strong that the republican authorities had been obliged to come to terms with them. During the year, such movements had also been able to extract significant concessions in Azerbaijan, Georgia, Armenia and Moldavia, and to a greater or lesser extent a situation of 'dual power' had been created in these, as in the Baltic republics. In the Ukraine, Shcherbitsky had finally been ousted, *Rukh* was making headway and the banned Ukrainian national churches were pressing for legalization; in Central Asia, especially Uzbekistan, national movements were also gathering force and Islam was winning greater toleration; there was no end in sight to the Armenian-Azerbaijani conflict over Nagornyi Karabakh; the Tatars, Bashkirs and other nations without Union republics of their own were campaigning for an end to this anomaly; the Soviet Germans had stepped up their campaign for the restoration of an autonomous German republic; the Russians themselves were mobilizing and creating new organizations and institutions.

The list seemed endless. Small wonder then, that in November KGB chief Vladimir Kriuchkov[120] and Gorbachev both stressed that the preservation of the Party's monopoly on power was essential because the Party was the only political force capable of counteracting 'centrifugal forces'.[121]

In the final weeks of 1989, even this hitherto inviolable Leninist principle was openly challenged. On 13 November, the USSR Supreme Soviet narrowly defeated a motion for the question of the Party's leading role to be discussed at the upcoming new session of the Congress of People's Deputies. In order to maintain the pressure, Sakharov and other leading democratic radicals proceeded to call for a general strike on this issue. In the meantime, on 7 December, the Lithuanians made history when their Supreme Soviet voted overwhelmingly to remove the provision in their republic's constitution guaranteeing the Party's leading role.[122] That same week the Party's political supremacy was also assailed in the Armenian and Estonian Supreme Soviets. When the new session of the Congress of People's Deputies convened on 12 December, a bid by democratic deputies to schedule a debate on the question of removing Article 6 from the Soviet Constitution, which guarantees the Party's monopoly on power, was voted down by 1,139 votes to 839, with 56 abstentions.[123]

Having beaten back for the time being this challenge by democratic forces, the Gorbachev leadership was almost immediately confronted with another situation that it had sought to avoid. On 20 December, the Lithuanian Communist Party went ahead and decided by a vote of 855 to 160 to declare its independence from the CPSU. Gorbachev promptly expressed his 'alarm and concern' and announced that a special plenum of the CPSU Central Committee was being called to discuss the crisis. In a telephone call to the leader of the breakaway Lithuanian party, Brazauskas, he warned that the Lithuanian act of defiance would cause a 'chain reaction'.[124]

Meanwhile, at the Congress of People's Deputies, Gorbachev pressed for the establishment of a constitutional oversight committee to ensure that republican laws and constitutions complied with the USSR Constitution. Baltic deputies and members of the Inter-regional group, who were still shaken by the death earlier that month of Andrei Sakharov, opposed this, for they saw it as a means of preserving Moscow's control over the republics. On 21 December Iurii Afanas'ev read out a statement that had been signed by

140 members of the Inter-regional group opposing the 'decreed leading role of the Party' and attempts to preserve the imperial structures. The signatories stated:

> We are against the submission of the national republics to a strong centre, that is, against the unitary, imperial state created by Stalin and preserved to the present. We consider it necessary to work out as soon as possible a new treaty on the Soviet Union as a free and voluntary union of sovereign republics, according to the formula of strong republics and the centre created by them. At the basis of the Soviet Union there must be the right of any people to self-determination, right up to secession.[125]

On 23 December the Soviet leader's anger at the way things were going exploded. He was provoked by a Ukrainian deputy from the Donbass, Valentin Karas'ov, who attempted to raise again the question of the Party's leading role and who, on being rudely interrupted by Gorbachev, asked: 'Doesn't Romania teach us anything?'[126] Soviet television showed the Soviet leader lashing out at the Inter-regional group, affirming that he remained 'a communist, a convinced communist', and going on to denounce 'the secessionists that exist in all republics'. He told the Congress that

> today, to exercise self-determination through secession is to blow apart the Union, to pit peoples against one another and to sow discord, bloodshed and death.

But there was another side to Gorbachev's diatribe; it revealed a bit more about the Soviet leader's 'Russianness' and how he understood things. In defending the Soviet federation, Gorbachev stressed that the unity of the Soviet peoples should not be viewed as something that had arisen 'only during the last 70 years', and that it reflected a process of unification that had been going on for centuries and in which the Russian people had played 'an outstanding role'. Ignoring what Marx and Lenin had thought about tsarist colonial conquests and practices, the Soviet leader argued that the Russian people had generously taken other peoples 'under their wing'. He then launched into a passionate defence of the Russians and their character, and even cited Dostoevsky to this end. As a nation, Gorbachev maintained, the Russians have manifested 'a huge store of internationalism, benevolence and humanism' and 'they are not to blame for what has happened' to the peoples of the Soviet Union.[127]

For all his bluster, Gorbachev himself was to admit on the final day of the Congress, 24 December, that compromises had had to be worked out.[128] A formula had to be devised before the formation of a constitutional oversight committee was approved. There were other tense moments too. When the findings of the commission dealing with the issue of the Molotov–Ribbentrop Pact were finally made public on 22 December, a number of deputies still insisted that the document was a fabrication. A somewhat watered-down resolution condemning the agreement was, however, passed the following day.[129] On 24 December, the Congress also condemned the violent crack-down on demonstrators in Tbilisi in April 1989, but not before some 200 deputies had walked out in protest against a speech by a deputy procurator general defending what had occurred.[130]

There was no denying how serious the situation had become. In his concluding remarks at the Congress, Gorbachev referred to national relations as 'the most complicated topic' of all, though he maintained that changes to the Soviet Constitution would improve matters.[131] Moreover, the Novosti Press Agency carried out a survey of the deputies at the Congress and revealed that they considered inter-ethnic conflicts to be the most serious danger facing the Soviet Union, with economic problems coming a close second.[132]

In this charged atmosphere, the Central Committee plenum convened on 25 December to discuss the insubordination of the Lithuanian communists. As was expected, Gorbachev delivered a scathing attack on the Lithuanian communists, accusing them of having created a 'schism', of having dealt a blow 'to our hopes and plans for renewing socialist society in the spirit of humanism and democracy' and of having become a 'hostage of the separatists'. He declared their decision, even though it had been carried by a five to one majority, illegal and invalid. 'No part of the Soviet Communist Party,' he insisted in his report, 'has the right to decide the question about its independent existence on the basis of its own programme and rules, without taking into account the position of the Soviet Communist Party as a whole.' He was even more scathing in his denunciation of *Sajudis* and other 'secessionist' and 'anti-socialist' independent groups in Lithuania, including the Lithuanian Catholic Church. Indeed, from his general assessment of the situation, or rather 'political struggle', in the republic, he might just as well have been ruling out the Lithuanian nation's right to national self-determination as he was the Lithuanian Communist Party's right to go its own way.

'The ideas of national separatism were always alien to the spirit of socialist internationalism, which is the core of the foundation of the Soviet multinational state,' Gorbachev stressed. Castigating 'nationalists', 'separatists' and 'national communists', he affirmed that the Soviet Party and state leadership would 'not permit the break-up of the federal state' and warned that there should be no 'illusions' on this score concerning the 'intentions or capabilities of the central government'. It was necessary, he elaborated, 'to define clearly the limits beyond which one cannot go, because going beyond them' meant the destruction of the federation and of *perestroika*.

One such limitation is the impossibility of rejecting the single structure of the Communist Party. Otherwise our Party would turn into an amorphous federalist club consisting of separate independent party groups. Isn't it clear that if we cross this line, we will wittingly be heading toward the disintegration of the USSR. . .?

Even though in one breath Gorbachev denied the non-Russians the right to national self-determination, in the other he again spoke about his commitment to overhauling and strengthening 'our free and voluntary union'. What was noteworthy this time, though, was that the Soviet leader actually acknowledged that what had existed until now had been a 'centralized, unitary' state and went on to make the rather startling claim that 'none of us yet has any experience of living in a federation'. The peoples of the USSR, he explained, would have to be won over anew to the idea of the federation. What was called for was not 'command and force', but the restoration of 'mutual trust' and for the nations of the USSR to be convinced of the 'advantages of integration'. Here the Soviet leader even recalled Lenin's precept, which he paraphrased as: 'it is better for the centre to "overdo" concessions to the non-Russians [*natsionalam*] than to "underdo" them.'

There was one other striking feature about Gorbachev's report. Breaking with previous practice, the Soviet leader made no attempt to justify the continued existence of the Soviet multinational state in terms of the advantages of socialism and of the Soviet Union being a new model society. Instead he came out with a new argument that appeared to be aimed as much at foreign opinion as it was at domestic:

> The existence of a unitary, strong and powerful Soviet Union is the pressing need of the time, and of the whole existing complex system of international security. No one can be interested in this system's disintegration which is fraught with the destabilization of the political situation in Europe and the world. This is also understood in foreign countries by politicians and the public.[133]

The two-day emergency plenum saw heated exchanges between moderates and those advocating a tough line against the Lithuanians, including 'the dissolution of the Lithuanian Party organization and the creation of an organizational committee to run the republic on a temporary basis'.[134] Hardly surprisingly, the plenum failed to resolve the problem and decided instead to postpone its decision on what to do until Gorbachev and other Party leaders visited Lithuania. As for the Lithuanian 'secessionists', with republican elections fast approaching and the Lithuanian public demonstrating their support for the break with the CPSU, Brazauskas and his colleagues stuck to their guns.[135] Meanwhile, on 27 December, the Latvian Supreme Soviet followed the example of Lithuania and voted to abolish the Communist Party's guaranteed right to rule.[136]

While it was nonplussed by the Lithuanian Party's break and the move towards a multi-party system in the Baltic republics generally, the Gorbachev leadership had to face yet more complications in the nationality sphere. In the case of one of them, it was itself responsible for creating further tension. On 1 December, the day on which Gorbachev met with the Pope in the Vatican, the Ukraine's Council for Religious Affairs announced that Ukrainian Catholic communities would be allowed to register with the authorities. But this announcement fell well short of formally recognizing and rehabilitating the Ukrainian Catholic Church; it also left unresolved the issue of the return of Ukrainian Catholic churches and property that had been seized in 1946 and handed over to the Russian Orthodox Church. Confusion spread: 'Russian Orthodox' parishes in Western Ukraine began en masse declaring their allegiance to the Ukrainian Catholic Church and Ukrainian Catholics began demanding the return, and in some cases, peacefully occupying, former Ukrainian Catholic cathedrals and churches; the Moscow Patriarchate and clergy loyal to it responded by protesting about the Ukrainian Catholic actions, depicting them as a wave of 'violence' and 'terror'; the central media by and large took the side of the Moscow Patriarchate; and the local authorities sat it out.[137]

The overthrow of the Ceauşescu regime in Romania in the second half of December took everyone by surprise and raised new questions about Moldavia's future. Until now, Moldavian national rights activists had faced a dilemma: whether to seek independence or reunification with Romania. While Romania had been under the control of a harsh dictatorship, the second option had been less attractive. With the democratic revolution in Romania, however, it seemed only a matter of time before Moldavians would start reviewing their ties with their western neighbour. In fact, as the fighting in Bucharest was coming to an end, the leader of the Moldavian Popular Front, Ion Hardica, told the *Guardian*'s correspondent: 'our relationship with Romania is like that between the two Germanies'.[138] At the end of December the new Moldavian Party leader Luchinskii was calling for the opening of the Romanian–Moldavian border on the West German–East German model.[139]

The border issue also came up elsewhere. In November 1989, the Azerbaijanis began a campaign 'to open the border' with Iranian Azerbaijan. At the end of December it culminated in unrest and clashes along the 790-kilometre-long Soviet–Iranian frontier: Soviet Azerbaijanis destroyed watchtowers, barbed-wire fences and border obstacles, and one person was reported to have been killed.[140] This new wave of unrest took place against the background of another serious incident elsewhere in Azerbaijan: on 29 December, thousands of demonstrators stormed the Party headquarters in Dzhalilabad to protest the 'unlimited power' of local officials. The police opened fire: one person was reported to have been killed and dozens injured.[141] On 30 December, tens of thousands demonstrated in Baku in solidarity with the Dzhalilabad protesters.[142]

Meanwhile, the Russian nationalist backlash also continued to gather force. The growing strength of Russian reaction, chauvinism and anti-Semitism had been manifested at the sixth plenum of the Board of the RSFSR Writers' Union, which was held in mid-November. One of the speakers,

Ivan Shestopal, put the case quite bluntly: the Fatherland was in danger. Not the socialist one, but the 'Russian' one 'in which we have lived together for a thousand years'.[143] The way in which Russian imperial nationalism and opposition to reform were increasingly becoming fused was highlighted at the end of December when a group of ten Russian nationalist organizations issued a joint election platform. They demanded more rights for the Russians, opposed concessions to the 'secessionists', rejected Gorbachev's economic reforms, deplored the impact of Western ideas, and called for a restoration of traditional communist values and 'the rebirth of the real Russia'.[144]

Within the Party itself there were more than enough hardliners and Russian nationalists who were unhappy at the way things were going. Moreover, during the summer and autumn there had been calls for the establishment of new, distinctly Russian institutions, including the creation of a separate Russian Communist Party within the CPSU. The Gorbachev leadership had gone quite a way towards meeting these demands and had agreed to the establishment of a variety of new RSFSR bodies, including a republican Ministry of Internal Affairs, as well as an all-Russian Komsomol and all-Russian Trade Union Council. It rejected, however, the idea of a separate Russian Party organization and instead only settled for the creation of a Russian Bureau in the CPSU Central Committee. As one analyst put it: the creation of this body at a plenum of the Central Committee on 9 December reflected 'an unstable compromise between Russian nationalists, hardline Party apparatchiks, and Mikhail Gorbachev himself'.[145]

Into the nineties

This then was the turbulent state of the national question in the Soviet Union at the beginning of the new decade. It was, of course, only one of the numerous serious problems that had made the domestic and foreign situation so complex and difficult for Moscow to deal with. The economic crisis at home persisted, worker unrest and self-organization was on the rise, and cynicism and apathy, not to mention outright opposition to reform, were widespread. *Glasnost'* had not only loosened tongues, reduced censorship and restored some of the uncomfortable truth about the past, but also contributed to a slow but gradual politicization of Soviet society. Nothing seemed sacred any more, not even Lenin and the leading role of the Party. Meanwhile, in Eastern and Central Europe, a dramatic but mainly peaceful revolution was unfolding. One after another, in Poland, Hungary, East Germany, Bulgaria, Czechoslovakia and Romania, the bankruptcy of the communist parties had been exposed. Nations that for so long had been Soviet satellite states were finally breaking free from Moscow's gravitational pull. In short, in both the Soviet Union and Eastern Europe things were happening that only a few years ago would have seemed impossible.

As far as the short term was concerned, though, much depended on the outcome of the important battles that had to be fought during the forthcoming months. The elections to republican legislatures and local councils, that were due to take place between December and the spring of 1990, presented the forces for change with a major opportunity. The results would also give a clearer picture of how strong the respective Russian democratic and conservative camps were. The republican Supreme Soviets that had defied Moscow had to show that they could stand their ground. The Lithuanian Communist Party still had to see if it could really get away with breaking loose from the CPSU. At the beginning of 1990 the Baltic republics were due to go over to economic self-management despite all the problems that this entailed. And, of course, during 1990 the Soviet Constitution was going to be amended and a Party Congress had been called for later on in the year.

At the beginning of the 1990s the Union was in a state of disunion, though the Kremlin still refused to call it that. As Poland, Hungary, East Germany, Czechoslovakia, Bulgaria and Romania were all in their different ways reasserting their own sovereignty and thereby contributing to the dissolution of the outer Soviet empire, Moscow was endeavouring to hold the inner Soviet empire together. 'The Soviet Union is not disintegrating,' the head of the KGB, Vladimir Kriuchkov, had felt compelled to stress in his major speech in November for the 72nd anniversary of the Bolshevik Revolution. 'It is searching for and finding new ways of renewal.'[146] The question was whether the processes of democratization and decolonization would prevail, or whether the Kremlin would resort to old ways of 'renewing' the empire.

Conclusion

The collapse of the huge Russian Empire in 1917 raised the hopes of its many disparate subject peoples; at last, it seemed, their national rights would be respected. Many non-Russian activists realized that their national movements were weak and unprepared as a result of the repressive policies and enforced Russification that had been pursued by St Petersburg. They limited their aspirations, therefore, to the hope that the destruction of tsarist autocracy would pave the way for some sort of federal arrangement in a democratized multinational state.

The Russian Provisional Government, however, was not keen to further the dissolution of the imperial patrimony, and procrastinated. After the Bolsheviks seized power at the end of 1917 many of the non-Russian nations attempted to set up their own independent states. Some, like the Poles, Finns, Lithuanians, Latvians and Estonians, succeeded. But the others were prevented from severing their bonds with Russia by, ironically, the very party that had championed the right of national self-determination and secession: the predominantly Russian, urban-based Bolsheviks.

Lenin and his colleagues had little sympathy for national movements unless they could be utilized as political weapons in the revolutionary struggle. National loyalties, they believed, were a bourgeois vestige that would be supplanted by a higher form of consciousness: 'proletarian internationalism'. They were convinced that the larger and more centralized the state, the better. Before 1917, Lenin had stressed that his party favoured a 'uniform language' and the 'assimilation of nations', by which he meant 'the shedding of national features, and the absorption by another nation', as long as this social digestion or 'fusion' was not 'founded on force or privilege'.[1]

On obtaining power, Lenin and the Bolsheviks did not hesitate to use force, terror and deception to consolidate and extend their rule over Russians and non-Russians alike. Gradually, most of the non-Russian territories that had been held by the Romanovs were reconquered.

The intention was not to restore the Russian Empire, but to create the world's first workers' state; but right from the outset it was clear that among the Bolsheviks and their supporters there was no shortage of Russian great-power chauvinists. Their attitude alarmed the relatively small band of non-Russian communists. Lenin realized that these new Russifiers masquerading as internationalists would alienate non-Russian sympathizers. Moreover, as the strength of the non-Russian national movements also became apparent, he began to acknowledge that force alone would not suffice to hold the new Soviet polity together, and that the non-Russians would have to be won over with concessions. This imperative was linked with the urgent need to conciliate the peasantry and allow economic recovery to take place. As Stalin, Lenin's pupil as regards the national question, put it in October 1920:

> Central Russia, that hearth of world revolution, cannot hold out long without the assistance of the border regions, which abound in raw materials, fuel and foodstuffs.[2]

Forced by harsh political realities to review his approach to the 'national problem', Lenin opted for federation and toleration of 'national development' as temporary expedients, even though he had rejected both on principle before 1917.

The non-Russians were subsequently offered an implicit national contract. In essence, they were promised 'sovereign' statehood and equality within a federal structure. Specifically, they were guaranteed the right to develop their cultures and make full use of their native languages, as well as to train and rely on native cadres in their republics; in short to complete the process of building their nation-states within the Soviet federal framework. Furthermore, the imperial Russian legacy was to be disowned, Russian chauvinism kept in check and Russification prohibited.

There were those like Stalin who would have preferred not to yield so much to the non-Russians. But Lenin's solution prevailed, at least for a time. Not surprisingly, the non-Russians attached great importance to this implicit arrangement, which they referred to in shorthand as the 'Leninist principles' of nationality policy. Later, when they were deprived of other 'lawful' means of defending their national rights, they were to use Lenin's last instructions as a shield against the assimilationist attitudes derived from Lenin's earlier writings.

So what precisely was the nature of the Soviet multinational state that was forged by Lenin? Clearly, it differed in more than just name from the Russian Empire. The non-Russians secured recognition and significant concessions; formally there was no longer any ruling nation. But the crucial feature about the new federation of supposedly 'free and equal' peoples was that power was concentrated in the unitary ruling Communist Party, which was dominated by Russians. Ukrainian and Georgian *communists*, realizing how much power Moscow and the Russian cadres had retained, vainly pressed for a confederation rather than a federation. Lenin himself grew increasingly alarmed by the strength of Russian chauvinism in the Party; on his deathbed, he lamented that the state which he had built was ending up more 'Russian' than Soviet.

'We must in all conscience admit,' he warned, that

> the apparatus we call ours is, in fact, still quite alien to us; it is a bourgeois and tsarist hotch-potch . . . There is no doubt that the infinitesimal percentage of Soviet and sovietized workers will drown in that tide of chauvinistic Great-Russian riffraff like a fly in milk.[3]

For a time during the 1920s, Moscow more or less observed the national contract and Russian chauvinism was kept under control. After this brief but important period of national revival, consolidation and development for the non-Russians, the national contract was unilaterally abrogated by the Stalin leadership. In 1939 Stalin even went so far as to collude with Hitler for the purposes of territorial aggrandizement.

As Zbigniew Brzezinski put it, if under the tsars Russia had been a prison of nations, under Stalin the Soviet Union came to resemble 'a graveyard of nations'.[4] Of all, that is, except one. Although the Russians were subjected to Stalin's Terror, they were nevertheless elevated to a privileged position as the USSR's leading nation. As Lenin had warned in his Testament (with the example of Stalin in mind), Russified non-Russian *apparatchiks* became more Russian in their zeal than the Russians themselves.[5] The Stalin regime made good use of this servile denationalized element. At the time of Stalin's death, although lip-service still continued to be paid to the national contract, Russian supremacy was scarcely concealed and the Soviet Union was indeed a 'Soviet Russian' empire.

Like Lenin before him, Stalin was quite aware of the nature and potency of the national problem. He relied on a combination of terror and Great-Russian chauvinism to keep the non-Russians subdued. Beria in his abortive quest for power wooed the non-Russians with the prospect of a restoration of the 'national contract'. Then, for a brief period between 1956 and 1958, Khrushchev proclaimed a restoration of 'Leninist principles' in nationalities policy. Before he started backtracking, he decentralized the economy, extended republican powers and permitted a measure of what would now be called *glasnost'* on the national question.

During Khrushchev's last years in power, the Kremlin embarked on a major programme of cultural engineering designed to mould a new 'Soviet' man in the Russian cultural image. The rationale was that modernization and social mobilization, together with camouflaged Russification and the inter-mixing of populations, would eliminate non-Russian nationalisms and break down national identities. Under Brezhnev, the process of de-Stalinization was halted, discussion of nationality problems suppressed and recentralization and Russification were pursued. The Brezhnev-Suslov concept of 'the Soviet people' was in fact a variation on Khrushchev's melting-pot scheme, designed to produce a 'Soviet' amalgam with a distinct Russian flavour and colour.

But, as Andropov and Chernenko indirectly began to acknowledge, the very policies that were supposed to eradicate non-Russian nationalism had the reverse effect. Far from diminishing, national consciousness and assertiveness grew. Indeed, by the mid 1980s, when the USSR found itself in a deep economic and social crisis, the national problem, though still largely concealed from sight, had in fact become more acute and complex.

Inadvertently, by loosening controls in order to facilitate economic modernization, Gorbachev let the genie out of the bottle. Just as on the previous occasion when controls had been relaxed (by Khrushchev in 1956–58), the non-Russians began airing their grievances and calling on the Kremlin to honour the terms of the original national contract, on the basis of which the Soviet Union was supposedly founded. Just as non-Russian dissidents had for years insisted that for them the idea of human rights was inseparable from that of national rights, so the new defenders of national rights stressed that there could be no genuine democratization without substantive changes in nationalities policy or, more precisely, in the nature of the imperial relationship between the Russians and the non-Russians.

As for the level of unity or disunity in the USSR after almost seven decades of Soviet rule, *glasnost'* revealed that the national problem in the USSR exists on two planes: the vertical and the horizontal. The first is the critical one and involves relations between the Russians and the non-Russians. The other, which was highlighted by the Armenian–Azerbaijani flare-up over Nagornyi Karabakh, concerns the friction and tensions between some neighbouring non-Russian peoples.

The Gorbachev leadership was extremely reluctant to review and alter Soviet nationalities policy. In fact, it was pushed along by pent-up forces from below. At first, it restricted itself to making minimal adjustments and talking about the need for more tact. There was no acknowledgement on its part of the need to offer the non-Russians a new deal. Meanwhile the non-Russians became more frustrated and radicalized. At the 19th Party Conference it was back to basics: picking up where the Ukrainians and Georgians had left off in 1923, the Balts headed a new push by the non-Russians to obtain 'in the definition of the character of the [Soviet] Union', as Stalin had put it, 'something midway between a confederation and a federation, with a leaning towards confederation'.[6]

Since then, as *glasnost'* and democratization have continued, so the USSR's imperial crisis has deepened. With the emergence of more and more of the bitter truth about the Stalin era and the Brezhnev years of 'stagnation', Moscow has had to face serious challenges to the legitimacy of Soviet rule in quite a few of the non-Russian republics. Moreover, the bankruptcy and rapid collapse of communist rule in most of Eastern Europe has also further undermined the Soviet Communist Party's claim to a monopoly on power. Not only is there growing pressure in the Soviet Union for the repeal of

Article 6 of the Soviet Constitution, which recognizes the 'leading role' of the Communist Party in Soviet society, but also the Lithuanian Communist Party has openly challenged the unitary nature of the monolithic party established by Lenin – the main element holding the USSR together.

In assessing the successes and failures of the Soviet Union as a multinational state it is important to remember some of the claims made by its creators, and to apply their own standards. The Bolsheviks claimed that they were building a completely new type of society in which equality and fraternity would prevail and there would be no basis for national problems. Lenin proclaimed these very ideals as he sent the Red Army in to destroy the governments set up by the non-Russians and as he shot or imprisoned fighters for the freedom of the non-Russian nations. Stalin, too, at the height of his Terror against the nations, claimed that the Soviet Union was a novel and superior form of multinational state in which the national problem had been solved. His successors perpetuated this myth.

The observation made by Ivan Dziuba in 1965 about the tsarist Russian Empire is, and was probably intended to be, just as applicable to the Soviet experience:

> Marx, Engels and Lenin considered Russian tsarist colonialism and oppression to be the most dreadful in the world, not least because it reached the peaks of hypocrisy and cynicism in using the noblest phraseology for the basest purpose and because it was so efficient at concealing the reality behind the outward appearance of things.[7]

In the early 1920s, both Lenin and Stalin wanted the Soviet multinational state to serve as a model that would attract other nations, especially, as Lenin put it, 'the hundreds of millions of people of Asia'. He warned:

> It would be unpardonable opportunism if, on the eve of the debut of the East, just as it is awakening, we undermined our prestige with its peoples, even if only by the slightest crudity or injustice towards our own non-Russian nationalities. The need to rally against the imperialists of the West, who are defending the capitalist world, is one thing . . . It is another when we ourselves lapse, even if only in trifles, into imperialist attitudes towards oppressed nationalities, thus undermining our principled sincerity. . .[8]

As we have seen, Moscow did lapse into imperialist attitudes towards the non-Russians, and it was not just in 'trifles'. Nevertheless, this did not stop the Soviet Union from posing as the champion of oppressed nations. In the early 1960s, while Ukrainians were being shot for daring to utter the word 'independence', Khrushchev promoted decolonization in Africa. Subsequently, Moscow backed the Palestinian Liberation Organization while denying the USSR's own 'Palestinians' – the Crimean Tatars – their homeland. Likewise with the Germans: abroad, the Kremlin was the patron of the German Democratic Republic; at home, it kept its German population stateless.

For his part, Stalin declared at the 12th Party Congress in 1923 that 'the system of singling out some nationalities and granting them privileges in order to cope with the rest' was perhaps attractive from the 'point of view of bureaucracy', but

> from the political point of view it means certain death to the state, for to violate the principle of equality of nations and to grant privileges to any one nationality means dooming one's national policy to certain failure.[9]

All the same, he and his successors proceeded to do just that: to single out the Russians as the Soviet Union's 'leading' nation and 'consolidating principle'.

The Soviet state did not die, and perhaps the most impressive thing about it has been that the Kremlin has managed to hold its vast heterogeneous domain together for so long. The means have been force and coercion, a sham ideology proclaiming commitment to equality and all-round progress, a unitary ruling party, a dominant majority nation, and a system of buying off and co-opting members of the non-ruling nations. This may have made for an effective nationalities policy, but it was hardly an enlightened way of managing national relations.

It also produced no end of contradictions. The Russians have maintained a political and cultural dominance, but though Moscow has closely controlled the economy, Russia herself has ended up economically worse off than quite a few of the larger non-Russian nations. The non-Russians feel they have been plundered and exploited; the Russians believe that their 'sacrifices' and 'help' have not been properly appreciated.

Or take, for example, the language question. Moscow has frequently boasted that Soviet scholars went out of their way to invent alphabets for some of the small 'backward' peoples. Yet, in the case of the Turkic peoples and the Moldavians, the Cyrillic script was imposed. Moreover, as a result of Soviet policies, many of the larger nations of the USSR ended up fearing for the very survival of their native languages. Another example is that of the attitude towards Soviet Jewry: the Soviet government went to the trouble of setting up a Jewish Autonomous Region in Birobidzhan, on the Chinese border, but, again, because of subsequent Soviet policies, the number of Jews who have left the Soviet Union far exceeds the total that has settled in this specially created Soviet 'Jewish' homeland.

The eruption of the national problem in the last years of the 1980s has exposed quite a few hitherto suppressed truths about the Soviet system, and shattered many illusions. Even the two arguments that were most frequently employed by supporters of the Soviet Union are no longer quite so convincing. It was frequently repeated that the unity of the Soviet peoples was demonstrated in the war against Fascism. But as is becoming clearer, what occurred in the war was a testimony not so much to the strength of Soviet unity as to the reaction against the brutality, racism and exploitation of the German invaders. Their ruthlessness and blind dogmatism alienated potential allies among the non-Russians and Russian anti-Stalinists.

An achievement that has also regularly been cited is the economic and social progress made under Soviet rule by 'formerly backward peoples'. But the problems and grievances now being aired by Central Asians or the native peoples of Siberia tell a different story: one of colonial exploitation through the cotton monoculture, ecological disaster, damage to spiritual life and the imposition of alien values.

What is happening in the Soviet Union, then, is not simply a case of 'nationalism' run wild, as some Soviet commentators still maintain. While ugly violent clashes have broken out between a number of non-Russian peoples, these dramatic, and in some cases historic, conflicts, however important to those affected, are ultimately side-shows. The main issue is the future of the Soviet empire and of the relationship between the Russians and the non-Russians. In the case of the Armenians and Azerbaijanis, for instance, the conflict over Nagornyi Karabakh has led both nations to review their attitude towards Moscow and their place in the USSR.

Because nationalism has become something of a dirty word in the West, it is important to recall that Lenin himself drew an important and valuable distinction between 'the nationalism of an oppressor nation' – he had in mind the Russians – 'and that of an oppressed nation; the nationalism of a big nation, and that of a small nation'.[10] From the point of view of the non-Russians, not only was the national contract violated and their national development trammelled, but also their territories were thoroughly exploited. They came to be used by the Russians as *lebensraum*, as a source of raw materials, and as a buffer zone against hostile powers. Deprived of the opportunity to have independent links with the outside world, their culture, history and achievements have been submerged in the Soviet Russian sea. Today, at a time when the USSR is in imperial decline, many of the non-Russian nations naturally look at the numerous former colonies that have gained their independence, at the peaceful de-Sovietization of Eastern and Central Europe, and await the day when they too can join the family of free nations.

This is how the eminent Ukrainian historian Mykhailo Braichevs'kyi put it at the inaugural congress of the Ukrainian restructuring movement *Rukh* in September 1989:

> Today, it is probably clear to everyone that the union of republics, in the form it has assumed during the final quarter of this century, is very far from the ideal and requires a fundamental restructuring . . . We are faced with the question of the viability, expediency and necessity of such a colossal federation comprising one sixth of the earth's surface. Once, great pride was taken in this colossus and it was regarded as an enormous achievement of mankind. Now quite a different tonality

rules. Historical experience shows that it is the small nations which demonstrate the best standards of living: Belgium, the Netherlands, Sweden, Norway, Denmark, Iceland, Greece, etc. And the experience of our Baltic republics during their period of independent statehood also looks very instructive.

The colonial system has collapsed; once subjugated people – large and small – have achieved independence . . . If nowadays not only traditional teenies like Luxembourg, Andorra or San Marino, but also such tots as Mauritius or Barbados exist safely, and no one threatens them or intends to conquer them – then why cannot the 50-million-strong Ukraine, or small Estonia, exist as fully independent states? In what way is the Ukraine with her inexhaustible resources worse than 50-million-strong Britain, and 4-million-strong Azerbaijan worse than 4-million-strong Norway?. . .

Today it is no secret to anyone that it is essential to dissolve the Stalinist-Brezhnevist Union and to replace it (were this deemed expedient) by an association of independent states . . . on the basis of full voluntariness and sovereignty not limited by anything . . . we will have to recognize as a condition *sine qua non* the total inadmissibility in principle of the existence not only of a 'strong' centre but altogether of any centre whatsoever. There must be no Constitution of the USSR. There must be no all-Union government . . . Instead of all that only one co-ordinating agency is needed, created on the basis of strict parity.[11]

Braichevs'kyi's views resembled Sakharov's position just before his death as regards the need to transform the USSR into a loose democratic confederation; but he went a step further than Sakharov in his rejection of the very idea of a 'Soviet Constitution' or new national contract.

The crucial question is how the majority of Russians will react to all this, and how the 'Russian problem' will develop. One of the things that the non-Russians had going for them at the end of the 1980s was that the 'centre' was itself divided, and that the Russians seemed confused about their own role, image and future. Democratic and pro-Western forces had emerged, but powerful reactionary forces were also crystallizing. With the gradual decline of the ruling ideology, Russian nationalism loomed as the only power capable of preventing the dissolution of the empire. What is at stake for Russian nationalists is not only the loss of territory and the trappings of imperial power, but also the possible loss of superpower status. After all, they could probably learn to live without the Baltic republics, but where would 'Russia' be without, say, the Ukraine? On the other hand, as many non-Russians and some Russians argue, a democratic Russia free from the burden of empire surely could better apply itself to the pressing problems and needs of the Russian people.

With the imperial and ideological decay of the Soviet Union advancing, there are at least four possible scenarios for the 1990s. First, the gradual break-up of the empire. Second, the creation of some sort of Soviet Commonwealth that would resemble a loose confederation. Third, a genuine federalization or 'Yugoslavization' of the USSR. And fourth, the restoration of an authoritarian Russian empire as a result of a takeover by Russian chauvinists and reactionaries. Whatever the case, after the momentous changes in Eastern Europe, the Soviet empire looks even more latently unstable and even more of an anachronism. One thing is clear: genuine democratization and the preservation of empire, however disguised, are incompatible.

Appendix

National structure of the USSR in early 1990

In the 1989 census, 102 nations and ethnic groups were identified in the Soviet Union; 16 of these had populations of less than 5,000. The principle of 'the equality and sovereignty of the peoples of Russia' proclaimed immediately after the October 1917 Bolshevik Revolution (pp. 18–19 above) was soon discarded when it came to creating the national territorial units which were largely finalized by 1936. Instead of equality, a hierarchical structure came about, consisting of several tiers.

The top tier was occupied by the 15 Union Republics: namely the Russian Soviet Federative Socialist Republic (RSFSR) and 14 other Soviet Socialist Republics (SSRs). Their privileges, not shared by the lower tiers, included, according to the 1977 Constitution, the right to free secession from the USSR and to enter into relations with foreign states. The arbitrary membership rules of this exclusive club were devised by Stalin, though apparently not codified officially. In order to qualify, the national unit had to have a common boundary with a foreign state (this was meant to lend credibility to the right to secession), and to have a minimum population of one million. Sometimes a third rule is mentioned: that more than half of its population had to belong to the 'titular' nationality. However, the numbers of the Kazakhs (since the collectivization holocaust), Kirghiz and Karelians were below half of the total populations of their respective SSRs. In the case of the short-lived (March 1940–July 1956) Karelo-Finnish SSR, however, the republic's population was only around half a million; this breach of the second rule illustrates the arbitrariness of their application.

The second tier consisted of 20 Autonomous Soviet Socialist Republics (ASSRs) which were subordinate to, and included in the territory of, some of the Union Republics. The RSFSR possessed 16 ASSRs, for which reason it was termed 'federative'; this rank was denied, though, to the three SSRs which had one or two ASSRs each. Like the SSRs, the ASSRs had their own constitutions.

Next were the Autonomous Regions (*oblast'*), also translated into English as Provinces (see the map on pp. xii–xiii); like the ASSRs, they were contained within some of the SSRs, but did not have their own constitutions. There were five such regions within the RSFSR, and one each in three other SSRs.

The lowest administrative form of national life was embodied by 10 National Districts (*okrug*), also translated as National Regions or Areas; since 1977, the term 'National' had been replaced by 'Autonomous'. They were all in the

RSFSR; unlike the units in the two preceding tiers, they were subordinate to certain Russian administrative subdivisions (either regions or 'areas') of the RSFSR rather than directly to the RSFSR central administration. Most of them were in the north, bordering on the Arctic Ocean.

These territorial units cater for some 60 nations and ethnic groups; some units contain more than one 'titular' nationality, while a couple of nationalities occupy more than one unit. Their territories can be seen on the maps on pp. xii–xiii, 365–7. A number of small ethnic groups, like the Shor, Evens or Veps, who number 16, 12 (in 1979), and 13,000 respectively, are more or less dispersed among other peoples, and have no national territorial units of their own; as such, they are even 'less equal than others'. The Crimean Tatars, whose Crimean ASSR was abolished by the end of World War II, had for decades been an 'un-nation'; in the 1989 census results, though, they were at last listed separately, numbering 265,739. In the 1979 census, only 132,272 Crimean Tatars were enumerated, although there must obviously have been about 200,000; the missing 60,000 were no doubt registered as 'plain' (i.e. Volga) Tatars. In the event, however, in the published 1979 results all these figures were lumped together as 'Tatars', the Crimean Tatars remaining unmentionable. The largest national group without its own territory, though, were the Soviet Germans, numbering over two million. Their Volga-German ASSR was, ironically, the first non-Russian autonomous republic to be created in the RSFSR shortly after the Revolution.

Other Soviet citizens without territorial units who were treated almost like 'foreigners' were those whose co-nationals 'live primarily outside the USSR'; some of the larger groups among them were Poles (1,126,137), Koreans (437,335) Bulgarians (378,790), Greeks (357,975), Kurds (152,952),[1] and Turks (207,369).[2] This latter figure includes hardly any natives of Turkey (Ottomans), the bulk of it representing Meskhetians (sometimes also called 'Meskhetian Turks') who are still denied their own distinct identity in the list of nationalities recognized for census purposes.

The Union Republics

As has been seen, the Soviet Union originally comprised the RSFSR, the Transcausasian SFSR, and the Ukrainian and Byelorussian SSRs. More SSRs were soon added in Central Asia: the Turkestan ASSR (then within the RSFSR), the Khorezm Soviet People's Republic (until 1920 the independent Khivan Khanate) and the Bukhara People's Soviet Republic (until 1920 the Bukharan Emirate) were repartitioned on ethnic principles, creating the Turkmen SSR and the Uzbek SSR in 1925. The latter contained the Tadzhik Autonomous SSR, which was separated from the Uzbek SSR and elevated to the rank of a full SSR in 1929. The Kirghiz ASSR was renamed the Kazak (*sic*) ASSR later in 1925, and in 1936 it became the Kazakh SSR, while the Kara-Kirghiz Autonomous Region, which had been incorporated into it during repartitioning, separated from the Kazakh SSR to become the Kirghiz SSR. Also in 1936, the Transcausasian Federation was disbanded, and its constituent republics, the Georgian, Armenian and Azerbaijani SSRs, became members of the USSR in their own right.

As a consequence of the Molotov–Ribbentrop Pact, Estonian, Latvian, Lithuanian and Moldavian SSRs were added to the Soviet Union, and in March 1940, after Finland's defeat in the Winter War, the Karelian ASSR (which had been an autonomous region in 1920–3) was upgraded into the Karelo-Finnish SSR. The new SSR was expected to incorporate Finland, which the Soviet government hoped to annex; but because Finland retained its independence, the Karelo-Finnish SSR was stripped of its rank and name in 1956, and reverted to its original status.

Table 1 below lists the Union Republics existing at the beginning of 1990, together with their total population figures from the 1979 and 1989 censuses; the latter figures come from the preliminary results published in *Pravda* on 29 April 1989.[3] Table 2 gives the figures for the titular nations of the SSRs, including those living outside their republics, from the same censuses[4]. The smaller 'Total [USSR] population' figures in Table 2 represent 'permanent' population only.

TABLE 1

Population of USSR and of Union Republics,
1979 and 1989

	1979	1989	Percentage Increase
USSR	262,436,000	286,717,000	9.3
RSFSR	137,551,000	147,386,000	7.2
Ukrainian SSR	49,755,000	51,704,000	3.9
Byelorussian SSR	9,560,000	10,200,000	6.7
Moldavian SSR	3,947,000	4,341,000	10.0
Lithuanian SSR	3,398,000	3,690,000	8.6
Latvian SSR	2,521,000	2,681,000	6.3
Estonian SSR	1,466,000	1,573,000	7.3
Georgian SSR	5,015,000	5,449,000	8.7
Azerbaijani SSR	6,028,000	7,029,000	16.6
Armenian SSR	3,031,000	3,283,000	8.3
Uzbek SSR	15,391,000	19,906,000	29.3
Kirghiz SSR	3,529,000	4,291,000	21.6
Tadzhik SSR	3,801,000	5,112,000	34.5
Turkmen SSR	2,759,000	3,534,000	28.1
Kazakh SSR	14,684,000	16,538,000	12.6

TABLE 2
National Composition of Population of Soviet Union,
1979 and 1989
(Union-Republic Nationalities only)

	1979	1989	Percentage Increase
Total population of whom	262,084,654	285,688,965	9.0
Russians	137,397,089	145,071,550	5.6
Ukrainians	42,347,387	44,135,989	4.2
Uzbeks	12,455,978	16,686,240	34.0
Byelorussians	9,462,715	10,030,441	6.0
Kazakhs	6,556,442	8,137,878	24.1
Azerbaijanis	5,477,330	6,791,106	24.0
Armenians	4,151,241	4,627,227	11.5
Tadzhiks	2,897,697	4,216,693	45.5
Georgians	3,570,504	3,983,115	11.6
Moldavians	2,968,224	3,355,240	13.0
Lithuanians	2,850,905	3,068,296	7.6
Turkmen	2,027,913	2,718,297	34.0
Kirghiz	1,906,271	2,530,998	32.8
Latvians	1,439,037	1,459,156	1.4
Estonians	1,019,851	1,027,255	0.7

'The lesser breeds'
During the repartition of Central Asia, some nations were 'promoted' all the way from a lowly autonomous region to the heights of a union republic. A similar process can be found among the lesser formations. The fate of the Chechens and Ingush is typical of deported nations: their autonomous regions were created in 1922 and 1924 respectively, and amalgamated into one Chechen-Ingush ASSR in 1936; its subsequent destruction and restoration have been chronicled in this book. Some ASSRs were created early and survived as such for decades, such as the Bashkir (1919), Tatar (1920) and Abkhaz (1921) ASSRs. Others were first created as autonomous regions and promoted to an ASSR only later: the Udmurt, Mari and Iakut autonomous regions, all created in 1920, were 'promoted' to ASSRs in 1934, 1936 and 1922 respectively.

These promotions virtually stopped after 1936 and the eight remaining autonomous regions still had no promotion by early 1990.

It is noteworthy that the titular nations of ASSRs and autonomous regions were not identical with any titular nation of a union republic, apart from two exceptions: the Nagornyi Karabakh and Nakhichevan Autonomous Regions. Both were created in 1923; Nakhichevan was turned into an ASSR in 1924. An ancient

Armenian territory, it had been colonized relatively recently by the Azeri Turks (Azerbaijanis) who by 1926 comprised 84 per cent of its population, rising to 96 per cent by 1979. Nagornyi Karabakh, which has remained an autonomous region, was 89 per cent Armenian before the war, dropping to 80 per cent in 1970 and about 75 per cent in the late 1980s. Both units were attached to Azerbaijan when they were created; the Azerbaijani possession of Nagornyi Karabakh, however, ill accords with the principle of self-determination.

Apart from Karelia, there was just one other promotion after 1936: that of Tuva. Situated between Mongolia and Russia, Tannu-Tuva, as it was then known, had been a tsarist Russian protectorate since 1914. It proclaimed its independence in 1921 as a 'people's state', and in 1926 became the Tuva People's Republic. On 17 August 1944, Tuva petitioned to be admitted to the USSR (four years earlier, the three Baltic states had been made to do the same). A few weeks later, Tuva was quietly annexed and made an autonomous region, rather than a union republic, as would have befitted a recently independent state. In 1962 it became an ASSR.

Government system

Union republics and ASSRs had a system of ministries common with the central Union government, and some ministries independent from the Moscow centre. Many central ministries, however, had no restraining counterparts in the republics, and exercised unlimited control there. Over years and decades, their ministries changed; but the overall tendency was practically always towards greater centralization. In this way, the republics' prerogatives were whittled away, until in the late 1980s some 95 per cent of a typical republic's economy was controlled from Moscow. The arrival of *perestroika* then brought the prospect of far-reaching decentralization.

The 'parliament' of the Soviet Union, intended to be the highest agency of state power, was originally called the Central Executive Committee (CEC); in 1936 its name was changed to the Supreme Soviet. Since the final adoption of the first USSR Constitution in 1923, it has had a bicameral structure. In the first chamber, the Council of the Union, representation of the national units was proportionate to the size of their population. In the second chamber, the Council of Nationalities, the number of deputies was independent of the size of a unit, though dependent on its rank; thus, in accordance with the 1977 Constitution, the numbers of deputies to be elected were: 32 from each Union republic, 11 from each ASSR, 5 from each autonomous region, and one from each national (autonomous) district. The purview of this second chamber was supposed to include nationality affairs.

Significant changes in these structures are expected to occur in the 1990s.

THE WESTERN REPUBLICS

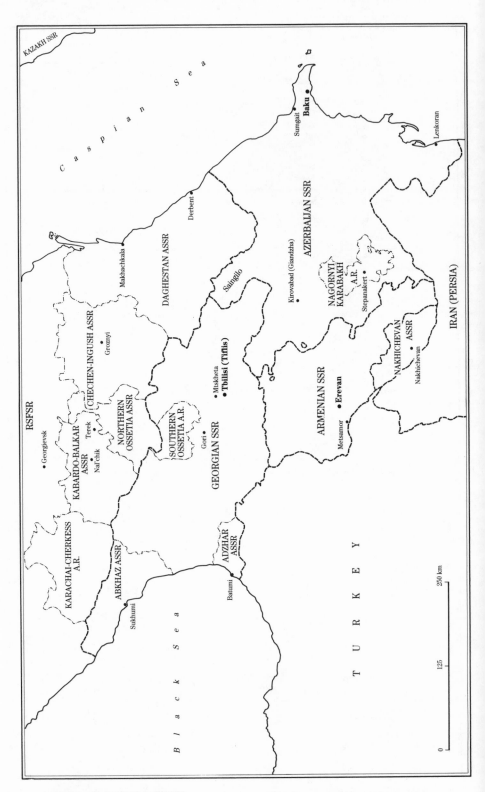

THE CAUCASUS

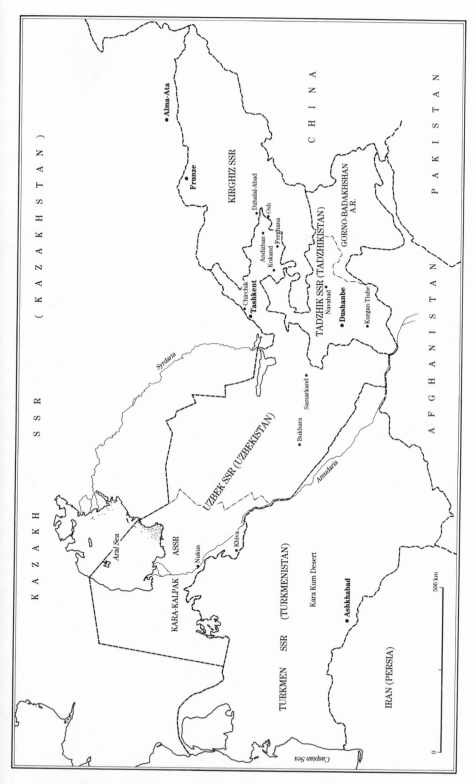

CENTRAL ASIA

Notes

1. Nations of the Russian Empire

1. V. Ianin, 'Zerkalo proshedshikh stoletii', *Nedelia* (Moscow), no. 43, 20–6 October 1986, p. 10.

2. M. N. Pokrovskii, 'Vozniknovenie Moskovskogo gosudarstva i "velikorusskaia narodnost' " ', *Istorik-marksist* (Moscow), no. 18–19, 1930, reprinted in Pokrovskii, *Russkaia istoriia s drevneishikh vremen*, vol. 1, Moscow, 1933, pp. 240–1.

3. Ibid., pp. 241–5.

4. M. N. Pokrovskii, *Izbrannye proizvedeniia: Kniga 1: Russkaia istoriia s drevneishikh vremen*, Moscow, 1966, p. 227.

5. Pokrovskii, 'Vozniknovenie . . .', pp. 236–7, 242, unambiguously identified Kievan Rus' with the Ukraine.

6. See, for instance, two articles by George Y. Shevelov, 'On Teofan Prokopovich as Writer and Preacher in His Kiev Period', *Harvard Slavic Studies*, vol. II, Cambridge, Mass., 1954, pp. 211–23, and 'Stefan Yavorsky and the Conflict of Ideologies in the Age of Peter I', *Slavonic and East European Review*, vol. 30, no. 74, 1951, pp. 40–62, and reprint, George Y. Shevelov, *Two Orthodox Ukrainian Churchmen of the Early Eighteenth Century: Teofan Prokopovych and Stefan Iavors'kyi*, Cambridge, Mass., 1985.

7. Marx's manuscript from the Institute of Social History in Amsterdam, published as Karl Marx, *Insemnări despre Români*, Bucharest, 1964, p. 30.

8. Julian Hale, *Ceauşescu's Rumania*, London, 1971, p. 183.

9. See Hugh Seton-Watson, *Decline of Imperial Russia, 1855–1914*, London, 1952.

10. F. Engels, 'What have the working classes to do with Poland? – II', *The Commonwealth*, no. 160, 31 March 1866, p. 5.

11. V. I. Lenin, *Collected Works*, Moscow and London, 1960–70, vol. 22, p. 342.

12. Karl Marx, *Die Inauguraladresse der internationalen Arbeiter-Association*, Stuttgart-Berlin, 1922, p. 29.

13. The London 1896 International Congress resolution is quoted in Lenin, *Collected Works*, vol. 20, pp. 430–1, and it stresses that 'This Congress declares that it stands for the full right of all nations to self-determination.'

14. Ibid., vol. 6, pp. 454–63.

15. Ibid., p. 454.

16. Ibid., vol. 19, p. 244.

17. Ibid., vol. 23, p. 52.

18. Ibid., vols 19, pp. 91, 542–3; 20, pp. 222, 425–9; 22, pp. 144–5, 333, 348; 23, pp. 48–57; 24, pp. 300, 338.

19. Ibid., vol. 24, p. 338.

20. Ibid., vol. 22, p. 146 (written January–February 1916, published in *Vorbote*, no. 2, April 1916).

21. Ibid., vol. 20, pp. 20–1, 40–2.

22. Ibid., vol. 26, pp. 175–6.

23. Ibid., vol. 22, p. 353. Lenin's policy in the nationalities question is discussed in detail by S. W. Page, 'Lenin and Self-determination', *Slavonic and East European Review*, vol. 28, no. 71, April 1950, pp. 342–58.

2. 1917 Revolutions: The Empire Breaks Up

1. *Istoriia Sovetskoi Konstitutsii (v dokumentakh): 1917–1956*, Moscow, 1957, pp. 57–8.

2. Lenin, *Collected Works*, vol. 26, p. 344.
3. *Lietuviu Balsas* (Voronezh), no. 86, 1917, quoted in V. Stanley Vardys (ed.), *Lithuania under the Soviets: Portrait of a Nation, 1940–65*, New York, 1965, p. 9.
4. 'Universal Ukrains'koi Tsentral'noi Rady', in *Ukrains'ka suspil'no-pol? tychna dumka v 20 stolitti: Dokumenty i materiialy*, vol. 1, ed. T. Hunchak and R. Sol'chanyk, (New York), 'Suchasnist', 1983, pp. 340–3.
5. I. I. Ul'ianov, *Kazaki i Sovetskaia respublika*, Moscow, 1929, p. 43.
6. Lenin, *Collected Works*, vol. 26, pp. 361–3.
7. Ibid., vol. 30, p. 270.
8. V. A. Antonov-Ovseenko, *Zapiski o grazhdanskoi voine*, vol. I, Moscow, 1924, p. 157.
9. I. S. Lubachko, *Belorussia under Soviet Rule: 1917–1957*, Lexington, Kentucky, 1972, pp. 18–23.
10. Lenin, *Collected Works*, vol. 26, pp. 423, 425.
11. *Istoriia Sovetskoi Konstitutsii*, pp. 142–58.
12. *Kommunisticheskaia partiia Ukrainy v rezoliutsiiakh . . . 1918–1956*, Kiev, 1958, p. 17.
13. Documents from the Archive of the CP of Lithuania, as quoted by M. I. Kulichenko, *Bor'ba Kommunisticheskoi partii za reshenie natsional'nogo voprosa v 1918–1920 godakh*, Kharkov, 1963, p. 40.
14. *Sotsialisticheskaia Sovetskaia Respublika Latvii v 1919 g. i inostrannaia interventsiia: Dokumenty i materialy*, vol. 1, Riga, 1959.
15. V. Knorin writing in *Zvezda*, 6 October 1918, as quoted in V. A. Krutalevich, *Rozhdenie Belorusskoi Sovetskoi Respubliki: . . . oktiabr' 1917– dekabr' 1918*, Minsk, 1975, p. 320.
16. A document from the Archive of the Central Committee of the CP of Byelorussia, as quoted by Kulichenko, *Bor'ba Kommunisticheskoi partii*, p. 54.
17. Lenin, *Collected Works*, vol. 28, p. 225. The text of the telegram was written by Stalin with additions by Lenin. Vacetis's name is given in the 5th Russian

edition, but not in the 4th (Russian or English), in which it is replaced by the name of the town, Serpukhov, where the HQ was situated (100 km south of Moscow).
18. V. Mickevičus-Kapsukas, 'Revoliutsiia v Litve (1918) i sozdanie Vremennogo revoliutsionnogo raboche-krest'ianskogo pravitel'stva', *Istorik-marksist*, no. 2–3, 1935, pp. 46–7.
19. A document from the Archive of the Central Committee of the CP of Lithuania, as quoted by Kulichenko, *Bor'ba Kommunisticheskoi partii*, p. 53.

3. 1919: Sovereign Soviet Republics

1. Kulichenko, *Bor'ba Kommunisticheskoi partii*, p. 249, quoting from the Central Party Archive of the Institute of Marxism-Leninism attached to the Central Committee of the CPSU (abbreviated as CPA IML), f. 17, op. 2, doc. 3, l. 1 (f. = fund, op. = file, doc. = document, l. = folio).
2. Kulichenko, *Bor'ba Kommunisticheskoi partii*, p. 250, quoting from the Party Archive of the Institute of Party History of the Central Committee of the Communist Party of Byelorussia (abbreviated as PA IIP Byel.), f. 4, op. 1, doc. 1, l. 20.
3. Kulichenko, *Bor'ba Kommunisticheskoi partii*, pp. 76–7, quoting from CPA IML, f. 3, op. 1, doc. 3589, l. 1; doc. 4671, l. 1; PA IIP Byel., f. 4, op. 1, doc. 1, l. 3.
4. *Leninskii sbornik*, vol. 34, Moscow, 1942, pp. 118–19.
5. Lenin, *Collected Works*, vol. 29, pp. 404–5.
6. *VIII s"ezd RKP(b), mart 1919 goda: Protokoly*, Moscow, 1959, p. 425.
7. Ibid., p. 286.
8. Ibid., pp. 52–6; Lenin, *Collected Works*, vol. 29, pp. 170–5.
9. *VIII s"ezd*, pp. 46–7.
10. Ibid., pp. 52–3; Lenin, *Collected Works*, vol. 29, pp. 171–4.
11. *VIII s"ezd*, pp. 80–1.
12. Ibid., p. 398.
13. *Obrazovanie Soiuza Sovetskikh Sotsialisticheskikh Respublik: Sbornik dokumentov*, Moscow, 1972, pp. 102–3, 483.

14. The texts of their letter and a lengthy memorandum are in I. Majstrenko, *Borot'bism: A Chapter in the History of Ukrainian Communism*, New York, 1954, pp. 136–8, 277–86.

15. Frantishek Silnitskii, *Natsional'naia politika KPSS v period s 1917 po 1922 god*, quoting from CPA IML, f. 17, op. 65, doc. 110, l. 63–4.

16. Silnitskii, *Natsional'naia politika*, quoting from CPA IML, f. 17, op. 65, doc. 110, l. 1, 12–13.

17. Lenin, *Collected Works*, vol. 42, p. 180.

18. Ibid., vol. 30, p. 471.

19. Ibid., vol. 30, pp. 163–4.

20. *KPSS v rezoliutsiiakh . . .*, 7th ed., vol. 1, Moscow, 1953, pp. 459–61.

21. R. P. Browder and Alexander F. Kerensky, *The Russian Provisional Government 1917: Documents*, vol. 1, Stanford, Ca, 1961, p. 370, doc. 332.

22. Kulichenko, *Bor'ba Kommunisticheskoi partii*, p. 406.

4. The Moslem Nations

1. *Dekrety Sovetskoi vlasti*, vol. 1, Moscow, 1957, pp. 113–14.

2. *Politika Sovetskoi vlasti po natsional'nym delam za tri goda: 1917–XI–1920*, Moscow, 1920, pp. 8–9.

3. Ibid., p. 9.

4. 'Soveshchanie po sozyvu Uchreditel'nogo S"ezda Tataro-Bashkirskoi Sovetskoi Respubliki', *Pravda*, 22 (9) May 1918; other articles on this subject, ibid., 18 (5)–21 (8) May, 23 (10) and 24 (11) May 1918.

5. A. Zevelev, *Iz istorii grazhdanskoi voiny v Uzbbekistane*, Tashkent, 1959, p. 441.

6. 'S"ezd musul'man-kommunistov v Moskve: Rech' t. Stalina', *Zhizn' natsional'nostei*, no. 3, 24 November 1918, p. 2. This speech of Stalin's is not in his *Works*, though his editorial 'Don't Forget the East', from the same issue, is in J. V. Stalin, *Works*, Moscow, 1952–5, vol. 4, pp. 174–6.

7. 'Rezoliutsiia po organizatsionnomu voprosu', *Zhizn' natsional'nostei*, 24 November 1918, p. 2; 'Otchet o mesiachnoi deiatel'nosti Tsentral'nogo Biuro musul'manskikh organizatsii RKP(b)', ibid., no. 7, 22 December 1918, p. 7.

8. *Dekrety Sovetskoi vlasti*, vol. 8, Moscow, 1976, pp. 220–1.

9. M. L. Murtazin, *Bashkiriia i bashkirskie voiska v grazhdanskuiu voinu*, Leningrad, 1927, p. 187.

10. P. Mostovenko, 'O bol'shikh oshibkakh v "Maloi" Bashkirii', *Proletarskaia revoliutsiia*, May 1928, no. 5 (76), p. 117; Murtazin, *Bashkiriia*, pp. 188ff.

11. F. Samoilov, 'Malaia Bashkiriia v 1918–1920 gg.', *Proletarskaia revoliutsiia*, December 1926, no. 12 (59), pp. 202–7; Mostovenko, 'O bol'shikh oshibkakh', pp. 109, 117.

12. Alexandre A. Bennigsen and S. Enders Wimbush, *Muslim National Communism in the Soviet Union: A Revolutionary Strategy for the Colonial World*, Chicago, 1979, pp. 66–7.

13. M. P—ch, 'V Krymu', *Zhizn' natsional'nostei*, no. 11, 28 May 1921, p. 4.

14. Mustafa Chokayev, 'Turkestan and the Soviet Regime', *Journal of the Royal Central Asian Society*, vol. 18 (1931), p. 406.

15. K. Zhitov and V. Krylova, *Pobeda Velikoi Oktiabr'skoi sotsialisticheskoi revoliutsii v Turkestane: Sbornik dokumentov*, Tashkent, 1947, p. 93, and G. Safarov, *Kolonial'naia revoliutsiia (Opyt Turkestana)*, Moscow, 1921, reprinted by the Society for Central Asian Studies, Reprint Series No. 4, with a second title-page, *The Colonial Revolution (The Case of Turkestan)*, Oxford, 1985, p. 109 (references are to the pages of the reprint whose pagination differs from that of the first edition); Safarov discusses the episode on pp. 106–10. In more recent publications, this excessively candid document is usually avoided.

16. Chokayev, 'Turkestan', p. 407. A French version, in Joseph Castagné, 'Le Turkestan depuis la Révolution russe

(1917–1921)', *Revue du monde musulman*, vol. 50, June 1922, p. 48 (also an offprint, Paris, 1922, p. 23), has 'au sujet de l'autonomie' instead of 'to self-determination'.

17. Chokayev, 'Turkestan', p. 408.
18. Vadim Chaikin, *K istorii rossiiskoi revoliutsii, vyp. 1: Kazn' 26 bakinskikh komissarov*, Moscow, 1922, p. 133.
19. *Ocherki istorii Kommunisticheskoi partii Turkestana*, vol. 2, Tashkent, 1959, p. 147.
20. *Istoriia Uzbekskoi SSR*, vol. 2, Tashkent, 1958, p. 58.
21. Cf. Safarov, *Kolonial'naia revoliutsiia*, pp. 121–2.
22. Ibid., pp. 124–5; G. Skalov, 'Sotsial'naia priroda basmachestva v Turkestane', *Zhizn' natsional'nostei*, no. 3–4 (Moscow, 1923), pp. 56–7.
23. Martha Brill Olcott, 'The Basmachi or Freemen's Revolt in Turkestan: 1918–24', *Soviet Studies*, vol. 33, July 1981, pp. 352–69; Safarov, *Kolonial'naia revoliutsiia*, pp. 133–4.
24. Zevelev, *Iz istorii grazhdanskoi voiny*, pp. 405, 407–9.
25. P. T. Alekseenkov, *Krest'ianskoe vosstanie v Fergane*, Tashkent, 1927, pp. 52–3.
26. Lenin, *Collected Works*, vol. 30, p. 138.
27. Zevelev, *Iz istorii grazhdanskoi voiny*, pp. 432–3, 436.
28. Ibid., pp. 440, 445–6.
29. Safarov, *Kolonial'naia revoliutsiia*, p. 177. Emphasis in his work.
30. Zevelev, *Iz istorii grazhdanskoi voiny*, pp. 448–50; Safarov, *Kolonial'naia revoliutsiia*, pp. 186–8.
31. There are discrepancies in the members' list between the two sources, Zevelev and Safarov.
32. Safarov, *Kolonial'naia revoliutsiia*, p. 188; Zevelev, *Iz istorii grazhdanskoi voiny*, p. 456.

5. National Contracts with the Non-Russians
1. *League of Nations Treaty Series*, vol. 11, nos 1–3, pp. 29–71.
2. Ibid., vol. 3, no. 2, pp. 105–37.

3. Ibid., vol. 2, no. 3, pp. 195–229.
4. S. E. Sef, *Bor'ba za Oktiabr' v Zakavkaz'i*, 'Zakkniga' (Tbilisi), 1932, p. 129.
5. Lenin, *Collected Works*, vol. 35, p. 443.
6. *Bor'ba za pobedu Sovetskoi vlasti v Azerbaidzhane, 1918–1920: Dokumenty i materialy*, Baku, 1967, p. 471; *Istoriia Sovetskoi Konstitutsii*, pp. 231–2.
7. Constantin Kandelaki, *The Georgian Question Before the Free World: Acts – Documents – Evidence*, Paris, 1953, pp. 12–13; Zourab Avalishvili, *The Independence of Georgia in International Politics, 1918–1921*, London, 1940, pp. 260–64, and the original edition of this work, in Russian, Z. Avalov, *Nezavisimost' Gruzii v mezhdunarodnoi politike, 1918–1921 g.g.: Vospominaniia. Ocherki*, Paris, 1924, pp. 285–9.
8. Kandelaki, *Georgian Question*, pp. 182–90.
9. Silnitskii, *Natsional'naia politika*, quoting from CPA IML, f. 80, op. 4, doc. 90. A somewhat different version was published in *Politika sovetskoi vlasti po natsional'nym delam*, p. 29.
10. Avalishvili, *Independence of Georgia*, pp. 281–6.
11. Ibid., p. 282.
12. Ibid., pp. 272, 275. (Italics in the Russian original, p. 301.)
13. *Istoriia Sovetskoi Konstitutsii*, pp. 240–6.
14. Ibid., p. 259.
15. Ibid., pp. 265–6, 299–300.
16. Lenin, 'Preliminary draft theses on the national and the colonial questions: For the Second Congress of the Communist International' (written in June 1920), in his *Collected Works*, vol. 31, p. 147.
17. Stalin, *Works*, vol. 5, pp. 16ff., 23–4.
18. *Desiatyi S''ezd Rossiiskoi Kommunisticheskoi partii: Stenograficheskii otchet (8–16 marta 1921 g.)*, Moscow, 1921, p. 110.
19. Ibid., pp. 113, 393.
20. S. I. Iakubovskaia, *Stroitel'stvo soiuznogo sovetskogo sotsialisticheskogo gosudarstva: 1922–1925 gg.*, Moscow, 1960, p. 124.

21. *Obrazovanie Soiuza*, pp. 295–6.
22. Silnitskii, *Natsional'naia politika*, quoting from CPA IML, f. 558, op. 2479, l. 146.
23. Lenin, *Polnoe sobranie sochinenii*, 5th ed., vol. 45, pp. 557–8.
24. Ibid., pp. 211–12. (Emphasis in the original.)
25. Ibid., pp. 211, 213, 682–7.
26. *Obrazovanie Soiuza*, pp. 299–300.
27. Lenin, *Polnoe sobranie sochinenii*, 5th ed., vol. 45, p. 214. (Emphasis in the original.) In Lenin's English-language *Collected Works*, vol. 33, p. 372, Kamenev's name is omitted (as it is also in the Russian 4th edition), and *Velikorusskomu shovinizmu*, 'Great-Russian chauvinism', is intentionally mistranslated as 'dominant nation chauvinism'.
28. *Obrazovanie Soiuza*, pp. 301–2.
29. Ibid., pp. 337–8; 89 per cent of delegates were communists.
30. *Dvenadtsatyi s"ezd RKP(b) 17–25 aprelia 1923 goda*, Moscow, 1968, p. 575. On their resignation, see p. 54 above.
31. *Obrazovanie Soiuza*, pp. 304–5.
32. Ibid., pp. 305–8.
33. Ibid., p. 347.
34. Ibid., pp. 300–1.
35. M. Kalinin, 'K X-mu s"ezdu sovetov', *Izvestia*, 17 December 1922, p. 1.
36. *Obrazovanie Soiuza*, p. 310.
37. Ibid., pp. 369, 501.
38. Ibid., pp. 370, 501.
39. Ibid., pp. 379–86, 501–2.
40. Lenin, *Collected Works*, vol. 36, pp. 605–11.
41. Ibid., pp. 606–11.
42. Ibid., p. 610.
43. Kh. Rakovskii, *Soiuz Sovetskikh Sotsialisticheskikh Respublik – novyi etap v sovetskom soiuznom stroitel'stve*, Kharkov, 1923, pp. 4–6.
44. *Dvenadtsatyi s"ezd*, pp. 495, 492.
45. Ibid., pp. 511–12.
46. Ibid., pp. 597–8.
47. Ibid., p. 879, note 247.
48. Ibid., pp. 503–4, 579–82, 576, 511, 516.
49. Ibid., p. 518.
50. Stalin, *Works*, vol. 5, pp. 269–70.
51. V. I. Ignat'ev, *Sovetskii stroi. Vypusk pervyi: Vozniknovenie i razvitie Konstitutsii Soiuza SSR*, Moscow, Leningrad, 1928, pp. 120, 138 (two versions prepared by the Moscow commission), and p. 129 (the Byelorussian SSR version, where the formula is implicit in Chapter 1). The original wording, *odno soiuznoe gosudarstvo*, can also be rendered as 'one union state'.
52. Ibid., pp. 123, 125–6, 144–6.
53. Ibid., pp. 127–8, 140–1, 146.
54. Stalin, *Works*, vol. 5, pp. 343–4. (Emphasis added.)
55. Ibid., p. 347.
56. *Obrazovanie Soiuza*, p. 420, and p. 503, note 137.
57. Ibid., pp. 423–5.
58. Ibid., p. 456; the text, pp. 456–72.

6. The National Contract Torn Up

1. Roy A. Medvedev, *Let History Judge: The Origins and Consequences of Stalinism*, New York, 1971; London, 1972, pp. 17–18.
2. Ibid., p. 17.
3. Lenin, *Collected Works*, vol. 36, pp. 594–5.
4. Ibid., p. 596.
5. *Kommunist*, 1956, no. 9, p. 15. The preface to the 1963 edition of that Congress's proceedings says, 'The delegations to the Congress considered it expedient/advisable (*priznali tselesoobraznym*) to leave . . .' rather than 'were in favour of leaving' (*Trinadtsatyi s"ezd RKP[b]: Mai 1924 goda*, Moscow, 1963, p. xxii).
6. Stalin, *Works*, vol. 5, pp. 335, 341.
7. Ibid., pp. 299–307.
8. *KPSS v rezoliutsiiakh* . . . , vol. 2, Moscow, 1970, pp. 488–94.
9. *Dvenadtsatyi s"ezd*, pp. 571, 597.
10. *Obrazovanie Soiuza*, p. 460.
11. Ibid., pp. 458, 465, 471, 460.
12. *Istoriia Sovetskoi Konstitutsii*, pp. 515–16. This article comes from the 1929 redaction, preserved also in the 1931 redaction.
13. Ibid., p. 532 (Article 13), p. 637 (Article 16).

14. Ibid., pp. 592–3 (Articles 20–3).
15. Ibid., p. 576.
16. *Ukraine: A Short Sketch of Economical, Cultural and Social Constructive Work of the Ukrainian Socialist Soviet Republic*, Kharkov, 1929, Chapter 6, 'The National and Cultural Development' (pp. 59–79).
17. Ibid., p. 71.
18. Ibid., pp. 72, 60, 75. Numbers of pupils in schools with the language of instruction other than Ukrainian were: Russian, 252,879; Yiddish, 68,836; Polish, 22,420; German, 33,579; Bulgarian, 5,758; others (Greek, Czech, Armenian, Tatar, Moldavian, Swedish and Assyrian), 10,278.
19. Ibid., p. 72.
20. Ibid., pp. 67, 75–6.
21. A. Bennigsen and Chantal Lemercier-Quelquejay, *Islam in the Soviet Union*, New York and London, 1967, p. 157.
22. A. Dzhunushev, *Iz istorii obrazovaniia Kirgizskoi Avtonomnoi Respubliki*, Frunze, 1966, pp. 73–4.
23. D. M. Malabaev, *Ukreplenie sovetov Kirgizii v period stroitel'stva sotsializma: 1917–1937*, Frunze, 1969, pp. 350–1; V. Lebedev, 'Delo Babakhanova–Khudaikulova', *Pravda*, 19 February 1927; 'Prigovor po delu Khudaikulova', *Pravda*, 24 February 1927.
24. G. Nekhoroshev, 'Eto nuzhno ne mertvym – zhivym . . .' (an interview with Eduard Beltov), *Knizhnoe obozrenie*, 17 June 1988, p. 7.
25. Alan W. Fisher, *The Crimean Tatars*, Stanford, 1978, pp. 140–3.
26. Stalin, *Works*, vol. 7, p. 71.
27. James E. Mace, *Communism and the Dilemmas of National Liberation: National Communism in Soviet Ukraine 1918–1933*, Cambridge, Mass., 1983, p. 282.
28. Since 1988, characterizations of this sort can often be found in the Soviet press (e.g. Raisa Skalii, 'Ne unykaty hostrykh problem', *Literaturna Ukraina*, no. 24, 16 June 1988, p. 2, col. 7) after over six decades of incessant vituperation against the *kulaks*.
29. Stalin, 'To Problems of Agrarian Policy in the USSR' (speech of

27 December 1929), in *Works*, vol. 12, pp. 147–78; *KPSS v rezoliutsiiakh . . .*, vol. 4, Moscow, 1970, pp. 383–6.
30. Roy Medvedev, 'The Suit Against Stalin', *Moscow News*, no. 48, 1988, p. 8.
31. V. Tikhonov, 'Chtoby narod prokormil sebia . . .', *Literaturnaia gazeta*, 3 August 1988, p. 10.
32. A. Solzhenitsyn, *The Gulag Archipelago*, 3 vols, London, 1974–8, vol. 1, p. 51.
33. Martha Brill Olcott, 'The Collectivization Drive in Kazakhstan', *The Russian Review*, vol. 40, no. 2, April 1981, p. 136; F. Lorimer, *The Population of the Soviet Union: History and Prospects*, Geneva, the League of Nations, 1946, p. 121; Andrew Cairns (Canadian economist who travelled in Kazakhstan and other areas during the years of famine), a 69-page report for the Foreign Office, in Public Record Office, London, FO 371/16329, 7 June 1932.
34. *Istoriia Sovetskoi Konstitutsii*, pp. 703–4.
35. Nikolai Tolstoy, *Victims of Yalta*, revised edn, London, 1979.
36. Medvedev, 'The Suit Against Stalin', p. 8.
37. Medvedev, *Let History Judge*, p. 16.
38. There is a chapter on the collectivization and famine in Mace, *Communism and the Dilemmas*, pp. 280–96; two recent book-length treatments of the subject are: Robert Conquest, *The Harvest of Sorrow: Soviet Collectivization and the Terror-Famine*, London, 1986; R. Serbyn and B. Kravchenko (eds), *Famine in Ukraine 1932–1933*, Edmonton, 1986. A particularly detailed 77-page account of the first year of the famine in the Ukraine, the Crimea and North Caucasus was prepared for the Foreign Office by Andrew Cairns (Public Record Office, FO 371/16329, June-July 1932); see also Marco Carynnyk et al., eds, *The Foreign Office and the Famine: British Documents on Ukraine and the Great Famine of 1932–1933*, Kingston, Ont., 1988.
39. 'Kollektivizatsiia: kak eto bylo'

(interview with V. Danilov), *Pravda*, 26 August 1988.

40. Victor Kravchenko, *I Chose Justice*, London, 1951, pp. 98–9.

41. Conquest, *The Harvest of Sorrow*, Chapter 8.

42. *Istoriia Sovetskoi Konstitutsii*, pp. 672–3.

43. Mace, *Communism and the Dilemmas*, p. 293; K. Mikhailov, 'Tsar'-golod', *Sobesednik* (Moscow), no. 49, November 1988, p. 12.

44. Interview with a Soviet Byelorussian writer in I. S. Lubachko, *Belorussia Under Soviet Rule*, p. 105.

45. Medvedev, *Let History Judge*, p. 93.

46. A. Orlov, *The Secret History of Stalin's Crimes*, London, 1954, p. 53.

47. A. I. Chugunov, 'Bor'ba s basmachestvom v Srednei Azii v 1931–1933 g.', *Istoriia SSSR*, 1972, no. 2, pp. 97–107; Malabaev, *Ukreplenie sovetov Kirgizii*, pp. 371–4, 393–6.

48. W. S. Ritter, 'The Final Phase in the Liquidation of Anti-Soviet Resistance in Tadzhikistan: Ibrahim Bek and the *Basmachi*, 1924–31', *Soviet Studies*, vol. 37, no. 4, October 1985, p. 488.

49. Olcott, 'The Basmachi', pp. 361–2 and note 61.

50. V. Chemerys, 'Syn komandarma', *Literaturna Ukraina*, no. 11, 17 March 1988, p. 3.

51. A. I. Zevelev *et al.*, *Basmachestvo: vozniknovenie, sushchnost', krakh*, Moscow, 1981, pp. 179–80.

52. O. Lacis, 'Problema tempov v sotsialisticheskom stroitel'stve', *Kommunist*, 1987, no. 18, p. 89.

53. Mary Kilbourne Matossian, *The Impact of Soviet Policies in Armenia*, Leiden, 1962, pp. 105–6.

54. Conquest, *Harvest of Sorrow*, Chapter 16.

55. M. Lewin, *Russian Peasants and Soviet Power: A Study of Collectivization*, New York, 1975, p. 508.

56. V. Chalikova, 'Arkhivnyi iunosha', *Neva*, 1988, no. 10, p. 158.

57. Nikolai Shmelev in a lecture at a research institute attached to the Central Committee, as summarized in *The Christian Science Monitor*, 16 June 1987.

58. Quoted in a speech of Akmal' Ikramov, First Secretary of the Uzbek CP, where he described the protesting national communists as 'bourgeois nationalists' (*Pravda Vostoka*, 16 January 1934). He and Chairman of the Uzbek Council of People's Commissars, Faizulla Khodzhaev, both loyal to Stalin, were themselves shot as 'bourgeois nationalists' being defendants in the monstrous Bukharin trial of 1938 (Robert Conquest, *The Great Terror: Stalin's Purge of the Thirties*, London, 1968, pp. 382–5, 423).

59. A. Zorin, '10 let sovetskoi Kirgizii', *Revoliutsionnyi vostok*, no. 6 (28), 1934, pp. 170–1.

60. G. Sannikov, 'Literaturnyi prazdnik Turkmenistana', *Revoliutsiia i natsional'nosti*, August 1934, no. 8 (54), pp. 46–7; G. Nepesov, *Pobeda sovetskogo stroia v severnom Turkmenistane (1917–1936)*, Ashkhabad, 1950, pp. 196–223, 299–356. Nepesov had to rewrite his book because it depicted Dzhunaid Khan (p. 70 above) and other resistance leaders in too favourable a light (the new version's title: *Velikii Oktiabr' i narodnye revoliutsii v severnom i vostochnom Turkmenistane*, Ashkhabad, 1958).

61. Teresa Rakowska-Harmstone, *Russia and Nationalism in Central Asia: The Case of Tadzhikistan*, Baltimore, 1970, pp. 40, 100–1.

62. I. Koshelivets', *Mykola Skrypnyk*, n.p. (Munich printed), 1972, p. 246.

63. M. Panchuk, 'Istorychna pam''iat'' – faktor perebudovy', *Literaturna Ukraina*, no. 27, 7 July 1988, p. 7; O. Musiienko, 'Hromadians'ka pozytsiia literatury i perebudova', *Literaturna Ukraina*, no. 7, 18 February 1988, p. 2.

64. Panchuk, 'Istorychna pam''iat''', p. 7.

65. Robert Conquest, *Stalin and the Kirov Murder*, London, 1989.

66. Medvedev, 'The Suit against Stalin', pp. 8–9.

67. Chalikova, 'Arkhivnyi iunosha', p. 158.

68. Conquest, *The Great Terror*, Appendix A: 'Casualty Figures', p. 533.

69. On the two dates, see ibid., pp. 468–9.
70. Mykhailo Slaboshpyts'kyi, 'Kolyms'kyi Vavilon i dolia: Anatoliu Kostenku – 80', *Literaturna Ukraina*, no. 33, 18 August 1988, p. 4.
71. *Kommunist* (Erevan), 15 November 1961 and 28 November 1963; Shelepin's speech in *XXII s"ezd Kommunisticheskoi partii Sovetskogo Soiuza*, vol. 2, Moscow, 1962, p. 404.
72. Medvedev, *Let History Judge*, p. 344; Walter Kolarz, *Russia and Her Colonies*, London, 1952, p. 133.
73. *Bakinskii rabochii*, 27 May 1956.
74. He was elected to the Central Committee in 1923 (*Dvenadtsatyi s"ezd*, p. 662). Though incriminated under interrogation by Tursun Khodzhaev in 1930 (E. Voskoboinikov and A. Zevelev, *Turkkomissiia VTsIK i SNK RSFSR i Turkbiuro TsK RKP(b) v bor'be za ukreplenie Sovetskoi vlasti v Turkestane*, Tashkent, 1951, pp. 94, 96), he was still active as Vice-Chairman of the RSFSR Council of People's Commissars in 1932, but was arrested in 1937, accused of 'nationalism', 'pan-Turkism' and 'treason', and executed on 10 February 1938 (*The Revolution in Central Asia as Seen by Muslim Bolsheviks*, Society for Central Asian Studies, Reprint Series, no. 3, Oxford, 1985, p. 11).
75. A. Altay, 'Kirgiziia During the Great Purge', *Central Asian Review*, 1964, vol. 12, no. 2, pp. 97–107.
76. Nepesov, *Pobeda sovetskogo stroia*, pp. 348–56; Langston Hughes, *I Wonder as I Wander*, New York, 1956, pp. 116–17; the author is an African-American poet who attended with Koestler one of the early trials – that of Atta Kurdov and others – in Ashkhabad in 1932.
77. Iurii Lavrinenko, *Rozstriliane vidrodzhennia: Antolohiia 1917–1933*, Paris, 1959, p. 12.
78. Nekhoroshev, 'Eto nuzhno'.
79. Il'ia Ehrenburg, 'Liudi, gody, zhizn', *Novyi mir*, no. 4, 1962, p. 28.
80. Nekhoroshev, 'Eto nuzhno'; Eduard Beltov, 'Naming the Repressed', *Moscow News*, no. 48, 1988, p. 8.

81. The decree of the CEC of the Moldavian ASSR of 15 March 1933 on the promulgation of the Latinized Moldavian alphabet is quoted in P. Mustiaţa, 'Do istorii rozvytku moldavs'koi literaturnoi movy u zv"iazku z latynizatsiieiu ii pys'ma', *Movoznavstvo*, no. 3–4, Kiev, 1935, pp. 98–9.
82. Aleksandr M. Nekrich, *The Punished Peoples*, New York, 1978, pp. 98–9; F. Beck and W. Godin, *Russian Purge and the Extraction of Confession*, London, 1951, p. 110.
83. Alex Weissberg, *Conspiracy of Silence*, London, 1952 (published in the US as *The Accused*), p. 326.
84. Beck and Godin, *Russian Purge*, p. 114.
85. Ibid., pp. 122–3.
86. Shirin Akiner, *Islamic Peoples of the Soviet Union*, London, 1983, pp. 208–15.
87. Alexander Uralov, *The Reign of Stalin*, London, 1953, pp. 140ff.; Aleksandr Uralov (A. Avtorkhanov), *Narodoubiistvo v SSSR: Ubiistvo chechenskogo naroda*, Munich, 1952, pp. 50–7.

7. Between Hitler and Stalin

1. *Dvenadtsatyi s"ezd*, p. 674.
2. 'Nota polpreda SSSR v Germanii t. Khinchuka germanskomu ministerstvu inostrannykh del', *Izvestia*, 24 June 1933. The claim was made in a memorandum submitted by the German delegation to the Economic Commission of the World Economic Conference in London (*The Times*, 17 June 1933, p. 12); the memorandum was, however, withdrawn within two days (*The Times*, 19 June 1933, p. 14).
3. *Manchester Guardian*, 18 March 1938, also in Jane Degras (ed.), *Soviet Documents on Foreign Policy*, vol. 3, Oxford, 1953, reprinted New York, 1978, p. 276.
4. A. Zhdanov, 'Angliiskoe i frantsuzskoe pravitel'stva ne khotiat ravnogo dogovora s SSSR', *Pravda*, 29 June 1939.
5. 'International Situation, 31 July 1939', *Parliamentary Debates* (Hansard), 350 H.C. Deb. 5s., London, 1939, col. 2099.

6. Public Record Office, FO 181/963/5. This document was published, apparently for the first time, in L. Y. Luciuk and B. S. Kordan, *Anglo-American Perspectives on the Ukrainian Question, 1938–1951: A Documentary Collection*, Kingston, Ont. – Vestal, N.Y., 1987, pp. 123–31, but with the wrong date, '17 December 1942' (and therefore misplaced in the chronological sequence of the documents) instead of the correct '17 December 1941'. Here and below, this document is quoted direct from the original in the Public Record Office.

7. 'Sovetsko-germanskoe khoziaistvennoe soglashenie', *Izvestia*, 10 April 1935; V. M. Molotov, *Stat'i i rechi 1935–1936*, Moscow, 1937, pp. 170–2.

8. Molotov's speech in *Tret'ia sessiia Verkhovnogo Soveta SSSR: 25–31 maia 1939 g.*, Moscow, 1939, p. 472.

9. Alfred Seidl (ed.), *Die Beziehungen zwischen Deutschland und der Sowjetunion, 1939–1941: Dokumente des Auswärtigen Amtes*, Tübingen, 1949, pp. 56–8.

10. Ibid., p. 66–9.

11. Degras, *Soviet Documents*, p. 359.

12. *Dvenadtsatyi s"ezd*, pp. 273–4 (italics in the original).

13. Ibid., p. 865, note 165.

14. M. Voslensky, 'The Soviet system: historical and theoretical evaluation', in A. Shtromas and M. A. Kaplan (eds), *The Soviet Union and the Challenge of the Future*, vol. 1, New York, 1988, p. 3.

15. For the view that Stalin's part in starting the war was very much greater, and much more sinister, than has been hitherto assumed, see Viktor Suvorov, *Icebreaker: Who Started the Second World War?*, London, 1990.

16. Both treaties were published at the time by the two governments, but without the Secret Additional Protocols. The Russian originals of the Secret Protocols have never been published; the German originals are available, together with the treaties themselves, in Seidl, *Beziehungen*, pp. 90–1, 125–6, and English translations (the treaties from Russian and the Protocols from German) in Degras, *Soviet Documents*, pp. 359–61, 377–9.

17. N. P. Vakar, *Belorussia: The Making of a Nation*, Cambridge, Mass., 1956, p. 156.

18. *Istoriia BSSR*, vol. 2, Minsk, 1961, p. 385.

19. *Istoriia Sovetskoi Konstitutsii*, pp. 809–10.

20. The text of the Treaty on the Transfer of Vilnius to Lithuania and on Soviet–Lithuanian Mutual Assistance of 10 October 1939 is in Degras, *Soviet Documents*, pp. 380–2. The Treaties with Latvia and Estonia are in *League of Nations Treaty Series*, vol. 198, pp. 223–9, 381–7. Molotov discusses the treaties in Degras, *Soviet Documents*, pp. 393–5, 446–7.

21. *Izvestia*, 1 November 1939; V. Molotov, *Soviet Peace Policy*, London, 1941, p. 36.

22. *Izvestia*, 16 May 1940.

23. M. Loginov, 'Kul't lichnosti chuzhd nashemu stroiu', *Molodoi kommunist*, 1962, no. 1, p. 53.

24. The full text of this conversation (in the course of which Molotov among other things predicted that the Soviet take-over of Europe would happen 'soon'), as remembered by Krėvė-Mickevičius, is found in US House of Representatives, *Third Interim Report of the Select Committee on Communist Aggression*, Washington, DC, 1954, pp. 341–4, and quoted by Vardys, *Lithuania Under the Soviets*. He reached the West, and ultimately the US, at the end of the war.

25. This is candidly admitted in Soviet sources; see I. Jankovski and O. Kuuli, 'Rahvas ja Revolutsioon', *Eesti Kommunist*, no. 7, July 1965, p. 27.

26. *Istoriia Sovetskoi Konstitutsii*, pp. 814–15.

27. Degras, *Soviet Documents*, p. 323.

28. *Istoriia Sovetskoi Konstitutsii*, pp. 812–13.

29. Degras, *Soviet Documents*, pp. 464–6.

30. Ibid., p. 466; Russian original in *Zasedaniia Verkhovnogo Soveta SSSR: Sed'maia sessiia*, Moscow, 1940, pp. 22ff.

31. Louis FitzGibbon, *Katyn*, London, 1971; also his *The Katyn Cover-Up*,

378 / *Notes*

London, 1972, *Unpitied and Unknown:*
Katyn . . . Bologoye . . . Dergachi,
London, 1975, and 'Katyn Massacre', *The*
Independent, 23 July 1988.
32. Jan T. Gross, *Revolution from Abroad:*
The Soviet Conquest of Poland's Western
Ukraine and Western Belorussia, Princeton,
NJ, 1988, pp. 193–202.
33. Stefan Szende, *The Promise Hitler*
Kept, London, 1945, pp. 124–5; I. Rassen,
Mir viln leben, New York, 1949, pp. 22–9;
Dr Mark Dvorzhetski, *Ierushalaim d'Lita*
im kamf un umkum, Paris, 1948, pp. 23–4;
I. Gar, *Umkum fun der iidisher Kovne*,
Munich, 1948, pp. 31–2.
34. Tania Fuks, *A vanderung iber*
okkupirte gebite, Buenos Aires, 1947,
p. 112.
35. Bohdan Krawchenko, *Social Change*
and National Consciousness in Twentieth-
Century Ukraine, Basingstoke and London,
1985, p. 155.
36. Ann Sheehy and Bohdan Nahaylo, *The*
Crimean Tatars, Volga Germans and
Meskhetians: Soviet Treatment of Some
National Minorities, 3rd edn (Minority
Rights Group, Report no. 6), London,
1980, pp. 17–19; R. Conquest, *The Nation*
Killers, London, 1970, pp. 59–63; Fred C.
Koch, *The Volga Germans in Russia and*
the Americas, from 1763 to the Present,
University Park, Pa, and London, 1977.
37. Algirdas M. Budreckis, *The Lithuanian*
National Revolt of 1941, Boston, 1968;
J. Pajanjis-Javis, *Soviet Genocide in*
Lithuania, New York, 1980.
38. Stasys Raštikis, *Kovose dėl Lietuvos*,
vol. 2, pp. 305–7, and *Lietuvių*
Enciklopedija, vol. 29, p. 178, quoted in
Vardys, *Lithuania Under the Soviets*, p. 72.
39. Romuald J. Misiunas and Rein
Taagepera, *The Baltic States: Years of*
Dependence 1940–1980, London, 1983,
pp. 46–7; William Tomingas, *The Soviet*
Colonization of Estonia, 'Kultuur'
(Toronto), 1973, pp. 275–7.
40. 'Vystuplenie po radio Predsedatelia
Gosudarstvennogo Komiteta Oborony
I. V. Stalina 3 iiulia 1941 goda', *Pravda*, 3
July 1941; Roy Medvedev, *On Stalin and*
Stalinism, Oxford, 1979, pp. 122–4; Isaac

Deutscher, *Stalin: A Political Biography*,
2nd edn, Harmondsworth, 1972, pp. 451–3.
41. *Pravda*, 8 November 1941, p. 1;
Deutscher, *Stalin*, pp. 457–9.
42. B. Volin, 'Velikii russkii narod',
Bol'shevik, no. 9, 1 May 1938, pp. 26–36.
43. Notable articles glorifying Russian
patriotism appeared in *Pravda*, in early
1942 alone, on 1 February (M. Mitin,
'Velikaia sila sovetskogo patriotizma'),
17 March and 2 May.
44. Public Record Office, FO 181/963/5.
45. General Petr Grigorenko, an interview
with Alex Alexiev, 12 March 1979, in Alex
Alexiev, *Soviet Nationalities in German*
Wartime Strategy, 1941–1945, Santa
Monica, Ca, 1982, p. 1.
46. Alexander Dallin, *German Rule in*
Russia, 1941–1945: A Study of Occupation
Policies, London, 1957, pp. 426–7.

8. Stalin's Last Years: The Terror Against
Nations
1. *Pravda* and *Izvestia*, 25 May 1945, p. 1,
and *Bol'shevik*, no. 10, May 1945, pp. 1–2.
(Emphasis added.)
2. This fact is reported in a Soviet source,
Stanislav Tel'niuk, ' "Slova siiaiut'
ametystamy . . .": Vidkrytyi lyst do
kryms'koho tataryna Seirana Useinova',
Literaturna Ukraina, no. 23, 8 June 1989,
p. 7.
3. On the deportation of these
nationalities, see Conquest, *Nation Killers*,
Sheehy and Nahaylo, *Crimean Tatars,*
Volga Germans and Meskhetians, and
Nekrich, *Punished Peoples*, who also gives
extensive details of the falsification and
suppression of the historical documentary
record relating to the Crimean Tatars on
pp. 167–76.
4. Medvedev, *Let History Judge*, pp. 491–
2; Nekrich, *Punished Peoples*, pp. 104–5.
5. V. Kubijovyč (ed.), *Ukraine: A Concise*
Encyclopaedia, vol. 1, Toronto, 1963,
p. 902.
6. Alexander Shtromas, 'The Baltic
States', in Robert Conquest (ed.), *The Last*
Empire: Nationality and the Soviet Future,
Stanford, Cal., 1986, p. 193.
7. N. S. Khrushchev, *The 'Secret' Speech*,

introd. Zhores and Roy Medvedev, Nottingham, 1976, p. 58.

8. Medvedev, *Let History Judge*, p. 485.

9. Nicholas Bethell, *The Last Secret: Forcible Repatriation to Russia, 1944–1947*, London, 1974; Tolstoy, *Victims of Yalta*; Mark R. Elliot, *Pawns of Yalta: Soviet Refugees and America's Role in Their Repatriation*, Urbana, Ill., 1982.

10. S. Swianiewicz, *Forced Labour and Economic Development: An Enquiry into the Experience of Soviet Industrialization*, Westport, Conn., 1985, pp. 43–5; Elliot, *Pawns of Yalta*, p. 2.

11. Boris A. Iakovlev, *Kontsentratsionnye lageri SSSR*, Munich, 1955, p. 23; Conquest, *The Great Terror*, p. 533.

12. For examples of warnings issued by Soviet partisans to collaborators, see John A. Armstrong (ed.), *Soviet Partisans in World War II*, Madison, Wisc., 1964, pp. 710–22.

13. B. Bociurkiw, 'The Uniate Church in the Soviet Ukraine: A Case Study in Soviet Church Policy', *Canadian Slavonic Papers*, vol. 7, 1965, pp. 89–113; Dennis J. Dunn, *The Catholic Church and the Soviet Government, 1939–1949*, New York, 1977, pp. 107–16.

14. German estimates are quoted from captured German military documents in a British War Office report of 13 December 1945, Public Record Office, FO 371/47957, published in Luciuk and Kordan, *Anglo-American Perspectives*, p. 173, and in *Journal of Ukrainian Studies*, vol. 6, no. 1(10), Spring 1981, p. 55. The Polish estimate is in Antoni B. Szcześniak and Wiesław Z. Szota, *Droga do nikąd: Działalność Organizacji Ukraińskich Nacjonalistów i jej likwidacja w Polsce*, Warsaw, 1973, p. 145.

15. The War Office report, as just quoted above.

16. Yuriy Tys-Krokhmaliuk, *UPA Warfare in Ukraine: Strategical, Tactical and Organizational Problems of Ukrainian Resistance in World War II*, New York, 1972, Chapter. 21; Strobe Talbott (ed. and transl.), *Khrushchev Remembers*, Boston and Toronto,\1970, London, 1971, pp. 140–1.

17. A. P. Kozlov, *Trevozhnaia sluzhba*, 2nd edn, Moscow, 1975, pp. 159–228. On the UPA, see also Yaroslav Bilinsky, *The Second Soviet Republic: The Ukraine After World War II*, New Brunswick, NJ, 1964, Chapter IV.

18. K. Girnius, 'Soviet Propagandists on the Partisan War in Lithuania', *RFE Research Situation Report*, Baltic Area SR/3, 22 March 1985, p. 27.

19. K. V. Tauras, *Guerrilla Warfare on the Amber Coast*, New York, 1962; V. Stanley Vardys, 'The Partisan Movement in Postwar Lithuania', *Slavic Review*, vol. 22, no. 3, September 1963, pp. 499–522, and in his *Lithuania Under the Soviets*, pp. 85–108; Thomas Remeikis, *Opposition to Soviet Rule in Lithuania, 1945–80*, Chicago, 1980; K. Girnius, 'The Opposition Movement in Postwar Lithuania', *Journal of Baltic Studies*, vol. 13, no. 1, spring 1982, pp. 66–73.

20. Vardys, 'The Partisan Movement', p. 501; his *Lithuania Under the Soviets*, p. 86.

21. By Simas Kudirka, the radio operator of a Soviet Lithuanian fishing boat, speaking at his 1970 trial for attempting to stay in the US (*A Chronicle of Current Events, Issues no. 19 and 20*, London, n.d., Issue no. 20, 2 July 1971 [Moscow], p. 233).

22. 'Na blago perestroiki i obnovleniia obshchestva' (an interview with Eismuntas), *Sovetskaia Litva*, 16 September 1988.

23. Misiunas and Taagepera, *The Baltic States*, pp. 81–91; Rein Taagepera, 'Soviet Documentation on the Estonian Pro-Independence Guerrilla Movement, 1945–1952', *Journal of Baltic Studies*, vol. 10, no. 2, summer 1979, pp. 91–106; Ādolfs Šilde, *Resistance Movement in Latvia*, Stockholm, 1972.

24. A list of 15 such incidents is provided in Volodymyr Kosyk, *Concentration Camps in the USSR*, London, 1962, p. 45. A Soviet source reports a 1943 strike against camp conditions; the strikers demanded to be sent to the front as an alternative. The authorities reacted by destroying the camp.

(V. Koval', 'Ioho nema . . .', *Literaturna Ukraina*, 19 October 1989, p. 8.)

25. On the role of the Ukrainians, see Paul Barton, 'The Strike Mechanism in Soviet Concentration Camps', *RFE Background Report*, No. 24, 15 June 1956, pp. 23–6; Alexander Solzhenitsyn, *The Gulag Archipelago*, vol. 3, London, 1978, pp. 235–7; Kosyk, *Concentration Camps*, pp. 48–55; Roland Gaucher, *Opposition in the USSR: 1917–1967*, New York, 1969, pp. 406, 408.

26. Bilinsky, *The Second Soviet Republic*, pp. 394–5.

27. *Kommunisticheskaia Partiia Kirgizii v rezoliutsiiakh i resheniiakh s"ezdov . . .*, pt 2, Frunze, 1968, p. 201.

28. *Sovetskaia Kirgiziia*, 11 July 1952, quoted by A. Bennigsen, 'The Muslim peoples of the Soviet Union and the Soviets. IV. The Political Problem', *Islamic Review*, vol. 43, no. 7, July 1955, pp. 33–4. The novel was published in 1935, 1937 and 1940; parts also appeared in *Literaturnaia gazeta*, 15 January 1947. The charges against it were withdrawn after Stalin's death, and the work was several times republished and extended.

29. Bennigsen, 'The Muslim peoples', p. 30. See note 50 to Chapter 6.

30. Leonard Schapiro, *The Communist Party of the Soviet Union*, 2nd edn, London, 1970, p. 540; Khrushchev, *'Secret' Speech*, p. 60; Michael Rywkin, *Moscow's Muslim Challenge: Soviet Central Asia*, New York, 1982, p. 101.

31. M. D. Bagirov, 'Starshii brat v sem'e sovetskikh narodov', *Kommunist*, no. 3, 1953, pp. 64–88; condensed translation in *CDSP*, vol. 5, no. 23, 18 July 1953, pp. 8–11.

32. Sh. V. Tsagareishvili (ed.), *Shamil' – stavlennik sultanskoi Turtsii i angliiskikh kolonizatorov*, Tbilisi, 1953.

33. *Manas: Kirgizskii narodnyi epos: Glavy iz 'Vekilogo pokhoda'*, Moscow, 1941.

34. 'V prezidiume Akademii nauk SSSR', *Vestnik Akademii nauk SSSR*, December 1950, p. 77.

35. Lowell Tillett, *The Great Friendship: Soviet Historians on the Non-Russian Nationalities*, Chapel Hill, NC, 1969, p. 158.

36. Kolarz, *Russia and Her Colonies*, p. 273.

37. M. A. Plotnikov, *Iangaal-Maa: Vogul'skaia poema*, Moscow-Leningrad, 1933, pp. 9–11, 39–40, quoted in Ivan Dzyuba, *Internationalism or Russification? A Study in the Soviet Nationalities Problem*, London, 1968, 1970, New York, 1974, pp. 71–2.

38. Max Hayward, *Writers in Russia: 1917–1978*, London, 1983, p. 104.

39. Joel Cang, *The Silent Millions: A History of the Jews in the Soviet Union*, London, 1969, and New York, 1970, Chapter 5.

40. 'Ob odnoi antipatrioticheskoi gruppe teatral'nykh kritikov', *Pravda*, 28 January 1949, p. 3, followed by articles in *Kul'tura i zhizn'*, 30 January, *Sovetskoe iskusstvo*, 19 February and 5 March, *Literaturnaia gazeta*, 12 February, 2 and 9 March, *Komsomol'skaia pravda*, 6 March, 'Kosmopolitizm – ideologicheskoe oruzhie amerikanskoi reaktsii', *Pravda*, 7 April, all of 1949, to mention but a few.

41. Khrushchev, *'Secret' Speech*, pp. 58–60, 84.

42. A. Avtorkhanov, *Zagadka smerti Stalina: Zagovor Beriia*, Frankfurt/M, 1976, p. 257.

43. ' "Narodyvsia i zhyv dlia dobra i liubovi": Nevidomi storinky shchodennykiv Oleksandra Dovzhenka', *Literaturna Ukraina*, no. 29, 21 July 1988, p. 3, entry dated 18 July 1954; also O. Dovzhenko, 'Storinky shchodennyka', *Dnipro*, no. 10, October 1988, p. 100.

44. A. L. Sachar, *A History of the Jews*, rev. ed., New York, 1972, p. 440; Y. Gilboa, *The Black Years of Soviet Jewry: 1939–1953*, Boston, 1971, pp. 146–256, 293–351; Ia. G. Frumkin *et al.* (eds), *Kniga o russkom evreistve 1917–1967*, New York, 1968, pp. 154–6; Nora Levin, *The Jews in the Soviet Union Since 1917: Paradox of Survival*, vol. 2, New York, 1988, pp. 527–50.

45. *Pravda*, 13 January 1953.

46. J. Lvavi, 'Jewish Agricultural

Settlement in the USSR', *Soviet Jewish Affairs*, no. 1, June 1971, p. 94.
47. Frumkin, *Kniga o russkom evreistve*, pp. 156–9.
48. Khrushchev, *'Secret' Speech*, pp. 62–3, 77–8, 84.
49. A. Antonov-Ovseyenko, *The Time of Stalin: Portrait of a Tyranny*, New York, 1983, p. 291.
50. Medvedev, *On Stalin and Stalinism*, p. 159.

9. Towards a Partial Restoration of the National Contract

1. Charles H. Fairbanks, Jr., 'National Cadres as a Force in the Soviet System: The Evidence of Beria's Career, 1949–53', in Jeremy R. Azrael, ed., *Soviet Nationality Policies and Practices*, New York, 1978, pp. 144–9.
2. Robert Conquest, *Power and Policy in the USSR: The Study of Soviet Dynastics*, London, 1961, p. 211.
3. *Pravda Ukrainy*, 13 June 1953.
4. *Sovetskaia Litva*, 18 June 1953; *Sovetskaia Latvia*, 28 June 1953.
5. Talbot, ed. and trans., *Khrushchev Remembers*, Boston and Toronto, 1970, pp. 329–30.
6. Ibid., p. 330.
7. AS 1042, as translated in George Saunders, ed., *Samizdat: Voices of the Soviet Opposition*, New York, 1974, pp. 427–40.
8. 'Ruki razviazany: razviazan li uzel?' *Sovetskaia molodezh'* (Riga), 24 September 1988, pp. 2 and 7.
9. Interview with Mykola Rudenko, Munich, January 1988.
10. *Dnipro*, no. 12, December 1962, p. 122.
11. Bociurkiw, 'The Uniate Church', p. 110, n. 91.
12. Osyp Zinkevych and Rev. Taras R. Lonchyna, *Martyrolohiia ukrains'kykh tserkov: Dokumenty, materiialy, khrystyians'kyi samvydav Ukrainy*, vol. II: *Ukrains'ka Katolyts'ka Tserkva*, Toronto and Baltimore, 1985, pp. 400–5.
13. Interview with Mykola Rudenko.

14. Fairbanks, Jr., 'National Cadres', pp. 173–4.
15. Misiunas and Taagepera, *The Baltic States*, pp. 127–8.
16. *Pravda*, 16 February 1958.
17. *Literaturnaia gazeta*, 24 February 1988.
18. V. Holubnychy, 'Ukraine Since World War II, 1945–62', in Kubijovyc, *Ukraine: A Concise Encyclopaedia*, p. 906.
19. *Pravda*, 8 August 1953.
20. Pravda, 9 December 1953.
21. *Bol'shaia Sovetskaia Entsiklopediia*, 1st ed., Moscow, vol. 59, 1935, p. 818.
22. *Pravda*, 12 January 1954.
23. *Pravda*, 27 February 1954.
24. *Pravda*, 12 January 1954.
25. Conquest, *Power and Policy*, pp. 68–9.
26. Walter Kolarz, *Communism and Colonialism*, London, 1964, p. 44.
27. B. Gafurov, 'V. I. Lenin i pobeda Sovetskoi vlasti v Srednei Azii', *Kommunist*, no. 6, April 1955, pp. 88–9.
28. N. Dzhandil'din, 'Nekotorye voprosy internatsional'nogo vospitaniia', *Kommunist*, no. 13, September 1959, p. 34.
29. On the Gulag at this time, see Paul Barton, 'Strikes in the Russian Camps', *Dissent*, III, No. 2, 1956, pp. 137–42; Paul Barton, *L'Institution Concentrationnaire en Russie 1930–57*, Paris 1959; Kosyk, *Concentration Camps in the USSR*.
30. Sheehy and Nahaylo, *National Minorities*, pp. 19–20.
31. See AS 1216, p. 5.
32. V. Stanley Vardys, *The Catholic Church, Dissent and Nationality in Soviet Lithuania*, New York, 1978, pp. 82–3.
33. Bociurkiw, 'Uniate Church', p. 109.
34. Tillett, *The Great Friendship*, pp. 196–9.
35. Holubnychy, 'Ukraine Since World War II', p. 907.
36. Khrushchev, *Secret Speech*, pp. 58, 60–61.
37. Leo Gruliow, ed., *Current Soviet Policies II: Documentary Record of the 20th Communist Party Congress and Its Aftermath*, New York, 1985, pp. 52–3.
38. Ibid., p. 88.
39. Ibid., p. 148.

40. *Kommunist*, no. 9, June 1956, pp. 22–6.

41. Interviews with Nougar Sharia, Karlo Inasaridze and Iakob Krikheli, Munich, November 1984. See also G. Charachaidze, 'Les emeutes de Tiflis et leur signification', *Est et Ouest*, no. 153, June 1956, pp. 15–17. The issue of the March 1956 protests in Georgia was to be taken up again in the Georgian press in the spring of 1988. See Elizabeth Fuller, 'Georgia, Stalin, and the Demonstrations of 1956', RL 190/88, 3 May 1988.

42. The arrests were reported in the Viennese press on 7 June 1956. *Facts on File*, XVI, no. 817, June 20–6, 1956, p. 206.

43. Joseph S. Berliner, *Factory and Manager in the USSR*, Cambridge, Mass., 1957, p. 302.

44. P. Nikitich, A. Tokombaev, K. Iudakhin, 'Zabytoe bogatstvo', *Literaturnaia gazeta*, 21 June 1956.

45. *Pravda vostoka*, 13 October 1956, as cited in P. Urban, 'The New Drive Against Nationalism in Turkestan', *The East Turkic Review*, no. 4, December 1960, pp. 14–15.

46. Lenin, *Collected Works*, vol. 30, pp. 163–4.

47. As cited in U. Hlybinny, 'Belorussian Culture After World War II', *Belorussian Review*, no. 6, 1958, pp. 55–6.

48. N. Dzhandil'din, 'O nekotorykh voprosakh razvitiia natsional'noi kul'tury', *Kommunist Kazakhstana*, no. 7, July 1957, pp. 15–22, as cited and summarized in H. Carrere d'Encausse, 'Linguistic Russification and Nationalist Opposition in Kazakhstan', *The East Turkic Review*, no. 1, 1958, pp. 96–100.

49. *Bakinskii rabochii*, 24 August 1956.

50. Walter Kolarz, 'The Nationalities Under Khrushchev: Gains and Losses', *Soviet Survey*, no. 24, April–June 1958, p. 64.

51. Allen Hetmanek, 'Kirgizstan and the Kirgiz', in Zev Katz, Rosemarie Rogers, Frederic Harned, eds., *Handbook of Major Soviet Nationalities*, New York, 1975, p. 256.

52. V. Borysenko, 'Ukrainian Opposition to the Soviet Regime 1956–59', *Problems of the Peoples of the USSR*, no. 6, 1960, p. 28; Bilinsky, *Second Soviet Republic*, p. 27.

53. *Literaturnaia gazeta*, 1 September 1956.

54. Kastus' Tarasaw, 'Ministerstva pryslala adkaz . . .', *Litaratura i mastatsva*, 19 December 1986, p. 4.

55. See John Soper, 'Central Asian Intellectuals Recall Khrushchev Era', RL 290/87, 29 July 1987.

56. Rolfs Ekmanis, *Latvian Literature Under the Soviets*, Belmont, Mass., 1978, pp. 226–7; excerpts from the poem are translated in Robert Conquest, ed., *Back to Life*, London, 1958, pp. 43–6.

57. Translated excerpts also in Conquest, *Back to Life*, pp. 38–40.

58. As cited in Borys Lewtyzkyj, *Politics and Society in Soviet Ukraine 1953–1980*, Edmonton, 1984, pp. 19–20.

59. Tillett, *The Great Friendship*, pp. 201–17.

60. Ekmanis, *Latvian Literature*, p. 184.

61. Bilinsky, *Second Soviet Republic*, p. 29.

62. Nekrich, *The Punished Peoples*, p. 135.

63. On the riots in Groznyi, see the references to them in two separate petitions addressed to the Soviet authorities in the mid-1960s by the Ukrainian political prisoners Sviatoslav Karavans'kyi and Mykhailo Masiutko. Karavans'kyi's comments are provided in Vyacheslav Chornovil, *The Chornovil Papers*, New York, 1968, p. 205; Masiutko's appear in Michael Browne, ed., *Ferment in the Ukraine*, London, 1971, p. 104. For an account of racial tensions in the restored Chechen-Ingush ASSR, see Nekrich, *Punished Peoples*, pp. 146–58.

64. Sheehy and Nahaylo, *National Minorities*, pp. 19–20; Kolarz, 'Nationalities', p. 59.

65. Sheehy and Nahaylo, *National Minorities*, p. 9.

66. Ibid., pp. 24–5.

67. See Remeikis, *Opposition to Soviet Rule in Lithuania*, pp. 65, 275–8.

68. Misiunas and Taagepera, *Baltic States*, pp. 130–1.

69. Kolarz, *Communism and Colonialism*, pp. 72–3.

70. V. Malanchuk, *Torzhestvo lenins'koi natsional'noi polityky (Komunistychna partiia – orhanizator rozv''iazannia natsional'noho pytannia v zakhidnykh oblastiakh URSR)*, Lviv, 1963, p. 564.

71. Bohdan Nahaylo, 'Four Decades of Resistance: An Interview with Danylo Shumuk', RL Supplement 7/87, 25 August 1987.

72. United Nations Special Committee on the Problem of Hungary, *Report of the Special Committee on the Problem of Hungary*, 2 vols., New York, 12 June 1957, vol. 2, pp. 172–5.

73. Conquest, *Back to Life*, pp. 18–20, 40.

74. See Carrère d'Encausse, 'Linguistic Russification', pp. 96–7.

75. AS 4494.

76. Saulius Girnius, 'The Arrest of Enn Tarto and the Crackdown on Baltic Dissent', RL 364/83, 29 September 1983.

77. Boris Weil, *Osobo opasnyi*, London, 1980, p. 227; Aleksandr Gidoni, *Solntse idet s zapada: kniga vospominanii*, Toronto, 1980, pp. 164, 210; Browne, *Ferment in the Ukraine*, pp. 104–5.

10. Khrushchev Changes Course Again

1. Tillett, *The Great Friendship*, pp. 217–21.

2. Lewytzkyj, *Soviet Ukraine*, pp. 31–2.

3. Leo Gruliow, ed., *Current Soviet Policies III: The Documentary Record of the Extraordinary 21st Congress of the Communist Party of the Soviet Union*, New York, 1960, pp. 104–5.

4. B. Gafurov, 'Uspekhi natsional'noi politiki KPSS i nekotorye voprosy internatsional'nogo vospitaniia', *Kommunist*, no. 11, August 1958, pp. 10–24.

5. *Pravda*, 14 November 1958.

6. Yaroslav Bilinsky, 'The Soviet Education Laws of 1958–59 and Soviet Nationality Policy', *Soviet Studies*, no. 2, October 1962, pp. 138–57; John Kolasky, *Education in Soviet Ukraine*, Toronto, 1968, Chapter 3. Unless otherwise indicated, the examples of opposition to

Thesis 19 that follow are taken from these two sources.

7. Roman Solchanyk, 'Language Politics in the Ukraine', in Isabelle T. Kreindler, ed., *Sociolinguistic Perspectives on Soviet National Languages: Their Past, Present and Future*, Berlin, 1985, p. 75.

8. See Aman Berdi Murat, 'Turkmenistan and the Turkmen', in Katz, *Major Soviet Nationalities*, p. 279; Gruliow, *Current Soviet Policies III*, p. 166.

9. Gruliow, *Current Soviet Policies III*, p. 54.

10. Ibid., pp. 50, 52.

11. Ibid., pp. 164–5.

12. G. O. Zimanas, 'Druzhba narodov SSSR i preodolenie perezhitkov burzhuaznogo natsionalizma', *Voprosy filosofii*, no. 1, 1958, pp. 27–38.

13. Gruliow, *Current Soviet Policies III*, pp. 104–6. On economic decentralization, localism and Central Asia, see A. V. Yurchenko, 'Economic Management and "Parochialism" in the Turkestan Republics', *The East Turkic Review*, II, no. 4, December 1960, pp. 3–12; Christian Duevel, 'The Way of "Obliteration": A Progress Report and Some Perspectives', *Problems of the Peoples of the USSR*, no. 20, winter 1963, pp. 12–13.

14. See Tillett, *The Great Friendship*, pp. 259–69.

15. *Literaturnaia gazeta*, 20 May 1959.

16. *Literaturnaia gazeta*, 21 May 1959.

17. Ibid.

18. Ibid.

19. Wolfgang Leonhard, *The Kremlin Since Stalin*, New York, 1962, p. 345.

20. Juris Dreifelds, 'Latvian National Demands and Group Consciousness Since 1959' in George W. Simmonds, ed., *Nationalism in the USSR and Eastern Europe in the Era of Brezhnev and Kosygin*, Detroit, 1977, p. 138.

21. Janis Peters, 'Veriu, ibo uchastvuiu', *Literaturnaia gazeta*, 5 November 1986. For details about the purge, see Misiunas and Taagepera, *The Baltic States*, pp. 134–41.

22. See Dzintra Bungs, 'Veteran Communist Interviewed by RFE', *RFE Research*, Baltic Area/8, 4 August 1988, pp. 15–18; 'Ruki razviazany', *Sovetskaia molodezh'*, 24 September 1988.

23. *V pomoshch' politicheskomu samoobrazovaniiu*, no. 1, January 1960, pp. 28–37, as cited in *CDSP*, XII, no. 5, pp. 16–17.

24. N. Dzandil'din, 'Nekotorye voprosy internatsional'nogo vospitaniia', *Kommunist*, no. 13, 1959, pp. 30–43.

25. A. V. Likholat, *Natsionalizm – vrag trudiashchikhsia*, Moscow, 1986, pp. 311–12.

26. P. Urban, 'The New Soviet Drive Against Nationalism in Turkestan', *The East Turkic Review*, II, no. 4, December 1960, pp. 22–3.

27. Hetmanek, 'Kirgizstan and the Kirgiz', p. 256.

28. Likholat, *Natsionalizm*, p. 312.

29. See ' "Nationalism" in the Soviet Muslim Republics', *Central Asian Review*, VII, no. 4, 1959, pp. 341–3; Teresa Rakowska-Harmstone, 'The Dilemma of Nationalism in the Soviet Union', in J. W. Strong, ed., *The Soviet Union Under Brezhnev and Kosygin: The Transition Years*, New York, 1971, pp. 122–3.

30. Rakowska-Harmstone, *Russia and Nationalism in Central Asia*, pp. 161–2, 175–6.

31. M. D. Kammari, 'Stroitel'stvo kommunizma i dal'neishee sblizhenie natsii v SSSR', *Voprosy filosofii*, no. 9, 1961, pp. 35–6. The idea of a 'Soviet people' was not new: it had been reflected in Russian wartime songs.

32. See Browne, *Ferment in the Ukraine*, pp. 104–5, 227–8; and Lewtyzkyj, *Soviet Ukraine*, pp. 27–8, and n. 54 on p. 39. In Lithuania, in 1957, two former political prisoners – Viktoras Petkus and Petras Paulitis – were among those known to have been arrested. See S. P. de Boer, E. J. Driessen and H. L. Verhaar, eds., *Biographical Dictionary of Dissidents in the Soviet Union, 1956–1975*, The Hague, 1982, pp. 435 and 419–20.

33. Weil, *Osobo opasnyi*, p. 260.

34. Gruliow, *Current Soviet Policies III*, p. 67.

35. The Latvian 'groups' are: the one led by Vilnis Kruklins, who was tried in 1960 (see *A Chronicle of Current Events*, no. 18, 5 March 1971, p. 115); Gunnar Astra's 'anti-Soviet organization' uncovered the following year (Aina Zarins, 'Crackdown on Latvian Dissidents Continues', RL 398/83, 26 October 1983); and the circle formed by Gunnars Rode (Aina Zarins, 'Latvian Dissident Renounces Soviet Citizenship for the Eleventh Time', RL 214/77, 14 September 1977). The Estonian case involved Enn Tarto who was arrested for a second time in 1962 along with four others (*USSR News Brief*, no. 17, 15 September 1983).

36. Zarins, 'Latvian Dissident'.

37. Information about ten of these groups can be found in Browne, *Ferment in the Ukraine*, pp. 227–31. The existence of two other groups has been reported by Danylo Shumuk. See Nahaylo, 'Interview with Danylo Shumuk', p. 14.

38. Browne, *Ferment in the Ukraine*, pp. 60–1.

39. Ibid., p. 37.

40. For details about this case, see ibid., pp. 16–19, 29–93; and Konstantyn Sawchuk, 'Opposition in the Ukraine: Seven Versus the Regime', *Survey*, XX, no. 1, winter 1974, pp. 36–46.

41. Browne, *Ferment in the Ukraine*, pp. 51 and 91.

42. Sheehy and Nahaylo, *National Minorities*, p. 9; Fisher, *The Crimean Tatars*, p. 176.

43. Weil, *Osobo opasnyi*, pp. 283–4.

44. Remeikis, *Opposition to Soviet Rule in Lithuania*, pp. 273–4.

45. Cang, *The Silent Millions*, Chapter 7.

46. Leonard Schroeter, *The Last Exodus*, Seattle, 1974, p. 24.

47. See Patricia Blake and Max Hayward, eds., *Half-way to the Moon: New Writings from Russia*, New York, 1964, pp. 30–1.

48. The text of the Party programme, with all amendments indicated, is published in Charlotte Saikowski and Leo Gruliow, eds., *Current Soviet Policies IV: The Documentary Record of the 22nd Congress of the Communist Party of the Soviet Union*, New York, 1962, pp. 1–33.

49. Saikowski and Gruliow, *Current Soviet Policies IV*, pp. 103–4.

50. Ibid., p. 103.

51. A. Avtorkhanov, 'What is New in Khrushchev's Nationality Policy', *Problems of the Peoples of the USSR*, no. 20, winter 1963, pp. 29–30; Duevel, 'The Way of Obliteration', pp. 5–6. See also Rakowska-Harmstone, *Russia and Nationalism*, p. 91.

52. Alec Nove, *An Economic History of the USSR*, London, 1968, p. 360; Rakowska-Harmstone, 'Dilemma of Nationalism', pp. 124–5.

53. See Grey Hodnett, 'The Debate Over Soviet Federalism', *Soviet Studies*, XVIII, April 1967, pp. 458–81, and 'What's in a Nation?' *Problems of Communism*, XVI, September–October 1967, pp. 2–15.

54. *Literaturnaia gazeta*, 6 February 1962. Cited by Jacob Orstein, 'Soviet Language Policy: Continuity and Change', in Erich Goldhagen, ed., *Ethnic Minorities in the Soviet Union*, New York, pp. 132–3.

55. Ivan Dzyuba, *Internationalism or Russification? A Study in the Soviet Nationalities Problem*, 3rd edn, New York, 1974, pp. 108–12.

56. Bohdan Krawchenko, *Social Change and National Consciousness in Twentieth-Century Ukraine*, Basingstoke, 1985, pp. 217–18.

57. See Bilinsky, *The Second Soviet Republic*, pp. 33–4.

58. Vasyl' Symonenko, *Bereh chekan'*, New York, 1965, p. 104. On the ferment in the Ukraine, see John Kolasky, *Two Years in Soviet Ukraine*, Toronto, 1970; Victor Swoboda, 'Cat and Mouse in the Ukraine', *Index on Censorship*, no. 1, 1973, pp. 81–9; and G. Luckyj, 'Turmoil in the Ukraine', *Problems of Communism*, XXVII, no. 4, July–August 1967, pp. 14–16.

59. *Chyrvonaia zmena*, 13 January 1963. See *Problems of the Peoples of the USSR*, no. 17, March 1963, p. 62.

60. Ibid., no. 20, winter 1963, pp. 54–5.

61. *Pravda Vostoka*, 27 June 1962. Cited in Allen Hetmanek, 'Intensified Campaign Against Nationalism in Soviet Central Asia', *Radio Liberty Dispatch*, 16 June 1962, p. 3.

62. F. Tabeev, 'Internatsional'noe vospitanie trudiashchikhsia i politicheskoe prosveshchenie', *Politicheskoe samoobrazovanie*, no. 1, 1963, pp. 75–84. See *Problems of the Peoples of the USSR*, no. 17, March 1963, p. 65.

63. See also Roman Shumliansky, ' "Watch Your Language!" Much Ado About Words in Georgia', *Problems of the Peoples of the USSR*, no. 20, winter 1963, pp. 35–44.

64. Michael Bourdeaux, *Patriarch and Prophets: Persecution of the Russian Orthodox Church*, London, 1975, pp. 30–1.

65. S. N. Pavlov, 'O sovremennom sostoianii russkoi pravoslavnoi tserkvi', *Sotsiologicheskie issledovaniia*, no. 4, July–August 1987, p. 41.

66. Alexandre Bennigsen and S. Enders Wimbush, *Muslims of the Soviet Empire*, Bloomington, 1986, p. 12.

67. Cang, *The Silent Millions*, p. 147.

68. Vardys, *Soviet Lithuania*, 1978, pp. 83–6.

69. *Gaisma*, no. 2, 1983.

70. See for example the 'exposé' on the underground life of the Ukrainian Catholic Church by Alla Trubnikova, 'Chemodan s dvoinym dnom', *Ogonek*, no. 46, 1963, pp. 30–1.

71. S. Andreev, *Pravda*, 19 March 1987. As cited in BBC Summary of World Broadcasts SU/8525/B/2, 25 March 1987.

72. John B. Dunlop, *The Faces of Contemporary Russian Nationalism*, Princeton, 1983, pp. 66–7.

73. Dimitry Pospielovsky, 'The Resurgence of Russian Nationalism in *Samizdat*', *Survey*, no. 1, winter 1973, p. 52.

74. Ludmilla Alexeyeva, *Soviet Dissent: Contemporary Movements for National, Religious, and Human Rights*, Middletown, Conn., 1985, pp. 123–34.

75. See Browne, *Ferment in the Ukraine*, pp. 233–4; *A Chronicle of Current Events*, no. 17, 31 December 1970, pp. 64–6; and Nina Strokata, 'Ukrains'kyi Natsional'nyi Front', *Suchasnist'*, June 1985, pp. 67–75. Strokata thinks that this group may have been formed before 1964.

76. For two different appraisals of

VSKhSON, see John. B. Dunlop, *The New Russian Revolutionaries*, Belmont, Mass., 1976, and Alexander Yanov, *The Russian Challenge and the Year 2000*, Oxford, 1987, Chapter 9.

77. Sheehy and Nahaylo, *National Minorities*, p. 10; Fisher, *The Crimean Tatars*, p. 177.

78. Sheehy and Nahaylo, *National Minorities*, p. 25.

79. Ibid., pp. 20–1.

80. Schroeter, *The Last Exodus*, p. 25. On the anti-Jewish campaign, see also Cang, *The Silent Millions*, Chapter 8; and William Korey, *The Soviet Cage: Anti-Semitism in Russia*, New York, 1973, pp. 78–82.

81. Cang, *The Silent Millions*, pp. 163–4.

82. Stephen Fischer-Galati, 'The Moldavian Soviet Republic in Soviet Domestic and Foreign Policy', in Roman Szporluk, ed., *The Influence of East Europe and the Soviet West on the USSR*, New York, 1975, pp. 244–5. On Mao's statement about Bessarabia, see William E. Griffith, *Sino–Soviet Relations, 1964–1965*, Cambridge, Mass., 1967, pp. 28–9.

11. Brezhnev and Kosygin Make Their Mark

1. See George W. Breslauer, *Khrushchev and Brezhnev as Political Leaders: Building Authority in Soviet Politics*, London, 1982, pp. 171–2.

2. Robert Conquest, *Soviet Nationalities Policy in Practice*, London, 1967, pp. 127–9; Lewytzkyj, *Soviet Ukraine*, pp. 95–6.

3. Based on an interview with Leon Mardirossian (Munich, May 1988), who participated in the demonstrations, and the account in Alexeyeva, *Soviet Dissent*, p. 123.

4. Mary Matossian, 'The Armenians', *Problems of Communism*, XVI, no. 5, September–October 1967, p. 68.

5. Hodnett, 'What's in a Nation?', p. 4.

6. Dunlop, *Faces of Russian Nationalism*, p. 38.

7. Ibid., p. 38; Pospielovsky, 'Resurgence of Russian Nationalism', pp. 52–3.

8. Bohdan Bociurkiw, 'Religion in the USSR after Khrushchev', in John W. Strong, ed., *The Soviet Union Under Brezhnev and Kosygin*, New York, 1971, pp. 137–8.

9. Peter Reddaway, 'Freedom of Worship and the Law', in Abraham Brumberg, ed., *In Quest of Justice*, London, 1970, pp. 65–6.

10. See the *samizdat* account of this meeting in Stephen F. Cohen, *An End to Silence: Uncensored Opinion in the Soviet Union from Roy Medvedev's Magazine 'Political Diary'*, New York, 1982, pp. 240–4.

11. Sheehy and Nahaylo, *National Minorities*, p. 10.

12. This account of the arrests and trials in the Ukraine is based on Bohdan Nahaylo, 'Beyond the Sinyavsky–Daniel' Case: the Twentieth Anniversary of the KGB Crackdown in the Ukraine', RL 288/85, 4 September 1985.

13. Browne, *Ferment in the Ukraine*, pp. 4–5.

14. This information was provided by the Ukrainian dissident Viacheslav Chornovil in a document published in the sixth issue of the *samizdat* journal, the *Ukrainian Herald*, dated March 1972. See *Ukrains'kyi visnyk: vypusk VI*, Paris, 1972, pp. 24–30.

15. AS 912; reprinted in Roman Kupchinsky, ed., *Natsional'nyi vopros v SSSR: sbornik dokumentov*, Munich, 1975, pp. 133–42.

16. Dzyuba, *Internationalism or Russification?*, pp. 213–14.

17. Ibid., pp. 13–14.

18. Ibid., p. 204.

19. Ibid., p. 6.

20. An English translation of Dziuba's address at Babii Iar can be found in Brumberg, *In Quest of Justice*, pp. 200–4.

21. Sheehy and Nahaylo, *National Minorities*, p. 10.

22. AS 1217 (this document is erroneously dated autumn 1965). For a brief discussion of Kaputikian's speech, see V. N. Dadrian, 'Sources of Armenian Unrest', *Problems of Communism*, XVI, no. 5, September–October 1967, p. 71.

23. Fischer-Galati, 'The Moldavian Soviet Republic', pp. 244–6.

24. *Pravda*, 30 March 1966.

25. *Pravda*, 2 April 1966.
26. *Pravda*, 30 March 1966, as translated in *CDSP*, XVIII, no. 16, pp. 8–9.
27. Hodnett, 'What's in a Nation?', pp. 4, 14–15.
28. Roman Szporluk, 'Nationalities and the Russian Problem in the USSR: an Historical Outline', *Journal of International Affairs*, 27, no. 1, 1973, p. 37.
29. *Vil'ne slovo*, 9 November 1968. See 'The Glitter of Celebrations – and the Somber Reality', RFE Research Paper, USSR/7, 10 January 1969, p. 5.
30. Chornovil, *The Chornovil Papers*, p. 210.
31. 'Rech' Vasilia Bykova na s"ezde Soiuza pisatelei Belorussii', *Grani*, XXI, no. 61, 1966, pp. 113–21.
32. Dadrian, 'Armenian Unrest', p. 71.
33. *V z"izd pys'mennykiv Ukrainy 16–19 lystopada 1966 roku*, Kiev, 1967, p. 59.
34. 'XXII s"ezd KPSS i zadachi izucheniia zakonomernostei razvitiia sovremennykh natsional'nykh iazykov Sovetskogo Soiuza', *Voprosy iazykoznaniia*, no. 1, 1962, pp. 5–6.
35. *V z"izd pys'mennykiv Ukrainy*, pp. 225–9.
36. Ibid., pp. 194–5.
37. Ibid., pp. 21–2, 24–5.
38. *Pravda*, 24 May 1967, as cited in *CDSP*, XIX, no. 22, p. 12.
39. 'How KGB Still Keeps a Grip on the Ukraine: Journalist Sent to Labour Camp for His Outcry Against Injustice', *The Times*, 7 February 1968; 'The Tomalin Winners', *Sunday Times*, 14 December 1975.
40. Browne, *Ferment in the Ukraine*, p. 159.
41. Ibid., p. 97.
42. Ibid., pp. 119–53.
43. On Karavans'kyi and his protest writings, see in Chornovil, *The Chornovil Papers*, pp. 166–221, especially pp. 198–207.
44. Interview with Aishe Seitmuratova, London, March 1980.
45. Sheehy and Nahaylo, *National Minorities*, p. 11; Fisher, *The Crimean Tatars*, pp. 178–81.
46. See Korey, *The Soviet Cage*, Chapter

7; Joshua Rubenstein, *Soviet Dissidents: Their Struggle for Human Rights*, Boston, 1980, p. 158.
47. Browne, *Ferment in the Ukraine*, p. 2.
48. AS 5225, p. 8.
49. Allen Hetmanek, 'Intensified Campaign Against Nationalism in Soviet Central Asia', *Radio Liberty Dispatch*, 16 June 1969, p. 3.
50. As cited in Alexandre Bennigsen and S. Enders Wimbush, *Mystics and Commissars: Sufism in the Soviet Union*, London, 1985, p. 51.
51. Pospielovsky, 'Russian Nationalism in Samizdat', p. 53; Alexander Yanov, *The Russian New Right: Right Wing Ideologies in the Contemporary USSR*, Berkeley, 1978, p. 13.
52. On the *derevenshchiki*, see Deming Brown, *Soviet Russian Literature Since Stalin*, Cambridge, 1978, Chapter 8; Geoffrey Hosking, *Beyond Socialist: Realism: Soviet Fiction Since Ivan Denisovich*, London, 1980, Chapter 3.
53. Andrei Amalrik, *Will the Soviet Union Survive Until 1984?*, revised edn, Harmondsworth, 1980, p. 41; Peter Reddaway, *Uncensored Russia: The Human Rights Movement in the Soviet Union*, London, 1972, pp. 430–1; Yanov, *The Russian New Right*, p. 13.
54. See Cohen, *An End to Silence*, pp. 171–4; Yanov, *The Russian New Right*, p. 12.
55. See Reddaway, *Uncensored Russia*, pp. 431–3.
56. *Pravda*, 11 April 1968; *Sovetskaia Rossiia*, 13 April 1968.
57. See Abraham Rothberg, *The Heirs of Stalin: Dissidence and the Soviet Regime, 1953–1970*, Ithaca, 1972, pp. 235–44.
58. Sheehy and Nahaylo, *National Minorities*, p. 14; see English text of the appeal in Reddaway, *Uncensored Russia*, pp. 249–52.
59. See Nekrich, *The Punished Peoples*, p. 155; Reddaway, *Uncensored Russia*, pp. 130–1, 253.
60. See English text of Grigorenko's speech on this subject in Brumberg, *In Quest of Justice*, pp. 208–13.

61. AS 100, p. 4.

62. On the *Chronicle*, see Reddaway, *Uncensored Russia*, and Mark Hopkins, *Russia's Underground Press: The Chronicle of Current Events*, New York, 1983.

63. Andrei Sakharov, *Progress, Coexistence and Intellectual Freedom*, New York, 1968, pp. 66, 54, 56–66.

64. See English text in Bohdan R. Bociurkiw, 'Political Dissent in the Soviet Union', *Studies in Comparative Communism*, vol. 3, no. 2, April 1979, pp. 145–8.

65. Yaroslav Bihun, ed., *Boomerang: The Works of Valentyn Moroz*, Baltimore-Paris, 1974, pp. 146–7.

66. See Grey Hodnett and Peter J. Potichnyj, *The Ukraine and the Czechoslovak Crisis*, Canberra, 1970.

67. For an account by one of the participants, see Natalia Gorbanevskaya, *Red Square at Noon*, Harmondsworth, 1973.

68. Reddaway, *Uncensored Russia*, p. 101.

69. See the brief history of the National Unification Party by one of its leading activists, Paruir Airikian, in *Russkaia mysl'*, 22 April 1988, p. 6; and in Alexeyeva, *Soviet Dissent*, pp. 124–5.

70. Reddaway, *Uncensored Russia*, pp. 257–62.

71. For further details about Moroz see Bihun, *Boomerang*.

72. Reddaway, *Uncensored Russia*, pp. 274–9; Sheehy and Nahaylo, *National Minorities*, p. 26.

73. Vardys, *Soviet Lithuania*, Chapters IX and X, and pp. 170–1.

74. Saunders, *Samizdat*, pp. 427–40.

75. Reddaway, *Uncensored Russia*, p. 295.

76. Anatole Shub, *The New Russian Tragedy*, New York, 1969, pp. 23–4, 104–5.

77. Reddaway, *Uncensored Russia*, p. 295–6.

78. Ibid., pp. 243–4.

79. Ibid., pp. 402–3.

80. Ibid., p. 403.

81. His case was mentioned by the Ukrainian political prisoner Yosyp Terelya in an open letter to Andropov written in 1976. Terelya met him in the early 1970s in the Sychovka prison psychiatric hospital. AS 2118. Translated in Yosyp Terelya, *Notes from a Madhouse*, Baltimore-Washington, 1977. See p. 9.

82. Frank Huddle, Jr., 'Azerbaijan and the Azerbaijanis', in Katz, *Handbook*, p. 206.

83. Korey, *The Soviet Cage*, Chapters 11, 12, 13, 14; Schroeter, *The Last Exodus*, Chapters 10–12.

84. Reddaway, *Uncensored Russia*, pp. 150–2.

85. AS 340. Published separately as *Programma Demokraticheskogo Dvizheniia Sovetskogo Soiuza*, Amsterdam, 1970.

86. Interview with Sergei Soldatov, London, September 1982.

87. See *Ukrains'kyi visnyk: vypusk VI*, pp. 140–2.

88. A. E. Levitin-Krasnov, *Rodnoi prostor: Demokraticheskoe dvizhenie. Vospominaniia, Chast' IV*, Frankfurt, 1981, pp. 246–51.

89. See Bohdan Nahaylo, 'Ukrainian Dissent and Opposition after Shelest', in Bohdan Krawchenko, ed., *Ukraine After Shelest*, Edmonton, 1983, p. 32.

90. Interview with Seitmuratova.

91. Amalrik, *Will the Soviet Union Survive Until 1984?*, pp. 59–61.

92. *International Herald Tribune*, 31 March 1969.

93. On this theme, see for example, 'Soviet Nationalities' Policies: Peking's Newest Propaganda Trick', *Radio Free Europe Research*, USSR/0257, 28 July 1969; Allen Hetmanek, 'The Turkic Peoples as Pawns in the Sino–Soviet Struggle', *Radio Liberty Dispatch*, 19 September 1969; Gretchen S. Brainerd, 'Soviets Intensify Propaganda to Moslem Nationalities in China', *Radio Liberty Dispatch*, 14 February 1972; Lewytzkyj, *Soviet Ukraine*, pp. 217–29.

94. V. Perevedentsev, *Literaturnaia gazeta*, 11 January 1967; as cited in *CDSP*, XIX, no. 2, p. 15.

95. V. Perevedentsev, *Literaturnaia gazeta*, 20 March 1968; as cited in *CDSP*, XX, no. 12, p. 9.

96. *Pravda*, 24 December 1967; as cited in *CDSP*, XIX, no. 51, p. 11.

97. 'Torzhestvo Leninskoi natsional'noi politiki', *Kommunist*, no. 13, September 1969, pp. 10–11.

98. Ibid., p.12.

99. *Entsyklopediia kibernetyky*, 2 vols., Kiev, 1973. See also Jaroslaw Pelenski, 'Shelest and His Period in Soviet Ukraine (1963–1972): A Revival of Controlled Ukrainian Autonomism', in Peter J. Potichnyj, ed., *Ukraine in the Seventies*, Oakville, Ontario, 1975, pp. 291–2.

100. P. Iu. Shelest, *Ukraino nasha radians'ka*, Kiev, 1970.

101. Vitalii Koval', ' "Sobor" i navkolo n'oho', *Dnipro*, no. 4, April 1988, p. 36.

102. M. Iu. Braichevs'kyi, *Pryiednannia chy vozz"iednannia?* in *Shyroke more Ukrainy: Documenty samvydavu z Ukrainy*, Paris-Baltimore, 1972, pp. 241–312, 235–7.

103. *Istoriia mist i sil Ukrains'koi RSR v dvadtsiaty shesty tomakh*, Kiev, 1967–74. For an overview of developments in the historiographical sphere under Shelest, see Pelenski, 'Shelest and His Period'.

104. Pelenski, 'Shelest and His Period', pp. 290–1.

105. V. Korets'kyi and V. Babii, 'Radians'ka bahatonatsional'na derzhava – uosoblennia iednosti i druzhby bratnikh respublik', *Radians'ke pravo*, no. 10, 1977, pp. 10–15. Pelenski, 'Shelest and His Period', p. 297.

106. James Critchlow, 'Nationalism in Uzbekistan in the Brezhnev Era', in Simmonds, *Nationalism in the USSR*, p. 312; James Critchlow, 'New Hint of National Communism in Central Asia', *Radio Liberty Dispatch*, 20 November 1969. Lenin's letter is quoted on p. 42 above.

107. Critchlow, 'Nationalism in Uzbekistan', p. 313. The appeal is quoted on p. 32 above.

108. See, for instance, Anna Procyk, 'The Search for a Heritage and the Nationality Question in Central Asia', in Edward Allworth, ed., *The Nationality Question in Central Asia*, New York, 1973, pp. 123–33; Teresa Rakowska-Harmstone, 'Nationalism in Soviet Central Asia' in Simmonds, *Nationalism in the USSR*, pp. 272–94;

Allen Hetmanek, 'National Renascence in Soviet Kazakhstan: The Brezhnev Era', in Simmonds, *Nationalism in the USSR*, pp. 295–305; David Nissman, 'Recent Developments in the Study of the Uzbek Central Asian Heritage', *Radio Liberty Research Paper*, no. 35, 1970.

109. Critchlow, 'Nationalism in Uzbekistan', p. 310; Reddaway, *Uncensored Russia*, pp. 392–3.

110. Her case was reported in the *Chronicle of Current Events*, no. 22, 10 November 1971, p. 29.

111. *Soviet Tojikistan*, 16 September 1970. See 'The Resurgence of Islam in Soviet Central Asia as Reflected in Soviet Media in the Summer of 1970', *Radio Liberty Dispatch*, 17 February 1971, p. 2.

112. See Alexander Yanov, *The Russian Challenge and the Year 2000*, Oxford, 1987, Chapter 10; Michael Scammell, 'Soviet Intellectuals Soldier On', *Survey*, 16, no. 1, winter 1971, p. 100.

113. Scammell, 'Soviet Intellectuals', p. 100.

114. Jonathan Harris, 'The Dilemma of Dissidence', *Survey*, 16, no. 1, winter 1971, p. 121.

115. Peter Reddaway, 'Policy Towards Dissent Since Khrushchev', in T. H. Rigby, Archie Brown and Peter Reddaway, eds., *Authority, Power and Policy in the USSR*, New York, 1980, pp. 165–6.

116. Yanov, *The Russian Challenge*, p. 113.

117. On *Veche*, see, for example, Yanov, *The Russian Challenge*, Chapter 11; Dunlop, *Faces of Russian Nationalism*; D. P. Hammer, 'Vladimir Osipov and the *Veche* Group (1971–1974): A Page from the History of Political Dissent', *Russian Review*, XLIII, no. 4, October 1984, pp. 355–75; Peter J. S. Duncan, 'The Fate of Russian Nationalism: The *Samizdat* Journal *Veche* Revisited', *Religion in Communist Lands*, 16, no. 1, spring 1988, pp. 36–53.

118. For an English translation of this document, see 'A Word to the Nation', *Survey*, 17, no. 3, summer 1971, pp. 191–9.

119. *Pravda*, 31 March 1971, as cited in

CDSP, XXIII, no. 14, p. 3.
120. Ibid.

12. Forging the Soviet People

1. *Izvestia*, 17 April 1971. For analysis of the results, see Roman Szporluk, 'The Nations of the USSR in 1970', *Survey*, 17, no. 4, 1971, pp. 67–100; Rein Taagepera, 'The 1970 Census: Fusion or Crystallization of Nationalities?' *Soviet Studies*, October 1971, pp. 216–21; J. A. Newth, 'The 1970 Soviet Census', *Soviet Studies*, October 1972, pp. 200–22.
2. For data, see Roman Solchanyk, 'Russian Language and Soviet Politics', *Soviet Studies*, XXXIV, no. 1, January 1982, p. 26.
3. See Roman Szporluk, 'Recent Trends in Soviet Policy Towards Printed Media in the Non-Russian Languages', RL Supplement, 7 November 1984.
4. V. Guseinov and V. Korchagin, 'Voprosy trudovykh resursov', *Voprosy ekonomiki*; cited in *CDSP*, XXIII, no. 18, p. 7.
5. B. Urlanis, 'Nasha obshchaia biografiia', *Literaturnaia gazeta*, 28 April 1971.
6. E. Bagramov, 'Razvitie i sblizhenie sotsialisticheskikh natsii', *Pravda*, 16 July 1971; cited in *CDSP*, XXIII, no. 28, p. 8.
7. Ruslan O. Rasiak, ' "The Soviet People": Multiethnic Alternative or Ruse?' in Edward Allworth, ed., *Ethnic Russia: The Dilemma of Dominance*, New York, 1980, p. 166.
8. Brian D. Silver, 'The Status of National Minority Languages in Soviet Education: An Assessment of Recent Changes', *Soviet Studies*, XXVI, no. 1, January 1974, p. 40.
9. E. Mordionov, 'Aktual'nye problemy razvitiia mezhnatsional'nykh otnoshenii v SSSR', *Voprosy filosofii*, no. 6, 1971, pp. 27–8.
10. *Pravda*, 16 July 1971; *CDSP*, XXIII, no. 28, p. 8. (Emphasis added.)
11. V. P. Sherstobitov, 'Obrazovanie SSSR i istoricheskie sud'by narodov nashei strany', *Istoriia SSSR*, no. 3, May–June 1972, pp. 20–41, as cited in *CDSP*, XXIV, no. 44, p. 15.
12. *Istoriia SSSR*, no. 3, May–June 1972, pp. 139–45, as cited in *CDSP*, XXIV, no. 44, pp. 14–15.
13. See Hetmanek, 'Kirgizstan and the Kirgiz', pp. 257–8, and 'Nationality and the Power Struggle', *Soviet Analyst*, 2, no. 4, 15 February 1973, p. 4.
14. Sheehy and Nahaylo, *National Minorities*, p. 26.
15. M. Suslov, 'Obshchestvennye nauki – boevoe oruzhie partii v stroitel'stve kommunizma', *Kommunist*, no. 1, January 1972, p. 24.
16. Reddaway, 'Policy Towards Dissent', p. 172; Hopkins, *Russia's Underground Press*, Chapter 3.
17. Peter Reddaway, 'The Development of Dissent and Opposition' in Archie Brown and Michael Kaser, eds, *The Soviet Union Since the Fall of Khrushchev*, New York, 1975, p. 137.
18. On these developments, see Nahaylo, 'Ukrainian Dissent and Opposition', pp. 30–5; 'The Braychevsky Case: Retractions in the Ukraine', *RFER*, 16 May 1973; *Ukrainian Herald 7–8*, pp. 12–28, 137–8; Bohdan R. Bociurkiw, 'Soviet Nationalities Policy and Dissent in the Ukraine', *The World Today*, May 1974, pp. 214–26.
19. Christian Dueval, 'An Unprecedented Plenum of the CPSU Central Committee', *Radio Liberty Dispatch*, 3 May 1972, p. 4; Lowell Tillett, 'Ukrainian Nationalism and the Fall of Shelest', *Slavic Review*, vol. 34, no. 4, December 1975, pp. 752–67.
20. For details about the extent of the purge, see *Ukrainian Herald 7–8*, pp. 125–61; Roman Solchanyk, 'Politics and the National Question in the Post-Shelest Period', in Krawchenko, *Ukraine After Shelest*, pp. 6–9.
21. Tillett, 'Fall of Shelest', p. 752.
22. *Zhovten'*, no. 2, 1988, p. 86, and no. 4, p. 62; *Molod' Ukrainy*, 3 May 1988, p. 4. Shelest was to surface again in the summer of 1988 when he was interviewed by *Stroitel'naia gazeta* on the eve of the 19th Party Conference. See Bohdan Nahaylo, 'Disgraced Ukrainian Party Leader Petro Shelest Reappears after Fifteen Years – A Slap in the Face for

Shcherbitsky?' RL 293/88, 29 July 1988.
23. *Argumenty i fakty*, no. 2, 1989, pp. 14–20. See also his later, more detailed interview in *Kyiv*, no. 10, 1989, pp. 90–110.
24. For general details, see Nahaylo, 'Ukrainian Dissent and Opposition', pp. 35–6; *Ukrainian Herald 7–8*, pp. 138–40. On Pliushch's case, see his illuminating autobiography: *History's Carnival: A Dissident's Biography*, New York, 1979.
25. A S 2307. Reprinted as V. Stus, 'Ia obvynuvachuiu' (dated 1975), in Roman Kupchyns'kyi, *Pohrom v Ukraini*, [Munich], 1980, pp. 40–4.
26. *Ukrainian Herald 7–8*, pp. 131–2.
27. Hetmanek, 'National Renascence in Soviet Kazakhstan', p. 303. See also Anna Procyk, 'The Search for a Heritage and the Nationality Question in Central Asia' in Allworth, *The Nationality Question in Soviet Central Asia*, p. 124.
28. On the aftermath of the 'General Pogrom', see *Ukrainian Herald 7–8*, pp. 131–54; and Solchanyk, 'Politics and the National Question'. In the spring of 1988 a Ukrainian writer charged that in 1973 a 'taboo was placed on all Ukrainian historiography and historical novels'. See Roman Ivanychuk, 'Dukhovne zdorov''ia i nihilistychnyi virus', *Kyiv*, no. 4, April 1988, p. 119.
29. See 'Soviet Socialist Republic – Georgian Style', *Soviet Analyst*, 3, no. 18, 5 September 1974, pp. 5–7; Peter Reddaway, 'The Georgian Orthodox Church: Corruption and Renewal', *Religion in Communist Lands*, 3, nos. 4–5, July–October 1975, p. 15.
30. 'Stamping Out Shelestism', *Soviet Analyst*, 2, no. 12, 7 June 1973, p. 3.
31. *Handbook of Central Asia*, monograph prepared for the Bureau of Social Science Research, American University, Washington, DC, 1956, p. 402.
32. Nancy Lubin, *Labour and Nationality in Soviet Central Asia: An Uneasy Compromise*, London, 1984, p. 164.
33. Christian Dueval, 'Nationalist Rumblings in Georgia', *Radio Liberty Dispatch*, 10 May 1972.
34. See Reddaway, 'The Georgian

Orthodox Church', and *A Chronicle of Current Events*, no. 32, 17 July 1974, pp. 46–8.
35. Vardys, *Soviet Lithuania*, Chapter XI; *The Chronicle of the Catholic Church in Lithuania: Underground Journal of Human Rights Violations, 1, nos. 1–9, 1972–74*, Chicago, 1981.
36. Vardys, *Soviet Lithuania*, pp. 144–5.
37. Ibid., p. 175, n. 21.
38. Ibid., pp. 173–81; and Remeikis, *Opposition to Soviet Rule in Lithuania*, pp. 118–20.
39. See Aina Zarins, 'Dissent in the Baltic Republics: A Survey of Grievances and Hopes', RL 496/76, 14 December 1976, pp. 8–10; and A S 1892.
40. See Bohdan Nahaylo, 'The Tenth Anniversary of the Death of the Buddhist Scholar Bidia Dandaron in a Soviet Labour Camp', RL 412/84, 25 October 1984.
41. A. Iakovlev, 'Protiv antiistorizma', *Literaturnaia gazeta*, 15 November 1972, as cited in *CDSP*, XXIV, no. 47, pp. 1–7. (Emphasis added.)
42. *Pravda*, 25 November 1972. See *CDSP*, XXIV, no. 47, p. 1.
43. *International Herald Tribune*, 21 December 1972.
44. A S 1775. Reprinted in *Vol'noe slovo*, no. 17–18, 1975, pp. 19–51.
45. As translated by Dunlop in *Faces of Russian Nationalism*, pp. 231–2. The Iakovlev affair and *Veche*'s responses are discussed by Dunlop in the same work on pp. 227–33, and by Yanov in *The Russian Challenge*, pp. 120–3.
46. *Veche*'s response to Iakovlev, for instance, referred to 'international cosmopolitan [that is, Jewish] forces', as being among the 'enemies of Russia'. *Vol'noe slovo*, no. 17–18, p. 51.
47. *Pravda*, 22 December 1972, as cited in *CDSP*, XXIV, no. 51, pp. 3–20.
48. Aleksandra E. Pavlova, 'The Party and the Classes in a Developed Socialist Society', *Znanie* pamphlet, No. 10, 1972 (History and CPSU Policy series), p. 5, as cited by Christian Duevel in ' "Accelerated" or "Gradual"

Assimilation', *Radio Liberty Dispatch*, 9 January 1973.

49. *CDSP*, XXIV, no. 51, pp. 8, 17–18.

50. V. Kistanov, 'Leninskaia natsional'naia politika i ekonomicheskoe raionirovanie v SSSR', *Voprosy ekonomiki*, no. 12, 1972, pp. 56–65. For a discussion of the implications of this article, see 'Moscow Redraws the Map', *Soviet Analyst*, 2, no. 16, 2 August 1973, p. 4.

51. D. Malabaev and M. Dzhanuzakov, 'Berech' i ukrepliat' velikoe bratstvo', *Sovetskaia Kirgizia*, 7 December 1972.

52. See Duevel, ' "Accelerated" or "Gradual" Assimilation'; Michael Rywkin, 'The Code Words and Catchwords of Brezhnev's Nationality Policy', RL 331/76, 29 June 1976, pp. 2–3.

53. Christian Duevel, 'USSR Government Official Contradicts "Voprosy Ekonomiki" on Boundary Issue', *Radio Liberty Dispatch*, 19 January 1973.

54. Christian Duevel, 'Mazurov at Odds with Suslov – on the Nationality Question', *Radio Liberty Dispatch*, 15 January 1974.

55. *Pravda*, 16 August 1973.

56. 'Internatsionalizm sovetskogo naroda', *Kommunist*, no. 13, September 1973, p. 6.

57. See the interview with Chingiz Aitmatov, 'Tsena prozreniia', *Ogonek*, no. 28, July 1987, p. 8; Janis Peters, 'Podlinnyi internatsionalizm predpolagaet . . .', *Literaturnaia gazeta*, 18 November 1987, pp. 1 and 3.

58. *Sovetskaia pedagogika*, no. 3, 1973, p. 108, as cited in 'Russian in Kindergarten – New Ideas in Internationalist Education', *Radio Free Europe Research*, 11 July 1973, p. 4.

59. For an account of these developments, see Solchanyk, 'Russian Language and Soviet Politics', pp. 25–8.

60. *Russkii iazyk: ego rol' v razvitii i ukreplenii sovetskogo obshchestva i mezhdunarodnogo sotrudnichestva*, Moscow, 1977, p. 22.

61. Iu. Desheriev, cited in Solchanyk, 'Russian Language and Soviet Politics', p. 25.

62. Leokadiia Drobizheva, 'My zhivem v mnogonatsional'noi strane', *Moskovskie*

novosti, no. 22, 31 May 1987, p. 7.

63. Iurii Badzo, 'An Open Letter to the Presidium of the Supreme Soviet of the USSR and the Central Committee of the CPSU', Part 2, *Journal of Ukrainian Studies* (Toronto), no. 17, winter 1984, p. 62; Solchanyk, 'Russian Language and Soviet Politics', p. 36.

64. Oles' Honchar, 'To zvidky zh vzialasia "zvizda Polyn"?' *Literaturna Ukraina*, 7 October 1987, p. 3; Oles' Gonchar, 'Otkuda iavilas' "zvezda Polyn"?' *Literaturnaia gazeta*, 9 December 1987, p. 2. Note that the Russian version was abridged.

65. Roman Szporluk, 'Policy Towards Printed Media in the Non-Russian Languages'.

66. Marko Horbach, 'I shche odyn zasib rusyfikatsii', *Vitrazh* (London), no. 4, summer 1978, pp. 31–3.

67. *Pravda*, 25 September 1973, as cited in *CDSP*, XXV, no. 39, p. 5.

68. *Pravda Ukrainy*, 5 October 1973, p. 2.

69. George B. Hewitt, 'Georgian: A Noble Past, a Secure Future', in Kreindler, *Sociolinguistic Perspectives*, p. 174.

70. Rywkin, 'Code Words', p. 5.

71. *Pravda*, 29 February 1976, as cited in *CDSP*, XXVIII, no. 13, p. 15.

72. *Pravda*, 27 February 1976, as cited in *CDSP*, XXVIII, no. 10, p. 12.

73. See Nahaylo, 'Ukrainian Dissent and Opposition', pp. 37–40. For an example of one of the renunciations of Soviet citizenship, see V. Chornovil, 'I renounce my citizenship', *Index on Censorship*, 5, no. 1, spring 1976, p. 62.

74. AS 3059.

75. *A Chronicle of Current Events*, no. 34, 31 December 1974, p. 14.

76. Peter Reddaway, 'Soviet Union: Dirty Tricks in Georgia', *Index on Censorship*, 5, no. 1, spring 1976, p. 73.

77. Alexeyeva, *Soviet Dissent*, p. 116.

78. For the text of Dzhaparidze's speech, see 'USSR: The Georgian Language', *Index on Censorship*, 5, no. 4, winter 1976, pp. 75–6.

79. AS 2869; 'The Recent Protests in Georgia', RL 401/76, 31 August 1976;

'Georgia: Explosive Republic', *Soviet Analyst*, 6, no. 3, 10 February 1977, pp. 5–7; 'Publicity Given to Recent Trials in the Georgian SSR', RL 42/77, 23 February 1977.

80. Alexeyeva, *Soviet Dissent*, pp. 128–30.

81. *Zaria Vostoka*, 27 April 1973; as cited in *CDSP*, XXV, no. 16, p. 5.

82. Roman Solchanyk and Ann Sheehy, 'Kapitonov on Nationality Relations in Georgia', RL 125/78, 1 June 1978.

83. Nekrich, *Punished Peoples*, pp. 158–66.

84. These developments are surveyed by Zarins in 'Dissent in the Baltic Republics'.

85. AS 1724.

86. Reproduced in *A Chronicle of Human Rights in the USSR*, no. 22, July–September 1976, p. 34.

87. Reddaway, 'Development of Dissent and Opposition', pp. 140–1; Alexeyeva, *Soviet Dissent*, pp. 181–91.

88. Sheehy and Nahaylo, *National Minorities*, p. 23.

89. *A Chronicle of Current Events*, no. 31, 17 May 1974, pp. 152–5.

90. Reuters, 11 December 1974; *Financial Times*, 12 December 1974.

91. See Ivan Maistrenko, *Natsional'naia politika KPSS*, Munich, 1978, p. 209.

92. See 'Selected Quotations on the Nationality Problem in the USSR', RL 16/76, 9 January 1976.

93. Valery Chalidze, *To Defend These Rights: Human Rights and the Soviet Union*, New York, 1974, pp. 164, 167.

94. Andrei Sakharov, *My Country and My World*, New York, 1976, p. 97.

95. AS 2364.

96. Reddaway, 'Development of Dissent and Opposition', p. 144.

97. Hammer, 'Vladimir Osipov and the *Veche* Group', pp. 364–5.

98. Peter J. S. Duncan, 'The Fate of Russian Nationalism: The *Samizdat* Journal *Veche* Revisited', *Religion in Communist Lands*, 16, no. 1, spring 1988, pp. 50–2.

99. See Frederique Diat, 'Olzhas Sulejmanov: "Az i ja" ', *Central Asian Survey*, 3, no. 1, 1984, pp. 101–21; and Ignacy Szenfeld, 'Olzhas Suleimanov

Under Fire from Neoslavophile Critics', RL 137/76, 15 March 1976.

100. *Conference on Security and Cooperation in Europe: Final Act*, Helsinki, 1975, pp. 80–1.

101. See Nahaylo, 'Ukrainian Dissent and Opposition', pp. 43–8. Many of the documents of the Ukrainian Helsinki monitoring group are available in English translation in Lesya Verba and Bohdan Yasen, eds., *The Human Rights Movement in Ukraine: Documents of the Ukrainian Helsinki Group 1976–1980*, Baltimore, 1980.

102. Remeikis, *Opposition to Soviet Rule in Lithuania*, pp. 144–52; 'Documents Issued by Lithuanian Helsinki Group', RL 242/77, 19 October 1977.

103. Alexeyeva, *Soviet Dissent*, p. 115.

104. AS 3059.

105. AS 3074. On the group and its leader, see Bohdan Nahaylo, 'Eduard Arutyunyan (1926–1984): Leader of the Armenian Helsinki Group and Political Prisoner', RL 53/85, 18 February 1985.

13. Acceleration Amid 'Stagnation'

1. See Elizabeth C. Sheetz, 'Recent Discussions of Leninist Nationality Policy: Domestic and International Implications', RL 473/76, 17 November 1976, p. 3, n. 9.

2. Kenneth Farmer, 'The USSR Academy of Sciences' Council on Nationality Problems Formulates its Five-year Plan', RL 393/76, 24 August 1976, p. 5.

3. *Letter to a Russian Friend: A 'Samizdat' Publication from Byelorussia*, London, Association of Byelorussians in Great Britain, 1979, p. 34.

4. AS 3087.

5. AS 3086.

6. AS 3085.

7. AS 3160. See also AS 3161, and Raymond Anderson, 'The Armenians Ask Moscow for Help, Charging Azerbaijan with Bias', *New York Times*, 10 December 1977.

8. *Pravda*, 5 June 1977, *CDSP*, XXIX, no. 23, p. 8.

9. Ibid. For a fuller assessment of the draft, see Elizabeth C. Sheetz, 'The Draft of the New Soviet Constitution: Republican Rights Versus Central Rights', RL 137/77, 6 June 1977.

10. *Pravda*, 8 October 1977, *CDSP*, XXIX, no. 41, p. 7.

11. See Ann Sheehy, 'The Nationwide Discussion of the Draft Constitution: Republican Rights, Federal Authority, and the Nationality Question', RL 226/77, 3 October 1977.

12. *Pravda*, 5 October 1977, *CDSP*, XXIX, no. 39, p. 5.

13. *Pravda*, 12 June 1977.

14. Ann Sheehy, 'The National Languages and the New Constitutions of the Transcaucasian Republics', RL 97/78, 3 May 1978; Elizabeth Fuller, 'The Transcaucasian Republics During the Brezhnev Era', RL 13/83, 7 January 1983, pp. 9–10.

15. Craig R. Whitney, 'Dispute in Caucasus Mirrors Soviet Ethnic Mosaic', *New York Times*, 25 June 1978. See also, Roman Solchanyk and Ann Sheehy, 'Kapitonov on Nationality Relations in Georgia', RL 125/78, 1 June 1978, and Ann Sheehy, 'Recent Events in Abkhazia Mirror the Complexities of National Relations in the USSR', RL 141/78, 26 June 1978.

16. *Jerusalem Post*, 5 September 1978.

17. Vladimir Petrov, 'Another Slanderous Allegation by HSINHUA', TASS, 13 December 1978. See also Nigel Wade, 'Soviet "Ethnic Uprising" ', *Daily Telegraph*, 13 December 1978.

18. *A Chronicle of Current Events*, no. 51, 1 December 1978, pp. 114–28.

19. *Bulletin d'Information/News Brief* (Brussels), no. 18/19, 1979, p. 7; see the remarks by Andrei Braun at a plenum of the Central Committee of the Kazakh Communist Party devoted to the national question, *Kazakhstanskaia pravda*, 7 June 1988.

20. Yurii Orlov *et al.*, 'On Prisoners in Soviet Camps', *Survey*, spring 1979, p. 79.

21. The *samizdat* materials issued by the prisoners in connection with this protest action are of considerable interest. See AS 3647, and *A Chronicle of Current Events*,

no. 52, 1 March 1979, pp. 54–7.

22. *A Chronicle of Current Events*, no. 53, 1 August 1979, p. 83.

23. See AS 3256, and 'A "Russian Dream" from Prison Camp', *Soviet Analyst*, 13 July 1978, pp. 5–7.

24. For an illuminating discussion of the language question, see Solchanyk, 'Russian Language and Soviet Politics', pp. 23–42.

25. See *ELTA Information Bulletin* (New York), August 1979, pp. 1–3; Kestutis Girnius, 'The Draft Recommendations of the Tashkent Conference: A New Wave of Russification?', RL 188/79, 19 June 1979; Jonas Papartis, 'The Eleventh Issue of the Unofficial Lithuanian Journal *Perspektyvos*', RL 343/79, 13 November 1979; Romuald J. Misiunas, 'The Fifteenth Issue of the Unofficial Journal *Ausra*', RL 366/79, 12 December 1979; and Jonas Papartis, 'The Nineteenth Issue of the Unofficial Lithuanian Journal *Ausra*', RL 183/80, 20 May 1980.

26. AS 3937.

27. On Badz'o, see Roman Senkus, 'Iurii Badzo: A Biographical Note', *Journal of Ukrainian Studies*, no. 16, summer 1984, pp. 70–3.

28. See *A Chronicle of Current Events*, no. 60, 31 December 1980, pp. 65–8.

29. AS 4167. For an English translation and commentary, see Elizabeth Fuller, 'Appeal for the Retention of the Georgian Language in Academic Life', RL 484/80, 17 December 1980.

30. For an English translation of the text, see Juri Estam and Jaan Pennar, 'Estonian Intellectuals Express Their Views on Causes of Recent Demonstrations in Open Letter', RL 477/80, 15 December 1980.

31. Roman Szporluk, 'Why Some Soviet Sociologists are Alarmed', *New York Times*, 27 August 1977; Anastasia Gelischanov, 'Demographic Policy: A Touchy Subject in the USSR', RL 316/81, 13 August 1981; Solchanyk, 'Russian Language and Soviet Politics', pp. 23–4.

32. G. I. Litvinova, 'Vozdeistvie gosudarstva i prava na demograficheskie protsessy', *Sovetskoe gosudarstvo i pravo*, no. 1, 1978, p. 135; as cited by

Gelischanov, RL 316/81, p. 2. See also Sergei Voronitsyn, 'For and Against a Differentiated Demographic Policy in the Soviet Union', RL 99/80, 6 March 1980.
33. Robert G. Kaiser, *Russia: The Power and the People*, New York, 1976, p. 60.
34. See Ann Sheehy, 'Language Affiliation Data from the Census of 1979', RL 130/80, 2 April 1980; M. N. Rutkevich, 'Dvuiazychie – vazhnyi faktor razvitia novoi istoricheskoi obshchnosti', *Istoriia SSSR*, no. 4, 1981, pp. 22–32.
35. '. . . A problemy ostaiutsia', *Argumenty i fakty*, no. 35, 1988, pp. 1–2. For background on the problem, see Ann Sheehy, 'Language Problems in the Soviet Armed Forces', RL 196/78, 11 September 1978.
36. Peter Duncan, 'Ideology and the National Question: Marxism-Leninism and the Nationality Policy of the Communist Party of the Soviet Union', paper presented to the conference on ideology in the USSR, organized by the Communist Politics Group of the Political Studies Association of the United Kingdom, and held at the School of Slavonic and East European Studies, University of London, 17 to 19 May 1985, p. 17.
37. See Roman Solchanyk, 'Molding the "Soviet People": The Role of Ukraine and Belorussia', *Journal of Ukrainian Studies*, no. 14, summer 1983, pp. 3–18.
38. Badzo, 'Open Letter', *Journal of Ukrainian Studies*, no. 17, p. 70.
39. See, for example, Aleksandr I. Solzhenitsyn, *The Mortal Danger: How Misconceptions about Russia Imperil the West*, London, 1980.
40. John B. Dunlop, *The New Russian Nationalism*, Washington, 1985, pp. 12–13.
41. On the Glazunov affair, see Dunlop. *Faces of Russian Nationalism*, pp. 59–60.
42. See Sergei Voronitsyn, 'The 600th Anniversary of the Battle of Kulikovo Pole', RL 299/80, 26 August, 1980; Dunlop, *The New Russian Nationalism*, pp. 9, 21–2.
43. John B. Dunlop, '*Mnogaya leta*: Advocate of a Russian Church–Soviet State Concordat', *Religion in Communist Lands*,

11, no. 2, summer 1983, pp. 146–160.
44. Peter Reddaway, *Problems of Communism*, November–December 1983, p. 10.
45. AS 4779. For an English translation of the text, see Remeikis, *Opposition to Soviet Rule in Lithuania*, pp. 659–63. This appeal was supported by a number of Russian dissidents, including Sakharov. See *ELTA Information Bulletin*, March–April, 1983, p. 20.
46. AS 4452.
47. AS 3857.
48. See V. Stanley Vardys, 'Polish Echoes in the Baltic', *Problems of Communism*, July–August 1983, p. 25.
49. AS 4327. For an English translation, see *ELTA Information Bulletin*, March–April, 1980.
50. On the activity of the Catholic Committee, see Kestutis and Saulius Girnius, 'Five Years of the Catholic Committee in Lithuania: Its Achievements and Dispersal', RL 431/83, 11 November 1983.
51. For the text of the appeal and details about the campaign, see *Chronicle of the Catholic Church in Lithuania*, no. 41, 1 January 1980, pp. 33–8, *Chronicle of the Catholic Church in Lithuania*, no. 72, 8 December 1986, pp. 51–4.
52. On Pope John Paul II's influence on Lithuania and Western Ukraine, see Kestutis Girnius, 'Relations between the Kremlin and the Vatican as Mirrored in Lithuania', RL 190/83, 11 May 1983; and Ivan Hvat, 'The Ukrainian Catholic Church, the Vatican and the Soviet Union during the Pontificate of Pope John Paul II', *Religion in Communist Lands*, no. 3, 1983, pp. 264–80.
53. On the situation in the Ukraine at this time, see Bohdan Nahaylo, 'Ukraine: Moscow's Recalcitrant Republic', *Soviet Analyst*, 17 August 1983, pp. 1–2.
54. AS 3919. On Chornovil and the conditions of his exile in Iakutia, see 'The Persecution of a Ukrainian Patriot', and 'Racial Tensions in Yakutia', *Soviet Analyst*, 17 December 1980, pp. 4–8. For another report about the disturbances in

Iakutia, see *Bulletin d'Information/News Brief*, no. 18/19, 1979, p. 7.

55. AS 4164, 4070, 4071. For translations, see 'Declaration of the Ukrainian Patriotic Movement', *Freedom Appeals* (New York), no. 5, May–June 1980, pp. 12–15.

56. *A Chronicle of Current Events*, no. 62, 14 July 1981, pp. 55–9.

57. See AS 4897 and 4898; and Ivan Hvat, 'Group Formed to Defend Catholics' Rights in Ukraine', RL 220/83, 6 June 1983.

58. The details are provided in *A Chronicle of Current Events*, no. 63, 31 December 1981, pp. 79–82.

59. See Alexeyeva, *Soviet Dissent*, pp. 117–19; Elizabeth Fuller, 'New *Samizdat* Document Gives Details of Georgian Demonstrations', RL 360/81, 11 September 1981, and 'Nationalist Protest in Georgia', RL 28/82, 19 January 1982.

60. Alexeyeva, *Soviet Dissent*, pp. 131–2.

61. AS 4644.

62. Allen Hetmanek, 'Spillover Effects of Religious Broadcasts in Iran on Soviet Muslims', RL 142/80, 14 April 1980.

63. Elizabeth Fuller, 'Transcaucasian KGB Chief Warns Against Ideological Subversion', RL 5/81, 5 January 1981.

64. Dimitrii Bezuglyi, 'S pozitsii boitsa', *Zhurnalist*, no. 1, 1981, pp. 46–8; as cited in Bennigsen and Wimbush, *Mystics and Commissars*, p. 51.

65. Ibid.

66. For details, see Ann Sheehy, 'North Ossetian First Secretary Fired', RL 25/82, 18 January 1982.

67. *Guardian*, 6 December 1980; David Satter, 'Moscow Concerned about Tension in Moslem Region', *Financial Times*, 8 January 1981.

68. *Vesti iz SSSR* (Munich), no. 19, 1982, p. 8.

69. Bess Brown, 'Profitable Unofficial Religious Publishing Operation Uncovered in Tashkent', RL 420/82, 20 October 1982.

70. *Vesti iz SSSR*, no. 5, 1984, p. 3.

71. Chingiz Aitmatov, 'I dol'she veka dlitsia den', *Novyi mir*, no. 11, 1980, pp. 3–185. The novel has been published in

English as *The Day Lasts More than a Hundred Years*, London, 1983.

72. Ann Sheehy, 'Uzbek Novel Found Ideologically Unsound', RL 337/82, 20 August 1982.

73. *Pravda*, 24 February 1981; as cited in *CDSP*, XXXIII, no. 8, p. 6.

74. Ann Sheehy, 'Non-Russian Periodical Press to be Available on Subscription Throughout the Soviet Union', RL 335/82, 19 August 1982.

75. L. L. Rybakovskii and N. V. Tarasova, 'Vzaimodeistvie migratsionnykh i etnicheskikh protsessov', *Sotsiologicheskie issledovaniia*, no. 4, 1982, pp. 29–30. On the question of 'due representation' in the Central Asian republics, see Bess Brown, 'The National Composition of the Governments of the Central Asian Republics', RL 313/82, 4 August 1982.

76. *Pravda*, 24 February 1981; as cited in *CDSP*, XXXIII, no. 8, p. 6.

77. *Pravda*, 25 March 1982; as cited in *CDSP*, XXXIX, no. 12, pp. 4–6. On Brezhnev's speech in Tashkent, see also Bess Brown, 'Brezhnev Mixes Praise and Criticism of Uzbekistan in Tashkent Speech', RL 140/82, 25 March 1982.

78. For a useful discussion of this problem, see Boris Rumer, 'Central Asia's Cotton: The Picture Now', *Central Asian Survey*, 6, no. 4, 1987, pp. 75–88.

79. *Pravda*, 25 March 1982; as cited in *CDSP*, XXXIX, no. 12, pp. 4–6.

80. *Pravda*, 25 February 1982; as cited in *CDSP*, XXXIII, no. 11, p. 9.

81. On 'Sibaral', see Philip P. Micklin, 'Soviet Water Diversion Plans: Implications for Kazakhstan and Central Asia', *Central Asian Survey*, 1, no. 4, April 1983, pp. 9–43; Sergei Voronitsyn, 'Renewed Polemics over Siberian Water Diversion Scheme', RL 154/82, 6 April 1982.

82. *Pravda*, 24 February 1981; as cited in *CDSP*, XXXIII, no. 8, p. 7.

83. *Kommunist*, no. 14, September 1982; as cited in *CDSP*, XXXIII, no. 49, pp. 4–5.

84. M. I. Kulichenko, *Rastsvet i sblizhenie natsii v SSSR. Problemy teorii i metodologii*, Moscow, 1981, pp. 213–14; as cited by Roman Solchanyk in 'Soviet Language Policy: Two Steps Forward, One Step Back?', RL 47/82, 28 January 1982.

85. See, for example, Roman Solchanyk, 'The Ukrainian Party *Aktiv* on Ideological Work', RL 204/79, 3 July 1979, and 'Shcherbitsky and the Ukrainian Cultural Intelligentsia Meet "to Exchange Ideas" ', RL 455/81, 13 November 1981.

86. Elizabeth Fuller, 'Large Scale Measures to Improve the Teaching of the Georgian Language', RL 157/80, 28 April 1980.

87. Ann Sheehy, 'Why Shouldn't Russians Learn the Vernacular?', RL 18/82, 14 January 1982; 'Estonian-language Olympiad Instituted for Pupils of Russian Schools in Estonia', RL 66/82, 10 February 1982; and 'Problems of Teaching Estonian in Tallinn's Russian-language Schools', RL 135/82, 23 March 1982.

88. Juri Estam, 'Open Letter from Estonian Intellectuals', RL 432/82, 28 October 1982.

89. Roman Solchanyk, 'Latvian Party Leader Discusses Language Policy', RL 297/82, 23 July 1982.

90. Paul A. Goble, 'Managing the Multinational USSR', *Problems of Communism*, July–August 1985, pp. 79–83. See also Martha Brill Olcott, 'Yuri Andropov and the National Question', *Soviet Studies*, XXXVII, no. 1, January 1985, pp. 103–17.

91. See Ann Sheehy, 'Andropov and the Merging of Nations', RL 516/82, 22 December 1982, pp. 3–5.

92. P. I. Kosolapov, 'Klassovye i natsional'nye otnosheniia na etape razvitogo sotsializma', in *Vospityvat' ubezhdennykh patriotov-internatsionalistov*, Moscow, 1982, p. 155.

93. Dunlop, *The New Russian Nationalism*, pp. 15–16.

94. See Serge Schmemann, 'Pro-Hitler Rally Fails in Moscow', *The New York Times*, 29 April 1982; Bohdan Nahaylo, 'The Protests in Pushkin Square', *Encounter*, March 1983, pp. 62–3; Julia Wishnevsky, 'Neo-Nazis in the Soviet Union', RL 226/85, 11 July 1985.

14. Andropov and Chernenko Keep up the Pressure

1. *Pravda*, 22 December 1982.

2. *Pravda*, 13 January 1983.

3. *Pravda*, 22 December 1982.

4. See V. I. Kozlov, *Natsional'nosti SSSR*, Moscow 1982, p. 287.

5. *Pravda*, 13 January 1982.

6. *Pravda*, 22 December 1982.

7. *Pravda*, 16 June 1983; as cited in *CDSP*, XXXV, no. 25, pp. 1–8.

8. *Pravda*, 15 June 1983; as cited in *CDSP*, XXXV, no. 24, pp. 2–10, 24.

9. See Ann Sheehy, 'Politburo Discusses Improving the Teaching of Russian', RL 221/83, 7 June 1983; Roman Solchanyk, 'Ukrainian Ministry of Education Takes Further Steps to Improve the Teaching of Russian', RL 400/83, 27 October 1983.

10. This was reiterated by K. Khanazarov in *Pravda*, 10 June 1983, pp. 2–3. English translation in *CDSP*, XXXV, no. 23, pp. 7–8.

11. *Pravda*, 21 February 1982, p. 1.

12. See, for example, Bess Brown, 'Measures to Integrate Central Asians into the Soviet Armed Forces Discussed in Uzbekistan', RL 93/83, 23 February 1983; and *Pravda Vostoka*, 15, 21, and 22 May 1983 (see *CDSP*, XXXV, no. 22, pp. 1–5). For a broader discussion of this problem and its implications, see Sergei Zamascikov, 'The Role of the Military in the Social Integration of Ethnic Muslims in the USSR', RL 477/83, 23 December 1983.

13. See Solchanyk, RL 400/83.

14. *Qazagstan Aielideri*, no. 2, 1982, pp. 12–13; as cited by Charles Carlson in 'Kazakh Writers Wistful About Greater Cultural Autonomy in Yakutia', RL 347/83, 16 September 1983, p. 8.

15. Ann Sheehy, 'Olzhas Suleimanov Elected First Secretary of Writers' Union of Kazakhstan', RL 114/84, 20 March 1984.

16. N. Mironov, *Pravda*, 27 January 1984. English translation in *CDSP*, XXXVI, no. 4, pp. 22–3.

17. See Roostam Sadri, 'Anti-Islamic Propaganda in the Tatar ASSR', RL 87/83, 21 February 1983; Ann Sheehy,

'Concern in Tatar ASSR about Nuclear Power Station to be Built on Kama River', RL 222/83, 7 June 1983.

18. Ann Sheehy, 'Usubaliev Scores Kirghiz Historians and Cultural Figures for Nationalistic Errors', RL 216/83, 1 June 1983.

19. See Julia Wishnevsky, ' "Anti-Zionist Committee" Formed in the Soviet Union', RL 170/83, 26 April 1983, and 'The Curtain Falls on Jewish Emigration', RL 232/183, 15 June 1983.

20. Alexeyeva, *Soviet Dissent*, pp. 132–3.

21. Elizabeth Fuller, 'Ten Georgians Sentenced for Protesting Against Celebrating Bi-centennial of Russian–Georgian Treaty', RL 129/84, 26 March 1984.

22. See Vardys, 'Polish Echoes in the Baltic', p. 32.

23. Saulius Girnius, 'The Arrest of Enn Tarto and the Crackdown on Baltic Dissent', RL 364/83, 29 September 1983; Alexeyeva, *Soviet Dissent*, pp. 103–4.

24. *Pravda*, 11 April 1984; as cited in *CDSP*, XXXVI, no. 15, p. 4.

25. A. F. Dashdamirov, 'Sil'nee krovnykh uz . . .', *Literaturnaia gazeta*, 25 January 1984.

26. Genrikas Zimanas, 'Rzhavchina mozhet raz"edat' stal' ', *Zhurnalist*, no. 8, 1984, pp. 22–4.

27. G. T. Tavadov, 'K kharakteristike sovremennogo etapa natsional'nykh otnoshenii v SSSR', *Nauchnyi kommunizm*, no. 5, 1984, pp. 33–9. For further discussion of this article, see Roman Solchanyk, 'Soviet Author on Contradictions in the National Question', RL 416/84, 30 October 1984.

28. Timur Kocaoglu, 'Uzbek Scholar Criticizes Indifference Towards National Culture', RL 85/84, 24 February 1984.

29. Ann Sheehy, 'Belorussian Scholar Upholds Importance of Nationhood and National Languages', RL 204/84, 23 May 1984.

30. S. L. Tykhvins'kyi, 'Aktual'ni problemy radians'koi istorychnoi nauky i deiaki pytannia vdoskonalennia pidhotovky i atestatsii naukovykh kadriv', *Ukrains'kyi*

istorychnyi zhurnal, no. 2, 1985, pp. 5–27. For an analysis, see Roman Solchanyk, 'Guidelines for Soviet Historians on the National Question – Russian and Non-Russian', RL 165/85, 20 May 1985.

31. For further details, see Ann Sheehy, 'Call for More Education and Publications in Russian in the Non-Russian Republics', RL 121/85, 17 April 1985.

32. See Ann Sheehy, 'Major Anti-corruption Drive in Uzbekistan', RL 324/84, 30 August 1984, and 'Progress of Anti-corruption Campaign in Uzbekistan Reviewed', RL 457/84, 29 November 1984.

33. *Izvestia*, 4 November 1984, p. 3.

34. Ann Sheehy, 'Ideological Shortcomings in Recent Uzbek Literary Works Come Under Fire', RL 28/85, 29 January 1985.

35. On Kukk's case, and Estonian national dissent until 1983 generally, see Rein Taagepera, *Softening without Liberalization in the Soviet Union*, Lanham, MD, 1984.

36. Bohdan Nahaylo, 'Oleksii Tykhy – The Martyrization of a Ukrainian Patriot', RL 213/84, 28 May 1984; 'Yurii Lytvyn's Suicide: The Final Protest of an Indomitable Ukrainian Dissident', RL 408/84, 24 October 1984.

37. Bohdan Nahaylo, 'Ukrainian Political Prisoner Ivan Sokul's'ky Said to Have Recanted', RL 161/84, 19 April 1984, and 'Imprisoned Ukrainian Helsinki Monitor Oles' Berdnyk Pardoned after Recanting', RL 284/84, 23 July 1984; Roman Solchanyk, 'Soviet Press Alleges Recantation by Longtime Ukrainian Political Prisoner', RL 241/85, 23 July 1985.

38. *Russkaia mysl'*, 24 July 1987.

39. Bohdan Nahaylo, 'Eduard Arutyunyan (1926–1984): Leader of the Armenian Helsinki Group and Political Prisoner', RL 53/85, 18 February 1985.

40. AS 5415; UPI, 30 March 1984.

41. On this subject, see Roman Solchanyk, 'Poland and the Soviet West', in S. Enders Wimbush, ed., *Soviet Nationalities in Strategic Perspective*, Beckenham, Kent, 1985, pp. 158–80.

42. See Ivan Hvat, *Chronicle of the Ukrainian Catholic Church in the Ukraine,*

RL 3/85, 7 January 1985; and Bohdan Nahaylo, 'The Church Rumbling Beneath the Kremlin', *The Times*, 12 January 1985.
43. See, for example, 'Lithuanian *Samizdat* on Soviet Casualties in Afghanistan', RL 299/82, 26 July 1982; Julia Wishnevsky, 'References to Afghanistan in *Samizdat*', RL 143/84, 6 April 1984; Bohdan Nahaylo, 'Ukrainian *Samizdat* Journal Gives Details of Casualties in Afghanistan', RL 9/85, 10 January 1985.
44. K. Chernenko, 'Na uroven' trebovanii razvitogo sotsializma. Nekotorye aktual'nye problemy teorii, strategii i taktiki KPSS', *Kommunist*, no. 18, December 1984, pp. 3–21.
45. M. S. Gorbachev, *Zhivoe tvorchestvo naroda*: Doklad na Vsesoiuznoi nauchno-prakticheskoi konferentsii 'Sovershenstvovanie razvitogo sotsializma i ideologicheskaia rabota partii v svete reshenii iiun'skogo (1983g.) Plenuma TSK KPSS', 10 dekabria 1984 goda, Moscow, 1985.

15. Gorbachev and the Advent of *Glasnost'*
1. *Pravda*, 24 April 1985; as translated in *CDSP*, XXXVII, no. 17, p. 6.
2. Mikhail Gorbachev, *Perestroika: New Thinking for Our Country and the World*, London, 1987, p. 120.
3. *Pravda*, 30 January, p. 2.
4. *Sovetskaia Rossiia*, 26 January 1988, p. 2.
5. TASS in English, 8 May 1985.
6. *Soviet Television*, 25 June 1986. See Bohdan Nahaylo, 'Gorbachev's Slip of the Tongue in Kiev', RL 221/85, 3 July 1985.
7. Radio Moscow, 27 March 1985.
8. Sergei Iur'enen, '80-letie Mikhaila Sholokhova: Za fasadom iubileinykh torzhestv', *Radio Svoboda: Materialy issledovatel'skogo otdela*, RS 111/85, 18 June, 1985; see also Vera Tolz, 'Soviet Literary Critic Lauds Stalin', RL 178/85, 29 May 1985.
9. *Krasnaia zvezda*, 7 November 1985.
10. *Guardian*, 17 May 1985.
11. As translated in *CDSP*, XXXVIII, no. 44, pp. 19–20.
12. *Kommunist* (Erevan) and *Izvestia*, 2 June 1985.

13. As translated in *CDSP*, XXXVII, no. 25, pp. 10–12.
14. See Ann Sheehy, 'Slav Elected First Secretary of Tashkent City Party Committee', RL 333/85, 3 October 1985; 'Slav Presence Increased in Uzbek Party Buro and Secretariat', RL 94/86, 24 February 1986.
15. See Elizabeth Fuller, 'Georgian Muslims Deported by Stalin Permitted to Return', RL 32/86, 14 January 1986; 'Deportation of Meskhetians Discussed in Georgian Press', RL 168/88, 12 April 1986.
16. *USSR News Brief* (Munich), no. 9, 1985, p. 1.
17. On Stus, who was elected an honorary member of the English centre of the International PEN club, see Nadia Svitlychna, 'The Death of Vasyl' Stus', *Index on Censorship*, no. 2, 1986, pp. 34–6.
18. *L'Humanité*, 8 February 1986, pp. 13–17; the interview was also published that day in *Sovetskaia Rossiia*.
19. *Pravda*, 26 October 1985.
20. See Roman Solchanyk, 'Two Soviet Scholars Oppose Silence on Concept of Merger (*Sliyanie*) of Nations', RL 125/86, 10 March 1986.
21. As summarized in *The Monitoring Report*, BBC (Caversham), Second Series, no. 8213, 21 March 1986, p. 1.
22. Evgenii Evtushenko, 'Kabychegonevyshlisty', *Pravda*, 9 September 1985.
23. Evgenii Evtushenko, 'Fuku', *Novyi mir*, no. 9, 1985, pp. 3–58.
24. *Literaturnaia gazeta*, 18 December 1985. For the full text of his speech, see *New York Times*, 18 December 1985.
25. *Literaturnaia gazeta*, 18 December 1985, pp. 4–9; as translated in *CDSP*, XXXVIII, no. 1, p. 10.
26. *Sovetskaia Rossiia*, 20 December 1985, p. 3.
27. *Pravda*, 12 February 1986, p. 2. On the opposition to the river diversion projects, see Nicolai N. Petro, ' "The Project of the Century": A Case Study of Russian National Dissent', *Studies in Comparative Communism*, XX, nos. 3/4, autumn/winter

1987, pp. 235–52; Robert G. Darst, Jr., 'Environmentalism in the USSR: The Opposition to the River Diversion Projects', *Soviet Economy*, 4, no. 3, July–September 1988, pp. 223–523.

28. Toomas Ilves, 'Party Congress Focuses on Nationality Problem', *RFER*, Baltic Area/2, 4 March, pp. 7–10.

29. Joseph Seagram, 'The Status of Islam in the USSR as Reflected in Speeches at the Republican Party Congresses', RL 120/86, 7 March 1986.

30. *Pravda Vostoka*, 31 January 1986; as translated in *CDSP*, XXXVIII, no. 6, pp. 11–14.

31. *Pravda Vostoka*, 2 February 1986. See also Joseph Seagram, 'Teaching of Russian Discussed at Party Congresses in Muslim Republics of the USSR', RL 131/86, 13 March 1986.

32. *Pravda Vostoka*, 31 January 1986. Ironically, Usmankhozhaev himself was soon arrested and tried for corruption.

33. *Pravda*, 26 February 1986; translated in *CDSP*, XXXVIII, no. 8, pp. 22–3.

34. *Pravda*, 26 February 1986; translated in *CDSP*, XXXVIII, no. 10, pp. 8–10.

35. Ibid.

36. *Pravda*, 28 February 1986.

37. Reuters, 4 March 1986; *Financial Times*, 5 March 1986.

38. *Pravda Vostoka*, 4, 5 and 6 April 1986.

39. *Pravda Vostoka*, 16 and 17 May 1986.

40. V. Makarov, 'Splochenie mnogonatsional'nogo voinskogo kollektiva', *Voennyi vestnik*, no. 9, 1985, pp. 6–9; Ann Sheehy, 'Problems in Recruiting Non-Slavs into Officer Corps', RL 383/87, 28 September 1987.

41. Iu. Bromlei, 'Sovershenstovovanie natsional'nykh otnoshenii v SSSR', *Kommunist*, no. 8, 1986, pp. 78–86.

42. *Literaturnaia gazeta*, 16 April 1986, p. 7.

43. Toomas Ilves, 'Estonian Writers' Union Congress Calls for Greater Freedom', *RFER*, Baltic Area/4, 18 July 1986, pp. 7–11; 'What the Writers' Union Congress Really Talked About', *RFER*, Baltic Area/6, 25 September 1986, pp. 3–6.

44. Toomas Ilves, 'An Open Letter of Protest from Estonian Scientists', *RFER*, Baltic Area/4, 18 July 1986, pp. 5–6.

45. Ann Sheehy, 'Concern in Tatar ASSR About Nuclear Power Station to be Built on Kama River', RL 222/83, 7 June 1983.

46. Elizabeth Fuller, 'Is Armenia on the Brink of an Ecological Disaster?', RL 307/86, 5 August 1986.

47. *Christian Science Monitor*, 4 February 1988, pp. 1 and 9.

48. Liubov Kovalevs'ka, 'Ne pryvatna sprava: do vsesoiuznoi narady z problem postachannia', *Literaturna Ukraina*, 27 March 1986, p. 1. See also Bohdan Nahaylo, 'Unsatisfactory Conditions at Chernobyl' Nuclear Power Station Previously Admitted in Soviet Press', RL 176/86, 30 April 1986.

49. Roman Solchanyk, 'Pre-Chernobyl' Premonitions at the Ukrainian Academy of Sciences', RL 360/86, 10 September 1986.

50. David R. Marples, *Chernobyl and Nuclear Power in the USSR*, New York, 1986, p. 8.

51. *Literaturna Ukraina*, 12 June 1986. See Roman Solchanyk, 'The Ukrainian Writers' Congress: A Spirited Defense of the Native Language', RL 247/86, 24 June 1986.

52. See Roman Solchanyk, 'Ukrainian Writer Lambasts "Great-Power Chauvinism" and "Home-Grown Russifiers" ', RL 270/86, 24 June, 1986.

53. *New York Times*, 30 June 1986.

54. The speeches delivered at the congress were published in an abridged form in *Literaturnaia gazeta*, 2 July 1986.

55. *Pravda*, 14 August 1986, p. 1.

56. *Pravda*, 20 August 1986, p. 1.

57. D. I. Ziuzin, 'Varianty sotsial'no-ekonomicheskogo razvitiia sredneaziatskogo regiona', *Sotsiologicheskie issledovaniia*, no. 4, 1986, pp. 17–25; see also Anne Bohr, 'Current Trends in Central Asian Labor Distribution', RL 508/87, 22 December 1987.

58. Radio Moscow, in Russian, 6 August 1986.

59. *Literaturnaia gazeta*, 2 July 1986, p. 7. For a discussion of these developments, see Roman Solchanyk, 'Russian History,

Russian Nationalism, and Soviet "Politics" ', RL 327/86, 1986.

60. Bohdan Nahaylo, 'The Millennium of the Christianization of Kievan Rus': An Interview with Professor Frank Sysyn', RL 393/87, 28 September 1987, and 'Moscow Manipulates the Millennium', *The American Spectator*, March 1988, pp. 16–18.

61. Saulius Girnius, 'Government Prepares for the Catholic Anniversary', *RFER*, Baltic Area SR/1, 28 January 1987, pp. 25–8.

62. See Oxana Antic, 'A New Phase in the Struggle Against "Religious" Communists', RL 18/87, 14 January 1987.

63. *Pravda Vostoka*, 25 November 1987, p. 1.

64. See Toomas Ilves, 'Arguments Over the Future of the Estonian Language', *RFER*, Baltic Area SR/3, 20 May 1986, p. 13.

65. *Litaratura i mastatstva*, 19 September 1986. See Roman Solchanyk, 'Criticism of Status of the Native Language in Belorussia's Schools', RL 365/86, 28 September 1986.

66. Roman Solchanyk, 'Letters to Byelorussian Weekly Evidence Strong Support for Native Language', RL 425/86, 9 November 1986.

67. *Litaratura i mastatstva*, 31 October 1986. For a discussion of Sadowski's letter, see Roman Solchanyk, 'Byelorussian Ministry of Education Accused of Sabotaging the Native Language', RL 434/86, 10 November 1986.

68. For an English translation of the letter, see *Letters to Gorbachev: New Documents from Soviet Byelorussia*, London, The Association of Byelorussians in Great Britain, 1987, 18pp. See also Roman Solchanyk, 'A Letter to Gorbachev: Byelorussian Intellectuals on the Language Question', RL 142/87, 20 April 1987; Toomas Ilves, 'Protest from Byelorussian Intellectuals to Gorbachev Published in Estonia', *RFER*, Baltic Area/4, 15 June 1987, pp. 9–11.

69. Mykola Zhulyns'kyi, 'Vymiry liuds'koi pam"iati', *Literaturna Ukraina*,

18 September 1986, pp. 3 and 5.

70. *Literaturna Ukraina*, 27 November 1986. See Roman Solchanyk, 'Ukrainian Writer Calls for Ukrainization', RL 467/86, 11 December 1986.

71. See Dzintra Bungs, 'The Baltic Question at the Chautauqua Conference', *RFER*, Baltic Area SR/7, 27 October 1986, pp. 15–18; 'After the Jurmala Conference: Imperfect *Glasnost'* ', *RFER*, Baltic Area/8, 9 December 1986, pp. 23–8; Toomas Ilves, 'The Chautauqua Conference in the Estonian Press', *RFER*, Baltic Area/7, 27 October 1986, p. 13; Saulius Girnius, 'Lithuanian Press on the Chautauqua Conference', *RFER*, Baltic Area/7, 27 October 1986, pp. 35–6.

72. See Dzintra Bungs, 'No Improvement in the Status of the Latvian Language', *RFER*, Baltic Area SR/1, 28 January 1987.

73. See Toomas Ilves, 'Estonian Press Breaks Nationality Discord Taboo', *RFER*, Baltic Area/1, 28 January 1987, pp. 3–5.

74. *Literaturnaia gazeta*, 26 November 1986, p. 2.

75. As cited by Bungs in 'No Improvement in the Status of the Latvian Language', pp. 23–4.

16. *Glasnost'* but no *Perestroika*

1. Novosti article by Askar Nurmanov for *Pogled* (Sofia), 21 December 1986, p. 10.

2. Ann Sheehy, 'Do Kazakhs Now Outnumber Russians in Kazakhstan?', RL 65/87, 19 February 1987.

3. APN in English, 22 December 1986.

4. Walker's report appeared in the *Guardian* on 30 December 1986. Replying to *Izvestia*'s criticism, Walker pointed out in the *Guardian* on 8 January 1987 that: 'openness about the riots in Kazakhstan has been in remarkably short supply in the Soviet press, save for the initial announcements by TASS . . .'

5. Reuters, 8 January, and *Washington Post*, 9 January 1987.

6. *Kazakhstanskaia pravda*, 4 February 1987.

7. AP, 18 February, and *Washington Post*, 19 February 1987.

8. *Izvestia*, 7 June 1988, p. 2. For a percipient discussion of the Kazakh protests and their significance, see S. Enders Wimbush, 'The Alma-Ata Riots', *Encounter*, June 1987, pp. 62–8.
9. *Izvestia*, 19 January 1987, p. 3.
10. John Soper, 'Problems in the Kazakh Educational System', RL 488/87, 2 December 1987.
11. Radio Budapest, 9 February 1987.
12. *Literaturnaia gazeta*, 12 May 1987.
13. *Druzhba narodov*, May 1988, p. 252.
14. *Kazakhstanskaia pravda*, 7 and 11 January, and 4 February 1987.
15. *Komsomol'skaia pravda*, 18 July 1987.
16. Reuters, 20 January 1987.
17. Radio Moscow, 25 December 1986.
18. *Literatura un maksla*, 1 January 1987. See Dzintra Bungs, 'Dispute Over the Latvian Language Continues', *RFER*, Baltic Area/2, 20 March 1987, p. 25.
19. *Izvestia*, 2 January 1987.
20. Ann Sheehy, 'Anti-Natal Policy for Tajikistan', RL 56/87, 2 February 1987. On 13 February 1987, TASS said that the Soviet population was growing too slowly and that measures were being taken to speed up growth rates.
21. Bess Brown, 'Kazakhstan in 1987 – the Year After Alma Ata', RL 5/88, 23 December 1987; Reuters, 20 January 1987. It is worth noting that in Georgia a Commission for Coordination and Further Development of Inter-Nationality Ties and Internationalist Upbringing of Workers had existed since at least 1982. *Kommunisti*, 7 February 1982.
22. Bess Brown, 'Upgrading the Role of Kazakh in Public Life', RL 418/87, 16 October 1987.
23. Brown, 'Kazakhstan in 1987'.
24. *Pravda*, 4 February 1988.
25. TASS in English, 27 January 1987.
26. John Soper, 'Local Press Coverage of Confrontations Involving Young People in Central Asia', RL 193/87, 30 April 1987; *Central Asian News Letter*, 6, no. 3, July 1987; Bess Brown, 'Religion in Tajikistan – A Tough Nut for the Ideologists', RL 7/88, 28 December 1987.
27. *Sovetskaia Moldaviia*, 22 February and 31 May 1987. See Bohdan Nahaylo, 'National Ferment in Moldavia', RL 32/88, 24 January 1988.
28. *Literaturna Ukraina*, 12 March 1987. See Roman Solchanyk, 'Ukrainian Writers Press for Obligatory Study of Native Language', RL 119/87, 24 March 1987.
29. *Literaturna Ukraina*, 5 March 1987. See Roman Solchanyk, 'Far-reaching Language Demands in Ukraine', RL 117/87, 23 March 1987.
30. Radio Moscow, 19 February 1987.
31. Toomas Ilves, 'Criticism of Russification Escalates', *RFER*, Baltic Area/3, 8 May 1987, pp 5–6.
32. *New York Times*, 18 April 1987.
33. P. Volobuev, 'Velikii Oktiabr' i istoricheskie sud'by nashei Rodiny', *Pravda*, 27 March 1987; O. Trubachev, 'Slaviane. Iazyk i istoriia', *Pravda*, 28 March 1987. See Roman Solchanyk, 'Shcherbitsky on Nationalism and Religion', RL 137/87, 6 April 1987.
34. For details, see Julia Wishnevsky, 'The Emergence of "Pamyat" and "Otechestvo" ', RL 342/87, 26 August 1987.
35. Julia Wishnevsky, 'Soviet Cultural Figures at Berlin Academy of Arts', RL 100/87, 12 March 1987; Ilves, 'Protest from Byelorussian Intellectuals to Gorbachev Published in Estonia'.
36. *Sovetskaia Belorussiia*, 27 March 1987. See Roman Solchanyk, 'Party Leader in Byelorussia Rejects Criticism About Status of Byelorussian Language', RL 180/87, 7 May 1987.
37. *Literaturnaia gazeta*, 6 May 1987.
38. *Pravda*, 2 April 1987; TASS, 18 April 1987; Radio Moscow and Reuters, 30 April 1987. For examples of earlier reports about cross-border raids by the Afghan resistance, see Reuters, 29 April 1982; and AFP, 16 January 1985.
39. *Literaturnaia gazeta*, 13 and 20 May 1987.
40. Silva Kaputikian, 'Rodina – bol'shaia i malaia', *Pravda*, 7 May 1987, pp. 3 and 6.
41. *Moskovskie novosti*, 31 May 1987, p. 13.
42. *Edasi*, 29 May 1987. See Toomas Ilves,

'A Scathing Attack on Language Policy', *RFER*, Baltic Area SR/5, 17 July 1987, pp. 3–6.

43. 'Tsena prozreniia', *Ogonek*, no. 26, July 1987, pp. 4–9.

44. Dzintra Bungs, 'Environmentalists Make Some Headway', *RFER*, Baltic Area Survey SR/1, 28 January 1987, pp. 17–20.

45. Toomas Ilves, 'Growing Opposition and Unrest Over Massive Mining Project', *RFER*, Baltic Area/4, 15 June 1987, pp. 5–8.

46. See Bohdan Nahaylo, 'Mounting Opposition in the Ukraine to Nuclear Energy Program', RL Supplement 1/88, 24 February 1988.

47. Elizabeth Fuller, 'Armenian Authorities Appear to Yield to "Ecological Lobby" ', RL 130/87, 30 March 1987; 'Armenian Journalist Links Air Pollution and Infant Mortality', RL 275/87, 14 July 1987.

48. Elizabeth Fuller, 'Georgian Intellectuals Oppose Mountain Railway Construction Project', RL 368/87, 25 August 1987.

49. Ann Sheehy, 'Highly Toxic Defoliant Finally Banned?' RL 157/87, 23 April 1987, and 'Steps Taken to Combat High Infant Mortality in Central Asia', RL 278/87, 14 July 1987.

50. *Literaturnaia gazeta*, 6 May 1985. For more details about the problem, see James Critchlow, 'The Politburo's Efforts to Deal with the Aral Sea Disaster', RL 447/88, 28 September 1988.

51. Soviet Television, 2 April 1987.

52. Antero Pietila, 'Estonia's Fear of Russian Dominance Underscores Ethnic Tensions', *Baltimore Sun*, 5 May 1987.

53. Dzintra Bungs, 'The "Grasshoppers" Strike', *RFER*, Baltic Area/4, 15 June 1987, pp. 17–20.

54. *Sovetskaia Latviia*, 7 August 1987. See Dzintra Bungs, 'Nationality Relations Commission Formed', *RFER*, Baltic Area SR/5, 17 July 1987, pp. 7–8.

55. See Nahaylo, 'National Ferment in Moldavia'; Ann Sheehy, 'Moldavians Gain Some Language Concessions', RL 353/87, 27 August 1987.

56. *Literaturnaia Rossiia*, 24 July 1987. For more details, see Ann Sheehy, 'Buryats Regain Primary Education in Native Language', RL 355/87, 31 August 1987.

57. DPA, 22 December 1987.

58. UPI, 4 January 1988.

59. *Kazakhstanskaia pravda*, 3 June 1987; *Sovetskaia Kirgiziia*, 9 January 1988.

60 *Kul'tura i zhyttia*, 1 February 1987. See Roman Solchanyk, 'Ukrainian Youth to be "Internationalized" ', RL 62/87, 9 February 1987.

61. *Sovetskaia Litva*, 2 April 1987.

62. *Pravda*, 3 June 1987.

63. Roman Solchanyk, 'Ukrainian Writers Told to Moderate Their Stand on Language Question', RL 250/87, 30 June 1987.

64. *Literaturna Ukraina*, 9 July 1987.

65. See Roman Solchanyk, 'Catastrophic Language Situation in Major Ukrainian Cities', RL 286/87, 15 July 1987; 'Statistical *Glasnost'*: Data on Language and Education in the Ukraine', RL 152/87, 15 April 1987.

66. *Literaturna Ukraina*, 9 July 1987. Solchanyk, RL 286/87.

67. Roman Solchanyk, 'An Open Letter to Gorbachev from Byelorussia', RL 344/87, 19 August 1987.

68. *Sovetskaia Belorussiia*, 7 July 1987. For details, see Roman Solchanyk, 'Language Question in Belorussia's Schools "Solved"?', RL 400/8, 22 July 1987.

69. *Pravda*, 14 August 1987. (Emphasis added.)

70. Soviet Television, 8 August 1987.

71. See Dzintra Bungs, 'The Demonstration of 14 June 1987', *RFER*, Baltic Area/6, 29 August 1987, pp. 5–8; 'Soviet Press on the Demonstration: Searching for an Explanation', *RFER*, Baltic Area/6, 29 August 1987, pp. 9–14.

72. Toomas Ilves, 'Banned Novel on Mass Deportations Published', *RFER*, Baltic Area/7, 28 October, 1987, pp. 3–5.

73. See Ann Sheehy, 'Crimean Tatar Commission Works Against Background of Continuing Protests', RL 405/87, 13 October 1987.

74. Juris Kaza, 'Baltic Protests to Mark Nazi Pact', the *Guardian*, 17 August 1987;

AFP, 24 August 1987; Toomas Ilves, 'The Baltic Demonstrations: Gorbachev's Problem', *RFER*, RAD Background Report/157 (Baltic Area), 11 September 1987; Dzintra Bungs, 'The Latvian Demonstration of 23 August 1987', *RFER*, Baltic Area/7, 28 October 1987, p. 20; Saulius Girnius, 'The Lithuanian Press on the Baltic Demonstrations', *RFER*, Baltic Area/7, 28 October 1987, pp. 21–5.

75. Toomas Ilves, 'Protest Letter from Leaders of Cultural Unions', *RFER*, Baltic Area SR/1, 21 January 1988, pp. 7–10.

76. See Roman Solchanyk, 'Ukrainian Party Adopts Action Program on the National Question', RL 350/87, 26 August 1987; 'Ukrainian Writers' Union Adopts "Counterresolution" on the National Question', RL 420/87, 19 October 1987.

77. See their appeal to Pope John Paul II: AS 6097. See also UPI and AP, 19 August 1987.

78. *Moscow News*, No. 37, September 1987, p. 13.

79. *Istoriia SSSR*, No. 6, 1987, p. 117.

80. *Sovetskaia Moldaviia*, 3 October 1987.

81. *Istoriia SSSR*, no. 6, 1987, pp. 115–19; A. Khantsevich, 'Delikatnaia tema?', *Komsomol'skaia pravda*, 10 January 1988, p. 1. For more details on the developments in Moldavia, see Nahaylo, 'National Ferment in Moldavia'.

82. *Pravda*, 11 September 1987; as translated in *CDSP*, XXXIX, no. 37, pp. 7–8.

83. 'Vremia', Soviet Television, 7 September 1987.

84. *Pravda*, 4 October 1987. For the implications of this change for Kazakhstan, see Bess Brown, 'Kazakhstan Loses Control of Its Nonferrous Metallurgy', RL 410/87, 9 October 1987.

85. *News from Ukraine*, no. 48, November 1987, p. 4.

86. Toomas Ilves, 'Conformist Communists Propose Turning Estonia into Closed Economic Zone', *RFER*, Baltic Area/7, 28 October 1987, pp. 11–13.

87. Juris Kaza, 'Latvian Call for Greater Freedom', *Guardian*, 7 October 1987.

88. Toomas Ilves, 'Estonia', *RFER*,

RAD Background Report/250 (Eastern Europe), 30 December 1987, p. 17. Also, interview with Tiit Madisson and Heiki Ahonen, Munich, August 1988.

89. Dzintra Bungs, 'Latvia', *RFER*, RAD Background Report/250 (Eastern Europe), 30 December 1987, p. 32.

90. *Guardian*, 13 October 1987; AP, 18 October 1987; *Moskovskie novosti*, 18 October 1987.

91. See Ann Sheehy, 'Commission Makes Cultural Concessions to Crimean Tatars', RL 459/87, 23 October 1987.

92. Elizabeth Fuller, 'Mass Demonstration in Armenia Against Environmental Pollution', RL 421/87, 18 October 1987.

93. Elizabeth Fuller, 'Armenians Demonstrate for Return of Territories from Azerbaijan', RL 441/87, 20 October 1987. On the origins and activities of the Nagornyi Karabakh Committee, see Felicity Barringer and Bill Keller, 'For Gorbachev, a Major Test of Change Explodes in Armenia', *New York Times*, 11 March 1988. For details about the Armenian appeals between 1985 and 1987, see Igor Muradyan's *samizdat* account in AS 6227.

94. Bohdan Nahaylo, ' "Informal" Ukrainian Culturological Club Under Attack', RL 477/87, 23 November 1987.

95. For details, see Bohdan Nahaylo, 'Representatives of Non-Russian National Movements Establish Coordinating Committee', RL 283/88, 22 June 1988.

96. Bohdan Nahaylo, 'Political Demonstration in Minsk Attests to Byelorussian National Assertiveness', RL 481/87, 26 November 1987; 'More Signs of Greater National Assertiveness by Byelorussians', RL 22/88, 18 January 1988.

97. Bohdan Nahaylo, ' "Informal" Byelorussian Patriotic Groups Hold First Conference', RL 47/88, 31 January 1988.

98. TASS, 30 October 1987.

99. TASS, 2 November 1987.

100. Martin Walker, 'The Heat's On in the Kitchen at Camelot on Ice', *Guardian*, 23 December 1987.

101. *Pravda*, 30 December 1987. The problem of 'national nihilism' and 'super-

internationalism' had been raised again by
Janis Peters in *Literaturnaia gazeta* on
18 November 1987.

17. Crisis in the Empire
1. *Pravda*, 19 February 1988.
2. *Pravda*, 18 February 1988.
3. *Russkaia mysl'*, 11 March 1988, p. 4;
AS 6172, pp. 6–7.
4. Toomas Ilves, 'Estonians Announce
Alternative Party and Platform', *RFER*,
Baltic Area/2, 16 February 1988, pp. 7–10.
5. Reuters, 8 December 1987.
6. Elizabeth Fuller, 'Georgian Press
Attacks "Unofficial" Group and its
Journal', RL 38/88, 3 February 1988;
'Georgian Press Launches New Attack on
Noted Dissident', RL 114/88, 10 March
1988.
7. See AS 6227, pp. 18, 23–29; Barringer
and Keller, *New York Times*, 11 March
1988; and Elizabeth Fuller, 'A Preliminary
Chronology of Recent Events in Armenia
and Azerbaijan', RL 101/88, 15 March 1988.
8. Ann Sheehy, 'Soviet Media Coverage
of Recent Events in Armenia and
Azerbaijan', RL 109/88; *Izvestia*,
24 February 1988.
9. Fuller, RL 101/88.
10. *La Repubblica*, 6–7 March 1988.
11. *Ibid.*
12. Reuters, 5 March and *Sunday
Telegraph*, 6 March 1988.
13. Toomas Ilves, 'Independence Day
Against the Backdrop of Rising National
Consciousness', *RFER*, Baltic Area/3, 24
March 1988.
14. AP, 5 March; Reuters, 6 March;
AFP, 22 March 1988.
15. Reuters, 7 March 1988.
16. *Pravda*, 16 March 1988. For details on
the visit, see Roman Solchanyk,
'Gorbachev in Yugoslavia: The National
Question', RL 123/88, 20 March 1988.
17. TASS, 16 March 1988.
18. *Pravda*, 16 March 1988, as cited in
Solchanyk, RL 123/88.
19. Elizabeth Fuller, 'Attitudes Harden
As Gorbachev's Nagorno-Karabakh
Deadline Approaches', RL 121/88,
22 March 1988.

20. TASS, 23 March 1988. See also
Elizabeth Fuller 'Whither the Nagorno-
Karabakh Campaign?' RL 149/88,
30 March 1988.
21. Philip Hanson and Elizabeth Teague,
'The Nagorno-Karabakh Package', RL 132/
88, 29 March 1988.
22. AS 6192, p. 19; on the crackdown, see
Fuller, 149/88.
23. Gary Lee, 'Armenian Protest Has
Become Nationalist Cause', *Washington
Post*, 30 March 1988.
24. AS 6192.
25. AS 6192, pp. 15–16.
26. For more details on the Andreeva
case, see Kevin Devlin, '*L'Unita* on the
"Secret History" of Andreeva Letter', RL
215/88, 26 May 1988.
27. *Literaturnaia gazeta*, 10 February
1988, p. 3.
28. Novosti, 25 March 1988.
29. *Literaturnaia gazeta*, 9 March 1988,
pp. 2–9. On Iakubov's speech, see also
Anne Bohr, 'Head of Uzbek Writers'
Union Criticizes Moscow's Economic
Diktat', RL 146/88, 22 March 1988.
30. Novosti, 4 March 1988.
31. E. V. Tadevosian, 'Demokratizm
natsional'noi politiki KPSS', *Voprosy istorii
KPSS*, no. 3, 1988, pp. 18–33.
32. *Druzhba narodov*, no. 5, 1988,
pp. 237–42.
33. *Kommunist*, no. 7, 1988, p. 10.
34. *Kommunist*, no. 8, 1988, p. 23.
35. *Literaturnaia gazeta*, 9 March 1988, p. 9.
36. *Pravda*, 14 April 1988, p. 2.
37. *Pravda*, 18 April 1988, p. 3.
38. William J. Eaton, 'Glasnost Rekindles
Nationalist Feelings in the Baltic', *Los
Angeles Times*, 21 February 1988.
39. TASS and Radio Moscow,
10 February 1988.
40. Reuters, 21 February 1988; Antero
Pietila, 'Estonians Seek Independent
Economy', *Baltimore Sun*,
22 February 1988.
41. Novosti (in English), 4 March 1988.
42. *Morning Star*, 24 March 1988, pp. 6–7.
43. For the text of the first resolution, see
Molodezh' Estonii, 13 May 1988. For more
details, see Toomas Ilves, 'Cultural Unions

Adopt Resolution on Nationality Reforms', 'The Cultural Unions' Resolution to the Leaderships of the ECP and ESSR', and 'Unprecedented Openness at Creative Unions' Plenum', *RFER*, Baltic Area/6, 3 June 1988, pp. 3–6, 7–14 and 15–19.

44. Jiri Pehe, 'Independent Movements in Eastern Europe (An Annotated Survey)'; *RFER*, RAD Background Report/228, 17 November 1988, p. 5.

45. Bill Kellar, 'Gorbachev Advisor Urges Popular Front as Alternative Party', *New York Times*, 24 May 1988, and the interview with Zaslavskaia in *Izvestia*, 4 June 1988, p. 3. For further details, see Vera Tolz, 'Creation of the Democratic Union: "Informal Groups" Take Initiative into Their Own Hands', RL 189/88, 10 May 1988.

46. AP, 21 June 1988.

47. Gary Lee, 'Soviet Group Forms Party to Dilute Communist Rule', *Washington Post*, 9 May 1988.

48. *Russkaia mysl'*, 24 June and 25 July 1988; Roman Solchanyk, 'Democratic Front to Promote *Perestroika* Formed in the Ukraine', RL 324/88, 17 July 1988, and 'Lvov Authorities Begin Criminal Proceedings Against Activists', RL 327/88, 26 July 1988.

49. Grigore Singurel, 'Moldavia on the Barricades of *Perestroika*', *Report on the USSR*, no. 8, 1989, pp. 35–6.

50. Vladimir Socor, 'The Moldavian Democratic Movement: Structure, Program, and Initial Impact', *Report on the USSR*, no. 8, 1989, p. 30.

51. Saulius Girnius, 'An Overview of Developments in the Baltic Republics in 1988', *RFER*, RAD Background Report/112, 22 June 1988, pp. 4–6 and 'The "Lithuanian Restructuring Movement" ', *RFER*, Baltic Area/8, 4 August 1988, pp. 19–23.

52. For the text of the Latvian demands, see *Sovetskaia Latviia*, 11 June 1988. See also Dzintra Bungs, 'Cultural Leaders Call for Greater National Sovereignty', and 'People's Front Planned', *RFER*, Baltic Area SR/7, 13 July 1988, pp. 15–19 and 31–2.

53. Bohdan Nahaylo, 'Representatives of Non-Russian National Movements Establish Coordinating Committee', RL 283/88, 22 June 1988.

54. AS 6217, pp. 24–6.

55. Toomas Ilves, 'Vote to Restore Estonian Flag and Decree Estonian as Official Language', *RFER*, Baltic Area/7, 13 July 1988, pp. 9–10.

56. Toomas Ilves, 'Party First Secretary Replaced by Native Estonian', and 'Massive Demonstrations', *RFER*, Baltic Area/7, 13 July 1988, pp. 3–6 and 7–8.

57. Saulius Girnius, 'Massive Rally in Vilnius', *RFER*, Baltic Area/7, 13 July 1988, pp. 33–5.

58. Dzintra Bungs, 'The Latvian Communist Party Leadership's Platform', *RFER*, Baltic Area/7, 13 July 1988, pp. 21–6.

59. Elizabeth Fuller, 'New Demonstrations in Armenia and Azerbaijan Exemplify Polarization of Views Over Nagorno-Karabakh', RL 220/88, 20 May 1988, and 'Party Secretaries Replaced in Armenia and Azerbaijan', RL 255/88, 24 May 1988.

60. *Sovetskaia Latviia*, 11 June 1988, p. 2.

61. TASS, 9 June 1988.

62. AP, 26 June 1988.

63. Ann Sheehy, 'Kazakh Minister Defends Territorial Integrity of Kazakhstan', RL 264/88, 15 June 1988.

64. *Pravda*, 25 June 1988, p. 3; Ann Sheehy, 'Tajiks Question Republican Frontiers', RL 366/88, 11 August 1988.

65. TASS, 29 April 1988 and Radio Moscow, 30 April 1988.

66. Soviet Television, 11 June 1988.

67. Bohdan Nahaylo, 'Ukrainian Catholic Issue Overshadows Start of Moscow Patriarchate's Millennial Celebration', RL 230/88, 6 June 1988.

68. Bohdan Nahaylo, 'Ukrainians Object to Moscow Patriarchate's Depiction of Millennium Jubilee as Solely "Russian" Affair', RL 476/88, 12 October 1988.

69. John Soper, 'Kirghiz and Uzbek Writers Express Their Views in Connection with Party Conference', RL 309/88, 12 July 1988, and Lois Olden, 'Uzbek Writers

Defend Their Republic Against
Accusations of Nationalism', RL 285/88,
23 June 1988.
70. *Izvestia*, 22 April 1988, p. 2.
71. TASS, 29 June 1988.
72. Soper, RL 309/88.
73. *Pravda*, 29 June 1988, pp. 2–7.
74. *Pravda*, 1 July 1988, p. 3.
75. *Pravda*, 30 June 1988, p. 7.
76. *Pravda*, 1 July 1988, p. 5.
77. *Pravda*, 2 July 1988.
78. *Pravda*, 1 July 1988.
79. *Pravda*, 2 July 1988.
80. *Sovetskaia Estonia*, 7 July 1988, p. 2.
81. *Pravda*, 5 July 1988, p. 3.

18. Waiting for Gorbachev
1. Saulius Girnius, 'Massive Rally in
Vilnius', *RFER*, Baltic Area SR/7, 13 July
1988, pp. 33–5.
2. Solchanyk, 'Democratic Front to
Promote *Perestroika* Formed in the
Ukraine'.
3. *Literaturna Ukraina*, 18 July 1988,
pp. 1–2.
4. Singurel, 'Moldavia on the Barricades
of *Perestroika*', p. 36.
5. Soviet Television, 19 July 1988;
Pravda, 20 July 1988. See also Bill Keller,
'Gorbachev, on TV, Leads Opposition to
Armenian Nationalists', *New York Times*,
20 July 1988.
6. Soviet Television, 19 July 1988;
Pravda, 20 July 1988.
7. *Pravda*, 30 July 1988.
8. Esther Fein, 'Interior Ministry Troops
Given Greater Powers', *New York Times*,
27 August 1989.
9. AP, 2 August 1988.
10. Bohdan Nahaylo, 'Lvov Authorities
Resort to Old Methods in Breaking Up
Unauthorized Meetings and Religious
Services', RL 355/88, 13 August 1988;
Literaturna Ukraina, 30 November 1989,
p. 5.
11. Kathleen Mihalisko, 'Byelorussian
Activists are Charged with Violating Law
on Unauthorized Assemblies', RL 418/88,
8 September 1988.
12. *Sovetskaia Latvia*, 12 August 1988.
13. *Pravda*, 13 August 1988.

14. *Sovetskaia Latvia*, 12 August, and
Sovetskaia Litva, 14 August 1988. What
Iakovlev did not add was that Lenin, in his
Testament, had in fact viewed such a
concession to the non-Russians as a 'step
backwards' necessitated by the all-
important task of maintaining and
strengthening 'the union of socialist
republics'. Lenin, *Collected Works*, vol. 36,
pp. 609–10.
15. *Sovetskaia Litva*, 16 August 1988.
16. Dzintra Bungs, 'The Baltic Republics
Demand Greater National Rights', *RFER*,
RAD BR/214, 25 October 1988.
17. Saulius Girnius, 'Police Disperse
Demonstrations', *RFER*, Baltic Area
SR/11, 5 October 1988, pp. 23–5.
18. Michael Dobbs, 'Estonians Focus on
Own Revolution', *Washington Post*,
2 October 1988.
19. Bill Keller, 'Popular Front Meets;
Seeks Capitalist-Style Economy', *New York
Times*, 2 October 1989; Michael Dobbs,
'Estonians Call for New Freedoms',
Washington Post, 3 October 1988.
20. Rupert Cornwell, 'Latvian
Nationalists Slip Kremlin Leash',
Independent, 10 October 1988; Xan Smiley,
'Baltic Challenge Soft-Pedalled by
Gorbachev', *Daily Telegraph*, 24 October
1988.
21. Saulius Girnius, 'Congress of the
Lithuanian Restructuring Movement',
RFER, Baltic Area SR/12, 28 October
1988.
22. *Kommunist*, no. 11, July 1988,
pp. 21–5.
23. *Europeo* (Milan), 13 September 1988.
24. Tanjug, 7 August 1988.
25. Leokadiia Drobizheva, 'Kontseptsiia
natsional'nogo stroitel'stva', *Moskovskie
novosti*, no. 38, 1988.
26. Ann Sheehy, 'Republican Rights and
the Proposed Amendments to the
Constitution', RL 497/88, 10 November
1988.
27. The events are summarized by
Toomas Ilves in his review of events in
Estonia during 1988. See *RFER*, RAD
BR/251, 30 December 1988, pp. 21–2.
28. Saulius Girnius, 'Baltic Condemnation

of Proposed Changes to the Soviet Constitution', *RFER*, RAD BR/227, 17 November 1988. See also his review of events in Lithuania during 1988: *RFER*, BR/251, 30 December 1988, pp. 36–7.

29. TASS, 23 November 1988; Rupert Cornwell, 'Georgians Say No to Moscow's Reforms', *Independent*, 25 November 1988.

30. *Literaturna Ukraina*, 24 November 1988, p. 2.

31. UPI, 24 November; Reuters, 25 November 1988.

32. TASS, 26 November and Soviet Television, 27 November 1988; Vincent J. Schodolski, 'Gorbachev Addresses Nation on Soviet Ethnic Strife', *Chicago Tribune*, 28 November 1988.

33. TASS, 29 November 1988. For a very useful overview of these developments, see Ann Sheehy, 'The First Stage of Gorbachev's Reform of the Political System and the Non-Russian Republics', RL 520/88, 2 December 1988.

34. *Izvestia*, 15 January 1989.

35. *Pravda*, 8 January 1989.

36. *Pravda*, 13 January 1989.

37. *Literaturnaia Rossiia*, 6 January 1989, p. 5.

38. See John B. Dunlop, 'Two Noteworthy Russian Nationalist Initiatives', *Report on the USSR*, no. 21, 1989, pp. 1–4. In this article, Dunlop also discusses the newly formed Foundation for Slavic Writing and Slavic Cultures, a pan-Slavic organization founded in March 1989 by conservative Russian nationalists.

39. See Douglas Smith, 'Moscow's "Otechestvo": A Link Between Russian Nationalism and Conservative Opposition to Reform', *Report on the USSR*, no. 30, 1989, pp. 6–9. Smith discusses another new Russian nationalist organization, the Union for the Spiritual Revival of the Fatherland, in his 'Formation of New Russian Nationalist Group', *Report on the USSR*, no. 27, 1989, pp. 5–8.

40. *Izvestia*, 21 December 1988, p. 2.

41. Kestutis Girnius, 'A Dispute over Education Between Lithuania and the Central Authorities', *RFER*, Baltic Area/2, 13 February 1989, pp. 17–21.

42. See Socor, *The Moldavian Democratic Movement*.

43. See Elizabeth Fuller, 'Abkhaz-Georgian Relations Remain Strained', *Report on the USSR*, no. 10, 1989, pp. 25–27, and 'New Abkhaz Campaign for Secession from Georgian SSR', *Report on the USSR*, no. 14, 1989, pp. 27–8.

44. Timur Kocaoglu, 'Uzbek Students Call for Uzbek to be Made the Republican State Language', *Report on the USSR*, no. 8, 1989, pp. 21–2.

45. See Ann Sheehy, 'Uzbeks Requesting Further Reduction of Cotton Target', *Report on the USSR*, no. 8, 1989, pp.19–21.

46. Annette Bohr, 'Soviet Muslims Demonstrate in Tashkent', *Report on the USSR*, no. 8, 24 February 1989, pp. 22–4.

47. Soviet Television, 22 February 1989; *Pravda*, 24 February 1989.

48. *Radians'ka Ukraina*, 22 February 1989.

49. See Elizabeth Fuller and Goulnara Ouratadze, 'Georgian Leadership Changes in Aftermath of Demonstrators' Deaths', *Report on the USSR*, no. 16, 21 April 1989, pp. 28–31; Vera Tolz, 'The USSR This Week', *Report on the USSR*, no. 17, 28 April 1989, p. 26.

50. See Hon-Thor Dahlburg, 'Baltic Nationalists Press Demands for Economic Freedom', *Independent*, 15 May 1989.

51. Soviet Television, 30 May 1989.

52. Annette Bohr, 'New Information on May Riots in Ashkhabad and Nebit-Dag', *Report on the USSR*, no. 29, 21 July 1989, pp. 40–1.

53. Annette Bohr, 'Violence Erupts in Uzbekistan', *Report on the USSR*, no. 24, 16 June 1989, pp. 23–6; Ann Sheehy, 'Social and Economic Background to Recent Events in Fergana Valley', *Report on the USSR*, no. 27, 7 July 1989, pp. 21–3.

54. David Remnik, 'Moslem Feud Blamed in Riots', *Washington Post*, 22 June 1989.

55. Ann Sheehy, 'Interethnic Disturbances in Western Kazakhstan', *Report on the USSR*, no. 27, 7 July 1989, pp. 11–14.

56. Elizabeth Fuller, 'Georgian Writers'

Union Issues Secession Ultimatum', *Report on the USSR*, no. 29, 21 July 1989, p. 28.

57. Vladimir Socor, 'Rallies in Kishinev Mourn Soviet Annexation, Escalate National Demands', *Report on the USSR*, no. 29, 21 July 1989, pp. 21–4.

58. Saulius Girnius, 'The Lithuanian Komsomol Congress', *Report on the USSR*, no. 34, 25 August 1989, pp. 21–3.

59. Jonathan Steele, 'The Crazy Quilt of Pluralism', *Guardian*, 3 July 1989; Kestutis Girnius, 'Lithuanian Communist Party Edges towards Independence', *Report on the USSR*, no. 40, 6 October 1989, pp. 15–17.

60. Jonathan Steele, 'The Crazy Quilt of Pluralism', *Guardian*, 3 July 1989; Kathleen Mihalisko, 'Byelorussian Popular Front Holds Founding Congress in Vilnius', *Report on the USSR*, no. 28, 14 July 1989, pp. 13–16.

61. *Pravda*, 2 July 1989.

62. *Pravda*, 21 July 1989.

63. TASS, 26 July 1989. For further details see Bill Kellar, 'Moscow Endorses Plan of Baltic Economic Experimentation', *New York Times*, 28 July 1989, and David Remnik, 'Baltic Republics to Control Own Economy', *Washington Post*, 28 July 1989.

64. *Ogonek*, no. 31, July 1989, pp. 26–7.

65. *Literaturnaia gazeta*, 7 June 1989, p. 5 and 14 June 1989, pp. 3 and 5.

66. *Izvestia TsK KPSS*, no. 6, 1989, p. 6.

67. See Mirza Mikhaeli and William Reese, 'The Popular Front in Azerbaijan and its Program', *Report on the USSR*, no. 43, 25 August 1989, pp. 29–32.

68. *Pravda*, 27 August 1989.

69. Cited in Scott Shane, 'Kremlin Keeps up Diatribe Against Nationalist Movements', *Baltimore Sun*, 29 August 1989.

70. See Dzintra Bungs, 'Statement of the Baltic Popular Front Organizations to the Peoples of the USSR', *Report on the USSR*, no. 37, 15 September 1989, pp. 18–19.

71. AFP, 18 September 1989.

72. See Vladimir Socor, 'Politics of the Language Question Heating Up in Soviet Moldavia', *Report on the USSR*, no. 36,

8 September 1989, pp. 33–6, and 'Moldavian Proclaimed Official Language in the Moldavian SSR', *Report on the USSR*, no. 38, 22 September 1989, pp. 13–15; TASS, 2 September 1989.

73. *Washington Post*, 30 August 1989 and TASS, 31 August 1989.

74. Rupert Cornwell, 'The Popular Front is Running Things Now', *Independent*, 18 September 1989.

75. See Jonathan Steele, 'Ukrainians Launch Freedom Front', *Guardian*, 9 September 1989; Michael Dobbs, 'Ukrainian Launch Autonomy Movement', *Washington Post*, 9 September 1989; Reuters, 9 September 1989.

76. Reuters, 18 September 1989; Michael Dobbs, 'Catholic Ukrainians Demand Legalization of Disbanded Church', *Washington Post*, 18 September 1989; Masha Hamilton, 'Thousands of Ukrainian Catholics Pray in Show of Strength', *Los Angeles Times*, 18 September 1989.

77. Scott Shane, 'New Group of Russian Workers Fights Economic Reform', *Baltimore Sun*, 14 September 1989; Vera Tolz, 'Creation of The United Front of Workers of Russia: Further Consolidation of Antireform Forces', *Report on the USSR*, no. 39, 29 September 1989, pp. 11–13; Reuters, 15 October 1989.

78. Soviet Television, 17 September 1989.

79. AFP, 18 September 1989.

80. TASS, 15 September 1989.

81. See Ann Sheehy, 'Russian Share of Population Down to 50.8 Percent', *Report on the USSR*, no. 42, 20 October 1989, pp. 1–5.

82. TASS, 19 September 1989; *Pravda*, 20 September 1989.

83. Ann Sheehy, 'Voting Power of the Non-Russian Republics in the CPSU Central Committee', *Report on the USSR*, no. 39, 29 September 1989, pp. 6–7.

84. *Pravda*, 21 September 1989.

85. *Pravda*, 22 September 1989.

86. See Suzanne Crow, 'Soviet Conscripts Fall Victim to Ethnic Violence', *Report on the USSR*, no. 26, 3 November 1989, pp. 8–9; James Critchlow, 'Uzbek Army Recruits Believed Murdered to Avenge Fergana

Killings', *Report on the USSR*, no. 44,
3 November 1989, pp. 23–5.
87. See the interview with Colonel-General Anatolii Kleimanov in *Krasnaia zvezda*, 29 October 1989.
88. *Pravda*, 22 September 1989.
89. *Pravda*, 21 September 1989.
90. *Pravda*, 22 September 1989.
91. AP, 31 October 1989.
92. *Pravda*, 21 and 22 September 1989.
93. Soviet Television, 20 September 1989; *Pravda*, 22 September 1989.
94. *Le Progrès*, 26 September 1989.
95. Bill Keller, 'Lithuanian Legislature Calls Soviet Annexation Illegal', *New York Times*, 23 September 1989.
96. Reuters, 29 September 1989; Scott Shane, 'Soviet Cover-up of Illegal Baltic Pact Finding Charged', *Baltimore Sun*, 30 September 1989.
97. TASS, 5 October 1989; Bill Kellar, 'Azerbaijan Peace Comes by Means of Pact', *New York Times*, 13 October 1989.
98. AFP, 19 October 1989.
99. AP, 31 October 1989; UPI, 2 November 1989.
100. Reuters, 23 October 1989.
101. Jeff Sallot, '1,000 Men in Baltics Spurn Draft into Soviet "Army of Occupation" ', *Toronto Globe and Mail*, 2 November 1989; Esrher Fein, 'Kremlin Confronted on Baltic Recruits', *New York Times*, 30 September 1989.
102. Soviet Television, 24 October 1989.
103. Radio Moscow, Soviet Television, AP, 22 October 1989.
104. Michael Parks, 'Lithuanian Parliament OKs Independence Referendum', *Los Angeles Times*, 4 November 1989; Reuters, 5 November 1989.
105. UPI, 5 November 1989; Reuters, 6 November 1989.
106. AP, 4 November 1989; Michael Parks, 'Armenia Opposition Unites to Oust Communist Party', *Los Angeles Times*, 6 November 1989.
107. Reuters, 7 November 1989.
108. Reuters and AP, 7 November 1989; Michael Dobbs, 'Protesters Disrupt Soviet Revolution Day Celebration', *Washington Post*, 8 November 1989.
109. Radio Moscow, 9 November 1989.
110. Vladimir Socor, 'Mass Protests and "Exceptional Measures" in Kishinev', *Report on the USSR*, no. 46, 17 November 1989, pp. 21–4.
111. Reuters, 19 November 1989.
112. Reuters, 10 November 1989.
113. Fen Montaigne, 'Latvia Claims Right to Veto Laws from Moscow', *Knight-Ridder Newspapers*, 12 November 1989.
114. TASS and AFP, 12 November 1989; Reuters, 13 November 1989.
115. Reuters, 16 November 1989.
116. AP, 17 November 1989.
117. Reuters, 17 November 1989.
118. AP and Reuters, 18 November 1989.
119. AP, 19 November 1989; Scott Shane, 'Georgia Reasserting Its Right to Secede from Soviet Union', *Baltimore Sun*, 20 November 1989.
120. *Pravda*, 5 November 1989.
121. Soviet Television, 16 November 1989; TASS, 17 November 1989.
122. John Rettie, 'Lithuania Defiantly Votes to Cut the Party Down to Size', *Guardian*, 8 December 1989.
123. Francis X. Clines, 'Testy Gorbachev Tangles with Party Congress', *New York Times*, 13 December 1989.
124. AP, 21 December 1989; Esther B. Fein, 'Gorbachev Calls Emergency Meeting', *New York Times*, 22 December 1989; Michael Parks, 'Gorbachev Calls Meeting to Discuss Lithuanian Secession', *Los Angeles Times*, 22 December 1989.
125. Soviet Television, 21 December 1989.
126. *Izvestia*, 24 December 1989; the exchange between Karas'ov and Gorbachev was translated by David Remnik in his 'Gorbachev Accuses Nationalist Groups', *Washington Post*, 24 December 1989.
127. Soviet Television, 23 December 1989; *Izvestia*, 24 December 1989.
128. *Pravda*, 25 December 1989.
129. TASS in English, 23 and 24 December; Reuters, 24 December 1989.
130. AP, 24 December 1989.
131. *Pravda*, 25 December 1989.

132. APN in English, 28 December 1989.

133. *Pravda*, 26 December 1989.

134. Ibid. See also Rupert Cornwell, 'Gorbachev Caught on the Horns of the Lithuanian Dilemma', *Independent*, 27 December 1989.

135. On 27 December tens of thousands of Lithuanians rallied in Vilnius to express their support for the Lithuanian Communist Party's split with the CPSU. Reuters, 27 December 1989.

136. AP, 28 December 1989.

137. See Roman Solchanyk, 'Church and State Split on Ukrainian Catholic Issue', *Report on the USSR*, 2, no. 1, 5 January 1990, pp. 10–12; Kathleen Mihalisko, 'The Ukrainian Catholics and the Russian Orthodox Church: The Unfolding Conflict in Western Ukraine', *Report on the USSR*, 2, no. 1, 5 January 1990, pp. 12–14.

138. John Rettie, 'Moldavia Stirs Over Historic Romanian Ties', *Guardian*, 29 December 1989 and 'Moldavians Call Rally to Press Case for Independence', *Guardian*, 28 December 1989. See also Anatol Lieven, 'Moldavians Cross Soviet Border They Want to See Erased', *The Times*, 2 January 1990.

139. AFP, 31 December 1989.

140. Reuters, 2 and 5 January 1990.

141. Reuters, AP and UPI, 30 December, and Reuters, 31 December 1989; UPI, 2 January 1990; David Remnik, 'Soviets Reinforce Troops Near Iranian Border', *Washington Post*, 4 January 1990.

142. Reuters, 31 December 1989.

143. Excerpts from the speeches appear in *Ogonek*, no. 48, November 1989, pp. 6–8 and 31.

144. *Sovetskaia Rossiia*, 30 December 1989; Reuters and AFP, 30 December 1989. '

145. Alexander Rahr, 'Gorbachev and the Russian Party Buro', *Report on the USSR*, no. 1, 5 January 1990, p. 1.

146. *Pravda*, 5 November 1989.

Conclusion

1. Lenin, *Collected Works*, vol. 20, pp. 35 and 27.

2. Stalin, *Works*, vol. 4, p. 363.

3. Lenin, *Collected Works*, vol. 36, p. 606.

4. *Newsweek*, 18 December 1989, p. 56.

5. Lenin, *Collected Works*, vol. 36, p. 608.

6. Stalin, *Works*, vol. 5, p. 343.

7. Dzyuba, *Internationalism or Russification?*, p. 86.

8. Lenin, *Collected Works*, vol. 36, pp. 610–11.

9. Stalin, *Works*, vol. 5, p. 260.

10. Lenin, *Collected Works*, vol. 36, p. 607.

11. *Literaturna Ukraina*, 12 October 1989, p. 6.

Appendix

1. A few months after the census, the figure of 'over 200,000 Kurds in the USSR today' was mentioned by N. F. Bugai, 'K voprosu o deportatsii narodov SSSR v 30–kh–40–kh godakh', *Istoriia SSSR*, no. 6, November–December 1989, p. 141.

2. The figures are from Gosudarstvennyi komitet SSSR po statistike, *Natsional'nyi sostav naseleniia: Chast' II*, Moscow, 1989, pp. 4–5.

3. Ann Sheehy, 'Preliminary Results of the All-Union Census Published', *Report on the USSR*, 19 May 1989, p. 3.

4. Ann Sheehy, 'Russian Share of Soviet Population Down to 50.8 Per Cent', *Report on the USSR*, 20 October 1989, p. 2, and *Natsional'nyi sostav*, p. 3.

Select Bibliography

Aitmatov, Chingiz, *The Day Lasts More Than a Hundred Years*, London and Sydney, 1983.

Akiner, Shirin, *Islamic Peoples of the Soviet Union*, London, 1983; 2nd ed., 1987.

Alexeyeva, Ludmilla, 'Unrest in the Soviet Union', *The Washington Quarterly*, vol. 13, no. 1, Winter 1990.

   Soviet Dissent: Contemporary Movements for National, Religious, and Human Rights, Middletown, Conn., 1985.

Allworth, Edward, *Ethnic Russia: The Dilemma of Dominance*, New York, 1980.

   (ed.), *The Nationality Question in Central Asia*, New York, 1973.

   (ed.), *Soviet Nationality Problems*, New York, 1971.

Altay, A., 'Kirgiziia during the Great Purge', *Central Asian Review*, 1964, vol. 12, no. 2.

Avalishvili, Zourab, *The Independence of Georgia in International Politics, 1918–1921*, London, 1940.

Azrael, Jeremy R. (ed.), *Soviet Nationality Policies and Practices*, New York, 1978.

Badzo, Iurii, 'An Open Letter to the Presidium of the Supreme Soviet of the USSR and the Central Committee of the CPSU', *Journal of Ukrainian Studies* (Toronto), no. 17, Winter 1984.

Barghoorn, F., *Soviet Russian Nationalism*, New York, 1956.

Bennigsen, Alexandre A. and Marie Broxup, *The Islamic Threat to the Soviet State*, London and Canberra, 1983.

   and Chantal Lemercier-Quelquejay, *Islam in the Soviet Union*, New York and London, 1967.

   and S. Enders Wimbush, *Muslim National Communism in the Soviet Union: A Revolutionary Strategy for the Colonial World*, Chicago, 1979.

   and S. Enders Wimbush, *Muslims of the Soviet Empire: A Guide*, Bloomington, 1986.

   and S. Enders Wimbush, *Mystics and Commissars: Sufism in the Soviet Union*, London, 1985.

Besançon, Alain, 'The Nationalities Issue in the USSR', *Survey*, vol. 30, no. 4 (131), June 1989.

Bethell, Nicholas, *The Last Secret: Forcible Repatriation to Russia, 1944–1947*, London, 1974.

Bilinsky, Yaroslav, *The Second Soviet Republic: The Ukraine after World War II*, New Brunswick, N.J., 1964.

Bociurkiw, Bohdan, 'The Uniate Church in the Soviet Ukraine: A Case Study in Soviet Church Policy', *Canadian Slavonic Papers*, 1965, vol. VII.

Brown, Archie and Michael Kaser (eds.), *The Soviet Union since the Fall of Krushchev*, New York, 1975.

Browne, Michael (ed.), *Ferment in the Ukraine*, London, 1971.

Brumberg, Abraham (ed.), *In Quest of Justice*, London, 1970.

Budreckis, Algirdas M., *The Lithuanian National Revolt of 1941*, Boston, 1968.

Burg, Steven L., 'The Soviet Union's Nationalities Question', *Current History*, vol. 88, no. 540, October 1989.

Cang, Joel, *The Silent Millions: A History of the Jews in the Soviet Union*, London, 1969, and New York, 1970.

Caroe, Olaf, *Soviet Empire: The Turks of Central Asia and Stalinism*, New York, 1967.

Carrère d'Encausse, Hélène, 'Linguistic Russification and Nationalist Opposition in Kazakhstan', *The East Turkic Review*, 1958, no. 1.

Decline of an Empire: The Soviet Socialist Republics in Revolt, New York, 1975.

Carynnyk, Marco *et al.* (eds.), *The Foreign Office and the Famine: British Documents on Ukraine and the Great Famine of 1932–33*, Kingston, Ont., 1988.

Chalikova, Viktoriia, 'Arkhivnyi iunosha', *Neva*, 1988, no. 10.

Chokayev, Mustafa, 'Turkestan and the Soviet regime', *Journal of the Royal Central Asian Society*, 1931, vol. 18.

Chornovil, Vyacheslav, *The Chornovil Papers*, New York, 1968.

Clem, Ralph S. (ed.), *The Soviet West: Interplay between Nationality and Social Organization*, New York, 1975.

Cohen, Stephen F., *An End to Silence: Uncensored Opinion in the Soviet Union from Roy Medvedev's Magazine 'Political Diary'*, New York, 1982.

Connor, Walker, *The National Question in Marxist-Lenninist Theory and Strategy*, Princeton, 1984.

Conquest, Robert (ed.), *Back to Life*, London, 1958.

(ed.), *The Last Empire: Nationality and the Soviet Future*, Stanford, Calif., 1986.

(ed.), *Soviet Nationalities Policy in Practice*, London, 1967.

The Great Terror: Stalin's Purge of the Thirties, London, 1968; 2nd edn, Harmondsworth, 1971 and London, 1973.

The Harvest of Sorrow: Soviet Collectivization and the Terror-Famine, London, 1986.

The Nation Killers, London, 1970.

Power and Policy in the USSR: The Study of Soviet Dynastics, London, 1961.

Dallin, Alexander, *German Rule in Russia, 1941–1945: A Study of Occupation Policies*, London, 1957.

Degras, Jane (ed.), *Soviet Documents on Foreign Policy*, 3 vols., Oxford, 1953, reprinted New York, 1978.

Dekrety Sovetskoi vlasti, Moscow, 1957– (in progress).

Dunlop, John B., *The Faces of Contemporary Russian Nationalism*, Princeton, 1983.

The New Russian Nationalism, Washington, 1985.

Dunn, Dennis J., *The Catholic Church and the Soviet Government, 1939–1949*, New York, 1977.

Dvenadtsatyi s"ezd RKP (b) 17–25 aprelia 1923 goda, Moscow, 1968.

Dzyuba, Ivan, *Internationalism or Russification? A Study in the Soviet Nationalities Problem*, London, 1968, 2nd ed., 1970, New York, 1974.

Ekmanis, Rolfs, *Latvian Literature Under the Soviets 1940–1975*, Belmont, Mass., 1978.

Elliot, Mark R., *Pawns of Yalta: Soviet Refugees and America's Role in Their Repatriation*, Urbana, Ill., 1982.

Fisher, Alan W., *The Crimean Tatars*, Stanford, 1978.

Frumkin, Ia. G. *et al.* (eds.), *Kniga o russkom evreistve 1917–1967*, New York, 1968.

Gaucher, Roland, *Opposition in the USSR: 1917–1967*, New York, 1969.

Gilboa, Yehoshua A., *The Black Years of Soviet Jewry: 1939–1953*, Boston, 1971.

Goldhagen, Erich (ed.), *Ethnic Minorities in the Soviet Union*, New York, 1968.

Gross, Jan T., *Revolution from Abroad: The Soviet Conquest of Poland's Western Ukraine and Western Belorussia*, Princeton, 1988.

Gruliow, Leo (ed.), *Current Soviet Policies III: The Documentary Record of the Extraordinary 21st Congress of the Communist Party of the Soviet Union*, New York, 1960.

Hajda, Lubomyr, 'The Nationalities Problem in the Soviet Union', *Current History*, October 1988.

Hopkins, Mark, *Russia's Underground Press: The Chronicle of Current Events*, New York, 1983.

Iakovlev, Boris A., *Kontsentratsionnye lageri SSSR*, Munich, 1955.

Istoriia Sovetskoi Konstitutsii (v dokumentakh): 1917–1956, Moscow, 1957.

Kamenetsky, Ihor, *Nationalism and Human Rights: Processes of Modernization in the USSR*, Littleton, Colo., 1977.

Karklins, Rasma, *Ethnic Relations in the USSR: The Perspective from Below*, Boston, 1986.

Katz, Zev, Rosemarie Rogers, and Frederic Harned (eds.), *Handbook of Major Soviet Nationalities*, New York, 1975.

Khrushchev, Nikita S., *The 'Secret' Speech*, introd. Zhores and Roy Medvedev, Nottingham, 1976.

Kolarz, Walter, 'The Nationalities under Khrushchev: Gains and Losses', *Soviet Survey*, no. 24, April–June 1958.

Communism and Colonialism, London, 1964.

Russia and Her Colonies, London, 1952.

Korey, William, *The Soviet Cage: Anti-Semitism in Russia*, New York, 1973.

Koshelivets', Ivan, *Mykola Skrypnyk*, n.p. [Munich printed], 1972.

Kosyk, Volodymyr, *Concentration Camps in the USSR*, London, 1962.

KPSS v rezoliutsiiakh . . ., Moscow (several editions).

Krawchenko, Bohdan (ed.), *Ukraine after Shelest*, Edmonton, 1983.

Social Change and National Consciousness in Twentieth-Century Ukraine, Basingstoke and London, 1985.

Kreindler, Isabelle T. (ed.), *Sociolinguistic Perspectives on Soviet National Languages: Their Past, Present and Future*, Berlin, 1985.

Kubijovyč, Volodymyr (ed.), *Ukraine: A Concise Encyclopaedia*, vol. 1, Toronto, 1963.

Kulichenko, Mikhail I., *Bor'ba Kommunisticheskoi partii za reshenie natsional'nogo voprosa v 1918–1920 godakh*, Kharkov, 1963.

Kupchinsky, Roman, *Natsional'nyi vopros v SSSR: sbornik dokumentov*, Munich, 1975.

Lapidus, Gail W., 'Gorbachev's Nationalities Problem', *Foreign Affairs*, vol. 68, no. 4, Fall 1989.

League of Nations Treaty Series, vols. 2, 3, 11, 198.

Lenin, V. I., *Collected Works*, Moscow and London, 1960–70.

Levin, Nora, *The Jews in the Soviet Union since 1917: Paradox of Survival*, 2 vols., New York, 1988.

Lewin, Moshe, *Russian Peasants and Soviet Power: A Study of Collectivization*, New York, 1975.

Lewytzkyj, Borys, *Die sowjetische Nationalitätenpolitik nach Stalins Tod (1953–1970)*, Munich, 1970.

Politics and Society in Soviet Ukraine: 1953–1980, Edmonton, 1984.

Lieven, Dominic, *Gorbachev and the Nationalities*, Conflict Studies no. 216, London (The Centre for Security and Conflict Studies), 1988.

Low, A. D., *Lenin on the National Question*, New York, 1958.

Lubachko, Ivan S., *Belorussia under Soviet Rule: 1917–1957*, Lexington, Kentucky, 1972.

Lubin, Nancy, *Labour and Nationality in Soviet Central Asia: An Uneasy Compromise*, London and Basingstoke, 1984.

Luciuk, Lubomyr Y., and Bohdan S. Kordan, *Anglo-American Perspectives on the Ukrainian Question, 1938–1951: A Documentary Collection*, Kingston, Ont. and Vestal, N.Y., 1987.

Luckyj, George S. N. (ed.), *Discordant Voices: The Non-Russian Soviet Literatures*, Oakville, 1975.

Mace, James E., *Communism and the Dilemmas of National Liberation: National Communism in Soviet Ukraine 1918–1933*, Cambridge, Mass., 1983.

Majstrenko, Ivan, *Borot'bism: A Chapter in the History of Ukrainian Communism*, New York, 1954.

Natsional'naia politika KPSS, Munich, 1978.

Malabaev, D. M., *Ukreplenie sovetov Kirgizii v period stroitel'stva sotsializma: 1917–1937*, Frunze, 1969.

Marples, David R., *Chernobyl and Nuclear Power in the USSR*, New York, 1986.

Matossian, Mary Kilbourne, *The Impact of Soviet Policies in Armeniz*, Leiden, 1962.

Medvedev, Roy A., *Let History Judge: The Origins and Consequences of Stalinism*, New York, 1971 – London, 1972; 2nd ed., New York, 1989.

On Stalin and Stalinism, Oxford, 1979.

Misiunas, Romuald J. and Rein Taagepera, *The Baltic States: Years of Dependence 1940–1980*, London, 1983.

Motyl, Alexander J., *Will the Non-Russians Rebel? State, Ethnicity and Stability in the USSR*, Ithaca., N.Y., and London, 1987.

Nahaylo, Bohdan P., 'Dziuba's *Internationalism or Russification?* Revisited: A Reappraisal of Dziuba's Treatment of Leninist Nationalities Policy', *Journal of Ukrainian Graduate Studies*, vol. 2, no. 2, Fall 1977.

'Nationalities', in Martin McCauley (ed.), *The Soviet Union Under Gorbachev*, London, 1987.

'The Non-Russians: alive, if not well', *Index on Censorship*, vol. 9, no. 4, August 1980.

'Why the Empire's subjects are restless', *Index on Censorship*, vol. 18, no. 5, May–June 1989.

Nekrich, Aleksandr M., *The Punished Peoples*, New York, 1978.

Nepesov, G., *Pobeda sovetskogo stroia v severnom Turkmenistane (1917–1936)*, Ashkhabad, 1950.

Obrazovanie Soiuza Sovetskikh Sotsialisticheskikh Respublik: Sbornik dokumentov, Moscow, 1972.

Olcott, Martha Brill, 'The Collectivization Drive in Kazakhstan', *The Russian Review*, vol. 40, no. 2, April 1981.

'Gorbachev's National Dilemma', *Journal of International Affairs*, vol., 42, no. 2, Spring 1989.

'Yuri Andropov and the "National Question"', *Soviet Studies*, vol. 37, no. 1, 1985.

Pajanjis-Javis, J., *Soviet Genocide in Lithuania*, New York, 1980.

Park, A., *Bolshevism in Turkestan*, New York, 1957.

Pipes, Richard, *The Formation of the Soviet Union: Communism and Nationalism 1917–1923*, Cambridge, Mass., rev. ed., 1964.

Politika Sovetskoi vlasti po natsional'nym delam za tri goda: 1917–XI–1920, Moscow, 1920.

Pospielovsky, Dimitry, 'The Resurgence of Russian Nationalism in *Samizdat*', *Survey*, no. 1, Winter 1973.

Potichnyj , Peter J. (ed.), *Ukraine in the Seventies*, Oakville, Ont., 1975.

Problems of Communism, vol. XVI, September–October 1967, Special Issue: Nationalities and Nationalism in the USSR.

vol. XXXVIII, July–August 1989 [articles on nationalities in the USSR].

Rakowska-Harmstone, Teresa, 'The Dialectics of Nationalism in the USSR', *Problems of Communism*, vol. XXIII, May–June 1974.

'The Dilemma of Nationalism in the Soviet Union', in J. W. Strong (ed.), *The Soviet Union under Brezhnev and Kosygin: The Transition Years*, New York, 1971.

Russia and Nationalism in Central Asia: The Case of Tadzhikistan, Baltimore, 1970.

Rauch, Georg von, *The Baltic States: The Years of Independence 1917–1940*, London, 1974.

Reddaway, Peter, *Uncensored Russia: The Human Rights Movement in the Soviet Union*, London, 1972.

Remeikis, Thomas, *Opposition to Soviet Rule in Lithuania, 1945–80*, Chicago, 1980.

The Revolution in Central Asia as Seen by Muslim Bolsheviks, Society for Central Asian Studies, Reprint Series, no. 3, Oxford, 1985.

RFE/RL, *Glasnost and Empire: National Aspirations in the USSR*, Munich, Washington D.C., New York, 1989.

Rigby, T. H., Archie Brown and Peter Reddaway (eds.), *Authority, Power and Policy in the USSR*, New York, 1980.

Rywkin, Michael, *Moscow's Muslim Challenge: Soviet Central Asia*, New York, 1982.

Safarov, Georgy I., *Kolonial'naia revoliutsiia (Opyt Turkestana)*, Moscow, 1921, reprinted by the Society for Central Asian Studies, Reprint Series, no. 4, with a second title-page, *The Colonial Revolution (The Case of Turkestan)*, Oxford, 1985.

Saunders, George (ed.), *Samizdat: Voices of the Soviet Opposition*, New York, 1974.

Schroeter, Leonard, *The Last Exodus*, Seattle, 1974.

Seidl, Alfred (ed.), *Die Beziehungen zwischen Deutschland und der Sowjetunion, 1939–1941: Dokumente des Auswärtigen Amtes*, Tübingen, 1949.

Shcherbak, Iurii, *Chernobyl: A Documentary Story* (translated from the Ukrainian by Ian Press), Basingstoke, 1989.

Sheehy, Ann and Bohdan Nahaylo, *The Crimean Tatars, Volga Germans and Meskhetians: Soviet Treatment of Some National Minorities*, 3rd ed. (Minority Rights Group, Report no. 6), London, 1980.

Shtromas, Alexander and Morton A. Kaplan (eds.), *The Soviet Union and the Challenge of the Future*, vol. 3: *Ideology, Culture, and Nationality*, New York, 1989.

Silde, Adolfs, *Resistance Movement in Lativia*, Stockholm, 1972.

Silnitskii, Frantisek, *Natsional'naia politika KPSS v period s 1917 po 1922 god*, Munich, 1981.

Simmonds, George W. (ed.), *Nationalism in the USSR and Eastern Europe in the Era of Brezhnev and Kosygin*, Detroit, 1977.

Simon, Gerhard, *Nationalismus und Nationalitatenpolitik in der Sowjetunion*, Baden-Baden, 1986.

Solchanyk, Roman, 'Russian Language and Soviet Politics', *Soviet Studies*, XXXIV, no. 1, January 1982.

Solzhenitsyn, Alexander, *The Gulag Archipelago*, 3 vols, London, 1974–8.

Stalin, J. V., *Works*, Moscow, 1952–55.

Survey, vol. 24, no. 3, Summer 1979 [articles on problems of empire].

Swianiewicz, Stanislaw, *Forced Labour and Economic Development: An Enquiry into the Experience of Soviet Industrialization*, Westport, Conn., 1985.

Swoboda, Victor, 'Cat and mouse in the Ukraine', *Index on Censorship*, vol. 2, no. 1, Spring 1973.

Swoboda, Victor and Ann Sheehy, *Ethnic Pressures in the Soviet Union*, Conflict Studies no. 30, London (Institute For the Study of Conflict), December 1972.

Szporluk, Roman (ed.), *The Influence of East Europe and the Soviet West on the USSR*, New York, 1975.

Taagepera, Rein, *Softening Without Liberalization in the Soviet Union: The Case of Juri Kukk*, Lanham, Md, 1984.

Talbott, Strobe (ed. and transl.), *Khrushchev Remembers*, Boston and Toronto, 1970, London, 1971.

Tillett, Lowell, *The Great Friendship: Soviet Historians on the Non-Russian Nationalities*, Chapel Hill, N.C., 1969.

Tolstoy, Nikolai, *Victims of Yalta*, revised ed., London, 1979.

Tomingas, William, *The Soviet Colonization of Estonia*, 'Kultuur' [Toronto], 1973.

Ukrainian Herald, Issue 7–8: Ethnocide of Ukranians in the USSR, Baltimore–Paris–Toronto, 1976.

Vakar Nicholas P., *Belorussia: The Making of a Nation*, Cambridge, Mass., 1956.

Vardys, V. Stanley (ed.), *The Catholic Church, Dissent and Nationality in Soviet Lithuania*, New York, 1978.

Lithuania under the Soviets: Portrait of a Nation, 1940–65, New York, 1965.

Weil, Boris, *Osobo opasnyi*, London, 1980.

Wimbush, Ender S., *Soviet Nationalities in Strategic Perspective*, London and Sydney, 1985.

Yanov, Alexander, *The Russian Challenge and the Year 2000*, Oxford, 1987.

The Russian New Right, Berkeley, 1978.

Zevelev, A. I., *Iz istorii grazhdanskoi voiny v Uzbekistane*, Tashkent, 1959.

Index